Michael and Mollie Hardwick have been working together as authors, dramatists for the stage, television and radio, and directors of plays for a number of years, one of which was almost wholly devoted to compiling the present work. Together or individually they have written over seventy books, ranging from other standard works of literary reference to best-selling novels. Their ten books about Charles Dickens include the two novels based on the major ITV drama series *Dickens of London*, on which they have acted as advisers. Born respectively in Leeds and Manchester, Michael and Mollie Hardwick, who are husband and wife, live in Highgate Village, London, in a book-crammed 18th-century house with two cats, Bellamy and Hudson, named from the characters of *Upstairs, Downstairs*, with which the Hardwicks have been so closely associated as writers.

Compiled by Michael and Mollie Hardwick

The Charles Dickens
Encyclopedia

Futura Publications Limited

An Omega Book

An Omega Book

First published in this form in 1976
by Futura Publications Limited
Originally published by
Osprey Publishing Ltd

Illustrations drawn by
Hablôt Knight Browne ('Phiz')
George Cruikshank
George Cattermole
Marcus Stone, R.A.
R. Seymour

ISBN 0 8600 7741 1
Printed in Great Britain by
Hazell Watson & Viney Ltd
Aylesbury, Bucks

Futura Publications Limited
110 Warner Road
Camberwell, London SE5

PREFACE

SOME day, inevitably, someone will produce a complete concordance to the works of Charles Dickens. One hears already of an American computer test-run on one of the novels which, at a cost of tens of thousands of dollars, has counted the commas. Our aim has been more modest and, we believe, more realistic; to provide the most comprehensive 'companion' to the works that has yet been attempted, but to include in it only the sort of information that we can imagine being of use or entertaiment to someone.

The most substantial part of the work, 'The People', we can claim is virtually exhaustive. There are more than 2,000 entries and they cover every named character in the stories, with the exception of some to whom mere allusion is made by, say, Mrs. Nickleby casting about for a memory. Nearly all are accompanied by a quotation illustrative of appearance, character, habit, manner of speaking, and so forth, which has been selected to be of genuine value to those who use the book as a tool, as well as to amuse.

It will be seen that we have confined ourselves to those works which are to be found in the usual 'complete' sets of Charles Dickens's writings: in other words, mostly the work of his imagination, as opposed to the straight reporting, critical essays, and campaigning pamphleteering. This has meant taking in those pieces from periodicals such as *Household Words* that are familiar in volume form as *Reprinted Pieces*, comprising both imaginative sketches and straight journalism; but we have glanced only in passing at *Miscellaneous Papers, American Notes* and *Pictures from Italy* which include no made-up stories, and have ignored the *Memoirs of Joseph Grimaldi*, which Dickens and his father merely edited and added to. We have touched upon the poetry briefly – the less said about Dickens as poet, the better – but have included the plays, for all their

inferiority, since they appear in some full editions.

Both the sections dealing with Dickens's circle and the places associated with his life and works are selective, and the selection is ours, based on our notion of what will prove useful or entertaining. Someone, somewhere, will deplore an omission. We can only answer that, even with half a million words at our disposal, some things had to go; and Dickens wrote over five million words.

We have dealt with Dickens's own life in the form of a Time Chart, in the belief that to have written exhaustively about it in essay form would not have shown up the sequence of related dates and facts in the quick-reference way this book requires. A chart of dates and events, however, can offer only a conjectural picture of the man as personality and character; and while a good deal more about him can be deduced from a study of what he wrote, we believe that this preface might be no bad place in which to add an impression or two of Charles Dickens which will summon him from behind the scenes.

His childhood nurse, for instance, remembered him as 'a lively boy of good, genial, open disposition . . . a terrible boy to read'. The latter was perhaps due in part to his physical delicacy and slightness of frame, though his schoolmaster's sister thought him 'a very handsome boy, with long curly hair of a light colour'. A schoolfellow at Wellington House saw him as 'full of animation and animal spirits'. All these descriptions add up to that given by his friend and biographer, John Forster, of Dickens the young man on the brink of fame.

A look of youthfulness first attracted you, and then a candour and openness of expression which made you sure of the qualities within. The features were very good. He had a capital forehead, a firm nose with full wide nostrils, eyes wonderfully beaming with intellect and running over with humour and cheerfulness, and a rather prominent mouth strongly marked with sensibility . . . the hair so scant and grizzled in later days was then of a rich brown and luxurious abundance, and the bearded face of his last two decades had hardly a vestige of hair or whisker; but there was that in the face as I first recollect it which no time could change, and which remained implanted on it unalterably to the last. This was the quickness, keenness and practical power, the eager, restless, energetic outlook on each several feature, and so much of a man of action and business in the world. Light and motion flashed from every part of it. *It was as if made of steel*, was said of it . . . by a most original and delicate observer, the late Mrs. Carlyle. 'What a face is his to meet in a drawing-room!' wrote Leigh Hunt to me, the morning after I made them known to each other. 'It has the life and soul in it of fifty human beings.'

Such, for many years, was the outward man. At first a dandy, with a taste for bright clothes and jewellery, he became with prosperity more sober in appearance, and, as middle age came on and troubles increased, the thick hair receded and the smooth face took on premature lines and wrinkles, while the beard and moustache added apparent years to his age. Within, he never varied. With a terrifying, daemonic energy which compelled him to wear himself out, he had the capacity for work and play of fifty human beings, as Hunt might have added. When he was not writing novels he was engaged in journalism, or in dashing off long vivacious letters, or walking huge distances, or playing with his children, or producing and acting in amateur theatricals, or travelling on a reading tour. The two latter activities were necessary to him as release for that part of

him which yearned to act rather than write; and yet he was no Bohemian in spirit. His meticulous passion for tidiness and order was the bane of his family. A byword for generosity, he yet had a streak in him which made a perceptive woman friend remark that while Thackeray was the gentlest-hearted, most generous, most loving of men, 'Dickens, whose whole mind went to almost morbid tenderness and sympathy, was infinitely less plastic, less self-giving, less personally sympathetic.'

From this trait, perhaps, came the failures of his personal life in connection with his wife, his family and other women. 'My father never understood women,' said the daughter who married the wrong man to get away from home; and it is a truism to add that it is only the comic women in his stories who spring to real life. Nor did he understand as young men the sons he had idolised when they were babies. One after another, as they failed to come up to his high ideals, they were sent as far away as possible to work out their destinies. It was a contradiction as strange as that which compelled him to write of London as if he loved it, to yearn for it in foreign places, and yet to loathe its squalor while mentally wallowing in it. He was in no way a countryman, yet it was in a country house in Kent, the dream-house of his boyhood, that he spent the last portion of his life.

'Whatever the word "great" means,' said G. K. Chesterton, 'Dickens was what it means.' Our personal tribute to him, if one may be permitted, is that after all the time and labour expended on preparing this book, a seemingly endless task of selection, checking, revision, re-checking, proof-reading, and all the rest of it, we can still sit down to read Charles Dickens's works with a certainty of enjoyment greater than any other writer can give us.

Michael and Mollie Hardwick

This new edition incorporates corrections to a small number of errors in the original, kindly pointed out by perceptive readers. For reasons of economy, the extensive selection of quotations from the works has had to be excluded, though the hardback edition containing these remains available. In any case, the most satisfying source of quotations from the works of Charles Dickens remains the works of Charles Dickens.

Michael and Mollie Hardwick 1976

ACKNOWLEDGEMENTS

We acknowledge with gratitude the help of the following people in preparing this book: Mr. John Greaves, Hon. Secretary of the Dickens Fellowship and Miss Marjorie Pillers, Curator of the Dickens House, London, for providing information and helping to settle debatable points of 'fact'; Miss Alison Hodgson, for her admirably relentless editing of the MS and assistance with the proof-reading; Miss Ann Hoffmann, for compiling the demanding Indexes; Mrs. Margaret Morton, for typing well over half a million words with less than a dozen mistakes; and Mr. Roger Cleeve of Osprey Publishing, on whose initiative this work was undertaken, and whose co-operation and understanding have been all that the authors could have desired.

CONTENTS

A NOTE ON TYPOGRAPHY
AND ABBREVIATIONS

TYPOGRAPHY

ALL references to titles of books and plays are given in italic script, and to magazine articles, book chapters, short stories, essays, poems and songs, in quotation marks. Thus 'No Thoroughfare' refers to the short story, *No Thoroughfare* to the play based upon it.

ABBREVIATIONS

The following abbreviations are used in this work

'At Dusk'	'To be Read at Dusk'
Boz	*Sketches by Boz*
Chuzzlewit	*The Life and Adventures of Martin Chuzzlewit*
Copperfield	*The Personal History of David Copperfield*
Curiosity Shop	*The Old Curiosity Shop*
Dombey	*Dealings with the Firm of Dombey and Son*
Dorrit	*Little Dorrit*
Drood	*The Mystery of Edwin Drood*
Expectations	*Great Expectations*
Humphrey	*Master Humphrey's Clock*
Mudfog	*The Mudfog and other Sketches*
Mutual Friend	*Our Mutual Friend*
Nickleby	*The Life and Adventures of Nicholas Nickleby*
Nightingale's Diary	*Mr Nightingale's Diary*
Pickwick	*The Posthumous Papers of the Pickwick Club*
Reprinted	*Reprinted Pieces*
Rudge	*Barnaby Rudge*
'Silverman'	'George Silverman's Explanation'
Twist	*The Adventures of Oliver Twist*
Two Apprentices	*The Lazy Tour of Two Idle Apprentices*
Two Cities	*A Tale of Two Cities*
Uncommercial	*The Uncommercial Traveller*
Young Couples	*Sketches of Young Couples*
Young Gentlemen	*Sketches of Young Gentlemen*

ALPHABETICAL LIST OF WORKS
COVERED BY THIS ENCYCLOPEDIA

This list gives all the writings of Dickens covered by this encyclopedia, each followed by the date(s) of journal or serial publication (if applicable) and of first known bound publication. Short stories and articles are posted up to the titles of the collections in which they appear. More detailed publishing history will be found in 'The Works' section.

David Copperfield, The Personal History of May 1849–Nov. 1850; 1850

'Detective Police, The' 27 July and 10 Aug. 1850; 1858 in *Reprinted*

'Dinner at Poplar Walk, A' see 'Mr. Minns and his Cousin' below

'Doctor Marigold' Dec. 1865; 1871 in *Christmas Stories*

'Doctors' Commons' 11 Oct. 1836; 1836 in *Boz*

Dombey and Son, Dealings with the Firm of Oct. 1846–Apr. 1848; 1848

'Domestic Young Gentleman, The' 1838 in *Young Gentlemen*

'Down with the Tide' 5 Feb. 1853; 1858 in *Reprinted*

'Drunkard's Death, The' 1836 in *Boz*

'Dullborough Town' 30 June 1860; 1860 in *Uncommercial*

'Early Coaches' 19 Feb. 1835; 1836 in *Boz*

'Egotistical Couple, The' 1840 in *Young Couples*

'Election for Beadle, The' 14 July 1835; 1836 in *Boz*

'Familiar Epistle from a Parent to a Child' Feb. 1839; post-1880 editions of *Mudfog*

'First of May, The' 31 May 1836; 1836 in *Boz*

'Flight, A' 30 Aug. 1851; 1858 in *Reprinted*

'Fly-leaf in a Life, A' 22 May 1869; 1890 in *Uncommercial*

'Formal Couple, The' 1840 in *Young Couples*

'Four Sisters, The' 18 June 1835; 1836 in *Boz*

'Full Report of the First Meeting of the Mudfog Association' Oct. 1837; 1880 in *Mudfog*

'Full Report of the Second Meeting of the Mudfog Association' Sept. 1838; 1880 in *Mudfog*

'Funny Young Gentleman, The' 1838 in *Young Gentlemen*

'George Silverman's Explanation' Jan.–Mar. 1868; uncertain

'Ghost of Art, The' 20 July 1850; 1858 in *Reprinted*

'Gin-shops' 7 Feb. 1835; 1836 in *Boz*

'Going into Society' Dec. 1858; 1871 in *Christmas Stories*

Great Expectations 1 Dec. 1860–3 Aug. 1861; 1861

'Great Tasmania's Cargo, The' 21 Apr. 1860; 1860 in *Uncommercial*

'Great Winglebury Duel, The' 1836 in *Boz*

'Greenwich Fair' 16 Apr. 1835; 1836 in *Boz*

'Hackney-coach Stands' 31 Jan. 1835; 1836 in *Boz*

'Half-pay Captain, The' see 'Curate, The' above

Hard Times 1 Apr.–12 Aug. 1854; 1854

'Haunted House, The' Dec. 1859; 1871 in *Christmas Stories*

'Haunted Man and the Ghost's Bargain, The' Dec. 1848; 1852 in *Christmas Books*

'His General Line of Business' 28 Jan. 1860; 1860 in *Uncommercial*

'Holiday Romance' Jan.–May 1868; uncertain

'Holly-Tree, The' Dec. 1855; 1871 in *Christmas Stories*

'Horatio Sparkins' Feb. 1834; 1836 in *Boz*

'Hospital Patient, The' 6 Aug. 1836; 1836 in *Boz*

'Hunted Down' 20 Aug.–3 Sept. 1859; 1861

'In the French-Flemish Country' 12 Sept. 1863; 1865 in *Uncommercial*

Is She His Wife? 1837 (?)

'Italian Prisoner, The' 13 Oct. 1860; 1860 in *Uncommercial*

'Ladies' Societies, The' 20 Aug. 1835; 1836 in *Boz*

Lamplighter, The 1879

'Lamplighter's Story, The' 1841

'Last Cab-driver, and the First Omnibus Cad, The' 1 Nov. 1835; 1836 in *Boz*

Lazy Tour of Two Idle Apprentices, The 3–31 Oct. 1857; 1890

Life of Our Lord, The 1934

'Little Dinner in an Hour, A' 2 Jan. 1869; 1875 in *Uncommercial*

Little Dorrit Dec. 1855–June 1857; 1857

'London Recreations' 17 Mar. 1835; 1836 in *Boz*

'Long Voyage, The' 31 Dec. 1853; 1858 in *Reprinted*

'Loving Couple, The' 1840 in *Young Couples*

'Lying Awake' 30 Oct. 1852; 1858 in *Reprinted*

'Making a Night of it' 18 Oct. 1835; 1836 in *Boz*

Martin Chuzzlewit, The Life and Adventures of Jan. 1843–July 1844; 1844

Master Humphrey's Clock 4 Apr. 1840–
4 Dec. 1841; 1840–1

'Medicine Men of Civilisation' 26 Sept.
1863; 1865 in *Uncommercial*

'Meditations in Monmouth-street' 24
Sept. 1836; 1836 in *Boz*

'Message from the Sea, A' Dec. 1860;
1871 in *Christmas Stories*

'Military Young Gentleman, The' 1838
in *Young Gentlemen*

Miscellaneous Papers 1838–69; 1908

'Misplaced Attachment of Mr. John
Dounce, The' 25 Oct. 1835; 1836 in *Boz*

'Miss Evans and the Eagle' 4 Oct. 1835;
1836 in *Boz*

'Mistaken Milliner, The. A Tale of
Ambition' 22 Nov. 1835; 1836 in *Boz*

'Monument of French Folly, A' 8 Mar.
1851; 1858 in *Reprinted*

'Mr. Barlow' 16 Jan. 1869; 1875 in *Uncommercial*

'Mr. Minns and his Cousin' (first title 'A
Dinner at Poplar Walk') 1 Dec. 1833;
1836 in *Boz*

Mr. Nightingale's Diary 1851

'Mr. Robert Bolton – the "gentleman
connected with the press" ' Aug. 1838;
1880 in *Mudfog*

'Mrs. Joseph Porter' Jan. 1834; 1836 in
Boz

'Mrs. Lirriper's Legacy' Dec. 1864; 1871
in *Christmas Stories*

'Mrs. Lirriper's Lodgings' Dec. 1863;
1871 in *Christmas Stories*

Mudfog and Other Sketches, The Jan.
1837–Feb. 1839; 1880

'Mugby Junction' Dec. 1866; 1871 in
Christmas Stories

Mystery of Edwin Drood, The Apr.–Sept.
1870; 1870

'New Year, The' 3 Jan. 1836; 1836 in *Boz*

'Nice Little Couple, The' 1840 in *Young
Couples*

*Nicholas Nickleby, The Life and Adven-
tures of* Apr. 1838–Oct. 1839; 1839

'Night Walks' 21 July 1860; 1860 in *Uncommercial*

'No. 1 Branch Line: The Signal-man', a
chapter of 'Mugby Junction' q.v., above

'No Thoroughfare' Dec. 1867; 1871 in
Christmas Stories

'Noble Savage, The' 11 June 1853; 1858
in *Reprinted*

'Nobody's Story' Dec. 1853; 1858 in
Reprinted, 1871 in *Christmas Stories*

'Nurse's Stories' 8 Sept. 1860; 1860 in
Uncommercial

'Old Couple, The' 1840 in *Young Couples*

Old Curiosity Shop, The 25 Apr. 1840
6 Feb. 1841; 1841

'Old Lady, The' see 'Curate, The' above

'Old Stage-coaching House, An' 1 Aug.
1863; 1865 in *Uncommercial*

Oliver Twist, The Adventures of Feb.
1837–Mar. 1839; 1838

'Omnibuses' 26 Sept. 1834; 1836 in *Boz*

'On an Amateur Beat' 27 Feb. 1869; 1875
in *Uncommercial*

'On Duty with Inspector Field' 14 June
1851; 1858 in *Reprinted*

'Our Bore' 9 Oct. 1852; 1858 in *Reprinted*

'Our English Watering-place' 2 Aug. 1851;
1858 in *Reprinted*

'Our French Watering-place' 4 Nov.
1854; 1858 in *Reprinted*

'Our Honourable Friend' 31 July 1852;
1858 in *Reprinted*

Our Mutual Friend May 1864–Nov. 1865;
1865

'Our Next-door Neighbour' 1836 in *Boz*

'Our Parish' 28 Feb.–20 Aug. 1835; 1836
in *Boz*

'Our School' 11 Oct. 1851; 1858 in
Reprinted

'Our Vestry' 28 Aug. 1852; 1858 in
Reprinted

'Out-and-out Young Gentleman, The'
1838 in *Young Gentlemen*

'Out of the Season' 28 June 1856; 1858 in
Reprinted

'Out of Town' 29 Sept. 1855; 1858 in
Reprinted

'Pantomime of Life, The' Mar. 1837;
1880 in *Mudfog*

'Parish Engine, The' see 'Beadle, The'
above

'Parliamentary Sketch, A' 7 Mar. and 11
Apr. 1835; 1836 in *Boz*

'Parlour Orator, The' 13 Dec. 1835; 1836
in *Boz*

'Passage in the Life of Mr. Watkins Tottle,
A' Jan. and Feb. 1835; 1836 in *Boz*

'Pawnbroker's Shop, The' 30 June 1835;
1836 in *Boz*

'Perils of Certain English Prisoners, The'
Dec. 1857; 1871 in *Christmas Stories*

THE WORKS

**LISTED IN ORDER OF FIRST
APPEARANCE IN ANY FORM: SERIALS BY FIRST
INSTALMENT, COLLECTIONS BY EARLIEST
INDIVIDUAL PIECE**

CONTENTS OF 'THE WORKS'

THE WORKS

SKETCHES BY BOZ

Dickens's first published writings, beginning with 'A Dinner at Poplar Walk' (later re-titled 'Mr. Minns and his Cousin') which appeared in the *Monthly Magazine* in December 1833. Other sketches subsequently appeared in this magazine and in the *Morning Chronicle, Evening Chronicle*, and *Bell's Life in London*. Dickens's pseudonym in the latter publication was Tibbs. The 'Boz' used elsewhere derived from the adenoidal pronunciation of the name Moses by which his younger brother Augustus was known in the family. The first collected series of *Sketches by Boz* appeared in February 1836 and the second in December, both published by Macrone. The first complete edition, embodying further pieces, was published in 1839 by Chapman & Hall. Published in the U.S.A. in two volumes, 1837 (Carey, Lea & Blanchard, Philadelphia).

The *Sketches* are a mixture of descriptive pieces of journalism, whose titles generally convey their subject, fictional portraits, and short stories, of varying quality but replete with hints of the Dickens-to-come, and valuable in their reflection of contemporary manners and conditions. Looking back in 1850, Dickens wrote in a Preface to the first cheap edition: 'They comprise my first attempts at authorship – with the exception of certain tragedies achieved at the mature age of eight or ten, and represented with great applause to overflowing nurseries. I am conscious of their often being extremely crude and ill-considered, and bearing obvious marks of haste and inexperience.'

OUR PARISH

A series of character sketches: 'The Beadle. The Parish Engine. The Schoolmaster'; 'The Curate. The Old Lady. The Half-pay Captain'; 'The Four Sisters'; 'The Election for Beadle'; 'The Broker's Man'; 'The Ladies' Societies'; 'Our Next-door Neighbour'.

SCENES

Portrayals of London life, owing much to Dickens's habit of tramping the streets at all hours of the night: 'The Streets – Morning'; 'The Streets – Night'; 'Shops and their Tenants'; 'Scotland-yard'; 'Seven Dials'; 'Meditations in Monmouth-street'; 'Hackney-coach Stands'; 'Doctors' Commons'; 'London Recreations'; 'The River'; 'Astley's'; 'Greenwich Fair'; 'Private Theatres'; 'Vauxhall-gardens by Day'; 'Early Coaches'; 'Omnibuses'; 'The Last Cab-driver, and the First Omnibus Cad'; 'A Parliamentary Sketch'; 'Public Dinners'; 'The First of May'; 'Brokers' and Marine-store Shops'; 'Gin-shops'; 'The Pawnbroker's Shop'; 'Criminal Courts'; 'A Visit to Newgate'.

CHARACTERS

Reflections about types, some of them in the form of short stories: 'Thoughts about People' – Dickens considers a humble clerk, rich bachelors, carefree apprentices; 'A Christmas Dinner' – a typical family gathering; 'The New Year' – Tupple, the perfect guest, attends a quadrille party given by Dobble, a fellow clerk in a government office; 'Miss Evans and the Eagle' – Samuel Wilkins takes J'mima Ivins to the Eagle Pleasure Gardens in the City Road and gets into a fight; 'The Parlour Orator' – a public-house know-all; 'The Hospital Patient' – a dying girl refuses to accuse her lover of beating her; 'The Misplaced Attachment of Mr. John Dounce' – a well-to-do widower is attracted by a pretty young oyster-bar keeper, is cut by his friends and relatives and refused by his young woman, and ends up married to his cook; 'The Mistaken Milliner. A Tale of Ambition' – Miss Amelia Martin disastrously fancies herself as a concert singer; 'The Dancing Academy' – Augustus Cooper takes a course of dancing lessons with Signor Billsmethi and finds himself sued for breach of promise by Miss Billsmethi; 'Shabby-genteel People' – an old reader in the British Museum typifies his kind; 'Making a Night of it' – two City clerks, Potter and Smithers, spend their quarter's salary on a one-night spree; 'The Prisoners' Van' – two young prostitute sisters are seen leaving Bow Street for Cold Bath Fields prison.

TALES

Twelve short stories: 'The Boardinghouse' – the arrival of Mrs. and the Misses Maplesone at Mrs. Tibbs's boardinghouse brings upheaval to the lives of the gentlemen boarders; 'Mr. Minns and his Cousin' – Augustus Minns, a fastidious bachelor, is pestered into visiting his deplorable cousin, Octavius Budden, and wishes he had stayed at home; 'Sentiment' – Lavinia Brook Dingwall is sent to the Misses Crumptons' educational establishment to remove her from the attentions of Theodosius Butler, who turns out to be the Misses Crumpton's cousin and a guest at their half-yearly ball; 'The Tuggses at Ramsgate' – the newly-rich Tuggs family are fleeced by two confidence tricksters, Captain and Belinda Waters; 'Horatio Sparkins' – the snobbish Malderton family bask in the acquaintance of the mysteriously aristocratic Horatio Sparkins, who proves to be a draper's assistant named Smith; 'The Black Veil' – a surgeon is pressed by a woman to visit a dying man, but finds himself confronted with the corpse of an executed criminal, her son; 'The Steam Excursion' – Percy Noakes organises a steam-packet excursion on the Thames, which is a great success until the weather turns rough; 'The Great Winglebury Duel' – Alexander Trott, trying to get himself arrested in order to avoid having to fight a duel with Horace Hunter, his rival for Emily Brown, is mistaken for Lord Peter, who has an assignation with the wealthy Julia Manners, and she finds him agreeable enough to marry instead; 'Mrs. Joseph Porter' – the Gattletons' private theatricals are ruined by their rival Mrs. Joseph Porter, who eggs on Mrs. Gattleton's erudite brother Thomas to keep correcting the players; 'A Passage in the Life of Mr. Watkins Tottle' – in return for the payment of his debts by Gabriel Parsons, Watkins Tottle agrees to marry Miss Lillerton and let Parsons share the advantage of her private income, but it emerges that she is engaged to the Revd. Charles Timson, who Tottle thinks is going to conduct the ceremony, and Tottle drowns himself in the Regent's Canal; 'The Bloomsbury Christening' – Nicodemus Dumps, a misanthropic bachelor, gets his own back for having to attend the christening of the baby of his nephew, Charles Kitterbell, by making a speech full of baleful prophecies about the child's future and sending Mrs. Kitterbell into hysterics; 'The Drunkard's Death' – Warden, whose drunkenness has caused his wife's death from grief and driven his sons from home, unintentionally betrays one of them to the police to face execution for murder, is deserted at long last by his loyal daughter, and drowns himself in the Thames.

THE POSTHUMOUS PAPERS OF THE PICKWICK CLUB

Dickens's first novel. Writing began in London in February 1836, at 15 Furnival's Inn, and continued at 48 Doughty Street; completed October 1837. First publication in England in monthly numbers, 31 March 1836 to 30 October 1837. Issued complete by Chapman & Hall, November 1837. First American publication 1836–7 by Carey, Lea & Blanchard, Philadelphia, in five volumes, each including four of the original parts.

In 1836 Chapman & Hall invited Dickens to provide the text for a series of 'Cockney sporting-plates of a superior sort' by the artist Robert Seymour. Dickens objected to their proposal for sketches concerning the activities of a 'Nimrod Club' on the grounds that he was no sportsman and that the idea was an old one. 'My views being deferred to, I thought of Mr. Pickwick, and wrote the first number.' The appearance and some characteristics of Pickwick himself were based on a 'fat old beau', John Foster, of Richmond. The early numbers were received quietly, but soon reviews became warm and the public enthusiastic as the original scrappy form gave place to a continuous story with developing characters and a humour previously unknown in English literature. The appearance of Sam Weller sealed the triumph of the book. Traces of the influence of Smollett, Fielding, and Defoe are noticeable in the writing, and the plot bears evidence of Dickens's wide travels as a parliamentary reporter and of his early experience of a debtors' prison, while Jingle, the actor, is an aspect of Dickens the actor *manqué*.

The Pickwick Club as a body makes an early and brief appearance, at one of its London meetings. Thereafter the central figures of the book are its President, the middle-aged, stout, jovial, and naïf Samuel Pickwick, a retired gentleman who sets out on a tour of investigation of scientific and cultural matters, and the three friends who accompany him: Nathaniel Winkle, who fancies himself as a sportsman but fails dismally to justify his pretensions; Augustus Snodgrass, melancholy and romantic in the fashionable Byronic manner (the period of the story is 1827–31); and the somewhat older Tracy Tupman, a plump bachelor amorist.

Their first adventure occurs at Rochester, where the cowardly Winkle is mistakenly challenged to a duel, the real offending party being Alfred Jingle, a strolling player. Jingle joins the party; it is the first of his mischievous appearances in Mr. Pickwick's life.

At a military review in Chatham the Pickwickians meet Mr. Wardle, a country squire, his daughters Bella and Emily, his spinster sister Rachael, and their servant Joe, an immensely fat and greedy youth with a tendency to sleep on his feet. An invitation from Wardle takes the party down to his Kentish manor at Dingley Dell, where the unfortunate Winkle, taken out shooting, misses his bird and shoots Tupman in the arm. Rachael Wardle, on the lookout for a husband, evinces great emotion at the incident, and a romantic association springs up between her and Tupman. But Jingle, who has again come on the scene, cuts out Tupman and elopes with Rachael to London, where Wardle and Pickwick find the pair about to marry by special licence. Jingle is bribed to abandon Rachael.

At the White Hart Inn, Borough, where the couple are staying, Pickwick meets the lively young Cockney Sam Weller, self-taught, voluble, and irrepressible, who is working as Boots. Pickwick decides to take Sam into his service as valet and servant; but his attempts to announce this to his landlady, the widowed Mrs. Bardell, are interpreted by that lady as a proposal of marriage to herself, and the other three Pickwickians arrive to see her fainting in the horrified Pickwick's arms.

They travel on to Eatanswill and witness the humours of an election. Once more Jingle appears, this time masquerading as a captain. Pickwick follows him to Bury St. Edmunds, proposing to unmask him. With the aid of his servant, the lugubrious Job Trotter, Jingle entices Pickwick into the grounds of a girls' boarding-school by night. Pickwick's intentions are gravely misunderstood by the teachers and pupils.

After a pleasant visit to Dingley Dell, the Pickwickians return to London and Pickwick is disturbed to learn that Mrs. Bardell, under the influence of the rascally lawyers Dodson and Fogg, has instituted an action for breach of promise against him. He journeys to Ipswich, where at the Great White Horse he finds himself by mistake in the bedroom of a lady just about to become engaged to the jealous Mr. Peter Magnus, who challenges him to a duel. The lady reports them to the magistrate Nupkins, but Pickwick clears his name and incidentally finds that Jingle is in Ipswich attempting to marry Miss Nupkins under false pretences. Pickwick unmasks him, and with his friends returns for a happy visit to Dingley Dell, enjoying country sports and pastimes and attending the wedding of Bella Wardle to Mr. Trundle.

Other romantic affairs are on hand: Winkle is in love with Arabella Allen, a friend of Emily Wardle, with whom Snodgrass is infatuated. Arabella's brother Ben, a medical student, turns up at Dingley

Dell with his friend Bob Sawyer, also a suitor for Arabella's hand.

There follows the hearing of the Bardell and Pickwick breach of promise case. Pickwick's defence is shattered by the inept testimony of Winkle and the eloquence of Mrs. Bardell's counsel, Serjeant Buzfuz. Mrs. Bardell is awarded £750 damages, which Pickwick refuses to pay. He takes refuge from his troubles at Bath, where he experiences the niceties of spa society, Sam attends a 'swarry' of snobbish footmen, and Mr. Winkle is seriously compromised by being found at midnight, clad only in his nightshirt, with the pretty Mrs. Dowler in her sedan-chair. Pickwick and Sam rescue him, and he meets Arabella Allen once again in Bristol. Sam Weller continues his courtship of Mary, Arabella's pretty maid.

Again in London, Pickwick is imprisoned in the Fleet for non-payment of damages. Sam gets himself imprisoned to remain in company with his master by a trick worked with his father, Tony Weller, a stout coachman who has married a widow addicted to piety and tea-drinking in the company of the Reverend Mr. Stiggins, a hypocritical drunken parson.

In the Fleet Pickwick meets again Jingle and Job Trotter, penniless, starving, and distressed. He befriends them generously and obtains their release and a passage to Demerara where they may start a new life. Mrs. Bardell arrives in the Fleet, sent there by Dodson and Fogg for non-payment of costs. Pickwick pays the costs for her on condition that she agrees to forgo his damages.

His final adventures are all connected with romance. Winkle has secretly married Arabella, and Pickwick reconciles both Winkle's father and Ben Allen to the match. Snodgrass and Emily Wardle are bent on elopement, because of Wardle's attitude to their engagement, but Pickwick brings father and daughter together and all misunderstandings are sorted out.

The Pickwick Club is dissolved. Pickwick retires to a neat villa in Dulwich, with Sam and Mary as his servants; they, too, marry. Tony Weller is now a widower, and has at last taken his revenge upon the Reverend Mr. Stiggins by ducking him in a horse-trough.

SUNDAY UNDER THREE HEADS

Sub-titled 'As it is: As Sabbath Bills would make it: As it might be made', this pamphlet was written for Chapman & Hall to publish in 1836, with three illustrations by Hablôt K. Browne. It is a sharp and early attack on advocates of more rigid observance of the Sabbath.

THE VILLAGE COQUETTES

Written in 1836 at Furnival's Inn, London, it was produced on 6 December 1836. It played in repertory for nineteen performances, afterwards transferring to Edinburgh. First published in 1836 by Richard Bentley, and in 1837 by Bradbury & Evans.

It had been suggested to Dickens by John Hullah, a young composer, that they should combine their talents. The resulting comic opera in two acts was accepted by Braham, lessee of the St. James's Theatre. The audience's reception was enthusiastic, but the press in general criticised the libretto.

Two village maidens, Lucy Benson and her cousin Rose, are respectively betrothed to George Edmunds and John Maddox. But at Harvest Home time the two girls transfer their attentions to Squire Norton and his friend the Honourable Sparkins Flam. The Squire tries to persuade Lucy to elope with him, and her father overhears him and banishes him from his farm, but later relents. Flam's proposed abduction of Rose is likewise foiled, and the rustic sweethearts are finally reconciled.

THE STRANGE GENTLEMAN

Written in 1836 at Furnival's Inn, London, and produced at the St. James's Theatre on 29 September the same year, it ran for sixty nights. First published in 1836 or 1837 by Chapman & Hall. It is based on the *Boz* tale, 'The Great Winglebury Duel'.

The Strange Gentleman arrives at a posting-house on the way to Gretna

Green and demands a private room. He has been challenged to a duel by Horatio Tinkles, his rival for the hand of Emily Brown; but Tinkles does not know that the Strange Gentleman, in reality Walter Trott, has never set eyes on Emily, their betrothal having been arranged by his father. Two young ladies, Fanny and Mary, arrive, on the way to Gretna Green. They imagine that Trott is Fanny's admirer, disguised. Miss Julia Dobbs is also en route for Gretna to marry a young lord, and in her turn mistakes Trott for him. Complications follow, Julia loses her lord and Trott his Emily, but they console each other and depart for Gretna together.

IS SHE HIS WIFE? OR, SOMETHING SINGULAR

Written early in 1837, at Furnival's Inn, London, this comic burletta was produced at the St. James's Theatre on 6 March in the same year. No author's name appeared on the playbill, but a later playbill attributed it to 'Boz'. No English publication date is known, nor does Forster mention it. But in 1876 James R. Osgood, a publisher of Boston, Mass., bought a printed copy from an English collector, who had in turn bought it from the stock of the theatrical bookseller T. H. Lacy. He paid £6 for the thirty-page pamphlet, and reprinted it in Boston in 1877. In 1879 the business premises of Osgood & Co. were destroyed by fire, and the original copy with them.

The newly-married Mr. Lovetown becomes indifferent to his wife who, to provoke his jealousy, pretends to a passion for Felix Tapkins, a bachelor neighbour. Overhearing her amorous soliloquy in which she regrets that an unnamed 'he' is not married, Tapkins assumes she is not really Lovetown's wife. Another couple, the Limburys, come on the scene. Lovetown flirts with the vain Mrs. Limbury, rousing the rage of her jealous husband, and a farrago of misunderstandings ensues.

THE MUDFOG AND OTHER SKETCHES

Three papers from *Bentley's Miscellany*, 1837–38.

The first, 'The Public Life of Mr. Tulrumble', January 1837, concerns the débâcle which ensues when the vain new mayor of Mudfog, Nicholas Tulrumble, persuades 'Bottle-nosed' Ned Twigger, the town drunkard, to grace his electoral procession in a full suit of brass armour. The other two are 'Full Report of the First Meeting of the Mudfog Association for the Advancement of Everything', October 1837, satirising the earnest scientists, sociologists, and statisticians who delivered papers at the annual meetings of the British Association for the Advancement of Science, founded in 1831, and a similar report, 'Full Report of the Second Meeting of the Mudfog Association for the Advancement of Everything', published September 1838.

Three further pieces are included with the *Mudfog Sketches*: 'The Pantomime of Life', March 1837, drawing parallels between everyday life and that of the stage; 'Some Particulars Concerning a Lion', May 1837, about the antics of a literary lion at a party; and 'Mr. Robert Bolton', August 1838, about a 'gentleman connected with the press' who regales an admiring audience in the Green Dragon, near Westminster Bridge, with an anecdote about a baker who assaults his wife and boils his protesting son in the washhouse copper.

All the above pieces were collected together for the first time in book form by Richard Bentley & Son in 1880 under the title *The Mudfog Papers, etc.*

'Familiar Epistle from a Parent to a Child', Dickens's valedictory to the *Miscellany*, was added in later editions.

THE ADVENTURES OF OLIVER TWIST
or, The Parish Boy's Progress

Dickens's second novel, written in part concurrently with *Pickwick*. First publication in monthly numbers in the new *Bentley's Miscellany*, published by Richard Bentley, 31 January (February issue) 1837 to March 1839; written mainly at 48 Doughty Street, London. Published in three volumes, 1838, with illustrations by Cruikshank. The third edition, with Preface dated Devonshire Terrace, March

1841, published by Chapman & Hall. First publication in America 1837: first and second chapters only, included in the second volume of *Tales and Sketches from Bentley's Miscellany* (these included various other writings of Dickens, including 'Public Life of Mr. Tulrumble', 'Mudfog Association', etc.), published by Carey, Lea & Blanchard. The entire work was published in 1838 in the American reprint of *Bentley's Miscellany*, published in New York by William and Jemima Walker.

In *Oliver Twist* Dickens embarked upon a straightforward storyline after the multi-plots of *Pickwick*. It is the first work in which he directly attacks social institutions, in this case the workhouse system of which Oliver is a victim. Dickens's travels as a reporter had shown him much of this particular evil, and he was able at the same time to dwell on the criminal world of London which he delighted to explore. The book is full of youthful melodrama: the villains are incredibly black and the good people improbably white, but the figure of Fagin is one of Dickens's immortals, touched with a strange sympathy, perhaps because he fascinated his author more than he repelled him. 'The Jew,' he wrote to Forster, '. . . is such an out and outer that I don't know what to make of him.'

Oliver Twist was in general liked, though it did not command the adulation given to *Pickwick*. There were comments on the 'lowness' of the subject, and some Jewish readers thought Fagin a libel upon their race.

In the workhouse of a provincial town seventy-five miles north of London a young woman who has arrived in an exhausted condition gives birth to a boy, and dies. The child is named Oliver Twist and put into the workhouse orphanage, presided over by the ill-natured Mrs. Corney. When he is nine, the beadle, Bumble, transfers him to the workhouse itself and he is set to picking oakum. When Oliver is chosen as the speaker for the other half-starved boys and asks for more of the gruel which is their staple fare, the authorities decide it is time to put him to a trade.

He becomes apprenticed to Sowerberry, an undertaker, his small frame and delicate appearance making him suitable for acting as a mute at children's funerals. But when Noah Claypole, another apprentice, insults his dead mother, Oliver attacks him and is cruelly punished by the Sowerberrys. He runs away to London, and in Barnet meets with a boy thief, Jack Dawkins, 'The Artful Dodger', a member of a pickpocket gang run by Fagin, a Jew. Fagin decides to use the uncomprehending Oliver, whom he instructs in the picking of pockets, and sends him out with the Dodger and another boy, Charley Bates. Oliver is horrified to see them pick the pocket of an old gentleman, Mr. Brownlow, at a bookstall, runs away, and is captured and taken before a magistrate; but the bookstall-keeper has seen the true robbers and exculpates Oliver.

Oliver is taken to Mr. Brownlow's house in Pentonville, where the housekeeper, Mrs. Bedwin, nurses him through an illness. He is treated with kindness and affection for the first time in his life, and is happy. But Fagin plots to recapture him, for while the boy is free his secrets are in danger. He engages Bill Sikes, a brutal robber, and Nancy, his mistress, also a member of the gang, to bring Oliver back.

Their stratagem is successful, and Sikes takes Oliver by night to Chertsey to carry out a robbery on the house of a Mrs. Maylie. When the alarm is given Sikes takes fright and escapes, and Oliver is shot and wounded. Mrs. Maylie and her adopted niece, Rose, take him in, listen to his story, and believe it. He settles with them, becoming a household favourite.

Rose is suddenly stricken with a serious illness. Mrs. Maylie's son, Harry, arrives, and on her recovery begs her to marry him. She refuses because she is nameless, having been adopted from a baby-farm by Mrs. Maylie. During his idyllic life with the Maylies Oliver catches glimpses of Monks, a sinister man who is in league with Fagin to recapture him. In Fagin's den they lay plots to do this; but Nancy, overhearing them and feeling compassion for the child, tells Rose about the conspiracy, without giving away the gang. Rose and her adviser, Dr. Losberne, promise Nancy that if Monks is brought to justice Fagin and Sikes shall not be in any danger of arrest.

Fagin has set Noah Claypole, now his tool, to follow Nancy and spy on her as she meets Rose and Mr. Brownlow on the steps of London Bridge. He reports the conversation to Fagin, who repeats it to Sikes. Sikes, maddened by Nancy's supposed treachery, rushes back to his own room, awakens her from sleep and clubs her to death.

He takes flight into the country north of London, driven from place to place by fear and conscience. Then, feeling that London is after all the safest place in which to conceal himself, he returns to his old haunts. He has been followed by his ill-treated but faithful dog, Bullseye, and has attempted to drown it, but it has escaped and returns to the gang's headquarters. Sikes arrives there to be greeted with horror and loathing by those of the gang who have escaped a police raid in which Fagin and Noah Claypole have been arrested. Charley Bates gives the alarm; Sikes attempts to escape across the roofs in order to drop into Folly Ditch below, but falls with a rope round his neck, and hangs himself. The dog, which has followed its brutal master even to this point, leaps for the dead man's shoulders and falls to death below.

Fagin is executed, appealing to Oliver in the condemned cell to save him. The Dodger is transported, Charley Bates sees the error of his ways and becomes a reformed character, and Noah Claypole escapes justice by turning King's evidence.

The plot against Oliver is unravelled by Mr. Brownlow, to whom Oliver has now been restored. Monks, otherwise Edward Leeford, is Oliver's half-brother, their father having seduced and promised marriage to Agnes, Oliver's mother, while still married to Leeford's mother. The provisions of the father's will leave money to Oliver on condition that he maintains a spotless reputation, and for this reason Monks has tried to keep the boy in Fagin's gang in order to discredit him and inherit the full sum himself. It is now discovered that Oliver's dead mother and Rose Maylie were sisters, and that Rose is, after all, legitimate.

Monks receives his share of the legacy, goes to America, and dies there in prison. Mr. and Mrs. Bumble (for the pompous beadle has married the orphanage matron) are proved to have been in the plot against Oliver, lose their positions of trust, and become workhouse inmates. Oliver is adopted by Mr. Brownlow, and Rose marries Harry Maylie, who for her sake has given up a promising political career to become a country clergyman, in whose church a memorial is raised to Oliver's mother, Agnes.

SKETCHES OF YOUNG GENTLEMEN

Twelve character sketches of types, written in 1838 for publication that year in volume form by Chapman & Hall: 'The Bashful Young Gentleman'; 'The Out-and-out Young Gentleman'; 'The Very Friendly Young Gentleman'; 'The Military Young Gentleman'; 'The Political Young Gentleman'; 'The Domestic Young Gentleman'; 'The Censorious Young Gentleman'; 'The Funny Young Gentleman'; 'The Theatrical Young Gentleman'; 'The Poetical Young Gentleman'; 'The "Throwing-off" Young Gentleman'; 'The Young Ladies' Young Gentleman'.

THE LIFE AND ADVENTURES OF NICHOLAS NICKLEBY

Dickens's third novel. He began it at 48 Doughty Street, London, in February 1838, and finished it during the family summer holiday at 40 Albion Street, Broadstairs in September 1839. It was published by Chapman & Hall in twenty monthly parts, the first appearing on 31 March 1838 (dated April). Issued complete in October 1839. First American publication begun 1838, in parts, by Carey, Lea & Blanchard, Philadelphia; completed in 1839 by Lea & Blanchard, successors of the old firm. Also published by James Turney of New York.

As a child, Dickens had heard of the notorious Yorkshire boarding schools, to which unwanted boys were sent to be out of the way, and where they were terribly ill-treated; an account of the trial of a Yorkshire schoolmaster for the death of such a boy remained in his mind. In 1838 he and Hablôt K. Browne ('Phiz', who illustrated *Nickleby*) travelled to Yorkshire to investigate the schools at first-hand, and met Shaw, the original of Mr. Squeers. Dickens subsequently stated that 'Mr. Squeers and his school are faint and feeble pictures of an existing reality'.

At the time when he had first heard of them, he says that his head was 'full of Partridge, Strap, Tom Pipes, and Sancho Panza'; and *Nickleby*, intended to be mainly propagandist, turned out, in fact, to be a picaresque, lively, humorous novel with a hero whose adventures echo those of Dickens's own childhood heroes. As in *Pickwick*, there are evidences of the influence of Fielding, Defoe, and Smollett. The Crummles family are an exuberant outburst of Dickens's love for, and knowledge of, the theatre, especially the provincial theatre, and he sets their headquarters in his birthplace, Portsmouth. The novel contains entertaining satires on snobbery and greed.

The widowed Mrs. Nickleby comes up to London from Devon to seek financial help from her brother-in-law, Ralph Nickleby, a money-lender, for herself and her children, Nicholas, aged nineteen, and his younger sister Kate. The miserly Ralph takes an immediate dislike to Nicholas, though he feels a grudging affection for Kate. He finds the two women a lodging in a decrepit house in Thames Street, settles Kate as an assistant to Madame Mantalini, a dressmaker in the West End, and dispatches Nicholas to Yorkshire to teach at Mr. Wackford Squeers's 'Academy', Dotheboys Hall.

Squeers is a coarse, brutal man with a wife and son to match, and a daughter, Fanny, as ugly as himself, who develops a sentimental passion for the handsome Nicholas, and is jealous of his polite attentions to her pretty friend, Matilda Price, who is engaged to a big, bluff Yorkshireman, John Browdie. Nicholas remains impervious to Fanny's charms. His anger is awakened by the cruelty and starvation imposed upon Squeers's miserable pupils, and particularly upon Smike, a poor drudge whose wits have become enfeebled by deprivation. Smike runs away, is caught, and is rescued by Nicholas from receiving a savage beating. The beating is, instead, administered by Nicholas to Squeers, after which Nicholas leaves for London. Smike catches up with him and begs to be his companion.

In London, Nicholas and Smike are befriended by Ralph's clerk, Newman Noggs, an eccentric, kindly alcoholic, who has come down in the world and disapproves of his hard master. Nicholas becomes tutor to the daughters of one of Newman's neighbours, Mr. Kenwigs, a turner in ivory, who aspires to gentility.

Kate is unhappy at Madame Mantalini's establishment. Her youthful beauty has attracted the jealousy of Miss Knag, a senior assistant, and the attentions of the flamboyant Mr. Mantalini, to the annoyance of his wife. She is dismissed. Ralph tries to sell Kate as mistress to one of his noble clients, introducing her at a dinner party to Sir Mulberry Hawk and Lord Frederick Verisopht. Kate takes a situation as companion to the snobbish and hypochondriacal Mrs Wititterley.

Nicholas quarrels with Ralph and decides to turn his back on London. Travelling coastwards with Smike, he meets the actor-manager of the Theatre Royal, Portsmouth, Vincent Crummles, who persuades Nicholas to join his company as actor and dramatist, but Nicholas returns to London in response to a letter from Newman Noggs. He overhears a conversation between Hawk and Verisopht in which Kate's name is mentioned insultingly, and beats Hawk, injuring him seriously. Hawk later kills Verisopht in a duel, fought over Kate's reputation. Nicholas, his mother and Kate go to lodge with Miss La Creevy, a miniature-painter. In search of work at a registry office, Nicholas meets the elderly twin brothers

Cheeryble, a philanthropic pair who engage him as a clerk and place the Nickleby family in a rural cottage at Bow, at a low rent.

Nicholas calls upon the Kenwigses, his one-time employers, to break the news that his Portsmouth friend, the actress Henrietta Petowker, has married Mr. Lillyvick, uncle of Mrs. Kenwigs. The Kenwigs family had expectations from Lillyvick, and are devastated by the news.

Smike is recaptured in the street by Squeers and imprisoned at Squeers's lodging, from which he is rescued by John Browdie, who is honeymooning with Matilda in London. Squeers then conspires with Ralph to pass off a man named Snawley as Smike's long-lost father, but they are foiled by Nicholas and John.

Nicholas falls in love with Madeline Bray, daughter of an ailing debtor in the Rules of the King's Bench. Ralph Nickleby is planning to marry her off to Arthur Gride, an old money-lender who possesses a deed concerning some property due to Madeline. Madeline promises to marry Gride in return for the payment of her father's debts. But on the wedding morning Bray dies of heart failure and Nicholas takes Madeline home to Bow, where Mrs. Nickleby and Kate nurse her through an illness.

The Cheerybles discover that Madeline is heiress to a fortune. Nicholas finds this a barrier between himself and Madeline, just as Kate, proposed to by the Cheerybles' nephew Frank, refuses him because he is so much wealthier than herself. Smike, who has never recovered from the privations of Dotheboys Hall, dies, confessing at the last to Nicholas his hopeless love for Kate.

The old brothers sort out the financial difficulties of the two young couples, and they are married on the same day. A few weeks later the Cheerybles' old clerk, Tim Linkinwater, marries Miss La Creevy.

Ralph receives a terrible shock in the news that Smike was his own son, the result of a secret marriage. At the same time his plotting with Gride is brought to light. From remorse and rage that Nicholas, his hated nephew, has rescued and be-friended his son, and the desire to thwart his enemies, he hangs himself from a hook in the attic which had been one of Smike's only memories of childhood.

Squeers is transported. At Dotheboys Hall a riot breaks out at the news, and the school disbands in confusion.

SKETCHES OF YOUNG COUPLES

Eleven sketches of marital relationships, inspired by Queen Victoria's impending marriage, written in 1840 for publication as a book that year by Chapman & Hall: 'The Young Couple'; 'The Formal Couple'; 'The Loving Couple'; 'The Contradictory Couple'; 'The Couple Who Dote Upon Their Children'; 'The Cool Couple'; 'The Plausible Couple'; 'The Nice Little Couple'; 'The Egotistical Couple'; 'The Couple Who Coddle Themselves'; 'The Old Couple'.

MASTER HUMPHREY'S CLOCK

Written at 1 Devonshire Terrace, Marylebone, Broadstairs, Brighton and Windsor, it was published in 88 weekly numbers, beginning in April 1840, and ending in December 1841. Published in three single volumes by Chapman & Hall on 15 October 1840, 12/15 April 1841, and 15 December 1841. First American publication simultaneously with British edition by Lea & Blanchard, Philadelphia, in monthly parts.

Dickens designed *Master Humphrey's Clock* as a work on original lines: 'the best general idea of the plan of the work might be given perhaps by reference to the *Tatler*, the *Spectator*, and Goldsmith's *Bee*; but it would be far more popular both in the subjects of which it treats and its mode of treating them.' The work was to introduce a little club or knot of characters whose stories were to run throughout, to reintroduce Pickwick and Sam Weller, and to contain humorous essays and contemporary comments, satires on administration in imaginary countries, and papers on old London.

In fact, the plan proved unsatisfactory. The story of *The Old Curiosity Shop*, at first intended to be merely an episode, took over Dickens's imagination and became a full-length novel serialised within the *Master Humphrey* frame. *Barnaby Rudge* followed later, and at the conclusion of it *Master Humphrey* was abandoned.

The linked tales of Master Humphrey, a crippled old man who addresses his readers from the chimney-corner beside his beloved grandfather clock, are supposedly derived from 'a pile of dusty papers' stored in the clock itself. They include stories told to Joe Toddyhigh in the Guildhall by the giants Gog and Magog, Jack Redburn's tale of a murderer's confession, the story of John Podgers told by Mr. Pickwick, an anecdote of Bill Binder, told by Sam Weller, Tony Weller's account of his grandson, the hairdresser's story, another of Sam's tales, and miscellaneous anecdotes.

THE OLD CURIOSITY SHOP

Dickens's fourth novel. Begun in March 1840, finished in January 1841, and written at 1 Devonshire Terrace, Marylebone, and at Broadstairs. Published in *Master Humphrey's Clock*, 25 April 1840 to 6 February 1841, and as a single volume on 15 December 1841. First American publication simultaneously with British publication, in monthly parts, by Lea & Blanchard, Philadelphia.

Dickens's first idea was that it should be a 'little child-story' to be included among the 'Personal Adventures of Master Humphrey', and an early form of the title was *The Curiosity Dealer and the Child*. It was to have finished the *Master Humphrey* sequence of stories, but grew in importance until it became a full-length novel which, with *Barnaby Rudge*, dwarfed the other stories into mere anecdotes. Forster says that it was conceived 'with less direct consciousness of design on his own part than I can remember in any other instance throughout his career,' and that it was, in his opinion, 'a story which was to add largely to his popularity, more than any other of his works to make the bond between himself and his readers one of personal attachment.'

The character of Little Nell took hold of the public's imagination as none of Dickens's creations had yet done, and

obsessed the author. 'All night I have been pursued by the child,' he wrote, 'and this morning I am unrefreshed and miserable.' His final killing-off of Nell (who was probably an idealised version of Mary Hogarth) reduced him to tears and drew protests from his distressed public.

Master Humphrey begins as the narrator of the story, but fades out after chapter 3. He is walking at dusk in Covent Garden when a child asks him the way to her home. He leads her there, and finds that she is Nelly Trent, who keeps house for her grandfather, the keeper of an old curiosity shop. Nell's profligate brother, Fred, is jealous of her closeness to their grandfather and fears that she may inherit all his money, in spite of the old man's repeated assurances that he is poor. Fred plans to marry Nelly to his dissipated friend, Dick Swiveller, so that he may share in the fortune.

The old man is, in fact, a compulsive gambler whose obsessional desire it is to win a fortune for Nell. By borrowing money he falls into the clutches of the sinister dwarf, Daniel Quilp, who lives on Tower Hill with his pretty young wife and inimical mother-in-law, Mrs. Jiniwin. Quilp's legal adviser is Sampson Brass, a shady lawyer who shares his practice in Bevis Marks with his hard-favoured sister Sally. Quilp persuades the ailing old man that his shop-boy, Kit Nubbles, whom Quilp hates, had been spying on him, to reveal his gambling habits, and Kit is summarily dismissed, to his distress, for he is devoted to Nell. The old man's furniture and possessions are sold up by Quilp to regain the money borrowed from him. Terrified of Quilp and Brass, and on the verge of senility since his recent illness, He persuades Nelly to leave the house secretly with him by night and go as far away as they can from Quilp.

Their long journey from London into the Midlands forms the main thread of the story. They meet two travelling showmen, Codlin and Short, and for a time accompany them and their Punch and Judy show, but begin to sense that Codlin suspects there may be a reward offered for the revelations of their whereabouts. The old man and the child move on.

Their next encounter is with Mrs. Jarley and her travelling waxworks show. She takes a fancy to Nell, and trains her to deliver little lectures on the waxworks to the public. Grandfather's gambling mania once again overcomes him; he falls into the hands of card-sharpers, and steals money from Nell. To save him, she makes him resume their wanderings.

The journey now becomes rougher and more exhausting. They travel part of the way along a canal in a barge, with drunken bargees. They arrive at an industrial town in the Midlands, where an eccentric furnace-keeper takes pity on them and lets them sleep on warm ashes by the furnace. As they wander on through the Black Country Nell feels the effects of their privations, but remains brave and cheerful, guiding her grandfather through ugly scenes, including a Chartist riot. By now they are at the point of starvation. Suddenly they encounter an old friend – a schoolmaster whom they met earlier in their travels, who had then lost a favourite pupil by death, and welcomed Nell as a replacement for him. He takes them to a village where he has been appointed clerk and schoolmaster, and establishes them in a peaceful home, a curious little house near the ancient church.

In London, Quilp is trying to track down the pair, as is (for benevolent reasons) the brother of the old man, who has, without revealing his name, taken a lodging at Sampson Brass's house. Also at Brass's is Dick Swiveller, employed as a clerk. He is highly suspicious of Sampson's and Sally's activities with Quilp. He befriends the twelve-year-old servant of the Brasses, a down-trodden drudge whom he calls 'The Marchioness' and introduces to the pleasures of beer, bread, and cribbage. (The little girl is, in fact, the illegitimate child of Quilp and Sally, but Dickens merely hints at this.) The lodger gets to know Kit Nubbles, and through him finds a clue to Nell's whereabouts. Kit is now employed by Mr. and Mrs. Garland at Finchley, where he is becoming enamoured of their pretty young maid,

Barbara, and is able to support his widowed mother and small brothers. Quilp still hates him, and through Brass fakes a theft-charge against him and has him imprisoned. Dick Swiveller gives evidence on Kit's behalf and looks after the boy's distressed mother, for which Brass dismisses him. Dick is taken suddenly and seriously ill, and remains in danger and delirium for three weeks before returning to consciousness to find that the Marchioness has established herself in his lodgings and has nursed him through his fever. In gratitude and affection he promises to bring her up and educate her, for an aunt has died and left him a comfortable annuity.

Quilp, who has already teased his wife and mother-in-law by pretending to be dead, dies in reality while flying from justice; for the Marchioness has overheard the plotting of Brass, Sally, and Quilp to incriminate Kit, and Brass has been arrested. Quilp is drowned in the marshes near his riverside lair.

Nell's great-uncle and Kit follow up the clues they have obtained, and with Mr. Garland arrive at the village where Nell and her grandfather have been staying – but they are too late. Nell's health has been declining steadily, and just before they arrive she has died, peacefully and happily. Her grandfather, driven crazy with sorrow, cannot believe in her death, and is unable to recognise his brother. Shortly afterwards he dies on her grave.

Sampson Brass is struck off the Rolls, and finishes up a convict. Sally sinks into poverty and oblivion. Quilp's widow marries again. The Marchioness's education proceeds so well that when she is nineteen, 'good-looking, clever, and good-humoured', Dick marries her. Because of her mysterious origins he has given her the name of Sophronia Sphynx. Kit marries Barbara, and Nell's great-uncle travels in the steps of the two dead wanderers, rewarding those who had been kind to them.

BARNABY RUDGE
A Tale of the Riots of 'Eighty

Dickens's fifth novel. Begun at 48 Doughty Street in January 1839, and finished at

Windsor in November 1841. The novel was commissioned by the publisher Richard Bentley, to follow *Oliver Twist* in *Bentley's Miscellany*. In May 1840 the contract was transferred to Chapman & Hall. The first number was published in *Master Humphrey's Clock* in February 1841, the last in November 1841. Published in book form in December, with illustrations by 'Phiz' and others. First American publication 1841–2 in monthly parts by Lea & Blanchard, Philadelphia.

This was Dickens's first historical novel, the only other being *A Tale of Two Cities*. Intended to centre on the anti-Catholic riots instigated by Lord George Gordon in 1780, and to show the brutality of the capital punishment system of the time, the book was largely taken over by its lighter characters, Grip the raven (based on Dickens's own pet bird), the Varden family, and the two Willets. Gordon and the riots are dutifully dealt with, but other scenes remain more vividly in the reader's mind.

On a March night of 1775, at the Maypole Inn, Chigwell, Essex, a story is told by Solomon Daisy, parish clerk and bell-ringer, of the events of twenty-two years earlier, to the very night. Reuben Haredale, owner of The Warren, the local manor-house, had been found murdered in his bedroom, with a cash-box missing. The steward, Rudge, and the gardener were not to be found, but later in the year the body of Rudge was discovered, with a knife-wound in the breast. The corpse was recognisable only by its clothes and belongings.

The day after the murder a child was born to Mrs. Rudge. This is Barnaby Rudge, who has grown up a gentle, slightly dim-witted boy, whose imagination is as fantastic as his appearance. His companion and confidant is a talking raven, Grip. His mother is menaced and shadowed by a mysterious stranger, who has heard the story told at the Maypole, and on the same night has committed a highway robbery, wounding and taking the purse of Edward Chester, a young gentleman in love with Emma Haredale,

niece of the murdered man. Edward is rescued by Gabriel Varden, a Clerkenwell locksmith.

Edward's father, John Chester, is the lifelong enemy of Geoffrey Haredale, Emma's uncle and brother to the murdered man. Chester, 'a man without heart and without principle', wishes Edward to marry a rich heiress, and opposes the Haredale match, as does Geoffrey Haredale. Apart from his hatred of Chester, Haredale is a Roman Catholic, and does not wish his niece to marry a Protestant.

We are introduced at length to the Varden household. Bluff, cheerful Gabriel has a wife whose sole interest in life seems to be the Protestant Manual, a tome which she reads constantly. It is her disposition to be jolly when other people are miserable, and miserable when other people are jolly, and she is supported in this as in all things by her maid, the vinegary spinster Miggs. Dolly, the Vardens' only child, is a pretty coquette, much eyed by Gabriel's apprentice, Sim Tappertit, a conceited youth with revolutionary notions. But Dolly is being seriously courted by Joe Willet, son of the landlord at the Maypole. Dolly's father approves of Joe, but her mother affects to disdain him, and Chester, for his own purposes, succeeds in coming between the two young people. Joe decides to join the army, and comes to say goodbye to Dolly, who pretends to be unaffected by the parting. After Joe has left for America, Dolly becomes companion to Emma Haredale, whose friend she has been from childhood.

Five years pass. Lord George Gordon, the Protestant fanatic, begins his 'No Popery' movement and incites a mob to riot in London. The Rudges are now in London, where Mrs. Rudge hopes to hide from her persecutor. Barnaby and Hugh, the wild, gipsy-like ostler of The Maypole, join the rioters. The mob surges out to Chigwell, and The Warren is burnt because the Haredales are Catholics. Emma and Dolly are kidnapped, taken to London, and kept as prisoners. Hugh and Sim Tappertit both covet Dolly, and Gashford, Lord George's secretary, has designs on Emma. Dennis, the hangman of Newgate, and Stagg, a blind man, are also concerned in the affair.

Barnaby is captured and imprisoned in Newgate. He is joined there by a man who proves to be his own father, Rudge, who twenty-eight years before had murdered Reuben Haredale and his gardener, and has since been in hiding, sometimes supplied with money by his wife. The rioters break into Newgate and release the prisoners. Barnaby and his father are recaptured and sentenced to death. Meanwhile, Emma and Dolly have been rescued by Geoffrey Haredale, Edward Chester, and Joe Willet – Joe less one arm, lost while fighting in the Savannahs.

Barnaby is pardoned, by the intercession of Gabriel Varden, but his father is hanged, as are Maypole Hugh and Dennis, the hangman of Newgate, who has been one of the rioters and has constantly gloated over the prospect of hanging others. John Chester (now knighted) discovers that Hugh was his bastard son. Chester and Haredale fight a duel: Chester is killed and Haredale goes abroad.

Dolly tells Joe that she repents the foolish pride which kept her from telling him that she loved him, five years before. They marry, and Joe takes over the Maypole, which has been pillaged by the rioters. The shock has left old Willet in a state of stupefaction, in which he remains for the rest of his life.

Emma and Edward marry and go to the West Indies. Barnaby and his mother go to live on the farm of the Maypole, and Barnaby's wits improve in these happy conditions. Miggs, disappointed that the now reformed Mrs. Varden no longer requires her services, becomes a female turnkey at Bridewell. Sim Tappertit's pride and glory, his legs, were crushed in the riots; he becomes a shoe-black, and marries the widow of a rag-and-bone merchant.

THE LAMPLIGHTER'S STORY

First published in 1841 in *The Pic Nic Papers*, a work in three volumes edited by Dickens and illustrated by George Cruikshank and 'Phiz' for the benefit of the widow and children of John Macrone, publisher of *Sketches by Boz*. The story was adapted from an unacted farce by Dickens, *The Lamplighter*.

Tom Grig, a lamplighter, is persuaded by an eccentric astrologer that he is destined to marry the old man's niece. Mooney, another scientist, predicts that Tom will die in two months' time, and the lamplighter resigns himself to the marriage. Just in time, a mistake is found in the calculations and it emerges that Tom will live to a ripe old age. He refuses the niece and the astrologer takes a mystical revenge.

AMERICAN NOTES
for General Circulation

Written mainly at Broadstairs between August and October 1842. Published in October 1842 in two volumes by Chapman & Hall. First publication in America 1842, by Wilson & Co., New York, as an extra number of *Brother Jonathan*.

The outcome of Dickens's visit to America in the first half of 1842, the *Notes* were based largely on the letters written by him to John Forster describing his American experiences. In the Preface he claimed that they were 'a record of the impressions I received from day to day ... and sometimes (but not always) of the conclusions to which they, and after-reflection on them, have led me.' He proposed to tell the truth, at the risk of offending persons who thought their country perfect, while acknowledging the hospitality he had received in America and the friends he had made.

Four editions were sold in England before the end of the year, but feeling in America ran high at Dickens's adverse comments on such matters as prison systems, the prevalence of pigs on Broadway, the corruption of the House of Representatives, and the universal habit of spitting. His views on international copyright had been highly unpopular, and his opinions on slavery even more so. In *American Notes* he reinforced them by the reproduction of actual advertisements, gruesome to a degree, about missing slaves.

THE LIFE AND ADVENTURES OF MARTIN CHUZZLEWIT

Dickens's sixth novel. Begun December 1842 or early January 1843, at Devonshire Terrace, London; written there and at Broadstairs; finished June 1844. Commissioned by Chapman & Hall after the termination of *Master Humphrey's Clock*, the first number was published in January 1843, the last in July 1844. Published in one volume, July 1844, by Chapman & Hall. First American publication 1844 (Harper & Bros., New York) in seven parts.

Dickens first conceived this as *The Life and Adventures of Martin Chuzzlewig, his family, friends and enemies. Comprising all his wills and his ways. With an historical record of what he did and what he didn't. The whole forming a complete key to the house of Chuzzlewig.* It was to have opened in Cornwall, which Dickens had just visited. Title, setting, and scheme for the book changed as Dickens was taken over by the character of Pecksniff from the moment he appeared in chapter 2. Forster says that 'the notion of taking Pecksniff for a type of character was really the origin of the book; the design being to show, more or less by every person introduced, the number and variety of humours and vices that have their root in selfishness.' In November 1843 Dickens wrote to Forster that 'I think *Chuzzlewit* in a hundred points immeasurably the best of my stories.' Early sales were disappointing, but later they became next to those of *Pickwick* and *Copperfield*. The American scenes, the fruit of his visit in 1842, provoked considerable anger and criticism across the Atlantic: 'made them all stark staring raving mad across the water,' said Dickens.

The novel's popularity rests largely on the more-than-lifesize figures of Pecksniff and Sairey Gamp, the Chuzzlewit interest being comparatively pale.

The story begins at the house of Mr. Pecksniff, a Salisbury architect. His monumental hypocrisy is revealed to the reader at once. His moralising is admired and echoed by his daughters, Charity and Mercy, playfully known as Cherry and Merry. Charity, the elder, is plain and vinegary; Mercy, a pretty frivolous giggler. Both are on the look-out for husbands, possibly from the ranks of their father's apprentices, who in fact are responsible for all the designs for which he takes the credit.

One, John Westlock, has been dismissed for speaking his mind. Still with Pecksniff, and blindly devoted to him, is Tom Pinch, a simple, young-old creature. A new apprentice is expected – young Martin Chuzzlewit. Martin is the grandson of another Martin, rich and eccentric, at this time lying ill in the local inn, the Blue Dragon, with the orphaned Mary Graham as his companion. Mary and young Martin are in love, to the displeasure of old Martin, who wanted to bring the match about his own way, and feels thwarted that his grandson has taken the initiative. Tom Pinch, seeing Mary in the church, falls in love with her.

Mr. Pecksniff takes his daughters to London, to stay at Mrs. Todgers's boarding-house. They encounter old Martin and his cousin, Anthony Chuzzlewit, and Anthony's son Jonas, a cold-hearted villain. At Todgers's, Merry is a great success with the gentlemen boarders. Jonas makes overtures to both sisters, raising Cherry's matrimonial hopes. Old Martin asks Pecksniff to dismiss his grandson, telling him of the young man's forbidden engagement to Mary. Pecksniff, hoping to profit by old Martin's wealth, agrees. When they return to Salisbury, Martin is dismissed summarily. He decides to emigrate to America, a country which must be in need of young architects, and takes with him Mark Tapley, the cheerful ostler of the Blue Dragon. Mark is an optimist who feels that his life is altogether too comfortable at the Dragon, and wants to experience circumstances in which his ability to be 'jolly' will be severely tested. When Martin leaves, Tom Pinch gives him his last half-sovereign and Mary sends him her diamond ring. He pays no particular regard to either present.

Anthony Chuzzlewit dies, in circumstances suggesting poison. Jonas, to Cherry's fury, proposes to Merry, who accepts him in a spirit of wilful coquetry. Jonas becomes a director of the Anglo-Bengalee Disinterested Loan and Life Insurance Company, a swindle organised and run by one Tigg Montague, alias Montague Tigg, a sharper. Tigg sees possibilities of blackmail in Jonas, and unearths details which suggest that Jonas has killed his father by poison. Jonas, who has by this time turned the laughing Merry into a bullied, beaten wife, is fear-ridden.

Pecksniff has now apparently ingratiated himself with old Martin, who, with Mary, is living in his house. But when Pecksniff makes advances to Mary she turns for help to Tom Pinch, and for the first time Tom sees his master clearly. Pecksniff accuses Tom of having made improper proposals to Mary himself, and dismisses him. Tom goes to London, renews acquaintance with John Westlock, removes his sister Ruth from a disagreeable situation as governess, and settles with her in an Islington lodging.

Meanwhile Mrs. Sairey Gamp, nurse and midwife, has entered the story. Lewsome, a doctor's assistant who has sold poison to Jonas, falls seriously ill and is nursed by Mrs. Gamp and her friend Betsey Prig, who annoys her greatly by casting doubts upon the existence of Sairey's much-quoted friend Mrs. Harris.

In America, young Martin finds that the rosy picture he had had of the place was a false one. At first welcomed into New York society, he is coldly treated when he admits that he travelled over as a steerage passenger. The 'thriving city' of Eden, for which he had hoped to design fine municipal buildings, is no more than a fever-ridden swamp. He becomes seriously ill, and Mark, having nursed him for weeks, falls ill himself. Martin's selfishness begins to leave him under the influence of Mark's devotion. They return to England, and see the laying of the corner-stone of a new building, with Pecksniff, the supposed architect, present. Martin recognises the design for one of his own. They go to call on Tom and Ruth Pinch in Islington, and hear how Tom has been given a situation

as secretary and librarian by a mysterious employer. They visit Salisbury, where Martin tries to see his grandfather, but is foiled by Pecksniff.

Jonas, still hounded by Tigg, who has set Nadgett, a private detective, to watch him, travels to Wiltshire, leaving Merry to cover up for him during his absence. He waylays Tigg, murders him, and buries him in a wood. Back in London, he is visited by old Martin, John Westlock, Mark Tapley, and the now recovered Lewsome. Lewsome accuses Jonas of the murder of his father; but Anthony Chuzzlewit's old clerk, Chuffey, reveals that he discovered Jonas's intentions, and that Anthony died of a broken heart on learning the truth of his son's wickedness.

Jonas, relieved, orders them all out; but Nadgett appears with a band of officers and arrests him for the murder of Tigg. The chief officer is Chevy Slyme, a relative of the Chuzzlewits and a friend of Tigg. Jonas tries to bribe him for time in which to commit suicide. Slyme refuses, but Jonas manages to poison himself in the coach on the way to gaol.

The story ends happily for most parties. Young Martin's selfishness is cured, as well as old Martin's pride: 'the curse of our house has been the love of self,' he says. The two are reconciled, and Martin is openly betrothed to Mary. John Westlock and Ruth Pinch follow their example, as do Mark and Mrs. Lupin, the widowed landlady of the Blue Dragon. Cherry Pecksniff is less fortunate. At the point of marriage to her, Augustus Moddle, a young gentleman of Todgers's, finds he cannot face it, for he was desperately in love with her sister; and he leaves her on the wedding morning.

Pecksniff is exposed and struck down by old Martin. He deteriorates into a 'drunken, squalid, begging-letter-writing man', with his shrewish daughter beside him. Old Martin (who is revealed to have been Tom's mysterious employer) takes Merry under his wing. Tom Pinch goes to live with Ruth and John after their marriage, remaining a life-long bachelor who is a particular favourite with Mary's small daughter.

CHRISTMAS BOOKS

Five of Dickens's long stories with a Christmas theme, collected in one volume in 1852. The *Christmas Books* were reprinted in so many forms in the U.S.A. that it is impossible to ascribe all the first publications. 'A Christmas Carol' was first published by Carey & Hart, Philadelphia, in 1844, and 'The Chimes' by Lea & Blanchard, Philadelphia, in 1845.

Dickens stated in the Preface, 'My purpose was, in a whimsical kind of masque, which the good humour of the season justified, to awaken some loving and forbearing thoughts, never out of season in a Christian land.' 'A Christmas Carol' has always been the most popular of the *Christmas Books*, followed by 'The Cricket on the Hearth' and 'The Chimes'. 'The Haunted Man' and 'The Battle of Life' are generally considered to be inferior to his normal standards. Of 'The Battle of Life' *Tait's Edinburgh Magazine* for January 1847 said: 'If Mr. Dickens really believes that a modest and discreet young lady could leave a ballroom on a winter night; make off with the greatest rake in the parish . . .': then follows a string of improbabilities in the plot, concluding with the reviewer's observation that he has nothing to say to any credulous readers 'except that the engravings of the volume are well executed'.

A CHRISTMAS CAROL
IN PROSE
BEING
A Ghost Story of Christmas

Begun in October 1843, written at Devonshire Terrace, London, and finished before the end of November. It was published in December in one volume by Chapman & Hall, with eight illustrations by John Leech.

Ebenezer Scrooge, a curmudgeonly miser, survivor of the partnership of Scrooge and Marley, spends a surly Christmas Eve reviling the institution of Christmas and all its merriment. That night he is visited by the ghost of his old partner, Marley, who tells him that three Spirits will visit him in turn so that he

may have the chance of escaping Marley's own fate, to wander round the world in chains. The Spirits of Christmas Past, Christmas Present, and Christmas Yet to Come duly visit Scrooge, showing him the happiness he might have enjoyed, the happiness poor folk such as his own clerk Bob Cratchit do enjoy at Christmas, and what the future will be unless he mends his ways. He awakes a reformed character on Christmas morning.

THE CHIMES
A Goblin Story
OF SOME BELLS
THAT RANG AN OLD YEAR OUT
AND A NEW YEAR IN

First published in one volume in December 1844 by Chapman & Hall, with illustrations by Maclise, Leech, Doyle, and Stanfield. One of Dickens's own favourites, it was designed as 'a plea for the poor'. It was written in 1844 at the Palazzo Peschiere, Genoa, in October and the beginning of November.

Toby Veck, a poor ticket-porter, whose daughter Meg is engaged to marry Richard, a young blacksmith, falls asleep on New Year's Eve while reading a newspaper, and dreams that the chimes in the church bell-tower above him summon him to join them. They blame him for his own shortcomings, and show him what man's callousness, pride, and hypocrisy can do to poor people such as himself. He sees the little niece of a Chartist, Lilian Fern, turn prostitute through poverty, and his own daughter prepare to drown herself and her baby in her despair. He awakes to find morning and the New Year Bells ringing a message of hope.

THE CRICKET ON THE HEARTH
A Fairy Tale of Home

Written in October 1845 and first published in one volume in December, by Bradbury & Evans, with illustrations by Maclise, Stanfield, Landseer, Doyle, and Leech. Its sales at first were double those of 'A Christmas Carol' and 'The Chimes': Dickens had succeeded in his design to 'put everybody in a good temper, and make such a dash at people's fenders and arm-chairs as hasn't been made for many a long day.'

John Peerybingle, the slow, sturdy carrier, is much older than his little wife Dot, but she is devoted to him. She has 'a very doll' of a baby tended by the nurse Tilly Slowboy. Their neighbours are Caleb Plummer, a poor toymaker, and his blind daughter Bertha, whom he has amiably deceived in letting her think that they are rich, and that their ill-tempered landlord and employer, Tackleton, is a model of charm. Another neighbour is May Fielding, forced by her snobbish mother into an engagement to Tackleton, though her heart is with Caleb's son Edward, long vanished overseas. A deaf old stranger arrives and misunderstandings ensue when Dot is seen alone with him, minus his white wig; but the Cricket on the Hearth, the little household god, reassures John that Dot is faithful and all will be well. The disguised man is Edward Plummer; he and May are reunited, Bertha is happy to know the truth at last, and all ends with a dance.

THE BATTLE OF LIFE
A Love Story

Written in Lausanne, Switzerland, in September–October 1846. Published in one volume in December 1846, with illustrations by Maclise, Stanfield, Doyle, and Leech.

Doctor Jeddler, a philosopher, has two daughters, Marion and Grace. He regards life as a great joke. On the eve of her wedding to Alfred Heathfield, the Doctor's ward Marion runs away, supposedly with a spendthrift young man, Michael Warden. When she has been gone some time her sister Grace marries Alfred. Marion returns, and reveals that she ran away because she knew that Grace loved Alfred, and sacrificed her own happiness for her sister's. But she has not been with Warden, having spent the intervening years with an aunt in the country. There is a sub-plot concerning the servant Clemency Newcome and her future husband Benjamin Britain.

THE HAUNTED MAN
AND
THE GHOST'S BARGAIN
A fancy for Christmas Time

Begun at Broadstairs in the autumn of 1847 and completed at Brighton in the winter of 1848. Published by Bradbury & Evans in December 1848. Illustrated by Stanfield, Tenniel, Frank Stone and Leech.

Redlaw, a chemist and lecturer, lives at an ancient institution for students. One night he is brooding over the past when the Swidgers, who keep the Lodge, enter to decorate his room for Christmas. They point out a brighter side of life to him. When they depart he is visited by an awful ghostly likeness of himself. It offers him the power to forget his sorrows without cancelling his knowledge and mental powers; and the power also to communicate this to others. He does so, with shocking results, depriving those he meets of their past. At last he prays the phantom to return; it does so, accompanied by the shade of Milly Swidger, a great influence for good, who tells him that it is a good thing to remember wrong 'that we may forgive it'.

PICTURES FROM ITALY

Written from December 1845 to February 1846 at 1 Devonshire Terrace, London. First published in the *Daily News*, January to March 1846, with the title *Travelling Letters written on the Road*. Originally illustrated by Samuel Palmer. Published, with five additional chapters, by Bradbury & Evans 'for the Author' in 1846 as *Pictures from Italy*. First American publication 1846, under the title *Travelling Letters written on the Road*, by Wiley & Putnam, New York. Issued later as *Pictures from Italy* in Wiley & Putnam's Library of Choice Reading.

Dickens's impressions of his Italian tour of 1844–5, largely based on letters written home to John Forster. Full of enjoyment and considerably less critical of Italian institutions than he had been of American ones, Dickens deals many swingeing blows at the Catholicism he found everywhere; as when, touring the Vatican, he remarks, 'I freely acknowledge that when I see a Jolly Young Waterman representing a cherubim (sic) or a Barclay and Perkins's drayman depicted as an Evangelist, I see nothing to commend or admire in the performance.'

Places visited include Rome, Naples, Carrara, Pisa, Florence, and Genoa.

Dealings with the Firm
of
DOMBEY AND SON,
Wholesale, Retail and for Exportation

Dickens's seventh novel, begun on 27 June 1846 at the Villa Rosemont, Lausanne, and continued in London, Paris, and Broadstairs. Completed in March 1848. First published in monthly numbers, October 1846 to April 1848. Issued complete by Bradbury & Evans, 1848. Illustrated by 'Phiz'. First American publication begun in parts in 1846 by Wiley & Putnam, New York, seventeen parts bearing their imprint, and the last two, in 1848, that of John Wiley.

Dickens's first notion was that *Dombey* was to do with pride what its predecessor, *Chuzzlewit*, had done with selfishness; but, says his biographer, John Forster, 'this limit he soon overpassed'. As the characters took over the thesis slipped behind. After writing the first four chapters, Dickens told Forster 'I design to show Mr. Dombey with that one idea of the Son taking firmer and firmer possession of him, and swelling and bloating his pride to a prodigious extent.' His professed plan for the book seems to have worked out almost precisely, except that he originally thought it a good idea to ruin the career of Walter Gay 'to show how the good turns into bad by degrees'. He was persuaded to reserve Walter for a happier future. He was particularly nervous that Dombey might be caricatured in the illustrations, and tried hard to get 'Phiz', the artist, to meet Dombey's living physical prototype, an unidentifiable 'Mr. A.'

Though he had decided from the first to 'slaughter' little Paul, in order to bring about the later workings of the plot, the actual death harrowed Dickens as the deaths of his child-angels usually did. 'There was but one small chapter more to write,' says Forster, 'in which he and his little friend were to part company for ever; and the greater part of the night of the day on which it was written, Thursday the 14th, he was wandering desolate and sad about the streets of Paris.' Dickens's readers were similarly affected, Lord Jeffrey writing to him from Edinburgh 'I have so cried and sobbed over it last night, and again this morning.'

The first number of *Dombey* outstripped the sale of the first *Chuzzlewit* by more than twelve thousand copies, and it continued to sell in large numbers.

Paul Dombey, senior, is the proud, stiff-necked head of a large London mercantile firm. He is gratified when his meek wife presents him with a son, Paul, six years after the birth of their only other child, Florence. Mrs. Dombey dies, unable to obey the advice of her brisk sister-in-law Mrs. Chick to Make an Effort. Dombey dedicates himself to the upbringing of little Paul as inheritor of and partner in the firm. A wet-nurse is hired, Polly Toodle, wife of a railway employee in Camden Town. Her maternal influence upon the orphaned children is a good one; sensing Florence's loneliness, she brings the child as much into contact with her baby brother as possible. Dombey insists that Polly be known as Richards, and that while in his employ she shall be separated from her own five children and her husband. But seeing the beneficial effect of Polly's nursing on Paul, he condescends to find her eldest son Robin, known as Biler, a place in the Charitable Grinders' school.

Paul is christened, his godmother being Miss Lucretia Tox, a timid, genteel spinster who hopes to capture her neighbour Major Joey Bagstock as a husband.

Polly and Florence's sharp-tongued maid, Susan Nipper, take Florence and Paul to Camden Town for an outing, as Polly is suffering from separation from her family. Returning home, the party is scattered by an alarm of 'Mad Bull!' and Florence, lost in the streets, is captured by an evil old woman calling herself Good Mrs. Brown, who robs her of her clothes and sends her out in rags. Florence wanders the City in search of her father's business premises, and is rescued by Walter Gay, a boy employed by Dombey's. Walter is struck by her childish beauty. He restores her to her father, who thanks him coldly. Polly is dismissed for taking Paul into the contaminating airs and society of Camden Town.

Miss Tox begins to hope that Dombey, in his solitary condition, will consider her as his second wife.

Paul has never recovered from the loss of Polly in infancy, and at five is a delicate child. He is sent with Florence to Brighton, where they lodge with the formidable Mrs. Pipchin.

Walter Gay, now a young man, lives with his uncle, Solomon Gills, a ships' instrument dealer, whose shop is known as the Wooden Midshipman from the wooden effigy above the door. His great friend is Captain Ned Cuttle, a one-handed retired seaman lodging with the widowed Mrs. MacStinger, who keeps a matrimonial eye upon him, as Miss Tox does upon Mr. Dombey. Sol Gills gets into debt and has his stock seized by a broker; Walter and Captain Cuttle seek a loan from Dombey, and receive it, Dombey pointing out to Paul how good it is to be rich and to be able to bestow charity. Paul is sent to school at Dr. Blimber's, a forcing-house where he is the youngest boy and the pet of the staff and his fellow-pupils. His particular friend is Mr. Toots, the eldest pupil, a young gentleman whose mental powers have become somewhat atrophied by over-study. Toots becomes the adorer of Florence. Paul is unable to cope with the arduous lessons imposed on him, becomes more and more frail, and faints at an end-of-term party. He is taken home to London.

Meanwhile the Carker brothers have appeared in the story. John is a junior clerk at Dombey's, who once robbed the firm, escaped dismissal, but was demoted to a minor post. James Carker, Dombey's manager, is a smiling villain who hates his brother and is secretly contemptuous of

Dombey. Anxious to get Walter Gay out of his way, he finds him a position in Barbados. Before sailing in the *Son and Heir* Walter is summoned to Paul's bedside, where he is joined by Polly Toodle and Florence. Paul dies in Florence's arms. Walter and Florence take an affectionate leave of each other and Walter sails for Barbados.

Dombey, broken by the death of his son, becomes more and more cold and indifferent towards Florence. She leads a lonely life, her only companions Susan Nipper and Diogenes, a dog Paul was fond of at Blimber's, brought to her by Toots.

Dombey goes to Leamington with Major Bagstock, who introduces him to Edith Granger, a beautiful young widow who matches him in coldness. She is accompanied by her vain, coquettish old mother, 'Cleopatra' Skewton, who urges Edith to accept the proposal from Dombey which is certainly imminent. Edith does so, cold-bloodedly bartering her beauty and accomplishments for wealth and position. Miss Tox is devastated by Dombey's marriage. An affectionate friendship springs up between Edith and Florence, discouraged by Dombey, who goads Edith in vain to neglect the girl as he does.

The *Son and Heir* is missing. Sol Gills disappears from his shop, gone to seek news of his nephew. Captain Cuttle furtively leaves Mrs. MacStinger's, and moves into the Wooden Midshipman to take charge in his friend's absence. He is hampered by the presence of Rob Toodle, whom James Carker has set as a spy upon Sol Gills. Mrs. MacStinger discovers Captain Cuttle, but is pacified by his friend Jack Bunsby, whom she ultimately marries.

'Good Mrs. Brown' reappears on the scene. She had told an ominous fortune for Edith before her marriage. She proves to be the mother of Alice Brown, or Marwood, a handsome woman of Edith's type who returns home after years as a convict. Alice is the cast-off mistress of James Carker; befriended by James's sister Harriet and his brother John, she throws their charity in their faces with curses. Alice and her mother keep a close watch on James.

James Carker and Edith elope. Through the spying of Mrs. Brown and Rob, Dombey discovers that they have fled to Dijon. Florence attempts to console him, but he strikes her down with an angry blow. She rushes from the house and takes refuge with Captain Cuttle, who cares for her tenderly. He seems in a strangely disturbed state of mind, and throws out a series of hints leading to the telling of a story about a lost ship from which one passenger was saved: Walter appears at the door, and she flies into his arms, to the joy of Captain Cuttle.

In Dijon, Edith is alone at the hotel. Carker appears; she rejects his advances, telling him that she has eloped with him to be revenged upon him and her husband for the insults they have put upon her. Dombey arrives, Edith escapes, and Carker flies. Dombey pursues him back to England, catches up with him at a country railway station, and sees him cut to pieces by a train in an attempt to avoid his pursuer.

Sol Gills returns to the Midshipman in time for the wedding of Florence and Walter, who then go abroad. Toots is consoled by Susan Nipper, and marries her. The House of Dombey fails. Dombey, a lonely, broken man, sits in his darkened house and meditates suicide. He is saved by the sudden appearance of Florence, returned from abroad, to offer him the love he once rejected and to tell him that she has a son – another Paul. At last her father's reserve is broken. He allows Florence to take him home with her, and spends the rest of his life in quiet happiness with Florence and her family.

THE PERSONAL HISTORY OF DAVID COPPERFIELD

Dickens's eighth novel. Begun at Devonshire Terrace, London, in February 1849, continued at Bonchurch, Isle of Wight, and Broadstairs, and completed at Devonshire Terrace in October 1850. It was the last of his books to be written there. First number published May 1849, last number November 1850. A dinner in honour of it was given at the Star and Garter, Richmond, in June 1850. Published by Bradbury & Evans. First published as a single volume, November 1850. First published in America 1849–50 (Lea & Blanchard, Philadelphia) in twenty parts.

'Whether I shall turn out to be the hero of my own life, or whether that station will be held by anybody else, these pages must show.' The opening words of the novel are indicative of its autobiographical quality. Dickens had at one time contemplated an autobiography, but chose instead to incorporate much of himself in fictional form.

John Forster is careful to state in his biography that 'too much has been assumed ... of the full identity of Dickens with his hero'; but certainly a good deal of Dickens's character and experience went into the book. In it he was able to write out of his heart the bitterness of his childhood servitude in the blacking warehouse, only slightly disguised, and his youthful adoration for Maria Beadnell, here presented as Dora. Dora's unsatisfactoriness as a housekeeper, and Agnes's efficient perfection, are probably an allegory of Dickens's irritation with his wife, and his admiration of her sister, Georgina Hogarth. His own career as law reporter and successful writer is faithfully reproduced. 'The story carried him along,' says Forster. The strength of the author's feeling and his close self-identification with the narrator make *Copperfield* the least involved and most convincing of his novels. There are fewer caricatures than in previous books: the character of Micawber, over which Dickens dwelt with obvious enjoyment, was so close to his own father in personality that, overdrawn as he appears to be, he never becomes one of the great grotesques, like Mrs. Gamp or Pecksniff. When writing the final chapter Dickens wrote to Forster: 'Oh, my dear Forster, if I were to say half of what *Copperfield* makes me feel tonight, how strangely, even to you, I should be turned inside out! I seem to be sending some part of myself into the Shadowy World.'

The book surpassed in popularity,

though not in sales, all its predecessors except *Pickwick*.

Awaiting the birth of her child at the Rookery, Blunderstone, Suffolk, the widowed young Mrs. Copperfield receives a surprise visit from her dead husband's aunt, the eccentric Betsey Trotwood. When the child is born, and proves to be a boy, Miss Trotwood departs in dudgeon, for she does not approve of the male sex. David's early childhood is happy; he is the pet of his gay, pretty young mother and her devoted servant Clara Peggotty. Then Mrs. Copperfield begins to receive attentions from Edward Murdstone, a saturnine bachelor. David is sent with Peggotty to her brother Daniel, at Great Yarmouth.

Daniel, a bluff, genial fisherman, lives with his niece Emily (known as Little Em'ly), her cousin Ham, and the gloomy Mrs. Gummidge in an upturned boat which David finds the most fascinating dwelling possible. He feels a childish love for Em'ly.

When David returns home he finds his mother and Murdstone married. His life darkens. Murdstone is a harsh stepfather, and his sister Jane equally unsympathetic; she takes over the running of the household from David's mother. Failing to satisfy Murdstone in the learning of his lessons, David is beaten, bites Murdstone's hand, and is imprisoned in his room before being sent away to boarding school at Blackheath. The carrier who conveys him, Mr. Barkis, is struck by Peggotty's charms, and sends her the message 'Barkis is willin' ' by David.

Salem House's headmaster is the sadistic Mr. Creakle, a flogger. Through innocent betrayal by David an assistant master, Mr. Mell, is dismissed. David becomes the protégé of James Steerforth, an older boy, handsome and arrogant.

In the next term, David hears that his mother has died after the birth of her child, also dead. Peggotty is dismissed by the Murdstones and accepts Barkis's proposal of marriage. David is taken away from school and sent to work in a warehouse, washing and labelling wine-bottles.

He is humiliated and wretched, his troubles being slightly alleviated by the family with whom he lodges, the Micawbers. Mr. Micawber is a hopelessly improvident optimist, always confident that something will turn up; his devoted wife supports him in everything and avers that she will never desert him.

When conditions at the warehouse become intolerable, and the Micawbers leave London, David runs away to take refuge at Dover with Miss Trotwood, his great-aunt whom he has never met but who is the only relative he knows of. At the beginning of the journey he is robbed of his luggage and money, and has to travel to Dover on foot, selling his clothes to buy food: he arrives exhausted. Miss Trotwood, who is astonished to see him, soon reveals a kind heart under a forbidding exterior. She takes counsel with Mr. Dick, her slightly simple lodger, and decides to fight for the custody of the boy. The Murdstones arrive to claim David back, but Miss Trotwood routs them.

David's life now takes a turn for the better. He is sent to Canterbury, to a well-run school with a benevolent headmaster, Dr. Strong; he lodges there with Mr. Wickfield, a solicitor, and his young daughter Agnes. Wickfield's clerk is Uriah Heep, a sly, hypocritical youth, who frequently affirms himself to be 'very 'umble'. Heep gradually gains influence over the weak, bottle-addicted Wickfield. There is a shadow in Dr. Strong's life, too: his young wife Annie may be too fond of her cousin Jack Maldon.

David leaves school and in London meets Steerforth again. He visits Steerforth's mother at her home in Highgate, where she lives with her companion, the sharp-tongued Rosa Dartle. David and Steerforth go to Yarmouth, where they find celebrations in progress for the engagement of Ham and Little Em'ly. Steerforth becomes instantly popular, using all his charm on people whom he secretly despises as peasants, though he is impressed with Em'ly's beauty.

Agnes warns David against Steerforth, but he takes no notice of her. By now he has met another old schoolfellow, the comic Tommy Traddles, who is reading for the Bar. David himself now has to choose a profession, decides to become a proctor, a species of solicitor, and is articled to the firm of Spenlow and Jorkins. He falls in love at first sight with Spenlow's daughter, Dora. Dora's chaperone is Miss Murdstone.

Hearing that Barkis is seriously ill, David goes to Yarmouth. Barkis dies; and on Daniel Peggotty's home a worse sorrow falls, for Little Em'ly elopes with Steerforth. Daniel vows to find her, and sets out on their trail. When David calls upon Mrs. Steerforth, taking Daniel with him, he finds her adamant that she will never encourage Steerforth to marry Em'ly, and that if he does not get rid of the girl she will forbid him her house. Rosa Dartle reveals depths of jealous rage.

David becomes secretary to Dr. Strong, now living in Highgate; and Mr. Micawber takes up a clerk's post at Canterbury in the firm of Wickfield and Heep – for Uriah has now wormed his way into a partnership. He is also meddling in the affairs of the Strong household, and has ambitions to marry Agnes.

Dora's father dies suddenly, and after a decent interval Dora and David become officially engaged. Their marriage is idyllic at first, until Dora's deficiencies as a housekeeper become apparent. She is delightful but quite incompetent. Daniel Peggotty and David discover Em'ly in London, through the agency of a prostitute, Martha Endell. Steerforth, tiring of Em'ly, has tried to pass her on to his servant Littimer, and she has found her way back to England alone. Daniel plans to take her to Australia.

At Canterbury, Uriah Heep's villainy is exposed, and he is firmly dealt with by Traddles, in his legal capacity. Micawber's affairs are put in order: Miss Trotwood reveals that the death of the husband who long ago deserted her and has since sponged on her relieves her of a great burden, and she also discovers that she has not, after all, lost the bulk of her property through Mr. Wickfield. She offers to finance the emigration of the Micawbers.

After the birth of a still-born child, Dora dies. In a great storm at sea, off Yarmouth, Ham loses his life trying to save a passenger, who proves to be Steerforth, also drowned. David, stricken and sorrowful, goes abroad for three years. He returns with the realisation that he has always loved Agnes. Miss Trotwood leads him to believe that Agnes has 'an attachment', and the resultant questioning precipitates a mutual confession of love. The impecunious Traddles marries his sweetheart, Sophy Wackles; Littimer and Heep are found in a model prison, both model prisoners.

David and Agnes are married. Years later, they are visited by Daniel Peggotty, with good news of the Australian emigrants.

MISCELLANEOUS PAPERS FROM HOUSEHOLD WORDS

A posthumous selection of non-fiction pieces by Dickens published in *The Examiner*, *Household Words* and *All the Year Round* between 1838 and 1869, collected by B. W. Matz and first published in volume form in the National Edition of Dickens's works by Chapman & Hall in 1908.

REPRINTED PIECES

Thirty-one of Dickens's essays from *Household Words*, the weekly journal founded and edited by him which first appeared on 30 March 1850, and was last published on 28 May 1859, upon its absorption by *All the Year Round*, were published by Chapman & Hall as a collection entitled *Reprinted Pieces* in 1858. Five of the pieces – 'A Christmas Tree', 'The Poor Relation's Story', 'The Child's Story', 'The Schoolboy's Story' and 'Nobody's Story' – were subsequently incorporated in *Christmas Stories*. The twenty-six remaining *Reprinted Pieces* are:

'The Long Voyage' – the wreck of the *Halsewell* East Indiaman: 'The Begging-letter Writer'; 'A Child's Dream of a Star' – a dead child, become an angel, waits for her brother to join her; 'Our English Watering-place' – Broadstairs; 'Our French Watering-place' – Boulogne;

'Bill-sticking'; ' "Births: Mrs. Meek, of a Son" '; 'Lying Awake'; 'The Ghost of Art' – a meeting with a male model; 'Out of Town' – impressions of Pavilionstone (Folkestone); 'Out of the Season' – staying at (presumably) Broadstairs, author walks to (presumably) Deal; 'A Poor Man's Tale of a Patent' – a smith's difficulties in getting his invention patented; 'The Noble Savage' – author debunks the delusion that savage peoples are virtuous, happy, and noble; 'A Flight' – by rail and steam-packet from London to Paris; 'The Detective Police' – author visits criminal establishments, escorted by Scotland Yard detectives under 'Inspector Wield', a pseudonym for Inspector Charles F. Field; 'Three "Detective" Anecdotes' – again involving Inspector Field, these are: 1. 'The Pair of Gloves'; 2. 'The Artful Touch'; 3. 'The Sofa'; 'On Duty with Inspector Field' – a night tour of unsavoury London; 'Down with the Tide' – a visit to the Thames Police; 'A Walk in a Workhouse'; 'Prince Bull. A Fairy Tale' – an allegory on British inefficiency and humiliation in the Crimean War; 'A Plated Article' – conditions in the Staffordshire potteries; 'Our Honourable Friend' – the hypocrisy of Members of Parliament; 'Our School' – Wellington House Academy, Hampstead Road, London; 'Our Vestry' – playing at parish politics; 'Our Bore'; 'A Monument of French Folly' – English slaughterhouses ironically compared with French abbatoirs.

CHRISTMAS STORIES

A posthumous collection, first published by Chapman & Hall in 1871 as part of the Charles Dickens Edition of his works, commenced 1867, under the editorship of his son Charley. It comprises some of the stories which Dickens habitually wrote each Christmas for *Household Words* and *All the Year Round* over the period 1850–67. Five of them – 'A Christmas Tree', 'The Poor Relation's Story', 'The Child's Story', 'The Schoolboy's Story' and 'Nobody's Story' – had originally been included in *Reprinted Pieces*. There were no illustrations. They were repub-

lished in America in so many forms that it is not possible to define first publication there.

'A Christmas Tree' – reflections upon the delights and macabre fantasies engendered by the Christmas tree and its decorations; 'What Christmas is as we grow Older'; 'The Poor Relation's Story' – Michael, the Poor Relation, tells of his happiness with his wife and children in his Castle, but admits finally that it is all a Castle in the Air; 'The Child's Story' – a grandfather's journey through life; 'The Schoolboy's Story' – Old Cheeseman, a Latin master despised by pupils and fellow masters at a boarding-school, acquires a fortune and marries his only friend, an assistant matron; 'Nobody's Story' – a parable of the life and death of an unknown working man; 'The Seven Poor Travellers' – a story told by the narrator to the Six Poor Travellers who inhabit Watts's Charity, Rochester, one Christmas Eve, about Richard Doubledick who joins the army hoping to get killed, but finds redemption from despair and dissipation through the death of his officer, Captain Taunton, and regains his lost love; 'The Holly-Tree' – a traveller detained at the Holly-Tree inn when his coach becomes snowbound ruminates upon types of inn he has known, is told by the Boots of two children's attempt to elope to Gretna Green, and finds that the love whom he had thought had left him for his friend is his after all; 'The Wreck of the Golden Mary' – the sailing ship *Golden Mary*, California-bound, strikes an iceberg and founders, and the survivors endure twenty-seven days in small boats, during which several, including the child 'Golden Lucy', die; 'The Perils of Certain English Prisoners' – Gill Davis, former private of the Royal Marines, tells how the small English community on Silver-Store Island, off the Mosquito Coast, held out against pirate attack; 'Going into Society' – Chops, a fairground dwarf, achieves his ambition of entering society upon winning a lottery, is fleeced of his money, returns to his showman employer, Toby Magsman, and dies; 'The Haunted House' –

the narrator and a group of friends spend several nights investigating the haunting of a house, but he discovers that the ghost of Master B. is that of his own childhood; 'A Message from the Sea' – Captain Jorgan brings a message about an inheritance from one of his sailors who is believed drowned, and helps to rid the man's family of a long-standing suspicion of guilt; 'Tom Tiddler's Ground' – a traveller tries to persuade a filthy hermit to reform, without success; 'Somebody's Luggage' – a head waiter passes off two manuscripts to *All the Year Round* as his own work: the story of how 'Monsieur the Englishman' befriends an orphan child in France, and the story of a pavement artist; 'Mrs. Lirriper's Lodgings' – Mrs. Lirriper, a lodging-house keeper, tells how she takes in an unmarried couple, and after the man absconds and the woman dies she brings up their boy, Jemmy, herself; 'Mrs. Lirriper's Legacy' – Mrs. Lirriper goes to France to find Jemmy's father dying, and allows Jemmy to believe his own romanticised version of his background; 'Doctor Marigold' – a travelling showman loses his wife and daughter and adopts a deaf-and-dumb girl, who marries a deaf-and-dumb husband but produces a perfect child (see also 'No. 1 Branch Line: The Signalman' below); 'Mugby Junction' – a traveller known as Barbox Brothers arrives at Mugby: he is moved by the fortitude of Phoebe, invalid daughter of Lamps, the porter; in a nearby town he meets the child of his old love; the Boy at Mugby Junction recounts the grim secrets of railway refreshment-room practices; and the narrator hears the ghost story of 'No. 1 Branch Line: The Signal-man' which, together with 'Doctor Marigold' (see above) was later republished under the title 'Two Ghost Stories'; 'No Thoroughfare', written with Wilkie Collins, and subsequently dramatised by him – the quest for the true identity of Walter Wilding, a London vintner, leads to his death and the attempted murder of his partner, George Vendale, by Jules Obenreizer, with whose niece Vendale is in love. The girl saves Vendale, who proves to be the real Wilding, and Obenreizer is killed. 'No

Thoroughfare' was dramatised by Collins alone in 1867, but is often included in collections of Dickens's plays.

A CHILD'S HISTORY OF ENGLAND

Begun at 1 Devonshire Terrace, London, in October 1850 and finished at Boulogne in September 1853. Published as a serial in *Household Words* between January 1851 and December 1853. Published by Bradbury & Evans in three volumes in 1852, 1853, 1854, with frontispieces by F. W. Topham, and in complete form, with dedication to his own children, in 1854.

Told in language which for that period was easy reading for children, the *History* covers the centuries between 55 B.C. and 1689, when William and Mary were established on the throne, the Protestant religion was established in England, and 'England's great and glorious Revolution was complete'. The years from then up to the date of writing are crisply summarised in one chapter, ending with 'GOD SAVE THE QUEEN!' Dickens's view of history is highly individual and violently prejudiced, with a strong Protestant bias throughout. Henry VIII is described as 'one of the most detestable villains that ever drew breath,' and James I referred to as His Sowship.

MR. NIGHTINGALE'S DIARY

This farce was privately printed in 1851, no author or publisher being given. First published in America in 1877 by James R. Osgood & Co., late Ticknor & Fields, Boston.

In one act, it was written for the Guild of Literature and Art founded by Dickens and Bulwer-Lytton for the benefit of impoverished authors and artists. The first charity performance of it was given at Devonshire House on 27 May 1851. Though generally thought of as being solely the work of Dickens, it had started out as a farce by Mark Lemon, but Dickens contributed so much humour to it that it came to be looked upon as his own. He acted in it, playing five characters, one of them a version of Mrs. Gamp. Mr. Gabblewig of the Middle Temple arrives at a Malvern inn disconsolate because his future father-in-law, Mr. Nightingale, does not approve of his verbosity. Nightingale, a hypochondriac, arrives at Malvern with his daughter Rosina to take the cure. In order to get round Nightingale, Gabblewig, working against an impoverished actor, Slap, Nightingale's brother-in-law, assumes a variety of comic disguises, aided by Rosina, and wins her in the end.

BLEAK HOUSE

Dickens's ninth novel. Begun November 1851 at Tavistock House, London, and completed at Boulogne in August 1853. Published March 1852 to September 1853 by Bradbury & Evans. Illustrated by 'Phiz'. Published as a single volume, September 1853. First publication in America 1852–3 (Harper & Bros., New York) in twenty parts; also in *Harper's Magazine*.

The idea of the story came to Dickens in August 1851 at Broadstairs, while staying at the seaside villa then known as Fort House, now Bleak House. It nagged at him until he felt 'a torment of desire to be anywhere but where I am,' and longed to rush off to Switzerland. But removal from Devonshire Terrace to Tavistock House prevented the writing of the first words until November. The book was intended to illustrate the evils caused by long-drawn-out suits in the Courts of Chancery, known to Dickens from his youthful days in association with the law; and to point out the terrible condition of the uneducated poor, as exemplified in the person of Jo the crossing-sweeper. Various titles combining the two themes were proposed: *The Solitary House that was always shut up. Tom-all-Alone's. The Ruined (House, Building, Factory, Mill) that got into Chancery and never got out.* These and others were abandoned, and the Jo thread occupies a lesser part of the story than Dickens had at first intended. The book is full of allegory. The pervading London fog represents the miasma surrounding the victims of Chancery and the terrible London slums and graveyards.

Bleak House is the only full-length novel in which Dickens uses a woman as first-person narrator, a device not wholly successful because of the aura of mock-modesty with which Esther Summerson surrounds herself: 'the too conscious unconsciousness of Esther,' as Forster says, and he comments fairly enough on the dark humours of the lesser characters, 'The Guppys, Weevles, Snagsbys, Chadbands, Krooks, and Smallweeds, even the Kenges, Vholeses, and Tulkinghorns, are much too real to be pleasant.' *Bleak House*, in fact, marked the end of Dickens's great comic inventions.

A hearing of the suit of Jarndyce and Jarndyce, in the High Court of Chancery before the Lord Chancellor, begins the story. Mr. Tulkinghorn, the Dedlock family's lawyer, visits Sir Leicester and Lady Dedlock at their town house and reports some new developments in the case, producing an affidavit at the sight of which Lady Dedlock becomes faint; she recognises the writing as that of her one-time lover.

Esther Summerson begins her own story. Illegitimate, brought up by a stern aunt, she is educated at the cost of her guardian, John Jarndyce, and after six years is summoned by his lawyers, Kenge and Carboy, to become companion to his ward, Ada Clare. In London she meets Ada, a pretty, winning girl, and her young cousin, Richard Carstone, who are obviously in love. Jarndyce has taken the young people into his home while the case is being heard in Chancery; it has dragged on for years. Jarndyce is sceptical of its success, but the optimistic Richard believes that it will make his fortune. The two wards and Esther meet Miss Flite, a whimsically mad old lady, also a victim of Chancery; and spend the night at the house of Mrs. Jellyby, who neglects her family and devotes all her time and energy to the cause of African natives. Miss Flite introduces them to her landlord, Krook, a drunken and eccentric old rag-and-bottle merchant.

Esther soon becomes the efficient housekeeper ('Dame Durden' is Jarndyce's affectionate name for her) of Bleak House, near St. Albans, and the close friend of Ada and Richard. Her advice is sought by both and by Jarndyce. She meets Harold Skimpole, delightful, artistic, irresponsible, 'a mere child', as he is fond of saying, in money matters. Richard unwisely pays a debt for which Skimpole has been arrested.

The link between Lady Dedlock and Esther is now made apparent. Mr. Guppy, a lawyer's clerk from Kenge and Carboy's, has become infatuated with Esther. Visiting the Dedlocks' country house, Chesney Wold, in Lincolnshire, he is struck by the familiar appearance of Lady Dedlock in her portrait, though he cannot pin-point the resemblance. He visits Esther, proposes to her, and is refused.

Tulkinghorn makes inquiries about the writer of the affidavit which had such a marked effect on Lady Dedlock. He discovers the man, a law-writer calling himself Nemo, to be a lodger at Krook's; but calling there, finds Nemo dead of poison. No papers of his are to be found. Jo, a young crossing-sweeper, gives evidence at the inquest, for Nemo had been his only friend. Tulkinghorn reports to the Dedlocks what has happened, and Lady Dedlock affects indifference.

Richard decides to become a surgeon, is soon bored, and chooses first the Law, then the Army, confident all the time that when the suit in Chancery is settled he will be rich and able to marry Ada. Esther falls in love with Allan Woodcourt, a young doctor whom she meets through Miss Flite. Jo reports to Tulkinghorn how a veiled lady has given him money for showing her the grave of Nemo; shown a similarly dressed woman in Tulkinghorn's chambers, he identifies the dress but does not recognise the wearer. She is, in fact, Hortense, Lady Dedlock's French maid, who has turned against her because she is jealous of her lady's preference for another maid, Rosa. Tulkinghorn is using her, and George Rouncewell, son of the housekeeper at Chesney Wold, to obtain information about Nemo with which to blackmail Lady Dedlock.

Guppy calls on Lady Dedlock and tells her that he has deduced that Esther is her daughter; that Esther's name is really Hawdon, and that Nemo was a pseudonym for Captain Hawdon.

Esther and her little maid Charley visit Jenny, a brickmaker's wife, and find Jo there, suffering with a feverish illness. They take him back to Bleak House, but he runs away in the night. Charley has caught smallpox from him. Esther nurses her, catches the disease herself, and emerges from it badly scarred. She renounces all thought of Allan Woodcourt. For the first time she meets Lady Dedlock, who tells her, after a tender interview, that they must never again meet for fear of their relationship being revealed. Guppy, on seeing Esther's changed face, loses interest in her.

The pursuit of Hawdon's papers goes on. Guppy and a friend, expecting a packet of them to be handed over by Krook, find him dead of spontaneous combustion. Tulkinghorn obtains from George Rouncewell a specimen of Hawdon's writing; he promises Lady Dedlock that he will not expose her without previous warning, provided that she does not leave Chesney Wold, as she proposes. He himself is being harried by Hortense, who insists that he finds her a new post in exchange for the help she has given him. After another interview with Lady Dedlock, Tulkinghorn is found the next morning shot dead in his chambers. George Rouncewell is arrested for his murder, but Mr. Bucket, a detective, discovers that it has been committed by Hortense, and arrests her.

Lady Dedlock disappears. She has been told by Guppy that not only he but several other people incidental to the story (Smallweed, Chadband, Mrs. Snagsby) know her secret. Bucket, with Esther, sets out in pursuit of her, but they are misled because she has changed clothes with Jenny. At last they find her, dead on the step of the sordid burial-ground where Hawdon lies.

The suit in Chancery has dragged to its close; costs have swallowed up the whole of the estate. Richard Carstone has drifted out of the Army and is lodging, ill and restive, at Symond's Inn. He has unfairly blamed John Jarndyce for all his troubles.

Ada secretly marries him, and only tells Esther her secret when she knows herself pregnant. Richard is reconciled to Jarndyce, and dies.

Jarndyce, who proposed to Esther after the loss of her beauty, and was accepted, now sees that she loves Allan Woodcourt, who has attended Jo in his last illness and befriended the dying Richard. Allan declares his love to Esther, but she refuses him. Jarndyce takes her to see Allan's future home, which he has called Bleak House, and tells her that this is the Bleak House of which she is to be mistress. He gives her, cheerfully and nobly, to Allan, relinquishing his own claims.

The story has also followed the fortunes of Caddy, Mrs. Jellyby's daughter, her dancing-master husband Prince Turveydrop and his pompous, selfish father; of Snagsby the law-stationer and his jealous wife; of Charley Neckett, the orphan who becomes Esther's maid; of the soldier Bagnet and his family; of Boythorn, Jarndyce's temperamental friend; and of the maid Rosa and the Rouncewell family.

TO BE READ AT DUSK

First published in 1852 in *The Keepsake*, an annual formerly edited by Lady Blessington. It was reprinted as an individual pamphlet in 1852.

There are two sombre stories in one: the tragedy of an English bride, narrated by a Genoese courier, and a ghostly legend recounted by his German counterpart.

HARD TIMES
For These Times

Dickens's tenth novel. Begun January 1854 at Tavistock House, written there and at Boulogne, where it was finished at about the end of July 1854. It was the first of his novels to be serialised in *Household Words*, between April and August 1854, but without illustrations. Published as an illustrated complete novel in August 1854, with a dedication to Thomas Carlyle, by Bradbury & Evans. The first cheap edition, 1865, had a frontispiece by A. Boyd Houghton. Fred Walker contributed four drawings to the Library Edition. First published in America 1854–5, by Harper & Bros., New York.

The shortest of Dickens's novels, it was the most difficult to write because of the limited space at his disposal in *Household Words*; but it more than doubled the circulation of his journal. It was meant to be, he said, a satire 'against those who see figures and averages, and nothing else – the representatives of the wickedest and most enormous vice of this time; the men who, through long years to come, will do more to damage the really useful truths of political economy than I could do (if I tried) in my whole life.' Because of its brevity it contained none of the embellishments, humorous or sentimental, of his earlier novels, and hardly any grotesquerie. Even the circus scenes appear perfunctory. It has the air of being a tract against materialism rather than a story told for its own sake, and Dickens's extremely poor ear for local dialect makes the dialogue of the Lancashire characters hard reading. There is a general dryness about it which suggests overwork and exhaustion in its author.

Thomas Gradgrind's family is ruled by Fact, and the school in Coketown, a northern industrial town, over which he presides is also dominated by it. He is displeased with Sissy Jupe, a circus clown's daughter, because of her unrealistic upbringing; and appalled when he finds his own children, Louisa and Tom, trying to see something of Sleary's Circus, where Jupe works. He and Josiah Bounderby, proud self-made man, banker, merchant, and owner of the Coketown mills, decide that Sissy had better be removed from the school, and are about to tell her so when they find that her father is missing. Gradgrind offers her a home, on condition that she holds no further communication with the circus people.

Tom is a weak, easily influenced boy, Louisa a dreamy, dissatisfied girl. Sensing Louisa's attraction for Bounderby, Tom decides to get at that powerful man through her.

Stephen Blackpool, a mill-hand married to a drunken, dissolute wife, is in love with Rachael, a fellow-worker. He consults Bounderby about the possibility of divorcing his wife, and finds it impossible under the existing laws. He meets a strange old woman outside Bounderby's house, who asks searching questions about its owner. Rachael nurses Stephen's wife and prevents her from taking poison. They are resigned to a life apart so long as his wife lives.

Gradgrind tells Louisa that Bounderby has asked for her in marriage. In spite of the disparity of their years and characters, she accepts. Bounderby shocks his aristocratically-related housekeeper, Mrs. Sparsit, with the news.

Louisa's marriage is unhappy. She tolerates the attentions of James Harthouse, a languid man of the world who has political business with Bounderby. He sees Louisa's love for her brother, and pretends an interest in Tom, whom he influences in turn.

Bounderby's Bank is robbed, and Stephen Blackpool suspected. He has been discharged from Bounderby's mill for failing to support a strike of operatives, and is generally in bad odour. Bitzer, clerk at the Bank, gives evidence against him. Louisa suspects Tom's guilt, and maintains her suspicions in spite of Harthouse's persuasions to the contrary. Mrs. Sparsit spies upon Louisa and Harthouse; when she discovers that they are meeting alone at Bounderby's country house she follows them, and overhears Harthouse's attempted seduction of Louisa. Louisa hurries back to Coketown, followed by Mrs. Sparsit, hopeful of collecting more evidence. But Louisa has gone to her father, to confess her temptation and take refuge with him. Her confession moves him to the point of realising his mistakes in her upbringing. Bounderby follows her to Gradgrind's, and decides that they would be better apart. Sissy Jupe goes to Harthouse's hotel, and tells him to have no further hope of Louisa.

Stephen has left Coketown in search of work, and Bounderby offers a reward for his capture. Sissy and Rachael find Stephen's hat near a disused mine-shaft, and Stephen himself at the bottom of the shaft, seriously injured. Dying, he asks Gradgrind to clear his name, hinting that Tom, his son, can tell him how.

Mrs. Sparsit, intent on malice, finds the so-called Mrs. Pegler, whom Stephen had met outside Bounderby's house. She proves to be Bounderby's unacknowledged mother, whose very existence contradicts all his fabrications about his hard, sordid childhood, deserted and thrown on the world by his mother as a baby. Bounderby is deflated.

Gradgrind learns from Louisa and Sissy that Tom was the bank-robber, and that he is hiding with Sleary's Circus. They find him there, and Sleary disguises him as a circus performer. His escape is nearly foiled by the spying of Bitzer, but Sleary and his accomplished horse and dog effect Tom's flight.

Tom dies abroad, sending a loving and penitent message to Louisa from his death-bed. Louisa does not re-marry, but matures into the woman she might have been earlier but for her harsh rearing. Rachael remains single and faithful to Stephen's memory, but Sissy marries. Gradgrind lives into old age, 'making his facts and figures subservient to Faith, Hope and Charity'.

LITTLE DORRIT

Dickens's eleventh novel. Begun at Tavistock House, London, May 1855, and written there, at Folkestone, Boulogne and Paris. Finished in May or June 1857 in London. Published by Bradbury & Evans in monthly parts between December 1855 and June 1857. Published complete in June 1857. Illustrated by 'Phiz'. First publication in America 1855-7 by Harper & Bros., New York, in *Harper's Magazine*.

The first title Dickens chose was *Nobody's Fault*, as his original idea had been to weave the story round a man 'who should bring about all the mischief in it, lay it all on Providence, and say at every fresh calamity, "Well, it's a mercy, however, nobody was to blame you know!" ' He abandoned this for a plot in which the characters 'came together, in a chance way, as fellow-travellers' and later were connected. He was, in fact, less sure of the outline of *Dorrit* than he had been about any previous book. It is a dark novel, with a preponderance of characters who are failures in life. There is little light relief beyond Flora Finching, Mr. F's Aunt and young John Chivery, who is in the main a pathetic figure. Arthur Clennam and Little Dorrit are stock figures from Dickens's cupboard: Little Dorrit might be Little Nell risen from the tomb. The core of the story is the Marshalsea Prison, the scene of Dickens's early humiliation when his father was imprisoned there.

The public bought the book with enthusiasm, but *Blackwood's Magazine* condemned it as 'twaddle', and the *Edinburgh Review* complained of Dickens's lack of originality in basing fictional events upon real ones, and criticised him for slandering real people in his descriptions of the Circumlocution Office.

In a Marseilles prison the villainous Rigaud tells his companion, Cavalletto, that he is there for murdering his wife for her money. He is sent for trial. Also in Marseilles is Arthur Clennam, who has been in business with his father in the East for twenty years, and is now returning to England, his father having died. He is in quarantine with the Meagles family: Mr. Meagles, a retired banker, his cheerful wife, his pretty daughter known as 'Pet', and her maid, nicknamed 'Tattycoram'. Tattycoram is wildly jealous of the attentions paid by everyone to Pet, and finds a sympathiser in Miss Wade, a coldly detached fellow-passenger.

Back in London, Arthur receives a chilly welcome from his mother, Mrs. Clennam, an invalid obsessed by her gloomy religion, who lives alone but for two old servants, Jeremiah Flintwinch and his wife Affery. Arthur tells his mother that he feels his father has been guilty of dishonesty in business, and she replies that she will cast him out with her curse if he speaks of the matter again. He hands over his share of the business to Flintwinch.

Arthur meets the girl who sews for Mrs. Clennam. Christened Amy, she is known as Little Dorrit, and is the younger daughter of William Dorrit, 'The Father of the Marshalsea'. Little Dorrit was born in the prison and has grown up there. Precociously mature, she supports her father, her brother Edward, known as 'Tip', and her sister Fanny, keeping her work a secret from the old man. Through William Dorrit's brother Frederick, Arthur is introduced to the family; because of his interest in the girl he seeks a way of releasing Dorrit. But his inquiries at the Circumlocution Office about Dorrit's creditors meet with no success. He meets Daniel Doyce, an engineer and inventor, who is to become his partner, and the Plornishes of Bleeding Heart Yard. Rigaud, now free, reappears in the story.

Arthur meets Flora Finching, once Flora Casby, his early love. She is now middle-aged, fat, voluble, and silly. Disillusioned, Arthur visits the Meagles family and wonders whether or not to allow himself to fall in love with Pet, but decides against it. Fanny Dorrit is pursued by Edmund Sparkler, son of the chill, fashionable Mrs. Merdle, and stepson of her banker husband, but she is too proud to encourage him in view of his mother's opposition. Besides, she tells her sister, 'he is almost an idiot'. Little Dorrit herself is in love with Arthur, but does not let him suspect it. Pet Meagles has formed an attachment to Henry Gowan, an artist of independent means, and marries him. Rigaud arrives at Mrs. Clennam's house, calling himself Blandois.

Pancks, a rent-collector, discovers that William Dorrit is heir-at-law to a great unclaimed estate, and is free to leave the Marshalsea, a rich man. With his family Dorrit sets out on foreign travels. In Switzerland they meet the newly-married Gowans. Later in the journey they are joined by Fanny's suitor, Sparkler, and his mother, and by Blandois. They are also accompanied by the formidable Mrs. General, chaperone to the Misses Dorrit, who has matrimonial designs on William. Fanny marries Sparkler. Merdle offers to assist William to invest his wealth, and the offer is accepted. Dorrit's failing mind reverts to his Marshalsea years, with embarrassing results when he addresses the guests at Mrs. Merdle's party; ten days later he dies, his brother Frederick dying at his bedside.

Arthur Clennam goes to Calais to interview Miss Wade, who is accompanied by Tattycoram, who has run away to her. She refuses to give him any information about Blandois, with whom he saw her in London, but hands him a written explanation of her own background. Back in London, he encounters Cavalletto, who tells him all he knows of the criminal past of Rigaud, alias Blandois, and Arthur passes this on to Mrs. Clennam, but she refuses to accept the truth. Arthur hears from Affery of the strange noises she hears at night in the house: 'rustlings and stealings about, tremblings. . . .'

The banker Merdle commits suicide, his bank fails, and Arthur finds himself ruined. Arrested for debt and taken to the Marshalsea, he is conducted to Little Dorrit's old room by young John Chivery, son of the Turnkey and the adorer of Little Dorrit. She visits Arthur in prison, and offers him all her wealth, which he refuses.

Blandois reveals to Mrs. Clennam that he knows her secret: Arthur is not her child, but the son of a woman whom her husband loved, but was forced to give up by family pressure. Mrs. Clennam removed the baby from his mother and brought him up as her own, in a spirit of revenge upon his parents, 'that the child might work out his release in bondage and hardship'. She has, Blandois knows, suppressed the codicil of a will by which Little Dorrit would inherit two thousand guineas. He threatens that if she will not accept his terms he will deliver the papers to Arthur. Mrs. Clennam is shocked out of her invalid chair. She rushes from the house to the Marshalsea, where Little Dorrit is watching over Arthur in an illness. Little Dorrit promises to return with her to plead with Blandois; but as they approach the house, it crumbles and disintegrates, burying Blandois in its debris. The strange noises heard by Affery had been intimations of the rot and decay which were to bring the house down at last.

Mr. Meagles calls on Miss Wade in France, to beg her to give up important papers left with her by Blandois. She refuses, but when he returns to England Tattycoram appears with the papers. She has followed him, and now confesses how much she has grown to fear Miss Wade's power over her, and that she has come to realise that she is being trained to become what Miss Wade is – a self-destroyer and a destroyer of others. She begs to come back to the Meagles family, who accept her joyfully.

Arthur, recovered, is released from the Marshalsea by the agency of Daniel Doyce and Meagles. Little Dorrit tells him that she has no fortune to offer him: she knows now that the Dorrit fortunes were dissipated, like his own, by the fraudulent Merdle. Nothing any longer stands in the way of their marriage, which takes place in the church next to the Marshalsea, where Little Dorrit had been christened.

A strong sub-theme in the novel concerns the Circumlocution Office, satirising red-tape administration: 'The most important department under Government . . . the Circumlocution Office was beforehand with all the public departments in the art of perceiving – How Not to Do It.' The family of Barnacle helps to administer it, Lord Decimus Barnacle being a master of the afore-named art; other members are Clarence, 'the born idiot of the family', Tite, Ferdinand, and William. A figure of hypocrisy is Christopher Casby, Flora Finching's father. Flora's aunt-in-law, 'Mr. F's Aunt', is the chief eccentric of the book, given to the utterance of startling irrelevancies. The Merdles and their pretensions are the target Dickens sets up for his attack on snobbery.

THE LAZY TOUR OF TWO IDLE APPRENTICES

First published in *Household Words* in October 1857, and written jointly by Dickens and Wilkie Collins, it is an account of a trip made by them to the North of England in the autumn of 1857. They call themselves respectively Thomas Idle and Francis Goodchild, after the characters in Hogarth's series of pictures.

Its first appearance in book form was in 1890 when Chapman & Hall printed it with 'No Thoroughfare' and 'The Perils of Certain English Prisoners' in a single volume, illustrated by Arthur Layard. The most notable episodes of the *Tour* are the ghost story told of a Lancaster inn, and a lively account of a race-meeting at Doncaster.

A TALE OF TWO CITIES

Dickens's twelfth novel. Written at Tavistock House, London, and Gad's Hill from March 1859. The first instalment appeared on 30 April 1859 in the first number of *All the Year Round*, the new weekly journal published by Chapman & Hall and conducted by Dickens which superseded and absorbed *Household Words*. The last instalment was on 26 November, and the story was published by Chapman & Hall in the same month as a complete novel, illustrated by 'Phiz'. First published in America 1859 by Harper & Bros., New York, in *Harper's Weekly*.

The idea occurred to Dickens when acting in *The Frozen Deep* with his amateur company in the summer of 1857. He had difficulty in getting down to the writing, and in finding a title. Among those he suggested to John Forster were *One of these Days*, *The Doctor of Beauvais*, and *Buried Alive*. He did not start writing it until March 1859. He was scrupulous in getting his historical details right and making a thorough study of the background to the French Revolution, and perhaps this very thoroughness led to the curiously un-Dickensian remoteness about the book, and a woodenness in its characters. There are only three strong themes: the imprisonment and recurrent amnesia of Doctor Manette; the heartless behaviour of the women spectators at the guillotine, linked with the revenge of the peasantry for their wrongs; and the self-sacrifice of Sydney Carton, the dominant figure of the book.

There is little humour, Jerry Cruncher's anathematising of his praying wife being repetitive and inferior to any of the 'humours' of comic characters in previous

books, and Miss Pross being used in the end as an instrument of drama. The *Saturday Review* anatomised the book scathingly, remarking that 'whenever Mr. Dickens writes a novel, he makes two or three comic characters just as he might cut a pig out of a piece of orange peel.'

The book was popularised by a dramatisation, *The Only Way*, produced at the Lyceum Theatre in 1899, starring John Martin Harvey.

The story opens in 1775. The states of England and France are described and compared, and the scene set for the French Revolution.

Jarvis Lorry, agent for Tellson's Bank in London, receives on his way to Paris a mysterious message, to which he sends back the answer RECALLED TO LIFE. At a Dover inn he meets by appointment Lucie Manette, French-born but brought up in England. Lorry tells her that her father, the physician Dr. Alexandre Manette, is not dead, as she supposed, but has been for many years a prisoner, for a State offence, in the Bastille, from where he has now been released. He takes her to the house in Paris where her father has been lodged. Defarge, a wine-shop keeper with a handsome, dominant wife, leads them to him: he is sitting at a bench, making shoes, a vacant-faced, prematurely white-haired man whose voice is unused to speaking and whose memory has apparently gone. Lucie tries to make him recognise her, with little success. She and Lorry take him back to England.

Five years later, in London, Jerry Cruncher, odd-jobber at Tellson's and 'resurrectionist' by night of dead bodies for medical purposes, is sent to the Old Bailey with a note for Lorry, grumbling as he departs about his pious wife's habit of 'flopping', as he describes her frequent bouts of prayer for his soul. The Court is trying a treason case: a young Frenchman, Charles Darnay (whose true name is St. Evrémonde), is accused of spying. He is acquitted after his counsel, Mr. Stryver, has pointed out that identification is unreliable evidence when one man can resemble another as much as the prisoner resembles another lawyer present in court, Sydney Carton. Lorry and the Manettes, who have been witnesses at the trial, congratulate Charles.

Carton is a dissolute, irresponsible character, who could have been a brilliant lawyer, but who aspires no higher than to do hack work for the more pushing Stryver. Carton and Charles visit the Manettes at their Soho home. Dr. Manette is now restored to health and sanity and lives happily with Lucie and her eccentric companion, Miss Pross.

The action moves to France. Driving in his carriage, the Marquis St. Evrémonde, Charles's uncle, runs over and kills the child of a peasant. That evening Charles visits him; the next morning the Marquis is found murdered, an act of vengeance by the child's father.

In England again, Charles, Carton, and Stryver all hope to marry Lucie Manette. Lorry advises Stryver not to propose to her. Charles speaks to Dr. Manette, who gives him his blessing. Carton tells Lucie of his love for her, but says that he knows she cannot return it, and that he is not worthy of her. He gives her a solemn assurance that for her, or anybody dear to her, he would do anything; that he is 'a man who would give his life, to keep a life you love beside you!'

In Paris, an English spy calling himself John Barsad arrives at the wine-shop and tells Monsieur and Madame Defarge that Charles Darnay is to marry Lucie Manette; and in England, on the evening before the wedding, Dr. Manette tells Lucie that he is entirely happy in the outcome. But after the couple have left for their honeymoon, a prison story about the discovery of a hidden paper, once told to him by Charles, comes back to his mind, and with it his amnesia. He goes back to his old employment of making shoes, to the distress of Lorry and Miss Pross who, when he returns to his senses, destroy his bench, tools, and leather.

In Paris the Revolution has broken out, the people of St. Antoine rise, and Defarge is their leader in the siege of the Bastille. The governor is captured and decapitated by Madame Defarge, herself

a leader of the revolutionary women. The mob burns the castle of the late Marquis St. Evrémonde and Gabelle, his tax and rent collector, is imprisoned in L'Abbaye, Paris. He writes to Charles begging for help. Charles leaves for Paris, as does Lorry, who is on business for Tellson's. Lorry warns Charles that he will be in danger when he reaches France, which proves to be the case. He has barely reached Paris when he is flung into the prison of La Force. Defarge, who befriended Dr. Manette after his release from the Bastille, refuses to help him.

Lucie, with her baby daughter, Miss Pross, and her father, follows him to Paris, full of apprehension, having heard of his imprisonment. When they arrive at Tellson's Lorry is shocked, both by their news and their presence there. Dr. Manette assures him that by virtue of his once having been a Bastille prisoner he can help Charles. The revolutionaries accept him and lead him to La Force, while Lorry places Lucie, little Lucie and Miss Pross in lodgings. They receive a note from the Doctor saying that Charles is safe. Madame Defarge does not respond to Lucie's gratitude for the note, and the aggressively British Miss Pross takes an instant dislike to the Frenchwoman.

Dr. Manette does not return for four days, during which time eleven hundred prisoners have been killed. Charles has been spared, but all Dr. Manette's efforts to get him released are fruitless. Every day, for a year and three months, Lucie fears to hear that her husband is to go to the guillotine. Her father tells her that there is a window in the prison from which Charles can see her if she stands at a certain point in the street. From that time she goes there every day, often with her child, horrified to see the fearful Carmagnole, expressing bloodthirsty hatred of aristocrats, danced in the streets.

Charles is called before the Tribunal, and on the testimony of Dr. Manette, Gabelle, and Lorry is acquitted and carried home in triumph; but he is almost immediately re-arrested at the instigation of the Defarges, and by the denunciation of 'one other', he is told.

Miss Pross, shopping with Jerry Cruncher, meets her brother Solomon, known as John Barsad in France, once a spy in the pay of the English Government, now a turnkey at the Conciergerie. Sydney Carton arrives on the scene, recognises Pross, and takes him to the office of Tellson's bank, in company with another prison officer. Jerry recognises the latter as Roger Cly, once Charles's servant and a witness against him at his trial. Carton persuades Barsad/Pross that he will give him away to the Conciergerie officials as a spy in the pay of England unless he allows Charles's family and friends access to him, should he be sentenced to death. He threatens also to denounce Cly, a threat backed up by Jerry, whose recognition of Cly came about because he had opened the coffin after Cly's fake funeral, and found it empty.

Once again before the Tribunal, Charles hears the identity of the 'one other' accuser. A paper has been found beneath the floor of Dr. Manette's old prison cell, setting out how he came to be imprisoned. In 1757 he had been summoned to a country house outside Paris to attend a young woman raving in delirium of 'my husband, my father, and my brother', and counting repeatedly up to twelve. Another patient was a young man who, in the hearing of the Marquis St. Evrémonde and his brother, told him that the girl was his sister, who as a bride was coveted by the younger St. Evrémonde. Her husband refusing to 'lend' her, the nobles literally worked him to death, and then St. Evrémonde took her away and raped her. Her brother challenged the rapist to a duel, and was fatally wounded, cursing the Marquis and his brother with a cross marked in blood. Some days later the girl died.

Manette had been visited at home by the wife of the Marquis St. Evrémonde, with her son, young Charles. She wished to make reparation for the wrongs done to the dead girl's family; she believed there was a young sister. Later Dr. Manette had been abducted and imprisoned at the behest of the Marquis. He wrote down his story and buried it beneath the floor.

Charles, as a St. Evrémonde, is condemned on this evidence to die in two days. Carton, drinking in Defarge's wine-shop, overhears Madame Defarge and other conspirators plotting the complete extermination of the St. Evrémonde family, and Madame's revelation that she herself was the little sister of the girl and boy attended by Dr. Manette. This has been her motivation in the pursuit of Charles and all who bear his name. Dr. Manette, distracted at having been the innocent cause of Charles's condemnation, returns to his old illusion that he is still making shoes in the Bastille.

Carton gives Lorry his own passport enabling him to leave Paris, and another allowing Lucie and the child to leave, telling him to get her, the Doctor and himself out of the city as soon as possible. Lorry obeys.

In the prison, during the early hours of the morning of his execution, Charles is visited by Carton, who commands him to change clothes with him and write a note referring to an old promise. Charles does not understand him, but obeys. Carton drugs him, puts on his discarded clothes, and orders Solomon Pross to carry Carton away, telling the guards that St. Evrémonde's visitor has fainted. He takes Charles's place and because of the great likeness between the two is not detected.

Madame Defarge and her fellow-revolutionaries decide to have Lucie and the child denounced. Madame goes to Lucie's lodging, to be confronted by Miss Pross, determined to play for time and cover Lucie's retreat. Neither she nor Madame can understand a word the other says, yet a fierce battle of wills takes place between them. Madame Defarge draws a pistol, struggles with Miss Pross and is shot. Miss Pross, deafened for ever by the noise of the pistol, hurries from the house and sets out with Jerry Cruncher for England.

Sydney Carton's last day has come. Still in the character of Charles, he is taken to the guillotine in a tumbril, comforting a little sempstress who is to die with him. For the first time Madame Defarge is not there with her knitting, to watch the executions.

In his last moments Carton sees vengeance falling on the revolutionaries, and his sacrifice justified by the safety and happiness of Darnay and his family: for he has kept his old promise to Lucie to save a life dear to her. 'It is a far, far better thing that I do, than I have ever done; it is a far, far better rest that I go to than I have ever known.'

HUNTED DOWN

First published in the *New York Ledger*, 20 and 27 August and 3 September 1859, and in *All the Year Round* 4 and 11 August 1860. The American version was illustrated with seven woodcuts. The first publication in separate form in England was as an 89-page pamphlet issued by John Camden Hotten, London, 1870, and including an account of the Wainewright poisoning case on which Dickens had founded the story. An earlier edition appeared in America in 1861.

Julius Slinkton is suspected of having poisoned one of his nieces for her insurance money. Meltham, an actuary of the insurance company, who had been in love with the girl, determines to trap Slinkton into betraying himself. 'Disappearing' as Meltham and reappearing as Alfred Beckwith, a seemingly excessive drinker, he strikes up a friendship with Slinkton and persuades the latter to insure him heavily, anticipating that he will attempt to dispose of him too. Slinkton is meanwhile working on his other niece, Margaret Niner, but she is saved from her sister's fate and Slinkton, unmasked, poisons himself. Miss Niner marries a nephew of Sampson, chief manager of the insurance company. Meltham, his task achieved, dies of his broken heart.

THE UNCOMMERCIAL TRAVELLER

A series of essays and sketches from life, written as articles for *All the Year Round* between 1860 and 1869. The first edition in volume form was published by Chapman & Hall in December 1860, comprising seventeen pieces. A subsequent edition, in 1865, added eleven more papers, and the posthumous edition of 1875 was enlarged by eight more. All these, with one final addition, make up the volume which is part of any 'complete' edition of Dickens's works.

The Uncommercial Traveller introduces himself as a faceless representative of what he might term 'the great house of Human Interest Brothers', setting forth from his rooms in Covent Garden to wander in city and country, observing 'many little things, and some great things, which, because they interest me, I think may interest others.' Most of his titles are self-explanatory: 'His General Line of Business'; 'The Shipwreck'; 'Wapping Workhouse'; 'Two Views of a Cheap Theatre'; 'Poor Mercantile Jack' – seamen's haunts in Liverpool; 'Refreshments for Travellers' – the difficulty of getting a good cheap meal in England; 'Travelling Abroad' – Paris, Strasbourg, Switzerland; 'The Great Tasmania's Cargo' – the Uncommercial Traveller is appalled by the condition of soldiers returned from the Crimea; 'City of London Churches'; 'Shy Neighbourhoods' – ruminations chiefly about birds and dogs; 'Tramps'; 'Dullborough Town' – the Uncommercial Traveller revisits his boyhood home (Chatham); 'Night Walks'; 'Chambers' – impressions of the Inns of Court; 'Nurse's Stories' – macabre tales recalled from childhood; 'Arcadian London' – the West End; 'The Italian Prisoner' – the Uncommercial Traveller transports an immense bottle of wine from Italy, a released prisoner's debt of gratitude to an English benefactor; 'The Calais Night Mail' – by train and night packet from London to Paris; 'Some Recollections of Mortality' – the Uncommercial Traveller visits the Paris morgue and recalls a drowning in the Regent's Canal and his experience as a Coroner's juror; 'Birthday Celebrations'; 'The Short-Timers' – he sees demonstrated the Half-Time system of educating the children of the poor; 'Bound for the Great Salt Lake' – a visit to a Mormon emigrant ship; 'The City of the Absent' – weekend wanderings in the City of London; 'An Old Stage-coaching House' – the effect of the railway upon an old coaching inn; 'The Boiled Beef of

New England' – a 'Cooking Depot' for the working classes of Whitechapel; 'Chatham Dockyard'; 'In the French-Flemish Country' – mainly describing a visit to a Fair; 'Medicine Men of Civilisation' – funerals and other absurd ceremonies of western society; 'Titbull's Alms-Houses' – the Uncommercial Traveller visits some almshouses in the East End of London, probably the Vintners' Almshouses, Mile End Road; 'The Ruffian' – the Uncommercial Traveller calls for harsher sentences for ruffianly behaviour, and tries to enforce a clause of the Police Act for himself; 'Aboard Ship' – travelling to New York in the Cunard steamship *Russia*; 'A Small Star in the East' – visits to poor workers' homes and to the East London Children's Hospital, Ratcliff; 'A Little Dinner in an Hour' – the Uncommercial Traveller and a friend dine disastrously at a seaside inn; 'Mr. Barlow' – thoughts about the pedantic tutor in the well-known children's book *The History of Sandford and Merton* by Thomas Day, published in parts 1783–9; 'On an Amateur Beat' – wanderings amongst London's deprived areas, a further visit to the East London Children's Hospital, and an investigation of lead-mills; 'A Fly-leaf in a Life' – overwork and its consequences; 'A Plea for Total Abstinence' – those who advocate abstinence from drink should abstain from other, generally accepted, excesses.

GREAT EXPECTATIONS

Dickens's thirteenth novel. Begun at Gad's Hill Place, October 1860, continued at 3 Hanover Terrace, Regent's Park, and Gad's Hill in June 1861. The first instalment appeared in *All the Year Round* on 1 December 1860, and it was published weekly until 3 August 1861. In August it was published by Chapman & Hall in three volumes, and in 1862 in one volume, the latter illustrated by Marcus Stone. First published in America in 1861 by Harper & Bros., New York, in *Harper's Weekly*.

Dickens got his 'very fine, new, and grotesque idea' for the book while working on *The Uncommercial Traveller*. He could see 'the whole of a serial revolving on it, in a most singular and comic manner'. He had, apparently, a clear scheme for the plot in his head before he began it, and went so far as to re-read *David Copperfield* to make sure he was not repeating himself in his autobiographical vein; for the new book was to be highly subjective without reproducing actual details of its author's youth, other than geographical ones. It is a greater novel than *Copperfield* by reason of its close integration, and lack of subplot and 'orange-peel-pig' comics; it bears every sign of Dickens's own outlook on life and intense feeling for his characters. The folly of pretended gentility, the impossibility of manipulating a human being into becoming a different personality for one's own pleasure (Magwitch and Pip, Miss Havisham and Estella), the ease with which wealth can corrupt, and the essential goodness of simplicity (Joe Gargery), all bear witness to Dickens's own state of mind and reveal much about him. Estella has been much praised as Dickens's first real young woman character, but in fact she lacks the life of his next two feminine juveniles, Bella Wilfer and Rosa Bud, and serves mainly to illustrate Miss Havisham's tragic mistake. Pip's sufferings from her coldheartedness may have been Dickens's own at Ellen Ternan's failure to reciprocate his autumn passion. Pip is the first 'hero' to have a real personality; to know himself as Nickleby, Chuzzlewit, Clennam, and even Copperfield do not. The lighter characters, Herbert Pocket, Wemmick, the Wopsles, and Uncle Pumblechook, are wholly credible as well as amusing.

Little Philip Pirrip, known as Pip, lives in the Kent marshes with his shrewish sister and her husband, the simply, kindly blacksmith, Joe Gargery. The story opens in a country churchyard, where Pip is terrified by the appearance of an escaped convict who threatens him with awful vengeance unless some food and a file for his fetters are obtained smartly. Pip manages to hide some of his own supper, steals more food from the pantry and, after an encounter with a different, younger convict, finds the original one and leaves him filing off his irons.

The convicts are later captured by soldiers. Pip's convict chivalrously says it was he who stole the food, and Pip is too afraid to confess the truth. Pip is sent for by Miss Havisham, of Satis House in the local market town, taken there by his Uncle Pumblechook, a corn-chandler, and conducted to Miss Havisham by her companion, Estella, a proud, beautiful young girl. Miss Havisham is a middle-aged woman whose whim it is to live perpetually in the bridal dress she wore on the day she was jilted by her lover, surrounded by the debris of the wedding-feast. She hates all the male sex, and has sent for Pip to enjoy the sight of him being tormented by Estella. On another visit he meets a 'pale young gentleman', Herbert Pocket, one of Miss Havisham's many relations, with whom he has a fight.

When Pip is old enough to become an apprentice blacksmith, Miss Havisham gives Joe twenty-five guineas as a premium for him. Mrs. Gargery is attacked and severely injured by an unknown hand. Pip is sure that her attacker was Orlick, an uncouth journeyman of Joe's. Mrs. Gargery's injuries have left her an invalid, and Joe takes a young orphan, Biddy, as his housekeeper. Pip tells Biddy of his longing to be a gentleman. He is disgusted and unhappy at the smithy, he says, without telling her that his ambitions are centred on Estella; but Biddy guesses as much.

Jaggers, a lawyer from London whom Pip has seen at Miss Havisham's, informs Joe and Pip that Pip has Great Expectations from an unknown benefactor, whose name he must never try to find out. He is always to be known as Pip, and will be brought up as a gentleman. His indentures are cancelled, he buys new clothes, says farewell to Miss Havisham, and goes to London, where he calls on Jaggers at his office in Little Britain. Wemmick, Jaggers's clerk, takes Pip to Barnard's Inn, where he meets Herbert, the son of Matthew Pocket, Miss Havisham's cousin, who is to be his tutor. Pip recognises Herbert as the boy he once fought at Satis House. They become close friends, and

are to share chambers at the Inn. Pip is also friendly with Wemmick, who takes him to tea at his home, a curious little residence known as the Castle, at Walworth, presided over by his Aged Parent, almost totally deaf but cheerful and contented.

Herbert tells Pip Miss Havisham's story, mentioning that the man who jilted her had extracted from her large sums of money, in which her half-brother was thought to have shared; and that Estella's origins are unknown. Pip becomes increasingly sure that his Expectations are from Miss Havisham. Jaggers invites him to dinner: Wemmick advises him to look closely at Jaggers's housekeeper, 'a wild beast tamed'. She proves to be about forty, with a striking face, and Jaggers draws the company's attention to her remarkably strong wrists. Pip takes a dislike to a boorish young man called Bentley Drummle, who is present.

Miss Havisham summons Pip to the old town. Orlick, he finds, is now her porter. He is reunited with Estella, home from being educated in France, grown up and more beautiful than ever. Pip is puzzled by a resemblance to somebody he cannot identify. Miss Havisham begs him, with wild insistence, to love Estella, however much she may hurt him. Soon after, Pip receives a note from Estella saying that she is coming to London. He meets her and escorts her to Richmond. She is friendly but cool, leaving Pip with the realisation that he is unhappy both with and without her.

Pip's sister dies just before Pip comes of age. He receives from Jaggers five hundred pounds, the gift of his anonymous benefactor. He visits Estella several times, and reproaches her for encouraging the attentions of Bentley Drummle.

One night Pip has a visitor; he is horrified to recognise the convict from his childhood. The man announces himself as Abel Magwitch, alias Provis, and shocks Pip by revealing that he, not Miss Havisham, is the founder of Pip's fortunes, in gratitude for the help given him long ago. He has got rich sheep-farming in Australia, and devoted all his wealth to Pip: 'Yes, Pip, dear boy, I've made a gentleman of you!' If his return to England were known, it would be death to him, he tells Pip and Herbert. They agree to hide him. He tells them the story of his life and association with a man called Compeyson, the other convict seen by the child Pip, and with Arthur Havisham, Miss Havisham's half-brother. When Magwitch and Compeyson were jointly tried for felony, Compeyson was let off with a seven-year sentence because of his gentlemanly appearance and speech, Magwitch receiving fourteen years.

Pip visits Miss Havisham and tells of his discovery, asking her to continue to help Herbert, whom he has set up in business. Confessing his love to Estella, he hears that she is to marry Drummle. With a final protestation of love, he rushes away and back to London.

Magwitch and he have been watched. Magwitch has been taken to a safer place, at the house where Herbert's fiancée, Clara Barley, lives with her father, near the Pool of London. A plan is arranged for Magwitch to escape by boat to a foreign vessel. Pip visits Miss Havisham, who is deeply distressed at the realisation of what she has done to him and to Estella. What she tells him of Estella's first coming to her confirms his belief that Jaggers's housekeeper is Estella's mother; he later learns that this is true, that she is a murderess whom Jaggers has saved, and that Magwitch is Estella's father. Miss Havisham's clothes catch fire; Pip saves her from burning, but she soon dies of her injuries.

Pip is summoned to a night appointment at the old lime-kiln on the marshes. He finds Orlick there, lying in wait for the man he deludedly imagines to be his old enemy, his rival for Biddy's affections and the favourite of the forge. He admits to attacking Pip's sister out of hatred for Pip, and threatens to kill Pip and burn his body in the lime-kiln. It is he who has tracked down Magwitch in Pip's chambers, and he is in league with Compeyson to prevent Magwitch's escape. But Pip is rescued in the nick of time.

The operation of rescuing Magwitch is begun. The boat in which Pip and Herbert are taking Magwitch down the river to board a foreign steamer is commanded to stop by an officer's boat, in which is Compeyson. The steamer runs them down, Compeyson is drowned, and Magwitch is severely hurt. He is brought to trial, and convicted, but is too ill for imprisonment. Pip visits him in the prison hospital; a new relationship springs up between them. Pip now feels for him tenderness and gratitude, and shame at his own former attitude. Magwitch dies, Pip giving him at the last news that his daughter, whom he thought dead, lives.

Pip becomes seriously ill. He rouses from delirium to find that Joe has been nursing him for weeks. As with Magwitch, his feelings change to remorse, for since becoming a 'gentleman' he has viewed poor Joe snobbishly, and been ashamed of him in public. His Great Expectations have done him no good; he is glad to be rid of them. After Joe has left, not waiting for thanks, Pip decides to go down to the country and ask Biddy to marry him, for long ago she seemed fond of him. He arrives to find that it is the wedding-day of Biddy and Joe.

He sells up, pays his many creditors, and leaves England to join Herbert Pocket in business in the East. Returning eleven years later, he pays a nostalgic evening visit to the site of Satis House. Walking in the garden is Estella. She is a widow, after an unhappy married life, from which she has learnt understanding and sympathy at last. She asks Pip to be her friend, and leave her. But as the evening mists rise and the light grows, he can see no shadow of another parting from her.

OUR MUTUAL FRIEND

Dickens's fourteenth novel. Begun in November 1863 at Gad's Hill; written there, at 57 Gloucester Place, Marylebone, and at 16 Somers Place, Hyde Park; finished at Gad's Hill about October 1865. First number published by Chapman & Hall on 1 May 1864; last number November 1865; the complete work in two volumes published in the same month. Illustrated by Marcus Stone. First American publication 1864–5 by Harper & Bros., New York, in *Harper's Magazine*.

Dickens chose the title for the book four years before he began to write it. He wrote to Forster of the leading themes. The many handbills he had seen describing persons drowned in the river suggested the 'ghastly calling' of the long-shore men Hexam and Riderhood. The idea of the 'living dead', which he perhaps intended to use again in *Drood*, provided the character of Rokesmith, supposed dead and 'retaining the singular view of life and character so imparted'. The Lammles were suggested by the notion of two people marrying each other for their money and finding out their mistake after marriage. The Veneerings exemplified his idea of 'new' people, 'bran new, like the furniture and the carriages – shining with varnish, and just home from the manufacturers'. An uneducated father with an educated son, whom Leech and he had seen, became Charley Hexam and his father; and Riah, the impossibly saintly old Jew, was a sop to those who had objected to Fagin as a disgrace to Judaism. The taxidermist's shop of Mr. Venus was found for him by Marcus Stone in Monmouth Street, St. Giles's.

The writing was slow, delayed by personal worries and by the illness which was beginning to trouble him. He was carrying some of the manuscript when involved in the Staplehurst railway disaster, and wrote a humorous 'postscript in lieu of preface' about the experiences of his characters in the accident.

Our Mutual Friend is, like *Little Dorrit*, a novel of failures and a parable of the corruption money brings. The society in which his middle-class characters move is a hollow one, superficially glittering; boredom, pretence, and pride invest it. The pretended greed of Boffin is painfully like the real thing. Venus's profession is grisly, Silas Wegg is mutilated. The recovery of corpses is the trade of Riderhood and Hexam. Abbey Potterson is the least genial of Dickens's innkeepers, Pleasant

Riderhood that rarity in his novels, a thoroughly ugly young woman. Yet among the pessimism and satire there are fine things: the unforgettable figure of the pretty, psychic dwarf, Jenny Wren, the savagely jealous Bradley Headstone, the astonishing reality of the heroine with refreshing weaknesses, Bella Wilfer.

Jesse Hexam, called 'Gaffer', lives by retrieving dead bodies from the Thames. His partner is Roger 'Rogue' Riderhood. Hexam and his daughter Lizzie find the body of a man in the river, and he refuses to share any reward he may get from it with Riderhood.

At the 'bran-new house in a bran-new quarter of London' live the Veneerings, a parvenu couple. At a dinner given by them, Mortimer Lightwood, a young solicitor, tells the story of John Harmon, a 'dust contractor' who made his fortune from the mountains of ordure piled up at Battle Bridge in north London. He turned his young son, John, out of doors after the boy had protested against his father's treatment of his sister, and the boy went abroad to make his own living. Harmon died, making the condition of his son's inheritance that he should marry Bella Wilfer, daughter of a clerk. Lightwood receives a note to say that the dead body of young John Harmon has been found in the Thames, and goes with his friend Eugene Wrayburn to Hexam's, encountering a young man calling himself Julius Handford, on the same errand.

Julius Handford is, in fact (though this is not revealed until half way through the novel), young John Harmon himself. On his way back from the Cape he had found himself so mistrustful of the destiny that awaited him that he arranged with the ship's third mate, who resembled him physically, to exchange clothes and identities. By this means he would be able to inspect Bella Wilfer from a distance and decide whether or not he would claim his inheritance and marry her. Should he not claim, the money would go to Mr. Nicodemus 'Noddy' Boffin, a confidential servant of his father's. Boffin and his wife befriended John in his unhappy childhood, and he is reluctant to deprive them of the legacy.

When they reached England the third mate drugged and robbed Harmon, but was himself attacked by other men at the lodging-house. Both he and Harmon were thrown into the river. The third mate drowned; his body was recovered and mistaken for Harmon's, but Harmon dragged himself out and recovered.

Now officially dead, he decides to go through with his plan to live under an alias. Calling himself John Rokesmith, he goes to lodge with 'Rumty' Wilfer, a clerk in Veneering's employ, who lives with his temperamental wife, and his daughters, Bella and Lavinia. He finds Bella pretty, but vain, spoilt, and over-fond of money.

Mr. Boffin is now manager of the Harmon Estates. He and his wife, far from rejoicing in their legacy, are grieved by the discovery of the body of the supposed John, and offer a reward of £10,000 for the arrest of his murderer. Mrs. Boffin decides to adopt an orphan, to take the place of the little John Harmon she loved, who shall in turn be given John's name. They also decide to ask Bella Wilfer to come and live with them, which she does with alacrity, delighted to leave her family, though she is deeply attached to her put-upon little father. At the Wilfers' they meet John 'Rokesmith', to whom Boffin refers as Our Mutal Friend. John becomes Boffin's secretary. Mrs. Boffin, when John enters their house, is haunted by the faces of old Harmon and his son and daughter.

The Boffins propose to adopt Johnny, the small grandson of Betty Higden, a child-minder, but he dies in the Children's Hospital. Betty is afraid of being taken to the workhouse, leaves home, and dies of exhaustion.

In parallel with the story of John and Bella runs that of Lizzie, Hexam's daughter. Handsome and intelligent, she attracts the attention of Wrayburn, and also of Bradley Headstone, her young brother's schoolmaster. When her father is accidentally drowned, after being accused of the murder of the supposed John Harmon, Lizzie goes to live in Westminster with a little crippled girl, Fanny Cleaver, known as Jenny Wren, who supports her drunken father by making dolls' dresses. Jenny is a whimsical, precocious child, and something of a visionary. When Headstone's importunities become too much for her Lizzie seeks the help of Riah, a kindly old Jew, who finds her a job at a paper-mill outside London.

In the world of fashion, John Harmon is being discussed by the Veneerings. They tell Boffin that his secretary is an adventurer. John proposes marriage to Bella, but she scornfully tells him that she intends to marry money. Boffin has secretly recognised his secretary as John Harmon, and in order to change Bella's worldly point of view he pretends to persecute John. He also pretends to become a miser, and abuses John for his supposed neglect of the Estate. Finally John is dismissed. Bella, in sympathy, goes with him. They are married, in the name of Rokesmith, for Bella still does not know her lover's identity, and after an idyllic wedding-breakfast at Greenwich, shared by Bella's father, settle down in a cottage at Blackheath.

Wrayburn has sought and found Lizzie. But he has been followed by Headstone, who considers Wrayburn to be the cause of Lizzie's rejection of him, and is madly jealous. He tracks down Wrayburn, and watches him keep an appointment with Lizzie on the river-bank, during which Lizzie refuses Wrayburn's love on account of the difference in their social status. Headstone imagines the interview to be an amorous one, and after Lizzie and Wrayburn have parted he attacks Wrayburn, wounds him severely, and throws him into the river. Lizzie rescues him and nurses him, and when he appears to be dying promises to marry him. Headstone, who thinks him dead, hears the news of the forthcoming wedding from the clergyman who is to perform it, and falls into a fit. Later he encounters Riderhood, who is blackmailing him. They struggle by the river and are both drowned.

John 'Rokesmith' meets Mortimer Lightwood, whom he has so far managed to avoid, as being the one person who would recognise him. He does so, and the secret is out. John takes Bella and their baby to their new home in London. Mrs. Boffin tells Bella how she came to recognise John, and why Boffin pretended to be harsh and miserly.

A will is found which appears to leave old Harmon's wealth to the Crown, and a later one naming the Boffins. Boffin generously makes over the money to John and Bella, retaining only 'Harmon's Jail', the home of his old employer, now renamed 'Boffin's Bower' by Mrs. Boffin.

Into the main plots are woven many other threads: the loveless marriage for money of the Lammles; the humours of Silas Wegg the one-legged ballad-monger and Mr. Venus the taxidermist; the pompous Podsnap, his equine-faced wife, and their gauche daughter Georgiana; Miss Emma Peecher, a little teacher at Headstone's school and his devoted adorer; Miss Abbey Potterson, formidable hostess of the Six Jolly Fellowship Porters, a Thames-side tavern, Pleasant Riderhood the pawnbroker; Sloppy the orphan, Betty Higden's mangle-turner; Twemlow, the Veneerings' humble friend and hanger-on; Fascination Fledgeby the money-broker. All their stories are interdependent.

GEORGE SILVERMAN'S EXPLANATION

First published in the American *Atlantic Monthly* in January, February, and March 1868 and in England in *All the Year Round* in February the same year.

George Silverman, an orphan, is brought up by Brother Hawkyard and other fanatical Nonconformists in Lancashire. He becomes a clergyman and secretary to Lady Fareway, with whose daughter Adelina, his pupil, he falls in love. When he self-sacrificingly contrives Adelina's marriage to another pupil, Granville Wharton, Lady Fareway believes Silverman has acted out of self-interest, dismisses him, and pursues him vengefully for some years before he finds peace.

HOLIDAY ROMANCE

Written for an American children's magazine, *Our Young Folks*, and first published there January–May 1868, and in England, in *All the Year Round*, in January–April 1868. The American edition had four illustrations by John (later Sir John) Gilbert.

Purportedly edited by William Tinkling, aged eight, it is in four parts, each supposedly written by a small child. William Tinkling, the eight-year-old editor, tells of his 'marriage' to Nettie Ashford, aged seven. He and Lieutenant-Colonel Robin Redforth, aged nine, try to rescue Nettie and Robin's bride, Alice Rainbird, aged seven, from imprisonment in the school of the Misses Drowvey and Grimmer. The plan fails and Tinkling is court-martialled. Alice Rainbird's story is of the Princess Alicia, eldest child of King Watkins the First. Her godmother, the Fairy Grandmarina, gives her a Magic Fishbone, which will bring her anything she wants. Alicia uses the wish to save her father's fortunes and is rewarded by her fairy godmother with a magnificent wedding to Prince Certainpersonio. Robin Redforth's romance concerns Captain Boldheart, intrepid master of the schooner *Beauty*, and his tussles with the Latingrammar master, the treacherous commander of the *Scorpion*. The final romance, by Nettie Ashford, tells of Mrs. Orange and Mrs. Lemon, children in charge of grown-ups who 'are never allowed to sit up to supper, except on their birthdays.'

THE MYSTERY OF EDWIN DROOD

Dickens's fifteenth novel, left unfinished at his death. Begun at Gad's Hill in October 1869, and written there and at 5 Hyde Park Place, London; the last words written at Gad's Hill on 8 June 1870. First instalment published on 1 April 1870, and the sixth in September 1870, by Chapman & Hall, with illustrations by Luke Fildes (the 'Green Cover' designed, and some unused drawings made, by Charles Collins). First published in America, April to October 1870, as a serial in a monthly Dickens Supplement to *Harper's Weekly*. Also published by Fields, Osgood & Co., Boston, April–September 1870. It first appeared in book form in England in August 1870.

Dickens outlined to Forster several ideas for what he little realised was to be his last novel. 'Two people – boy or girl, or very young, going apart from one another, pledged to be married after many years – at the end of the book. The interest to arise out of the tracing of their separate ways, and the impossibility of telling what will be done with that impending fate.' This he discarded for a 'very curious and new idea' about the murder of a nephew by an uncle, who would review his own career in the condemned cell as though it were somebody else's. The murderer was to discover the utter needlessness of the murder soon after its commission, and was to be discovered by means of a gold ring found uncorroded in quicklime.

Exactly half the numbers of the book had been written when Dickens died. It is impossible to deduce with any certainty what the outcome of the mystery was to be; whether he had changed the scheme mentioned to Forster or not. What exists seems to make Jasper so inescapably the murderer that there is not much interest in the plot. 'If Edwin Drood is dead, there is not much mystery about him,' commented G. K. Chesterton. Many volumes have been devoted to conjecture, but no completely satisfactory solution has ever been suggested.

The writing is unlike anything Dickens had done before, as though, in his last year of life, he had slipped into a new, fresh style, in complete contrast to the heaviness and complexity of the preceding novel, *Our Mutual Friend*. It might be described as the literary equivalent of architectural High Gothic, with many passages of poetic prose and the most vivid scenic descriptions Dickens had yet produced. It is as though he were writing the narrative to accompany a film as it unrolled itself in his mind. He had never conveyed so clearly the essence of his beloved Rochester before. The Cathedral dominates the story as no building has previously done in his works. London has receded to a 'gritty' place; but the Law and its practice are no longer portrayed with Dickens's usual contempt. Mr. Grewgious is a man with a heart and (it seems)

some detective ability; Staple Inn has flowers and birds instead of the cats and bugs of early disgusted descriptions of the Inns of Court. Crisparkle is his first likeable clergyman, Rosa his most real and living girl, more vital even than Bella Wilfer. When the book suddenly stops, the reader is left with a feeling of disappointment and loss. 'It is certainly one of his most beautiful works, if not the most beautiful of all,' said Longfellow.

In the Prologue, written like the telling of a dream, a man lies on a squalid broken bed in an opium den, lost in a vision of eastern pageantry. As he wakes from his stupor, the bedpost becomes the tower of an English cathedral: the cathedral of Cloisterham.

The dreamer is John Jasper, music-master and choirmaster of the cathedral. He is a dark, pale man of sombre manner. He welcomes to his rooms in the cathedral gatehouse his nephew Edwin Drood, only a few years younger than himself, a cheerful youth with whom he seems on the best and most affectionate of terms. Edwin, a student engineer, has been engaged since childhood to Rosa Bud, his father having expressed the dying wish that his son should marry the daughter of his old friend. Both are now orphans. Edwin's guardian is Jasper, Rosa's is Mr. Hiram Grewgious, a lawyer of Staple Inn.

Edwin has come down to see Rosa on her birthday. She is a pupil at Miss Twinkleton's Academy, where she receives Edwin somewhat pettishly, telling him how it irks her to be so teased about their engagement. They quarrel. Edwin treats her casually and calls her 'Pussy'. But Jasper has other and deeper feelings. As though trying to tell Edwin something without words, he confesses that he is unhappy, unfulfilled, in his cathedral work – that 'even a poor monotonous chorister and grinder of music – in his niche – may be troubled with some stray sort of ambition, aspiration . . .' – and bids Edwin take it as a warning. Edwin obviously fails to understand him.

Canon Crisparkle, a brisk, sporting young bachelor clergyman, receives visitors at his mother's house in Minor Canon Corner. They are Neville and Helena Landless, twins from Ceylon, dark, handsome, and with an untamed air. Neville is to be Crisparkle's pupil, Helena to attend Miss Twinkleton's. She becomes friendly with Rosa. A musical party is held at which Rosa sings to Jasper's accompaniment, wavers under his passionate, hypnotic gaze, and faints. Neville is attracted to Rosa and antagonistic to Edwin, who treats her far too lightly, he thinks; and Edwin seems more attracted to Helena than to Rosa. On the way home the two young men quarrel, a quarrel subtly fed by Jasper as he entertains them later. Neville's fiery temper is roused, and Jasper dwells on its violence to Crisparkle.

Grewgious visits Rosa to discuss the marriage settlement, and she asks him if her engagement could be broken without any forfeit on either side. He replies that it was 'merely a wish' on the part of Edwin's father and hers, and is not a binding contract. But he does not sense the feeling behind her query.

Edwin calls on Grewgious in London, and receives from him a tactfully veiled lecture on his light-minded attitude towards Rosa, whom he does not seem to value enough: Grewgious was in love with her dead mother, whom he sees again in Rosa. He gives Edwin a ring taken from her dead finger, charging him to give it to Rosa on the day their betrothal is finally and solemnly settled; but if Edwin has doubts, or if there is anything wrong between them, Edwin is to bring the ring back to him.

Edwin goes down to Cloisterham for Christmas, having been invited by Jasper to become reconciled with Neville at his rooms. When he meets Rosa, they walk by the river, and she tells him that she feels they should only be friends, not lovers, for they have not voluntarily chosen each other and will never be happy. Edwin, touched and saddened, agrees; but they decide not to tell Jasper yet, for his heart (Edwin believes) is set on the union. Rosa looks strangely at him. Their parting kiss is seen by Jasper.

Jasper goes on a night tour of the cathedral with Durdles, the sexton, plying him with strong drink as they go, until Durdles falls into a stupor and seems to hear the clink of keys and footsteps going away from him. Jasper seems deeply interested in Durdles's ability to detect, by tapping the masonry, bodies, or other objects lying within ancient tombs. He is angered by the attentions of an urchin, Deputy, whose job it is to stone Durdles if he catches him out after ten o'clock and drive him home.

On Christmas Eve, Neville prepares for a walking-tour he intends to make next day. He leaves the house with his bundle and a stout, heavy stick. Edwin wanders about the town until it is time to go to Jasper's, calls at a jeweller's to have his watch repaired, and mentions to the man that he wears no jewellery but his watch, chain, and shirt-pin. He meets the old woman who is the proprietress of the opium den in London frequented by Jasper. She asks him for money and warns him that if his name is Eddy he is in grave danger. John Jasper goes to the rendezvous singing, with a great black scarf wound in a loop over his arm.

That night a terrible gale of wind blows, tearing off the hands of the cathedral clock and damaging the tower. Jasper rushes among the spectators of the damage exclaiming that Edwin has vanished after walking down to the river with Neville the previous night. Neville is pursued, brought back, and taken before the Mayor. He angrily declares his innocence. A day and night search is instituted for Edwin, and Crisparkle, bathing early in the river, finds his watch and shirt-pin, seeming drawn to them by a kind of magnetism. Grewgious visits Jasper, finds him exhausted after hours of futile search, and apparently deeply despondent. Grewgious's manner to him is notably abrupt. He informs Jasper that the engagement between Edwin and Rosa had been broken off before Edwin's disappearance. Jasper swoons. Days afterwards, when no trace other than the jewellery has yet been found of Edwin, Jasper shows Crisparkle an entry in his diary vowing to track down the murderer of his 'dear dead boy'.

Six months later, Neville Landless is living in chambers in Staple Inn, near Grewgious, driven away from Cloisterham by suspicion and rumour. He is ill and worried. Crisparkle visits him and Grewgious, who points out that Jasper is lurking outside, possibly keeping a watch on Neville. Neville receives a visit from a neighbour, Mr. Tartar, a handsome, lively young man who has resigned from the Royal Navy on coming into property. Tartar befriends him.

After the end of the summer term, Rosa has been left alone at Miss Twinkleton's. Jasper joins her in the garden, and makes a wild declaration of love to her, swearing to hound Neville to his death if she will not love him. Rosa is terrified. That night she goes up to London and tells Grewgious her story. He finds a temporary lodging for her at Furnival's Inn. Next morning Crisparkle arrives, and Helena, who is now staying with Neville. Tartar calls, and Crisparkle and he greet each other as once master and fag in schooldays. Tartar and Rosa are instantly attracted to one another, and he gallantly offers her the use of his chambers. From Tartar's, Rosa goes to lodge with Mrs. Billickin, and Miss Twinkleton comes up to chaperone her, though she and Mrs. Billickin are natural enemies. Tartar disappears from the scene, and Rosa pines.

A new face appears in Cloisterham: Dick Datchery, a sturdy man of indeterminate age with somewhat odd-looking white hair. He takes the lodgings beneath Jasper's, and appears very inquisitive about all the recent doings in Cloisterham. He enlists Deputy as spy or reporter, and questions people, including Jasper, notching up successes in chalk on his cupboard door. The opium woman arrives on the track of Jasper; Datchery directs her to the cathedral.

Jasper, meanwhile, has visited her in London and in an opium trance has related an apparently symbolical journey he has made repeatedly, in imagination,

always in the same way and with the same companion; but when it was made in fact, it was 'the poorest of all. No struggle, no consciousness of peril, no entreaty – and yet I never saw *that* before. . . .'

The story breaks off as Datchery, having seen the opium woman into the cathedral, falls to his breakfast with an appetite.

Minor characters are Mr. Honeythunder, the pompous and bigoted District Philanthropist, who is the Landlesses' guardian; Mr. Sapsea, the equally pompous Mayor of Cloisterham; and Bazzard, Grewgious's mysterious clerk, thought by many Dickensians to be the disguised Datchery.

THE LAMPLIGHTER

On the crest of his *Pickwick* fame, Dickens was invited in 1838 by William Macready to write a play for him. The result was *The Lamplighter*, a farce, which Dickens completed in November and read to the actor-manager and his company. The piece was rehearsed, but never performed, as Macready, pressed by his actors, asked Dickens to withdraw it. The text is included in volumes of Dickens's plays. He made use of the plot in the story entitled 'The Lamplighter's Story'.

THE LIFE OF OUR LORD

Written in 1846 at the Villa Rosemont, Lausanne. Never intended for publication, it was however published in 1934, by Associated Newspapers.

John Forster describes this as 'an abstract, in plain language for the use of his children, of the narrative in the Four Gospels. . . . Allusion was made, shortly after his death, to the existence of such a manuscript, with expression of a wish that it might be published; but nothing would have shocked himself so much as any suggestion of that kind. The little piece was of a peculiarly private character; written for his children, and exclusively and strictly for their use only.'

THE PEOPLE

AN ALPHABETICAL LIST
OF ALL THE NAMED CHARACTERS IN
DICKENS'S WORKS

THE PEOPLE

'Aaron': Wrayburn's slighting name for Riah. *'If Mr. Aaron,' said Eugene . . . 'will be good enough to relinquish his charge to me, he will be quite free for any engagement he may have at the Synagogue' (Mutual Friend).*

Adams: Head-boy at Dr. Strong's. *He looked like a young clergyman, in his white cravat, but he was very affable and good-humoured (Copperfield).*

Adams: Sampson's clerk ('Hunted Down').

Adams, Captain, and **Westwood:** Seconds to Verisopht and Hawk in their duel. *Both utterly heartless, both men upon town, both thoroughly initiated in its worst vices, both deeply in debt, both fallen from some higher estate, both addicted to every depravity for which society can find some genteel name and plead its most depraving conventionalities as an excuse, they were, naturally, gentlemen of unblemished honour themselves, and of great nicety concerning the honour of other people (Nickleby).*

Adams, Jack: Subject of one of Cousin Feenix's anecdotes. *'Jack – little Jack – man with a cast in his eye, and slight impediment in his speech – man who sat for somebody's borough. We used to call him in my parliamentary time W. P. Adams, in consequence of his being Warming Pan for a young fellow who was in his minority' (Dombey).*

Adams, Jane: The Fieldings' housemaid who takes her friend Anne in to see the wedding preparations. *Comes all out of breath to redeem a solemn promise of taking her in, under cover of the confusion, to see the breakfast table spread forth in state, and – sight of sights! – her young mistress ready dressed for church (Young Couples – 'Young Couple').* She appears again, widowed and living in an alms-house, in *Young Couples – 'Old Couple'.*

Admiralty: Naval magnate, guest at Merdle's *(Dorrit).*

Affery: Maiden name of Mrs. Jeremiah Flintwinch, by which she is still known in Mrs. Clennam's service. *Lived in terror of her husband and Mrs. Clennam, the clever ones (Dorrit).*

African Knife-Swallower, The: Member of the Crummleses' theatrical company. *Looked and spoke remarkably like an Irishman (Nickleby).*

'Aged, The': Wemmick's father. *A very old man in a flannel coat : clean, cheerful, comfortable, and very well cared for, but intensely deaf (Expectations).*

'Aggerawayter': See **Cruncher, Mrs.** *(Two Cities).*

Agnes: Mrs. Bloss's maid, admired by Tibbs. *In a cherry-coloured merino dress, open-work stockings, and shoes with sandals : like a disguised Columbine (Boz – 'Boarding-House').*

Akerman: Head jailer at Newgate at the time of the Gordon Riots. He was a real character, of humane disposition. *'I have a good many people in my custody.' He glanced downward, as he spoke, into the jail : and the feeling that he could see into the different yards, and that he overlooked everything which was hidden from their view by the rugged walls, so lashed and goaded the mob, that they howled like wolves (Rudge).*

Akershem, Sophronia: A predatory friend of the Veneerings. She marries Lammle, believing him to be wealthy. *Mature young lady; raven locks, and complexion that lights up well when well-powdered – as it is – carrying on considerably in the captivation of mature young gentleman (Mutual Friend).*

Alice: Youngest of the Five Sisters of York (q.v.). *If the four elder sisters were lovely, how beautiful was the youngest, a fair creature of sixteen ! The blushing tints in the soft bloom on the fruit, or the delicate painting on the flower, are not more exquisite than was the blending of the rose* *and lily in her gentle face, or the deep blue of her eye. The vine, in all its elegant luxuriance, is not more graceful than were the clusters of rich brown hair that sported round her brow (Nickleby).*

Alice, Mistress: A sixteenth century bowyer's daughter, heroine of Magog's tale. *Mistress Alice, his only daughter, was the richest heiress in all his wealthy ward. Young Hugh had often maintained with staff and cudgel that she was the handsomest. To do him justice, I believe she was (Humphrey).*

Alicia, Princess: Eldest child of King Watkins the First and god-daughter of the Fairy Grandmarina in Alice Rainbird's romantic tale. She marries Prince Certainpersonio ('Holiday Romance').

Alick: Young passenger who dances on the Gravesend steam packet. *Alick, who is a damp earthy child in red worsted socks, takes certain small jumps upon the deck, to the unspeakable satisfaction of his family circle (Boz – 'The River').*

Alicumpaine, Mrs.: A juvenile friend of the Oranges in Nettie Ashford's romantic tale ('Holiday Romance').

Allen, Arabella: Ben's sister who secretly marries Winkle. *A young lady with black eyes, an arch smile, and a pair of remarkably nice boots with fur round the top (Pickwick).*

Allen, Benjamin: Arabella's brother, drinking companion of Bob Sawyer, his fellow medical student. *A coarse, stout, thick-set young man, with black hair cut rather short, and a white face cut rather long. He was embellished with spectacles, and wore a white neckerchief. Below his single-breastéd black surtout, which was buttoned up to his chin, appeared the usual number of pepper-and-salt coloured legs, terminating in a pair of imperfectly polished boots. Although his coat was short in the sleeves, it disclosed no vestige of a linen wristband; and although there was quite enough of his face to admit of the encroachment of a shirt collar, it was not graced by the smallest approach to that appendage. He presented, altogether, rather a mildewy appearance, and emitted a fragrant odour of full-flavoured Cubas (Pickwick).*

Alphonse: The Wittiterly's page. *A little page; so little, indeed, that his body would not hold, in ordinary array, the number of small buttons which are indispensable to a page's costume, and they were consequently obliged to be stuck on four abreast. . . . If ever an Alphonse carried plain Bill in his face and figure, that page was the boy (Nickleby).*

'Altro': Pancks's nickname for Cavaletto, from his habit of frequently using the Italian word, meaning 'certainly' (Dorrit).

Amelia: Sister of Jane, two marriageable girls displayed by their mamma at the Ramsgate library gambling tables. *'Nice figure, Amelia,' whispered the stout lady to a thin youth beside her (Boz – 'Tuggses at Ramsgate').*

Amelia: Wife of Bill, a criminal, and supplicant to Jaggers for him (Expectations).

America Junior: Of Messrs. Hancock & Floby, Dry Goods Store, No. 47, Bunker Hill Street. Name and address to which Putnam Smif wishes Martin Chuzzlewit to address his letter of reply (Chuzzlewit).

'Analytical Chemist': Simile for the Veneerings' butler. *The retainer goes round, like a gloomy Analytical Chemist; always seeming to say, after 'Chablis, sir?' – 'You wouldn't if you knew what it's made of'(Mutual Friend).*

Anderson, John and Mrs. John: A couple of self-respecting tramps. *Monarchs could not deprive him of his hard-earned character. Accordingly, as you come up with this spectacle of virtue in distress, Mrs. Anderson rises, and with a decent curtsey presents for your consideration a certificate from a Doctor of Divinity, the reverend the Vicar of Upper Dodgington, who informs his Christian friends and all whom it may concern that the bearers, John Anderson and his lawful wife, are persons to whom you cannot be too liberal (Uncommercial – 'Tramps').*

Angelica: A former sweetheart of the Uncommercial Traveller. *O, Angelica,* *what has become of you, this present Sunday morning when I can't attend to the sermon; and, more difficult question than that, what has become of Me as I was when I sat by your side?* (Uncommercial – 'City of London Churches').

Anglo-Bengalee Disinterested Loan and Life Assurance Company: Fraudulent company promoted by Montague Tigg, with David Crimple as secretary. *'What,' asked the secretary . . . 'will be the paid-up capital, according to the next prospectus?' 'A figure of two, and as many oughts after it as the printer can get into the same line,' replied his friend. 'Ha, ha!'* (Chuzzlewit).

Anne: A housemaid at Dombey's. Marries Towlinson, the footman (Dombey).

Anne: Housemaid friend of Jane Adams, who takes her in to see Emma Fielding's wedding preparations. *Heaven alone can tell in what bright colours this marriage is painted upon the mind of the little housemaid at number six, who has hardly slept a wink all night with thinking of it, and now stands on the unswept door-steps leaning upon her broom, and looking wistfully towards the enchanted house. Nothing short of omniscience can divine what visions of the baker, or the greengrocer, or the smart and most insinuating butterman, are flitting across her mind – what thoughts of how she would dress on such an occasion, if she were a lady – of how she would dress, if she were only a bride* (Young Couples – 'Young Couple'). She is referred to again in *Young Couples* – 'Old Couple' as having married a man who ill-treated her and having died in Lambeth workhouse.

Anny: One of the old paupers attending Agnes Fleming's deathbed *(Twist)*.

Antonio: Spanish guitarist in a London sailors' lodging-house. *The look of the young man and the tinkling of the instrument so change the place in a moment to a leaf out of Don Quixote, that I wonder where his mule is stabled* (Uncommercial – 'Poor Mercantile Jack').

'Archbishop of Greenwich': Simile for the head waiter at Rokesmith's and Bella

Wilfer's wedding breakfast. *A solemn gentleman in black clothes and a white cravat, who looked much more like a clergyman than the clergyman, and seemed to have mounted a great deal higher in the church: not to say, scaled the steeple. This dignitary, conferring in secrecy with John Rokesmith on the subject of punch and wines, bent his head as though stooping to the Papistical practice of receiving auricular confession. Likewise, on John's offering a suggestion which didn't meet his views, his face became overcast and reproachful, as enjoining penance (Mutual Friend).*

'Artful Dodger, The': See **Dawkins, John** *(Twist)*.

Ashford, Nettie: William Tinkling's 'bride', aged 'half-past six', and author of the romantic tale of the Oranges and Mrs. Alicumpaine. *We were married in the right-hand closet in the corner of the dancing-school, where first we met, with a ring (a green one) from Wilkingwater's toy-shop* ('Holiday Romance').

Atherfield, Mrs.: Passenger in the *Golden Mary* with her daughter Lucy. *A bright-eyed, blooming young wife who was going out to join her husband in California, taking with her their only child, a little girl of three years old, whom he had never seen* (Christmas Stories – 'Golden Mary').

Atherfield, Lucy: Mrs. Atherfield's daughter. She dies in the long-boat after the wreck. *As the child had a quantity of shining fair hair, clustering in curls all about her face, and as her name was Lucy, Steadiman gave her the name of the Golden Lucy* (Christmas Stories – 'Golden Mary').

Augustus: The pet dog dissected by Professors Muff and Nogo in their hotel room. *The deceased was named, in affectionate remembrance of a former lover of his mistress, to whom he bore a striking personal resemblance, which renders the circumstances additionally affecting (Mudfog).*

Aunt, Mr. F's: See **Mr. F's Aunt** *(Dorrit)*.

'Avenger, The': See **Pepper** *(Expectations)*.

Ayresleigh: A debtor whom Pickwick meets while under arrest at Namby's. *A middle-aged man in a very old suit of black, who looked pale and haggard, and paced up and down the room incessantly (Pickwick).*

B., Master: The ghost of the haunted house, really a manifestation of the lost youth of John, the narrator. *The young spectre was dressed in an obsolete fashion: or rather, was not so much dressed as put into a case of inferior pepper-and-salt cloth, made horrible by means of shining buttons. I observed that these buttons went, in a double row, over each shoulder of the young ghost, and appeared to descend his back. He wore a frill round his neck. His right hand (which I distinctly noticed to be inky) was laid upon his stomach; connecting this action with some feeble pimples on his countenance, and his general air of nausea, I concluded this ghost to be the ghost of a boy who had habitually taken a great deal too much medicine (Christmas Stories – 'Haunted House').*

Babley, Richard: See Dick, Mr. *(Copperfield).*

Bachelor, The: An old gentleman who is kind to Little Nell and her grandfather at a village they visit in their wanderings. He proves to be brother to Abel Garland's father. *The little old gentleman was the active spirit of the place, the adjuster of all differences, the promoter of all merry-makings, the dispenser of his friend's bounty, and of no small charity of his own besides; the universal mediator, comforter, and friend. None of the simple villagers had cared to ask his name, or, when they knew it, to store it in their memory. Perhaps from some vague rumour of his college honours which had been whispered abroad on his first arrival, perhaps because he was an unmarried, unencumbered gentleman, he had been called the bachelor (Curiosity Shop).*

Badger, Bayham: A doctor cousin of Kenge, practising at Chelsea, to whom Richard Carstone is articled. *A pink, fresh-faced, crisp-looking gentleman, with a weak voice, white teeth, light hair, and surprised eyes: some years younger, I should say, than Mrs. Bayham Badger. He admired her exceedingly, but principally, and to begin with, on the curious ground (as it seemed to us) of her having had three husbands. We had barely taken our seats, when he said to Mr. Jarndyce quite triumphantly, 'You would hardly suppose that I am Mrs. Bayham Badger's third!' (Bleak House).*

Badger, Mrs. Bayham: Badger's wife, widow of Captain Swosser, R.N., and of Professor Dingo. *She was surrounded in the drawing-room by various objects, indicative of her painting a little, playing the piano a little, playing the guitar a little, playing the harp a little, singing a little, working a little, reading a little, writing poetry a little, and botanising a little. She was a lady of about fifty, I should think, youthfully dressed, and of a very fine complexion. If I add, to the little list of her accomplishments, that she rouged a little, I do not mean that there was any harm in it (Bleak House).*

Bagman, The: Narrator of 'The Bagman's Story' and 'The Bagman's Uncle' at the Peacock, Eatanswill. *A stout, hale personage of about forty, with only one eye – a very bright black eye, which twinkled with a roguish expression of fun and good humour (Pickwick).*

Bagman's Uncle, The: See Martin, Jack *(Pickwick).*

Bagnet, Malta and Quebec: The Bagnets' elder and younger small daughters, sisters of Woolwich. *Not supposed to have been actually christened by the names applied to them, though always so called in the family, from the places of their birth in barracks (Bleak House).*

Bagnet, Matthew ('Lignum Vitae'): Bassoon player in a theatre orchestra and proprietor of a musical instrument shop in London. He helps George Rouncewell in his financial and other difficulties. *An ex-artilleryman, tall and upright, with shaggy eyebrows, and whiskers like the fibres of a cocoa-nut, not a hair upon his head, and a torrid complexion. His voice, short, deep, and resonant, is not at all* *unlike the tones of the instrument to which he is devoted. Indeed, there may be generally observed in him an unbending, unyielding, brass-bound air, as if he were himself the bassoon of the human orchestra (Bleak House).*

Bagnet, Mrs. Matthew: Bagnet's strong-minded wife. She reunites Mrs. Rouncewell with George. *Not at all an ill-looking woman. Rather large-boned, a little coarse in the grain, and freckled by the sun and wind which have tanned her hair upon the forehead; but healthy, wholesome, and bright-eyed. A strong, busy, active, honest-faced woman of from forty-five to fifty. Clean, hardy, and so economically dressed (though substantially), that the only article of ornament of which she stands possessed appears to be her wedding-ring; around which her finger has grown to be so large since it was put on, that it will never come off again until it shall mingle with Mrs. Bagnet's dust (Bleak House).*

Bagnet, Woolwich: The Bagnets' young son, brother of Malta and Quebec. *Young Woolwich is the type and model of a young drummer (Bleak House).*

Bagstock, Major Joseph: Neighbour to Miss Tox and toady to Dombey. *A wooden-featured, blue-faced major, with his eyes starting out of his head, in whom Miss Tox recognised, as she herself expressed it, 'something so truly military.' || 'Joey B., sir,' the major would say, with a flourish of his walking-stick, 'is worth a dozen of you. If you had a few more of the Bagstock breed among you, sir, you'd be none the worse for it. Old Joe, sir, needn't look far for a wife even now, if he was on the look-out; but he's hard-hearted, sir, is Joe – he's tough, sir, tough, and de-vilish sly!' After such a declaration wheezing sounds would be heard; and the major's blue would deepen into purple, while his eyes strained and started convulsively (Dombey).*

Bailey, Captain: David Copperfield's rival at the Larkinses' ball. *I take Miss Larkins out. I take her sternly from the side of Captain Bailey. He is wretched, I have no doubt; but he is nothing to me. I have been wretched, too (Copperfield).*

Bailey, Benjamin: A small boy, page at Todgers's, later taken into partnership by Sweedlepipe. Also known as Uncle Ben, Uncle, Barnwell and other nicknames. *The gentlemen at Todgers's had a merry habit, too, of bestowing upon him, for the time being, the name of any notorious malefactor or minister; and sometimes when current events were flat, they even sought the pages of history for these distinctions; as Mr. Pitt, Young Brownrigg, and the like. || A small boy with a large red head, and no nose to speak of (Chuzzlewit).*

Balderstone, Thomas (Uncle Tom): Mrs. Gattleton's rich brother. *He was one of the best-hearted men in existence: always in a good temper, and always talking. It was his boast that he wore top-boots on all occasions, and had never worn a black silk neckerchief; and it was his pride that he remembered all the principal plays of Shakespeare from beginning to end – and so he did. The result of this parrot-like accomplishment was, that he was not only perpetually quoting himself, but that he could never sit by, and hear a misquotation from the 'Swan of Avon' without setting the unfortunate delinquent right (Boz – 'Mrs. Joseph Porter').*

Balim: A young ladies' young gentleman. *Seated upon the ground, at the feet of a few young ladies who were reclining on a bank; he was so profusely decked with scarfs, ribands, flowers, and other pretty spoils, that he looked like a lamb – or perhaps a calf would be a better simile – adorned for the sacrifice. One young lady supported a parasol over his interesting head, another held his hat, and a third his neckcloth, which in romantic fashion, he had thrown off; the young gentleman himself, with his hand upon his breast, and his face moulded into an expression of the most honeyed sweetness, was warbling forth some choice specimens of vocal music in praise of female loveliness, in a style so exquisitely perfect, that we burst into an involuntary shout of laughter, and made a hasty retreat (Young Gentlemen – 'Young Ladies' Young Gentleman').*

Bamber, Jack: Narrator of the 'Tale of the Queer Client'. *A little yellow high-*

shouldered man. . . . *There was a fixed grim smile perpetually on his countenance; he leant his chin on a long skinny hand, with nails of extraordinary length; and as he inclined his head to one side, and looked keenly out from beneath his ragged grey eyebrows, there was a strange, wild slyness in his leer, quite repulsive to behold (Pickwick).* He reappears in *Humphrey.*

Banger, Captain: Vestryman, of Wilderness Walk (*Reprinted* – 'Our Vestry').

Bangham, Mrs.: Attendant at Amy Dorrit's birth in the Marshalsea. *Mrs. Bangham, charwoman and messenger, who was not a prisoner (though she had been once), but was the popular medium of communication with the outer world, had volunteered her services as fly-catcher and general attendant. The walls and ceiling were blackened with flies. Mrs. Bangham, expert in sudden device, with one hand fanned the patient with a cabbage leaf, and with the other set traps of vinegar and sugar in gallipots; at the same time enunciating sentiments of an encouraging and congratulatory nature, adapted to the occasion (Dorrit).*

Banks, Major: Retired East India Director: a disguise assumed by Meltham to outwit Julius Slinkton. *An old man, whose head was sunk on his breast, and who was enveloped in a variety of wrappers* ('Hunted Down').

Bantam, Angelo Cyrus: Master of the Ceremonies at Bath. *A charming young man of not much more than fifty, dressed in a very bright blue coat with resplendent buttons, black trousers, and the thinnest possible pair of highly-polished boots. A gold eye-glass was suspended from his neck by a short broad black ribbon; a gold snuff-box was lightly clasped in his left hand; gold rings innumerable glittered on his fingers; and a large diamond pin set in gold glistened in his shirt frill. He had a gold watch, and a gold curb-chain with large gold seals; and he carried a pliant ebony cane with a heavy gold top. His linen was of the very whitest, finest, and stiffest; his wig of the glossiest, blackest, and curliest. His snuff was prince's mixture; his scent bouquet du roi. His features were*

contracted into a perpetual smile; and his teeth were in such perfect order that it was difficult at a small distance to tell the real from the false (Pickwick).

Baps: Dancing-master at Dr. Blimber's school. *A very grave gentleman, with a slow and measured manner of speaking (Dombey).*

Baps, Mrs.: Baps's wife (*Dombey*).

Baptista, Giovanni: Genoese courier who narrates the story of Clara and Signor Dellombra ('At Dusk').

Baptiste: Soldier billeted on the water-carrier in the French town where Langley lodges. *Sitting on the pavement in the sunlight, with his martial legs asunder, and one of the Water-carrier's spare pails between them, which (to the delight and glory of the heart of the Water-carrier coming across the Place from the fountain, yoked and burdened) he was painting bright-green outside and bright-red within (Christmas Stories –* 'Somebody's Luggage').

Bar: Legal magnate, guest at Merdle's. *With his little insinuating Jury droop, and fingering his persuasive double eye-glass (Dorrit).*

Barbara: The Garlands' housemaid. She marries Kit Nubbles. *Very tidy, modest and demure, but very pretty too (Curiosity Shop).*

Barbara's Mother: Mother of the Garlands' servant. *Didn't she look genteel, standing there with her gloves on (Curiosity Shop).*

Barbary, Miss: Esther Summerson's stern aunt at Windsor who brings her up in childhood. Sister to Lady Dedlock. *She was a good, good woman! She went to church three times every Sunday, and to morning prayers on Wednesdays and Fridays, and to lectures whenever there were lectures; and never missed. She was handsome; and if she had ever smiled, would have been (I used to think) like an angel – but she never smiled. She was always grave and strict. She was so very good herself, I thought, that the badness of other people made her frown all her life (Bleak House).*

Barbary, Mrs. Captain, of Cheltenham: Horse-owner who sells her mount for spite, through Captain Maroon, because it had run away with her *(Dorrit)*.

Barbox Brothers: A financial house off Lombard Street taken over and closed down by Jackson (q.v.). *The firm of Barbox Brothers had been some offshoot or irregular branch of the Public Notary and bill-broking tree. It had gained for itself a griping reputation before the days of Young Jackson, and the reputation had stuck to it and to him. . . . But he did at last effect one great release. . . . With enough to live on (though, after all, with not too much), he obliterated the firm of Barbox Brothers from the pages of the Post-Office Directory and the face of the earth, leaving nothing of it but its name on two portmanteaus (Christmas Stories – 'Mugby Junction').*

Bardell, Mrs. Martha: Pickwick's landlady in Goswell Street and his opponent in the celebrated lawsuit for breach of promise. Mother of Tommy. *Mrs. Bardell – the relict and sole executrix of a deceased custom-house officer – was a comely woman of bustling manners and agreeable appearance, with a natural genius for cooking, improved by study and long practice, into an exquisite talent (Pickwick).*

Bardell, Tommy: Mrs. Bardell's small son. *Clad in a tight suit of corduroy, spangled with brass buttons of a very considerable size (Pickwick).*

Bark: Lodging-house keeper and receiver of stolen goods in Wentworth Street, Whitechapel, visited by the narrator and Inspector Field. *Bark is a red villain and a wrathful, with a sanguine throat that looks very much as if it were expressly made for hanging, as he stretches it out, in pale defiance, over the half-door of his hutch. Bark's parts of speech are of an awful sort – principally adjectives. I won't, says Bark, have no adjective police and adjective strangers in my adjective premises! I won't, by adjective and substantive! Give me my trousers, and I'll send the whole adjective police to adjective and substan-* *tive! Give me, says Bark, my adjective trousers! I'll put an adjective knife in the whole bileing of 'em (Reprinted – 'On Duty with Inspector Field').*

Barker, Mrs.: A lady of whom the censorious young gentleman's opinion is sought. *It is forthwith whispered about, that Mr. Fairfax (who, though he is a little prejudiced, must be admitted to be a very excellent judge) has observed something exceedingly odd in Mrs. Barker's manner (Young Gentlemen – 'Censorious Young Gentleman').*

Barker, Fanny: See Brown, Fanny ('Lamplighter's Story').

Barker, Phil: A thieving frequenter of the Three Cripples. *'I've got Phil Barker here : so drunk, that a boy might take him' (Twist).*

Barker, William (also Bill Boorker or Aggerawatin' Bill): The first London omnibus cad, or conductor. *When the appearance of the first omnibus caused the public mind to go in a new direction, and prevented a great many hackney-coaches from going in any direction at all . . . his active mind at once perceived how much might be done in the way of enticing the youthful and unwary, and shoving the old and helpless, into the wrong buss, and carrying them off, until, reduced by despair, they ransomed themselves by the payment of sixpence a-head, or, to adopt his own figurative expression in all its native beauty, 'till they was rig'larly done over, and forked out the stumpy' (Boz – 'First Omnibus Cad').*

Barkis: The Yarmouth carrier. Suitor, and eventually husband, of Clara Peggotty. *The carrier had a way of keeping his head down, like his horse, and of drooping sleepily forward as he drove, with one of his arms on each of his knees. I say 'drove', but it struck me that the cart would have gone to Yarmouth quite as well without him, for the horse did all that; and as to conversation, he had no idea of it but whistling. || 'Barkis is willin'' (Copperfield).*

Barley, Clara: Old Bill Barley's daughter. Herbert Pocket's fiancée, later wife, who arranges for Magwitch, under the name of Campbell, to wait in her father's house near London Bridge until he can be smuggled abroad. *A very pretty, slight, dark-eyed girl of twenty or so. . . . She really was a most charming girl, and might have passed for a captive fairy, whom that truculent Ogre, Old Barley, had pressed into his service (Expectations).*

Barley, Old Bill ('Gruff and Grim'): Clara's father, a retired ship's purser. '*I am afraid he is a sad old rascal,*' said Herbert, smiling, '*but I have never seen him. Don't you smell rum? He is always at it.*' *. . . As we passed Mr. Barley's door, he was heard hoarsely muttering within, in a strain that rose and fell like the wind, the following Refrain; in which I substitute good wishes for something quite the reverse.* '*Ahoy! Bless your eyes, here's old Bill Barley, bless your eyes. Here's old Bill Barley on the flat of his back, by the Lord. Lying on the flat of his back, like a drifting old dead flounder, here's your old Bill Barley, bless your eyes. Ahoy! Bless you*' *(Expectations).*

Barnacle, Lady: Wife of Lord Decimus Tite Barnacle. See **Bilberry, Lady Jemima** *(Dorrit)*.

Barnacle, Clarence (Barnacle, Junior): Tite Barnacle's empty-headed son, employed in the Circumlocution Office. *Had a youthful aspect, and the fluffiest little whisker, perhaps, that ever was seen. Such a downy tip was on his callow chin, that he seemed half fledged like a young bird; and a compassionate observer might have urged, that if he had not singed the calves of his legs, he would have died of cold. He had a superior eye-glass dangling round his neck, but unfortunately had such flat orbits to his eyes, and such limp little eyelids, that it wouldn't stick in when he put it up, but kept tumbling out against his waistcoat buttons with a click that discomposed him very much (Dorrit).*

Barnacle, Lord Decimus Tite: Tite Barnacle's uncle, Minister of Circumlocution. *Had risen to official heights on the wings of one indignant idea, and that was, My Lords, that I am yet to be told that it behoves a Minister of this free country to* set bounds to the philanthropy, to cramp the charity, to fetter the public spirit, to contract the enterprise, to damp the independent self-reliance, of its people. That was, in other words, that this great statesman was always yet to be told that it behoved the Pilot of the ship to do anything but prosper in the private loaf and fish trade ashore, the crew being able, by dint of hard pumping, to keep the ship above water without him. On this sublime discovery, in the great art How not to do it, Lord Decimus had long sustained the highest glory of the Barnacle family; and let any ill-advised member of either House but try How to do it, by bringing in a Bill to do it, that Bill was as good as dead and buried when Lord Decimus Tite Barnacle rose up in his place (Dorrit).*

Barnacle, Ferdinand: Private secretary to Lord Decimus Tite Barnacle. *A vivacious, well-looking, well-dressed, agreeable young fellow – he was a Barnacle, but on the more sprightly side of the family. . . . This touch and go young Barnacle had 'got up' the Department in a private secretaryship, that he might be ready for any little bit of fat that came to hand; and he fully understood the Department to be a politico-diplomatic hocus pocus piece of machinery, for the assistance of the nobs in keeping off the snobs. This dashing young Barnacle, in a word, was likely to become a statesman, and to make a figure (Dorrit).*

Barnacle, Tite: Nephew to Lord Decimus Tite Barnacle and one of his senior officials in the Circumlocution Office. *Mr. Barnacle dated from a better time, when the country was not so parsimonious, and the Circumlocution Office was not so badgered. He wound and wound folds of white cravat round his neck, as he wound and wound folds of tape and paper round the neck of the country. His wristbands and collar were oppressive, his voice and manner were oppressive. He had a large watchchain and bunch of seals, a coat buttoned up to inconvenience, a waistcoat buttoned up to inconvenience, an unwrinkled pair of trousers, a stiff pair of boots. He was altogether splendid, massive, overpowering, and impracticable. He seemed to have been* *sitting for his portrait to Sir Thomas Law-rence all the days of his life (Dorrit).*

Barnacle, William, M.P.: One of the parliamentary Barnacles present at the wedding of Henry Gowan and Minnie Meagles. *Who had made the ever-famous coalition with Tudor Stiltstalking, and who always kept ready his own particular recipe for How not to do it; sometimes tapping the Speaker, and drawing it fresh out of him, with a 'First, I will beg you, sir, to inform the House what Precedent we have for the course into which the honourable gentleman would precipitate us' (Dorrit).*

Barney: Jewish waiter at the Three Cripples, Saffron Hill. *Younger than Fagin, but nearly as vile and repulsive in appearance . . . whose words : whether they came from the heart or not : made their way through the nose (Twist).*

Barroneau, Madame Henri: An inn-keeper's widow, beautiful and wealthy, married by Rigaud. He is charged with her murder, which he represents as suicide, but is acquitted. *'Even when I wanted any little sum of money for my personal expenses, I could not obtain it without collision – and I, too, a man whose character it is to govern! One night, Madame Rigaud and myself were walking amicably – I may say like lovers – on a height overhanging the sea. An evil star occasioned Madam Rigaud to advert to her relations; I reasoned with her on that subject, and remonstrated on the want of duty and devotion manifested in her allow-ing herself to be influenced by their jealous animosity towards her husband. Madame Rigaud retorted; I retorted. Madame Rigaud grew warm; I grew warm and provoked her. . . . At length, Madame Rigaud, in an access of fury that I must ever deplore, threw herself upon me with screams of passion (no doubt those that were overheard at some distance), tore my clothes, tore my hair, lacerated my hands, trampled and trod the dust, and finally leaped over, dashing herself to death upon the rocks below' (Dorrit).*

Barsad, John: See Pross, Solomon *(Two Cities).*

Barton, Jacob: Mrs. Malderton's brother, a social embarrassment to the *nouveau riche* family. *A large grocer; so vulgar, and so lost to all sense of feeling, that he actually never scrupled to avow that he wasn't above his business : 'he'd made his money by it, and he didn't care who know'd it' (Boz – 'Horatio Sparkins').*

Bates, Belinda: Close friend of the sister of John, the narrator, and a member of the party visiting the haunted house. *A most intellectual, amiable, and delightful girl. . . . She has a fine genius for poetry, combined with real business earnestness, and 'goes in' – to use an expression of Alfred's – for Woman's mission, Woman's rights, Woman's wrongs, and everything that is woman's with a capital W, or is not and ought to be, or is and ought not to be (Christmas Stories – 'Haunted House').*

Bates, Charley: Member of Fagin's gang. *Charley Bates exhibited some very loose notions concerning the rights of property, by pilfering divers apples and onions from the stalls at the kennel sides, and thrusting them into pockets which were so surprisingly capacious, that they seemed to undermine his whole suit of clothes in every direction (Twist).*

Battens: A Titbull's pensioner. *A viru-lent old man . . . who had a working mouth which seemed to be trying to masticate his anger and to find that it was too hard and there was too much of it (Uncommercial – 'Titbull's Alms-Houses').*

Bayton: A poor man whose wife is buried by Bumble's parish *(Twist).*

Bayton, Mrs.: Bayton's wife, a victim of starvation *(Twist).*

Bazzard: Grewgious's clerk, and an aspiring playwright. *A pale, puffy-faced, dark-haired person of thirty with big dark eyes that wholly wanted lustre, and a dis-satisfied doughy complexion, that seemed to ask to be sent to the baker's, this attendant was a mysterious being, possessed of some strange power over Mr. Grewgious. As though he had been called into existence, like a fabulous Familiar, by a magic spell which had failed when required to dismiss him, he stuck tight to Mr. Grewgious's*

stool, although Mr. Grewgious's comfort
and convenience would manifestly have
been advanced by dispossessing him. A
gloomy person with tangled locks, and a
general air of having been reared under the
shadow of that baleful tree of Java which
has given shelter to more lies than the
whole botanical kingdom, Mr. Grewgious,
nevertheless, treated him with unaccountable consideration (Drood).

Beadle, Harriet ('Tattycoram'): Taken
from the Foundling Hospital to become
Pet Meagles's maid, she is influenced by
Miss Wade to run away and join her, but
returns penitently. *A sullen, passionate
girl! Her rich black hair was all about her
face, her face was flushed and hot, and as
she sobbed and raged, she plucked at her
lips with an unsparing hand. || 'She was
called in the Institution, Harriet Beadle —
an arbitrary name, of course. Now, Harriet, we changed into Hattey, and then into
Tatty, because, as practical people, we
thought even a playful name might be a
new thing to her, and might have a soften-
ing and affectionate kind of effect, don't
you see? As to Beadle, that I needn't say
was wholly out of the question. If there is
anything that is not to be tolerated on any
terms, anything that is a type of Jack-in-
office insolence and absurdity, anything that
represents in coats, waistcoats, and big
sticks, our English holding-on by nonsense,
after every one has found it out, it is a
beadle. . . . The name of Beadle being out
of the question, and the originator of the
Institution for these poor foundlings having
been a blessed creature of the name of
Coram, we gave that name to Pet's little
maid. At one time she was Tatty, and at one
time she was Coram, until we got into a
way of mixing the two names together, and
now she is always Tattycoram' (Dorrit).*

Beadwood, Ned: One of Miss Mowcher's
allusions. *'Have I got all my traps? It
seems so. It won't do to be like long Ned
Beadwood, when they took him to church
"to marry him to somebody," as he says,
and left the bride behind' (Copperfield).*

Bear, Prince: Prince Bull's adversary,
symbolising Russia in the Crimean War
(Reprinted – 'Prince Bull').

Beatrice: See **Tresham, Beatrice**
(*Christmas Stories* – 'Mugby Junction').

Beaver, Nat: Captain of a merchantman,
an old shipmate of Jack Governor, who
brings him on his visit to the haunted
house. *A thick-set, wooden face and figure,
and apparently as hard as a block all over,
proved to be an intelligent man, with a
world of watery experiences in him, and
great practical knowledge (Christmas
Stories – 'Haunted House').*

Bebelle: Pet name of Gabrielle, the
orphan baby befriended by Corporal
Théophile and adopted by Langley. *A
mere baby, one might call her, dressed in
the close white linen cap which small French
country children wear (like the children in
Dutch pictures), and in a frock of home-
spun blue, that had no shape except where
it was tied round her little fat throat. So
that, being naturally short and round all
over, she looked behind, as if she had been
cut off at her natural waist, and had had
her head neatly fitted on it (Christmas
Stories – 'Somebody's Luggage').*

Beckwith, Alfred: Identity assumed by
Meltham after he has circulated reports
of his death, so as to be able to hunt
down Julius Slinkton. *A man with all the
appearances of the worst kind of drunkard,
very far advanced upon his shameful way
to death ('Hunted Down').*

Becky: Barmaid at the Red Lion, Hampton, where Bill Sikes and Oliver Twist
pause on their way to burgle Mrs. Maylie's (*Twist*).

Bedwin, Mrs.: Brownlow's housekeeper.
*A motherly old lady, very neatly and pre-
cisely dressed (Twist).*

Begs, Mrs. Ridger: See **Micawber,
Emma** (*Copperfield*).

Belinda: A love-sick young woman who
writes to Master Humphrey for help in
tracing her elusive swain. *Heavens! into
what an indiscretion do I suffer myself to
be betrayed! To address these faltering lines
to a total stranger, and that stranger one
of conflicting sex! – and yet I am precipitated into the abyss, and have no power of
self-snatchation (forgive me if I coin that*

phrase) from the yawning gulf before me (Humphrey).

Bell, Knight, M.R.C.S.: Speaker at the anatomy and medicine session at the first meeting of the Mudfog Association. *Exhibited a wax preparation of the interior of a gentleman who in early life had inadvertently swallowed a door-key. It was a curious fact that a medical student of dissipated habits, being present at the* post mortem *examination, found means to escape unobserved from the room, with that portion of the coats of the stomach upon which an exact model of the instrument was distinctly impressed, with which he hastened to a locksmith of doubtful character, who made a new key from the pattern so shown to him. With this key the medical student entered the house of the deceased gentleman, and committed a burglary to a large amount, for which he was subsequently tried and executed (Mudfog).*

Bella: Miss Pupford's housemaid (*Christmas Stories* – 'Tom Tiddler's Ground').

Bella and Emily: Young prostitutes observed entering the prisoners' van at Bow Street. *The elder could not be more than sixteen, and the younger of whom had certainly not attained her fourteenth year. That they were sisters, was evident, for the resemblance which still subsisted between them, though two additional years of depravity had fixed their brand upon the elder girl's features, as legibly as if a red-hot iron had seared them. They were both gaudily dressed, the younger one especially; and, although there was a strong similarity between them in both respects, which was rendered the more obvious by their being handcuffed together, it is impossible to conceive a greater contrast than the demeanour of the two presented. The younger girl was weeping bitterly – not for display, or in the hope of producing effect, but for very shame; her face was buried in her handkerchief; and her whole manner was but too expressive of bitter and unavailing sorrow* (Boz – 'Prisoners' Van').

Belle: Scrooge's former sweetheart. *A fair young girl in a mourning-dress: in whose eyes there were tears* (*Christmas Books* – 'Christmas Carol').

Beller, Henry: Convert reported to the committee of the Brick Lane Branch of the United Grand Junction Ebenezer Temperance Association. *For many years toast-master at various corporation dinners, during which time he drank a great deal of foreign wine; may sometimes have carried a bottle or two home with him; is not quite certain of that, but is sure if he did, that he drank the contents. Feels very low and melancholy, is very feverish, and has a constant thirst upon him; thinks it must be the wine he used to drink (cheers). Is out of employ now; and never touches a drop of foreign wine by any chance (tremendous plaudits) (Pickwick).*

Belling: Pupil at Dotheboys Hall. *On the trunk was perched – his lace-up half-boots and corduroy trousers dangling in the air – a diminutive boy, with his shoulders drawn up to his ears (Nickleby).*

Bellows, Brother: Legal magnate, guest at Merdle's *(Dorrit).*

'Belltott': See Tott, Mrs. Isabella (*Christmas Stories* – 'English Prisoners').

Belvawney, Miss: Member of the Crummleses' theatrical company. *Seldom aspired to speaking parts, and usually went on as a page in white silk hose, to stand with one leg bent, and contemplate the audience, or to go in and out after Mr. Crummles in stately tragedy (Nickleby).*

Ben: A waiter at Rochester. *I would trust Ben, the waiter, with untold gold; but there are strings in the human heart which must never be sounded by another, and drinks that I make myself are those strings in mine* (*Christmas Stories* – 'Seven Poor Travellers').

Ben: Mail-coach guard at Hatfield whom Bill Sikes overhears tell of Nancy's murder *(Twist).*

Bench: Magisterial magnate, guest at Merdle's *(Dorrit).*

Benjamin: Officer of the Prentice Knights *(Rudge).*

Benjamin, Thomas: Plaintiff in a divorce suit successfully conducted by Spenlow and David Copperfield. *Had taken out his marriage licence as Thomas only; suppres-*

sing the Benjamin, in case he should not find himself as comfortable as he expected. Not *finding himself as comfortable as he expected, or being a little fatigued with his wife, poor fellow, he now came forward, by a friend, after being married a year or two, and declared that his name was Thomas Benjamin, and therefore he was not married at all. Which the Court confirmed, to his great satisfaction (Copperfield).*

Benson, Lucy: Old Benson's daughter, Young Benson's sister. She flirts with Squire Norton, but recognises the dangers in time and returns to her humble sweetheart, George Edmunds *(Village Coquettes).*

Benson, Old: Father of Lucy and Young Benson. A small farmer *(Village Coquettes).*

Benson, Young: Old Benson's son, Lucy's brother *(Village Coquettes).*

Benton, Miss: Master Humphrey's housekeeper, briefly loved by Tony Weller. She marries Slithers. *Miss Benton, hurrying into her own room and shutting herself up, in order that she might preserve that appearance of being taken by surprise which is so essential to the polite reception of visitors (Humphrey).*

Berinthia (Berry): Miss Pipchin's middle-aged niece and drudge. *Possessing a gaunt and iron-bound aspect, and much afflicted with boils on her nose (Dombey).*

Berry: See **Berinthia** *(Dombey).*

Bet, or Betsy: Prostitute and friend to Nancy. She is driven mad by the ordeal of identifying Nancy's body. *Gaily, not to say gorgeously attired, in a red gown, green boots, and yellow curl-papers (Twist).*

Betley: One of Mrs. Lirriper's first lodgers. *Which at that time had the parlours and loved his joke (Christmas Stories – 'Mrs. Lirriper's Lodgings').*

Betsey: Nurse to the two Master Britains *(Christmas Books – 'Battle of Life').*

Betsey Jane: Mrs. Wickam's cousin, whom she cites in warning Berry not to allow little Paul Dombey to attach himself too closely to her. *'She took fancies to people; whimsical fancies, some of them;*

others, affections that one might expect to see – only stronger than common. They all died' (Dombey).*

Betsy: Mrs. Raddle's maid. *A dirty slipshod girl in black cotton stockings, who might have passed for the neglected daughter of a superannuated dustman in very reduced circumstances (Pickwick).*

Bevan: A kind man from Massachusetts whom Martin Chuzzlewit meets at Pawkins's Boarding-House, New York. He subsequently lends Martin money to enable him and Mark Tapley to return to England. *A middle-aged man with a dark eye and a sunburnt face, who had attracted Martin's attention by having something very engaging and honest in the expression of his features (Chuzzlewit).*

Bevan, Mrs.: Former neighbour of Mrs. Nickleby. *'I recollect dining once at Mrs. Bevan's, in that broad street round the corner by the coachmaker's, where the tipsy man fell through the cellar-flap of an empty house nearly a week before the quarter-day, and wasn't found till the new tenants went in – and we had roast pig there. It must be that, I think, that reminds me of it, especially as there was a little bird in the room that would keep on singing all the time of dinner – at least, not a little bird, for it was a parrot, and he didn't sing exactly, for he talked and swore dreadfully' (Nickleby).*

Beverley: See **Loggins** *(Boz* – 'Private Theatres').*

Bib, Julius Washington Merryweather: A boarder at the National Hotel in America where Martin Chuzzlewit stays before embarking for Eden. *'A gentleman in the lumber line, sir, and much esteemed' (Chuzzlewit).*

Biddy: Wopsle's great-aunt's granddaughter. She is devoted to Pip, but he is blind to her affection and does not decide to ask her to marry him until too late – her wedding day to Joe Gargery. *She was an orphan like myself; like me, too, had been brought up by hand. She was most noticeable, I thought, in respect of her extremities; for, her hair always wanted brushing, her hands always wanted wash-*

ing, and her shoes always wanted mending and pulling up at heel. This description must be received with a week-day limitation. On Sundays she went to church elaborated (Expectations).

Bigby, Mrs.: Mrs. Meek's mother. *In my opinion she would storm a town, single-handed, with a hearth-broom, and carry it. I have never known her to yield any point whatever, to mortal man. She is calculated to terrify the stoutest heart (Reprinted –* 'Births, Mrs. Meek, of a Son').

Bigwig Family: A large and wealthy family devoted to directing the destinies of their inferiors. *Composed of all the stateliest people thereabouts, and all the noisiest (Christmas Stories –* 'Nobody's Story').

Bilberry, Lady Jemima: First daughter by the second marriage of the fifteenth Earl of Stiltstalking with the Honourable Clementina Toozellem. Married, in 1797, to Lord Decimus Tite Barnacle *(Dorrit).*

'Biler': See Toodle, Robin *(Dombey).*

Bilkins: The 'only' authority on taste. *Never took any notice that we can find out, of our French watering-place. Bilkins never wrote about it, never pointed out anything to be seen in it, never measured anything in it, always left it alone. For which relief, Heaven bless the town and the memory of the immortal Bilkins likewise! (Reprinted –* 'Our French Watering-place').

Bill: Criminal being defended by Jaggers. Husband of Amelia *(Expectations).*

Bill: Former turnkey at the Fleet Prison who figures in Sam Weller's tale of the little dirty-faced man in the brown coat *(Pickwick).*

Bill: Grave-digger who buries Mrs. Bayton *(Twist).*

Bill, Aggerawatin': See Barker, William *(Boz –* 'First Omnibus Cad').

Bill, Black: Prisoner in Newgate visited by Pip and Wemmick *(Expectations).*

Bill, Uncle: Life and soul of a party at a public tea-garden. *Observe the inexpressible delight of the old grandmother, at Uncle Bill's splendid joke of 'tea for four :*

bread-and-butter for forty.' . . . The young man is evidently 'keeping company' with Uncle Bill's niece : and Uncle Bill's hints – such as 'Don't forget me at the dinner, you know,' 'I shall look out for the cake, Sally,' 'I'll be godfather to your first – wager it's a boy,' and so forth, are equally embarrassing to the young people, and delightful to the elder ones (Boz – 'London Recreations').

Billickin, Mrs.: Widowed cousin of Grewgious with whom Rosa Bud lodges in Bloomsbury after fleeing from Jasper's attentions. *Personal faintness, and an overpowering personal candour, were distinguishing features of Mrs. Billickin's organisation. She came languishing out of her own exclusive back parlour, with the air of having been expressly brought-to for the purpose, from an accumulation of several swoons (Drood).*

Billsmethi, Master: Billsmethi's son. *When everybody else was breathless, danced a hornpipe, with a cane in his hand, and a cheese-plate on his head, to the unqualified admiration of the whole company (Boz –* 'Dancing Academy').

Billsmethi, Miss: Billsmethi's daughter. She partners Augustus Cooper in his dancing lessons, courts him, and finally sues him for breach of promise. *A young lady, with her hair curled in a crop all over her head, and her shoes tied in sandals all over her ankles (Boz –* 'Dancing Academy').

Billsmethi, Signor: of the 'King's Theatre'. Proprietor of a dancing academy near Gray's Inn Lane. *The Signor was at home, and what was still more gratifying, he was an Englishman! Such a nice man – and so polite! (Boz –* 'Dancing Academy').

Bilson and Slum: Commercial house, of Cateaton Street, City of London, employing Tom Smart as traveller *(Pickwick).*

Bintrey: Walter Wilding's solicitor. He helps to expose Obenreizer and prove Vendale's identity. *A cautious man, with twinkling beads of eyes in a large overhanging bald head, who inwardly but* *intensely enjoyed the comicality of open-ness of speech, or hand, or heart* (Christmas Stories – 'No Thoroughfare'.)

Bishop: Ecclesiastical magnate, guest at Merdle's. *Jauntily stepping out a little with his well-shaped right leg, as though he said to Mr. Merdle 'don't mind the apron; a mere form!' (Dorrit).*

Bit, Charley: A theatre-going Boots, one of the characters assumed by Mr. Gab-blewig (q.v.) in order to unmask Slap (*Nightingale's Diary*).

Bitherstone, Master: A boarder at Mrs. Pipchin's. *Master Bitherstone, whose relatives were all in India, and who was required to sit, between the services, in an erect position with his head against the parlour wall neither moving hand nor foot, suffered so acutely in his young spirits that he once asked Florence on a Sunday night, if she could give him any idea of the way back to Bengal (Dombey).*

Bitzer: A pupil at Gradgrind's, later a porter at Bounderby's Bank. *He held the respectable office of general spy and infor-mer in the establishment. || His cold eyes would hardly have been eyes, but for the short ends of lashes which, by bringing them into immediate contrast with something paler than themselves, expressed their form. His short-cropped hair might have been a mere continuation of the sandy freckles on his forehead and face. His skin was so unwholesomely deficient in the natural tinge, that he looked as though, if he were cut, he would bleed white (Hard Times).*

Black, Mrs.: A pert and flouncing pupil of Mrs. Lemon in Nettie Ashford's romantic tale ('Holiday Romance').

Black and Green: Police constables who accompany the narrator and Inspector Field to thieves' lodgings in Wentworth Street, Whitechapel. *Imperturbable Black opens the cab-door; Imperturbable Green takes a mental note of the driver (Re-printed – 'On Duty with Inspector Field').*

'Black Lion, The': Landlord of a White-chapel inn frequented by Joe Willet. *This Lion or landlord, – for he was called both man and beast, by reason of his having instructed the artist who painted his sign, to convey into the features of the lordly brute whose effigy it bore, as near a counterpart of his own face as his skill could compass and devise . . . stood indebted, in no small amount, to beer; of which he swigged such copious draughts, that most of his faculties were utterly drowned and washed away, except the one great faculty of sleep, which he retained in surprising perfection (Rudge).*

Blackey: A beggar lodging in the Old Farm House, Borough, visited by the narrator and Inspector Field. *Has stood near London bridge these five-and-twenty years, with a painted skin to represent disease (Reprinted – 'On Duty with Inspector Field').*

Blackpool, Stephen: A power-loom weaver in Bounderby's mill. Unable to divorce his drunken wife and marry Rachael, hounded by his workmates for refusing to join a union, and suspected of bank robbery, he falls down a disused pit shaft and is killed. *It is said that every life has its roses and thorns; there seemed, however, to have been a misadventure or mistake in Stephen's case, whereby some-body else had become possessed of his roses, and he had become possessed of the same somebody else's thorns in addition to his own. He had known, to use his words, a peck of trouble. He was usually called Old Stephen, in a kind of rough homage to the fact (Hard Times).*

Blackpool, Mrs. Stephen: Stephen's wife. *A disabled, drunken creature, barely able to preserve her sitting posture by steadying herself with one begrimed hand on the floor, while the other was so purposeless in trying to push away her tangled hair from her face, that it only blinded her the more with the dirt upon it. A creature so foul to look at, in her tatters, stains and splashes, but so much fouler than that in her moral infamy, that it was a shameful thing even to see her (Hard Times).*

Bladud, Prince: Mythical founder of Bath, whose legend Pickwick reads while visiting that city *(Pickwick).*

Blake, 'Warmint': An out-and-out young gentleman. *Upon divers occasions* has distinguished himself in a manner that would not have disgraced the fighting man (*Young Gentlemen* – 'Out-and-out Young Gentleman').

Blandois: See **Rigaud** (*Dorrit*).

Blank: Exhibitor in the display of models and mechanical science at the second meeting of the Mudfog Association. *Exhibited a model of a fashionable annual, composed of copper-plates, gold leaf, and silk boards, and worked entirely by milk and water (Mudfog).*

Blanquo, Pierre: Swiss guide accompanying Our Bore. *Pierre Blanquo : whom you may know, perhaps? – our bore is sorry you don't, because he's the only guide deserving of the name* (*Reprinted* – 'Our Bore').

Blathers: Bow Street officer investigating the burglary at Mrs. Maylie's. *A stout personage of middle height, aged about fifty : with shiny black hair, cropped pretty close ; half-whiskers, a round face, and sharp eyes (Twist).*

Blaze and Sparkle: Fashionable London jewellers. *'If you want to address our people, sir,' say Blaze and Sparkle the jewellers – meaning by our people, Lady Dedlock and the rest – 'you must remember that you are not dealing with the general public' (Bleak House).*

Blazo, Colonel Sir Thomas: Jingle's opponent in a single-wicket cricket match in the West Indies. *'Won the toss – first innings – seven o'clock* A.M. *– six natives to look out – went in ; kept in – heat intense – natives all fainted – taken away – fresh half-dozen ordered – fainted also – Blazo bowling – supported by two natives – couldn't bowl me out – fainted too – cleared away the Colonel – wouldn't give in – faithful attendant – Quanko Samba – last man left – sun so hot, bat in blisters – ball scorched brown – five hundred and seventy runs – rather exhausted – Quanko mustered up last remaining strength – bowled me out – had a bath, and went out to dinner' (Pickwick).*

Blight: Lightwood's office factotum. *A dismal boy . . . the managing clerk, junior clerk, common-law clerk, conveyancing clerk, chancery clerk, every refinement and department of clerk (Mutual Friend).*

Blimber, Dr.: Principal of the Brighton boarding-school attended by Paul Dombey. *A portly gentleman in a suit of black, with strings at his knees, and stockings below them. He had a bald head, highly polished ; a deep voice ; and a chin so very double, that it was a wonder how he ever managed to shave into the creases. He had likewise a pair of little eyes that were always half shut up, and a mouth that was always half expanded into a grin, as if he had, that moment, posed a boy, and were waiting to convict him from his own lips. Insomuch that when the Doctor put his right hand into the breast of his coat ; and with his other hand behind him, and a scarcely perceptible wag of his head, made the commonest observation to a nervous stranger, it was like a sentiment from the sphynx, and settled his business (Dombey).*

Blimber, Mrs.: Dr. Blimber's wife. *Not learned herself, but she pretended to be, and that did quite as well. She said at evening parties, that if she could have known Cicero, she thought she could have died contented. It was the steady joy of her life to see the Doctor's young gentlemen go out walking, unlike all other young gentlemen, in the largest possible shirt-collars, and the stiffest possible cravats. It was so classical, she said (Dombey).*

Blimber, Cornelia: Dr. Blimber's daughter and a teacher in his school. *Miss Blimber, too, although a slim and graceful maid, did no soft violence to the gravity of the house. There was no light nonsense about Miss Blimber. She was dry and sandy with working in the graves of deceased languages. None of your live languages for Miss Blimber. They must be dead – stone dead – and then Miss Blimber dug them up like a ghoul (Dombey).*

Blinder, Mrs.: The Necketts' neighbour who looks after their children. *A good-natured-looking old woman, with a dropsy, or an asthma, or perhaps both (Bleak House).*

Blinder, Bill: Deceased ostler who left Tony Weller his lantern. *'The hostler as* *had charge o' them two vell-known piebald leaders that run in the Bristol fast coach, and vould never go to no other tune but a sutherly vind and a cloudy sky, which wos consekvently played incessant, by the guard, wenever they wos on duty' (Humphrey).*

Blinkins: Latin master at Our School. *A colourless doubled-up near-sighted man with a crutch, who was always cold, and always putting onions into his ears for deafness, and always disclosing ends of flannel under all his garments, and almost always applying a ball of pocket-handkerchief to some part of his face with a screwing action round and round. He was a very good scholar, and took great pains where he saw intelligence and a desire to learn; otherwise, perhaps not. Our memory presents him (unless teased into a passion) with as little energy as colour – as having been worried and tormented into monotonous feebleness – as having had the best part of his life ground out of him in a Mill of boys (Reprinted – 'Our School').*

Blockitt, Mrs.: Nurse to the first Mrs. Dombey. *A simpering piece of faded gentility, who did not presume to state her name as a fact, but merely offered it as a mild suggestion (Dombey).*

Blockson, Mrs.: The Knags' charwoman. *'As I had two twin children the day before yesterday was only seven weeks, and my little Charley fell down an airy and put his elber out, last Monday, I shall take it as a favior if you'll send nine shillings, for one week's work, to my house, afore the clock strikes ten tomorrow' (Nickleby).*

Blogg: Parish beadle who arranged Betty Higden's adoption of Sloppy *(Mutual Friend).*

Bloss, Mrs.: The wealthy widow of (and formerly cook to) a cork-cutter. She imagines herself an invalid, eats prodigiously and marries her fellow hypochondriac and boarder at Mrs. Tibbs's, Gobler. *There arrived a single lady with a double-knock, in a pelisse the colour of the interior of a damson-pie; a bonnet of the same, with a regular conservatory of artificial flowers; a white veil, and a green parasol, with a cobweb border. The visitor (who was very fat and red-faced) was shown into the drawing-room (Boz – 'Boarding-House').*

Blotton: A member of the Pickwick Club whose calling Pickwick 'humbug' occasions a debate upon the meaningful use of abuse *(Pickwick).*

Blower, Captain, R.N.: An ancient invalid, one of the characters assumed by Gabblewig in order to unmask Slap *(Nightingale's Diary).*

Blowers: Counsel appearing before the former Lord Chancellor. *The last Lord Chancellor handled it neatly, when, correcting Mr. Blowers the eminent silk gown who said that such a thing might happen when the sky rained potatoes, he observed, 'or when we get through Jarndyce and Jarndyce, Mr. Blowers'; – a pleasantry that particularly tickled the maces, bags, and purses (Bleak House).*

Blubb: Lecturer at the umbugology and ditch-waterisics session of the second meeting of the Mudfog Association. His subject is the skull of Greenacre, the murderer, but it proves to be a carved coconut. *Delivered a lecture upon the cranium before him, clearly showing that Mr. Greenacre possessed the organ of destructiveness to a most unusual extent, with a most remarkable development of the organ of carveativeness (Mudfog).*

Blumb, R.A.: Royal Academician taken by Our Bore to see 'the finest picture in Italy'. *And you never saw a man so affected in your life as Blumb was. He cried like a child! (Reprinted – 'Our Bore').*

Blunderbore, Captain: Officer of the Horse Marines who makes the profound observation that a one-eyed pony winks his eye and whisks his tail simultaneously *(Mudfog).*

Blunderum: Speaker at the zoology and botany session of the first meeting of the Mudfog Association. *Delighted the section with a most interesting and valuable paper 'on the last moments of the learned pig,' which produced a very strong impression on the assembly (Mudfog).*

Bob: Turnkey at the Marshalsea who befriends William Dorrit and becomes godfather to Amy. *Time went on, and the turnkey began to fail. His chest swelled, and his legs got weak, and he was short of breath. The well-worn wooden stool was 'beyond him,' he complained. He sat in an arm-chair with a cushion, and sometimes wheezed so, for minutes together, that he couldn't turn the key. When he was overpowered by these fits, the debtor often turned it for him (Dorrit).*

Bobbo: Schoolfellow of the hero of Jemmy Lirriper's tale. *'The cleverest and bravest and best-looking and most generous of all the friends that ever were'* (Christmas Stories – 'Mrs. Lirriper's Lodgings').

Bobby, Lord: See Mizzler, Marquis of *(Curiosity Shop).*

Bobster: Cecilia Bobster's father. *Of a violent and brutal temper (Nickleby).*

Bobster, Cecilia: The girl whom Newman Noggs mistakes for Madeline Bray and arranges for Nicholas to meet clandestinely *(Nickleby).*

Bocker, Tom: Orphan suggested by Milvey for adoption by the Boffins. *'I doubt, Frank,' Mrs. Milvey hinted, after a little hesitation, 'if Mrs. Boffin wants an orphan quite nineteen, who drives a cart and waters the roads' (Mutual Friend).*

Boffer: Ruined stockbroker whose probable suicide is the subject of a bet between Flasher and Simmery. *'I'm very sorry he has failed,' said Wilkins Flasher, Esquire. 'Capital dinners he gave.' 'Fine port he had too,' remarked Mr. Simmery (Pickwick).*

Boffin, Nicodemus ('Noddy' or 'The Golden Dustman'): Former confidential servant and foreman to John Harmon's father, who left him a fortune on his death. He and his wife are Bella Wilfer's benefactors and enable John Harmon to marry her. *A broad, round-shouldered, one-sided old fellow in mourning, coming comically ambling towards the corner, dressed in a pea overcoat, and carrying a large stick. He wore thick shoes, and thick leather gaiters, and thick gloves like a hedger's. Both as to his dress and to* *himself, he was of an overlapping rhino-ceros build, with folds in his cheeks, and his forehead, and his eyelids, and his lips, and his ears; but with bright, eager, childishly-inquiring grey eyes, under his ragged eyebrows, and broad-brimmed hat. A very odd-looking old fellow altogether (Mutual Friend).*

Boffin, Mrs. Nicodemus (Henrietta): Boffin's wife who befriends Bella Wilfer. *A stout lady of rubicund and cheerful aspect, dressed (to Mr. Wegg's consternation) in a low evening dress of sable satin, and a large velvet hat and feathers. 'Mrs. Boffin, Wegg,' said Boffin, 'is a high-flyer at Fashion. And her make is such, that she does it credit' (Mutual Friend).*

Bogles, Mrs.: A former landlady of the Uncommercial Traveller, who recalls a party given at her boarding-house. *On which occasion Mrs. Bogles was taken in execution by a branch of the legal profession who got in as the harp, and was removed (with the keys and subscribed capital) to a place of durance, half an hour prior to the commencement of the festivities (Uncommercial – 'Refreshments for Travellers').*

Bogsby, James George: Landlord of the Sol's Arms, Chancery Lane. *A highly respectable landlord (Bleak House).*

Boiler, The Revd. Boanerges: A boring preacher whose services the Uncommercial Traveller was compelled to attend as a child. *I have sat under Boanerges when he has specifically addressed himself to us – us, the infants – and at this present writing I hear his lumbering jocularity (which never amused us, though we basely pretended that it did), and I behold his big round face, and I look up the inside of his outstretched coat-sleeve as if it were a telescope with the stopper on, and I hate him with an unwholesome hatred for two hours (Uncommercial – 'City of London Churches').*

Bokum, Mrs.: Friend and bridesmaid to Mrs. MacStinger. *He learnt from this lady that she was the widow of a Mr. Bokum, who had held an employment in the Custom House; that she was the dearest friend of Mrs. MacStinger, whom she considered a pattern for her sex (Dombey).*

Bolder: Pupil at Dotheboys Hall. *An unhealthy-looking boy, with warts all over his hands (Nickleby).*

Boldheart, Captain: Piratical captain of the schooner *Beauty* and hero of Robin Redforth's romantic tale. *Considering himself spited by a Latin-grammar master, demanded the satisfaction due from one man of honour to another. Not getting it, he privately withdrew his haughty spirit from such low company, bought a second-hand pocket pistol, folded up some sandwiches in a paper bag, and made a bottle of Spanish liquorice-water, and entered on a career of valour* ('Holiday Romance').

Boldwig, Captain: Landowner near Dingley Dell who finds Pickwick sleeping off the effects of punch on his land and consigns him in a wheelbarrow to the pound. *A little fierce man in a stiff black neckerchief and blue surtout, who, when he did condescend to walk about his property, did it in company with a thick rattan stick with a brass ferrule, and a gardener and sub-gardener with meek faces, to whom (the gardeners, not the stick) Captain Boldwig gave his orders with all due grandeur and ferocity: for Captain Boldwig's wife's sister had married a Marquis, and the Captain's house was a villa, and his land 'grounds,' and it was all very high, and mighty, and great (Pickwick).*

Bolo, Miss: Pickwick's card partner at Bath Assembly Rooms. *If he played a wrong card, Miss Bolo looked a small armoury of daggers (Pickwick).*

Bolter, Mrs.: See **Charlotte** *(Twist).*

Bolter, Morris: See **Claypole, Noah** *(Twist).*

Bolton, Robert: The 'gentleman connected with the press' who tells tall stories to admiring listeners at the Green Dragon, Westminster Bridge. *An individual who defines himself as 'a gentleman connected with the press,' which is a definition of peculiar indefiniteness (Mudfog –* 'Mr. Robert Bolton').

Bones, Banjo and Mrs. Banjo: Entertainers in a sailors' 'singing-house'. *The celebrated comic favourite, Mr. Banjo Bones, looking very hideous with his* blackened face and limp sugar-loaf hat; beside him, sipping rum-and-water, Mrs. Banjo Bones, in her natural colours – a little heightened *(Uncommercial –* 'Poor Mercantile Jack').

Bonney: Promoter of the United Metropolitan Improved Hot Muffin and Crumpet Baking and Punctual Delivery Company. *A pale gentleman in a violent hurry, who, with his hair standing up in great disorder all over his head, and a very narrow white cravat tied loosely round his throat, looked as if he had been knocked up in the night and had not dressed himself since (Nickleby).*

Boodle, Lord: A friend of Dedlock. *Of considerable reputation with his party, who has known what office is, and who tells Sir Leicester Dedlock with much gravity, after dinner, that he really does not see to what the present age is tending (Bleak House).*

Boorker, Bill: See **Barker, William** *(Boz –* 'First Omnibus Cad').

Boots: See **Cobbs** *(Christmas Stories –* 'Holly-Tree').

Boots: Frequent guest, with Brewer, at the Veneerings', and one of Veneering's election campaign workers *(Mutual Friend).*

Boozey, William: Captain of the foretop in the schooner *Beauty*, commanded by Captain Boldheart, who saves him from drowning ('Holiday Romance').

Boozle: Actor approached to take over from Flimkins at the Surrey Theatre, but declines *(Young Gentlemen –* 'Theatrical Young Gentleman').

Borum, Mrs.: Patron of Crummles's productions and mother of six children, including **Augustus, Charlotte** and **Emma** *(Nickleby).*

'Bottle-Nosed Ned': See **Twigger, Edward** *(Mudfog).*

Bottles: Deaf stable-man employed by John. *I kept him in my service, and still keep him, as a phenomenon of moroseness not to be matched in England (Christmas Stories –* 'Haunted House').

Bouclet, Madame: Langley's landlady in France. *A compact little woman of thirty-*

five or so (*Christmas Stories* – 'Some-body's Luggage').

Bounderby, Josiah: Coketown banker and manufacturer, son of Mrs. Pegler. He marries Louisa Gradgrind. *A big, loud man, with a stare, and a metallic laugh. A man made out of a coarse material, which seemed to have been stretched to make so much of him. A man with a great puffed head and forehead, swelled veins in his temples, and such a strained skin to his face that it seemed to hold his eyes open, and lift his eyebrows up. A man with a per-vading appearance on him of being inflated like a balloon, and ready to start. A man who could never sufficiently vaunt him-self a self-made man. A man who was always proclaiming, through that brassy speaking-trumpet of a voice of his, his old ignorance and his old poverty. A man who was the Bully of humility (Hard Times).*

Bounderby, Mrs. Josiah (Louisa): See Gradgrind, Louisa *(Hard Times)*.

Bowley, Lady: Sir Joseph's wife. *A stately lady in a bonnet (Christmas Books* – 'Chimes').

Bowley, Master: The Bowleys' son, aged twelve. *'Sweet boy! We shall have this little gentleman in Parliament now … before we know where we are. We shall hear of his successes at the poll; his speeches in the House; his overtures from Governments; his brilliant achievements of all kinds; ah! we shall make our little orations about him in the Common Council, I'll be bound' (Christmas Books* – 'Chimes').

Bowley, Sir Joseph, M.P.: An elderly Member of Parliament, father of Master Bowley. *'I do my duty as the Poor Man's Friend and Father; and I endeavour to educate his mind, by inculcating on all occasions the one great moral lesson which that class requires. That is, entire Depen-dence on myself. They have no business whatever with – with themselves. If wicked and designing persons tell them otherwise, and they become impatient and discontented, and are guilty of insubordinate conduct and black-hearted ingratitude; which is undoubtedly the case; I am their*

Friend and Father still. It is so Ordained. It is in the nature of things' (*Christmas Books* – 'Chimes').

Bowyer, The: Mistress Alice's father and Hugh Graham's master in Magog's story. *An honest Bowyer who dwelt in the ward of Cheype, and was rumoured to possess great wealth. Rumour was quite as infal-lible in those days as at the present time, but it happened then as now to be some-times right by accident. It stumbled upon the truth when it gave the old Bowyer a mint of money (Humphrey).*

Boxer: John Peerybingle's dog. *Every-body knew him, all along the road – especially the fowls and pigs, who when they saw him approaching, with his body all on one side, and his ears pricked up in-quisitively, and that knob of a tail making the most of itself in the air, immediately withdrew into remote back settlements, without waiting for the honour of a nearer acquaintance. He had business everywhere; going down all the turnings, looking into the wells, bolting in and out of all the cottages, dashing into the midst of all the Dame-schools, fluttering all the pigeons, magnifying the tails of all the cats, and trotting into the public-houses like a regular customer. Wherever he went, somebody or other might have been heard to cry, 'Halloa! Here's Boxer!' (Christmas Books* – 'Cricket').

'Boy at Mugby, The': See Ezekiel (*Christmas Stories* – 'Mugby Junction').

Boythorn, Lawrence: An old friend of Jarndyce and litigating neighbour of Dedlock. *There was a sterling quality in his laugh, and in his vigorous healthy voice, and in the roundness and fulness with which he uttered every word he spoke, and in the very fury of his superlatives, which seemed to go off like blank cannons and hurt nothing. … . He was not only a very handsome old gentleman – upright and stalwart as he had been described to us – with a massive grey head, a fine composure of face when silent, a figure that might have become corpulent but for his being so con-tinually in earnest that he gave it no rest, and a chin that might have subsided into a double chin but for the vehement emphasis* in which it was constantly required to assist; but he was such a true gentleman in his manner, so chivalrously polite, his face was lighted by a smile of so much sweetness and tenderness, and it seemed so plain that he had nothing to hide, but showed himself exactly as he was (Bleak House).

Brandley, Mrs.: A widow with whom Estella lodges at Richmond. The lady with whom Estella was placed, Mrs. Brandley by name, was a widow, with one daughter several years older than Estella. The mother looked young and the daughter looked old; the mother's complexion was pink, and the daughter's was yellow; the mother set up for frivolity, and the daughter for theology (Expectations).

Brass, Sally: Sampson Brass's sister and partner, probably mother of 'The Marchioness' (q.v.) by Quilp. His clerk, assistant, housekeeper, secretary, confidential plotter, adviser, intriguer, and bill of cost increaser, Miss Brass – a kind of amazon at common law. . . . A lady of thirty-five or thereabouts, of a gaunt and bony figure, and a resolute bearing, which if it repressed the softer emotions of love, and kept admirers at a distance, certainly inspired a feeling akin to awe in the breasts of those male strangers who had the happiness to approach her. . . . In complexion Miss Brass was sallow – rather a dirty sallow, so to speak – but this hue was agreeably relieved by the healthy glow which mantled in the extreme tip of her laughing nose. Her voice was exceedingly impressive – deep and rich in quality, and, once heard, not easily forgotten. . . . In mind she was of a strong and vigorous turn, having from her earliest youth devoted herself with uncommon ardour to the study of the law; not wasting her speculation upon its eagle flights, which are rare, but tracing it attentively through all the slippery and eel-like crawlings in which it commonly pursues its way (Curiosity Shop).

Brass, Sampson: Quilp's legal adviser, who eventually turns evidence against him, but is jailed for his part in the plot against Kit Nubbles. An attorney of no very good repute, from Bevis Marks in the City of London; he was a tall, meagre man, with a nose like a wen, a protruding forehead, retreating eyes, and hair of a deep red. He wore a long black surtout reaching nearly to his ankles, short black trousers, high shoes, and cotton stockings of a bluish-grey. He had a cringing manner, but a very harsh voice; and his blandest smiles were so extremely forbidding, that to have had his company under the least repulsive circumstances, one would have wished him to be out of temper that he might only scowl (Curiosity Shop).

Bravassa, Miss: Member of the Crummleses' theatrical company. The beautiful Miss Bravassa, who had once had her likeness taken 'in character' by an engraver's apprentice, whereof impressions were hung up for sale in the pastry-cook's window, and the greengrocer's, and at the circulating library, and the box-office, whenever the announce bills came out for her annual night (Nickleby).

Bray, Madeline: Slave to her misanthropic father, she is rescued by his death from having to marry Gride, and eventually marries Nicholas Nickleby. A young lady who could be scarcely eighteen, of very slight and delicate figure, but exquisitely shaped. . . . She raised her veil, for an instant, while she preferred the inquiry, and disclosed a countenance of most uncommon beauty, though shaded by a cloud of sadness, which, in one so young, was doubly remarkable (Nickleby).

Bray, Walter: A bankrupt widower, embittered and selfish, father to Madeline whom he tries to marry off to Gride, one of his principal creditors. He was scarce fifty, perhaps, but so emaciated as to appear much older. His features presented the remains of a handsome countenance, but one in which the embers of strong and impetuous passions were easier to be traced than any expression which would have rendered a far plainer face much more prepossessing. His looks were very haggard, and his limbs and body literally worn to the bone, but there was something of the old fire in the large sunken eye notwithstanding, and it seemed to kindle afresh as he struck a thick stick, with which he seemed to have supported himself in his seat, impatiently on the floor twice or thrice, and called his daughter by her name (Nickleby).

Brewer: Frequent guest, with Boots, at the Veneerings', and one of Veneering's election campaign workers (Mutual Friend).

Brick, Jefferson: War correspondent of the New York Rowdy Journal. A small young gentleman of very juvenile appearance, and unwholesomely pale in the face; partly, perhaps, from intense thought, but partly, there is no doubt, from the excessive use of tobacco, which he was at that moment chewing vigorously. He wore his shirt-collar turned down over a black ribbon; and his lank hair, a fragile crop, was not only smoothed and parted back from his brow, that none of the Poetry of his aspect might be lost, but had, here and there, been grubbed up by the roots; which accounted for his loftiest developments being somewhat pimply (Chuzzlewit).

Brick, Mrs. Jefferson: Brick's wife. 'Pray,' said Martin, 'who is that sickly little girl opposite, with the tight round eyes?' (Chuzzlewit).

Briggs: Paul Dombey's room-mate at Dr. Blimber's school. Sat looking at his task in stony stupefaction and despair – which it seemed had been his condition ever since breakfast-time (Dombey).

Briggs, Mr. and Mrs.: Friends of the egotistical couple (Young Couples – 'Egotistical Couple').

Briggs, Mrs.: Mother of two sons, **Samuel**, an attorney, and **Alexander**, articled to his brother, and three daughters, **Julia**, **Kate**, and another. Their chief preoccupation is trying to gain ascendancy over the **Tauntons** (q.v.). Between the Briggses and the Tauntons there existed a degree of implacable hatred, quite unprecedented. The animosity between the Montagues and Capulets, was nothing to that which prevailed between these two illustrious houses. . . . If the Miss Briggses appeared in smart bonnets, the Miss Tauntons eclipsed them with smarter. If Mrs. Taunton appeared in a cap of all the hues

of the rainbow, Mrs. Briggs forthwith mounted a toque, with all the patterns of the kaleidoscope. If Miss Sophia Taunton learnt a new song, two of the Miss Briggses came out with a new duet. The Tauntons had once gained a temporary triumph with the assistance of a harp, but the Briggses brought three guitars into the field, and effectually routed the enemy. There was no end to the rivalry between them (Boz – 'Steam Excusion').

Britain, Benjamin (Little Britain): Dr. Jeddler's manservant, later husband of Clemency Newcome, father of two sons, and an infant daughter 'Little Clem' and landlord of the Nutmeg Grater inn. A small man, with an uncommonly sour and discontented face. || 'I was hid for the best part of two years behind a bookstall, ready to fly out if anybody pocketed a volume: and after that, I was light porter to a stay and mantua-maker, in which capacity I was employed to carry about, in oilskin baskets, nothing but deceptions – which soured my spirits and disturbed my confidence in human nature (Christmas Books – 'Battle of Life').

Brittles: Servant at Mrs. Maylie's. A lad of all-work: who, having entered her service a mere child, was treated as a promising young boy still, though he was something past thirty (Twist).

Brobity, Miss: See Sapsea, Mrs. Ethelinda (Drood).

Brogley: Secondhand dealer and broker who takes possession of Sol Gills's business in execution of a debt. A moist-eyed, pink-complexioned, crisp-haired man, of a bulky figure and an even temper – for that class of Caius Marius who sits upon the ruins of other people's Carthages, can keep up his spirits well enough (Dombey).

Brogson: Dinner guest at the Buddens'. An elderly gentleman in a black coat, drab knee-breeches, and long gaiters (Boz – 'Mr. Minns and his Cousin').

Brook Dingwall, Cornelius, M.P.: Father of Lavinia and Frederick. Very haughty, solemn, and portentous. He had, naturally, a somewhat spasmodic expression of countenance, which was not rendered the less remarkable by his wearing an extremely stiff cravat. He was wonderfully proud of the M.P. attached to his name, and never lost an opportunity of reminding people of his dignity. He had a great idea of his own abilities, which must have been a great comfort to him, as no one else had (Boz – 'Sentiment').

Brook Dingwall, Mrs. Cornelius: Brook Dingwall's wife, mother of Lavinia and Frederick (Boz – 'Sentiment').

Brook Dingwall, Frederick: The Brook Dingwalls' infant son, brother of Lavinia. One of those public nuisances, a spoiled child, was playing about the room, dressed after the most approved fashion – in a blue tunic with a black belt a quarter of a yard wide, fastened with an immense buckle – looking like a robber in a melodrama, seen through a diminishing glass (Boz – 'Sentiment').

Brook Dingwall, Lavinia: Daughter of the Brook Dingwalls and sister to Frederick. She is sent to the Misses Crumpton's establishment to quench her ardour for Edward M'Neville Walter (see **Butler, Theodosius**). One of that numerous class of young ladies, who, like adverbs, may be known by their answering to a commonplace question, and doing nothing else (Boz – 'Sentiment').

Brooker: Ralph Nickleby's former clerk, turned criminal. He knows that Nickleby is the father of Smike, and tries to blackmail him, but fails. A spare, dark, withered man . . . with a stooping body, and a very sinister face rendered more ill-favoured by hollow and hungry cheeks deeply sunburnt, and thick black eyebrows, blacker in contrast with the perfect whiteness of his hair; roughly clothed in shabby garments, of a strange and uncouth make; and having about him an indefinable manner of depression and degradation (Nickleby).

Brooks: One of five occupants of a bed at Dotheboys Hall (Nickleby).

Brooks: Former fellow-lodger of Sam Weller. A pieman. 'Wery nice man he was – reg'lar clever chap, too – make pies out o' anything, he could. "What a number o' cats you keep, Mr. Brooks," says I, when I'd got intimate with him. "Ah," says he, "I do – a good many," says he. "You must be wery fond o' cats," says I. "Other people is," says he, a winkin' at me; "they an't in season till the winter, though," says he. "Not in season!" says I. "No," says he, "fruits is in, cats is out" ' (Pickwick).

Browdie, John: A blunt Yorkshire corn factor who becomes friends with Nicholas Nickleby while he is at Dotheboys Hall. He marries Matilda Price. The expected swain arrived, with his hair very damp from recent washing, and a clean shirt, whereof the collar might have belonged to some giant ancestor, forming, together with a white waistcoat of similar dimensions, the chief ornament of his person . . . something over six feet high, with a face and body rather above the due proportion than below it (Nickleby).

Brown: Performer on the violoncello at the Gattletons' private theatricals (Boz – 'Mrs. Joseph Porter').

Brown: Friend of Mrs. Nubbles, whom she offers as testifier to her statements. Supposed to be then a corporal in the East Indies, and who could of course be found with very little trouble (Curiosity Shop).

Brown: Greedy, gout-ridden pupil of Mrs. Lemon in Nettie Ashford's romantic tale ('Holiday Romance').

Brown: Member of the Mudfog Association (Mudfog).

Brown, the three Misses: Three spinster sisters in 'our parish' whose admiration for the young curate spurs them to charitable works. The curate preached a charity sermon on behalf of the charity school, and in the charity sermon aforesaid, expatiated in glowing terms on the praiseworthy and indefatigable exertions of certain estimable individuals. Sobs were heard to issue from the three Miss Brown's pew; the pew-opener of the division was seen to hurry down the centre aisle to the vestry door, and to return immediately, bearing a glass of water in her hand. A low moaning ensued; two more pew-openers rushed to the spot, and the three Miss

Browns, each supported by a pew-opener, were led out of the church, and led in again after the lapse of five minutes with white pocket-handkerchiefs to their eyes, as if they had been attending a funeral in the church-yard adjoining (Boz – 'Our Parish', 'Ladies' Societies').

rown, Mrs. ('Good Mrs. Brown'): Mother of Alice Marwood. She briefly abducts Florence Dombey and steals her clothes. *A very ugly old woman, with red rims round her eyes, and a mouth that mumbled and chattered of itself when she was not speaking. She was miserably dressed, and carried some skins over her arm. She seemed to have followed Florence some little way at all events, for she had lost her breath ; and this made her uglier still, as she stood trying to regain it : working her shrivelled yellow face and throat into all sorts of contortions (Dombey).*

Brown, Mrs.: Hostess of the party at which Griggins's antics offend everyone. *They were surprised at Mrs. Brown's allowing it (Young Gentlemen – 'Funny Young Gentleman').*

Brown, Alice: See **Marwood, Alice** *(Dombey).*

Brown, Conversation: Colleague of Lord Feenix's Parliamentary days. *Four bottle man at the Treasury Board (Dombey).*

Brown, Fanny: Stargazer's niece whom he wishes to marry Tom Grig *(Lamplighter).* In 'The Lamplighter's Story', the subsequent prose version of this farce, she is renamed Fanny Barker.

Brown of Muggleton: Maker of Rachael Wardle's shoes, through which Jingle is tracked down in the nick of time *(Pickwick).*

Brown and O'Brien: Passengers on the Gravesend steam packet with an eye for the young ladies. *Mr. Brown or Mr. O'Brien, as the case may be, remarks in a low voice that he has been quite insensible of late to the beauties of nature – that his whole thoughts and wishes have centred in one object alone – whereupon the young lady looks up, and failing in her attempt to appear*

unconscious, looks down again (Boz – 'The River').

Browndock, Miss: One of Mrs. Nickleby vaguely-recalled connections. *'Your poor dear papa's cousin's sister-in-law – a Miss Browndock – was taken into partnership by a lady that kept a school at Hammer-smith, and made her fortune in no time at all. I forget, by the bye, whether that Miss Browndock was the same lady that got the ten thousand pounds prize in the lottery, but I think she was' (Nickleby).*

Brownlow: Gentleman who befriends Oliver Twist, who has been accused of picking his pocket. He establishes his true identity and eventually adopts him as his son. *A very respectable-looking personage, with a powdered head and gold spectacles. He was dressed in a bottle-green coat with a black velvet collar ; wore white trousers ; and carried a smart bamboo cane under his arm (Twist).*

Bucket, Inspector: The detective officer employed by Tulkinghorn and later by Dedlock. He is instrumental in clearing up the prolonged case of Jarndyce and Jarndyce. *Mr. Snagsby is dismayed to see . . . a person with a hat and stick in his hand, who was not there when he himself came in, and has not since entered by the door or by either of the windows. There is a press in the room, but its hinges have not creaked, nor has a step been audible upon the floor. Yet this third person stands there, with his attentive face, and his hat and stick in his hands, and his hands behind him, a composed and quiet listener. He is a stoutly built, steady-looking, sharp-eyed man in black, of about the middle-age (Bleak House).*

Bucket, Mrs.: Bucket's wife. She helps her husband find Tulkinghorn's mur-derer. *A lady of a natural detective genius, which if it had been improved by profes-sional exercise, might have done great things, but which has paused at the level of a clever amateur (Bleak House).*

Bud, Rosa: Also known as **Rosebud** and **Pussy.** A pupil at Miss Twinkleton's, betrothed to Drood at their fathers' wish. *A blooming schoolgirl . . . her flowing* *brown hair tied with a blue riband, and her beauty remarkable for a quite childish, almost babyish, touch of saucy discontent, comically conscious of itself.* || *'You're very welcome, Eddy. . . . No, I can't kiss you, because I've got an acidulated drop in my mouth'* (Drood).

Budden, Alexander Augustus: Small son of Octavius and Amelia and godson by proxy of Augustus Minns. *Habited in a sky-blue suit with silver buttons; and possessing hair of nearly the same colour as the metal* (Boz – 'Mr. Minns and his Cousin').

Budden, Octavius: Father of Alexander Augustus and cousin to Augustus Minns. A wealthy retired corn-chandler living near Stamford Hill. *He always spoke at the top of his voice, and always said the same thing half a dozen times* (Boz – 'Mr. Minns and his Cousin').

Budden, Mrs. Octavius (Amelia): Budden's wife, mother of Alexander Augustus (Boz – 'Mr. Minns and his Cousin').

Budger, Mrs.: Tupman's partner in a quadrille at the Bull, Rochester. *A little old widow, whose rich dress and profusion of ornament bespoke her a most desirable addition to a limited income* (Pickwick).

Buffer, Dr.: Member of the Mudfog Association (Mudfog).

Buffle: Father of Robina. Tax-collector resented by Mrs. Lirriper and Major Jackman. They become friends with the Buffles after taking them in when their house burns down. *Mr. Buffle's manners when engaged in his business were not agreeable. To collect is one thing, and to look about as if suspicious of the goods being gradually removing in the dead of the night by a back door is another, over taxing you have no control but suspecting is voluntary* (Christmas Stories – 'Mrs. Lirriper's Legacy').

Buffle, Mrs.: Buffle's wife, Robina's mother, whose superior air is resented by Mrs. Lirriper. *It was considered besides that a one-horse pheayton ought not to have elevated Mrs. Buffle to that height* (Christmas Stories – 'Mrs. Lirriper's Legacy').

Buffle, Robina: The Buffles' daughter, in love with George. *It was whispered that Miss Buffle would go either into a consumption or a convent she being so very thin and off her appetite* (Christmas Stories – 'Mrs. Lirriper's Legacy').

Buffum, Oscar: A boarder at the National Hotel, in America, where Martin Chuzzlewit stays before embarking for Eden (Chuzzlewit).

Buffy, The Right Hon. William, M.P.: A friend of Dedlock. *Contends across the table with some one else, that the shipwreck of the country – about which there is no doubt; it is only the manner of it that is in question – is attributable to Cuffy* (Bleak House).

Bulder, Colonel: Officer commanding the Rochester garrison. *Colonel Bulder, in full military uniform, on horseback, galloping first to one place and then to another, and backing his horse among the people, and prancing, and curvetting, and shouting in a most alarming manner, and making himself very hoarse in the voice, and very red in the face, without any assignable cause or reason whatever* (Pickwick).

Bulder, Mrs. and Miss: Colonel Bulder's wife and daughter, present at the charity ball at the Bull, Rochester (Pickwick).

Bule, Miss: Leader of society, though aged only eight or nine, at Miss Griffin's school. *Struggling with the diffidence so natural to, and charming in, her adorable sex* (Christmas Stories – 'Haunted House').

Bull, Prince: A mighty prince – symbolising England at the time of the Crimean War – hampered by a tyrannical godmother and the Civil Service Establishment. *He had gone through a great deal of fighting, in his time, about all sorts of things, including nothing; but, had gradually settled down to be a steady, peaceable, good-natured, corpulent, rather sleepy Prince. . . . This good Prince had two sharp thorns in his pillow, two hard knobs in his crown, two heavy loads on his mind, two unbridled nightmares in his sleep,* *two rocks ahead in his course. He could not by any means get servants to suit him, and he had a tyrannical old godmother, whose name was Tape (Reprinted – 'Prince Bull').*

Bullamy: Porter at the Anglo-Bengalee Disinterested Loan and Life Assurance Company's offices. *A wonderful creature, in a vast red waistcoat and a short-tailed pepper-and-salt coat – who carried more conviction to the minds of sceptics than the whole establishment without him. . . . People had been known to apply to effect an insurance on their lives for a thousand pounds, and looking at him, to beg, before the form of proposal was filled up, that it might be made two (Chuzzlewit).*

Bull-dogs, The United: Name adopted by the Prentice Knights (q.v.) when older members' indentures expired *(Rudge).*

Bullfinch: Friend of the Uncommercial Traveller who makes the disastrous suggestion that they dine at the Temeraire, at the seaside resort of Namelesston. *An excellent man of business (Uncommercial – 'A Little Dinner in an Hour').*

Bullman: Plaintiff in Bullman and Ramsey, the case discussed at length by Dodson and Fogg's clerks while Pickwick awaits attention *(Pickwick).*

Bullock: See **Tipkins against Bullock** *(Copperfield).*

Bull's Eye: Bill Sikes's dog. *A white shaggy dog, with his face scratched and torn in twenty different places (Twist).*

Bulph: A pilot with whom Crummles lodges in Portsmouth *(Nickleby).*

Bumble: Beadle of the parish workhouse where Oliver Twist is born. He marries the matron, Mrs. Corney, but they are eventually dismissed and end their days as workhouse inmates. *A fat man, and a choleric . . . Mr. Bumble had a great idea of his oratorical powers and his importance (Twist).*

Bumble, Mrs.: See **Corney, Mrs.** *(Twist).*

Bumple, Michael: Complainant against Sludberry for brawling *(Boz – 'Doctors' Commons').*

Bung: A broker's assistant who defeats Spruggins in election for beadle of 'Our Parish'. *There was a serenity in the open countenance of Bung – a kind of moral dignity in his confident air – an 'I wish you may get it' sort of expression in his eye – which infused animation into his supporters, and evidently dispirited his opponents (Boz – 'Election for Beadle'. See also Boz – 'Broker's Man').*

Bunkin, Mrs.: Neighbour quoted by Mrs. Sanders as having told her that Pickwick was engaged to Mrs. Bardell. *Mrs. Bunkin which clear-starched (Pickwick).*

Bunsby, Captain Jack: Master of the *Cautious Clara,* much admired by Captain Cuttle whom he rescues from the matrimonial designs of Mrs. Mac-Stinger; though at sacrifice of himself, for she carries him off in forcible marriage. *Immediately there appeared, coming slowly up above the bulk-head of the cabin, another bulk-head – human, and very large – with one stationary eye in the mahogany face, and one revolving one, on the principle of some lighthouses. This head was decorated with shaggy hair, like oakum, which had no governing inclination towards the north, east, west, or south, but inclined to all four quarters of the compass, and to every point upon it. The head was followed by a perfect desert of chin, and by a shirt-collar and neckerchief, and by a dreadnought pilot-coat, and by a pair of dreadnought pilot-trousers, whereof the waistband was so very broad and high, that it became a succedaneum for a waistcoat; being ornamented near the wearer's breastbone with some massive wooden buttons, like backgammon men As the lower portions of these pantaloons became revealed, Bunsby stood confessed (Dombey).*

Burton, Thomas: Convert reported to the committee of the Brick Lane Branch of the United Grand Junction Ebenezer Temperance Association. *Purveyor of cat's meat to the Lord Mayor and Sheriffs, and several members of the Common Council (the announcement of this gentleman's name was received with breathless interest). Has a wooden leg; finds a* *wooden leg expensive, going over the stones; used to wear second-hand wooden legs, and drink a glass of hot gin-and-water regularly every night – sometimes two (deep sighs). Found the second-hand wooden legs split and rot very quickly; is firmly persuaded that their constitution was undermined by the gin-and-water (prolonged cheering). Buys new wooden legs now, and drinks nothing but water and weak tea. The new legs last twice as long as the others used to do, and he attributes this solely to his temperate habits (triumphant cheers) (Pickwick).*

Butcher, William: John's friend, who advises him to patent his invention. *A Chartist. Moderate. He is a good speaker. He is very animated (Reprinted – 'Poor Man's Tale of a Patent').*

Butcher, The Young: David Copperfield's adversary in Canterbury. *He is the terror of the youth of Canterbury. There is a vague belief abroad, that the beef suet with which he anoints his hair gives him unnatural strength, and that he is a match for a man. He is broad-faced, bull-necked young butcher, with rough red cheeks, an ill-conditioned mind, and an injurious tongue. His main use of this tongue, is, to disparage Doctor Strong's young gentlemen. He says, publicly, that if they want anything he'll give it 'em (Copperfield).*

Butler, Theodosius: Author, under the pseudonym Edward M'Neville Walter, of the pamphlet 'Considerations on the Policy of Removing the Duty on Bees'-wax', with which he gains the favour of Cornelius Brook Dingwall, M.P., and the heart of his daughter Lavinia. *One of those immortal geniuses who are to be met with in almost every circle. They have, usually, very deep, monotonous voices. They always persuade themselves that they are wonderful persons, and that they ought to be very miserable, though they don't precisely know why. They are very conceited, and usually possess half an idea; but, with enthusiastic young ladies, and silly young gentlemen, they are very wonderful persons. The individual in person, Mr. Theodosius, had written a pamphlet containing some very weighty considera-tions on the expediency of doing something or other; and as every sentence contained a good many words of four syllables, his admirers took it for granted that he meant a good deal (Boz – 'Sentiment').*

Buxom Widow, The: Landlady of an inn on the Marlborough Downs wooed by Tom Smart and Jinkins in 'The Bagman's Story'. (See Bagman, The). *A buxom widow of somewhere about eight and forty or thereabouts, with a face as comfortable as the bar (Pickwick).*

Buzfuz, Serjeant: Mrs. Bardell's counsel in the trial of Bardell and Pickwick. *Serjeant Buzfuz then rose with all the majesty and dignity which the grave nature of the proceedings demanded . . . pulled his gown over his shoulders, settled his wig, and addressed the jury (Pickwick).*

Callow: One of many doctors consulted by Our Bore. *Said, 'Liver!' and prescribed rhubarb and calomel, low diet, and moderate exercise (Reprinted – 'Our Bore').*

Calton: Boarder at Mrs. Tibbs's. He courts Mrs. Maplesone, but when he fails to marry her is successfully sued for breach of promise. *A superannuated beau – an old boy. He used to say of himself that although his features were not regularly handsome, they were striking. They certainly were. It was impossible to look at his face without being reminded of a chubby street-door knocker, half-lion half-monkey; and the comparison might be extended to his whole character and conversation. . . . He had never been married; but he was still on the look-out for a wife with money. He had a life interest worth about* 300*l. a year – he was exceedingly vain, and inordinately selfish. He acquired the reputation of being the very pink of politeness, and he walked round the Park, and up Regent Street, every day (Boz –* 'Boarding-House').

Camilla: Raymond's wife, Matthew Pocket's sister. *Very much reminded me of my sister, with the difference that she was older, and (as I found when I caught sight of her) of a blunter cast of features. Indeed, when I knew her better I began to* think it was a Mercy she had any features at all, so very blank and high was the dead wall of her face (*Expectations*).

Campbell: See Magwitch, Abel (*Expectations*).

Cape: Performer on the violin at the Gattletons' private theatricals (*Boz* – 'Mrs. Joseph Porter').

Capper: The narrator's friend who introduces him to Mincin. (*Young Gentlemen* – 'Very Friendly Young Gentleman').

Captain, The: A Member of Parliament. *The spare, squeaking old man, who sits at the same table, and who, elevating a little cracked bantam sort of voice to its highest pitch, invokes damnation upon his own eyes or somebody else's at the commencement of every sentence he utters. 'The Captain', as they call him, is a very old frequenter of Bellamy's, much addicted to stopping 'after the House is up' (an inexpiable crime in Jane's eyes), and a complete walking reservoir of spirits and water* (*Boz* – 'Parliamentary Sketch').

Captain, The Half-pay: A neighbour of the Old Lady. *He is an old naval officer on half-pay, and his bluff and unceremonious behaviour disturbs the old lady's domestic economy, not a little* (*Boz* – 'Half-pay Captain').

Carker, Harriet: Sister of John and James Carker and later wife to Mórfin. She is Alice Marwood's only friend and tends her at death. *On her beauty there has fallen a heavier shade than Time of his unassisted self can cast, all-potent as he is – the shadow of anxiety and sorrow, and the daily struggle of a poor existence. But it is beauty still; and still a gentle, quiet, and retiring beauty that must be sought out, for it cannot vaunt itself; if it could, it would be what it is, no more* (*Dombey*).

Carker, James: Brother of John and Harriet. Manager and confidential assistant to Dombey, with whose second wife he elopes to France. Tracked down through the agency of Mrs. Brown, whose daughter had been his mistress, he is pursued back to England by Dombey and is killed by a train. *Thirty-eight or forty years old, of a florid complexion,* and with two unbroken rows of glistening teeth, whose regularity and whiteness were quite distressing. It was impossible to escape the observation of them, for he showed them whenever he spoke; and bore so wide a smile upon his countenance (a smile, however, very rarely, indeed, extending beyond his mouth), that there was something in it like the snarl of a cat. He affected a stiff white cravat, after the example of his principal, and was always closely buttoned up and tightly dressed. His manner towards Mr. Dombey was deeply conceived and perfectly expressed. He was familiar with him, in the very extremity of his sense of the distance between them. 'Mr. Dombey, to a man in your position from a man in mine, there is no show of subservience compatible with the transaction of business between us, that I should think sufficient. I frankly tell you, sir, I give it up altogether' (*Dombey*).

Carker, John: Brother of James and Harriet. Junior clerk at Dombey and Son's and known as Mr. Carker the Junior, though he is James's elder. He had been tempted into embezzlement when young but kept on by Dombey, whom he helps financially after inheriting James's fortune on his death. *He was not old, but his hair was white; his body was bent, or bowed as if by the weight of some great trouble: and there were deep lines in his worn and melancholy face. The fire of his eyes, the expression of his features, the very voice in which he spoke, were all subdued and quenched, as if the spirit within him lay in ashes. He was respectably, though very plainly dressed, in black; but his clothes, moulded to the general character of his figure, seemed to shrink and base themselves upon him, and to join in the sorrowful solicitation which the whole man from head to foot expressed, to be left unnoticed, and alone in his humility* (*Dombey*).

Carlavero, Giovanni: Wine-shopkeeper on the Mediterranean coast of Italy, who persuades the Uncommercial Traveller to convey a huge bottle of wine to a friend in England who has helped him. *A well-favoured man of good stature and* *military bearing, in a great cloak. . . . As his striking face is pale, and his action is evidently that of an enfeebled man, I remark that I fear he has been ill. It is not much, he courteously and gravely answers, though bad while it lasts : the fever (Uncommercial –* 'Italian Prisoner').

Carlo: One of Jerry's performing dogs. *The lucky individual whose name was called, snapped up the morsel thrown towards him, but none of the others moved a muscle (Curiosity Shop).*

Carolina: Clara's maid, admired by Baptista. *La belle Carolina, whose heart was gay with laughter : who was young and rosy* ('At Dusk').

Caroline: Wife of one of Scrooge's debtors (*Christmas Books –* 'Christmas Carol').

Carstone, Richard: Ward in Chancery under John Jarndyce's guardianship. He secretly marries his cousin and fellow ward, Ada Clare, but his involvement in the case of Jarndyce and Jarndyce undermines his health and causes his death. *A handsome youth, with an ingenuous face, and a most engaging laugh. . . . He was very young ; not more than nineteen then, if quite so much (Bleak House).*

Carter: President of the mechanical science session at the first meeting of the Mudfog Association *(Mudfog).*

Carton, Captain George (later Admiral Sir George Carton, Bart.): Officer commanding the expedition against the pirates at Silver-Store Island. He marries Marion Maryon. *With his bright eyes, brown face, and easy figure (Christmas Stories –* 'English Prisoners').

Carton Sydney: Dissolute barrister who prepares Stryver's law cases for him. He falls in love with Lucie Manette but sacrifices his life to save Charles Darnay by means of their physical resemblance. *Sydney Carton, idlest and most unpromising of men, was Stryver's great ally. What the two drank together between Hilary Term and Michaelmas, might have floated a king's ship. . . . They prolonged their usual orgies late into the night, and Carton was rumoured to be seen at broad day, going home stealthily and unsteadily to his lodgings, like a dissipated cat. At last, it began to get about, among such as were interested in the matter, that although Sydney Carton would never be a lion, he was an amazingly good jackal (Two Cities).*

Casby, Christopher: Flora Finching's father. An apparently benign, but grasping landlord of slum properties, including Bleeding Heart Yard, whose extortionate methods are exposed by his employee, Pancks. *Patriarch was the name which many people delighted to give him. Various old ladies in the neighbourhood spoke of him as The Last of the Patriarchs. So grey, so slow, so quiet, so impassionate, so very bumpy in the head, Patriarch was the word for him. He had been accosted in the streets, and respectfully solicited to become a Patriarch for painters and for sculptors (Dorrit).*

Cavalletto, John Baptist ('Altro'): Italian refugee imprisoned with Rigaud, whom he later helps to track down in London. *A sunburnt, quick, lithe, little man, though rather thick-set. Earrings in his brown ears, white teeth lighting up his grotesque brown face, intensely black hair clustering about his brown throat, a ragged red shirt open at his brown breast. Loose, seamanlike trousers, decent shoes, a long red cap, a red sash round his waist, and a knife in it (Dorrit).*

Caveton: A 'throwing off' young gentleman. *Sometimes the throwing-off young gentleman happens to look in upon a little family circle of young ladies who are quietly spending the evening together, and then indeed he is at the very height and summit of his glory ; for it is to be observed that he by no means shines to equal advantage in the presence of men as in the society of over-credulous young ladies, which is his proper element (Young Gentlemen –* ' "Throwing-off" Young Gentleman').

Celia: See **Joseph and Celia** (*Uncommercial –* 'City of the Absent').

Certainpersonio, Prince: Alicia's bridegroom in Alice Rainbird's romantic tale ('Holiday Romance').

Chadband, The Revd. Mr.: A hypo-critical clergyman who is drawn into the Smallweeds' scheme for blackmailing Dedlock. Marries Mrs. Rachael. *A large yellow man, with a fat smile, and a general appearance of having a good deal of train oil in his system. . . . Mr. Chadband moves softly and cumbrously, not unlike a bear who has been taught to walk upright. He is very much embarrassed about the arms, as if they were inconvenient to him, and he wanted to grovel; is very much in a per-spiration about the head; and never speaks without first putting up his great hand, as delivering a token to his hearers that he is going to edify them (Bleak House).*

Chadband, Mrs.: Chadband's wife, formerly Mrs. Rachael, Esther Summer-son's nurse. *A stern, severe-looking silent woman (Bleak House).*

Chancery Prisoner, The: A wretched debtor whose death Pickwick witnesses in the Fleet. *A tall, gaunt, cadaverous man, in an old great-coat and slippers: with sunken cheeks, and a restless, eager eye. His lips were bloodless, and his bones sharp and thin. God help him! the iron teeth of con-finement and privation had been slowly filing him down for twenty years (Pick-wick).*

Chaplain, Drunken: A fellow prisoner of Pickwick in the Fleet. *Fastened his coat all the way up to his chin by means of a pin and a button alternately, had a very coarse red face, and looked like a drunken chaplain; which, indeed, he was (Pick-wick).*

Charker, Corporal Harry: Gill Davis's comrade in the Royal Marines, killed in the fight with pirates. *Besides being able to read and write like a Quarter-master, he had always one most excellent idea in his mind. That was, Duty (Christmas Stories – 'English Prisoners').*

Charles and Louisa: A cool couple. *The cool couple are seldom alone together, and when they are, nothing can exceed their apathy and dulness: the gentleman being for the most part drowsy, and the lady silent. If they enter into conversation, it is usually of an ironical or recriminatory nature (Young Couples – 'Cool Couple').*

Charles, Old: A highly respected waiter, believed to have made a fortune at it, but found at his death to possess nothing. *Long eminent at the West Country Hotel, and by some considered the Father of the Waitering (Christmas Stories – 'Some-body's Luggage').*

Charley: Pot-boy at the Magpie and Stump. *A shambling pot-boy, with a red head (Pickwick).*

Charley: Narrator of the story. Suppos-ing himself jilted by Angela Leath, he sets off for America, is snowed-up at the Holly-Tree Inn in Yorkshire, and dis-covers in time that his love is true to him, after all. *I am a bashful man. Nobody would suppose it, nobody ever does suppose it, nobody ever did suppose it, but I am naturally a bashful man (Christmas Stories – 'Holly-Tree').*

Charley: Chatham marine-store dealer to whom David offers his jacket for half-a-crown during his tramp from London to Dover. *'Oh, my lungs and liver,' cried the old man, 'no! Oh, my eyes, no! Oh, my limbs, no! Eighteenpence. Goroo!' (Copperfield).*

Charley: See Neckett, Charlotte *(Bleak House).*

Charlotte: Schoolfellow of Miss Wade who makes her jealously infatuated with her. *I loved that stupid mite in a pas-sionate way that she could no more deserve, than I can remember without feeling ashamed of, though I was but a child. She had what they called an amiable temper, an affectionate temper. She could distribute, and did distribute pretty looks and smiles to every one among them. I believe there was not a soul in the place, except myself, who knew that she did it purposely to wound and gall me! (Dorrit).*

Charlotte: One of the two daughters of John, the narrator. *Her husband run away from her in the basest manner, and she and her three children live with us (Reprinted – 'Poor Man's Tale of a Patent').*

Charlotte: Sowerberry's maidservant, later, as 'Mrs. Bolter', Noah Claypole's mistress and associate in crime. *A slat-*

ternly girl, in shoes down at heel, and blue worsted stockings very much out of repair (Twist).

Charlotte: Edward's wife and mother of James and Charlotte. *She now lets down her back hair, and proceeds to brush it; preserving at the same time an air of conscious rectitude and suffering virtue, which is intended to exasperate the gentleman – and does so (Young Couples – 'Contradictory Couple').*

Charlotte, Miss: See **James and Charlotte** (*Young Couples* – 'Contradictory Couple').

Cheeryble, Charles: First of the twin brothers to meet Nicholas Nickleby, whose benefactors they become. Self-made merchants, they are models of benevolence, notably to the Nicklebys, Madeline Bray, and their nephew Frank. *A sturdy old fellow in a broad-skirted blue coat, made pretty large, to fit easily, and with no particular waist; his bulky legs clothed in drab breeches and high gaiters, and his head protected by a low-crowned broad-brimmed white hat, such as a wealthy grazier might wear. He wore his coat buttoned; and his dimpled double-chin rested in the folds of a white neckerchief – not one of your stiff-starched apoplectic cravats, but a good, easy, old-fashioned white neckcloth that a man might go to bed in and be none the worse for. But what principally attracted the attention of Nicholas, was the old gentleman's eye, – never was such a clear, twinkling, honest, merry, happy eye, as that. And there he stood, looking a little upward, with one hand thrust into the breast of his coat, and the other playing with his old-fashioned gold watch-chain; his head thrown a little on one side, and his hat a little more on one side than his head (but that was evidently accident; not his ordinary way of wearing it), with such a pleasant smile playing about his mouth, and such a comical expression of mingled slyness, simplicity, kind-heartedness, and good-humour, lighting up his jolly old face, that Nicholas would have been content to have stood there, and looked at him until evening, and to have forgotten, meanwhile, that there was such a thing as a*

soured mind or a crabbed countenance to be met with in the whole wide world (Nickleby).

Cheeryble, Edwin: Twin brother of Charles. *Something stouter than his brother; this, and a slight additional shade of clumsiness in his gait and stature, formed the only perceptible difference between them (Nickleby).*

Cheeryble, Frank: Nephew of Charles and Edwin. Marries Kate Nickleby and becomes a partner, with Nicholas, in the brothers' firm. *A sprightly, good-humoured, pleasant fellow, with much both in his countenance and disposition that reminded Nicholas very strongly of the kind-hearted brothers. His manner was as unaffected as theirs, and his demeanour full of that heartiness which, to most people who have anything generous in their composition, is peculiarly prepossessing. Add to this, that he was good-looking and intelligent, had a plentiful share of vivacity, was extremely cheerful (Nickleby).*

Cheeseman, Old: Pupil, then second Latin master, at the school, where he is always the butt of the boys. He marries his only friend there, Jane Pitts, a matron. *Old Cheeseman used to be called by the names of all sorts of cheeses – Double Glo'sterman. Family Cheshireman, Dutchman, North Wiltshireman, and all that. But he never minded it. And I don't mean to say he was old in point of years – because he wasn't – only he was called from the first, Old Cheeseman (Christmas Stories –* 'Schoolboy's Story').

Cheggs, Miss: Cheggs's sister (*Curiosity Shop*).

Cheggs, Alick: The market gardener who wins the hand of Sophy Wackles from Dick Swiveller (*Curiosity Shop*).

'Cherub, The': See **Wilfer, Reginald** (*Mutual Friend*).

Chester, Edward: Son of Sir John Chester, by whom he is disowned for persisting in courting Emma Haredale, whom he later saves from Gashford and marries. *A young man of about eight-and-twenty, rather above the middle height, and though of a somewhat slight figure,* *gracefully and strongly made. He wore his own dark hair, and was accoutred in a riding-dress, which together with his large boots (resembling in shape and fashion those worn by our Life Guardsmen at the present day), showed indisputable traces of the bad condition of the roads. But travel-stained though he was, he was well and even richly attired, and without being over-dressed looked a gallant gentleman (Rudge).*

Chester, Sir John: A suave but ruthless gentleman, father of Edward, whose marriage to Emma Haredale, daughter of his lifelong enemy, he tries unsuccessfully to thwart. Natural father of Hugh, the Maypole ostler. He is killed in a duel by Geoffrey Haredale. *He was a staid, grave, placid gentleman, something past the prime of life, yet upright in his carriage, for all that, and slim as a greyhound. He was well-mounted upon a sturdy chestnut cob, and had the graceful seat of an experienced horseman; while his riding gear, though free from such fopperies as were then in vogue, was handsome and well chosen. He wore a riding-coat of a somewhat brighter green than might have been expected to suit the taste of a gentleman of his years, with a short, black velvet cape, and laced pocket-holes and cuffs, all of a jaunty fashion; his linen, too, was of the finest kind, worked in a rich pattern at the wrists and throat, and scrupulously white (Rudge).*

Chestle: Kentish hop-grower who marries the eldest Miss Larkins *(Copperfield).*

Chib: Of Tucket's Terrace, father of the Vestry. *A remarkably hale old gentleman of eighty-two (Reprinted – 'Our Vestry').*

Chick, John: Dombey's brother-in-law. *A stout bald gentleman, with a very large face, and his hands continually in his pockets, and who had a tendency in his nature to whistle and hum tunes, which, sensible of the indecorum of such sounds in a house of grief, he was at some pains to repress at present. 'Don't you over-exert yourself, Loo,' said Mr. Chick, 'or you'll be laid up with spasms, I see. Right tol loor*

rul! Bless my soul, I forgot! We're here one day and gone the next!' (Dombey).

Chick, Mrs. John (Louisa): Wife of John Chick, sister to Dombey, and friend of Miss Tox until she becomes aware that the latter aspires to be the second Mrs. Dombey. *A lady rather past the middle age than otherwise, but dressed in a very juvenile manner, particularly as to the tightness of her bodice (Dombey).*

Chickenstalker, Mrs. Anne: General shopkeeper. She marries Tugby in Trotty's vision. *A good-humoured comely woman of some fifty years of age, or thereabouts (Christmas Books – 'Chimes').*

Chicksey, Veneering and Stobbles: Firm of drug dealers near Mincing Lane, City of London, where Reginald Wilfer is clerk and Hamilton Veneering is sole surviving partner. *Chicksey and Stobbles, his former masters, had both become absorbed in Veneering, once their traveller or commission agent: who had signalised his accession to supreme power by bringing into the business a quantity of plate-glass window and French-polished mahogany partition, and a gleaming and enormous door-plate (Mutual Friend).*

Chickweed, Conkey: Landlord of a public-house near Battle Bridge who, according to Blathers, faked the theft of all his money in order to raise more from sympathetic public benefits and subscriptions *(Twist).*

Chiggle: Renowned American sculptor of Elijah Pogram. *'Our own immortal Chiggle, sir, is said to have observed, when he made the celebrated Pogram statter in marble, which rose so much con-test and preju-dice in Europe, that the brow was more than mortal' (Chuzzlewit).*

Childers, jun. ('The Little Wonder of Scholastic Equitation'): Son of E. W. B. Childers and Josephine Sleary *(Hard Times).*

Childers, E. W. B.: Equestrian with Sleary's Circus who helps Tom Gradgrind escape arrest and leave the country. Married to Josephine Sleary. *His face, close-shaven, thin, and sallow, was shaded by a great quantity of dark hair, brushed* *into a roll all round his head, and parted up the centre. His legs were very robust, but shorter than legs of good proportion should have been. His chest and back were as much too broad, as his legs were too short. He was dressed in a Newmarket coat and tight-fitting trousers; wore a shawl round his neck; smelt of lamp-oil, straw, orange-peel, horses' provender, and sawdust; and looked a most remarkable sort of Centaur, compounded of the stable and the play-house. Where the one began, and the other ended, nobody could have told with any precision. This gentleman was mentioned in the bills of the day as Mr. E. W. B. Childers, so justly celebrated for his daring vaulting act as the Wild Huntsman of the North American Prairies (Hard Times).*

Chill, Uncle: Uncle of Michael, the Poor Relation. *Avarice was, unhappily, my uncle Chill's master-vice. Though he was rich, he pinched, and scraped, and clutched, and lived miserably* (*Christmas Stories* – 'Poor Relation').

Chillip, Dr.: Mrs. Copperfield's medical attendant at David's birth. *He was the meekest of his sex, the mildest of little men. He sidled in and out of a room, to take up the less space. He walked as softly as the Ghost in Hamlet, and more slowly. He carried his head on one side, partly in modest depreciation of himself, partly in modest propitiation of everybody else. It is nothing to say that he hadn't a word to throw at a dog. He couldn't have thrown a word at a mad dog. He might have offered him one gently, or half a one, or a fragment of one; for he spoke as slowly as he walked; but he wouldn't have been rude to him, and he couldn't have been quick with him, for any earthly consideration* (*Copperfield*).

Chinaman, Jack: Princess Puffer's rival opium-den keeper. *'Nobody but me (and Jack Chinaman t'other side the court; but he can't do it as well as me) has the true secret of mixing it'* (*Drood*).

Chips: Family of shipyard carpenters involved in a bargain with the Devil in a story told to the Uncommercial Traveller in his childhood by his nurse Mercy.

Chips the father had sold himself to the Devil for an iron pot and a bushel of tenpenny nails and half a ton of copper and a rat that could speak; and Chips the grandfather had sold himself to the Devil for an iron pot and a bushel of tenpenny nails and half a ton of copper and a rat that could speak; and Chips the great-grandfather had disposed of himself in the same direction on the same terms; and the bargain had run in the family for a long, long time. So, one day, when young Chips was at work in the Dock Slip all alone, down in the dark hold of an old Seventy-four that was haled up for repairs, the Devil presented himself (*Uncommercial* – 'Nurse's Stories').

Chirrup, Mr. and Mrs.: The nice little couple. *Mr. Chirrup has the smartness, and something of the brisk, quick manner of a small bird. Mrs. Chirrup is the prettiest of all little women, and has the prettiest little figure conceivable. She has the neatest little foot, and the softest little voice, and the pleasantest little smile, and the tidiest little curls, and the brightest little eyes, and the quietest little manner, and is, in short, altogether one of the most engaging of all little women, dead or alive. . . . Nobody knows all this better than Mr. Chirrup, though he rather takes on that he don't. Accordingly he is very proud of his better-half, and evidently considers himself as all other people consider him, rather fortunate in having her to wife* (*Young Couples* – 'Nice Little Couple').

Chitling, Tom: Member of Fagin's gang, recently out of prison. *He had small twinkling eyes, and a pock-marked face; wore a fur cap, a dark corduroy jacket, greasy fustian trousers, and an apron. His wardrobe was, in truth, rather out of repair; but he excused himself to the company by stating that his 'time' was only out an hour before; and that, in consequence of having worn the regimentals for six weeks past, he had not been able to bestow any affection on his private clothes* (*Twist*).

Chivery, John: Kindly but laconic non-resident turnkey at the Marshalsea. Father of Young John. *He had imbibed* a *professional habit of locking everything up. He locked himself up as carefully as he locked up the Marshalsea debtors. Even his custom of bolting his meals may have been a part of an uniform whole; but there is no question, that, as to all other purposes, he kept his mouth as he kept the Marshalsea door. He never opened it without occasion. When it was necessary to let anything out, he opened it a little way, held it open just as long as sufficed for the purpose, and locked it again (Dorrit).*

Chivery, Mrs. John: Chivery's wife and mother of Young John. Keeper of a tobacco-shop near the Marshalsea. *A comfortable looking woman, much respected about Horsemonger Lane for her feelings and her conversation (Dorrit).*

Chivery, Young John: John Chivery's son, in love with Amy Dorrit and Pancks's associate in restoring her family's fortunes. *Small of stature, with rather weak legs and very weak light hair. One of his eyes (perhaps the eye that used to peep through the keyhole) was also weak, and looked larger than the other, as if it couldn't collect itself. Young John was gentle likewise. But he was great of soul. Poetical, expansive, faithful (Dorrit).*

Choke, General Cyrus: American Militia officer, member of the Watertoast Association of United Sympathisers and of the Eden Land Corporation, in which he advises Martin Chuzzlewit to invest. *One very lank gentleman, in a loose limp white cravat, a long white waistcoat, and a black great-coat, who seemed to be in authority (Chuzzlewit).*

Chollop, Major Hannibal: Caller upon Martin Chuzzlewit at Eden. *A lean person in a blue frock and a straw hat, with a short black pipe in his mouth, and a great hickory stick, studded all over with knots, in his hand; who smoking and chewing as he came along, and spitting frequently, recorded his progress by a train of decomposed tobacco on the ground (Chuzzlewit).*

Chopper, Great-uncle: William Tinkling's great-uncle, present at the christening of his baby brother. *I said that ma had said afterwards (and so she had), that*

Great-uncle Chopper's gift was a shabby one . . . electrotyped, second-hand, and below his income ('Holiday Romance').

Chopper, Mrs.: Mrs. Merrywinkle's mother, who fosters her hypochondria. *A mysterious old lady who lurks behind a pair of spectacles, and is afflicted with a chronic disease, respecting which she has taken a vast deal of medical advice, and referred to a vast number of medical books, without meeting any definition of symptoms that at all suits her, or enables her to say, 'That's my complaint'* (Young Couples – 'Couple who Coddle Themselves').

Chops (real name **Stakes**, but also known as **Major Tpschoffki, of the Imperial Bulgraderian Brigade,** contracted to **Chopski**): Dwarf in Magsman's Amusements who wins a fortune and goes into society with disastrous results. *He was an un-common small man, he really was. Certainly not so small as he was made out to be, but where is your Dwarf as is? He was a most uncommon small man, with a most uncommon large Ed. . . . The kindest little man as never growed! Spirited, but not proud* (Christmas Stories – 'Going into Society').

'Chowley': See **MacStinger, Charles** *(Dombey)*.

Chowser, Colonel: A dinner guest of Ralph Nickleby *(Nickleby)*.

Christiana: Former sweetheart and imagined wife of Michael, the Poor Relation. *She was very beautiful, and very winning in all respects. . . . I never had loved any one but Christiana, and she had been all the world, and O far more than all the world, to me, from our childhood!* (Christmas Stories – 'Poor Relation').

Christina, Donna: One of Jingle's boasted thousands of conquests in Spain. Daughter of Don Bolaro Fizzgig (q.v.). *'Splendid creature – loved me to distraction – jealous father – high-souled daughter – handsome Englishman – Donna Christina in despair – prussic acid – stomach pump in my portmanteau – operation performed – old Bolaro in ecstasies – consent* to our union – join hands and floods of tears – romantic story – very.' 'Is the lady in England now, sir?' inquired Mr. Tupman, on whom the description of her charms had produced a powerful impression. 'Dead, sir,' said the stranger, applying to his right eye the brief remnant of a very old cambric handkerchief. 'Never recovered the stomach pump – undermined constitution – fell a victim' (Pickwick).

Christopher: Head-waiter at a London hotel coffee-house, 'author' and narrator of this collection of stories. Having come of a family of Waiters, and owning at the present time five brothers who are all Waiters, and likewise an only sister who is a Waitress (Christmas Stories – 'Somebody's Luggage').

Chuckster: Witherden's clerk and friend of Swiveller. Being a gentleman of cultivated taste and refined spirit, was one of that Lodge of Glorious Apollos whereof Mr. Swiveller was perpetual Grand (Curiosity Shop).

Chuffey: Clerk to Anthony Chuzzlewit and Son. A little blear-eyed, weazen-faced, ancient man came creeping out. He was of a remote fashion, and dusty, like the rest of the furniture; he was dressed in a decayed suit of black; with breeches garnished at the knees with rusty wisps of ribbon, the very paupers of shoe-strings; on the lower portion of his spindle legs were dingy worsted stockings of the same colour. He looked as if he had been put away and forgotten half-a-century before, and somebody had just found him in a lumber-closet (Chuzzlewit).

Chuzzlewit, Anthony: Old Martin's brother and father of Jonas. A Manchester warehouseman. The face of the old man so sharpened by the wariness and cunning of his life, that it seemed to cut him a passage through the crowded room (Chuzzlewit).

Chuzzlewit, Diggory: A Chuzzlewit ancestor. In the habit of perpetually dining with Duke Humphrey (i.e. going without his lunch) (Chuzzlewit).

Chuzzlewit, George: A gay bachelor cousin of old Martin. Claimed to be young but had been younger, and was inclined to corpulency, and rather overfed himself: to that extent, indeed, that his eyes were strained in their sockets, as if with constant surprise (Chuzzlewit).

Chuzzlewit, Jonas: Cruel and scheming son of Anthony, whose death he causes, and nephew of old Martin. He marries Mercy Pecksniff and ill-treats her, murders Tigg, and poisons himself after arrest. The education of Mr. Jonas had been conducted from his cradle on the strictest principles of the main chance. The very first word he learnt to spell was 'gain', and the second (when he got into two syllables), 'money'. . . . From his early habits of considering everything as a question of property, he had gradually come to look, with impatience, on his parent as a certain amount of personal estate, which had no right whatever to be going at large, but ought to be secured in that particular description of iron safe which is commonly called a coffin, and banked in the grave (Chuzzlewit).

Chuzzlewit, Martin, jun.: The central character, grandson of old Martin, who has brought him up expecting to become his heir, but turns him out for loving Mary Graham. After experiencing hardships – which temper his unlikeable nature – in London and America, in company with Mark Tapley, Martin returns to favour and marries Mary. He was young – one-and-twenty, perhaps – and handsome; with a keen dark eye, and a quickness of look and manner (Chuzzlewit).

Chuzzlewit, Martin, sen.: The rich old family head, brother of Anthony, cousin of George and grandfather of Martin jun. He manipulates those with designs upon his money, breaks Pecksniff, and eventually gives Martin jun. the hand of Mary Graham, old Martin's adopted daughter and constant companion. He was, beyond all question, very ill, and suffered exceedingly; not the less, perhaps, because he was a strong and vigorous old man, with a will of iron, and a voice of brass (Chuzzlewit).

Chuzzlewit, Mrs. Ned, and the **Misses:** Widow of a brother of old Martin. *Being almost supernaturally disagreeable, and having a dreary face and a bony figure and a masculine voice, was, in right of these qualities, what is commonly called a strong-minded woman. . . . Beside her sat her spinster daughters, three in number, and of gentlemanly deportment, who had so mortified themselves with tight stays, that their tempers were reduced to something less than their waists, and sharp lacing was expressed in their very noses* (*Chuzzlewit*).

Chuzzlewit, Toby: A Chuzzlewit ancestor whose deathbed reply that his father was 'The Lord No Zoo' is regarded as evidence in the family's claims to noble connections *(Chuzzlewit)*.

Cicero: A negro truckman, formerly a slave, encountered by Mark Tapley and Martin Chuzzlewit in New York. *'Ah!' said Mark in the same tone. 'Nothing else. A slave. Why, when that there man was young – don't look at him, while I'm a telling it – he was shot in the leg; gashed in the arm; scored in his live limbs, like crimped fish; beaten out of shape; had his neck galled with an iron collar, and wore iron rings upon his wrists and ankles. The marks are on him to this day. When I was having my dinner just now, he stripped off his coat, and took away my appetite'* (*Chuzzlewit*).

Clara: The English bride, mistress of Carolina, haunted by Dellombra. *Brooding in a manner very strange; in a frightened manner; in an unhappy manner; with a cloudy, uncertain alarm upon her* ('At Dusk').

Clare, Ada: Ward in Chancery under John Jarndyce's guardianship, and close friend to Esther Summerson. Left a pregnant widow by the death of her cousin, Richard Carstone, after their secret marriage, she returns to Jarndyce's care. *I saw in the young lady, with the fire shining upon her, such a beautiful girl!! With such rich golden hair, such soft blue eyes, and such a bright, innocent, trusting face! (Bleak House).*

Clark: A clerk at Dombey and Son's. *A stout man stood whistling, with his pen* behind his ear, and his hands in his pockets, as if the day's work were nearly done (Dombey).

Clark, Mrs.: Employer to whom the agency sends Madeline Bray. *'She'll have a nice life of it, if she goes there,' observed the fat lady (Nickleby).*

Clark, Betsy: Servant-girl in the Covent Garden district. *The servant of all work, who, under the plea of sleeping very soundly, has utterly disregarded 'Missis's' ringing for half an hour previously . . . awakes all of a sudden, with well-feigned astonishment, and goes downstairs very sulkily, wishing, while she strikes a light, that the principle of spontaneous combustion would extend itself to coals and kitchen range (Boz – 'The Streets – Morning').*

Clarke, Mrs. Susan: Widowed landlady of the Marquis of Granby, Dorking, whom Tony Weller marries. See **Weller, Mrs. Tony,** sen. *(Pickwick)*.

Clarkson: Counsel for Shepherdson and other criminals arrested by Sergeant Mith (*Reprinted* – 'Detective Police').

Clarriker: Shipping broker in whose firm Pip secretly buys an interest for Herbert Pocket. He himself obtains work in the firm after the loss of his fortunes. *A worthy young merchant or shipping-broker, not long established in business, who wanted intelligent help, and who wanted capital, and who in due course of time and receipt would want a partner (Expectations).*

Clatter: One of many doctors consulted by Our Bore. *The moment Clatter saw our bore, he said, 'Accumulation of fat about the heart!' (Reprinted – 'Our Bore').*

Claypole, Noah: Sowerberry's apprentice, later a criminal under the name **Morris Bolter.** It is after a fight with him that Oliver Twist runs away and falls into criminal company. Claypole, too, enters Fagin's service, spies on Nancy, and brings about her murder. *It is difficult for a large-headed, small-eyed youth, of lumbering make and heavy countenance, to look dignified under any circumstances; but it is more especially so, when super-added to these attractions are a red nose* and yellow smalls. . . . Noah was a charity-boy, but not a workhouse orphan. No chance-child was he, for he could trace his genealogy all the way back to his parents, who lived hard by; his mother being a washerwoman, and his father a drunken soldier (Twist).

Cleaver ('Mr. Dolls'): Fanny Cleaver's drunken father, known as 'Mr. Dolls' after the trade by which she supports him. 'Like his own father, a weak wretched trembling creature, falling to pieces, never sober. But a good workman too, at the work he does' (Mutual Friend).

Cleaver, Fanny ('Jenny Wren'): A crippled child, who supports her drunken father by making dolls' dresses. She becomes Lizzie Hexam's faithful friend. A child – a dwarf – a girl – a something. . . . The queer little figure, and the queer but not ugly little face, with its bright grey eyes, were so sharp, that the sharpness of the manner seemed unavoidable. As if, being turned out of that mould, it must be sharp (Mutual Friend).

Clennam, Mrs.: Adoptive mother of Arthur Clennam, the son of her husband and his mistress. She conducts all her affairs from the confinement of her room. On a black bier-like sofa in this hollow, propped up behind with one great angular black bolster, like the block at a state execution in the good old times, sat his mother in a widow's dress. She and his father had been at variance from his earliest remembrance. To sit speechless himself in the midst of rigid silence, glancing in dread from the one averted face to the other, had been the peacefullest occupation of his childhood. She gave him one glassy kiss, and four stiff fingers muffled in worsted (Dorrit).

Clennam, Arthur: Mrs. Clennam's adopted son. Becoming Doyce's partner, he speculates with Merdle, and is bankrupted and imprisoned in the Marshalsea, where he is tended by Amy Dorrit, whom he subsequently marries. A grave dark man of forty. || 'I am the son, Mr. Meagles, of a hard father and mother. I am the only child of parents who weighed, measured, and priced everything; for whom what could not be weighed, measured, and priced, had no existence. Strict people as the phrase is, professors of a stern religion, their very religion was a gloomy sacrifice of tastes and sympathies that were never their own, offered up as a part of a bargain for the security of their possessions. Austere faces, inexorable discipline, penance in this world and terror in the next – nothing graceful or gentle anywhere, and the void in my cowed heart everywhere – this was my childhood, if I may so misuse the word as to apply it to such a beginning of life' (Dorrit).

Clennam, Gilbert: Uncle of Mrs. Clennam's late husband. He leaves Frederick Dorrit or his niece £1,000 in his own will. Mrs. Clennam suppresses the information and Rigaud attempts to blackmail her in consequence (Dorrit).

'Cleopatra': See Skewton, The Hon. Mrs. (Dombey).

Clergyman, The: Clergyman of a village visited by Little Nell and her grandfather. A simple-hearted old gentleman, of a shrinking, subdued spirit, accustomed to retirement, and very little acquainted with the world (Curiosity Shop).

Clergyman, The: Guest at Dingley Dell who sings 'The Ivy Green' and narrates 'The Convict's Return'. A bald-headed old gentleman, with a good-humoured benevolent face. His Wife, also a guest, was a stout blooming old lady, who looked as if she were well skilled, not only in the art and mystery of manufacturing home-made cordials greatly to other people's satisfaction, but of tasting them occasionally very much to her own (Pickwick).

Cleverly, William and Susannah: Brother and sister, Mormon recruits aboard the emigrant ship Amazon (Uncommercial – 'Bound for the Great Salt Lake').

Click: Fellow lodger and friend of Tom. In the gas-fitting way of life. He is very good company, having worked at the theatres, and, indeed, he has a theatrical turn himself, and wishes to be brought out in the character of Othello; but whether on account of his regular work always black-

ing his face and hands more or less, I cannot say (Christmas Stories – 'Somebody's Luggage').

Click: A villain encountered by Inspector Field's party in Saint Giles's (*Reprinted – 'On Duty with Inspector Field'*).

Clickett ('The Orfling'): The Micawber's servant. *A dark-complexioned young woman, with a habit of snorting, who was servant to the family, and informed me, before half an hour had expired, that she was 'a Orfling', and came from St. Luke's workhouse, in the neighbourhood (Copperfield).*

Clickit, Mr. and Mrs.: Subjects of the Bobtail Widgers' praise. *The plausible lady immediately launches out in their praise. She quite loves the Clickits. Were there ever such true-hearted, hospitable, excellent people – such a gentle, interesting little woman as Mrs. Clickit, or such a frank, unaffected creature as Mr. Clickit? (Young Couples – 'Plausible Couple').*

Clip: A hairdresser, one of the admiring audience of the gentleman connected with the press at the Green Dragon, Westminster Bridge (*Mudfog – 'Mr. Robert Bolton'*).

Clissold, Lawrence: Clerk with Dringworth Bros. who stole £500 and laid the blame upon Tregarthen, a crime uncovered by the message from the sea (*Christmas Stories – 'Message from the Sea'*).

Clive: Official at the Circumlocution Office, to whom Wobbler refers Arthur Clennam (*Dorrit*).

Clocker: A grocer referred to in a story told to the narrator in a Kent coastal inn (*Reprinted – 'Out of the Season'*).

Clubber, Sir Thomas, Lady and the Misses: Commissioner of Chatham Dockyard and his family, present at the charity ball at the Bull, Rochester. *A great sensation was created throughout the room by the entrance of a tall gentleman in a blue coat and bright buttons, a large lady in blue satin, and two young ladies, on a similar scale, in fashionably-made dresses of the same hue (Pickwick).*

Cluppins, Mrs. Elizabeth: Mrs. Bardell's neighbour and friend, who testifies on her behalf at the trial. *A little brisk, busy-looking woman (Pickwick).*

Cly, Roger: Formerly servant to Charles Darnay, whom he betrays. Associate of Solomon Pross, and spy, who shams death and is given a mock burial to escape the revolutionary mob. *The virtuous servant, Roger Cly. . . . He had never been suspected of stealing a silver tea-pot; he had been maligned respecting a mustardpot, but it turned out to be only a plated one (Two Cities).*

Coavinses: Skimpole refers to Neckett (q.v.) as Coavinses (*Bleak House*).

Cobb, Tom: General chandler and postoffice keeper at Chigwell and *habitué* of the Maypole. *Beyond all question the dullest dog of the party (Rudge).*

Cobbey: Pupil at Dotheboys Hall. *'Oh!' said Squeers: 'Cobbey's grandmother is dead, and his uncle John has took to drinking, which is all the news his sister sends, except eighteenpence, which will just pay for that broken square of glass' (Nickleby).*

Cobbler, The: Prisoner in the Fleet for twelve years who rents Sam Weller a bed in his room. *He was a sallow man – all cobblers are; and had a strong bristly beard – all cobblers have. His face was a queer, good-tempered, crooked-featured piece of workmanship, ornamented with a couple of eyes that must have worn a very joyous expression at one time, for they sparkled yet. The man was sixty, by years, and Heaven knows how old by imprisonment, so that his having any look approaching to mirth or contentment, was singular enough. He was a little man, and, being half doubled up as he lay in bed, he looked about as long as he ought to have been without his legs. He had a great red pipe in his mouth, and was smoking, and staring at the rush light, in a state of enviable placidity (Pickwick).*

Cobbs: Boots at the Holly-Tree Inn, Yorkshire. Former under-gardener to Walmers. *Where had he been in his time? he repeated, when I asked him the question. Lord, he had been everywhere! And* *what had he been? Bless you, he had been everything you could mention a'most!* (*Christmas Stories* – 'Holly-Tree').

Cobby: Gigantic tramp observed by the Uncommercial Traveller eating meat-pie in a hedgerow with a lady. *It was on an evening in August, that I chanced upon this ravishing spectacle, and I noticed that, whereas the Giant reclined half concealed beneath the overhanging boughs and seemed indifferent to Nature, the white hair of the gracious Lady streamed free in the breath of the evening, and her pink eyes found pleasure in the landscape* (*Uncommercial* – 'Tramps').

Cocker, Indignation: A disgruntled patron of the Temeraire, Namelesston. *A severe diner, lately finished, perusing his bill fiercely through his eye-glass* (*Uncommercial* – 'A Little Dinner in an Hour').

Codger, Miss: An American literary celebrity at Pogram's levee at the National Hotel. *'To be presented to a Pogram,' said Miss Codger, 'by a Hominy, indeed, a thrilling moment is it in its impressiveness on what we call our feelings. But why we call them so, or why impressed they are, or if impressed they are at all, or if at all we are, or if there really is, oh gasping one! a Pogram or a Hominy, or any active principle to which we give those titles, is a topic, Spirit searching, light abandoned, much too vast to enter on, at this unlooked-for crisis'* (*Chuzzlewit*).

Codlin, Thomas: Partner of Short (alias Harris) in the Punch-and-Judy show which Little Nell and her grandfather accompany briefly. *He who took the money – had rather a careful and cautious look, which was perhaps inseparable from his occupation* (*Curiosity Shop*).

Coiler, Mrs.: The Matthew Pockets' neighbour. *A widow lady of that highly sympathetic nature that she agreed with everybody, blessed everybody, and shed smiles and tears on everybody, according to circumstances* (*Expectations*).

Coleshaw, Miss: Passenger in the *Golden Mary. A sedate young woman in black, some five years older (about thirty as I*

should say), who was going out to join a brother (*Christmas Stories* – 'Golden Mary').

Compact Enchantress, The: A French actress sharing a railway compartment with the narrator. *Twenty minutes' pause, by Folkestone clock, for looking at Enchantress while she eats a sandwich* (*Reprinted* – 'A Flight').

Compeyson: Miss Havisham's absconded fiancé. A criminal who drew Magwitch into crime. He informs about the attempt by Pip and Herbert Pocket to get Magwitch out of the country, and takes part in his arrest, but is drowned by Magwitch in the struggle. *'He set up fur a gentleman, this Compeyson, and he'd been to a public boarding-school and had had learning. He was a smooth one to talk, and was a dab at the ways of gentlefolks. He was good-looking, too. . . . He'd no more heart than an iron file, he was as cold as death, and he had the head of the Devil afore mentioned'* (*Expectations*).

Compeyson, Mrs. (Sally): Compeyson's wife. *'Which Compeyson kicked mostly'* (*Expectations*).

Conway, General: A political opponent of Lord George Gordon. (*Rudge*).

Cooper, Augustus: Young man in the oil and colour business who takes dancing lessons at Billsmethi's academy, is pursued by Miss Billsmethi and finally sued by her for breach of promise, having to buy himself off. *With a little money, a little business, and a little mother, who, having managed her husband and his business in his lifetime, took to managing her son and his business after his decease; and so, somehow or other, he had been cooped up in the little back-parlour behind the shop of week-days, and in a little deal box without a lid (called by courtesy a pew) at Bethel Chapel, on Sundays, and had seen no more of the world than if he had been an infant all his days* (*Boz* – 'Dancing Academy').

Copperfield, Mrs. Clara: David's young mother. Widowed before his birth, she marries Murdstone but is separated from David and ill-used by her husband and his sister, and dies of a broken heart. *When my mother is out of breath and rests herself in an elbow-chair, I watch her winding her bright curls round her fingers, and straightening her waist, and nobody knows better than I do that she likes to look so well, and is proud of being so pretty (Copperfield).*

Copperfield, David: The central figure and narrator of the story, the most nearly autobiographical of Dickens's novels. *Whether I shall turn out to be the hero of my own life, or whether that station will be held by anybody else, these pages must show. . . . It was declared by the nurse, and by some sage women in the neighbourhood who had taken a lively interest in me several months before there was any possibility of our becoming personally acquainted, first, that I was destined to be unlucky in life; and secondly, that I was privileged to see ghosts and spirits; both these gifts inevitably attaching, as they believed, to all unlucky infants of either gender, born towards the small hours on a Friday night (Copperfield).*

Copperfield, Mrs. David the First: See Spenlow, Dora *(Copperfield)*.

Copperfield, Mrs. David the Second: See Wickfield, Agnes *(Copperfield)*.

Coppernose: Exhibitor in the display of models and mechanical science at the second meeting of the Mudfog Association. He proposes creating an enclosed area, ten miles by four, for the exclusive use of young noblemen. *This delightful retreat would be fitted up with most commodious and extensive stables, for the convenience of such of the nobility and gentry as had a taste for ostlering, and with houses of entertainment furnished in the most expensive and handsome style. It would be further provided with whole streets of door-knockers and bell-handles of extra size, so constructed that they could be easily wrenched off at night, and regularly screwed on again, by attendants provided for the purpose, every day. There would also be gas lamps of real glass, which could be broken at a comparatively small expense per dozen, and a broad and handsome pavement for gentlemen to drive their cabriolets upon when they were humorously disposed − for the full enjoyment of which feat live pedestrians would be procured from the workhouse at a very small charge per head (Mudfog).*

Cornberry: Former fiancé of Julia Manners. *'Who was to have married you, and didn't, because he died first; and who left you his property unencumbered with the addition of himself,' suggested the mayor (Boz − 'Great Winglebury Duel').*

Corney, Mrs.: Matron of the workhouse where Oliver Twist was born, later married to Bumble and dismissed with him. *'It's no part of my duty to see all the old women in the house die, and I won't − that's more. Mind that, you impudent old harridans' (Twist).*

'Countess, The': See Grimwood, Eliza *(Reprinted − 'Three "Detective" Anecdotes').*

Cower: The Tuggses' solicitor whose clerk brings them the news that they are rich *(Boz − 'Tuggses at Ramsgate').*

Crackit, Toby ('Flash Toby'): Housebreaker, partner of Bill Sikes, who is hunted down to Crackit's house on Jacob's Island, Bermondsey, after murdering Nancy. *He was dressed in a smartly-cut snuff-coloured coat, with large brass buttons; an orange neckerchief; a coarse, staring shawl-pattern waistcoat; and drab breeches. Mr. Crackit (for he it was) had no very great quantity of hair, either upon his head or face; but what he had, was of a reddish dye, and tortured into long corkscrew curls, through which he occasionally thrust some very dirty fingers, ornamented with large common rings (Twist).*

Craddock, Mrs.: Pickwick's landlady at Royal Crescent, Bath *(Pickwick).*

Craggs, Thomas: Partner in Snitchey and Craggs, Dr. Jeddler's lawyers. *A cold, hard, dry man, dressed in grey and white, like a flint; with small twinkles in his eyes, as if something struck sparks out of them (Christmas Books − 'Battle of Life').*

Craggs, Mrs. Thomas: Craggs's wife and friend of Mrs. Snitchey. *Snitchey* and Craggs had each, in private life as in professional existence, a partner of his own. Snitchey and Craggs were the best friends in the world, and had real confidence in one another; but, Mrs. Snitchey, by a dispensation not uncommon in the affairs of life, was on principle suspicious of Mr. Craggs; and Mrs. Craggs was on principle suspicious of Mr. Snitchey (*Christmas Books* – 'Battle of Life').

Cratchit, Bob: Scrooge's clerk, father of Tiny Tim, Martha, Belinda and Peter. *His clerk, who in a dismal little cell beyond, a sort of tank, was copying letters. Scrooge had a very small fire, but the clerk's fire was so very much smaller that it looked like one coal. But he couldn't replenish it, for Scrooge kept the coal-box in his own room; and so surely as the clerk came in with the shovel, the master predicted that it would be necessary for them to part. Wherefore the clerk put on his white comforter, and tried to warm himself at the candle; in which effort, not being a man of a strong imagination, he failed* (*Christmas Books* – 'Christmas Carol').

Cratchit, Mrs. Bob: Bob's wife, mother of Martha, Belinda, Peter, and Tim (q.v.). *Dressed out but poorly in a twice-turned gown, but brave in ribbons, which are cheap and make a goodly show for sixpence* (*Christmas Books* – 'Christmas Carol').

Cratchit, Tim (Tiny Tim): The Cratchits' youngest son; brother of Martha, Belinda, and Peter. Speaker of the celebrated line, 'God bless us every one!' *Alas for Tiny Tim, he bore a little crutch, and had his limbs supported by an iron frame!* (*Christmas Books* – 'Christmas Carol').

Creakle: Proprietor and headmaster of Salem House school, near Blackheath, attended by David Copperfield and Steerforth. *Mr. Creakle's face was fiery, and his eyes were small, and deep in his head; he had thick veins in his forehead, a little nose, and a large chin. He was bald on the top of his head; and had some thin wet-looking hair that was just turning grey, brushed across each temple, so that the two sides interlaced on his forehead. But the circumstance about him which*

impressed me most, was, that he had no voice, but spoke in a whisper. . . . I should think there never can have been a man who enjoyed his profession more than Mr. Creakle did. He had a delight in cutting at the boys, which was like the satisfaction of a craving appetite. I am confident that he couldn't resist a chubby boy, especially; that there was a fascination in such a subject, which made him restless in his mind, until he had scored and marked him for the day. I was chubby myself, and ought to know* (*Copperfield*).

Creakle, Miss: The Creakles' daughter, widely believed to be in love with Steerforth. *I didn't think Miss Creakle equal to little Em'ly in point of beauty, and I didn't love her (I didn't dare); but I thought her a young lady of extraordinary attractions, and in point of gentility not to be surpassed. When Steerforth, in white trousers, carried her parasol for her, I felt proud to know him* (*Copperfield*).

Creakle, Mrs.: Creakle's wife. She breaks the news to David Copperfield of his mother's death. *Thin and quiet. . . . She was very kind to me* (*Copperfield*).

Crewler, Caroline, Sarah, Louisa, Margaret, and Lucy: Daughters of the Revd. and Mrs. Crewler, and sisters to Sophy and four other girls. *They were a perfect nest of roses; they looked so wholesome and fresh. They were all pretty* (*Copperfield*).

Crewler, The Revd. Horace: A penurious Devonshire curate, father of Sophy and nine other daughters. '*An excellent man, most exemplary in every way*' (*Copperfield*).

Crewler, Mrs. Horace: Crewler's wife, mother of 'ten, down in Devonshire', including Sophy, Caroline, Sarah, Louisa, Margaret, and Lucy. '*She is a very superior woman, but has lost the use of her limbs. Whatever occurs to harass her, usually settles in her legs*' (*Copperfield*).

Crewler, Sophy: The Crewlers' fourth daughter, sister to Caroline, Sarah, Louisa, Margaret, Lucy, and four others. She cares for them all and Traddles finds some difficulty in getting consent to marry her, but succeeds. *'It was rather a painful transaction, Copperfield, in my case. You see, Sophy being of so much use in the family, none of them could endure the thought of her ever being married. Indeed, they had quite settled among themselves that she never was to be married, and they called her the old maid' (Copperfield).*

Crimp: See **Crimple, David** *(Chuzzlewit).*

Crimple, David: A pawnbroker's clerk named Crimp, who changes his name upon becoming secretary of the Anglo-Bengalee Disinterested Loan and Life Assurance Company. *A smiling gentleman, of less pretensions and of business looks, whom he addressed as David. Surely not David of the – how shall it be phrased? – the triumvirate of golden balls? (Chuzzlewit).*

Crinkles: Exhibitor in the display of models and mechanical science at the second meeting of the Mudfog Association. *Exhibited a most beautiful and delicate machine, of little larger size than an ordinary snuff-box, manufactured entirely by himself, and composed exclusively of steel, by the aid of which more pockets could be picked in one hour than by the present slow and tedious process in four-and-twenty (Mudfog).*

Cripples: Proprietor of an academy for evening tuition in the building where Frederick and Fanny Dorrit lodge *(Dorrit).*

Cripples, Master: Cripples's son. *A little white-faced boy, with a slice of bread-and-butter, and a battledore (Dorrit).*

Cripps, Tom: Boy employed by Bob Sawyer to advertise the medical practice of Sawyer's, late Nockemorf's, by delivering the wrong medicines, thereby causing patients to send round to, and thus notice, the surgery. *In a sober grey livery and a gold-laced hat, with a small covered basket under his arm (Pickwick).*

Crisparkle, Mrs.: Crisparkle's mother. *What is prettier than an old lady – except a young lady – when her eyes are bright, when her figure is trim and compact, when her face is cheerful and calm, when her dress is as the dress of a china shepherdess: so dainty in its colours, so individually assorted to herself, so neatly moulded on her? Nothing is prettier, thought the good Minor Canon frequently, when taking his seat at table opposite his long-widowed mother. Her thought at such times may be condensed into the two words that oftenest did duty together in all her conversations: 'My Sept!' (Drood).*

Crisparkle, Canon Septimus: Minor Canon at Cloisterham Cathedral. Mentor of Neville Landless. *Mr. Crisparkle, Minor Canon, fair and rosy, and perpetually pitching himself head-foremost into all the deep running water in the surrounding country; Mr. Crisparkle, Minor Canon, early riser, musical, classical, cheerful, kind, good-natured, social, contented, and boy-like; Mr. Crisparkle, Minor Canon and good man, lately 'Coach' upon the chief Pagan high roads, but since promoted by a patron (grateful for a well-taught son) to his present Christian beat (Drood).*

Crofts: Harvey's barber *(Young Couples – 'Old Couple').*

Crookey: Attendant at Namby's lock-up. *In dress and general appearance looked something between a bankrupt grazier, and a drover in a state of insolvency (Pickwick).*

Cropley, Miss: Friend of Mrs. Nickleby at Exeter, whose brother had a place at court. *'It was the chief part of his duty to wear silk stockings, and a bag wig like a black watch-pocket' (Nickleby).*

Crowl: Fellow lodger of Newman Noggs. *A hard-featured square-faced man, elderly and shabby (Nickleby).*

Crummles, Ninetta ('The Infant Phenomenon'): The Crummleses' daughter, sister to Percy and Master Crummles. *The infant phenomenon, though of short stature, had a comparatively aged countenance, and had moreover been precisely the same age – not perhaps to the full extent of the memory of the* oldest inhabitant, but certainly for five good years. But she had been kept up late every night, and put upon an unlimited allowance of gin-and-water from infancy, to prevent her growing tall, and perhaps this system of training had produced in the infant phenomenon these additional phenomena (Nickleby).

Crummles, Master and Percy: The Crummleses' sons, brothers of Ninetta. A couple of boys, one of them very tall and the other very short, both dressed as sailors – or at least as theatrical sailors, with belts, buckles, pigtails, and pistols complete – fighting what is called in playbills a terrific combat, with two of those short broadswords with basket hilts which are commonly used at our minor theatres (Nickleby).

Crummles, Vincent: A touring actor-manager who employs and befriends Nicholas Nickleby and Smike. He saluted Nicholas, who then observed that the face of Mr. Crummles was quite proportionate in size to his body; that he had a very full under-lip, a hoarse voice, as though he were in the habit of shouting very much, and very short black hair, shaved off nearly to the crown of his head – to admit (as we afterwards learnt) of his more easily wearing character wigs of any shape or pattern. . . . He was very talkative and communicative, stimulated perhaps, not only by his natural disposition, but by the spirits and water he sipped very plentifully, or the snuff he took in large quantities from a piece of whitey-brown paper in his waistcoat pocket (Nickleby).

Crummles, Mrs. Vincent: Crummles's wife. A stout, portly female, apparently between forty and fifty, in a tarnished silk cloak, with her bonnet dangling by the strings in her hand, and her hair (of which she had a great quantity) braided in a large festoon over each temple (Nickleby).

Crumpton, Amelia and Maria: Spinster sisters who conduct Minerva House, a 'finishing establishment for young ladies'. Two unusually tall, particularly thin, and exceedingly skinny personages: very upright, and very yellow. Miss Amelia Crumpton owned to thirty-eight,

and Miss Maria Crumpton admitted she was forty; an admission which was rendered perfectly unnecessary by the self-evident fact of her being at least fifty. They dressed in the most interesting manner – like twins! and looked as happy and comfortable as a couple of marigolds run to seed. They were very precise, had the strictest possible ideas of propriety, wore false hair and always smelt very strongly of lavender (Boz – 'Sentiment').

Cruncher, Jerry, sen.: Father of Young Jerry. Tellson's Bank messenger and resurrectionist. He accompanies Jarvis Lorry and Miss Pross to Paris, where the horrors of the Revolution put an end to his fascination with death. He had eyes . . . of a surface black, with no depth in the colour or form, and much too near together – as if they were afraid of being found out in something, singly, if they kept too far apart. They had a sinister expression, under an old cocked hat like a three-cornered spittoon, and over a great muffler for the chin and throat, which descended nearly to the wearer's knees (Two Cities).

Cruncher, Mrs. Jerry, sen.: Jerry Cruncher's wife, mother of Young Jerry. A devout woman whose predilection for prayer irritates her husband into naming her 'Aggerawayter'. A woman of orderly and industrious appearance rose from her knees in a corner, with sufficient haste and trepidation to show that she was the person referred to (Two Cities).

Cruncher, Young Jerry: The Crunchers' son. A grisly urchin of twelve, who was his express image (Two Cities).

Crupp, Mrs.: David Copperfield's plump landlady at Buckingham Street, Adelphi, when he becomes an articled clerk. Mrs. Crupp was a martyr to a curious disorder called 'the spazzums', which was generally accompanied with inflammation of the nose, and required to be constantly treated with peppermint. . . . She came up to me one evening, when I was very low, to ask . . . if I could oblige her with a little tincture of cardamums mixed with rhubarb, and flavoured with seven drops of the essence of cloves, which was the best remedy for her complaint; – or, if I had not such a thing by me, with a little brandy, which was the next best (*Copperfield*). -

Crushton, The Hon. Mr.: Obsequious companion of Lord Mutanhed at Bath (*Pickwick*).

Curdle, Mr. and Mrs.: Patrons of Miss Snevellici's dramatic 'bespeak' in Portsmouth. *Mrs. Curdle was supposed, by those who were best informed on such points, to possess quite the London taste in matters relating to literature and the drama; and as to Mr. Curdle, he had written a pamphlet of sixty-four pages, post octavo, on the character of the Nurse's deceased husband in Romeo and Juliet, with an inquiry whether he really had been a 'merry man' in his life-time, or whether it was merely his widow's affectionate partiality that induced her so to report him. He had likewise proved, that by altering the received mode of punctuation, any one of Shakespeare's plays could be made quite different, and the sense completely changed; it is needless to say, therefore, that he was a great critic, and a very profound and most original thinker* (*Nickleby*).

Cute, Alderman: A pompous worthy, determined to 'put down' all talk of poverty and sickness. *Coming out of the house at that kind of light-heavy pace — that peculiar compromise between a walk and a jog-trot — with which a gentleman upon the smooth down-hill of life, wearing creaking boots, a watch-chain, and clean linen,* may *come out of his house : not only without any abatement of his dignity, but with an expression of having important and wealthy engagements elsewhere. . . . He was a merry fellow, Alderman Cute. Oh, and a sly fellow too! A knowing fellow. Up to everything. Not to be imposed upon. Deep in the people's hearts! He knew them, Cute did* (*Christmas Books* – 'Chimes').

Cutler, Mr. and Mrs.: Friends of the Kenwigses (*Nickleby*).

Cuttle, Captain Edward: An old seafaring friend of Sol Gills, whose shop he cares for during Sol's disappearance, eventually becoming his partner. Lodger with Mrs. MacStinger, whose matrimonial advances he narrowly evades. *A*

gentleman in a wide suit of blue, with a hook instead of a hand attached to his right wrist; very bushy black eyebrows; and a thick stick in his left hand, covered all over (like his nose) with knobs. He wore a loose black silk handkerchief round his neck, and such a very large coarse shirt collar, that it looked like a small sail. He was evidently the person for whom the spare wine-glass was intended, and evidently knew it; for having taken off his rough outer coat and hung up, on a particular peg behind the door, such a hard glazed hat as a sympathetic person's head might ache at the sight of, and which left a red rim round his own forehead as if he had been wearing a tight basin, he brought a chair to where the clean glass was, and sat himself down behind it. He was usually addressed as Captain, this visitor; and had been a pilot, or a skipper, or a privateer's-man, or all three perhaps; and was a very salt-looking man indeed.* || *'When found, make a note of'* (*Dombey*).

Dabber, Sir Dingleby: Portraitist, imagined by Mrs. Nickleby as the painter of Kate's portrait to be reproduced in annuals on her marriage to Sir Mulberry Hawk. *Perhaps some one annual, of more comprehensive design than its fellows, might even contain a portrait of the mother of Lady Mulberry Hawk, with lines by the father of Sir Dingleby Dabber. More unlikely things had come to pass. Less interesting portraits had appeared. As this thought occurred to the good lady, her countenance unconsciously assumed that compound expression of simpering and sleepiness which, being common to all such portraits, is perhaps one reason why they are always so charming and agreeable* (*Nickleby*).

Dadson, Mr. and Mrs.: Writing-master at the Misses Crumpton's and his wife. *The wife in green silk, with shoes and cap-trimmings to correspond : the writing-master in a white waistcoat, black knee-shorts, and ditto silk stockings, displaying a leg large enough for two writing-masters* (*Boz* – 'Sentiment').

Daisy, Solomon: Parish clerk and bell-ringer of Chigwell, Essex, and *habitué* of the village inn, the Maypole. *The little man . . . had little round black shiny eyes like beads; moreover this little man wore at the knees of his rusty black breeches, and on his rusty black coat, little queer buttons like nothing except his eyes; but so like them, that as they twinkled and glistened in the light of the fire, which shone too in his bright shoe-buckles, he seemed all eyes from head to foot (Rudge).*

'Dame Durden': See Summerson, Esther *(Bleak House).*

Dando: Head boatman at Searle's yard on the Thames. *Watch him, as taking a few minutes' respite from his toils, he negligently seats himself on the edge of a boat, and fans his broad bushy chest with a cap scarcely half so furry. Look at his magnificent, though reddish whiskers, and mark the somewhat native humour with which he 'chaffs' the boys and 'prentices, or cunningly gammons the gen'l'm'n into the gift of a glass of gin, of which we verily believe he swallows in one day as much as any six ordinary men, without ever being one atom the worse for it (Boz – 'The River').*

Danton: Friend of Kitterbell, introduced to Dumps at the christening party. *A young man of about five-and-twenty, with a considerable stock of impudence, and a very small share of ideas: he was a great favourite, especially with young ladies of from sixteen to twenty-six years of age, both inclusive. He could imitate the French-horn to admiration, sang comic songs most inimitably, and had the most insinuating way of saying impertinent nothings to his doting female admirers. He had acquired, somehow or other, the reputation of being a great wit, and accordingly, whenever he opened his mouth, everybody who knew him laughed very heartily (Boz – 'Bloomsbury Christening').*

Darby: Police constable who goes with Bucket and Snagsby to Tom-all-Alone's *(Bleak House).*

Darby, Mr. and Mrs.: Keepers of an unregistered lodging-house in the Liverpool dock area *(Uncommercial – 'Poor Mercantile Jack').*

Darnay, Charles: English identity of the exiled French aristocrat Charles St. Evrémonde. He marries Lucie Manette; later Sydney Carton saves him from the guillotine. *A young man of about five-and-twenty, well-grown and well-looking, with a sunburnt cheek and a dark eye. His condition was that of a young gentleman. He was plainly dressed in black, or very dark grey, and his hair, which was long and dark, was gathered in a ribbon at the back of his neck; more to be out of his way than for ornament. As an emotion of the mind will express itself through any covering of the body, so the paleness which his situation engendered came through the brown upon his cheek, showing the soul to be stronger than the sun (Two Cities).*

Dartle, Rosa: Mrs. Steerforth's companion. Jealously in love with Steerforth, she exacts bitter revenge on Little Em'ly for eloping with him. *She had black hair and eager black eyes, and was thin, and had a scar upon her lip. . . . I concluded in my own mind that she was about thirty years of age, and that she wished to be married. She was a little dilapidated – like a house – with having been so long to let (Copperfield).*

Datchery, Dick: The unidentified investigator who visits Cloisterham after Edwin Drood's disappearance to observe John Jasper. *A white-haired personage, with black eyebrows. Being buttoned up in a tightish blue surtout, with a buff waistcoat and grey trousers, he had something of a military air; but he announced himself at the Crozier (the orthodox hotel, where he put up with a portmanteau) as an idle dog who lived upon his means (Drood).*

David: The Cheeryble brothers' butler. *An ancient butler of apoplectic appearance, and with very short legs (Nickleby).*

David, Old: Assistant sexton at the village where Little Nell dies *(Curiosity Shop).*

Davis, Gill: Narrator of the story. *There I was, a-leaning over the bulwarks of the sloop Christopher Columbus, in the South American waters off the Mosquito shore: a subject of his Gracious Majesty King George of England, and a private in the*

Royal Marines (*Christmas Stories –* 'English Prisoners').

Dawes, Miss: The nurse who goaded Miss Wade into leaving the noble family in which she was governess. *A rosy-faced woman always making an obtrusive pretence of being gay and good-humoured, who had nursed them both, and who had secured their affections before I saw them. I could almost have settled down to my fate but for this woman (Dorrit).*

Dawkins, John or Jack ('The Artful Dodger'): Member of Fagin's gang who enlists Oliver Twist. He is transported for life for picking pockets. *He was a snub-nosed, flat-browed, common-faced boy enough; and as dirty a juvenile as one would wish to see; but he had about him all the airs and manners of a man. He was short of his age : with rather bow-legs, and little, sharp, ugly eyes. His hat was stuck on the top of his head so lightly, that it threatened to fall off every moment – and would have done so, very often, if the wearer had not had a knack of every now and then giving his head a sudden twitch, which brought it back to its old place again. He wore a man's coat, which reached nearly to his heels. He had turned the cuffs back, half-way up his arm, to get his hands out of the sleeves : apparently with the ultimate view of thrusting them into the pockets of his corduroy trousers; for there he kept them. He was, altogether, as roystering and swaggering a young gentleman as ever stood four feet six, or something less, in his bluchers (Twist).*

Daws, Mary: Kitchenmaid at Dombey's (*Dombey*).

Dawson: Surgeon who attends Mrs. Robinson's confinement. *Mr. Dawson, the surgeon, etc., who displays a large lamp with a different colour in every pane of glass, at the corner of the row (Boz –* 'Four Sisters').

Deaf Gentleman, The: A close companion of Master Humphrey, who never discovers his name or his story. *Whatever sorrow my dear friend has known, and whatever grief may linger in some secret corner of his heart, he is now a cheerful, placid, happy creature. Misfortune can*

never have fallen upon such a man but for some good purpose (*Humphrey*).

Dean of Cloisterham: *With a pleasant air of patronage, the Dean as nearly cocks his quaint hat as a Dean in good spirits may, and directs his comely gaiters towards the ruddy dining-room of the snug old red-brick house where he is at present, 'in residence' with Mrs. Dean and Miss Dean (Drood).*

Dedlock, Lady (Honoria): Sir Leicester's wife and natural mother of Esther Summerson by Captain Hawdon. She flies from home when her secret threatens to emerge and dies near Hawdon's grave in a squalid London burial-ground. *He married her for love. A whisper still goes about, that she had not even family; howbeit, Sir Leicester had so much family that perhaps he had enough, and could dispense with any more. But she had beauty, pride, ambition, insolent resolve, and sense enough to portion out a legion of fine ladies. Wealth and station, added to these, soon floated her upward; and for years, now, my Lady Dedlock has been at the centre of the fashionable intelligence, and at the top of the fashionable tree. How Alexander wept when he had no more worlds to conquer, everybody knows – or has some reason to know by this time, the matter having been rather frequently mentioned. My Lady Dedlock, having conquered her world, fell, not into the melting, but rather into the freezing mood. An exhausted composure, a worn-out placidity, an equanimity of fatigue not to be ruffled by interest or satisfaction, are the trophies of her victory. She is perfectly well-bred. If she could be translated to Heaven to-morrow, she might be expected to ascend without any rapture (Bleak House).*

Dedlock, Sir Leicester, Bart.: Owner of Chesney Wold. *Sir Leicester is twenty years, full measure, older than my Lady. He will never see sixty-five again, nor perhaps sixty-six, nor yet sixty-seven. He has a twist of the gout now and then, and walks a little stiffly. He is of a worthy presence, with his light grey hair and whiskers, his fine shirt-frill, his pure white waistcoat, and his blue coat with bright*

buttons always buttoned. He is cere-
monious, stately, most polite on every
occasion to my Lady, and holds her personal attractions in the highest estimation.
His gallantry to my Lady, which has never
changed since he courted her, is the only
little touch of romantic fancy in him (Bleak
House).

Dedlock, Volumnia: Dedlock's cousin
and beneficiary, living at Bath, who
keeps house for him after his wife's death.
A young lady (of sixty), who is doubly
highly related; having the honour to be a
poor relation, by the mother's side, to
another great family. Miss Volumnia,
displaying in early life a pretty talent for
cutting ornaments out of coloured paper,
and also for singing to the guitar in the
Spanish tongue, and propounding French
conundrums in country houses, passed the
twenty years of her existence between
twenty and forty in a sufficiently agreeable
manner. Lapsing then out of date, and
being considered to bore mankind by her
vocal performances in the Spanish language, she retired to Bath. . . . She has an
extensive acquaintance at Bath among
appalling old gentlemen with thin legs and
nankeen trousers, and is of high standing
in that dreary city. But she is a little
dreaded elsewhere, in consequence of an
indiscreet profusion in the article of rouge,
and persistency in an obsolete pearl necklace like a rosary of little bird's-eggs
(Bleak House).

Deedles: Eminent banker (Deedles
Brothers) and high officer of the Gold-
smiths' Company who commits suicide
in his counting-house, to the consternation of Alderman Cute. 'It's almost
enough to make one think, if one didn't
know better,' said Alderman Cute, 'that
at times some motion of a capsizing nature
was going on in things, which affected the
general economy of the social fabric.
Deedles Brothers!' (Christmas Books –
'Chimes').

Defarge, Ernest: Parisian wine-shop
keeper and revolutionary, custodian of
Dr. Manette after his release from the
Bastille. He produces the evidence which
condemns Darnay. A bull-necked, mar-

tial-looking man of thirty. . . . He was a
dark man altogether, with good eyes and a
good bold breadth between them. Good-
humoured looking on the whole, but
implacable-looking, too; evidently a man
of a strong resolution and a set purpose;
a man not desirable to be met, rushing
down a narrow pass with a gulf on either
side, for nothing would turn the man (Two
Cities).

Defarge, Madame Ernest (Thérèse):
Defarge's wife and a leader of women
revolutionaries. Killed in a struggle with
Miss Pross. A stout woman . . . with a
watchful eye that seldom seemed to look at
anything, a large hand heavily ringed, a
steady face, strong features, and great
composure of manner. . . . Madame
Defarge being sensitive to cold, was wrapped
in fur, and had a quantity of bright shawls
twined about her head, though not to the
concealment of her large earrings. Her
knitting was before her, but she had laid it
down to pick her teeth with a toothpick
(Two Cities).

Defresnier et Cie: Swiss wine exporters
employing Obenreizer as their London
agent (Christmas Stories – 'No Through-
fare').

Dellombra, Signor: Mysterious acquaintance of Clara's husband, whose
face haunts her. He was dressed in black,
and had a reserved and secret air, and he
was a dark, remarkable-looking man, with
black hair and a grey moustache ('At
Dusk').

Demented Traveller: One of the narrator's companions on a journey to
France. Demented Traveller, who has
been for two or three minutes watchful,
clutches his great-coats, plunges at the
door, rattles it, cries 'Hi!' eager to
embark on board of impossible packets, far
inland (Reprinted – 'A Flight').

Demple, George: A doctor's son, pupil
at Salem House (Copperfield).

Denham, Edmund: Assumed name of
the Tetterbys' student lodger, Edmund
Longford. He is evilly influenced by
Redlaw, and temporarily loses his grati-

tude for Milly's kindness in his illness (*Christmas Books* – 'Haunted Man').

Dennis, Ned: Hangman and a ringleader of the Gordon rioters, for which he is executed. *A squat, thickset personage, with a low, retreating forehead, a coarse shock head of hair, and eyes so small and near together, that his broken nose alone seemed to prevent their meeting and fusing into one of the usual size. A dingy handkerchief twisted like a cord about his neck, left its great veins exposed to view, and they were swoln and starting, as though with gulping down strong passions, malice, and ill-will. His dress was of threadbare velveteen – a faded, rusty, whitened black, like the ashes of a pipe or a coal fire after a day's extinction; discoloured with the soils of many a stale debauch, and reeking yet with pot-house odours. In lieu of buckles at his knees, he wore unequal loops of packthread; and in his grimy hands he held a knotted stick, the knob of which was carved into a rough likeness of his own vile face (Rudge).*

Deputy: Boy employed at the Travellers' lodging-house, Cloisterham. Paid tormentor of Durdles and ally of Datchery. Also known as 'Winks'. *A hideous small boy in rags flinging stones at him as a well-defined mark in the moonlight.* || '*I'm man-servant up at the Travellers' Twopenny in Gas Works Garding,*' this thing explains. '*All us man-servants at Travellers' Lodgings is named Deputy* (Drood).

Derrick, John: The narrator's servant in the interpolated tale 'To be Taken with a Grain of Salt' (*Christmas Stories* – 'Doctor Marigold').

Despair: One of Miss Flite's birds *(Bleak House).*

Dibabs, Jane: Lady whose example is instanced by Mrs. Nickleby in arguing that Madeline Bray might reasonably marry Gride. '*Jane Dibabs – the Dibabses lived in the beautiful little thatched white house one storey high, covered all over with ivy and creeping plants, with an exquisite little porch with twining honeysuckles and all sorts of things : where the earwigs used to fall into one's tea on a summer evening, and always fell upon their backs and kicked*

dreadfully, and where the frogs used to get into the rushlight shades when one stopped all night, and sit up and look through the little holes like Christians – Jane Dibabs, she married a man who was a great deal older than herself, and would marry him, notwithstanding all that could be said to the contrary, and she was so fond of him that nothing was ever equal to it' (*Nickleby).*

Dibble, Sampson and **Dorothy**: A very old couple of Mormon recruits, the man quite blind, aboard the emigrant ship *Amazon* (*Uncommercial* – 'Bound for the Great Salt Lake').

Dick: Sweetheart of Sally (**Sarah Goldstraw**) (*Christmas Stories* – 'No Thoroughfare').

Dick: Ostler at the Salisbury inn where Tom Pinch and Martin Chuzzlewit jun. meet *(Chuzzlewit).*

Dick: Guard of the coach taking Nicholas Nickleby and Squeers to Yorkshire *(Nickleby).*

Dick: Tim Linkinwater's blind blackbird. *There was not a bird of such methodical and business-like habits in all the world, as the blind blackbird, who dreamed and dozed away his days in a large snug cage, and had lost his voice, from old age, years before Tim first bought him. There was not such an eventful story in the whole range of anecdote, as Tim could tell concerning the acquisition of that very bird; how, compassionating his starved and suffering condition, he had purchased him, with the view of humanely terminating his wretched life; how he determined to wait three days and see whether the bird revived; how, before half the time was out, the bird did revive; and how he went on reviving and picking up his appetite and good looks until he gradually became what –* 'what you see him now, sir!' *– Tim would say, glancing proudly at the cage (Nickleby).*

Dick: Child workhouse inmate with Oliver Twist. *Pale and thin; his cheeks were sunken; and his eyes large and bright. The scanty parish dress, the livery of his misery, hung loosely on his feeble body; and his young limbs had wasted away, like those of an old man (Twist).*

Dick, Mr.: The name by which Richard Babley, Betsey Trotwood's lodger and protégé, insists upon being known. A mild eccentric, having had his mind disturbed by his sister's ill-treatment by her husband, he is a kind friend to David Copperfield and reconciles Dr. Strong and his wife with one another. *Grey-headed and florid : I should have said all about him in saying so, had not his head been curiously bowed – not by age ; it reminded me of one of Mr. Creakle's boys' heads after a beating – and his grey eyes prominent and large, with a strange kind of watery brightness in them that made me, in combination with his vacant manner, his submission to my aunt, and his childish delight when she praised him, suspect him of being a little mad. . . . He was dressed like any other ordinary gentleman, in a loose grey morning coat and waistcoat, and white trousers ; and had his watch in his fob, and his money in his pockets : which he rattled as if he were very proud of it (Copperfield).*

Diego, Don: *Don Diego de – I forget his name – the inventor of the last new Flying Machines* (*Reprinted –* 'A Flight').

Digby: See **Smike** (*Nickleby*).

Dilber, Mrs.: A laundress shown to Scrooge by the Ghost of Christmas Yet to Come (*Christmas Books –* 'Christmas Carol').

Dingo, Professor: Mrs. Bayham Badger's deceased second husband. *The Professor was yet dying by inches in the most dismal manner, and Mrs. Badger was giving us imitations of his way of saying, with great difficulty, 'Where is Laura? Let Laura give me my toast and water !' when the entrance of the gentlemen consigned him to the tomb (Bleak House).*

Dingwall: See **Brook Dingwall** (*Boz –* 'Sentiment').

Diogenes: Florence Dombey's dog, a present from Toots. *Diogenes was as ridiculous a dog as one would meet with on a summer's day ; a blundering, ill-favoured, clumsy, bullet-headed dog, continually acting on a wrong idea that there was an enemy in the neighbourhood, whom it was meritorious to bark at (Dombey).*

'Dismal Jemmy': See **Hutley, Jemmy** (*Pickwick*).

Diver, Colonel: Editor of the New York Rowdy Journal who introduces Martin Chuzzlewit to the Pawkins Boarding-House. *A sallow gentleman, with sunken cheeks, black hair, small twinkling eyes, and a singular expression hovering about that region of his face, which was not a frown, nor a leer, and yet might have been mistaken at the first glance for either. Indeed it would have been difficult, on a much closer acquaintance, to describe it in any more satisfactory terms than as a mixed expression of vulgar cunning and deceit (Chuzzlewit).*

Dobble Family: A clerk, his wife, son, and daughter, hosts at a New Year's Eve party. *The master of the house with the green blinds is in a public office ; we know the fact by the cut of his coat, the tie of his neckcloth, and the self-satisfaction of his gait – the very green blinds themselves have a Somerset House air about them (Boz –* 'New Year').

Dobbs, Julia: See **Manners, Julia** (*Strange Gentleman*).

Dodger, The Hon. Ananias: A millionaire, the story of whose acquisition of wealth at first bores and then relieves the narrator ('At Dusk').

Dodson: Dominant partner of Dodson and Fogg, Mrs. Bardell's attorneys. *A plump, portly, stern-looking man, with a loud voice (Pickwick).*

Do'em: Livery servant and accomplice in crime of Captain the Hon. Fitz-Whisker Fiercy (q.v.). *A most respectable servant to look at, who has grown grey in the service of the captain's family (Mudfog –* 'Pantomime of Life').

Dogginson: Vestryman. *Regarded in our Vestry as 'a regular John Bull' (Reprinted –* 'Our Vestry').

Dolloby: Kent Road old-clothes dealer who buys David Copperfield's waistcoat for ninepence during his walk to Dover. *He looked like a man of a revengeful dis-*

position, who had hung all his enemies, and was enjoying himself (Copperfield).

'Dolls, Mr.': See Cleaver *(Mutual Friend).*

Dombey, Florence (Floy): Dombey's unwanted daughter by his first wife. She becomes close friends with his second, is turned out of his house and taken in by Captain Cuttle. She marries Walter Gay and eventually persuades her broken father to accept the love she has always cherished for him. *If a book were read aloud, and there were anything in the story that pointed at an unkind father, she was in pain for their application of it to him; not for herself. So with any trifle of an interlude that was acted, or picture that was shown, or game that was played, among them. . . . How few who saw sweet Florence, in her spring of womanhood, the modest little queen of those small revels, imagined what a load of sacred care lay heavy in her breast! (Dombey).*

Dombey, Little Paul: The awaited son upon whom Dombey's hopes for the posterity of his firm and fortune are centred. Left motherless at birth, cared for by Polly Toodle and his sister Florence and doted upon by all who encounter him, the sickly child dies aged six. *He was a pretty little fellow; though there was something wan and wistful in his small face, that gave occasion to many significant shakes of Mrs. Wickam's head, and many long-drawn inspirations of Mrs. Wickham's breath. His temper gave abundant promise of being imperious in after-life; and he had as hopeful an apprehension of his own importance, and the rightful subservience of all other things and persons to it, as heart could desire. He was childish and sportive enough at times, and not of a sullen disposition; but he had a strange, old-fashioned, thoughtful way, at other times, of sitting brooding in his miniature arm-chair, when he looked (and talked) like one of those terrible beings in the fairy tales, who, at a hundred and fifty or two hundred years of age, fantastically represent the children for whom they have been substituted (Dombey).*

Dombey, Paul: Father of Florence and

Little Paul by his first wife, Fanny. Later married to Edith Granger. A wealthy London merchant, head of the firm of Dombey and Son. *Dombey was about eight-and-forty years of age . . . rather bald, rather red, and though a handsome well-made man, too stern and pompous in appearance to be prepossessing. . . . On the brow of Dombey, Time and his brother Care had set some marks, as on a tree that was to come down in good time – remorseless twins they are for striding through their human forests, notching as they go (Dombey).*

Dombey, Mrs. Paul the First (Fanny): Dombey's first wife, mother of Florence and of Paul, at whose birth she dies. *Mr. Dombey would have reasoned: That a matrimonial alliance with himself must, in the nature of things, be gratifying and honourable to any woman of common sense. That the hope of giving birth to a new partner in such a house, could not fail to awaken a glorious and stirring ambition in the breast of the least ambitious of her sex. That Mrs. Dombey had entered on that social contract of matrimony: almost necessarily part of a genteel and wealthy station, even without reference to the perpetuation of family firms: with her eyes fully open to these advantages. That Mrs. Dombey had had daily practical knowledge of his position in society. That Mrs. Dombey had always sat at the head of his table, and done the honours of his house in a remarkably ladylike and becoming manner. That Mrs. Dombey must have been happy. That she couldn't help it (Dombey).*

Dombey, Mrs. Paul the Second (Edith): Dombey's second wife, widow of Colonel Granger and daughter of the Hon. Mrs. Skewton. She elopes briefly with James Carker and after his death makes her home with her Cousin Feenix. *Very handsome, very haughty, very wilful, who tossed her head and drooped her eyelids, as though, if there were anything in all the world worth looking into, save a mirror, it certainly was not the earth or sky (Dombey).*

Donny, the Misses: Twin sisters, proprietors of Greenleaf, the boarding school near Reading attended by Esther Summerson *(Bleak House)*.

Dor, Madame: Obenreizer's housekeeper and ally of Marguerite. *She was a true Swiss impersonation . . . from the breadth of her cushion-like back, and the ponderosity of her respectable legs (if the word be admissible), to the black velvet band tied tightly round her throat for the repression of a rising tendency to goître; or, higher still, to her great copper-coloured gold ear-rings; or, higher still, to her head-dress of black gauze stretched on wire (Christmas Stories –* 'No Thoroughfare').

Dorker: Pupil who died at Dotheboys Hall. *'I remember very well, sir,' rejoined Squeers. 'Ah! Mrs. Squeers, sir, was as partial to that lad as if he had been her own; the attention, sir, that was bestowed upon that boy in his illness! Dry toast and warm tea offered him every night and morning when he couldn't swallow anything – a candle in his bed-room on the very night he died – the best dictionary sent up for him to lay his head upon – I don't regret it though. It is a pleasant thing to reflect that one did one's duty by him* (Nickleby).

Dornton, Sergeant: One of the Detective Force officers of Scotland Yard. *About fifty years of age, with a ruddy face and a high sunburnt forehead, has the air of one who has been a Sergeant in the army – he might have sat to Wilkie for the Soldier in the Reading of the Will. He is famous for steadily pursuing the inductive process, and, from small beginnings, working on from clue to clue until he bags his man* (Reprinted – 'Detective Police').

Dorrit, Amy (Little Dorrit): Daughter of William Dorrit, sister of Edward and Fanny. Born in the Marshalsea, she tends her father there, directs her brother's and sister's destinies, and succours Clennam, when he is a Marshalsea prisoner, eventually marrying him. *A pale, transparent face, quick in expression, though not beautiful in feature, its soft hazel eyes excepted. A delicately bent head, a tiny form, a quick little pair of busy hands, and a shabby dress.* || *She took the place of eldest of the three, in all things but precedence; was the head of the fallen family; and bore, in her own heart, its anxieties and shames. At thirteen, she could read and keep accounts – that is, could put down in words and figures how much the bare necessaries that they wanted would cost, and how much less they had to buy them with. She had been, by snatches of a few weeks at a time, to an evening school outside, and got her sister and brother sent to day schools. . . . She knew well – no one better – that a man so broken as to be the Father of the Marshalsea, could be no father to his own children (Dorrit).*

Dorrit, Edward ('Tip'): William Dorrit's son, brother to Amy and Fanny, an unstable character who ruins his health with drink. *Tip tired of everything. . . . His small second mother, aided by her trusty friend, got him into a warehouse, into a market garden, into the hop trade, into the law again, into an auctioneer's, into a brewery, into a stockbroker's, into the law again, into a coach office, into a waggon office, into the law again, into a general dealer's, into a distillery, into the law again, into a wool house, into a dry goods house, into the Billingsgate trade, into the foreign fruit trade, and into the docks. But whatever Tip went into, he came out of tired, announcing that he had cut it (Dorrit).*

Dorrit, Fanny: Sister to Amy and Edward. A ballet dancer who marries Edmund Merdle, proves heartless and neglects her children, who are cared for by Amy. *A pretty girl of a far better figure and much more developed than Little Dorrit, though looking much younger in the face when the two were observed together (Dorrit).*

Dorrit, Frederick: William's brother, uncle of Fanny, Edward and Amy. Ruined along with William, he is kept from the knowledge of a legacy under Gilbert Clennam's will and lives an outcast from the family, save Little Dorrit. *Naturally a retired and simple man, he had shown no particular sense of being ruined, at the time when that calamity fell upon him, further than that he left off washing himself when the shock was announced,* and never took to that luxury any more. He had been a very indifferent musical amateur in his better days; and when he fell with his brother, resorted for support to playing a clarionet as dirty as himself in a small Theatre Orchestra. It was the theatre in which his niece became a dancer; he had been a fixture there a long time when she took her poor station in it; and he accepted the task of serving as her escort and guardian, just as he would have accepted an illness, a legacy, a feast, starvation – anything but soap (Dorrit).

Dorrit, William ('Father of the Marshalsea'): Father of Amy, Edward and Fanny. A debtor in the Marshalsea Prison for twenty-five years, he is found to be heir to a fortune, but loses it and ruins his family afresh through speculating with Merdle. A very amiable and very helpless middle-aged gentleman, who was going out again directly. Necessarily, he was going out again directly, because the Marshalsea lock never turned upon a debtor who was not. He brought in a portmanteau with him, which he doubted its being worth while to unpack; he was so perfectly clear – like all the rest of them, the turnkey on the lock said – that he was going out again directly. He was a shy, retiring man; well-looking, though in an effeminate style; with a mild voice, curling hair, and irresolute hands – rings upon the fingers in those days – which nervously wandered to his trembling lip a hundred times, in the first half-hour of his acquaintance with the jail (Dorrit).

Doubledick, Richard: Hero of the story with which the narrator entertains the Six Poor Travellers, a tale of Doubledick's adventurous rise from dissolute private to reformed captain. He marries Mary Marshall. His object was to get shot; but he thought he might as well ride to death as be at the trouble of walking. . . . He was passed as Richard Doubledick; age, twenty-two; height, five foot ten; native place, Exmouth, which he had never been near in his life. There was no cavalry in Chatham when he limped over the bridge here with half a shoe to his dusty feet, so he enlisted into a regiment of the line, and

was glad to get drunk and forget all about it (Christmas Stories – 'Seven Poor Travellers').

Dounce, John: An 'old boy' who becomes infatuated with a barmaid in an oyster saloon, is first encouraged, then spurned by her, and in desperation offers marriage to several ladies. He eventually marries his own cook, who henpecks him. A retired glove and braces maker, a widower, resident with three daughters – all grown up and all unmarried – in Cursitor Street, Chancery Lane. He was a short, round, large-faced, tubbish sort of man, with a broad-brimmed hat, and a square coat; and had that grave, but confident, kind of roll, peculiar to old boys in general. Regular as clockwork – breakfast at nine – dress and tittivate a little – down to the Sir Somebody's Head – a glass of ale and the paper – come back again, and take daughters out for a walk – dinner at three – glass of grog and pipe – nap – tea – little walk – Sir Somebody's Head again – capital house – delightful evenings (Boz – 'Misplaced Attachment').

Dowdles, the two Misses: Proprietresses (or fellow pupils) of Kate Nickleby's school in Devonshire. 'Twenty-five young ladies, fifty guineas a-year without the et-ceteras, both the Miss Dowdles, the most accomplished, elegant, fascinating creatures' (Nickleby).

Dowler, Captain: A bombastic ex-army officer who becomes involved with Pickwick and his friends at Bath and quarrels violently with Winkle over Mrs. Dowler. A stern-eyed man of about five-and-forty, who had a bald and glossy forehead, with a good deal of black hair at the sides and back of his head, and large black whiskers. . . . He looked up from his breakfast as Mr. Pickwick entered, with a fierce and peremptory air, which was very dignified; and having scrutinised that gentleman and his companions to his entire satisfaction, hummed a tune, in a manner which seemed to say that he rather suspected somebody wanted to take advantage of him, but it wouldn't do (Pickwick).

Dowler, Mrs.: Dowler's wife, involved with Winkle in the misunderstanding over the sedan chair at Bath. *A rather pretty face in a bright blue bonnet (Pickwick).*

Doyce, Daniel: A neglected inventor whose partner Arthur Clennam becomes. Clennam speculates the firm's money with Merdle and loses everything, but Doyce sells his invention abroad and returns to reclaim Clennam. *He was not much to look at, either in point of size or in point of dress; being merely a short, square, practical looking man, whose hair had turned grey, and in whose face and forehead there were deep lines of cogitation, which looked as though they were carved in hard wood. He was dressed in decent black, a little rusty, and had the appearance of a sagacious master in some handicraft. He had a spectacle-case in his hand, which he turned over and over while he was thus in question, with a certain free use of the thumb that is never seen but in a hand accustomed to tools (Dorrit).*

Doylance, Old: Former schoolmaster of John, the narrator (*Christmas Stories – 'Haunted House'*).

Doze, Professor: A vice-president of the zoology and botany session at the first meeting of the Mudfog Association (*Mudfog*).

Drawley: A vice-president of the zoology and botany session at the second meeting of the Mudfog Association (*Mudfog*).

Dringworth Bros.: Of America Square, London. Employers of Clissold and Tregarthen (*Christmas Stories – 'Message from the Sea'*).

Drooce, Sergeant: Sergeant of Royal Marines in the sloop *Christopher Columbus. The most tyrannical non-commissioned officer in His Majesty's service* (*Christmas Stories – 'English Prisoners'*).

Drood, Edwin: John Jasper's nephew, betrothed to Rosa Bud under his father's will, whose disappearance is the Mystery of the novel. *'I am afraid I am but a shallow, surface kind of fellow, Jack, and that my headpiece is none of the best. But I needn't say I am young; and perhaps I shall not grow worse as I grow older. At all events, I hope I have something impressible*

within me, which feels – deeply feels – the disinterestedness of your painfully laying yourself bare, as a warning to me' (Drood).

Drowvey, Miss: Partner in Miss Grimmer's school in William Tinkling's romantic tale (*'Holiday Romance'*).

Drummle, Bentley ('The Spider'): Fellow boarder with Pip at Matthew Pocket's. Marries Estella, whom he ill-treats, and is killed by a horse which he has also used cruelly. 'The Spider' is Jaggers's nickname for him. *Bentley Drummle, who was so sulky a fellow that he even took up a book as if its writer had done him an injury, did not take up an acquaintance in a more agreeable spirit. Heavy in figure, movement, and comprehension – in the sluggish complexion of his face, and in the large awkward tongue that seemed to loll about in his mouth as he himself lolled about in a room – he was idle, proud, niggardly, reserved, and suspicious. He came of rich people down in Somersetshire, who had nursed this combination of qualities until they made the discovery that it was just of age and a blockhead (Expectations).*

Dubbley: Constable's assistant at Ipswich. *A dirty-faced man, something over six feet high, and stout in proportion (Pickwick).*

Duff: Bow Street officer investigating the burglary at Mrs. Maylie's. *A red-headed, bony man, in top boots; with a rather ill-favoured countenance, and a turned-up sinister-looking nose (Twist).*

Dull: A vice-president of the umbugology and ditchwaterisics session at the second meeting of the Mudfog Association (*Mudfog*).

Dumbledon: A favoured pupil at Our School. *An idiotic goggle-eyed boy, with a big head and half-crowns without end, who suddenly appeared as a parlour-boarder, and was rumoured to have come by sea from some mysterious part of the earth where his parents rolled in gold. He was usually called 'Mr.' by the Chief, and was said to feed in the parlour on steaks and gravy; likewise to drink currant wine. And he openly stated that if rolls and coffee* were ever denied him at breakfast, he would write home to that unknown part of the globe from which he had come, and cause himself to be recalled to the regions of gold. He was put into no form or class, but learnt alone, as little as he liked – and he liked very little – and there was a belief among us that this was because he was too wealthy to be 'taken down' (Reprinted – 'Our School').

Dumkins: Renowned batsman of the All-Muggleton Cricket Club. The redoubtable Dumkins (Pickwick).

Dummins: An out-and-out young gentleman, friend of Blake. 'Both Mr. Blake and Mr. Dummins are very nice sort of young men in their way, only they are eccentric persons, and unfortunately rather too wild!' (Young Gentlemen – 'Out-and-out Young Gentleman').

Dummy: A vice-president of the umbugology and ditchwaterisics session at the second meeting of the Mudfog Association (Mudfog).

Dumps, Nicodemus: Charles Kitterbell's uncle and reluctant godfather to the Kitterbells' first baby. He solaces himself by throwing the christening party into dismay with a speech full of gloomy prophecies. Mr. Nicodemus Dumps, or, as his acquaintance called him, 'long Dumps', was a bachelor, six feet high, and fifty years old : cross, cadaverous, odd, and ill-natured. He was never happy but when he was miserable; and always miserable when he had the best reason to be happy. The only real comfort of his existence was to make everybody about him wretched – then he might be truly said to enjoy life. He was afflicted with a situation in the Bank worth five hundred a year, and he rented a 'first-floor furnished', at Pentonville, which he originally took because it commanded a dismal prospect of an adjacent churchyard. He was familiar with the face of every tombstone, and the burial service seemed to excite his strongest sympathy. . . . He adored King Herod for his massacre of the innocents; and if he hated one thing more than another, it was a child. . . . He subscribed to the 'Society for the Suppression of Vice' for the pleasure

of putting a stop to any harmless amusements; and he contributed largely towards the support of two itinerant Methodist parsons, in the amiable hope that if circumstances rendered any people happy in this world, they might perchance be rendered miserable by fears for the next (Boz – 'Bloomsbury Christening').

Dundey, Dr.: Robber of a bank in Ireland, tracked down in America by Sergeant Dornton (Reprinted – 'Detective Police').

Dunkle, Dr. Ginery: Spokesman of the deputation of boarders waiting on the Hon. Elijah Pogram at the National Hotel in America where Martin Chuzzlewit stays before embarking for Eden. A very shrill boy (Chuzzlewit).

Dunstable: Village butcher whose name is invoked by Pumblechook to persuade Pip that he is lucky not to have been born a pig. 'Dunstable the butcher would have come up to you as you lay in your straw, and he would have whipped you under his left arm, and with his right he would have tucked up his frock to get a penknife from out of his waistcoat-pocket, and he would have shed your blood and had your life. No bringing up by hand then. Not a bit of it!' (Expectations).

Durdles: Cloisterham stonemason made drunk by John Jasper, who abstracts his keys to the burial vaults. In a suit of coarse flannel with horn buttons, a yellow neckerchief with draggled ends, an old hat more russet-coloured than black, and laced boots of the hue of his stony calling, Durdles leads a hazy, gipsy sort of life, carrying his dinner about with him in a small bundle, and sitting on all manner of tombstones to dine. This dinner of Durdles's has become quite a Cloisterham institution : not only because of his never appearing in public without it, but because of its having been, on certain renowned occasions, taken into custody along with Durdles (as drunk and incapable), and exhibited before the Bench of Justices at the townhall (Drood).

Dust: One of Miss Flite's birds (Bleak House).

Edkins: Loquacious member of Percy Noakes's committee for organising the steam excursion. *A pale young gentleman, in a green stock and spectacles of the same, a member of the Honourable Society of the Inner Temple* (*Boz* – 'Steam Excursion').

Edmunds: John Edmunds's father in the story of 'The Convict's Return'. '*A morose, savage-hearted, bad man : idle and dissolute in his habits ; cruel and ferocious in his disposition. Beyond the few lazy and reckless vagabonds with whom he sauntered away his time in the fields, or sotted in the alehouse, he had not a single friend or acquaintance ; no one cared to speak to the man whom many feared, and every one detested*' (*Pickwick*).

Edmunds, Mrs.: John Edmunds's mother in the story of 'The Convict's Return', killed by grief for her son and by her husband's ill-usage. '*Brute as he was, and cruelly as he had treated her, she had loved him once ; and the recollection of what he had been to her, awakened feelings of forebearance and meekness under suffering in her bosom, to which all God's creatures, but women, are strangers*' (*Pickwick*).

Edmunds, George: A farm labourer, sweetheart of Lucy Benson. She is temporarily enticed away from him by Squire Norton, but finally returns (*Village Coquettes*).

Edmunds, John: Central figure in the story of 'The Convict's Return', told by the clergyman at Dingley Dell. '*Many a look was turned towards him, and many a doubtful glance he cast on either side to see whether any knew and shunned him. There were strange faces in almost every house ; in some he recognised the burly form of some old schoolfellow – a boy when he last saw him – surrounded by a troop of merry children ; in others he saw, seated in an easy-chair at a cottage door, a feeble and infirm old man, whom he only remembered as a hale and hearty labourer ; but they had all forgotten him, and he passed on unknown*' (*Pickwick*).

Edson, Mr. and 'Mrs.' (Peggy): A young couple who take lodgings with Mrs. Lirriper. Edson abandons Peggy. Mrs. Lirriper prevents her drowning herself, but she dies giving birth to Jeremy Jackman Lirriper (q.v.). Years later Mrs. Lirriper is summoned to Edson's deathbed in France. *I did not quite take to the face of the gentleman though he was good-looking too but the lady was a very pretty young thing and delicate* (*Christmas Stories* – 'Mrs. Lirriper's Lodgings' and 'Mrs. Lirriper's Legacy').

Edward: Charlotte's husband, whose pleasure is in contradicting her. Father of James and Charlotte. *They return home from Mrs. Bluebottle's dinner-party, each in an opposite corner of the coach, and do not exchange a syllable until they have been seated for at least twenty minutes by the fireside at home, when the gentleman, raising his eyes from the stove, all at once breaks silence : 'What a very extraordinary thing it is,' says he, 'that you will contradict me, Charlotte!'* (*Young Couples* – 'Contradictory Couple').

Edward ('Eddard'): Donkey who responds to his owner's mentioning the name of Boffin by taking Wegg straight to Boffin's Bower. *The effect of the name was so very alarming, in respect of causing a temporary disappearance of Edward's head, casting his hind hoofs in the air, greatly accelerating the pace and increasing the jolting, that Mr. Wegg was fain to devote his attention exclusively to holding on, and to relinquish his desire of ascertaining whether this homage to Boffin was to be considered complimentary or the reverse* (*Mutual Friend*).

Edwards, Miss: Pupil-teacher at Miss Monflathers's school. *This young lady, being motherless and poor, was apprenticed at the school – taught for nothing – teaching others what she learnt, for nothing – boarded for nothing – lodged for nothing – and set down and rated as something immeasurably less than nothing, by all the dwellers in the house* (*Curiosity Shop*).

Edwin: Charley's supposed rival for Angela Leath. He proves to be engaged to her cousin Emmeline. *A bright-eyed fellow, muffled in a mantle* (*Christmas Stories* – 'Holly-Tree').

Eight Club: Club founded at Cloisterham by Sapsea. *We were eight in number ; we met at eight o'clock during eight months* *of the year; we played eight games of four-handed cribbage, at eightpence the game; our frugal supper was composed of eight rolls, eight mutton chops, eight pork sausages, eight baked potatoes, eight marrow-bones with eight toasts, and eight bottles of ale. There may, or may not, be a certain harmony of colour in the ruling idea of this (to adopt a phrase of our lively neighbours) reunion (Drood* fragment).

Ellis: Admirer of Rogers's oratory. *A sharp-nosed, light-haired man in a brown surtout reaching nearly to his heels, who took a whiff at his pipe, and an admiring glance at the red-faced man, alternately* (*Boz* – 'Parlour Orator').

Emile: Soldier billeted at the clockmaker's in the French town where Langley lodges. *Perpetually turning to of an evening, with his coat off, winding up the stock* (*Christmas Stories* – 'Somebody's Luggage').

Emilia: Mrs. Orange's baby in Nettie Ashford's romantic tale. *Mrs. Orange's baby was a very fine one, and real wax all over* ('Holiday Romance').

Emily: See **Bella and Emily** (*Boz* – 'Prisoners' Van').

Em'ly, Little: Daniel Peggotty's orphan niece and adopted daughter. On the eve of her marriage to Ham she elopes with Steerforth, who before long deserts her. She is eventually found by Daniel Peggotty and emigrates to Australia with him, Mrs. Gummidge and Martha Endell. *A most beautiful little girl . . . who wouldn't let me kiss her when I offered to, but ran away and hid herself (Copperfield).*

Emma: Waitress at an anglers' inn, gratefully recalled by Charley, the narrator. *The peerless Emma with the bright eyes and the pretty smile, who waited, bless her! with a natural grace that would have converted Blue-Beard* (*Christmas Stories* – 'Holly-Tree').

Emma: A maidservant at Dingley Dell. *Mr. Weller, not being particular at being under the mistletoe, kissed Emma and the other female servants, just as he caught them (Pickwick).*

Emmeline: Angela Leath's cousin, engaged to Edwin (*Christmas Stories* – 'Holly-Tree').

Endell, Martha: A former schoolmate of Little Em'ly, turned prostitute. She is saved and emigrates to Australia with the Peggottys. *'It's a poor wurem, Mas'r Davy,' said Ham, 'as is trod underfoot by all the town. Up street and down street. The mowld o' the churchyard don't hold any that the folk shrink away from, more'* (*Copperfield*).

'Englishman, Mr. The': See **Langley** (*Christmas Stories* – 'Somebody's Luggage').

Estella: Daughter of Magwitch and Molly, adopted by Miss Havisham who teaches her to hate and tantalise men. She marries Drummle, who ill-treats her, and separates from him. *'You must know,' said Estella, condescending to me as a brilliant and beautiful woman might, 'that I have no heart, . . . Oh! I have a heart to be stabbed in, or shot in, I have no doubt,' said Estella, 'and, of course, if it ceased to beat I should cease to be. But you know what I mean. I have no softness there, no – sympathy – sentiment – nonsense' (Expectations).*

Etc. Etc.: Applicant for a place in Master Humphreys' circle of friends. *'I am considered a devilish gentlemanly fellow, and I act up to the character. If you want a reference, ask any of the men at our club. Ask any fellow who goes there to write his letters, what sort of conversation mine is. Ask him if he thinks I have the sort of voice that will suit your deaf friend and make him hear, if he can hear anything at all. Ask the servants what they think of me. There's not a rascal among 'em, sir, but will tremble to hear my name' (Humphrey).*

Eugène: Soldier billeted at the tinman's in the French town where Langley lodges. *Cultivating, pipe in mouth, a garden four feet square, for the Tinman, in the little court behind the shop, and extorting the fruits of the earth from the same, on his knees, with the sweat of his brow* (*Christmas Stories* – 'Somebody's Luggage').

Evans: Plays the rôle of Roderigo in the Gattletons' private production of *Othello.*

Pronounced by all his lady friends to be 'quite a dear'. He looked so interesting, and had such lovely whiskers : to say nothing of his talent for writing verses in albums and playing the flute! (Boz – 'Mrs. Joseph Porter').

Evans, Mrs., and Tilly: Jemima's mother and sister (Boz – 'Miss Evans and the Eagle').

Evans, Jemima ('J'mima Ivins'): Shoe-binder and straw-bonnet maker, courted by Samuel Wilkins. In a white muslin gown carefully hooked and eyed, a little red shawl, plentifully pinned, a white straw bonnet trimmed with red ribbons, a small necklace, a large pair of bracelets, Denmark satin shoes, and open-worked stockings; white cotton gloves on her fingers, and a cambric pocket-handkerchief, carefully folded up, in her hand – all quite genteel and ladylike (Boz – 'Miss Evans and the Eagle').

Evans, Richard: A pupil at Marton's village school. 'An amazing boy to learn, blessed with a good memory, and a ready understanding, and moreover with a good voice and ear for psalm-singing, in which he is the best among us. Yet, sir, that boy will come to a bad end; he'll never die in his bed; he's always falling asleep in sermon-time' (Curiosity Shop).

Evenson, John: Boarder at Mrs. Tibb's. A stern-looking man, of about fifty, with very little hair on his head. . . . He was very morose and discontented. He was a thorough Radical, and used to attend a great variety of public meetings, for the express purpose of finding fault with every-thing that was proposed (Boz – 'Boarding-House').

'Exchange or Barter': Pupil at Salem House. I heard that one boy, who was a coal-merchant's son, came as a set-off against the coal-bill, and was called, on that account, 'Exchange or Barter' – a name selected from the arithmetic-book as expressing this arrangement (Copperfield).

Ezekiel: 'The boy at Mugby', narrator of the third chapter. I am the boy at what is called The Refreshment Room at Mugby Junction, and what's proudest boast is, that it never yet refreshed a mortal being (Christmas Stories – 'Mugby Junction').

F, Mr.: Abbreviation used by Flora Finching to refer to her late husband. See also **Mr. F's Aunt** (Dorrit).

Face-Maker, Monsieur The: Performer at a Flemish country fair. 'Messieurs et Mesdames, with no other assistance than this mirror and this wig, I shall have the honour of showing you a thousand charac-ters' (Uncommercial – 'In the French-Flemish Country').

Fagin: Receiver of stolen goods and leader of the gang of young thieves in London into which Oliver Twist is introduced. He informs Bill Sikes of Nancy's treachery, bringing about her murder, is in turn informed against by Noah Claypole, and hanged. A very old shrivelled Jew, whose villainous-looking and repulsive face was obscured by a quantity of matted red hair. He was dressed in a greasy flannel gown, with his throat bare. || 'We are very glad to see you, Oliver, very,' said the Jew. 'Dodger, take off the sausages; and draw a tub near the fire for Oliver. Ah, you're a staring at the pocket-handkerchiefs! eh, my dear! There are a good many of 'em, ain't there? We've just looked 'em out, ready for the wash; that's all, Oliver; that's all. Ha! ha! ha!' (Twist).

Fair Freedom: Prince Bull's lovely wife. She had brought him a large fortune, and had borne him an immense number of children, and had set them to spinning, and farming, and engineering, and soldiering, and sailoring, and doctoring, and lawyer-ing, and preaching, and all kinds of trades (Reprinted – 'Prince Bull').

Fairfax: A censorious young gentleman. Of music, pictures, books, and poetry, the censorious young gentleman has an equally fine conception. As to men and women, he can tell all about them at a glance (Young Gentlemen – 'Censorious Young Gentle-man').

Family Pet: Nickname of a criminal to whom Duff attributes the theft at Con-key Chickweed's (q.v.) (Twist).

Fan: Scrooge's sister, mother of Fred (*Christmas Books* – 'Christmas Carol').

Fanchette: Daughter of a Swiss innkeeper who nurses Our Bore (*Reprinted* – 'Our Bore').

Fang: Magistrate who sentences Oliver Twist to three months' hard labour on the unproven charge of picking Brownlow's pocket. *A lean, long-backed, stiff-necked, middle-sized man, with no great quantity of hair, and what he had, growing on the back and sides of his head. His face was stern, and much flushed. If he were really not in the habit of drinking rather more than was exactly good for him, he might have brought an action against his countenance for libel, and have recovered heavy damages (Twist).*

Fanny: A pretty girl, presumably the narrator's sweetheart. *One of the prettiest girls that ever was seen – just like Fanny in the corner there (Christmas Stories –* 'Child's Story').

Fareway: Lady Fareway's second son and Adelina's brother; no Christian name is given. George Silverman is his college tutor for a time and through him meets Lady Fareway, with unhappy consequences ('Silverman').

Fareway, Lady: Adelina's mother, widow of Gaston Fareway, Bart. She presents George Silverman to a living and appoints him Adelina's tutor, but dismisses him upon learning that he has married Adelina to Granville Wharton ('Silverman').

Fareway, Adelina: Pupil of George Silverman and daughter of his benefactor. She reciprocates his love, but allows him to ally her with Granville Wharton, whom she marries ('Silverman').

Fat Boy, The: See Joe *(Pickwick).*

'Father of the Marshalsea': See **Dorrit, William** *(Dorrit).*

Fee, Dr. W. R.: Member of the Mudfog Association *(Mudfog).*

Feeder, Mr., B.A.: Dr. Blimber's assistant and subsequent successor. Marries Cornelia Blimber. *A kind of human barrel-organ, with a little list of tunes at which he was continually working, over and over again, without any variation. He might have been fitted up with a change of barrels, perhaps, in early life, if his destiny had been favourable; but it had not been; and he had only one, with which, in a monotonous round, it was his occupation to bewilder the young ideas of Dr. Blimber's young gentlemen (Dombey).*

Feeder, The Revd. Alfred, M.A.: Brother of Feeder, B.A., whose marriage ceremony he conducts *(Dombey).*

Feenix, Lord (Cousin Feenix): Man-about-town cousin to Edith Dombey, whom he shelters after her flight from Dombey. *Cousin Feenix was a man about town, forty years ago; but he is still so juvenile in figure and in manner, and so well got up, that strangers are amazed when they discover latent wrinkles in his lordship's face, and crows' feet in his eyes; and first observe him, not exactly certain when he walks across a room, of going quite straight to where he wants to go (Dombey).*

Fendall, Sergeant: One of the Detective Force officers of Scotland Yard. *A light-haired, well-spoken, polite person, is a prodigious hand at pursuing private in-quiries of a delicate nature (Reprinted –* 'Detective Police').

Ferdinand, Miss: Inattentive fellow pupil of Rosa Bud at Miss Twinkleton's. *Miss Ferdinand, being apparently incor-rigible, will have the kindness to write out this evening, in the original language, the first four fables of our vivacious neighbour, Monsieur La Fontaine (Drood).*

Fern, Lilian: Will Fern's orphan niece. *'She's my brother's child: an orphan. Nine year old, though you'd hardly think it; but she's tired and worn out now' (Christmas Books –* 'Chimes').

Fern, Will: Uncle of Lilian, an unemployed countryman befriended by Toby Veck after being taken before the magistrates for sleeping rough in London. He turns out to be an old friend of Mrs. Chickenstalker. *A sun-browned, sinewy, country-looking man, with grizzled hair, and a rough chin (Christmas Books –* 'Chimes').

Féroce, Monsieur: Proprietor of bathing

machines at the narrator's French watering-place. *How he ever came by his name we cannot imagine. He is as gentle and polite a man as M. Loyal Devasseur himself; immensely stout withal; and of a beaming aspect. M. Féroce has saved so many people from drowning, and has been decorated with so many medals in consequence, that his stoutness seems a special dispensation of Providence to enable him to wear them (Reprinted – 'Our French Watering-place').*

Fezziwig: Scrooge's master in his apprentice days. *An old gentleman in a Welsh wig, sitting behind such a high desk, that if he been two inches taller he must have knocked his head against the ceiling (Christmas Books – 'Christmas Carol').*

Fezziwig, Mrs. and the Misses: Fezziwig's wife and daughters. *In came Mrs. Fezziwig, one vast substantial smile. In came the three Miss Fezziwigs, beaming and loveable (Christmas Books – 'Christmas Carol').*

Fibbitson, Mrs.: Fellow resident of Mrs. Mell in a Blackheath almshouse. *Another old woman in a large chair by the fire, who was such a bundle of clothes that I feel grateful to this hour for not having sat upon her (by mistake (Copperfield).*

Field, Inspector: Central figure of 'On Duty with Inspector Field'. He is based on a real-life figure, Inspector Charles F. Field, on whom Dickens also modelled Inspector Wield of 'Detective Police' and 'Three "Detective" Anecdotes' (*Reprinted*).

Fielding, Mrs.: May's mother. *A little querulous chip of an old lady with a peevish face, who, in right of having preserved a waist like a bedpost, was supposed to be a most transcendent figure; and who, in consequence of having once been better off, or of labouring under an impression that she might have been, if something had happened which never did happen, and seemed to have never been particularly likely to come to pass – but it's all the same – was very genteel and patronising indeed (Christmas Books – 'Cricket').*

Fielding, Emma: The bride. *'Looking like the sweetest picter,' in a white chip bonnet and orange flower, and all other elegancies becoming a bride (Young Couples – 'Young Couple').* She appears again in old age in 'Old Couple': *One or two dresses from the bridal wardrobe are yet preserved. They are of a quaint and antique fashion, and seldom seen except in pictures. White has turned yellow, and brighter hues have faded. Do you wonder, child? The wrinkled face was once as smooth as yours, the eyes as bright, the shrivelled skin as fair and delicate.*

Fielding, May: Friend of Dot Peerybingle. Persuaded to marry Tackleton, she jilts him on the wedding morning for her long-lost Edward Plummer. *May was very pretty. You know sometimes, when you are used to a pretty face, how, when it comes into contact and comparison with another pretty face, it seems for the moment to be homely and faded, and hardly to deserve the high opinion you have had of it. Now, this was not at all the case, either with Dot or May; for May's face set off Dot's, and Dot's face set off May's, so naturally and agreeably, that, as John Peerybingle was very near saying when he came into the room, they ought to have been born sisters – which was the only improvement you could have suggested (Christmas Books – 'Cricket').*

Fiery, Captain the Hon. Fitz-Whisker: Confidence trickster who buys goods on credit and disposes of them for cash through his 'servant', Do'em, *Struts and swaggers about with that compound air of conscious superiority and general bloodthirstiness which a military captain should always, and does most times, wear, to the admiration and terror of plebeian men. But the tradesmen's backs are no sooner turned, than the captain, with all the eccentricity of a mighty mind, and assisted by the faithful Do'em, whose devoted fidelity is not the least touching part of his character, disposes of everything to great advantage; for, although the articles fetch small sums, still they are sold considerably above cost price, the cost to the captain having been nothing at all (Mudfog – 'Pantomime of Life').*

Fikey: Secondhand carriage dealer and

forger of South-Western Railway debentures, taken by Inspector Wield (*Reprinted* – 'Detective Police').

Filer: Friend of Alderman Cute, preoccupied with statistics. *A low-spirited gentleman of middle age, of a meagre habit, and a disconsolate face; who kept his hands continually in the pockets of his scanty pepper-and-salt trousers, very large and dog's-eared from that custom; and was not particularly well brushed or washed* (*Christmas Books* – 'Chimes').

Filletoville: The Marquis of Filletoville's heir, from whose abduction the Bagman's Uncle rescues the beautiful lady. *A young gentleman in a powdered wig, and a sky-blue coat trimmed with silver, made very full and broad in the skirts, which were lined with buckram. . . . He wore knee breeches, and a kind of leggings rolled up over his silk stockings, and shoes with buckles; he had ruffles at his wrists, a three-cornered hat on his head, and a long taper sword by his side. The flaps of his waistcoat came half-way down his thighs, and the ends of his cravat reached to his waist* (*Pickwick*).

Finchbury, Lady Jane: Something of an artist. *'There's an uncommon good church in the village,' says cousin Feenix, thoughtfully; 'pure specimen of the Anglo-Norman style, and admirably well sketched too by Lady Jane Finchbury – woman with tight stays'* (*Dombey*).

Finches of the Grove: Club joined by Pip and Herbert Pocket, also frequented by Startop and Drummle. *The object of which institution I have never divined, if it were not that the members should dine expensively once a fortnight, to quarrel among themselves as much as possible after dinner, and to cause six waiters to get drunk on the stairs* (*Expectations*).

Finching, Mrs.: Friend of the plausible couple, the Widgers. *'Oh dear!' cries the plausible lady, 'you can-not think how often Bobtail and I have talked about poor Mrs. Finching – she is such a dear soul, and was so anxious that the baby should be a fine child – and very naturally, because she was very much here at one time, and*

there is, you know, a natural emulation among mothers (*Young Couples* – 'Plausible Couple').

Finching, Mrs. Flora: Christopher Casby's widowed daughter, once loved by Arthur Clennam, for whose sake she befriends Amy Dorrit. *Flora, always tall, had grown to be very broad too, and short of breath; but that was not much. Flora, whom he had left a lily, had become a peony; but that was not much. Flora, who had seemed enchanting in all she said and thought, was diffuse and silly. That was much. Flora, who had been spoiled and artless long ago, was determined to be spoiled and artless now. That was a fatal blow* (*Dorrit*).

Fips: Solicitor of Austin Friars, City of London, retained by old Martin Chuzzlewit to employ Tom Pinch as his librarian. *Small and spare, and looked peaceable, and wore black shorts and powder* (*Chuzzlewit*).

Fish: Sir Joseph Bowley's confidential secretary. *A not very stately gentleman in black* (*Christmas Books* – 'Chimes').

Fisher, Fanny: Mrs. Venning's daughter, living with her husband on Silver-Store Island. *Quite a child she looked, with a little copy of herself holding to her dress* (*Christmas Stories* – 'English Prisoners').

Fithers: See Slummery and Fithers (*Young Couples* – 'Plausible Couple').

Fitz Binkle, Lord and Lady: Chairman at a dinner of the Indigent Orphans' Friends' Benevolent Institution, and his wife. *'Lord Fitz Binkle, the chairman of the day, in addition to an annual donation of fifteen pound – thirty guineas* [*prolonged knocking: several gentlemen knock the stems off their wine-glasses, in the vehemence of their approbation*]. *Lady Fitz Binkle, in addition to an annual donation of ten pound – twenty pound'* [*protracted knocking and shouts of 'Bravo!'*] (*Boz* – 'Public Dinners').

Fitz-Marshall, Captain Charles: An alias used by Jingle (q.v.) at Eatanswill and Ipswich (*Pickwick*).

Fitz-Osborne, The Hon. Augustus

Fitz-Edward Fitz-John: Suggested by Flamwell to be the true identity of Horatio Sparkins (*Boz* – 'Horatio Sparkins').

Fitz-Sordust, Colonel: The garrison commander (*Young Gentlemen* – 'Military Young Gentleman').

Five Sisters of York, The: Subjects of a tale told by a passenger of a broken-down coach in which Squeers and Nicholas Nickleby are travelling to Yorkshire *(Nickleby)*.

Fixem: A broker, master of Bung. He uses the alias of Smith. *'Fixem (as we always did in that profession), without waiting to be announced, walks in'* (*Boz* – 'Broker's Man').

Fizkin, Horatio: Defeated Parliamentary candidate at Eatanswill. *The speeches of the two candidates, though differing in every other respect, afforded a beautiful tribute to the merit and high worth of the electors of Eatanswill. . . . Fizkin expressed his readiness to do anything he was wanted (Pickwick).*

Fizzgig, Don Bolaro: Spanish grandee, father of Jingle's conquest, Donna Christina (q.v.), who consents to the match too late, causing her death. *'And her father?' inquired the poetic Snodgrass. 'Remorse and misery,' replied the stranger. 'Sudden disappearance – talk of the whole city – search made everywhere – without success – public fountain in the great square suddenly ceased playing – weeks elapsed – still a stoppage – workmen employed to clean it – water drawn off – father-in-law discovered sticking head first in the main pipe, with a full confession in his right boot – took him out, and the fountain played away again, as well as ever' (Pickwick).*

Flabella, Lady: Heroine of a romantic novel read by Kate Nickleby to Mrs. Wititterly. *'The Lady Flabella, with an agitation she could not repress, hastily tore off the envelope and broke the scented seal. It was from Befillaire – the young, the slim, the low-voiced – her own Befillaire' (Nickleby).*

Fladdock, General. American Militia officer introduced to Martin Chuzzlewit at the Norrises' in New York. *The general, attired in full uniform for a ball, came darting in with such precipitancy, that, hitching his boot in the carpet, and getting his sword between his legs, he came down headlong, and presented a curious little bald place on the crown of his head to the eyes of the astonished company. Nor was this the worst of it ; for being rather corpulent and very tight, the general, being down, could not get up again, but lay there writhing and doing such things with his boots, as there is no other instance of in military history (Chuzzlewit).*

Flam, The Hon. Sparkins: Wastrel man-about-town, friend of Squire Norton. He plans to abduct Rose, but is thwarted by Martin Stokes *(Village Coquettes).*

Flamwell: Toadying friend to the Maldertons. *One of those gentlemen of remarkably extensive information whom one occasionally meets in society, who pretend to know everybody, but in reality know nobody. At Malderton's, where any stories about great people were received with a greedy ear, he was an especial favourite ; and, knowing the kind of people he had to deal with, he carried his passion of claiming acquaintance with everybody, to the most immoderate length. He had rather a singular way of telling his greatest lies in a parenthesis, and with an air of self-denial, as if he feared being thought egotistical (Boz – 'Horatio Sparkins').*

Flanders, Sally: Formerly the Uncommercial Traveller's nurse. He attends the funeral of her late husband, a small master builder. *The moment I saw her I knew that she was not in her own real natural state. She formed a sort of Coat of Arms, grouped with a smelling-bottle, a handkerchief, an orange, a bottle of vinegar, Flanders's sister, her own sister, Flanders's brother's wife, and two neighbouring gossips – all in mourning, and all ready to hold her whenever she fainted (Uncommercial – 'Medicine Men of Civilisation').*

'Flash Toby': See **Crackit, Toby** *(Twist).*

Flasher, Wilkins: Stockbroker who assists Tony Weller with his late wife's estate. *Wilkins Flasher, Esquire, was balancing himself on two legs of an office stool, spearing a wafer-box with a pen-knife, which he dropped every now and then with great dexterity into the very centre of a small red wafer that was stuck outside (Pickwick).*

Fledgeby ('Fascination Fledgeby'): Owner of the moneylending business of Pubsey and Co., run for him by Riah as a front for financial sharp practices. He has a hold upon Lammle, Wrayburn, Twemlow, and others, but is eventually thwarted by Lightwood. *Young Fledgeby had a peachy cheek, or a cheek compounded of the peach and the red red red wall on which it grows, and was an awkward, sandy-haired, small-eyed youth, exceeding slim (his enemies would have said lanky), and prone to self-examination in the articles of whisker and moustache. While feeling for the whisker that he anxiously expected, Fledgeby underwent remarkable fluctuations of spirits, ranging along the whole scale from confidence to despair. There were times when he started, as exclaiming, 'By Jupiter, here it is at last!' There were other times when, being equally depressed, he would be seen to shake his head, and give up hope (Mutual Friend).*

Fleetwood, Mr. and Mrs.: Participants in the steam excursion with their small son Alexander. *The latter was attired for the occasion in a nankeen frock, between the bottom of which and the top of his plaid socks, a considerable portion of two small mottled legs was discernible. He had a light blue cap with a gold band and tassel on his head, and a damp piece of gingerbread in his hand, with which he had slightly embossed his countenance (Boz – 'Steam Excursion').*

Fleming, Agnes: Oliver Twist's mother, Rose Maylie's sister. Having been seduced by Leeford, she dies giving birth to Oliver in a workhouse. *The pale face of a young woman was raised feebly from the pillow; and a faint voice imperfectly articulated the words, 'Let me see the child, and die' (Twist).*

Fleming, Rose: See Maylie. Rose *(Twist).*

Flimkins, Mr. and Mrs.: An acting couple at the Surrey Theatre (*Young Gentlemen* – 'Theatrical Young Gentleman').

Flintwinch, Ephraim: Jeremiah's brother and double, entrusted by Jeremiah with getting the Dorrit legacy documents out of England *(Dorrit).*

Flintwinch, Jeremiah: Mrs. Clennam's confidential clerk and later partner. *A short, bald old man, in a high-shouldered black coat and waistcoat, drab breeches, and long drab gaiters. He might, from his dress, have been either clerk or servant, and in fact had long been both. There was nothing about him in the way of decoration but a watch, which was lowered into the depths of its proper pocket by an old black ribbon, and had a tarnished copper key moored above it, to show where it was sunk. His head was awry, and he had a one-sided, crab-like way with him, as if his foundations had yielded at about the same time as those of the house, and he ought to have been propped up in a similar manner (Dorrit).*

Flintwinch, Mrs. Jeremiah: Jeremiah's wife. See Affery *(Dorrit).*

Flipfield: Friend of the Uncommercial Traveller, notable for his successful birthday parties. *There had been nothing set or formal about them; Flipfield having been accustomed merely to say, two or three days before, 'Don't forget to come and dine, old boy, according to custom'; – I don't know what he said to the ladies he invited, but I may safely assume it* not *to have been 'old girl' (Uncommercial – 'Birthday Celebrations').*

Flipfield, Miss: Sister of Flipfield and Tom Flipfield. *Held her pocket-handkerchief to her bosom in a majestic manner, and spoke to all of us (none of us had ever seen her before), in pious and condoning tones, of all the quarrels that had taken place in the family, from her infancy – which must have been a long time ago – down to that hour (Uncommercial – 'Birthday Celebrations').*

Flipfield, Mrs.: Flipfield's, Tom Flipfield's, and Miss Flipfield's mother. *With a blue-veined miniature of the late Mr. Flipfield round her neck, in an oval, resembling a tart from the pastrycook's* (*Uncommercial* – 'Birthday Celebrations').

Flipfield, Tom ('The Long Lost'): Brother of Miss Flipfield and of Flipfield, whose birthday party he wrecks by returning from 'the banks of the Ganges'. *He was an antipathetical being, with a peculiar power and gift of treading on everybody's tenderest place. They talk in America of a man's 'Platform'. I should describe the Platform of the Long-lost as a Platform composed of other people's corns, on which he had stumped his way, with all his might and main, to his present position* (*Uncommercial* – 'Birthday Celebrations').

Flite, Miss: A veteran suitor in Chancery who haunts the Law Courts. She is a tenant of Krook and makes friends with Esther Summerson and her companions. *A curious little old woman in a squeezed bonnet, and carrying a reticule, came curtseying and smiling up to us, with an air of great ceremony. . . . 'I was a ward myself. I was not mad at that time,' curtseying low, and smiling between every little sentence. 'I had youth and hope. I believe, beauty. It matters very little now. Neither of the three served, or saved me. I have the honour to attend Court regularly. With my documents. I expect a judgment. Shortly. On the Day of Judgment.'* She keeps a score of larks, linnets, and goldfinches in cages in her room. *'I began to keep the little creatures,' she said . . . 'with the intention of restoring them to liberty. When my judgment should be given. Ye-es! They die in prison, though'* (*Bleak House*).

Flopson: One of the Matthew Pockets' nursemaids (*Expectations*).

Flowers: Mrs. Skewton's maid. *At night, she should have been a skeleton, with dart and hour-glass, rather than a woman, this attendant; for her touch was as the touch of Death. The painted object shrivelled underneath her hand; the form collapsed, the hair dropped off, the arched dark eyebrows changed to scanty tufts of grey; the pale lips shrunk, the skin became cadaverous and loose; an old, worn, yellow nodding woman, with red eyes, alone remained in Cleopatra's place, huddled up, like a slovenly bundle, in a greasy flannel gown* (*Dombey*).

Fluggers: Member of Crummles's theatrical company. *'Old Fluggers, who does the heavy business you know'* (*Nickleby*).

Flummery: Speaker at the zoology and botany session of the second meeting of the Mudfog Association. *Exhibited a twig, claiming to be a veritable branch of that noble tree known to naturalists as the* SHAKESPEARE, *which has taken root in every land and climate, and gathered under the shade of its broad green boughs the great family of mankind* (*Mudfog*).

Fogg: Partner in Dodson and Fogg, Mrs. Bardell's attorneys. *An elderly, pimply-faced, vegetable-diet sort of man, in a black coat, dark mixture trousers, and small black gaiters: a kind of being who seemed to be an essential part of the desk at which he was writing, and to have as much thought or sentiment* (*Pickwick*).

Folair: Dancer and actor with Crummles's theatrical company. *A shabby gentleman in an old pair of buff slippers came in at one powerful slide* (*Nickleby*).

Foley: One of Feenix's numerous acquaintances (*Dombey*).

Folly: One of Miss Flite's birds (*Bleak House*).

Foreign Gentleman: Guest at the Podsnaps'. *There was a droll disposition, not only on the part of Mr. Podsnap, but of everybody else, to treat him as if he were a child who was hard of hearing* (*Mutual Friend*).

Formiville: See **Slap** (*Nightingale's Diary*).

Foxey, Dr.: Member of the Mudfog Association. *Nothing unpleasant occurred until noon, with the exception of Doctor Foxey's brown silk umbrella and white hat becoming entangled in the machinery while he was explaining to a knot of ladies the construction of the steam-engine* (*Mudfog*).

Francis, Father: See Voigt, Maître *(No Thoroughfare)*.

François: A waiter attending Carker and Edith Dombey at Dijon. *'François has flown over to the Golden Head for supper. He flies on these occasions like an angel or a bird' (Dombey)*.

Frank, Little: Child cousin and friend of Michael, the Poor Relation. *He is a diffident boy by nature; and in a crowd he is soon run over, as I may say, and forgotten. He and I, however, get on exceedingly well. I have a fancy that the poor child will in time succeed to my peculiar position in the family. We talk but little; still, we understand each other (Christmas Stories – 'Poor Relation')*.

Fred: Scrooge's nephew, son of Fan. *He had so heated himself with rapid walking in the fog and frost, this nephew of Scrooge's, that he was all in a glow: his face was ruddy and handsome; his eyes sparkled, and his breath smoked again (Christmas Books – 'Christmas Carol')*.

Frost, Miss: A girl at Our School. *Why a something in mourning, called 'Miss Frost', should still connect itself with our preparatory school, we are unable to say. We retain no impression of the beauty of Miss Frost – if she were beautiful; or of the mental fascinations of Miss Frost – if she were accomplished; yet her name and her black dress hold an enduring place in our remembrance (Reprinted – 'Our School')*.

G: The gentleman believed by Miss Pupford's pupils to be in love with her. *It is suspected by the pupil-mind that G is a short, chubby old gentleman, with little black sealing-wax boots up to his knees (Christmas Stories – 'Tom Tiddler's Ground')*.

Gabblewig: Lawyer suitor of Rosina Nightingale. Her uncle disapproves, thinking him a weak character, so he proves his strength by saving Mr. Nightingale from Slap's planned extortion, in the course of which he assumes disguises as Charley Bit, Mr. Poulter, Captain Blower, R.N., and a deaf sexton *(Nightingale's Diary)*.

Gabelle, Théophile: Postmaster and official on the St. Evrémonde estate. Denouncer of Charles Darnay. *A small Southern man of retaliative temperament (Two Cities)*.

Gabrielle: See Bebelle *(Christmas Stories – 'Somebody's Luggage')*.

Gallanbile, M.P.: Client of the General Agency Office. *'Fifteen guineas, tea and sugar, and servants allowed to see male cousins, if godly. Note. Cold dinner in the kitchen on the Sabbath, Mr. Gallanbile being devoted to the Observance question. No victuals whatever, cooked on the Lord's Day, with the exception of dinner for Mr. and Mrs. Gallanbile, which, being a work of piety and necessity, is exempted. Mr. Gallanbile dines late on the day of rest, in order to prevent the sinfulness of the cook's dressing herself' (Nickleby)*.

'Game Chicken, The': Pugilist who tutors Toots in the noble art. *Always to be heard of at the bar of the Black Badger, wore a shaggy white great-coat in the warmest weather, and knocked Mr. Toots about the head three times a week, for the small consideration of ten and six per visit (Dombey)*.

Gamfield: Chimney sweep who wishes to take Oliver Twist for his apprentice. *Whose villainous countenance was a regular stamped receipt for cruelty (Twist)*.

Gammon: One of Miss Flite's birds *(Bleak House)*.

Gamp, Mrs. Sarah (Sairey): Midwife and nurse who attends Anthony Chuzzlewit, Lewsome, and Chuffey, and is one of the causes of Jonas Chuzzlewit's exposure. *She was a fat old woman, this Mrs. Gamp, with a husky voice and a moist eye, which she had a remarkable power of turning up, and only showing the white of it. Having very little neck, it cost her some trouble to look over herself, if one may say so, at those to whom she talked. She wore a very rusty black gown, rather the worse for snuff, and a shawl and bonnet to correspond. . . . The face of Mrs. Gamp – the nose in particular – was somewhat red and swollen, and it was difficult to enjoy her society without becoming con-*

scious of a smell of spirits. *Like most persons who have attained to great eminence in their profession, she took to hers very kindly; insomuch, that setting aside her natural predilections as a woman, she went to a lying-in or a laying-out with equal zest and relish (Chuzzlewit).* See also **Harris, Mrs.**

Gander: A boarder at Todgers's. *Gander was of a witty turn (Chuzzlewit).*

Ganz, Dr.: Physician practising at Neuchâtel, whose testimony helps to prove George Vendale's identity (*Christmas Stories* – 'No Thoroughfare').

Gargery, Joe: Pip's blacksmith brother-in-law married to Pip's sister Georgiana Mary. He remains Pip's loyal friend, even after Pip, turning gentleman, comes to despise his unsophisticated ways. After his wife's death Joe marries Biddy and finds happiness. *A fair man, with curls of flaxen hair on each side of his smooth face, and with eyes of such a very undecided blue that they seemed to have somehow got mixed with their own whites. He was a mild, good-natured, sweet-tempered, easy-going, foolish, dear fellow – a sort of Hercules in strength, and also in weakness (Expectations).*

Gargery, Mrs. Joe (Georgiana Mary): Pip's sister, Joe's first wife. A neurotic shrew, she bullies the uncomplaining Joe and Pip. She is paralysed in an assault by Orlick, and dies. *My sister, Mrs. Joe, with black hair and eyes, had such a prevailing redness of skin, that I sometimes used to wonder whether it was possible she washed herself with a nutmeg-grater instead of soap. She was tall and bony, and almost always wore a coarse apron, fastened over her figure behind with two loops, and having a square impregnable bib in front, that was stuck full of pins and needles. She made it a powerful merit in herself, and a strong reproach against Joe, that she wore this apron so much (Expectations).*

Garland: Father of Abel and brother of 'The Bachelor' (q.v.). Friend and defender of Kit Nubbles. *A little fat placid-faced old gentleman (Curiosity Shop).*

Garland, Mrs.: Garland's wife. Mother of Abel. *A little old lady, plump and placid (Curiosity Shop).*

Garland, Abel: The Garlands' son, articled to Witherden and later his partner. *Had a quaint old-fashioned air about him, looked nearly of the same age as his father, and bore a wonderful resemblance to him in face and figure, though wanting something of his full, round cheerfulness, and substituting in its place, a timid reserve. In all other respects, in the neatness of the dress, and even in the club-foot, he and the old gentleman were precisely alike (Curiosity Shop).*

Gashford: Lord George Gordon's secretary. Would-be possessor of Emma Haredale. He eventually poisons himself. *Angularly made, high-shouldered, bony, and ungraceful. His dress, in imitation of his superior, was demure and staid in the extreme; his manner, formal and constrained. This gentleman had an overhanging brow, great hands and feet and ears, and a pair of eyes that seemed to have made an unnatural retreat into his head, and to have dug themselves a cave to hide in. His manner was smooth and humble, but very sly and slinking. He wore the aspect of a man who was always lying in wait for something that wouldn't come to pass; but he looked patient – very patient – and fawned like a spaniel dog (Rudge).*

Gaspard: Parisian labourer, murderer of Marquis St. Evrémonde, whose carriage had killed his child. *One tall joker . . . his head more out of a long squalid bag of a nightcap than in it, scrawled upon a wall with his finger dipped in muddy wine-lees – BLOOD (Two Cities).*

Gattleton: Of Rose Villa, Clapham Rise; head of a family 'infected with the mania for Private Theatricals'. He acts as prompter for their production of *Othello*. *A stock-broker in especially comfortable circumstances (Boz – 'Mrs. Joseph Porter').*

Gattleton, the Misses: The Gattletons' three daughters, sisters to Sempronius. Caroline plays Fenella and Lucina Desdemona in the family's private theatricals (*Boz* – 'Mrs. Joseph Porter').

Gattleton, Mrs.: Gattleton's wife, mother of Sempronius, Caroline, Lucina, and another daughter. *A kind, good-tempered, vulgar soul, exceedingly fond of her husband and children, and entertaining only three dislikes. In the first place, she had a natural antipathy to anybody else's unmarried daughters; in the second, she was in bodily fear of anything in the shape of ridicule; lastly – almost a necessary consequence of this feeling – she regarded, with feelings of the utmost horror, one Mrs. Joseph Porter over the way (Boz – 'Mrs. Joseph Porter').*

Gattleton, Sempronius: The Gattletons' son, brother to Caroline, Lucina, and another sister. He produces, and plays the title role in, their private presentation of *Othello. In consideration of his sustaining the trifling inconvenience of bearing all the expenses of the play, Mr. Sempronius had been, in the most handsome manner, unanimously elected stage-manager (Boz – 'Mrs. Joseph Porter').*

Gay, Walter: Nephew of Solomon Gills. A junior clerk employed by Dombey, who sends him abroad at James Carker's instigation, and he is thought lost in a shipwreck; but he returns and marries Florence Dombey. *A cheerful-looking, merry boy, fresh with running home in the rain; fair-faced, bright-eyed, and curly-haired (Dombey).*

Gazingi, Miss: Member of Crummles's theatrical company. *With an imitation ermine boa tied in a loose knot round her neck (Nickleby).*

General, Mrs.: A middle-aged widow engaged to impart gentility to the Dorrit girls. *In person, Mrs. General, including her skirts which had much to do with it, was of a dignified and imposing appearance; ample, rustling, gravely voluminous; always upright behind the proprieties. She might have been taken – had been taken – to the top of the Alps and the bottom of Herculaneum, without disarranging a fold in her dress, or displacing a pin. If her countenance and hair had rather a floury appearance, as though from living in some transcendently genteel Mill, it was rather because she was a chalky creation altogether, than because she mended her complexion with violet powder, or had turned grey. If her eyes had no expression, it was probably because they had nothing to express. If she had few wrinkles, it was because her mind had never traced its name or any other inscription on her face. A cool, waxy, blown-out woman, who had never lighted well (Dorrit).*

Gentleman in Small-clothes, The: A deranged old gentleman who woos Mrs. Nickleby over the garden wall. *The apparition of an old black velvet cap, which, by slow degrees, as if its wearer were ascending a ladder or pair of steps, rose above the wall dividing their garden from that of the next cottage . . . and was gradually followed by a very large head, and an old face in which were a pair of most extraordinary grey eyes: very wild, very wide open, and rolling in their sockets, with a dull languishing leering look, most ugly to behold (Nickleby).*

George: Member of a typical audience at Astley's. *The eldest son, a boy of fourteen years old, who was evidently trying to look as if he did not belong to the family (Boz – 'Astley's').*

George: Guard of the snowbound coach taking Charley to Liverpool. *The coachman had already replied, 'Yes, he'd take her through it,' – meaning by Her the coach, – 'if so be as George would stand by him.' George was the guard, and he had already sworn that he would stand by him (Christmas Stories – 'Holly-Tree').*

George: Buffle's articled clerk, in love with Robina (*Christmas Stories* – 'Mrs. Lirriper's Legacy').

George: Guard of the Yarmouth mail-coach taking David Copperfield to school. *'Take care of that child, George, or he'll burst!' (Copperfield).*

George: Mrs. Jarley's caravan driver, later her husband (*Curiosity Shop*).

George: A friend of the Kenwigs. *A young man, who had known Mr. Kenwigs when he was a bachelor, and was much esteemed by the ladies, as bearing the reputation of a rake (Nickleby).*

George, Aunt and **Uncle**: Hosts at Christmas dinner. *Aunt George at home dusting decanters and filling castors, and uncle George carrying bottles into the dining-parlour, and calling for corkscrews, and getting into everybody's way (Boz – 'Christmas Dinner').*

George, Mrs.: Friend and neighbour of Mrs. Quilp *(Curiosity Shop)*.

George, Trooper or **Mr.**: See **Rouncewell, George** *(Bleak House)*.

Georgiana : Cousin of Miss Havisham and one of the toadies surrounding her. *An indigestive single woman, who called her rigidity religion, and her liver love (Expectations).*

Ghost of Christmas Past: An apparition which shows Scrooge scenes and characters from his past life. *It was a strange figure – like a child : yet not so like a child as like an old man, viewed through some supernatural medium, which gave him the appearance of having receded from the view, and being diminished to a child's proportions. Its hair, which hung about its neck and down its back, was white as if with age ; and yet the face had not a wrinkle in it, and the tenderest bloom was on the skin. The arms were very long and muscular ; the hands the same, as if its hold were of uncommon strength. Its legs and feet, most delicately formed, were, like those upper members, bare. It wore a tunic of the purest white ; and round its waist was bound a lustrous belt, the sheen of which was beautiful. It held a branch of fresh green holly in its hand ; and, in singular contradiction of that wintry emblem, had its dress trimmed with summer flowers. But the strangest thing about it was, that from the crown of its head there sprung a bright clear jet of light, by which all this was visible ; and which was doubtless the occasion of its using, in its duller moments, a great extinguisher for a cap, which it now held under its arm (Christmas Books – 'Christmas Carol').*

Ghost of Christmas Present: An apparition which shows Scrooge present scenes, including the Cratchits' Christmas Day. *It was clothed in one simple green robe, or mantle, bordered with white fur. This garment hung so loosely on the figure, that its capacious breast was bare, as if disdaining to be warded or concealed by any artifice. Its feet, observable beneath the ample folds of the garment, were also bare ; and on its head it wore no other covering than a holly wreath, set here and there with shining icicles. Its dark brown curls were long and free ; free as its genial face, its sparkling eye, its open hand, its cheery voice, its unconstrained demeanour, and its joyful air. Girded round its middle was an antique scabbard ; but no sword was in it, and the ancient sheath was eaten up with rust (Christmas Books – 'Christmas Carol').*

Ghost of Christmas Yet to Come: An apparition which shows Scrooge prophetic scenes. *It was shrouded in a deep black garment, which concealed its head, its face, its form, and left nothing of it visible save one outstretched hand. But for this it would have been difficult to detach its figure from the night, and separate it from the darkness by which it was surrounded. He felt that it was tall and stately when it came beside him, and that its mysterious presence filled him with a solemn dread. He knew no more, for the Spirit neither spoke nor moved (Christmas Books – 'Christmas Carol').*

Gibbs, Villiam. A young hairdresser, obsessed with the beauty of one of the dummy figures in his shop window, in a tale told by Sam Weller. ' *"I never vill enter into the bonds of vedlock,"* he says, *"until I meet vith a young 'ooman as realises my idea o' that 'ere fairest dummy vith the light hair. Then, and not till then,"* he says, *"I vill approach the altar."* All the young ladies he know'd as had got dark hair told him this wos very sinful, and that he wos wurshippin' a idle ; but them as wos at all near the same shade as the dummy coloured up very much, and wos observed to think him a very nice young man' (Humphrey).*

Giggles, Miss: Inattentive fellow pupil of Rosa Bud at Miss Twinkleton's. *Responsible inquiries having assured us that it was but one of those 'airy nothings'* *pointed at by the Poet (whose name and date of birth Miss Giggles will supply within half an hour), we would now discard the subject (Drood).*

Gilbert, Mark: A London apprentice, initiate to the Prentice Knights, or United Bull-Dogs, and later close associate of Sim Tappertit. '*Mark Gilbert. Age, nineteen. Bound to Thomas Curzon, hosier, Golden Fleece, Aldgate. Loves Curzon's daughter. Cannot say that Curzon's daughter loves him. Should think it probable. Curzon pulled his ears last Tuesday week*' (*Rudge*).

Giles: Mrs. Maylie's butler at Chertsey. He wounds Oliver Twist with a pistol shot during the attempted burglary. *He had taken his station some half-way between the sideboard and the breakfast-table; and, with his body drawn up to its full height, his head thrown back, and inclined the merest trifle on one side, his left leg advanced, and his right hand thrust into his waistcoat, while his left hung down by his side, grasping a waiter, looked like one who laboured under a very agreeable sense of his own merits and importance* (*Twist*).

Gill, Mrs.: Frequent client of Mrs. Gamp in her capacity as midwife. ' "*Often and often have I heerd him say,*" I says to Mrs. Harris, meaning Mr. Gill, "*that he would back his wife agen Moore's almanack, to name the very day and hour, for ninepence farden*" ' (*Chuzzlewit*).

Gills, Solomon (Old Sol): Walter Gay's uncle. Ship's instrument-maker and proprietor of a shop in the City of London, The Wooden Midshipman (q.v.). He goes searching for Walter when he disappears at sea and returns to make Captain Cuttle his partner. *Solomon Gills himself (more generally called Old Sol) was far from having a maritime appearance. To say nothing of his Welsh wig, which was as plain and stubborn a Welsh wig as ever was worn, and in which he looked like anything but a Rover, he was a slow, quiet-spoken, thoughtful old fellow, with eyes as red as if they had been small suns looking at you through a fog; and a newly-awakened manner, such as he might*

have acquired by having stared for three or four days successively through every optical instrument in his shop, and suddenly come back to the world again, to find it green. The only change ever known in his outward man, was from a complete suit of coffee-colour cut very square, and ornamented with glaring buttons, to the same suit of coffee-colour minus the inexpressibles, which were then of a pale nankeen. He wore a very precise shirt-frill, and carried a pair of first-rate spectacles on his forehead, and a tremendous chronometer in his fob, rather than doubt which precious possession, he would have believed in a conspiracy against it on the part of all the clocks and watches in the City, and even of the very sun itself (Dombey).

Gimblet, Brother: An elderly drysalter who acts as chorus to the preaching of Verity Hawkyard ('Silverman').

Glamour, Bob: Regular drinker at the Six Jolly Fellowship Porters (*Mutual Friend*).

Glavormelly: A deceased fellow actor of Mr. Snevellici. '*You never saw my friend Glavormelly, sir!*' said Miss Snevellici's papa. '*Then you have never seen acting yet*' (*Nickleby*).

Glibbery: See **Gliddery, Bob** (*Mutual Friend*).

Gliddery, Bob: Potboy at the Six Jolly Fellowship Porters. (He is referred to as **Glibbery** early in the story, **Gliddery** later) (*Mutual Friend*).

Globson, Bully: Schoolmate of the Uncommercial Traveller. *A big fat boy, with a big fat head and a big fat fist, and at the beginning of that Half had raised such a bump on my forehead that I couldn't get my hat of state on, to go to church* (*Uncommercial* – 'Birthday Celebrations').

Glogwog, Sir Chipkins: One of the aristocratic acquaintances claimed by the egotistical couple (*Young Couples* – 'Egotistical Couple').

Glorious Apollos: A 'select convivial circle' of which Dick Swiveller is Perpetual Grand (*Curiosity Shop*).

Glubb, Old: An old man who wheeled

Paul Dombey along the parade at Brighton. '*He used to draw my couch. He knows all about the deep sea, and the fish that are in it, and the great monsters that come and lie on rocks in the sun, and dive into the water again when they're startled, blowing and splashing so, that they can be heard for miles*' (*Dombey*).

Gobler: Boarder at Mrs. Tibbs's. He marries his fellow boarder and hypochondriac, Mrs. Bloss, who admires his symptoms. *A lazy, selfish hypochondriac; always complaining and never ill. . . . He was tall, thin, and pale; he always fancied he had a severe pain somewhere or other, and his face invariably wore a pinched, screwed-up expression; he looked, indeed, like a man who had got his feet in a tub of exceedingly hot water, against his will* (*Boz* – 'Boarding-House').

Gog and **Magog:** Two giant figures in the Guildhall, City of London, which come to life and converse, overheard by Joe Toddyhigh. *These guardian genii of the City had quitted their pedestals, and reclined in easy attitudes in the great stained glass window. Between them was an ancient cask, which seemed to be full of wine; for the younger Giant, clapping his huge hand upon it, and throwing up his mighty leg, burst into an exulting laugh, which reverberated through the hall like thunder* (*Humphrey*). The figures, commemorating two survivors of a brood of giants, who had been made to serve as porters at the medieval palace formerly on the Guildhall site, were destroyed in the Great Fire and replaced by new ones over 14 ft. high (those of Dickens's time), which were in turn destroyed in an air raid in 1940. New figures replaced them in 1953.

'Golden Dustman, The': See Boffin, Nicodemus (*Mutual Friend*).

'Golden Lucy': See Atherfield, Lucy (*Christmas Stories* – 'Golden Mary').

Goldstraw, Mrs. Sarah: Wilding's new housekeeper, a widow, formerly a nurse at the Foundling Hospital known as Sally. She reveals the mistake in his identity. *A woman, perhaps fifty, but looking younger, with a face remarkable for placid cheerfulness, and a manner no less remarkable for its quiet expression of equability and temper. Nothing in her dress could have been changed to her advantage. Nothing in the noiseless self-possession of her manner could have been changed to her advantage* (*Christmas Stories* – 'No Thoroughfare' and dramatised version of 'No Thoroughfare').

Goodchild, Francis: One of the two apprentices. *Goodchild was laboriously idle and would take upon himself any amount of pains and labour to assure himself that he was idle; in short, had no better idea of idleness than that it was useless industry* (*Two Apprentices*).

Goodwin: Mrs. Pott's maid. *Attached to Mrs. Pott's person was a body-guard of one, a young lady whose ostensible employment was to preside over her toilet, but who rendered herself useful in a variety of ways, and in none more so than in the particular department of constantly aiding and abetting her mistress in every wish and inclination opposed to the desires of the unhappy Pott* (*Pickwick*).

Goody, Mrs.: An old parishioner whose grandchild, the Rev. Mr. Milvey suggests, might suit the Boffins for adoption. '*I don't think,*' said Mrs. Milvey, glancing at the Reverend Frank – '*and I believe my husband will agree with me when he considers it again – that you could possibly keep that orphan clean from snuff. Because his grandmother takes so,* many *ounces, and drops it over him. . . . And she is an inconvenient woman. I hope it's not uncharitable to remember that last Christmas Eve she drank eleven cups of tea, and grumbled all the time*' (*Mutual Friend*).

Gordon, Colonel: Kinsman and political opponent of Lord George Gordon (*Rudge*).

Gordon, Emma: Member of Sleary's Circus, subsequently married to a cheesemonger who admired her from the audience. *The most accomplished tightrope lady* (*Hard Times*).

Gordon, Lord George: President of the Protestant Association and leader of the anti-Popery 'Gordon Riots' of 1780. Arrested for high treason but acquitted. He died during imprisonment for libel in 1793. *About the middle height, of a slender make, and sallow complexion, with an aquiline nose, and long hair of reddish brown, combed perfectly straight and smooth about his ears, and slightly powdered, but without the slightest vestige of a curl. He was attired, under his great-coat, in a full suit of black, quite free from any ornament, and of the most precise and sober cut. The gravity of his dress, together with a certain lankness of cheek and stiffness of deportment, added nearly ten years to his age, but his figure was that of one not yet past thirty. As he stood musing in the red glow of the fire, it was striking to observe his very bright large eye, which betrayed a restlessness of thought and purpose, singularly at variance with the studied composure and sobriety of his mien, and with his quaint and sad apparel. It had nothing harsh or cruel in its expression: neither had his face, which was thin and mild, and wore an air of melancholy; but it was suggestive of an air of indefinable uneasiness, which infected those who looked upon him, and filled them with a kind of pity for the man: though why it did so, they would have had some trouble to explain (Rudge).*

Governor, Jack: Old friend of John, the narrator, and one of the party visiting the haunted house. *I have always regarded Jack as the finest-looking sailor that ever sailed. He is grey now, but as handsome as he was a quarter of a century ago – nay, handsomer. A portly, cheery, well-built figure of a broad-shouldered man, with a frank smile, a brilliant dark eye, and a rich dark eyebrow. I remember those under darker hair, and they look all the better for their silver setting. He has been wherever his Union namesake flies, has Jack (Christmas Stories – 'Haunted House').*

Gowan, Mrs.: Gowan's mother, widow of a 'Commissioner of nothing particular somewhere or other'. *A courtly old lady, formerly a Beauty, and still sufficiently well-favoured to have dispensed with the powder on her nose, and a certain impossible bloom under each eye. She was a little lofty (Dorrit).*

Gowan, Henry: A feckless artist who marries Minnie Meagles. *This gentleman looked barely thirty. He was well dressed, of a sprightly and gay appearance, a well-knit figure, and a rich dark complexion. . . . Mr. Henry Gowan, inheriting from his father, the Commissioner, that very questionable help in life, a small independence, had been difficult to settle; the rather, as public appointments chanced to be scarce, and his genius, during his earlier manhood, was of that exclusively agricultural character which applies itself to the cultivation of wild oats. At last he had decided that he would become a Painter (Dorrit).*

Gradgrind, Adam Smith: A younger son of Gradgrind *(Hard Times).*

Gradgrind, Jane: Gradgrind's younger daughter. *Little Jane, after manufacturing a good deal of moist pipe-clay on her face with slate-pencil and tears, had fallen asleep over vulgar fractions (Hard Times).*

Gradgrind, Louisa: Gradgrind's eldest child. She is married off to Bounderby, but runs home to her father after Harthouse's attempted seduction and, refusing to return to Bounderby, is disowned by him. *There was an air of jaded sullenness . . . particularly in the girl: yet, struggling through the dissatisfaction of her face, there was a light with nothing to rest upon, a fire with nothing to burn, a starved imagination keeping life in itself somehow, which brightened its expression. Not with the brightness natural to cheerful youth, but with uncertain, eager, doubtful flashes, which had something painful in them, analogous to the changes on a blind face groping its way. She was a child now, of fifteen or sixteen; but at no distant day would seem to become a woman all at once. Her father thought so as he looked at her. She was pretty. Would have been self-willed (he thought in his eminently practical way) but for her bringing-up (Hard Times).*

Gradgrind, Malthus: A younger son of Gradgrind *(Hard Times).*

Gradgrind, Thomas: Retired merchant of Coketown, father of Louisa, Tom, Adam Smith, Malthus and Jane. He blighted their youth by his emphasis of the superiority of fact to imagination. *The emphasis was helped by the speaker's square wall of a forehead, which had his eyebrows for its base, while his eyes found commodious cellarage in two dark caves, over-shadowed by the wall. The emphasis was helped by the speaker's mouth, which was wide, thin, and hard set. The emphasis was helped by the speaker's voice, which was inflexible, dry, and dictatorial. The emphasis was helped by the speaker's hair, which bristled on the skirts of his bald head, a plantation of firs to keep the wind from its shining surface, all covered with knobs, like the crust of a plum pie, as if the head had scarcely warehouse-room for the hard facts stored inside. The speaker's obstinate carriage, square coat, square legs, square shoulders – nay, his very neckcloth, trained to take him by the throat with an unaccommodating grasp, like a stubborn fact, as it was, – all helped the emphasis (Hard Times).*

Gradgrind, Mrs. Thomas: Gradgrind's wife. *A little, thin, white, pink-eyed bundle of shawls, of surpassing feebleness, mental and bodily; who was always taking physic without any effect, and who, whenever she showed a symptom of coming to life, was invariably stunned by some weighty piece of fact tumbling on her (Hard Times).*

Gradgrind, Tom ('The Whelp'): Gradgrind's eldest son. Feckless and dishonest as a result of his repressive upbringing, he robs Bounderby's Bank and throws the blame on Blackpool, but is found out and flees the country to escape arrest. *It was very remarkable that a young gentleman who had been brought up under one continuous system of unnatural restraint, should be a hypocrite; but it was certainly the case with Tom. It was very strange that a young gentleman who had never been left to his own guidance for five consecutive minutes, should be incapable at last of governing himself; but so it was with Tom. It was altogether unaccountable that a young gentleman whose imagination had been strangled in his cradle, should be still inconvenienced by its ghost in the form of grovelling sensualities; but such a monster, beyond all doubt, was Tom (Hard Times).*

Graham, Hugh: A sixteenth-century bowyer's apprentice in love with his master's daughter, Mistress Alice, in Magog's tale. *A bold young 'prentice who loved his master's daughter. There were no doubt within the walls a great many 'prentices in this condition, but I speak of only one (Humphrey).*

Graham, Mary: Companion to old Martin Chuzzlewit and eventual wife to young Martin. *She was very young; apparently no more than seventeen; timid and shrinking in her manner, and yet with a greater share of self-possession and control over her emotions than usually belongs to a far more advanced period of female life. . . . She was short in stature; and her figure was slight, as became her years; but all the charms of youth and maidenhood set if off, and clustered on her gentle brow. Her face was very pale, in part no doubt from recent agitation. Her dark brown hair, disordered from the same cause, had fallen negligently from its bonds, and hung upon her neck: for which instance of its waywardness, no male observer would have had the heart to blame it (Chuzzlewit).*

Grainger: Friend of Steerforth. Guest at David Copperfield's first bachelor dinner at Adelphi. *Very gay and lively (Copperfield).*

Gran, Mrs.: Jemmy Lirriper's name for Mrs. Lirriper in the story he makes up (*Christmas Stories* – 'Mrs. Lirriper's Legacy').

Grandfather, Little Nell's: See Trent (*Curiosity Shop*).

Grandmarina, Fairy: Princess Alicia's godmother in Alice Rainbird's romantic tale ('Holiday Romance').

Grandpapa and Grandmamma: Senior guests at Christmas dinner. *Grandpapa produces a small sprig of mistletoe from his pocket, and tempts the boys to*

kiss their little cousins under it – a proceeding which affords both the boys and
the old gentleman unlimited satisfaction,
but which rather outrages grandmamma's
ideas of decorum, until grandpapa says,
that when he was just thirteen years and
three months old, he kissed grandmamma
under a mistletoe too, on which the children clap their hands, and laugh very
heartily, as do aunt George and uncle
George; and grandmamma looks pleased,
and says, with a benevolent smile, that
grandpapa was an impudent young dog, on
which the children laugh very heartily
again, and grandpapa more heartily than
any of them (Boz – 'Christmas Dinner').

Granger, Edith: See Dombey, Mrs.
Paul the Second *(Dombey)*.

Grannett: Workhouse overseer admired
by Bumble and Mrs. Corney for his
treatment of a dying pauper. *'As he
wouldn't go away, and shocked the company very much, our overseer sent him out
a pound of potatoes and half a pint of
oatmeal. "My heart!" says the ungrateful
villain, "what's the use of this to me? You
might as well give me a pair of iron spectacles!" "Very good," says our overseer,
taking 'em away again, "you won't get
anything else here." "Then I'll die in the
streets!" says the vagrant . . . and he did
die in the streets. There's a obstinate pauper
for you'* (Twist).

Graymarsh: Pupil at Dotheboys Hall.
*'Graymarsh's maternal aunt,' said Squeers
. . . 'is very glad to hear he's so well and
happy, and sends her respectful compli-
ments to Mrs. Squeers, and thinks she
must be an angel. She likewise thinks Mr.
Squeers is too good for this world; but
hopes he may long be spared to carry on the
business. Would have sent the two pair of
stockings as desired, but is short of money,
so forwards a tract instead'* (Nickleby).

Grayper, Mr. and Mrs.: Mrs. Copperfield's neighbours at Blunderstone, at
whose house she meets Murdstone
(Copperfield).

**Grazinglands, Mr. and Mrs. (Ara-
bella):** A wealthy Midlands couple in
search of a meal in London. *Over the
whole, a young lady presided, whose
gloomy haughtiness as she surveyed the
street, announced a deep-seated grievance
against society, and an implacable deter-
mination to be avenged. From a beetle-
haunted kitchen below this institution,
fumes arose, suggestive of a class of soup
which Mr. Grazinglands knew, from
painful experience, enfeebles the mind,
distends the stomach, forces itself into the
complexion, and tries to ooze out at the
eyes* (Uncommercial – 'Refreshments for
Travellers').

Green: A law writer said to have known
the deceased Nemo better than anybody.
*Which son of Mrs. Green's appears, on
inquiry, to be at the present time aboard a
vessel bound for China, three months out,
but considered accessible by telegraph, on
application to the Lords of the Admiralty*
(Bleak House).

Green, Miss: Friend of the Kenwigses
(Nickleby).

Green, Police Constable: See Black
and Green *(Reprinted – 'On Duty with
Inspector Field')*.

Green, Lucy: See Specks, Mrs. Joe
(Uncommercial – 'Dullborough Town').

Green, Tom: The name taken by Joe
Willet as a soldier. *He was a gallant,
manly, handsome fellow, but he had lost
his left arm (Rudge)*.

Greenwood (also Joby): One-eyed tramp
said to have encountered the hooded
woman *(Christmas Stories – 'Haunted
House')*.

Greenwood, the Misses: Acquaintances
of Fairfax *(Young Gentlemen – 'Censorious Young Gentleman')*.

Gregory: Foreman packer at Murdstone
and Grinby's warehouse *(Copperfield)*.

Gregsbury, M. P.: A Member of Parliament to whom Nicholas Nickleby applies
for work. *A tough, burly, thick-headed
gentleman, with a loud voice, a pompous
manner, a tolerable command of sentences
with no meaning in them, and, in short,
every requisite for a very good member
indeed (Nickleby)*.

Grewgious, Hiram: Lawyer of Staple
Inn. Guardian of Rosa Bud, with whose

late mother he had been in love. Ardent defender of Neville Landless when he is suspected of Drood's murder. *He was an arid, sandy man, who, if he had been put into a grinding-mill, looked as if he would have ground immediately into high-dried snuff. He had a scanty flat crop of hair, in colour and consistency like some very mangy yellow fur tippet; it was so unlike hair, that it must have been a wig, but for the stupendous improbability of anybody's voluntarily sporting such a head. The little play of feature that his face presented, was cut deep into it, in a few hard curves that made it more like work; and he had certain notches in his forehead, which looked as though Nature had been about to touch them into sensibility or refinement, when she had impatiently thrown away the chisel, and said: 'I really cannot be worried to finish off this man; let him go as he is.' With too great length of throat at his upper end, and too much ankle-bone and heel at his lower; with an awkward and hesitating manner; with a shambling walk; and with what is called a near sight – which perhaps prevented his observing how much white cotton stocking he displayed to the public eye, in contrast with his black suit – Mr. Grewgious still had some strange capacity in him of making on the whole an agreeable impression (Drood).*

Grey, the Misses: Amelia and her sister, friends of Felix Nixon (*Young Gentlemen* – 'Domestic Young Gentleman').

Gride, Arthur: Co-creditor, with Ralph Nickleby, of Walter Bray, whose daughter Madeline he proposes to marry. Bray's death prevents it, Gride's housekeeper, Peg Sliderskew, makes off with the documents which give him power over many people, and he is eventually murdered by burglars. *A little old man of about seventy or seventy-five years of age, of a very lean figure, much bent, and slightly twisted. . . . His nose and chin were sharp and prominent, his jaws had fallen inwards from loss of teeth, his face was shrivelled and yellow, save where the cheeks were streaked with the colour of a dry winter apple; and where his beard had been, there lingered yet a few grey tufts,*

which seemed, like the ragged eyebrows, to denote the badness of the soil from which they sprung. The whole air and attitude of the form, was one of stealthy cat-like obsequiousness; the whole expression of the face was concentrated in a wrinkled leer, compounded of cunning, lecherousness, slyness, and avarice (Nickleby).*

Gridley ('The Man from Shropshire'): A ruined Chancery suitor constantly attempting to address the Lord Chancellor and being imprisoned for contempt. He dies evading arrest. *A tall sallow man with a careworn head, on which but little hair remained, a deeply lined face, and prominent eyes. He had a combative look; and a chafing, irritable manner, which, associated with his figure – still large and powerful, though evidently in its decline – rather alarmed me (Bleak House).*

Griffin, Miss: Principal of the school attended by Master B. *We knew Miss Griffin to be bereft of human sympathies (Christmas Stories* – 'Haunted House').

Grig, Tom: The lamplighter, believed by Stargazer to have been sent by destiny to fulfil a prediction of his. Thinking the old man will make him rich by his discovery of the philosopher's stone, Grig agrees to marry Stargazer's niece, Fanny Brown, but declines when the stone fails to materialise. Led to believe he has only weeks to live, he accepts the servant, Betsy Martin, recanting in the nick of time when he learns that he is actually destined for a ripe old age (*The Lamplighter*). The ending of 'The Lamplighter's Story', the subsequent prose version of this farce, is different, and Tom Grig does not escape entirely unscathed.

Griggins: Life and soul of Mrs. Brown's party. *Presented himself, amidst another shout of laughter and a loud clapping of hands from the younger branches. This welcome he acknowledged by sundry contortions of countenance, imitative of the clown in one of the new pantomimes, which were so extremely successful, that one stout gentleman rolled upon an ottoman in a paroxysm of delight, protesting, with many* *gasps, that if somebody didn't make that fellow Griggins leave off, he would be the death of him, he knew* (*Young Gentlemen* – 'Funny Young Gentleman').

Griggs: See Porkenham, Griggs, and Slummintowken Families *(Pickwick)*.

Grimble, Sir Thomas: Wealthy Yorkshire landowner with whom Mrs. Nickleby supposes Smike might have dined while at Dotheboys Hall. '*A very proud man, Sir Thomas Grimble, with six grown-up and most lovely daughters, and the finest park in the county.*' '*My dear mother!*' *reasoned Nicholas, 'do you suppose that the unfortunate outcast of a Yorkshire school was likely to receive many cards of invitation from the nobility and gentry in the neighbourhood?*' '*Really, my dear, I don't know why it should be so very extraordinary,*' *said Mrs. Nickleby. 'I know that when I was at school, I always went at least twice every half-year to the Hawkinses at Taunton Vale, and they are much richer than the Grimbles, and connected with them in marriage; so you see it's not so very unlikely, after all*' (*Nickleby*).

Grime, Professor: Member of the Mudfog Association. *Professor Grime having lost several teeth, is unable, I observe, to eat his crusts without previously soaking them in his bottled porter (Mudfog).*

Grimmer, Miss: School proprietress, with Miss Drowvey, in William Tinkling's romantic tale ('Holiday Romance').

Grimwig: Brownlow's friend, a lawyer, who tries in vain to persuade Brownlow that Oliver Twist is not to be trusted. *A stout old gentleman, rather lame in one leg, who was dressed in a blue coat, striped waistcoat, nankeen breeches and gaiters, and a broad-brimmed white hat, with the sides turned up with green. A very small-plaited shirt frill stuck out from his waistcoat; and a very long steel watch-chain, with nothing but a key at the end, dangled loosely below it. The ends of his white neckerchief were twisted into a ball about the size of an orange; the variety of shapes into which his countenance was twisted, defy description. He had a manner of*

screwing his head on one side when spoke; and of looking out of the corners of his eyes at the same time: which irresistibly reminded the beholder of a parrot (Twist).

Grimwood, Liza ('The Countess'): Young woman whose murder in her bedroom in the Waterloo Road was investigated by Inspector Wield. '*She was commonly called The Countess, because of her handsome appearance and her proud way of carrying of herself*' (*Reprinted* – 'Three "Detective" Anecdotes').

Grinder: Proprietor of a travelling stilt-act encountered by Little Nell and her grandfather. *Used his natural legs for pedestrian purposes and carried at his back a drum (Curiosity Shop).*

Grip: The ancient raven who constantly accompanies Barnaby Rudge. *After a short survey of the ground, and a few sidelong looks at the ceiling and at everybody present in turn, he fluttered to the floor, and went to Barnaby – not in a hop, or walk, or run, but in a pace like that of a very particular gentleman with exceedingly tight boots on, trying to walk fast over loose pebbles. Then, stepping into his extended hand, and condescending to be held out at arm's-length, he gave vent to a succession of sounds, not unlike the drawing of some eight or ten dozen of long corks, and again asserted his brimstone birth and parentage with great distinction (Rudge).*

Groffin, Thomas: Chemist, who tries in vain to be excused jury service in Bardell and Pickwick. '*I've left nobody but an errand-boy in my shop. He is a very nice boy, my Lord, but he is not acquainted with drugs; and I know that the prevailing impression on his mind is, that Epsom salts means oxalic acid; and syrup of senna, laudanum. That's all, my Lord*' (*Pickwick*).

Grogzwig: See Koëldwethout (*Nickleby*).

Grompus: Partner of an unwilling Georgiana Podsnap in a set of dances at her birthday party. *That complacent monster, believing that he was giving Miss Podsnap a treat, prolonged to the utmost stretch of possibility a peripatetic account* of an archery meeting; while his victim, heading the procession of sixteen as it slowly circled about, like a revolving funeral, never riased her eyes except once to steal a glance at Mrs. Lammle, expressive of intense despair (Mutual Friend).

Groper, Colonel: A boarder at the National Hotel, in America, where Martin Chuzzlewit stays before embarking for Eden (Chuzzlewit).

Groves, James: Rascally landlord of the Valiant Soldier inn. 'Honest Jem Groves, as is a man of unblemished moral character, and has a good dry skittle-ground. If any man has got anything to say again Jem Groves, let him say it to Jem Groves, and Jem Groves can accommodate him with a customer on any terms from four pound a side to forty' (Curiosity Shop).

Grub: President of the umbugology and ditchwaterisics session at the second meeting of the Mudfog Association (Mudfog).

Grub, Gabriel: The sexton stolen by goblins in Wardle's Christmas Eve story at Dingley Dell. 'An ill-conditioned, cross-grained, surly fellow – a morose and lonely man, who consorted with nobody but himself, and an old wicker bottle which fitted into his large deep waistcoat pocket – and who eyed each merry face, as it passed him by, with such a deep scowl of malice and ill-humour, as it was difficult to meet, without feeling something the worse for' (Pickwick).

Grubble, W.: Landlord of the Dedlock Arms, Chesney Wold. A pleasant-looking stoutish, middle-aged man, who never seemed to consider himself cosily dressed for his own fireside without his hat and top-boots, but who never wore a coat except at church (Bleak House).

Grudden, Mrs.: Member of Crummles's theatrical company. Assisted Mrs. Crummles in her domestic affairs, and took money at the doors, and dressed the ladies, and swept the house, and held the prompt book when everybody else was on for the last scene, and acted any kind of part on any emergency without ever learning it, and was put down in the bills under any

name or names whatever, that occurred to Mr. Crummles as looking well in print (Nickleby).

Grueby, John: Lord George Gordon's manservant, who tries to save his wayward master from himself and his provokers. He was a square-built, strong-made, bull-necked fellow, of the true English breed. . . . He was much older than the Maypole man, being to all appearance five-and-forty; but was one of those self-possessed, hard-headed imperturbable fellows, who, if they are ever beaten at fistycuffs, or other kind of warfare, never know it, and go on coolly till they win (Rudge).

'Gruff and Glum': Old Greenwich pensioner enchanted by Bella Wilfer as she arrives to marry John Rokesmith. Two wooden legs had this gruff and glum old pensioner, and, a minute before Bella stepped out of the boat, and drew that confiding little arm of hers through Rokesmith's, he had had no object in life but tobacco, and not enough of that (Mutual Friend).

'Gruff and Grim': Herbert Pocket's nickname for Old Bill Barley (q.v.) (Expectations).

Gruff and Tackleton: See Tackleton (Christmas Books – 'Cricket').

Grummer, Daniel: Constable at Ipswich who arrests Pickwick and Tupman. The elderly gentleman in the top-boots, who was chiefly remarkable for a bottle-nose, a horse voice, a snuff-coloured surtout, and a wandering eye (Pickwick).

Grummidge, Dr.: Speaker at the anatomy and medicine session of the second meeting of the Mudfog Association. Stated to the section a most interesting case of monomania, and described the course of treatment he had pursued with perfect success. The patient was a married lady in the middle rank of life, who, having seen another lady at an evening party in a full suit of pearls, was suddenly seized with a desire to possess a similar equipment, although her husband's finances were by no means equal to the necessary outlay (Mudfog).

Grundy: Fellow law clerk, and drinker, of Lowten (*Pickwick*).

Guard, The: The railway guard who sets Jackson down at Mugby Junction. *Glistening with drops of wet, and looking at the tearful face of his watch by the light of his lantern* (*Christmas Stories* – 'Mugby Junction').

Gubbins: Ex-churchwarden of Our Parish who presents an engraved silver inkstand to the curate. *Acknowledged by the curate in terms which drew tears into the eyes of all present – the very waiters were melted* (*Boz* – 'Curate').

Gulpidge, Mr. and Mrs.: Fellow dinner guests with David Copperfield at the Waterbrooks' (*Copperfield*).

Gummidge, Mrs.: Widow of Daniel Peggotty's partner and now his housekeeper. She emigrates to Australia with him, Martha Endell, and Little Em'ly. *'I an't what I could wish myself to be. . . . I had better go into the house and die. I am a lone lorn creetur', and had much better not make myself contrairy here'* (*Copperfield*).

Gunter: Medical student present at Bob Sawyer's party. *A gentleman in a shirt emblazoned with pink anchors* (*Pickwick*).

Guppy, Mrs.: Guppy's mother. *An old lady in a large cap, with rather a red nose and rather an unsteady eye, but smiling all over* (*Bleak House*).

Guppy, William: Clerk to Kenge and Carboy. He falls in love with Esther Summerson and 'files a declaration' to her, which, rejected at the time, he subsequently regrets ever having made. *A young gentleman who had inked himself by accident. || I scarcely knew him again, he was so uncommonly smart. He had an entirely new suit of glossy clothes on, a shining hat, lilac-kid gloves, a neckerchief of a variety of colours, a large hot-house flower in his button-hole, and a thick gold ring on his little finger. Besides which, he quite scented the dining-room with bear's-grease and other perfumery* (*Bleak House*).

Gusher: A missionary friend of Mrs. Pardiggle. *A flabby gentleman with a moist surface, and eyes so much too small for his moon of a face that they seemed to have been originally made for somebody else* (*Bleak House*).

Guster: The Snagsbys' maidservant. *A lean young woman from a workhouse (by some supposed to have been christened Augusta); who, although she was farmed or contracted for, during her growing time, by an amiable benefactor of the species resident at Tooting, and cannot fail to have been developed under the most favourable circumstances, 'has fits' – which the parish can't account for* (*Bleak House*).

Gwynn, Miss: Writing and ciphering governess at Westgate House school, Bury St. Edmunds (*Pickwick*).

Haggage, Dr.: A Marshalsea prisoner who brings Amy Dorrit into the world there. *The doctor was amazingly shabby, in a torn and darned rough-weather sea-jacket, out at elbows and eminently short of buttons (he had been in his time the experienced surgeon carried by a passenger ship), the dirtiest white trousers conceivable by mortal man, carpet slippers, and no visible linen* (*Dorrit*).

'Hamlet's Aunt': See Spiker, Mrs. Henry (*Copperfield*).

'Handel': Herbert Pocket's nickname for Pip. *'We are so harmonious, and you have been a blacksmith. . . . Would you mind Handel for a familiar name? There's a charming piece of music by Handel called the Harmonious Blacksmith'* (*Expectations*).

Handford, Julius: Alias used by John Harmon when viewing his own supposed corpse (*Mutual Friend*).

Hannah: Miss La Creevy's servant (*Nickleby*).

Hardy: Percy Noakes's great friend and fellow organiser of the steam excursion. *A stout gentleman of about forty . . . a practical joker, immensely popular with married ladies, and a general favourite with young men. He was always engaged in some pleasure excursion or other, and delighted in getting somebody into a scrape* on such occasions. He could sing comic songs, imitate hackney-coachmen and fowls, play airs on his chin, and execute concertos on the Jew's-harp. He always eat and drank most immoderately, and was the bosom-friend of Mr. Percy Noakes. He had a red face, a somewhat husky voice, and a tremendous laugh (Boz – 'Steam Excursion').

Haredale, Emma: Daughter of the murdered Reuben, niece of Geoffrey, who tries to discourage her suitor, Edward Chester. Edward rescues her from Gashford's clutches after the Gordon Riots, and they eventually marry. A lovely girl (Rudge).

Haredale, Geoffrey: A Roman Catholic gentleman living at 'The Warren', near the Maypole Inn, Chigwell. Uncle of Emma. He is widely suspected of having murdered his brother Reuben, but the burning of his house by the Gordon Rioters leads to his innocence being established. He kills his lifelong rival, Sir John Chester, in a duel and retires to a religious establishment abroad. A burly square-built man, negligently dressed, rough and abrupt in manner, stern, and, in his present mood, forbidding both in look and speech (Rudge).

Harker: Officer in charge of the jury in the interpolated tale 'To be taken with a Grain of Salt' (Christmas Stories – 'Dr. Marigold').

Harker, The Revd. John: Vicar of Groombridge Wells, martyred abroad for his faith, who provided a reference for Mrs. Miller to adopt Walter Wilding (Christmas Stories – 'No Thoroughfare').

Harleigh: Principal singer in the Gattletons' private production of the musical play Masaniello. Mr. Harleigh smiled and looked foolish – not an unusual thing with him – hummed 'Behold how brightly breaks the morning,' and blushed as red as the fisherman's night-cap he was trying on (Boz – 'Mrs. Joseph Porter').

Harmon: John Harmon's deceased father, a garbage contractor. 'He grew rich as a Dust Contractor, and lived in a hollow in a hilly country entirely composed of Dust. On his own small estate the growling old vagabond threw up his own mountain range, like an old volcano, and its geological formation was Dust. Coal-dust, vegetable-dust, crockery-dust, rough dust, and sifted dust – all manner of Dust' (Mutual Friend).

Harmon, John (alias Julius Handford, alias John Rokesmith): The central character of the story, who assumes other identities after his supposed murder, works for his late father's servant, Boffin, and lodges with the Wilfers, whose daughter Bella was to have become his bride under his father's will. He marries Bella, the Boffins discover his true identity, and he takes up his father's legacy. A dark gentleman. Thirty at the utmost. An expressive, one might say handsome, face. A very bad manner. In the last degree constrained, reserved, diffident, troubled (Mutual Friend).

Harmon, Mrs. John: See Wilfer, Bella (Mutual Friend).

Harriet: See Hopkins and Harriet: (Young Gentlemen – 'Bashful Young Gentleman').

Harris: Law stationer friend of Dounce (Boz – 'Misplaced Attachment').

Harris: Greengrocer at Bath in whose house the footmen's soirée is held (Pickwick).

Harris ('Short Trotters', 'Short', or 'Trotters'): Partner of Codlin in the Punch-and-Judy show which Little Nell and her grandfather accompany briefly. A little merry-faced man with a twinkling eye and a red nose, who seemed to have unconsciously imbibed something of his hero's character (Curiosity Shop).

Harris, Mrs.: Mrs. Gamp's imaginary friend, with whom she holds conversations upon all sorts of subjects. Betsey Prig's declaration that she does not believe Mrs. Harris exists is her culminating insult to Mrs. Gamp. A fearful mystery surrounded this lady of the name of Harris, whom no one in the circle of Mrs. Gamp's acquaintance had ever seen; neither did any human being know her place of residence, though Mrs. Gamp appeared on

*her own showing to be in constant com-
munication with her. There were conflicting rumours on the subject; but the preva-
lent opinion was that she was a phantom
of Mrs. Gamp's brain – as Messrs Doe
and Roe are fictions of the law – created
for the express purpose of holding visionary
dialogues with her on all manner of subjects, and invariably winding up with a
compliment to the excellence of her nature
(Chuzzlewit).*

Harrison: Orphan suggested by Milvey
for adoption by the Boffins. *'Oh, Frank!'
remonstrated his emphatic wife. . . . 'I
don't think Mrs. Boffin would like an
orphan who squints so much' (Mutual
Friend).*

Harry: Marton's favourite pupil. *A very
young boy; quite a little child. His hair
still hung in curls about his face, and his
eyes were very bright; but their light was of
Heaven, not earth (Curiosity Shop).*

Harry: Pedlar who offers to remove a
bloodstain from Bill Sikes's hat. *This was
an antic fellow, half pedlar and half
mountebank, who travelled about the
country on foot to vend hones, strops,
razors, washballs, harness-paste, medicine
for dogs and horses, cheap perfumery,
cosmetics, and such-like wares, which he
carried in a case slung to his back (Twist).*

Harry and Kate: A debtor in Solomon
Jacobs's sponging-house and his wife.
*A genteel-looking young man was talking
earnestly, and in a low tone, to a young
female, whose face was concealed by a
thick veil (Boz – 'Watkins Tottle').*

Harthouse, James: A friend of Gradgrind's who, visiting Coketown as a
Parliamentary candidate, attempts to
seduce Louisa Bounderby. *'Five-and-
thirty, good-looking, good figure, good teeth,
good voice, good breeding, well-dressed,
dark hair, bold eyes.'* || *Had tried life as
a Cornet of Dragoons, and found it a bore;
and had afterwards tried it in the train of
an English minister abroad, and found it a
bore; and had then strolled to Jerusalem,
and got bored there; and had then gone
yachting about the world, and got bored
everywhere (Hard Times).*

Harvey: Emma Fielding's bridegroom.
*There are two points on which Anne
expatiates over and over again, without
the smallest appearance of fatigue or
intending to leave off; one is, that she
'never see in all her life such a – oh such
an angel of a gentleman as Mr. Harvey'
(Young Couples – 'Young Couple'). He
appears again, in old age, in 'Old
Couple': How the old gentleman chuckles
over boyish feats and roguish tricks, and
tells long stories of a 'barring-out'
achieved at the school he went to: which
was very wrong, he tells the boys, and
never to be imitated of course, but which
he cannot help letting them know was very
pleasant too – especially when he kissed
the master's niece.*

Havisham, Miss: Once a beautiful
heiress, she had been jilted by Compeyson and has lived ever since in her bridal
dress amongst the decaying ruins of her
wedding feast at Satis House, Rochester,
where she has brought up her protégée
Estella to despise men. She pays for
Pip's apprenticeship and he believes her
his secret benefactor. He rescues her
from nearly burning to death; but when
she later dies she leaves almost all her
fortune to Estella. *She was dressed in
rich materials – satins, and lace, and silks
– all of white. Her shoes were white. And
she had a long white veil dependent from
her hair, but her hair was white. Some
bright jewels sparkled on her neck and on
her hands. . . . But, I saw that everything
within my view which ought to be white,
had been white long ago, and had lost its
lustre, and was faded and yellow. I saw
that the bride within the bridal dress had
withered like the dress, and like the
flowers, and had no brightness left but the
brightness of her sunken eyes. I saw that
the dress had been put upon the rounded
figure of a young woman, and that the
figure upon which it now hung loose, had
shrunk to skin and bone. Once, I had been
taken to see some ghastly waxwork at the
Fair, representing I know not what
impossible personage lying in state. Once,
I had been taken to one of our old marsh
churches to see a skeleton in the ashes of a*

rich dress, that had been dug out of a vault under the church pavement. Now, waxwork, and skeleton seemed to have dark eyes that moved and looked at me (Expectations).

Havisham, Arthur: Miss Havisham's deceased brother, who had been drawn into crime by Compeyson (Expectations).

Hawdon, Captain ('Nemo'): Penurious law-writer lodging at Krook's, where he dies. As a rakish young officer he had been Lady Dedlock's lover before her marriage, and is the father by her of Esther Summerson. He lies there, dressed in shirt and trousers, with bare feet. He has a yellow look in the spectral darkness of a candle that has guttered down, until the whole length of its wick (still burning) has doubled over, and left a tower of winding-sheet above it. His hair is ragged, mingling with his whiskers and his beard – the latter, ragged too, and grown, like the scum and mist around him, in neglect. Foul and filthy as the room is, foul and filthy as the air is, it is not easy to pereceive what fumes those are which most oppress the senses in it; but through the general sickliness and faintness, and the odour of stale tobacco, there comes into the lawyer's mouth the bitter, vapid taste of opium (Bleak House).

Hawk, Sir Mulberry: Man-about-town and would-be seducer of Kate Nickleby. He kills Verisopht in a duel and flees the country. Remarkable for his tact in ruining, by himself and his creatures, young gentlemen of fortune – a genteel and elegant profession, of which he had undoubtedly gained the head. With all the boldness of an original genius, he had struck out on an entirely new course of treatment quite opposed to the usual method; his custom being, when he had gained the ascendancy over those he took in hand, rather to keep them down than to give them their own way; and to exercise his vivacity upon them, openly, and without reserve. Thus, he made them butts, in a double sense, and while he emptied them with great address, caused them to ring with sundry welladministered taps, for the diversion of society (Nickleby).

Hawkins: Middle-aged baker successfully sued for breach of promise by Anastasia Rugg (Mutual Friend).

Hawkins, M.P.: A new Member of Parliament. When they praise the good looks of Mr. Hawkins, the new member, (the political young gentleman) says he's very well for a representative, all things considered, but he wants a little calling to account, and he is more than half afraid it will be necessary to bring him down on his knees for that vote on the miscellaneous estimates (Young Gentlemen – 'Political Young Gentleman').

Hawkinson, Aunt: An aunt of Georgiana Podsnap who left her a necklace which Georgiana gives to Mrs. Lammle to help her in financial difficulty (Mutual Friend).

Hawkyard, Brother Verity: George Silverman's self-appointed guardian. Preacher to an obscure Nonconformist congregation at West Bromwich ('Silverman').

Headstone, Bradley: Charley Hexam's headmaster. Loving Lizzie Hexam passionately, he tries to murder his rival, Wrayburn, is blackmailed by Riderhood and drowns with him in a struggle. Bradley Headstone, in his decent black coat and waistcoat, and decent white shirt, and decent formal black tie, and decent pantaloons of pepper and salt, with his decent silver watch in his pocket and its decent hair-guard round his neck, looked a thoroughly decent young man of six-and-twenty. He was never seen in any other dress, and yet there was a certain stiffness in his manner of wearing this, as if there were a want of adaptation between him and it, recalling some mechanics in their holiday clothes. . . . There was a kind of settled trouble in the face. It was the face belonging to a naturally slow or inattentive intellect that had toiled hard to get what it had won, and that had to hold it now that it was gotten. He always seemed to be uneasy lest anything should be missing from his mental warehouse, and taking stock to assure himself (Mutual Friend).

Heathfield, Alfred: Medical student and

ward of Dr. Jeddler, to whose daughter, Marion, he is engaged. She sacrifices him to her sister Grace. *The active figure of a handsome young man (Christmas Books –* 'Battle of Life').

Heep, Mrs.: Uriah's mother. *The dead image of Uriah, only short. She received me with the utmost humility, and apologised to me for giving her son a kiss, observing that, lowly as they were, they had their natural affections, which they hoped would give no offence to any one (Copperfield).*

Heep, Uriah: Wickfield's hypocritical clerk, later partner, who designs to marry Agnes Wickfield. He defrauds Wickfield, is unmasked by Micawber and sentenced to transportation for life. *Hardly any eyebrows, and no eyelashes, and eyes of a red-brown, so unsheltered and unshaded, that I remember wondering how he went to sleep. He was high-shouldered and bony; dressed in decent black, with a white wisp of a neckcloth; buttoned up to the throat; and had a long, lank, skeleton hand, which particularly attracted my attention. . . . It was no fancy of mine about his hands, I observed; for he frequently ground the palms against each other as if to squeeze them dry and warm, besides often wiping them, in a stealthy way, on his pocket-handkerchief. ||* ' "*Be umble, Uriah," says father to me, "and you'll get on. It was what was always being dinned into you and me at school; it's what goes down best. Be umble," says father, "and you'll do!" And really it ain't done bad!' (Copperfield).*

Helves, Captain: A specious military type, met by the Tauntons on a Gravesend packet (and therefore considered respectable), whom they bring with them on the steam excursion. His courtship of Julia Briggs is cut short by his arrest for embezzlement. *A lion – a gentleman with a bass voice and an incipient red moustache (Boz –* 'Steam Excursion').

Henrietta: Tom's sweetheart until she jilts him for another pavement-artist. *To say that Henrietta was volatile is but to say that she was woman. . . . She consented to walk with me. Let me do her the justice*

to say that she did so upon trial. '*I am not,*' said Henrietta, '*as yet prepared to regard you, Thomas, in any other light than as a friend; but as a friend I am willing to walk with you, on the understanding that softer sentiments may flow.*' We walked (Christmas Stories – 'Somebody's Luggage').

Henry: Pawnbroker's assistant. *The gentleman behind the counter, with the curly black hair, diamond ring, and double silver watch-guard (Boz –* 'Pawnbroker's Shop').

Henry: Cousin and eventual husband of Maria Lobbs in Sam Weller's tale of 'The Parish Clerk'. *The only eye-sore in the whole place' (Pickwick).*

Herbert, M.P.: Member of the House of Commons who points out that Lord George Gordon is present in the House with a blue cockade, signal of rebellion, in his hat, during the debate on the Catholic Emancipation question *(Rudge).*

Herschel, Mr. and Mrs. John: First cousin of John, the narrator, and his wife, who visit the haunted house with him. *So called after the great astronomer: than whom I suppose a better man at a telescope does not breathe. With him, was his wife: a charming creature to whom he had been married in the previous spring (Christmas Stories –* 'Haunted House').

Hexam, Charley: Son of Jesse, brother to Lizzie. He is obsessed with becoming 'respectable', which aim he pursues through the schoolmastering profession. *There was a curious mixture in the boy, of uncompleted savagery, and uncompleted civilisation. His voice was hoarse and coarse, and his face was coarse, and his stunted figure was coarse; but he was cleaner than other boys of his type; and his writing, though large and round was good; and he glanced at the backs of the books, with an awakened curiosity that went below the binding. Not one who can read, ever looks at a book, even unopened on a shelf, like one who cannot (Mutual Friend).*

Hexam, Jesse (Gaffer): Father of Charley and Lizzie, a seeker for, and robber of, corpses in the Thames. He eventually becomes one himself when about to be arrested on suspicion of murdering John Harmon. *A strong man with ragged grizzled hair and a sun-browned face . . . with no covering on his matted head, with his brown arms bare to between the elbow and the shoulder, with the loose knot of a looser kerchief lying low on his bare breast in a wilderness of beard and whisker, with such dress as he wore seeming to be made out of the mud that begrimed his boat, still there was business-like usage in his steady gaze (Mutual Friend).*

Hexam, Lizzie: Daughter of Jesse, sister to Charley. Her father's unwilling helper until his death, she is educated by Wrayburn. She refuses Headstone's passionate proposal, precipitating his attempted murder of Wrayburn, whom Lizzie at length marries. *A dark girl of nineteen or twenty (Mutual Friend).*

Heyling, George: The revengeful central figure of 'The Old Man's Tale About the Queer Client', told to Pickwick at the Magpie and Stump. *'The deepest despair, and passion scarcely human, had made such fierce ravages on his face and form, in that one night, that his companions in misfortune shrunk affrighted from him as he passed by. His eyes were bloodshot and heavy, his face a deadly white, and his body bent as if with age. He had bitten his under-lip nearly through in the violence of his mental suffering, and the blood which had flowed from the wound had trickled down his chin, and stained his shirt and neckerchief. No tear, or sound of complaint escaped him: but the unsettled look, and disordered haste with which he paced up and down the yard, denoted the fever which was burning within' (Pickwick).*

Heyling, Mrs. George (Mary): George Heyling's wife, whose death he devotes himself to avenging. *'The slight and delicate young woman was sinking beneath the combined effects of bodily and mental illness' (Pickwick).*

Hicks, Septimus: Boarder at Mrs. Tibbs's. He marries, but deserts, Matilda Maplesone. *A tallish, white-faced young man, with spectacles, and a black ribbon round his neck instead of a neckerchief – a most interesting person; a poetical walker of the hospitals, and a 'very talented young man.' He was fond of 'lugging' into conversation all sorts of quotations from Don Juan, without fettering himself by the propriety of their application (Boz – 'Boarding-House').*

Higden, Mrs. Betty: A poor child-minder and laundress from whom Mrs. Boffin wishes to adopt Johnny. *She was one of those old women, was Mrs. Betty Hidgen, who by dint of an indomitable purpose and a strong constitution fight out many years, though each year has come with its new knock-down blows fresh to the fight against her, wearied by it; an active old woman, with a bright dark eye and a resolute face, yet quite a tender creature too; not a logically-reasoning woman, but God is good, and hearts may count in Heaven as high as heads (Mutual Friend).*

Hilton: Master of the ceremonies at the Misses Crumpton's ball. *The popular Mr. Hilton (Boz – 'Sentiment').*

Holliday, Arthur: The fictitious name given by Dr. Speddie to the racegoer central figure in his story of the corpse in the hotel bed. *One of those reckless, rattle-pated, open-hearted, and open-mouthed young gentlemen, who possess the gift of familiarity in its highest perfection, and who scramble carelessly along the journey of life making friends, as the phrase is, wherever they go (Two Apprentices).*

Hominy, Mrs. Major: An American literary celebrity imposed upon Martin Chuzzlewit at the National Hotel where he stays before embarking for Eden. *A lady who certainly could not be considered young – that was matter of fact; and probably could not be considered handsome –but that was matter of opinion. She was very straight, very tall, and not at all flexible in face or figure. On her head she wore a great straw-bonnet, with trimmings of the same, in which she looked as if she had been thatched by an unskilful labourer (Chuzzlewit).*

Honeythunder, Luke: Professional philanthropist. Guardian of the Landless twins. *Always something in the nature of a Boil upon the face of society, Mr. Honey-thunder expanded into an inflammatory Wen in Minor Canon Corner. Though it was not literally true, as was facetiously charged against him by public unbelievers, that he called aloud to his fellow-creatures: 'Curse your souls and bodies, come here and be blessed!' still his philanthropy was of that gunpowderous sort that the difference between it and animosity was hard to determine (Drood).*

Hope: One of Miss Flite's birds *(Bleak House)*.

Hopkins: Candidate for election for beadle of 'Our Parish'. *'Hopkins for Beadle. Seven small children!!' (Boz –* 'Election for Beadle').

Hopkins, Captain: Fellow prisoner of Micawber in the King's Bench. *In the last extremity of shabbiness (Copperfield).*

Hopkins, Jack: A medical student present at Bob Sawyer's party. *He wore a black velvet waistcoat, with thunder-and-lightning buttons; and a blue striped shirt, with a white false collar (Pickwick).*

Hopkins and Harriet: The bashful young gentleman and his sister. *The bashful young gentleman then observes it is very fine weather, and being reminded that it has only just left off raining for the first time these three days, he blushes very much, and smiles as if he had said a very good thing. The young lady who was most anxious to speak, here inquires, with an air of great commiseration, how his dear sister Harriet is to-day; to which the young gentleman, without the slightest consideration, replies with many thanks, that she is remarkably well. 'Well, Mr. Hopkins!' cries the young lady, 'why, we heard she was bled yesterday evening, and have been perfectly miserable about her.' 'Oh, ah,' says the young gentleman, 'so she was. Oh, she's very ill, very ill indeed' (Young Gentlemen –* 'Bashful Young Gentleman').

Horse Guards: Military magnate, guest at Merdle's *(Dorrit)*.

Hortense: Lady Dedlock's maid, sup-planted by Rosa and dismissed. Failing to extort money from Tulkinghorn she murders him, but is brought to justice by Inspector and Mrs. Bucket. *My Lady's maid is a Frenchwoman of two-and-thirty, from somewhere in the southern country about Avignon and Marseilles – a large-eyed brown woman with black hair: who would be handsome, but for a certain feline mouth, and general uncomfortable tightness of face, rendering the jaws too eager, and the skull too prominent. There is something indefinably keen and wan about her anatomy; and she has a watchful way of looking out of the corners of her eyes without turning her head, which could be pleasantly dispensed with – especially when she is in an ill-humour and near knives. Through all the good taste of her dress and little adornments, these objections so express themselves, that she seems to go about like a very neat She-Wolf imperfectly tamed (Bleak House).*

Howler, The Revd. Melchisedech: Evangelical preacher who conducts Mrs. MacStinger's marriage to Captain Bunsby. *Having been one day discharged from the West India Docks on a false suspicion (got up expressly against him by the general enemy) of screwing gimlets into puncheons, and applying his lips to the orifice, had announced the destruction of the world for that day two years, at ten in the morning, and opened a front-parlour for the reception of ladies and gentlemen of the Ranting persuasion, upon whom, on the first occasion of their assemblage, the admonitions of the Reverend Melchisedech had produced so powerful an effect, that, in their rapturous performance of a sacred jig, which closed the service, the whole flock broke through into a kitchen below, and disabled a mangle belonging to one of the fold (Dombey).*

Hubble: Wheelwright friend of the Gargerys. *A tough high-shouldered stooping old man, of a sawdusty fragrance, with his legs extraordinarily wide apart: so that in my short days I always saw some miles of open country between them when I met him coming up the lane (Expectations).*

Hubble, Mrs.: Hubble's wife. *A little*

curly sharp-edged person in sky-blue, who held a conventionally juvenile position, because she had married Mr. Hubble – I don't know at what remote period – when she was much younger than he (Expectations).

Hugh: Ostler at the Maypole Inn, later a leader of the Gordon Riots, for which he is executed after his natural father, Sir John Chester, has refused to appeal for him. *A young man, of a hale athletic figure, and a giant's strength, whose sunburnt face and swarthy throat, overgrown with jet black hair, might have served a painter for a model. Loosely attired, in the coarsest and roughest garb, with scraps of straw and hay – his usual bed – clinging here and there, and mingling with his uncombed locks, he had fallen asleep in a posture as careless as his dress. The negligence and disorder of the whole man, with something fierce and sullen in his features, gave him a picturesque appearance (Rudge).*

Humm, Anthony: President of the Brick Lane Branch of the United Grand Junction Ebenezer Temperance Association. *A converted fireman, now a schoolmaster, and occasionally an itinerant preacher (Pickwick).*

Humphrey, Master: An amiable, deformed old semi-recluse, whose small circle of friends, romantics all, gather in his rooms each week to chat and read their compositions which they store in the case of his old clock. *I am not a churlish old man. Friendless I can never be, for all mankind are my kindred, and I am on ill terms with no one member of my great family. But for many years I have led a lonely, solitary life ; – what wound I sought to heal, what sorrow to forget, originally, matters not now ; it is sufficient that retirement has become a habit with me, and that I am unwilling to break the spell which for so long a time has shed its quiet influence upon my home and heart (Humphrey).* See also **Single Gentleman, The** *(Curiosity Shop).*

Hunt: Boldwig's head gardener *(Pickwick).*

Hunter, Horace: Alexander Trott's rival – and intended duelling opponent – for Emily Brown, whom he eventually marries. *'I've seen him hit the man at the Pall Mall shooting-gallery, in the second buttonhole of the waistcoat, five times out of every six, and when he didn't hit him there, he hit him in the head' (Boz – 'Great Winglebury Duel').* In the dramatised version, *The Strange Gentleman,* he is renamed Horatio Tinkles.

Hunter, Leo: Mrs. Hunter's husband. *A grave man (Pickwick).*

Hunter, Mrs. Leo: The Eatanswill poetess. *'She doats on poetry, sir. She adores it ; I may say that her whole soul and mind are wound up, and entwined with it. She has produced some delightful pieces herself, sir. You may have met her "Ode to an Expiring Frog," sir. . . . It created an immense sensation. It was signed with an "L" and eight stars, and appeared originally in a Lady's Magazine. It commenced*

> *"Can I view thee panting, lying*
> *On thy stomach, without sighing ;*
> *Can I unmoved see thee dying*
> > *On a log,*
> > *Expiring frog !"'*
> > *(Pickwick).*

Hutley Jemmy ('Dismal Jemmy'): Job Trotter's brother and Jingle's actor friend, who recounts 'The Stroller's Tale' at The Bull, Rochester. *A careworn looking man, whose sallow face, and deeply sunken eyes, were rendered still more striking than nature had made them, by the straight black hair which hung in matted disorder half way down his face. His eyes were almost unnaturally bright and piercing ; his cheekbones were high and prominent ; and his jaws were so long and lank, that an observer would have supposed that he was drawing the flesh of his face in, for a moment, by some contraction of the muscles, if his half-opened mouth and immovable expression had not announced that it was his ordinary expression (Pickwick).*

Hyppolite, Private: Soldier billeted at the perfumer's in the French town where

Langley lodges. *When not on duty, volunteered to keep shop while the fair Perfumeress stepped out to speak to a neighbour or so, and laughingly sold soap with his war-sword girded on him* (*Christmas Stories* – 'Somebody's Luggage').

Idle, Thomas: One of the two apprentices. *An idler of the unmixed Irish or Neapolitan type; a passive idler, a born-and-bred idler, a consistent idler, who practised what he would have preached if he had not been too idle to preach; a one entire and perfect chrysolite of idleness* (*Two Apprentices*).

Ikey: Assistant bailiff to Solomon Jacobs. *A man in a coarse Petersham great-coat, whity-brown neckerchief, faded black suit, gamboge-coloured top-boots, and one of those large-crowned hats, formerly seldom met with, but now very generally patronised by gentlemen and costermongers* (*Boz* – 'Watkins Tottle').

Ikey: Stable-boy at the inn near the haunted house. *A high-shouldered young fellow, with a round red face, a short crop of sandy hair, a very broad humorous mouth, a turned-up nose, and a great sleeved waistcoat of purple bars, with mother-of-pearl buttons, that seemed to be growing upon him, and to be in a fair way – if it were not pruned – of covering his head and overrunning his boots* (*Christmas Stories* – 'Haunted House').

'Infant Phenomenon, The': See Crummles, Ninetta *(Nickleby)*.

Inspector: The police officer investigating John Harmon's supposed murder. *His elbows learning on his desk, and the fingers and thumb of his right hand fitting themselves to the fingers and thumb of his left. Mr. Inspector moved nothing but his eyes (Mutual Friend)*.

Isaac: Associate of Jackson in apprehending Mrs. Bardell. *A shabby man in black leggings (Pickwick)*.

'Ivins, J'mima': See Evans, Jemina (*Boz* – 'Miss Evans and the Eagle').

Izzard: A boarder at the National Hotel, in America, where Martin Chuzzlewit stays before embarking for Eden *(Chuzzlewit)*.

Jack: Prisoner for an assault, which proves fatal, on his mistress. *A powerful, ill-looking young fellow* (*Boz* – 'Hospital Patient').

Jack: Driver of the London–Salisbury coach. *Of all the swells that ever flourished a whip, professionally, he might have been elected emperor (Chuzzlewit)*.

Jack: Mrs. Lupin's manservant *(Chuzzlewit)*.

Jack: Police officer assisting at the arrest of Jonas Chuzzlewit *(Chuzzlewit)*.

'Jack', The: Thames-side boatmen's helper, concerned in the attempt to smuggle Magwitch out of England. *A grizzled male creature, the 'Jack' of the little causeway, who was as slimy and smeary as if he had been low water-mark too (Expectations)*.

Jack, Dark: The species of coloured sailorman. *I should be very slow to interfere oppressively with Dark Jack, for, whenever I have had to do with him I have found him a simple and a gentle fellow* (*Uncommercial* – 'Poor Mercantile Jack').

Jack, Mercantile: The species of merchant sailorman. *Is the sweet little cherub who sits smiling aloft and keeps watch on the life of poor Jack, commissioned to take charge of Mercantile Jack, as well as Jack of the national navy? If not, who is? What is the cherub about, and what are we all about, when poor Mercantile Jack is having his brains slowly knocked out by penny-weights, aboard the brig Beelzebub, or the barque Bowie-knife – when he looks his last at the infernal craft, with the first officer's iron boot-heel in his remaining eye, or with his dying body towed overboard in the ship's wake, while the cruel wounds in it do 'the multitudinous seas incarnadine'?* (*Uncommercial* – 'Poor Mercantile Jack').

Jackman, Major Jemmy: Permanent lodger and friend of Mrs. Lirriper. He joins with her in adopting Jemmy Jackman Lirriper (q.v.). *A most obliging Lodger and punctual in all respects except one irregular which I need not particularly specify. . . . So much the gentleman that* though he is far from tall he seems almost so when he has his shirt-frill out and his frock coat on and his hat with the curly brims, and in what service he was I cannot truly tell you my dear whether Militia or Foreign, for I never heard him even name himself as Major but always simple 'Jemmy Jackman' (Christmas Stories – 'Mrs. Lirriper's Lodgings' and 'Mrs. Lirriper's Legacy').

Jackson: Also termed 'Young Jackson' and 'Barbox Brothers' (the firm he had come to control and closed down). Visiting Mugby Junction, he rediscovers his lost love, Beatrice Tresham, and hears the Signalman's story. A man within five years of fifty either way, who had turned grey too soon, like a neglected fire ; a man of pondering habit, brooding carriage of the head, and suppressed internal voice ; a man with many indications on him of having been too much alone (Christmas Stories – 'Mugby Junction').

Jackson: Former turnkey at the Marshalsea, whose brother's courting of the daughter of a prisoner, Captain Martin, William Dorrit cites as an example to Amy to encourage Young John Chivery's attentions (Dorrit).

Jackson: Chief clerk to Dodson and Fogg. An individual in a brown coat and brass buttons, whose long hair was scrupulously twisted round the rim of his napless hat, and whose soiled drab trousers were so tightly strapped over his Blucher boots, that his knees threatened every moment to start from their concealment (Pickwick).

Jackson, Mr. and Mrs.: Friends of the Plausible Couple (Young Couples – 'Plausible Couple').

Jackson, Michael: Inspector Bucket's imaginary informant about Lady Dedlock's visit to the brickmakers' cottage. 'A person of the name of Michael Jackson, with a blue velvetten waistocat with a double row of mother of pearl buttons' (Bleak House).

Jacobs, Solomon: A bailiff, to whose sponging-house in Cursitor Street Watkins Tottle is taken by Jacobs's assistant, Ikey, and from which he is released by Gabriel Parsons. The two friends soon found themselves on that side of Mr. Solomon Jacobs's establishment, on which most of his visitors were very happy when they found themselves once again – to wit, the outside (Boz – 'Watkins Tottle').

Jacques One, Two, Three, Four, and Five: Revolutionary associates whose ringleader, Jacques Four, is Defarge. The looks of all of them were dark, repressed, and revengeful. . . . They had the air of a rough tribunal (Two Cities).

Jaggers: Lawyer employed by both Miss Havisham and Magwitch. Employer of Molly (q.v.). He was a burly man of an exceedingly dark complexion, with an exceedingly large head and a corresponding large hand. He took my chin in his large hand and turned up my face to have a look at me by the light of the candle. He was prematurely bald on the top of his head, and had bushy black eyebrows that wouldn't lie down, but stood up bristling. His eyes were set very deep in his head, and were disagreeably sharp and suspicious (Expectations).

James: Twin brother of John, whose phantasm he sees ('At Dusk').

James: The Bayham Badgers' butler (Bleak House).

James: Mrs. Tibbs's male servant (Boz – 'Boarding-House').

James: Servant to Brook Dingwall. A red-hot looking footman in bright livery (Boz – 'Sentiment').

James: Son of John, the narrator. Went wild and for a soldier, where he was shot in India, living six weeks in hospital with a musket-ball lodged in his shoulder blade (Reprinted – 'Poor Man's Tale of a Patent').

James, Henry: Commander of the barque Defiance which found the wreckage of the brig Son and Heir (Dombey).

James and Charlotte, Master and Miss: Children of Edward and Charlotte. Present themselves after dinner, and being in perfect good humour, and finding their parents in the same amiable state, augur from these appearances half a glass of wine a-piece and other extraordinary indulgences (*Young Couples* – 'Contradictory Couple').

Jane: The Kitterbells' maidservant (*Boz* – 'Bloomsbury Christening').

Jane: Barmaid at Bellamy's restaurant in the Houses of Parliament. *The Hebe of Bellamy's. . . . Her leading features are a thorough contempt for the great majority of her visitors; her predominant quality, love of admiration, as you cannot fail to observe, if you mark the glee with which she listens to something the young Member near her mutters somewhat unintelligibly in her ear (for his speech is rather thick from some cause or other), and how playfully she digs the handle of a fork into the arm with which he detains her, by way of reply* (*Boz* – 'Parliamentary Sketch').

Jane: Sister of Amelia. Both are marriageable girls displayed by their mamma at the Ramsgate library gambling tables. *'Throw, Jane, my dear,' said the stout lady. An interesting display of bashfulness – a little blushing in a cambric handkerchief* (*Boz* – 'Tuggses at Ramsgate').

Jane: Miss Wozenham's maidservant (*Christmas Stories* – 'Mrs. Lirriper's Lodgings').

Jane: Pecksniff's maidservant (*Chuzzlewit*).

Jane: Mrs. Orange's maidservant ('Holiday Romance').

Jane: Sister of the fiancée of the old lord who admires Kate Nickleby at Madame Mantalini's *salon* (*Nickleby*).

Jane: The Pott's maidservant (*Pickwick*).

Jane: One of Wardle's maidservants (*Pickwick*).

Jane, Aunt: See **Robert, Uncle** (*Boz* – 'Christmas Dinner').

Janet: Betsey Trotwood's maidservant. Despite her professed aversion to matrimony she marries a tavern-keeper. *A pretty, blooming girl, of about nineteen or twenty, and a perfect picture of neatness. . . . She was one of a series of protégées whom my aunt had taken into her service expressly to educate in a renouncement of* mankind, and who had generally completed their abjuration by marrying the baker (*Copperfield*).

Jarber: Reader of the manuscript of this story (*Christmas Stories* – 'Going into Society').

Jargon: One of Miss Flite's birds (*Bleak House*).

Jarley, Mrs.: Proprietress of a travelling waxworks who befriends and employs Little Nell. Marries her driver, George. *A Christian lady, stout and comfortable to look upon, who wore a large bonnet trembling with bows* (*Curiosity Shop*).

Jarndyce, John: Bachelor guardian of his cousins Richard Carstone and Ada Clare, for whose companion he employs Esther Summerson. He proposes marriage to her, and is accepted, but when she is married it is to Allan Woodcourt. *It was a handsome, lively, quick face, full of change and motion; and his hair was a silvered iron-grey. I took him to be nearer sixty than fifty, but he was upright, hearty, and robust. || I felt that if we had been at all demonstrative, he would have run away in a moment* (*Bleak House*).

Jarndyce, Tom: See **Jarndyce and Jarndyce** (*Bleak House*).

Jarndyce and Jarndyce: The interminable Chancery suit which hangs over the whole story and those involved in it. *Jarndyce and Jarndyce drones on. This scarecrow of a suit has, in course of time, become so complicated, that no man alive knows what it means. The parties to it understand it least; but it has been observed that no two Chancery lawyers can talk about it for five minutes, without coming to a total disagreement as to all the premises. Innumerable children have been born into the cause; innumerable young people have married into it; innumerable old people have died out of it. Scores of persons have deliriously found themselves made parties in Jarndyce and Jarndyce, without knowing how or why; whole families have inherited legendary hatreds with the suit. The little plaintiff or defendant, who was promised a new rocking-horse when Jarndyce and Jarndyce should* be settled, has grown up, possessed himself of a real horse, and trotted away into the other world. Fair wards of court have faded into mothers and grandmothers; a long procession of Chancellors has come in and gone out; the legion of bills in the suit have been transformed into mere bills of mortality; there are not three Jarndyces left upon the earth, perhaps, since old Tom Jarndyce in despair blew his brains out at a coffee-house in Chancery Lane; but Jarndyce and Jarndyce still drags its weary length before the Court, perenially hopeless (Bleak House).

Jarvis: Wilding's clerk (Christmas Stories – 'No Thoroughfare', but not in the dramatised version).

Jasper, John: Lay Precentor at Cloisterham Cathedral and secret opium smoker. Uncle to Edwin Drood and jealously in love with Rosa Bud. At the point where the novel ends, unfinished, Jasper seems the likeliest candidate for Drood's supposed murderer. Mr. Jasper is a dark man of some six-and-twenty, with thick, lustrous, well-arranged black hair and whiskers. He looks older than he is, as dark men often do. His voice is deep and good, his face and figure are good, his manner is a little sombre. His room is a little sombre, and may have had its influence in forming his manner. It is mostly in shadow (Drood).

Jean Marie: An Alpine guide appearing in the dramatic version, but not the printed story (No Thoroughfare).

Jean Paul: An Alpine guide appearing in the dramatic version, but not the printed story (No Thoroughfare).

Jeddler, Dr. Anthony: Philosopher and widower father of Grace and Marion, and brother of Martha. Doctor Jeddler was, as I have said, a great philosopher, and the heart and mystery of his philosophy was, to look upon the world as a gigantic practical joke; as something too absurd to be considered seriously, by any rational man (Christmas Books – 'Battle of Life').

Jeddler, Grace and Marion: Elder and younger daughters of Dr. Jeddler. Marion is engaged to Alfred Heathfield, but pretends to elope with Warden, in reality taking refuge with Aunt Martha in order to enable Grace, whose love for Heathfield she has recognised, to marry him, which she does. It was agreeable to see the graceful figures of the blooming sisters, twined together, lingering among the trees, conversing thus, with earnestness opposed to lightness, yet, with love respondingly tenderly to love. . . . The difference between them, in respect of age, could not exceed four years at most; but, Grace, as often happens in such cases, when no mother watches over both (the Doctor's wife was dead), seemed, in her gentle care of her young sister, and in the steadiness of her devotion to her, older than she was; and more removed, in course of nature, from all competition with her, or participation, otherwise than through her sympathy and true affection, in her wayward fancies, than their ages seemed to warrant (Christmas Books – 'Battle of Life').

Jellyby: Mrs. Jellyby's husband. I was a little curious to know who a mild bald gentleman in spectacles was, who dropped into a vacant chair . . . and seemed passively to submit himself to Borrioboola-Gha, but not to be actively interested in that settlement (Bleak House).

Jellyby, Mrs.: A devotee of public causes, especially concerning Africa and the natives of Borrioboola-Gha, preoccupations which cause her to neglect herself and her family. She was a pretty, very diminutive, plump woman, of from forty to fifty, with handsome eyes, though they had a curious habit of seeming to look a long way off. As if – I am quoting Richard again – they could see nothing nearer than Africa! . . . Mrs. Jellyby had very good hair, but was too much occupied with her African duties to brush it. The shawl in which she had been loosely muffled, dropped on to her chair when she advanced to us; and as she turned to resume her seat, we could not help noticing that her dress didn't nearly meet up the back, and that the open space was railed across with a lattice-work of stay-lace – like a summer-house (Bleak House).

Jellyby, Caroline ('Caddy'): The Jellybys' eldest daughter and her mother's overworked amanuensis. Sister of 'Peepy'. She makes a happy marriage with Prince Turveydrop and has a deaf and dumb daughter. *A jaded and unhealthy-looking, though by no means plain girl, at the writing-table, who sat biting the feather of her pen, and staring at us. I suppose nobody ever was in such a state of ink. And, from her tumbled hair to her pretty feet, which were disfigured with frayed and broken satin slippers trodden down at heel, she really seemed to have no article of dress upon her, from a pin upwards, that was in its proper condition or its right place (Bleak House).*

Jellyby, 'Peepy': The Jellybys' neglected small son, brother of Caddy. *Everything the dear child wore, was either too large for him or too small. Among his other contradictory decorations he had the hat of a Bishop, and the little gloves of a baby. His boots were, on a small scale, the boots of a ploughman : while his legs, so crossed and recrossed with scratches that they looked like maps, were bare, below a very short pair of plaid drawers finished off with two frills of perfectly different patterns. The deficient buttons on his plaid frock had evidently been supplied from one of Mr. Jellyby's coats, they were extremely brazen and so much too large. Most extraordinary specimens of needlework appeared on several parts of his dress, where it had been hastily mended (Bleak House).*

Jem: Doorkeeper of Solomon Jacobs's sponging-house. *A sallow-faced red-haired sulky boy (Boz – 'Watkins Tottle').*

Jem: One of Wardle's farm hands *(Pickwick).*

Jemima: Polly Toodle's unmarried sister who cares for her children while she is in Dombey's service. *A younger woman not so plump, but apple-faced also, who led a plump and apple-faced child in each hand (Dombey).*

Jenkins: Sir Mulberry Hawk's manservant *(Nickleby).*

Jenkins: Acquaintance of the Contradictory Couple and the subject of one of their arguments. *'I appealed to Mr. Jenkins who sat next to me on the sofa in the drawing-room during tea –' 'Morgan, you mean,' interrupts the gentleman. 'I do not mean anything of the kind,' answers the lady (Young Couples – 'Contradictory Couple').*

Jenkins, Miss: Pianist at the Gattletons' private theatricals. *Miss Jenkins's talent for the piano was too well known to be doubted for an instant (Boz – 'Mrs. Joseph Porter').*

Jenkinson: A messenger for the Circumlocution Office. *Was eating mashed potatoes and gravy behind a partition by the hall fire (Dorrit).*

Jennings: Robe-maker friend of Dounce *(Boz – 'Misplaced Attachment').*

Jennings: Tulrumble's secretary. *Just imported from London, with a pale face and light whiskers (Mudfog).*

Jennings: One of five occupants of a bed at Dotheboys Hall *(Nickleby).*

Jennings, Miss: Fellow pupil of Rosa Bud at Miss Twinkleton's *(Drood).*

Jenny: Wife of a drunken brickmaker visited by Mrs. Pardiggle. She helps Lady Dedlock in her flight from home. *A woman with a black eye, nursing a poor little gasping baby (Bleak House).*

Jerry: Proprietor of a troupe of performing dogs, encountered by Little Nell and her grandfather in their travels. *A tall black-whiskered man in a velveteen coat (Curiosity Shop).*

Jilkins: Last of the many doctors consulted by Our Bore. *Jilkins then got up, walked across the room, came back, and sat down. His words were these. 'You have been humbugged. This is a case of indigestion, occasioned by deficiency of power in the Stomach. Take a mutton chop in half an hour, with a glass of the finest old sherry that can be got for money. Take two mutton chops to-morrow, and two glasses of the finest old sherry. Next day, I'll come again.' In a week our bore was on his legs, and Jilkins's success dates from that period! (Reprinted – 'Our Bore').*

Jingle, Alfred: An irresponsible strolling actor who throws in his lot with the Pickwickians, succeeds in embarrassing them extremely by eloping with Rachael

Wardle, masquerades as a Captain Fitz-Marshall, and becomes a prisoner in the Fleet, from where he is rescued by Pickwick, who sends him to Demerara to turn over a new leaf. *He was about the middle height, but the thinness of his body, and the length of his legs, gave him the appearance of being much taller. The green coat had been a smart dress garment in the days of swallow-tails, but had evidently in those times adorned a much shorter man than the stranger, for the soiled and faded sleeves scarcely reached to his wrists. It was buttoned closely up to his chin, at the imminent hazard of splitting the back; and an old stock, without a vestige of shirt collar, ornamented his neck. His scanty black trousers displayed here and there those shiny patches which bespeak long service, and were strapped very tightly over a pair of patched and mended shoes, as if to conceal the dirty white stockings, which were nevertheless distinctly visible. His long black hair escaped in negligent waves from beneath each side of his old pinched-up hat; and glimpses of his bare wrists might be observed between the tops of his gloves, and the cuffs of his coat sleeves. His face was thin and haggard; but an indescribable air of jaunty impudence and perfect self-possession pervaded the whole man (Pickwick).*

Jiniwin, Mrs.: Betsey Quilp's mother. *Resided with the couple and waged perpetual war with Daniel; of whom, notwithstanding, she stood in no slight dread (Curiosity Shop).*

Jinkins: Pawnbroker's customer. *An unshaven, dirty, sottish-looking fellow, whose tarnished paper-cap, stuck negligently over one eye, communicates an additionally repulsive expression to his very uninviting countenance (Boz – 'Pawnbroker's Shop').*

Jinkins: Senior boarder at Todgers's; a fish-salesman's book-keeper. *Of a fashionable turn, being a regular frequenter of the Parks on Sundays, and knowing a great many carriages by sight. He spoke mysteriously, too, of splendid women, and was suspected of having once committed himself with a countess (Chuzzlewit).*

Jinkins: Tom Smart's rival for the buxom widow in 'The Bagman's Story'. (See **Bagman, The.**) *'A tall man – a very tall man – in a brown coat and bright basket buttons, and black whiskers, and wavy black hair, who was seated at tea with the widow, and who it required no great penetration to discover was in a fair way of persuading her to be a widow no longer' (Pickwick).*

Jinkins, Mrs.: Jinkins's wife. *A wretched worn-out woman, apparently in the last stage of consumption, whose face bears evident marks of recent ill-usage, and whose strength seems hardly equal to the burden – light enough, God knows! – of the thin, sickly child she carries (Boz – 'Pawnbroker's Shop').*

Jinkinson: Barber and bear-keeper in a tale of Sam Weller's. *'Easy shavin' was his natur', and cutting' and curlin' was his pride and glory. His whole delight wos in his trade. He spent all his money on bears' (Humphrey).*

Jinks: Clerk to the magistrates at Ipswich. *A pale, sharp-nosed, half-fed, shabbily-clad clerk, of middle-age (Pickwick).*

Jip (short for **Gypsy**): Dora Spenlow's little dog. *I approached him tenderly, for I loved even him; but he showed his whole set of teeth, got under a chair expressly to snarl, and wouldn't hear of the least familiarity (Copperfield).*

Jo ('**Toughey**'): A boy crossing-sweeper. He is Hawdon's only mourner and shows Lady Dedlock her former lover's haunts, for which he is hounded by Tulkinghorn. He dies in George's Shooting-gallery. *Name, Jo. Nothing else that he knows on. Don't know that everybody has two names. Never heerd of sich a think. Don't know that Jo is short for a longer name. Thinks it long enough for him. He don't find no fault with it. Spell it? No. He can't spell it. No father, no mother, no friends. Never been to school. What's home? (Bleak House).*

Jobba: Speaker at the mechanical science session of the first meeting of the Mudfog Association. *Produced a forcing-machine* on a novel-plan, for bringing joint-stock railway shares prematurely to a premium. The instrument was in the form of an elegant gilt weatherglass, of most dazzling appearance, and was worked behind, by strings, after the manner of a pantomime trick, the strings being always pulled by the directors of the company to which the machine belonged (Mudfog).

Jobling, Dr. John: Medical attendant to Anthony Chuzzlewit and Lewsome, later medical officer of the Anglo-Bengalee Disinterested Loan and Life Assurance Company. He had a portentously sagacious chin, and a pompous voice, with a rich huskiness in some of its tones that went directly to the heart, like a ray of light shining through the ruddy medium of choice old burgundy. . . . Perhaps he could shake his head, rub his hands, or warm himself before a fire, better than any man alive; and he had a peculiar way of smacking his lips and saying, 'Ah!' at intervals while patients detailed their symptoms, which inspired great confidence. It seemed to express, 'I know what you're going to say better than you do; but go on, go on' (Chuzzlewit).

Jobling, Tony ('Weevle'): Snagsby's law writer and close friend of Guppy. Mr. Jobling is buttoned up closer than mere adornment might require. His hat presents at the rims a peculiar appearance of a glistening nature, as if it had been a favourite snail-promenade. The same phenomenon is visible on some parts of his coat, and particularly at the seams. He has the faded appearance of a gentleman in embarrassed circumstances; even his light whiskers droop with something of a shabby air (Bleak House).

Jobson, Jessie, Sophronia, Jessie Number Two, Matilda, William, Jane, Matilda Number Two, Brigham, Leonardo, and Orson: Mormon emigrants aboard the Amazon (Uncommercial – 'Bound for the Great Salt Lake').

Joby (also Greenwood): One-eyed tramp said to have encountered the hooded woman (Christmas Stories – 'Haunted House').

Jock: Boy at the little Cumberland inn where Idle's sprained ankle is treated. A white-headed boy, who, under pretence of stirring up some bay salt in a basin of water for the laving of this unfortunate ankle, had greatly enjoyed himself for the last ten minutes in splashing the carpet (Two Apprentices).

Jodd: A boarder at the National Hotel, in America, where Martin Chuzzlewit stays before embarking for Eden (Chuzzlewit).

Joe: Receiver of stolen goods, shown to Scrooge by the Ghost of Christmas Yet to Come. A grey-haired rascal, nearly seventy years of age (Christmas Books – 'Christmas Carol').

Joe: A labourer at the wharf where Florence Dombey meets Walter Gay after her ordeal with Good Mrs. Brown (Dombey).

Joe: Driver of the Cloisterham omnibus (Drood).

Joe: The fat boy, servant to Wardle. The fat boy rose, opened his eyes, swallowed the huge piece of pie he had been in the act of masticating when he last fell asleep, and slowly obeyed his master's orders – gloating languidly over the remains of the feast, as he removed the plates, and deposited them in the hamper (Pickwick).

Joe: Waiter at the hotel where Rose Maylie stays near Hyde Park (Twist).

Joe: Guard of the Dover mailcoach. He stood on his own particular perch behind the mail, beating his feet, and keeping an eye and a hand on the arm-chest before him, where a loaded blunderbuss lay at the top of six or eight loaded horse-pistols, deposited on a substratum of cutlass (Two Cities).

Joey: One of Miss Flite's birds (Bleak House).

Joey, Captain: Regular drinker at the Six Jolly Fellowship Porters (Mutual Friend).

John: Twin brother of James, to whom his phantasm appears as he lies dying ('At Dusk').

John: The Maldertons' multi-purpose manservant. *A man who, on ordinary occasions, acted as half-groom, half-gardener; but who, as it was important to make an impression on Mr. Sparkins, had been forced into a white neckerchief and shoes, and touched up, and brushed, to look like a second footman* (Boz – 'Horatio Sparkins').

John: The Parsonses' manservant (*Boz* – 'Watkins Tottle').

John: Narrator of the story and tenant of the haunted house. *I find the early morning to be my most ghostly time. Any house would be more or less haunted, to me, in the early morning; and a haunted house could scarcely address me to greater advantage than then* (Christmas Stories – 'Haunted House').

John: A riverside labourer on whom Florence Dombey takes pity when she is visiting the Skettles. Father of Martha. *A very poor man, who seemed to have no regular employment, but now went roaming about the banks of the river when the tide was low, looking out for bits and scraps in the mud (Dombey).*

John: The Lovetowns' servant *(Is She His Wife?).*

John: A bibulous pantomime clown whose death is the subject of 'The Stroller's Tale' told by Jem Hutley. *'Never shall I forget the repulsive sight that met my eye when I turned round. He was dressed for the pantomime, in all the absurdity of a clown's costume. The spectral figures in the Dance of Death, the most frightful shapes that the ablest painter ever portrayed on canvas, never presented an appearance half so ghastly. His bloated body and shrunken legs – their deformity enhanced a hundred fold by the fantastic dress – the glassy eyes, contrasting fearfully with the thick white paint with which the face was besmeared; the grotesquely ornamented head, trembling with paralysis, and the long, skinny hands, rubbed with white chalk – all gave him a hideous and unnatural appearance'* (Pickwick).

John: Waiter at the Saracen's Head, Towcester *(Pickwick).*

John: The narrator, a working-man who has to spend almost all his life-savings in various officials' fees in order to patent an invention. Father of James, Mary, Charlotte, and others. *I am a smith by trade. My name is John. I have been called 'Old John' ever since I was nineteen year of age, on account of not having much hair. I am fifty-six year of age at the present time, and I don't find myself with more hair, nor yet with less, to signify, than at nineteen year of age aforesaid* (Reprinted – 'Poor Man's Tale of a Patent').

John: Waiter at the St. James's Arms *(Strange Gentleman).*

John: Unemployed boilermaker in east London, visited by the Uncommercial Traveller. *It soon appeared that he was rather deaf. He was a slow, simple fellow of about thirty* (Uncommercial – 'Small Star in the East').

John: The Fieldings' manservant who finds Jane Adams showing Anne the wedding preparations, and claims a forfeit: *Mr. John, who has waxed bolder by degrees, pleads the usage at weddings, and claims the privilege of a kiss, which he obtains after a great scuffle* (Young Couples – 'Young Couple').

Johnny: Betty Higden's child grandson, whom the Boffins wish to adopt. He dies before they can succeed *(Mutual Friend).*

Johnson: Pupil at Dr. Blimber's. *Every young gentleman fastened his gaze upon the Doctor, with an assumption of the deepest interest. One of the number who happened to be drinking, and who caught the Doctor's eye glaring at him through the side of his tumbler, left off so hastily that he was convulsed for some moments, and in the sequel ruined Doctor Blimber's point (Dombey).*

Johnson: Nicholas Nickleby's stage name *(Nickleby).*

Johnson, John: Traveller to Gretna Green, with his intended bride Mary Wilson. He is detained at the St. James's Arms by lack of funds to pay his bill *(Strange Gentleman).*

Johnson, Tom: One of Feenix's numerous acquaintance. *Cousin Feenix, sitting in the mourning-coach, recognises innumerable acquaintances on the road, but takes no other notice of them, in decorum, than checking them off aloud as they go by, for Mr. Dombey's information, as 'Tom Johnson. Man with cork leg from White's. What are you here, Tommy? Foley on a blood mare. The Smalder girls –' and so forth (Dombey).*

Jollson, Mrs.: Mrs. MacStinger's predecessor at 9, Brig Place, India Docks *(Dombey)*.

Joltered, Sir William: President of the zoology and botany session at the second meeting of the Mudfog Association *(Mudfog)*.

Jonathan: Regular drinker at the Six Jolly Fellowship Porters *(Mutual Friend)*.

Jones: Employee of Blaze and Sparkle's. *'Our people, Mr. Jones,' said Blaze and Sparkle to the hand in question on engaging him, 'our people, sir, are sheep – mere sheep. Where two or three marked ones go, all the rest follow. Keep those two or three in your eye, Mr. Jones, and you have the flock'* (Bleak House).

Jones: Barrister's clerk friend of Dounce. *Rum fellow that Jones – capital company – full of anecdote!* (Boz – 'Misplaced Attachment').

Jones: Dinner guest at the Buddens'. *A little smirking man with red whiskers, sitting at the bottom of the table, who during the whole of dinner had been endeavouring to obtain a listener to some stories about Sheridan* (Boz – 'Mr. Minns and his Cousin').

Jones, George: Regular drinker at the Six Jolly Fellowship Porters *(Mutual Friend)*.

Jones, Mary: A victim of Ned Dennis, the hangman. *'A young woman of nineteen who come up to Tyburn with an infant at her breast, and was worked off for taking a piece of cloth off the counter of a shop in Ludgate Hill, and putting it down again when the shopman see her; and who had never done any harm before, and only*

tried to do that, in consequence of her husband having been pressed three weeks previous, and she being left to beg, with two young children – as was proved at the trial. Ha ha! – Well! That being the law and the practice of England, is the glory of England, an't it, Muster Gashford?' (Rudge).

Jones, Spruggins, and Smith's: Of Tottenham-court Road. The cut-price drapery of which Samuel Smith, alias Horatio Sparkins, is junior partner *(Boz – 'Horatio Sparkins')*.

Joper, Billy: Fellow member of Brooks's with Feenix. *'Man with a glass in his eye'* (Dombey).

Joram: Omer's assistant, later partner. He marries Minnie Omer, and becomes father of Joe and Minnie. *A good-looking young fellow (Copperfield).*

Joram, Mrs.: See **Omer, Minnie** *(Copperfield)*.

Joram, Joe and Minnie: The Jorams' children *(Copperfield)*.

Jorgan, Captain Silas Jonas: Native of Salem, Massachusetts, finder of Hugh Raybrock's message. *He had seen many things and places, and had stowed them all away in a shrewd intellect and a vigorous memory. He was an American born . . . but he was a citizen of the world, and a combination of most of the best qualities of most of its best countries (Christmas Stories – 'Message from the Sea').*

Jorkins: Junior partner in the law practice of Spenlow and Jorkins. *A mild man of a heavy temperament, whose place in the business was to keep himself in the background, and be constantly exhibited by name as the most obdurate and ruthless of men. || A large, mild, smooth-faced man of sixty, who took so much snuff that there was a tradition in the Commons that he lived principally on that stimulant, having little room in his system for any other article of diet (Copperfield).*

Joseph: Much respected head waiter at the Slamjam Coffee-house, London, E.C., to whom Christopher dedicates his essays. *Than which an individual more eminently deserving of the name of man,* or a more amenable honour to his own head and heart, whether considered in the light of a Waiter or regarded as a human being, do not exist (Christmas Stories – 'Somebody's Luggage').

Joseph and **Celia:** Charity children observed in a City churchyard. *They were making love – a tremendous proof of the vigour of that immortal article, for they were in the graceful uniform under which English Charity delights to hide herself* (*Uncommercial* – 'City of the Absent').

Jowl, Joe: A gambler under whose influence little Nell's grandfather falls. *A burly fellow of middle age, with large black whiskers, broad cheeks, a coarse wide mouth, and bull neck, which was pretty freely displayed as his shirt-collar was only confined by a loose red handkerchief (Curiosity Shop).*

Joy, Thomas: Friend of William Butcher with whom John lodges in London, and who helps him with his patent application. *A carpenter, six foot four in height, and plays quoits well* (*Reprinted* – 'Poor Man's Tale of a Patent').

Julia: The narrator's beloved (*Reprinted* – 'Ghost of Art').

Jupe, Signor: Sissy's father, a clown in Sleary's Circus. Thinking himself finished, he disappears with his dog, Merrylegs, and is never seen again. *Signor Jupe was that afternoon to 'elucidate the diverting accomplishments of his highly trained performing dog Merrylegs'. He was also to exhibit 'his astounding feat of throwing seventy-five hundred-weight in rapid succession backhanded over his head, thus forming a fountain of solid iron in mid-air, a feat never before attempted in this or any other country, and which having elicited such rapturous plaudits from enthusiastic throngs it cannot be withdrawn.' The same Signor Jupe was to 'enliven the varied performances at frequent intervals with his chaste Shakespearean quips and retorts'* (*Hard Times*).

Jupe, Cecilia (Sissy): Jupe's deserted daughter. Taken into Gradgrind's household, she proves a ministering angel and helps its members in their varying

troubles. *So dark-eyed and dark-haired, that she seemed to receive a deeper and more lustrous colour from the sun, when it shone upon her (Hard Times).*

Kags: A wanted man hiding at Toby Crackit's on Jacob's Island, Bermondsey, when Bill Sikes takes refuge there. *A robber of fifty years, whose nose had been almost beaten in, in some old scuffle, and whose face bore a frightful scar which might probably be traced to the same occasion. (Twist).*

Kate: See **Harry** and **Kate** (*Boz* – 'Watkins Tottle').

Kate: An orphan child whom Florence Dombey meets at Skettles's. *There came among the other visitors, soon after Florence, one beautiful girl, three or four years younger than she, who was an orphan child, and who was accompanied by her aunt (Dombey).*

Kate: Sister of Henry and cousin to Maria Lobbs in Sam Weller's story of 'The Parish Clerk'. *'An arch, impudent-looking, bewitching little person'* (*Pickwick*).

Kedgick, Captain: Landlord of the National Hotel in America where Martin Chuzzlewit stays before embarking for Eden *(Chuzzlewit).*

Kenge ('Conversation Kenge'): Solicitor, of Kenge and Carboy, employed by Jarndyce. Richard Carstone becomes articled to the firm. *A portly important-looking gentleman, dressed all in black, with a white cravat, large gold watch seals, a pair of gold eyeglasses, and a large seal-ring upon his little finger. . . . He appeared to enjoy beyond everything the sound of his own voice. I couldn't wonder at that, for it was mellow and full, and gave great importance to every word he uttered. He listened to himself with obvious satisfaction, and sometimes gently beat time to his own music with his head, or rounded a sentence with his hand. I was very much impressed by him – even then, before I knew that he formed himself on the model of a great lord who was his client, and that he was generally called Conversation Kenge (Bleak House).*

Kenwigs: Fellow lodger, with his family, of Noggs. Nicholas Nickleby is engaged to teach the Kenwigs children. *A turner in ivory, who was looked upon as a person of some consideration on the premises, inasmuch as he occupied the whole of the first floor, comprising a suite of two rooms (Nickleby).*

Kenwigs, Mrs. (Susan): Kenwigs's wife. *Quite a lady in her manners, and of a very genteel family, having an uncle who collected a water-rate; besides which distinction, the two eldest of her little girls went twice a week to a dancing-school in the neighbourhood, and had flaxen hair, tied with blue ribands, hanging in luxuriant pigtails down their backs; and wore little white trousers with frills round the ankles – for all of which reasons, and many more equally valid but too numerous to mention, Mrs. Kenwigs was considered a very desirable person to know, and was the constant theme of all the gossips in the street, and even three or four doors round the corner at both ends (Nickleby).*

Kenwigs, Morleena: The Kenwigs' eldest daughter. *Regarding whose uncommon Christian name it may be here remarked that it had been invented and composed by Mrs. Kenwigs previous to her first lying-in, for the special distinction of her eldest child, in case it should prove a daughter (Nickleby).*

Ketch, Professor John: Exhibitor of the skull of Greenacre at the umbugology and ditchwaterisics session of the second meeting of the Mudfog Association. *Remarking, on being invited to make any observations that occurred to him, 'that he'd pound it as that 'ere 'spectable section had never seed a more gamerer cove nor he vos' (Mudfog).*

Kettle, La Fayette: Secretary of the Watertoast Association of United Sympathisers whom Martin Chuzzlewit meets while travelling in America. *He was as languid and listless in his looks, as most of the gentlemen they had seen; his cheeks were so hollow that he seemed to be always sucking them in; and the sun had burnt him, not a wholesome red or brown, but dirty yellow. He had bright dark eyes, which he kept half closed; only peeping out of the corners, and even then with a glance that seemed to say, 'Now you won't overreach me : you want to, but you won't' (Chuzzlewit).*

Kibble, Jacob: Fellow-passenger of John Harmon from Cape Colony to England who gives evidence at the inquest on him. *An unctuous broad man of few words and many mouthfuls (Mutual Friend).*

Kidderminster: Childers's assistant in his riding act in Sleary's Circus. *A diminutive boy with an old face, who now accompanied him, assisted as his infant son : being carried upside down over his father's shoulder, by one foot, and held by the crown of his head, heels upwards, in the palm of his father's hand, according to the violent paternal manner in which wild huntsmen may be observed to fondle their offspring. Made up with curls, wreaths, wings, white bismuth, and carmine, this hopeful young person soared into so pleasing a Cupid as to constitute the chief delight of the maternal part of the spectators; but in private, where his characteristics were a precocious cutaway coat and an extremely gruff voice, he became of the Turf, turfy (Hard Times).*

Kidgerbury, Mrs.: One of David and Dora Copperfield's domestic trials. *The oldest inhabitant of Kentish town, I believe, who went out charing, but was too feeble to execute her conceptions of that art (Copperfield).*

Kimber: Dancing-master. A member of the Eight Club (q.v.) at Cloisterham. *A commonplace, hopeful sort of man, wholly destitute of dignity or knowledge of the world (Drood fragment).*

Kimmeens, Kitty: Pupil of Miss Pupford, whom Mr. Traveller takes to visit Tom Tiddler's Ground. *A self-helpful, steady little child is Miss Kitty Kimmeens : a dimpled child too, and a loving (Christmas Stories – 'Tom Tiddler's Ground').*

Kinch, Horace: Prisoner in the King's Bench, where he dies. *He was a likely man to look at, in the prime of life, well to* *do, as clever as he needed to be, and popular among many friends. He was suitably married, and had healthy and pretty children. But, like some fair-looking houses or fair-looking ships, he took the Dry Rot. The first strong external revelation of the Dry Rot in men, is a tendency to lurk and lounge; to be at street-corners without intelligible reason; to be going anywhere when met; to be about many places rather than at any; to do nothing tangible, but to have an intention of performing a variety of intangible duties to-morrow or the day after* (Uncommercial – 'Night Walks').

Kindheart: The Uncommercial Traveller's companion during a period of residence in Italy. *An Englishman of an amiable nature, great enthusiasm, and no discretion* (Uncommercial – 'Medicine Men of Civilisation').

King, Christian George: Pilot of the sloop *Christopher Columbus* on her arrival at Silver-Store Island, and her betrayer to the pirates. He is shot by Captain Carton. *I confess, for myself, that on that first day, if I had been captain of the Christopher Columbus, instead of private in the Royal Marines, I should have kicked Christian George King – who was no more a Christian than he was a King or a George – over the side, without exactly knowing why, except that it was the right thing to do* (Christmas Stories – 'English Prisoners').

Kitt, Miss: Girl with whom David Copperfield flirts at Dora Spenlow's birthday picnic when Red Whisker makes him jealous of Dora. *A young creature in pink, with little eyes* (Copperfield).

Kitten: Pordage's Vice-commissioner at Silver-Store Island. *A small, youngish, bald, botanical and mineralogical gentleman* (Christmas Stories – 'English Prisoners').

Kitterbell, Charles: Husband of Jemima and father of Frederick Charles William. Nephew of Nicodemus Dumps, whom he persuades, against his better judgement, to stand godfather to the child. *A small, sharp, spare man, with a very large*

head, and a broad, good-humoured countenance. He looked like a faded giant, with his head and face partially restored; and he had a cast in his eye which rendered it quite impossible for any one with whom he conversed to know where he was looking. His eyes appeared fixed on the wall, and he was staring you out of countenance. . . . In addition to these characteristics, it may be added that Mr. Charles Kitterbell was one of the most credulous and matter-of-fact little personages that ever took to himself a wife, and for himself a house in Great Russell Street, Bedford Square (Boz – 'Bloomsbury Christening').

Kitterbell, Mrs. Charles (Jemima): Kitterbell's wife, mother of Frederick Charles William. *A tall, thin young lady, with very light hair, and a particularly white face – one of those young women who almost invariably, though one hardly knows why, recall to one's mind the idea of a cold fillet of veal* (Boz – 'Bloomsbury Christening').

Kitterbell, Frederick Charles William: The Kitterbells' first baby, subject of the gloomy prognostications of his godfather, Nicodemus Dumps. *A remarkably small parcel . . . packed up in a blue mantle trimmed with white fur* (Boz – 'Bloomsbury Christening').

Klem, Miss: The Klems' daughter. *Apparently ten years older than either of them* (Uncommercial – 'Arcadian London').

Klem, Mr. and Mrs.: The woman who waits on the Uncommercial Traveller while he lodges with a Bond Street hatter, and her husband. Parents of Miss Klem. *An elderly woman labouring under a chronic sniff, who, at the shadowy hour of half-past nine o'clock of every evening, gives admittance at the street door to a meagre and mouldy old man whom I have never yet seen detached from a flat pint of beer in a pewter pot* (Uncommercial – 'Arcadian London').

Knag, Miss: Sister of Mortimer Knag. Forewoman and successor to Madam Mantalini. *A short, bustling, over-dressed female, full of importance. . . . Every now* and then, she was accustomed, in the torrent of her discourse, to introduce a loud, shrill, clear, 'hem!' the import and meaning of which, was variously interpreted by her acquaintance; some holding that Miss Knag dealt in exaggeration, and introduced the monosyllable, when any fresh invention was in course of coinage in her brain; others, that when she wanted a word, she threw it in to gain time, and prevent anybody else from striking into the conversation. It may be further remarked, that Miss Knag still aimed at youth, although she had shot beyond it, years ago; and that she was weak and vain, and one of those people who are best described by the axiom, that you may trust them as far as you can see them, and no farther (Nickleby).

Knag, Mortimer: Miss Knag's brother. A stationer and keeper of a circulating library off Tottenham Court Road. A tall lank gentleman of solemn features, wearing spectacles, and garnished with much less hair than a gentleman bordering on forty, or thereabouts, usually boasts (Nickleby).

Koëldwethout, Baron von, of Grogzwig: Hero of a tale told by a passenger of a broken-down coach in which Squeers and Nicholas Nickleby are travelling to Yorkshire. A fine swarthy fellow, with dark hair and large moustachios, who rode a-hunting in clothes of Lincoln green, with russet boots on his feet, and a bugle slung over his shoulder, like the guard of a long stage (Nickleby).

Koëldwethout, Baroness von: Koëldwethout's wife, daughter of Baron von Swillenhausen (Nickleby).

Krook, ('Lord Chancellor'): Rag-and-bone dealer and landlord to Miss Flite and Hawdon. Brother to Mrs. Smallweed. On the night that he is due to hand over to Jobling papers relating to Hawdon he disappears, leaving a room full of smoke and some ashes. He is assumed to have died by spontaneous combustion, about the possibility of which there has been much controversy since this story appeared. He was short, cadaverous, and withered; with his head sunk sideways between his shoulders, and the breath

issuing in visible smoke from his mouth, as if he were on fire within. His throat, chin and eyebrows were so frosted with white hairs, and so gnarled with veins and puckered skin, that he looked from his breast upward, like some old root in a fall of snow (Bleak House).

Kutankumagen, Dr.: Of Moscow. Speaker at the anatomy and medicine session of the first meeting of the Mudfog Association, who describes his treatment of a patient 'labouring under symptoms peculiarly alarming to any medical man' – perfect health and heartiness. By dint of powerful medicine, low diet, and bleeding, the symptoms in the course of three days perceptibly decreased. . . . At the present moment he was restored so far as to walk about, with the slight assistance of a crutch and a boy. It would perhaps be gratifying to the section to learn that he ate little, drank little, slept little, and was never heard to laugh by any accident whatever (Mudfog).

Kwakley: Speaker at the statistics session of the second meeting of the Mudfog Association. Stated the result of some most ingenious statistical inquiries relative to the difference between the value of the qualification of several members of Parliament as published to the world, and its real nature and amount (Mudfog).

La Cour, Capitaine de: Officer billeted at Madame Bouclet's (Christmas Stories – 'Somebody's Luggage').

La Creevy, Miss: A miniature painter, landlady and friend to the Nicklebys in London. She marries Tim Linkinwater. The wearer of the yellow head-dress, who had a gown to correspond, and was of much the same colour herself. Miss La Creevy was a mincing young lady of fifty (Nickleby).

Ladle, Joey: Head cellarman of Wilding and Co. He goes to Switzerland with Marguerite Obenreizer and they rescue Vendale. A slow and ponderous man, of the drayman order of human architecture, dressed in a corrugated suit and bibbed apron, apparently a composite of door-mat and rhinoceros-hide (Christmas Stories –

'No Thoroughfare' and dramatised version).

Lady Jane: Krook's cat. *A large grey cat leaped from some neighbouring shelf . . . and ripped at a bundle of rags with her tigerish claws, with a sound that it set my teeth on edge to hear. 'She'd do as much for any one I was to set her on,' said the old man. 'I deal in cat-skins among other general matters, and hers was offered to me. It's a very fine skin, as you may see, but I didn't have it stripped off!' (Bleak House).*

Lagnier: See **Rigaud** *(Dorrit)*.

Lambert, Miss: A partner of Hopkins in the quadrille. *The young lady, after several inspections of her bouquet, all made in the expectation that the bashful young gentleman is going to talk, whispers her, who is sitting next her, which whisper the bashful young gentleman immediately suspects (and possibly with very good reason) must be about him. (Young Gentlemen – 'Bashful Young Gentleman').*

Lammle, Alfred: A fortune-hunter inveigled by Veneering into marrying Sophronia Akershem in the belief that she is rich. *Too much nose in his face, too much ginger in his whiskers, too much torso in his waistcoat, too much sparkle in his studs, his eyes, his buttons, his talk, and his teeth (Mutual Friend).*

Lammle, Mrs. Alfred: See **Akershem, Sophronia** *(Mutual Friend)*.

'Lamps': Phoebe's father, employed at Mugby Junction. *'On Porter's wages, sir. But I am Lamps.' || He was a spare man of about the Barbox Brothers time of life, with his features whimsically drawn upward as if they were attracted by the roots of his hair. He had a peculiarly shining, transparent complexion, probably occasioned by constant oleaginous application; and his attractive hair, being cut short, and being grizzled, and standing straight up on end as if it in its turn were attracted by some invisible magnet above it, the top of his head was not very unlike a lamp-wick (Christmas Stories – 'Mugby Junction').*

Landless, Neville and Helena: Orphan twins from Ceylon, wards of Luke Honeythunder. Neville is coached by Crisparkle at Cloisterham, while Helena attends Miss Twinkleton's. Neville is attracted by Rosa and incurs Drood's hostility. He is arrested as Drood's suspected murderer. *An unusually handsome lithe young fellow, and an unusually handsome lithe girl; much alike; both very dark, and very rich in colour; she of almost the gypsy type; something untamed about them both; a certain air upon them of hunter and huntress; yet withal a certain air of being the objects of the chase, rather than the followers. Slender, supple, quick of eye and limb; half shy, half defiant; fierce of look; an indefinable kind of pause coming and going on their whole expression, both of face and form, which might be equally likened to the pause before a crouch or a bound (Drood).*

Landlord: Landlord of the Peal of Bells village inn who tells Mr. Traveller about Mopes. *With an asphyxiated appearance on him as one unaccustomed to definition (Christmas Stories – 'Tom Tiddler's Ground').*

Lane, Miss: Governess to the Borum children *(Nickleby)*.

Langdale: Distiller and vintner who shelters Haredale from the Gordon Rioters and has his premises ransacked and burnt. *The vintner – whose place of business was down in some deep cellars hard by Thames Street, and who was as purple-faced an old gentleman as if he had all his life supported their arched roof on his head (Rudge).*

Langley ('Mr. The Englishman'): Living misanthropically in France after disowning his daughter in England, he meets Corporal Théophile and Bebelle, and after the soldier's death adopts the child and returns to reconciliation with his daughter. *Now the Englishman, in taking his Appartement, – or, as one might say on our side of the Channel, his set of chambers, – had given his name, correct to the letter, LANGLEY. But as he had a British way of not opening his mouth very wide on foreign soil, except at meals, the Brewery* had been able to make nothing of it but *L'Anglais. So Mr. The Englishman he had become and he remained (Christmas Stories – 'Somebody's Luggage').*

'Larkey Boy, The': Prizefighter who gives the 'Game Chicken' a beating. *The Chicken himself attributed this punishment to his having had the misfortune to get into Chancery early in the proceedings, when he was severely fibbed by the Larkey One, and heavily grassed. But it appeared from the published records of that great contest that the Larkey Boy had had it all his own way from the beginning, and that the Chicken had been tapped, and bunged, and had received pepper, and had been made groggy, and had come up piping, and had endured a complication of similar strange inconveniences, until he had been gone into and finished (Dombey).*

Larkins: The eldest Miss Larkins's father. *A gruff old gentleman with a double chin, and one of his eyes immoveable in his head (Copperfield).*

Larkins, the eldest Miss: An object of David Copperfield's youthful infatuation. She marries Chestle. *The eldest Miss Larkins is not a little girl. She is a tall, dark, black-eyed, fine figure of a woman. The eldest Miss Larkins is not a chicken; for the youngest Miss Larkins is not that, and the eldest must be three or four years older. Perhaps the eldest Miss Larkins may be about thirty. . . . I picture Miss Larkins sinking her head upon my shoulder, and saying, 'Oh, Mr. Copperfield, can I believe my ears!' I picture Mr. Larkins waiting on me next morning, and saying, 'My dear Copperfield, my daughter has told me all. Youth is no objection. Here are twenty thousand pounds. Be happy!' (Copperfield).*

Larkins, Jem: Amateur actor, known as Horatio St. Julien. *That gentleman in the white hat and checked shirt, brown coat and brass buttons, lounging behind the stage-box on the O.P. side. . . . His line is genteel comedy – his father's coal and potato (Boz – 'Private Theatres').*

Latin-Grammar Master, The: Captain Boldheart's adversary, captain of the

Scorpion, in Robin Redforth's romantic tale ('Holiday Romance').

Lazarus: Brother of 'Habraham Latharuth', an arrested thief. He tries in vain to persuade Jaggers to defend the case. *I remarked this Jew, who was of a highly excitable temperament, performing a jig of anxiety under a lamp-post, and accompanying himself, in a kind of frenzy, with the words, 'Oh Jaggerth, Jaggerth, Jaggerth! all otherth ith Cag-Maggerth, give me Jaggerth!' (Expectations).*

Leath, Angela: Charley's sweetheart, and subsequent wife. *It happened in the memorable year when I parted for ever from Angela Leath, whom I was shortly to have married, on making the discovery that she preferred my bosom friend (Christmas Stories – 'Holly-Tree').*

Leaver: A vice-president of the display of models and mechanical science session at the second meeting of the Mudfog Association *(Mudfog).*

Leaver, Augustus and **Augusta:** A loving couple. *Mr. and Mrs. Leaver are pronounced by Mrs. Starling . . . to be a perfect model of wedded felicity. 'You would suppose,' says the romantic lady, 'that they were lovers only just engaged. Never was such happiness! They are so tender, so affectionate, so attached to each other, so enamoured, that positively nothing can be more charming!' (Young Couples – 'Loving Couple').*

Ledbrain, X.: Vice-president of the statistics session at the first meeting of the Mudfog Association. *Read a very ingenious communication, from which it appeared that the total number of legs belonging to the manufacturing population of one great town in Yorkshire was, in round numbers, forty thousand, while the total number of chair and stool legs in their houses was only thirty thousand, which, upon the very favourable average of three legs to a seat, yielded only ten thousand seats in all. From this calculation it would appear . . . that ten thousand individuals (one half of the whole population) were either destitute of any rest for their legs at all, or passed the whole of their leisure time in sitting upon boxes (Mudfog).*

Ledbrook, Miss: Member of Crummles's theatrical company *(Nickleby)*.

Leeford, Edward (alias **Monks**): Oliver Twist's villainous half-brother, son of Edwin Leeford. *The man who was seated there, was tall and dark, and wore a large cloak. . . . Mr. Bumble felt, every now and then, a powerful inducement, which he could not resist, to steal a look at the stranger : and that, whenever he did so, he withdrew his eyes, in some confusion, to find that the stranger was at that moment stealing a look at him. Mr. Bumble's awkwardness was enhanced by the very remarkable expression of the stranger's eye, which was keen and bright, but shadowed by a scowl of distrust and suspicion, unlike anything he had ever observed before, and repulsive to behold (Twist).*

Leeford, Edwin: Seducer of Agnes Fleming and father of Oliver Twist and Edward Leeford (alias Monks) *(Twist)*.

Lemon, Mrs.: Proprietress of a preparatory school for grown-ups in Nettie Ashford's romantic tale ('Holiday Romance').

Lenville, Thomas: Member of Crummles's theatrical company. *A dark-complexioned man, inclining indeed to sallow, with long thick black hair, and very evident indications (although he was close shaved) of a stiff beard, and whiskers of the same deep shade. His age did not appear to exceed thirty, though many at first sight would have considered him much older, as his face was long, and very pale, from the constant application of stage paint (Nickleby).*

Lenville, Mrs. Thomas: Lenville's wife, also a member of Crummles's theatrical company. *In a very limp bonnet and veil, decidedly in that way in which she would wish to be if she truly loved Mr. Lenville (Nickleby).*

Lewsome: A physician's young assistant induced by Jonas Chuzzlewit to supply poison for the attempted murder of Anthony Chuzzlewit. Mrs. Gamp, attending him in subsequent sickness, hears his delirious confession. *He was so wasted, that it seemed as if his bones would rattle when they moved him. His cheeks were sunken, and his eyes unnaturally large. He lay back in the easy-chair like one more dead than living ; and rolled his languid eyes towards the door when Mrs. Gamp appeared, as painfully as if their weight alone were burdensome to move (Chuzzlewit).*

Licensed Victualler, Mr.: Proprietor of a Liverpool sailors' 'singing-house'. *A sharp and watchful man, Mr. Licensed Victualler, the host, with tight lips and a complete edition of Cocker's arithmetic in each eye (Uncommercial –* 'Poor Mercantile Jack').

Life: One of Miss Flite's birds *(Bleak House)*.

Lightwood, Mortimer: Boffin's lawyer, much connected with the Harmon mystery. *A certain 'Mortimer', another of Veneering's oldest friends ; who never was in the house before, and appears not to want to come again, who sits disconsolate on Mrs. Veneering's left, and who was inveigled by Lady Tippins (a friend of his boyhood) to come to these people's and talk, and who won't talk (Mutual Friend).*

'Lignum Vitae': See **Bagnet, Matthew** *(Bleak House)*.

Lillerton, Miss: The spinster to whom Gabriel Parsons tries to marry off Watkins Tottle, for his own pecuniary advantage. She is already engaged to the Revd. Charles Timson, and marries him. *A lady of very prim appearance, and remarkably inanimate. She was one of those persons at whose age it is impossible to make any reasonable guess ; her features might have been remarkably pretty when she was younger, and they might always have presented the same appearance. Her complexion – with a slight trace of powder here and there – was as clear as that of a well-made wax-doll, and her face as expressive (Boz –* 'Watkins Tottle').

Lillyvick: Mrs. Kenwigs's uncle, a collector of water-rates. He marries Henrietta Petowker. *'The kindest-hearted man as ever was,' said Kenwigs. 'It goes to his heart, I believe, to be forced to cut the*

*water off, when the people don't pay,'
observed the bachelor friend (Nickleby).*

Lillyvick, Mrs.: See **Petowker, Henrietta** *(Nickleby).*

Limbkins: Chairman of the authorities of the parish in whose workhouse Oliver Twist is born. *At the top of the table, seated in an arm-chair rather higher than the rest, was a particularly fat gentleman with a very round, red face (Twist).*

Limbury, Peter and **Mrs. Peter:** Friends of the Lovetowns. Alfred Lovetown's flirtation with Mrs. Limbury infuriates Limbury but helps to restore his own wife's affection for him *(Is She His Wife?).*

Linderwood, Lieutenant: Officer commanding the Royal Marines in the sloop *Christopher Columbus (Christmas Stories – 'English Prisoners').*

Linkinwater, Miss: Tim Linkinwater's sister *(Nickleby).*

Linkinwater, Tim: The Cheeryble brothers' faithful old clerk, whom Nicholas Nickleby assists for some time. He befriends the Nickleby family and marries Miss La Creevy. *A fat, elderly, large-faced clerk, with silver spectacles and a powdered head (Nickleby).*

Linseed, Duke of: Writer of a begging letter to Boffin *(Mutual Friend).*

Linx, Miss: One of Miss Pupford's pupils who notes gentlemen's advances to her teacher at Tunbridge Wells. *A sharply observant pupil (Christmas Stories – 'Tom Tiddler's Ground').*

Lion: Henry Gowan's dog, poisoned by Rigaud. *A fine Newfoundland dog (Dorrit).*

Lirriper, Mrs. Emma: Narrator of the two stories. Keeper of a lodging-house at 81, Norfolk Street, Strand, London. She adopts, with Major Jackman, the child of Peggy Edson, who dies at her lodgings. *It was about the Lodgings that I was intending to hold forth and certainly I ought to know something of the business having been in it so long, for it was early in the second year of my married life that I*

lost my poor Lirriper and I set up at Islington directly afterwards and afterwards came here, being two houses and eight-and-thirty years and some losses and a deal of experience (Christmas Stories – 'Mrs. Lirriper's Lodgings' and 'Mrs. Lirriper's Legacy'). See also **Gran, Mrs.**

Lirriper, Jemmy Jackman: Peggy Edson's child, adopted by Mrs. Lirriper and Major Jackman after his mother's death following Edson's desertion. *We called him Jemmy, being after the Major his own godfather with Lirriper for a surname being after myself, and never was a dear child such a brightening thing in a Lodgings or such a playmate to his grandmother as Jemmy to this house and me, and always good and minding what he was told (upon the whole) (Christmas Stories – 'Mrs. Lirriper's Lodgings' and 'Mrs. Lirriper's Legacy').*

Lirriper, Dr. Joshua: Youngest brother of Mrs. Lirriper's deceased husband. *Doctor of what I am sure it would be hard to say unless Liquor, for neither Physic nor Music nor yet Law does Joshua Lirriper know a morsel of except continually being summoned to the County Court and having orders made upon him which he runs away from, and once was taken in the passage of this very house with an umbrella up and the Major's hat on, giving his name with the doormat round him as Sir Johnson Jones, K.C.B. in spectacles residing at the Horse Guards (Christmas Stories – 'Mrs. Lirriper's Legacy').*

List, Isaac: A gambler who fleeces Little Nell's grandfather and then induces him to rob Mrs. Jarley. *Stooping, and high in the shoulders – with a very ill-favoured face, and a most sinister and villainous squint (Curiosity Shop).*

Lithers, Thomas: Landlord of the Water-Lily Hotel at Malvern, the setting of the farce *(Nightingale's Diary).*

Littimer: Steerforth's manservant. He assists his master to elope with Little Em'ly and is offered her when Steerforth tires of her. Miss Mowcher reveals him to be a thief and he is transported. *He was* *taciturn, soft-footed, very quiet in his manner, deferential, observant, always at hand when wanted, and never near when not wanted; but his great claim to consideration was his respectability. . . . Nobody could have thought of putting him in a livery, he was so highly respectable. To have imposed any derogatory work upon him, would have been to inflict a wanton insult on the feelings of a most respectable man. And of this, I noticed the women-servants in the household were so intuitively conscious, that they always did such work themselves, and generally while he read the paper by the pantry fire (Copperfield).*

Little Dorrit: See Dorrit, Amy *(Dorrit).*

Little Em'ly: See Em'ly, Little *(Copperfield).*

Little Nell: See Trent, Nell *(Curiosity Shop).*

Lively: Receiver of stolen goods on Saffron Hill, from whom Fagin inquires Bill Sikes's whereabouts. *A salesman of small stature, who had squeezed as much of his person into a child's chair as the chair would hold (Twist).*

Liz: A brickmaker's wife, friend of Jenny *(Bleak House).*

Lobbs, Maria: The object of Nathaniel Pipkin's affections in Sam Weller's tale of 'The Parish Clerk'. She is cousin to Kate and also to Henry, whom she marries. *'A prettier foot, a gayer heart, a more dimpled face, or a smarter form, never bounded so lightly over the earth they graced, as did those of Maria Lobbs, the old saddler's daughter. There was a roguish twinkle in her sparkling eyes . . . and there was such a joyous sound in her merry laugh, that the sternest misanthrope must have smiled to hear it' (Pickwick).*

Lobbs, Old: The fiery father of Maria. *'Old Lobbs the great saddler, who could have bought up the whole village at one stroke of his pen, and never felt the outlay . . . old Lobbs, who it was well known, on festive occasions garnished his board with a real silver tea-pot, cream-ewer, and*

sugar-basin, which he was wont, in the pride of his heart, to boast should be his daughter's property when she found a man to her mind' (Pickwick).

Lobley: Ex-seaman. Tartar's man and boatman. *A jolly-favoured man, with tawny hair and whiskers, and a big red face. He was the dead image of the sun in old woodcuts, his hair and whiskers answering for rays all around him (Drood).*

Lobskini, Signor: Singing-master at the Misses Crumpton's. *The splendid tenor of the inimitable Lobskini (Boz – 'Sentiment').*

Loggins: Amateur actor, known as Beverley, who plays Macbeth *(Boz – 'Private Theatres').*

Long Eers, The Hon. and Revd.: Member of the Mudfog Association *(Mudfog).*

Longford, Edmund: See Denham, Edmund *(Christmas Books – 'Haunted Man').*

'Lord Chancellor': Krook's neighbours' nickname for him. His shop is called the Court of Chancery *(Bleak House).*

Lord Mayor, The: Lord Mayor of London during the Gordon Riots. The real-life incumbent of the office was the incompetent Alderman Kennet, a waiter turned vintner. *'I'm sure I don't know what's to be done. – There are great people at the bottom of these riots. – Oh dear me, what a thing it is to be a public character!' (Rudge).*

Lord Mayor Elect, The: Wholesale fruiterer, alderman, Sheriff, member of the worshipful Company of Pattenmakers, and subject of the Deaf Gentleman's narrative. *He was a very substantial citizen indeed. His face was like the full moon in a fog, with two little holes punched out for his eyes, a very ripe pear stuck on for his nose, and a wide gash to serve for a mouth. The girth of his waistcoat was hung up and lettered in his tailor's shop as an extraordinary curiosity. He breathed like a heavy snorer, and his voice in speaking came thickly forth, as if it were oppressed and stifled by feather-beds.*

He trod the ground like an elephant, and eat and drank like – like nothing but an alderman, as he was (Humphrey).

Lorn: Dr. Speddie's assistant, who may have been the revived 'corpse' from the story told by Speddie to Goodchild. *He was at least two-and-fifty; but, that was nothing. What was startling in him was his remarkable paleness. His large black eyes, his sunken cheeks, his long and heavy iron-grey hair, his wasted hands, and even the attenuation of his figure, were at first forgotten in his extraordinary pallor. There was no vestige of colour in the man (Two Apprentices).*

Lorry, Jarvis: Confidential clerk at Tellson's Bank who brings Dr. Manette back to England after his long imprisonment in the Bastille. *He wore an odd little sleek crisp flaxen wig, setting very close to his head : which wig, it is to be presumed, was made of hair, but which looked far more as though it were spun from filaments of silk or glass. . . . A face habitually suppressed and quieted, was still lighted up under the quaint wig by a pair of moist bright eyes that it must have cost their owner, in years gone by, some pains to drill to the composed and reserved expression of Tellson's Bank. He had a healthy colour in his cheeks, and his face, though lined, bore few traces of anxiety (Two Cities).*

Losberne, Mr.: Surgeon, friend to the Maylies, who treats the shot Oliver Twist and helps save him from arrest. *Known throughout a circuit of ten miles round as 'the doctor', had grown fat, more from good-humour than from good living ; and was as kind and hearty, and withal as eccentric an old bachelor, as will be found in five times that space, by any explorer alive (Twist).*

Louis: Murderer whose arrest was witnessed by the narrator at a Swiss inn (*Christmas Stories* – 'Holly-Tree').

Louis: A servant of the Uncommercial Traveller while visiting France. *A bright face looked in at the window (Uncommercial* – 'Travelling Abroad').

Louisa: See **Charles** and **Louisa** (*Young Couples* – 'Cool Couple').

Lovetown, Alfred and Mrs. Alfred: A young married couple who re-stimulate affection for one another by arousing mutual jealousy, Alfred flirting with Mrs. Limbury and his wife with Felix Tapkins (*Is She His Wife?*).

Lowfield, Miss: An admirer of Caveton. *A young lady who, truth to tell, is rather smitten with the throwing-off young gentleman* (*Young Gentlemen* – ' "Throwing-off" Young Gentleman').

Lowten: Perker's clerk, and *habitué* of the Magpie and Stump. *A puffy-faced young man (Pickwick).*

Loyal Devasseur, Monsieur: The narrator's landlord during his sojourns in France. *We doubt if there is, ever was, or ever will be, a man so universally pleasant in the minds of people as M. Loyal is in the minds of the citizens of our French watering-place. They rub their hands and laugh when they speak of him. Ah, but he is such a good child, such a brave boy, such a generous spirit, that Monsieur Loyal ! . . . A portly, upright, broad-shouldered, brown-faced man, whose soldierly bearing gives him the appearance of being taller than he is, look into the bright eye of M. Loyal, standing before you in his working-blouse and cap, not particularly well shaved, and, it may be, very earthy, and you shall discern in M. Loyal a gentleman whose true politeness is ingrain, and confirmation of whose word by his bond you would blush to think of (Reprinted* – 'Our French Watering-place').

Lucas, Solomon: Jewish theatrical costumier patronised by the Pickwickians for Mrs. Leo Hunter's fancy dress breakfast at Eatanswill. *His wardrobe was extensive – very extensive – not strictly classical perhaps, nor quite new, nor did it contain any one garment made precisely after the fashion of any age or time, but everything was more or less spangled ; and what can be prettier than spangles ! (Pickwick).*

Luffey: Leading player of Dingley Dell Cricket Club. *The highest ornament of Dingley Dell (Pickwick).*

Lumbey, Dr.: Mrs. Kenwigs's attendant at her last confinement. *Doctor Lumbey was popular, and the neighbourhood was prolific; and there had been no less than three other knockers muffled, one after the other, within the last forty-eight hours (Nickleby).*

Lummy Ned: Former guard of the Light Salisbury coach whose example in emigrating to America, recounted by William Simmons, inspires young Martin Chuzzlewit to follow suit *(Chuzzlewit).*

Lupin, Mrs.: Landlady of the Blue Dragon, near Salisbury, where Mark Tapley is ostler before joining Martin Chuzzlewit on his travels. When Mark returns he marries her and the inn is renamed The Jolly Tapley. *Just what a landlady should be: broad, buxom, comfortable, and good-looking, with a face of clear red and white, which, by its jovial aspect, at once bore testimony to her hearty participation in the good things of the larder and cellar, and to their thriving and healthful influences. She was a widow, but years ago had passed through her state of weeds, and burst into flower again (Chuzzlewit).*

Mac Coorts of Mac Coort: Great Highland family from which Mrs. Woodcourt states her late husband was descended *(Bleak House).*

Macey, Mr. and Mrs.: Marion Maryon's sister and her husband, residents of Silver-Store Island (*Christmas Stories – 'English Prisoners'*).

M'Choakumchild: Teacher in Gradgrind's school. *He and some one hundred and forty other schoolmasters, had been lately turned at the same time, in the same factory, on the same principles, like so many pianoforte legs. He had been put through an immense variety of paces, and had answered volumes of head-breaking questions. Orthography, etymology, syntax, and prosody, biography, astronomy, geography, and general cosmography, the sciences of compound proportion, algebra, land-surveying and levelling, vocal music, and drawing from models, were all at the ends of his ten chilled fingers. . . . If only he had learnt a little less, how infinitely* better he might have taught much more *(Hard Times).*

Mackin, Mrs.: Pawnbroker's customer. *A slipshod woman, with two flat-irons in a little basket (Boz – 'Pawnbroker's Shop').*

Macklin, Walker, and Pelow, Mesdames: London suburban housewives. *In the suburbs, the muffin-boy rings his way down the little street, much more slowly than he is wont to do; for Mrs. Macklin, of No. 4, has no sooner opened her little street-door, and screamed out 'Muffins!' with all her might, than Mrs. Walker, at No. 5, puts her head out of the parlour-window, and screams 'Muffins!' too; and Mrs. Walker has scarcely got the words out of her lips, than Mrs. Peplow, over the way, lets loose, Master Peplow, who darts down the street, with a velocity which nothing but buttered muffins in perspective could possibly inspire, and drags the boy back by main force (Boz – 'The Streets – Night').*

MacStinger, Mrs.: Captain Cuttle's domineering landlady at 9 Brig Place, India Docks. When her matrimonial intentions become too apparent he escapes, but she tracks him down and he is only rescued when Captain Bunsby makes himself her ultimate sacrifice. *A widow lady, with her sleeves rolled up to her shoulders, and her arms frothy with soap-suds and smoking with hot water (Dombey).*

MacStinger, Alexander: Mrs. MacStinger's younger son. *Alexander being black in the face with holding his breath after punishment, and a cool paving-stone being usually found to act as a powerful restorative in such cases (Dombey).*

MacStinger, Charles: Mrs. MacStinger's elder son. *Popularly known about the scenes of his youthful sports, as Chowley (Dombey).*

MacStinger, Juliana: Mrs. MacStinger's daughter. *One of the most frightful circumstances of the ceremony to the captain, was the deadly interest exhibited therein by Juliana MacStinger; and the fatal concentration of her faculties, with which that promising child, already the* *image of her parent, observed the whole proceedings. The captain saw in this a succession of man-traps stretching out infinitely; a series of ages of oppression and coercion, through which the seafaring line was doomed (Dombey).*

Maddox, John: Farm labourer, sweetheart of Rose *(Village Coquettes).*

Madgers, Winifred: One of Mrs. Lirriper's succession of maids. *She was what is termed a Plymouth Sister, and the Plymouth Brother that made away with her was quite right, for a tidier young woman for a wife never came into a house and afterwards called with the beautifullest Plymouth Twins (Christmas Stories – 'Mrs. Lirriper's Legacy').*

Madman, The: Author of the manuscript, lent to Pickwick by the clergyman at Dingley Dell, which frightens him when he reads it alone in his bedroom. *'I knew that madness was mixed up with my very blood, and the marrow of my bones; that one generation had passed away without the pestilence appearing among them, and that I was the first in whom it would revive. I knew it must be so: that so it always had been, and so it ever would be: and when I cowered in some obscure corner of a crowded room, and saw men whisper, and point, and turn their eyes towards me, I knew they were telling each other of the doomed madman; and I slunk away again to mope in solitude' (Pickwick).*

Madness: One of Miss Flite's birds *(Bleak House).*

Magg: Vestryman, of Little Winkling Street. *One of our first orators (Reprinted – 'Our Vestry').*

Maggy: Mrs. Bangham's granddaughter, befriended by Amy Dorrit and later employed by Mrs. Plornish. *She was about eight-and-twenty, with large bones, large features, large feet and hands, large eyes and no hair. Her large eyes were limpid and almost colourless; they seemed to be very little affected by light, and to stand unnaturally still. There was also that attentive listening expression in her face, which is seen in the faces of the blind; but she was not blind, having one tolerably serviceable eye. Her face was not exceedingly ugly, though it was only redeemed from being so by a smile; a good-humoured smile, and pleasant in itself, but rendered pitiable by being constantly there. A great white cap, with a quantity of opaque frilling that was always flapping about, apologised for Maggy's baldness, and made it so very difficult for her old black bonnet to retain its place upon her head that it held on round her neck like a gipsy's baby. A commission of haberdashers could alone have reported what the rest of her poor dress was made of; but it had a strong general resemblance to seaweed, with here and there a gigantic tea-leaf. Her shawl looked particularly like a tea-leaf, after long infusion (Dorrit).*

Magnus, Peter: Traveller with Pickwick in a coach to Ipswich, where Magnus is to propose to Miss Witherfield. Pickwick enters her bedroom by mistake that night and he and his friends are denounced by Magnus next day and arrested. *A red-haired man with an inquisitive nose and blue spectacles . . . who was an important-looking, sharp-nosed, mysterious-spoken personage, with a bird-like habit of giving his head a jerk every time he said anything (Pickwick).*

Magog: See **Gog and Magog** *(Humphrey).*

Magsman, Robert (Toby): Narrator of the story, a showman. *A Grizzled Personage in velveteen, with a face so cut up by varieties of weather that he looked as if he had been tattooed (Christmas Stories – 'Going into Society').*

Magwitch, Abel (alias **Provis**, alias **Campbell**): An escaped convict; grateful to Pip for befriending him, he returns secretly from Australia, a rich man, to reveal himself as Pip's secret benefactor. It emerges that he is the father of Estella by Molly. Trying to escape the country again, he drowns his betrayer, Compeyson, is sentenced to death, but dies in prison. The fortune he had intended for Pip goes to the Crown. *A fearful man, all in coarse grey, with a great iron on his leg. A man with no hat, and with broken* shoes, and with an old rag tied round his head. *A man who had been soaked in water, and smothered in mud, and lamed by stones, and cut by flints, and stung by nettles, and torn by briars; who limped and shivered, and glared and growled; and whose teeth chattered in his head as he seized me by the chin (Expectations).*

Malderton: Father of Thomas, Frederick, Teresa and Marianne. A *nouveau riche* City man who entertains Horatio Sparkins at his Camberwell home, believing him to be a notability. *A man whose whole scope of ideas was limited to Lloyd's, the Exchange, the India House, and the Bank. A few successful speculations had raised him from a situation of obscurity and comparative poverty, to a state of affluence. As frequently happens in such cases, the ideas of himself and his family became elevated to an extraordinary pitch as their means increased; they affected fashion, taste, and many other fooleries, in imitation of their betters, and had a very decided and becoming horror of anything which could, by possibility, be considered low. He was hospitable from ostentation, illiberal from ignorance, and prejudiced from conceit. Egotism and the love of display induced him to keep an excellent table: convenience, and a love of good things of this life, ensured him plenty of guests. He liked to have clever men, or what he considered such, at his table, because it was a great thing to talk about* (Boz – 'Horatio Sparkins').

Malderton, Mrs.: Malderton's wife, mother of Thomas, Frederick, Teresa, and Marianne. Sister of Jacob Barton. *A little fat woman* (Boz – 'Horatio Sparkins').

Malderton, Frederick: The Maldertons' elder son, brother of Thomas, Teresa, and Marianne. *In full-dress costume, was the very beau ideal of a smart waiter* (Boz – 'Horatio Sparkins').

Malderton, Marianne: The Maldertons' younger daughter, sister to Teresa, Frederick, and Thomas. *Engaged in netting a purse, and looking sentimental* (Boz – 'Horatio Sparkins').

Malderton, Teresa: The Maldertons' elder daughter, sister to Marianne, Frederick, and Thomas. *A very little girl, rather fat, with vermilion cheeks, but good-humoured, and still disengaged, although, do do her justice, the misfortune arose from no lack of perseverance on her part. In vain had she flirted for ten years; in vain had Mr. and Mrs. Malderton assiduously kept up an extensive acquaintance among the young eligible bachelors of Camberwell, and even of Wandsworth and Brixton; to say nothing of those who 'dropped in' from town* (Boz – 'Horatio Sparkins').

Malderton, Thomas: The Maldertons' younger son, brother to Frederick, Teresa, and Marianne. *With his white dress-stock, blue coat, bright buttons, and red watch-ribbon, strongly resembled the portrait of that interesting, but rash young gentleman, George Barnwell* (Boz – 'Horatio Sparkins').

Maldon, Jack: Mrs. Strong's cousin and admirer, who precipitates her temporary estrangement from her husband. *Mr. Jack Maldon shook hands with me; but not very warmly, I believed; and with an air of languid patronage, at which I secretly took great umbrage. But his languor altogether was quite a wonderful sight; except when he addressed himself to his cousin Annie (Copperfield).*

Mallard: Serjeant Snubbin's clerk. *An elderly clerk, whose sleek appearance, and heavy gold watch-chain, presented imposing indications of the extensive and lucrative practice of Mr. Serjeant Snubbin (Pickwick).*

Mallet: President of the display of models and mechanical science session at the second meeting of the Mudfog Association *(Mudfog).*

'Man from Shropshire, The': See **Gridley** *(Bleak House).*

Manette, Dr. Alexandre: Father of Lucie. Confined in the Bastille for eighteen years before the Revolution, then reunited with his daughter in London. The unwitting instrument of Darnay's condemnation to death. *He had a white beard, raggedly cut, but not very* long, a hollow face, and exceedingly bright eyes. The hollowness and thinness of his face would have caused them to look large, under his yet dark eyebrows and his confused white hair, though they had been really otherwise; but, they were naturally large, and looked unnaturally so. His yellow rags of shirt lay open at the throat, and showed his body to be withered and worn. He, and his old canvas frock, and his loose stockings, and all his poor tatters of clothes, had, in a long seclusion from direct light and air, faded down to such a dull uniformity of parchment-yellow, that it would have been hard to say which was which (Two Cities).

Manette, Lucie: Dr. Manette's daughter, loved by Sydney Carton; but she marries Charles Darnay, who is later saved from execution by Carton. His eyes rested on a short, slight, pretty figure, a quantity of golden hair, and pair of blue eyes that met his own with an inquiring look, and a forehead with a singular capacity (remembering how young and smooth it was), of lifting and knitting itself into an expression that was not quite one of perplexity, or wonder, or alarm, or merely of a bright fixed attention, though it included all the four expressions (Two Cities).

Mann, Mrs.: Matron of the branch workhouse where Oliver Twist lives until he is nine. The elderly female was a woman of wisdom and experience; she knew what was good for children; and she had a very accurate perception of what was good for herself. So, she appropriated the greater part of the weekly stipend to her own use, and consigned the rising parochial generation to even a shorter allowance than was originally provided for them. Thereby finding in the lowest depth a deeper still; and proving herself a very great experimental philosopher (Twist).

Manners, Julia: A wealthy spinster who elopes with Alexander Trott, mistaking him for her suitor, Lord Peter, and likes him enough to marry him. A buxom richly-dressed female of about forty (Boz – 'Great Winglebury Duel'). In the dramatised version, The Strange Gentleman, she is renamed Julia Dobbs.

Manning, Sir Geoffrey: One of Wardle's neighbouring landowners, on whose ground the shooting party takes place (Pickwick).

Mantalini, Alfred: An idler, philanderer and spendthrift, constantly sponging upon his wife, whom he bankrupts. His name was originally Muntle; but it had been converted, by an easy transition, into Mantalini: the lady rightly considering that an English appellation would be of serious injury to the business. He had married on his whiskers; upon which property he had previously subsisted, in a genteel manner, for some years; and which he had recently improved, after patient cultivation, by the addition of a moustache, which promised to secure him an easy independence: his share in the labours of the business being at present confined to spending the money (Nickleby).

Mantalini, Madame Alfred: A fashionable dressmaker in the West End of London, married to Mantalini, whose extravagance bankrupts her. A buxom person, handsomely dressed and rather good-looking, but much older than the gentleman in the Turkish trousers, whom she had wedded some six months before (Nickleby).

Maplesone, Mrs.: Mother of Matilda and Julia. She and her daughters come to board at Mrs. Tibbs's, where all are courted by the male boarders. Mrs. Maplesone successfully sues her beau, Calton, for a thousand pounds for breach of promise. An enterprising widow of about fifty; shrewd, scheming, and good-looking. She was amiably anxious on behalf of her daughters; in proof whereof she used to remark, that she would have no objection to marry again, if it would benefit her dear girls – she could have no other motive (Boz – 'Boarding-House').

Maplesone, Matilda and Julia: Elder and younger daughters of Mrs. Maplesone. Matilda marries Septimus Hicks, but is deserted by him; Julia marries Simpson, and deserts him. The 'dear girls' themselves were not at all insensible to the merits of 'a good establishment'. One of them was twenty-five; the other, three years younger. They had been at different watering-places, for four seasons; they had gambled at libraries, read books in balconies, sold at fancy fairs, danced at assemblies, talked sentiment – in short, they had done all that industrious girls could do – but, as yet, to no purpose (Boz – 'Boarding-House').

'Marchioness, The': The Brass family's ill-treated maidservant. Since she has no given name, Dick Swiveller calls her Sophronia Sphynx. He educates her, and eventually marries her. *A small slip-shod girl in a dirty coarse apron and bib, which left nothing of her visible but her face and feet. She might as well have been dressed in a violin-case (Curiosity Shop).*

Margaret: Winkle senior's maidservant *(Pickwick).*

Margaret, Aunt: Guest at Christmas dinner. *Grandmamma draws herself up, rather stiff and stately; for Margaret married a poor man without her consent, and poverty not being a sufficiently weighty punishment for her offence, has been discarded by her friends, and debarred the society of her dearest relatives (Boz –* 'Christmas Dinner').

Marigold, Dr.: The narrator, a cheap-jack showman. After the death of his daughter Sophy he adopts another Sophy (q.v.), who is deaf and dumb, and teaches her to help him. *I am at present a middle-aged man of a broadish build, in cords, leggings, and a sleeved waistcoat the strings of which is always gone behind. . . . I am partial to a white hat, and I like a shawl round my neck wore loose and easy, Sitting down is my favourite posture. If I have a taste in point of personal jewelry, it is mother-of-pearl buttons (Christmas Stories –* 'Doctor Marigold').

Marigold, Mrs.: Marigold's Suffolk-born wife, mother of Sophy, whom she ill-treats. She drowns herself. *She wasn't a bad wife, but she had a temper. If she could have parted with that one article at a sacrifice, I wouldn't have swopped her away in exchange for any other woman in England. Not that I ever did swop her*

away, for we lived together till she died, and that was thirteen year (Christmas Stories – 'Doctor Marigold').

Marigold, Little Sophy: Marigold's own daughter, ill-treated by his wife. She dies of fever, still a child. *She had a wonderful quantity of shining dark hair, all curling natural about her. It is quite astonishing to me now, that I didn't go tearing mad when I used to see her run from her mother before the cart, and her mother catch her by this hair, and pull her down by it, and beat her. . . . Yet in other respects her mother took great care of her. Her clothes were always clean and neat, and her mother was never tired of working at 'em. Such is the inconsistency in things (Christmas Stories –* 'Doctor Marigold').

Marigold, Willum: Dr. Marigold's late father. *Had been a lovely one in his time at the Cheap Jack work (Christmas Stories –* 'Doctor Marigold').

Marker, Mrs.: Client of the General Agency Office. ' "Mrs. Marker," ' said Tom, reading, ' "Russell Place, Russell Square; offers eighteen guineas; tea and sugar found. Two in family, and see very little company. Five servants kept. No man. No followers" ' (Nickleby).

Markham: Friend of Steerforth; guest at David Copperfield's first bachelor dinner at Adelphi. *He said it was no derogation from a man's dignity to confess that I was a devilish good fellow (Copperfield).*

Markleham, Mrs. ('The Old Soldier'): Annie Strong's mother. *Our boys used to call her the Old Soldier, on account of her generalship, and the skill with which she marshalled great forces of relations against the Doctor. She was a little, sharp-eyed woman, who used to wear, when she was dressed, one unchangeable cap, ornamented with some artificial flowers, and two artificial butterflies supposed to be hovering above the flowers (Copperfield).*

Marks, Will: John Podgers's nephew, hero of the dangerous adventures of Mr. Pickwick's tale. *A wild, roving young fellow of twenty who had been brought up* *in his uncle's house and lived there still, – that is to say, when he was at home, which was not as often as it might have been (Humphrey).*

Marley, Jacob: Scrooge's deceased partner, whose ghost visits him on Christmas Eve to warn him of the consequences of misanthropy. *Marley in his pigtail, usual waistcoat, tights and boots; the tassels on the latter bristling, like his pig-tail, and his coat-skirts, and the hair upon his head. The chain he drew was clasped about his middle. It was long, and wound about him like a tail; and it was made (for Scrooge observed it closely) of cash boxes, keys, padlocks, ledgers, deeds, and heavy purses wrought in steel. His body was transparent; so that Scrooge, observing him, and looking through his waistcoat, could see the two buttons on his coat behind (Christmas Books* – 'Christmas Carol').

Maroon, Captain: Creditor of Edward Dorrit. *A gentleman with tight drab legs, a rather old hat, a little hooked stick, and a blue neckerchief (Dorrit).*

Marshall, the Misses: Acquaintances of Fairfax (*Young Gentlemen* – 'Censorious Young Gentleman').

Marshall, Mary: Richard Doubledick's fiancée, eventually wife. *Slowly labouring, at last, through a long, heavy dream of confused time and place, presenting faint glimpses of army surgeons whom he knew, and of faces that had been familiar to his youth, – dearest and kindest among them, Mary Marshall's, with a solicitude upon it more like reality than anything he could discern, – Lieutenant Richard Doubledick came back to life (Christmas Stories* – 'Seven Poor Travellers').

Martha: The Parsonses' servant who had helped bring her master and mistress together (*Boz* – 'Watkins Tottle').

Martha: Daughter of John, the riverside labourer. *Ugly, misshapen, peevish, ill-conditioned, ragged, dirty – but beloved! (Dombey).*

Martha: Workhouse inmate who attends Agnes Fleming in giving birth to Oliver Twist. *Her body was bent by age; her limbs trembled with palsy; her face, distorted into a mumbling leer, resembled more the grotesque shaping of some wild pencil, than the work of Nature's hand (Twist).*

Martha, Aunt: Dr. Jeddler's sister, with whom Marion takes refuge when she pretends to have eloped (*Christmas Books* – 'Battle of Life').

Martin: A gamekeeper at Dingley Dell. *A tall rawboned gamekeeper (Pickwick).*

Martin: Ben Allen's aunt's coachman. *A surly-looking man with his legs dressed like the legs of a groom, and his body attired in the coat of a coachman (Pickwick).*

Martin, Captain: Former prisoner in the Marshalsea, who had encouraged his sister to accept attentions from the son of Jackson, a turnkey, an invented example held up by William Dorrit to Amy to influence her in favour of young John Chivery. *'Captain Martin (highly respected in the army) then unhesitatingly said, that it appeared to him that his – hem! – sister was not called upon to understand the young man too distinctly, and that she might lead him on . . . on her father's – I should say, brother's – account' (Dorrit).*

Martin, Miss: Cashier at the coffeehouse where Christopher works. *Miss Martin is the young lady at the bar as makes out our bills; and though higher than I could wish considering her station, is perfectly well-behaved (Christmas Stories* – 'Somebody's Luggage').

Martin, Amelia: Milliner and dressmaker with misplaced ambitions as a singer. *Pale, tallish, thin, and two-and-thirty – what ill-natured people would call plain, and police reports interesting (Boz* – 'Mistaken Milliner').

Martin, Betsy: The Stargazer family's servant. Believing he has only weeks to live, Tom Grig agrees to marry her, but hastily changes his mind on learning that he will live to a ripe old age (*Lamplighter*, and its short story version).

Martin, Betsy: Convert reported to the committee of the Brick Lane Branch of the United Grand Junction Ebenezer

Temperance Association. *Widow, one child, and one eye. Goes out charing and washing, by the day; never had more than one eye, but knows her mother drank bottled stout, and shouldn't wonder if that caused it (immense cheering). Thinks it not impossible that if she had always abstained from spirits, she might have had two eyes by this time (tremendous applause) (Pickwick).*

Martin, Jack: The Bagman's uncle, central figure of the story of that name. *'In personal appearance, my uncle was a trifle shorter than the middle size; he was a thought stouter too, than the ordinary run of people, and perhaps his face might be a shade redder. He had the jolliest face you ever saw, gentlemen: something like Punch, with a handsomer nose and chin; his eyes were always twinkling and sparkling with good humour; and a smile – not one of your unmeaning wooden grins, but a real, merry, hearty, good-tempered smile – was perpetually on his countenance. He was pitched out of his gig once, and knocked, head first, against a mile-stone. . . . I have heard my uncle say, many a time, that the man said who picked him up that he was smiling as merrily as if he had tumbled out for a treat, and that after they had bled him, the first faint glimmerings of returning animation, were, his jumping up in bed, bursting out into a loud laugh, kissing the young woman who held the basin, and demanding a mutton chop and a pickled walnut. He was very fond of pickled walnuts, gentlemen. He said he always found that, taken without vinegar, they relished the beer' (Pickwick).*

Martin, Tom: A fellow prisoner of Pickwick in the Fleet. *A gentleman prematurely broad for his years: clothed in a professional blue jean frock, and top-boots with circular toes (Pickwick).*

Martin Family: Friends of Mincin (*Young Gentlemen* – 'Very Friendly Young Gentleman').

Marton: A village schoolmaster who befriends Little Nell and her grandfather during their wanderings. *He had a kind face. In his plain old suit of black, he looked pale and meagre. They fancied, too,*

a lonely air about him and his house, but perhaps that was because the other people formed a merry company upon the green, and he seemed the only solitary man in all the place (Curiosity Shop).

Marwood, Alice: Alias of Alice Brown, daughter of 'Good Mrs. Brown' and discarded mistress of James Carker. She returns to England from transportation for theft, bent on revenge. *A solitary woman of some thirty years of age; tall; well-formed; handsome; miserably dressed. . . . As her hands, parting on her sun-burnt forehead, swept across her face, and threw aside the hindrances that encroached upon it, there was a reckless and regardless beauty in it: a dauntless and depraved indifference to more than weather: a carelessness of what was cast upon her bare head from heaven or earth (Dombey).*

Mary: Nupkins's housemaid, with whom Sam Weller falls in love on sight. She helps bring Winkle and Arabella Allen together and enters their service, but is eventually married to Sam and made Pickwick's housekeeper. *'Your master's a knowin' hand, and has just sent me to the right place,' said Mr. Weller, with a glance of admiration at Mary. 'If I wos master o' this here house, I should always find the materials for comfort vere Mary wos' (Pickwick).*

Mary: One of the two daughters of John, the narrator. *Comfortable in her circumstances, but water on the chest (Reprinted – 'Poor Man's Tale of a Patent').*

Mary Anne: A young woman presiding over the gambling at Ramsgate library (*Boz* – 'Tuggses at Ramsgate').

Mary Anne: Wemmick's maidservant. *A neat little girl (Expectations).*

Mary Anne: Miss Peecher's favourite pupil and household assistant. *The pupil had been, in her state of pupilage, so imbued with the class-custom of stretching out an arm, as if to hail a cab or omnibus, whenever she found she had an observation on hand to offer to Miss Peecher, that she often did it in their domestic relations (Mutual Friend).*

Mary and Sarah: Residents of Seven Dials who fight in the street. *A little crowd has collected round a couple of ladies, who having imbibed the contents of various 'three-outs' of gin-and-bitters in the course of the morning, have at length differed on some point of domestic arrangement, and are on the eve of settling the quarrel satisfactorily, by an appeal to blows (Boz – 'Seven Dials').*

Maryon, Captain: Captain of the sloop *Christopher Columbus.* Brother of Marion Maryon. *Brave and bold (Christmas Stories – 'English Prisoners').*

Maryon, Marion: Captain Maryon's sister, living on Silver-Store Island. Gill Davies loves and protects her, but she marries Captain Carton. *Marion Maryon. Many a time have I run off those two names in my thoughts, like a bit of verse. Oh many, and many a time! (Christmas Stories – 'English Prisoners').*

Mask, The: Masked cavalier who meets Will Marks near Putney and orders him to take a corpse to London, in Mr, Pickwick's tale. *A man pretty far advanced in life, but of a firm and stately carriage. His dress was of a rich and costly kind, but so soiled and disordered that it was scarcely to be recognised for one of those gorgeous suits which the expensive taste and fashion of the time prescribed for men of any rank or station (Humphrey).*

Matinter, the two Misses: Ladies at the ball at Bath Assembly Rooms. *Being single and singular, paid great court to the Master of the Ceremonies, in the hope of getting a stray partner now and then (Pickwick).*

Matron: The superintendent of Watts's Charity, where the Six Poor Travellers lodge. *A decent body, of a wholesome matronly appearance (Christmas Stories – 'Seven Poor Travellers').*

Maunders: An old showman, subject of a reminiscence by Vuffin. *'I remember the time when old Maunders had in his cottage in Spa Fields in the winter time, when the season was over, eight male and female dwarfs setting down to dinner every day, who was waited on by eight old giants in green coats, red smalls, blue cotton stockings, and high-lows' (Curiosity Shop).*

Mawls, Master: Fellow pupil of the narrator at Our School. *Generally speaking, we may observe that whenever we see a child intently occupied with its nose, to the exclusion of all other subjects of interest, our mind reverts, in a flash, to Master Mawls (Reprinted – 'Our School').*

Maxby: Fellow pupil of the narrator at Our School, rumoured to be favoured because the usher was 'sweet upon' one of his sisters *(Reprinted – 'Our School').*

Maxey, Caroline: One of Mrs. Lirriper's succession of servants. *A good-looking black-eyed girl was Caroline and a comely-made girl to your cost when she did break out and laid about her (Christmas Stories – 'Mrs. Lirriper's Lodgings').*

Mayday: Friend of the Uncommercial Traveller who gives daunting birthday parties. *The guests have no knowledge of one another except on that one day in the year, and are annually terrified for a week by the prospect of meeting one another again (Uncommercial – 'Birthday Celebrations').*

Maylie, Mrs.: Mother of Harry, adoptive aunt of Rose. She befriends Oliver Twist after he has been shot helping Bill Sikes to burgle her house at Chertsey. *Well advanced in years; but the high-backed oaken chair in which she sat, was not more upright than she. Dressed with the utmost nicety and precision, in a quaint mixture of by-gone costume, and some slight concessions to the prevailing taste, which rather served to point the old style pleasantly than to impair its effect, she sat, in a stately manner, with her hands folded on the table before her (Twist).*

Maylie, Harry: Mrs. Maylie's clergyman son. Marries Rose Maylie. *He seemed about five-and-twenty years of age, and was of the middle height; his countenance was frank and handsome; and his demeanour easy and prepossessing (Twist).*

Maylie, Rose: Adopted niece of Mrs. Maylie, she is really Rose Fleming, sister of Oliver Twist's deceased mother and a victim of the machinations of Monks. She marries Harry Maylie. *In the lovely bloom and springtime of womanhood; at that age, when, if ever angels be for God's good purposes enthroned in mortal forms, they may be, without impiety, supposed to abide in such as hers. She was not past seventeen. Cast in so slight and exquisite a mould; so mild and gentle; so pure and beautiful; that earth seemed not her element, nor its rough creatures her fit companions. The very intelligence that shone in her deep blue eye, and was stamped upon her noble head, seemed scarcely of her age, or of the world; and yet the changing expression of sweetness and good humour, the thousand lights that played about the face, and left no shadow there; above all, the smile, the cheerful, happy smile, were made for Home, and fireside peace and happiness (Twist).*

Meagles: Minnie's father, a retired banker who helps Clennam and Doyce. He and his wife adopt Harriet Beadle ('Tattycoram') from the Foundling Hospital. *With a whimsical good humour on him all the time (Dorrit).*

Meagles, Mrs.: Meagles's wife, mother of Minnie. *Comely and healthy, with a pleasant English face which had been looking at homely things for five-and-fifty years or more, and shone with a bright reflection of them (Dorrit).*

Meagles, Minnie ('Pet'): The Meagleses' daughter who marries Henry Gowan. *Pet was about twenty. A fair girl with rich brown hair hanging free in natural ringlets. A lovely girl, with a frank face, and wonderful eyes; so large, so soft, so bright, set to such perfection in her kind good head. She was round and fresh and dimpled and spoilt, and there was in Pet an air of timidity and dependence which was the best weakness in the world, and gave her the only crowning charm a girl so pretty and pleasant could have been without (Dorrit).*

'Mealy Potatoes': Boy employee with David Copperfield at Murdstone and Grinby's. *This youth had not been christened by that name, but . . . it had been bestowed upon him in the workhouse, on account of his complexion, which was pale or mealy (Copperfield).*

Meek, Augustus George: The Meeks' baby. *When I saw the announcement in the Times, I dropped the paper. I had put it in, myself, and paid for it, but it looked so noble that it overpowered me. (Reprinted – 'Births. Mrs. Meek, of a Son').*

Meek, George: The proud father of Augustus George. *I hope and believe I am a quiet man. I will go farther. I know I am a quiet man. My constitution is tremulous, my voice was never loud, and, in point of stature, I have been from infancy, small (Reprinted – 'Births. Mrs. Meek, of a Son').*

Meek, Mrs. George (Maria Jane): Meek's wife. Mother of Augustus George and daughter of Mrs. Bigby. *Far from strong, and is subject to headaches, and nervous indigestion (Reprinted – 'Births. Mrs. Meek, of a Son').*

Melchisedech: Solicitor in Clifford's Inn to whom Tulkinghorn refers Trooper George *(Bleak House).*

'Melia: Servant at Dr. Blimber's. *The young woman seemed surprised at his appearance, and asked him where his mother was. When Paul told her she was dead, she took her gloves off, and . . . gave him a kiss (Dombey).*

Mell, Mrs.: Mell's mother, residing in an almshouse at Blackheath *(Copperfield)*

Mell, Charles: Teacher at Salem House, dismissed because his mother lived in an almshouse. Latrr Dr. Mell of Colonial Salem-House Grammar School, Port Middlebay, Australia. *A gaunt, sallow young man, with hollow cheeks. . . . He was dressed in a suit of black clothes which were rather rusty and dry too, and rather short in the sleeves and legs; and he had a white neckerchief on, that was not over-clean (Copperfield).*

Mellows, J.: Landlord of the Dolphin's Head, the subject of the essay. *I found J. Mellows, looking at nothing, and apparently experiencing that it failed to raise his spirits (Uncommercial – 'Old Stage-coaching House').*

Melluka, Miss: Polly Tresham's doll, bought for her by Jackson. *Of Circassian descent, possessing as much boldness of beauty as was reconcilable with extreme feebleness of mouth, and combining a sky-blue silk pelisse with rose-coloured satin trousers, and a black velvet hat: which this fair stranger to our northern shores would seem to have founded on the portraits of the late Duchess of Kent* (*Christmas Stories* – 'Mugby Junction').

Meltham: Actuary of the Inestimable Life Assurance Company who devotes himself to the destruction of Julius Slinkton, whose niece, with whom Meltham had been in love, has been murdered by her uncle for her insurance money. Meltham assumes the identities of Alfred Beckwith and Major Banks in pursuing his vendetta, and helps to save Margaret Niner, another niece of Slinkton's, from being murdered also. His purpose achieved, he dies. '*He was at once the most profound, the most original, and the most energetic man I have ever known connected with Life Assurance*' ('Hunted Down').

Melvilleson, Miss M.: Singer at the Harmonic Meetings at the Sol's Arms, Chancery Lane. *She has been married a year and a half, though announced as Miss M. Melvilleson, the noted siren, and . . . her baby is clandestinely conveyed to the Sol's Arms every night to receive its natural nourishment during the entertainments* (*Bleak House*).

'Memory': Stryver's nickname for Sydney Carton (*Two Cities*).

'Mercury': The Dedlocks' footman. *Mercury, with his hands in the pockets of his bright peach-blossom small-clothes, stretches his symmetrical silk legs with the air of a man of gallantry* (*Bleak House*).

Mercy: The Uncommercial Traveller's childhood nurse and teller of gruesome tales. *This female bard – may she have been repaid my debt of obligation to her in the matter of nightmares and perspirations! – reappears in my memory as the daughter of a shipwright. Her name was Mercy, though she had none on me* (*Uncommercial* – 'Nurse's Stories').

Merdle, M.P.: Financier, banker, forger and thief. Speculation in his enterprises ruins Clennam, the Dorrits, and others, and he commits suicide. *Immensely rich; a man of prodigious enterprise; a Midas without the ears, who turned all he touched to gold. He was in everything good, from banking to building. . . . His desire was to the utmost to satisfy Society (whatever that was), and take up all its drafts upon him for tribute. He did not shine in company; he had not very much to say for himself; he was a reserved man, with a broad, overhanging, watchful head, that particular kind of dull red colour in his cheeks which is rather stale than fresh, and a somewhat uneasy expression about his coat-cuffs, as if they were in his confidence, and had reasons for being anxious to hide his hands* (*Dorrit*).

Merdle, Mrs.: Merdle's wife, mother of Edmund Sparkler by her first marriage. *The lady was not young and fresh from the hand of Nature, but was young and fresh from the hand of her maid. She had large unfeeling handsome eyes, and dark unfeeling handsome hair, and a broad unfeeling handsome bosom, and was made the most of in every particular. Either because she had a cold, or because it suited her face, she wore a rich white fillet tied over her head and under her chin. And if ever there were an unfeeling handsome chin that looked as if, for certain, it had never been, in familiar parlance, 'chucked' by the hand of man, it was the chin curbed up so tight and close by that laced bridle* (*Dorrit*).

Merrylegs: Signor Jupe's performing dog, which he takes with him when he decamps from Sleary's Circus. The dog eventually returns alone and dies (*Hard Times*).

Merrywinkle, Mr. and Mrs.: A couple who coddle themselves. *Mr. Merrywinkle is a rather lean and long-necked gentleman, middle-aged and middle-sized, and usually troubled with a cold in the head. Mrs. Merrywinkle is a delicate-looking lady, with very light hair, and is exceedingly subject to the same unpleasant disorder*

(*Young Couples* – 'Couple Who Coddle Themselves').

Mescheck, Aaron: Jewish confidence trickster tracked down by Sergeant Dornton to the Tombs prison, New York (*Reprinted* – 'Detective Police').

'Mesrour': Nickname given to Tabby in the Seraglio fantasy (*Christmas Stories* – 'Haunted House').

Micawber, Emma: The Micawbers' second child, sister to Wilkins junior and the twins and the baby. She becomes Mrs. Ridger Begs, of Port Middlebay, Australia. *In whom, as Mr. Micawber told us, 'her mother renewed her youth, like the phoenix' (Copperfield).*

Micawber, Wilkins, jun.: The Micawbers' eldest child, brother of Emma, and the twins and the baby. A talented singer. *'It was my hope when I came here,' said Mr. Micawber, 'to have got Wilkins into the Church : or perhaps I shall express my meaning more strictly, if I say the Choir. But there was no vacancy for a tenor in the venerable Pile for which this city is so justly eminent ; and he has – in short, he has contracted a habit of singing in public-houses, rather than in sacred edifices' (Copperfield).*

Micawber, Wilkins, sen.: Agent of Murdstone and Grinby, and David Copperfield's landlord while he is employed there. Moving optimistically from employment to employment – interrupted by a spell in the Marshalsea for debt – he remains David's staunch friend, unmasks Uriah Heep for a villain, and is rewarded by Betsey Trotwood and others who pay his debts and send him and his family to Australia, where he becomes a prominent resident of Middlebay. *A stoutish, middle-aged person, in a brown surtout and black tights and shoes, with no more hair upon his head (which was a large one, and very shining) than there is upon an egg, and with a very extensive face, which he turned full upon me. His clothes were shabby, but he had an imposing shirt-collar on. He carried a jaunty sort of a stick, with a large pair of rusty tassels to it ; and a quizzing-glass*

hung outside his coat, – for ornament (Copperfield).

Micawber, Mrs. Wilkins, Sen. (Emma): Micawber's wife and champion in all adversity. Mother of Wilkins junior, Emma, twins and a baby. *A thin and faded lady, not at all young, who was sitting in the parlour (the first floor was altogether unfurnished, and the blinds were kept down to delude the neighbours), with a baby at her breast. . . . I have known her to be thrown into fainting fits by the king's taxes at three o'clock, and to eat lamb-chops breaded, and drink warm ale (paid for with two teaspoons that had gone to the pawnbroker's) at four (Copperfield).*

Micawber twins: The Micawbers' third and fourth children. *I may remark here that I hardly ever, in all my experience of the family, saw both the twins detached from Mrs. Micawber at the same time. One of them was always taking refreshment (Copperfield).*

Michael: The Poor Relation. He represents himself to be Christiana's husband, John Spatter's partner and Little Frank's friend, but it is all his day-dream. *Sometimes, one of my relations or acquaintances is so obliging as to ask me to dinner. Those are holiday occasions, and then I generally walk in the Park. I am a solitary man, and seldom walk with anybody. Not that I am avoided becuase I am shabby; for I am not at all shabby, having always a very good suit of black on (or rather Oxford mixture, which has the appearance of black and wears much better) ; but I have got into a habit of speaking low, and being rather silent, and my spirits are not high, and I am sensible that I am not an attractive companion (Christmas Stories* – 'Poor Relation').

'Middlesex Dumpling': Prizefighter whose contest with the Suffolk Bantam was stopped by Nupkins. *'Bless my soul, ma'am, are you aware of the activity of our local magistracy? Do you happen to have heard, ma'am, that I rushed into a prizering on the fourth of May last, attended* by only sixty special constables; and, at the hazard of falling a sacrifice to the angry passions of an infuriated multitude, prohibited a pugilistic contest between the Middlesex Dumpling and the Suffolk Bantam?' (Pickwick).

Miff, Mrs.: Pew-opener at the church where Dombey marries Edith Granger and, later, Walter Gay marries Florence. *A vinegary face has Mrs. Miff, and a mortified bonnet, and eke a thirsty soul for sixpences and shillings. Beckoning to stray people to come into pews, has given Mrs. Miff an air of mystery; and there is reservation in the eye of Mrs. Miff, as always knowing of a softer seat, but having her suspicions of the fee (Dombey).*

Miggot: Parkle's laundress in Gray's Inn. *He had an idea which he could never explain, that Mrs. Miggot was in some way connected with the Church. When he was in particularly good spirits, he used to believe that a deceased uncle of hers had been a Dean (Uncommercial – 'Chambers').*

Miggs, Miss: The Vardens' disloyal servant and rival of Dolly Varden for Sim Tappertit, whom she follows to the Gordon Riots. Later a turnkey at Bridewell. *This Miggs was a tall young lady, very much addicted to pattens in private life; slender and shrewish, of a rather uncomfortable figure, and though not absolutely ill-looking, of a sharp and acid visage. As a general principle and abstract proposition, Miggs held the male sex to be utterly contemptible and unworthy of notice; to be fickle, false, base, sottish, inclined to perjury, and wholly undeserving. When particularly exasperated against them (which, scandal said, was when Sim Tappertit slighted her most) she was accustomed to wish with great emphsis that the whole race of women could but die off, in order that the men might be brought to know the real value of the blessings by which they set so little store; nay, her feeling for her order ran so high, that she sometimes declared, if she could only have good security for a fair, round number – say ten thousand – of young virgins following her example, she would, to spite man-kind, hang, drown, stab, or poison herself, with a joy past all expression (Rudge).*

Mike: Client of Jaggers, rebuked for producing an invented witness *(Expectations).*

Miles, Bob: A villain encountered by Inspector Field's party in Saint Giles's *(Reprinted* – 'On Duty with Inspector Field').

Miles, Owen: One of Master Humphrey's circle and inseparable compaion of Jack Redburn. *A most worthy gentleman . . . once a very rich merchant; but receiving a severe shock in the death of his wife, he retired from business, and devoted himself to a quiet, unostentatious life. He is an excellent man, of thoroughly sterling character: not of quick apprehension, and not without some amusing prejudices (Humphrey).*

Milkwash, John: A poetical young gentleman. *The favourite attitude of the poetical young gentleman is lounging on a sofa with his eyes fixed upon the ceiling, or sitting bolt-upright in a high-backed chair, staring with very round eyes at the opposite wall. When he is in one of these positions, his mother, who is a worthy affectionate old soul, will give you a nudge to bespeak your attention without disturbing the abstracted one, and whisper with a shake of the head, that John's imagination is at some extraordinary work or other, you may take her word for it. Hereupon John looks more fiercely intent upon vacancy than before, and suddenly snatching a pencil from his pocket, puts down three words, and a cross on the back of a card, sighs deeply, paces once or twice across the room, inflicts a most unmerciful slap upon his head, and walks moodily up to his dormitory (Young Gentlemen –* 'Poetical Young Gentleman').

Miller: A guest at Dingley Dell. *A little hard-headed, Ripstone-pippin-faced man (Pickwick).*

Miller, Jane Ann: Lime Tree Lodge, Groombridge Wells. Mrs. Wilding's married sister, who adopted Walter Wilding from the Foundling Hospital on her behalf *(Christmas Stories –* 'No

Thoroughfare'; not in dramatised version).

Millers: One of Mrs. Matthew Pocket's nursemaids *(Expectations)*.

Mills: Julia Mills's father. *Mr. Mills was not at home. I did not expect he would be. Nobody wanted him. Miss Mills was at home. Miss Mills would do (Copperfield).*

Mills, Julia: Dora Spenlow's pessimistic bosom friend. She goes to India and returns the disagreeable wife of a disagreeable rich man. *Comparatively stricken in years – almost twenty, I should say. . . . Miss Mills had had her trials in the course of a chequered existence . . . having been unhappy in a misplaced affection, and being understood to have retired from the world on her awful stock of experience, but still to take a calm interest in the unblighted hopes and loves of youth (Copperfield).*

Mills, Julia: Avid reader of romances contained in the library at our English watering-place. *She has left marginal notes on the pages, as 'Is not this truly touching? J.M.' 'How thrilling! J.M.' 'Entranced here by the Magician's potent spell. J.M.' She has also italicised her favourite traits in the description of the hero, as 'his hair, which was* dark *and* wavy, *clustered* in *rich profusion around a* marble brow, *whose lofty paleness bespoke the intellect within.' It reminds her of another hero. She adds, 'How like B.L. Can this be mere coincidence? J.M.'* (Reprinted – 'Our English Watering-Place').

Milvey, The Revd. Frank: Husband of Margaretta. Curate who introduces the Boffins to Betty Higden and marries Eugene Wrayburn to Lizzie Hexam. *He was quite a young man, expensively educated and wretchedly paid, with quite a young wife and half a dozen quite young children. He was under the necessity of teaching and translating from the classics, to eke out his scanty means, yet was generally expected to have more time to spare than the idlest person in the parish, and more money than the richest. He accepted the needless inequalities and in-*

consistencies of his life, with a kind of conventional submission that was almost slavish; and any daring layman who would have adjusted such burdens as his, more decently and graciously, would have had small help from him (Mutual Friend).

Milvey, Mrs. Frank (Margaretta): The Revd. Frank's wife. *A pretty, bright little woman, something worn by anxiety, who had repressed many pretty tastes and bright fancies, and substituted in their stead, schools, soup, flannel, coals, and all the week-day cares and Sunday coughs of a large population, young and old (Mutual Friend).*

Mim: A showman, exhibitor of the giant Pickleson, and stepfather of Sophy, whom he sells to Dr. Marigold for six pairs of braces. *A very hoarse man . . . a most ferocious swearer (Christmas Stories – 'Doctor Marigold').*

Mincin: A very friendly young gentleman; a medical man. *A gentleman who had been previously showing his teeth by the fireplace (Young Gentlemen – 'Very Friendly Young Gentleman').*

Minns, Augustus: Government clerk, at Somerset House, of private means. Cousin to Octavius Budden and proxy godfather to Alexander Augustus Budden. *A bachelor, of about forty as he said – of about eight-and-forty as his friends said. He was always exceedingly clean, precise, and tidy; perhaps somewhat priggish, and the most retiring man in the world. . . . There were two classes of created objects which he held in the deepest and most unmingled horror; these were dogs, and children. He was not unamiable, but he could, at any time, have viewed the execution of a dog, or the assassination of an infant, with the liveliest satisfaction. Their habits were at variance with his love of order; and his love of order was as powerful as his love of life (Boz – 'Mr. Minns and his Cousin').*

'Missis, Our': Formidable head of the Mugby Junction refreshment room. *You should hear Our Missis give the word, 'Here comes the Beast to be Fed!' and then you should see 'em indignantly skipping across the Line, from the Up to the*

*Down, or Wicer Warsaw, and begin to
pitch the stale pastry into the plates, and
chuck the sawdust sangwiches under the
glass covers, and get out the – ha, ha, ha!
– the sherry, – O my eye, my eye! – for
your Refreshment (Christmas Stories –*
'Mugby Junction').

Misty, X. X.: Speaker at the zoology and
botany session of the second meeting of
the Mudfog Association. *Communicated
some remarks on the disappearance of
dancing-bears from the streets of London,
with observations on the exhibition of
monkeys as connected with barrel-organs
(Mudfog).*

Mith, Sergeant: One of the Detective
Force officers of Scotland Yard. *A
smooth-faced man with a fresh bright
complexion, and a strange air of simplicity,
is a dab at housebreakers (Reprinted –*
'Detective Police').

Mithers, Lady: Client of Miss Mowcher.
'There's *a woman! How she wears! – and
Mithers himself came into the room where
I was waiting for her –* there's *a man!
How he wears! and his wig too, for he's had
it these ten years' (Copperfield).*

Mitts, Mrs.: A Titbull's pensioner. *She
had a way of passing her hands over and
under one another as she spoke, that was
not only tidy but propitiatory (Uncommercial –* 'Titbull's Alms-Houses').

Mivins ('The Zephyr'): A fellow prisoner of Pickwick in the Fleet. *A man in
a broad-skirted green coat, with corduroy
knee smalls and grey cotton stockings, was
performing the most popular steps of a
hornpipe, with a slang and burlesque
caricature of grace and lightness, which,
combined with the very appropriate character of his costume, was inexpressibly
absurd (Pickwick).*

Mizzler, Marquis of and Lord Bobby:
Subjects of an anecdote by which
Chuckster seeks to impress the Garlands. *He was in a condition to relate the
exact circumstances of the difference
between the Marquis of Mizzler and Lord
Bobby, which it appeared originated in a
disputed bottle of champagne, and not in a
pigeon-pie, as erroneously reported in the
newspapers (Curiosity Shop).*

Mobbs: Pupil at Dotheboys Hall.
'Mobbs's *mother-in-law,' said Squeers,
'took to her bed on hearing that he
wouldn't eat fat, and has been very ill
ever since. She wishes to know, by an
early post, hwere he expects to go to, if he
quarrels with his vittles; and with what
feelings he could turn up his nose at the
cow's liver broth, after his good master
had asked a blessing on it' (Nickleby).*

Moddle, Augustus: The 'youngest
gentleman' boarder at Todgers's. Falls
hopelessly in love with Mercy Pecksniff, but she marries Jonas Chuzzlewit
and Moddle transfers his affection to her
sister Charity, whom he jilts in the nick
of time and goes to America. *The
youngest gentleman blew his melancholy
into a flute. He didn't blow much out of it,
but that was all the better. If the two Miss
Pecksniffs and Mrs. Todgers had perished
by spontaneous combustion, and the sere-
nade had been in honour of their ashes, it
would have been impossible to surpass the
unutterable despair expressed in that one
chorus, 'Go where glory waits thee!' It was
a requiem, a dirge, a moan, a howl, a wail,
a lament, an abstract of everything that is
sorrowful and hideous in sound (Chuzzlewit).*

Model, The: A gloomy artists' model
encountered by the narrator on a Thames
steamboat. '*I sets to the profession for a
bob a-hour. . . . When I don't set for a
head, I mostly sets for a throat and a pair
of legs' (Reprinted –* 'Ghost of Art').

Molly: Mother of Estella by Magwitch,
she had been tried for murder but successfully defended by Jaggers, who has
since employed her as housekeeper. *She
was a woman of about forty, I supposed –
but I may have thought her younger than
she was. Rather tall, of a lithe nimble
figure, extremely pale, with large faded
eyes, and a quantity of streaming hair. I
cannot say whether any diseased affection
of the heart caused her lips to be parted as
if she were panting, and her face to bear
a curious expression of sadness and flutter;
but I know that I had been to see Macbeth
at the theatre, a night or two before, and
that her face looked to me as if it were all*

disturbed by fiery air, like the faces I had seen rise out of the Witches' cauldron (Expectations).

Monflathers, Miss: Proprietress of a select school for young ladies whose pupils visit Jarley's waxwork show. Was of rather uncertain temper, and lost no opportunity of impressing moral truths upon the tender minds of the young ladies (Curiosity Shop).

Monks: See Leeford, Edward (Twist).

Montague, Julia: Singer who shares the bill with Amelia Martin at White Conduit. Solo, Miss Montague (positively on this occasion only) – 'I am a Friar' – (enthusiasm) (Boz – 'Mistaken Milliner').

Montague, Tigg: See Tigg, Montague (Chuzzlewit).

Moon: One of many doctors consulted by Our Bore. Moon, whom half the town was then mad about (Reprinted – 'Our Bore').

Mooney: Beadle officiating at the Coroner's Inquest on Hawdon. Hopes to read in print what 'Mooney, the active and intelligent beadle of the district,' said and did; and even aspires to see the name of Mooney as familiarly and patronisingly mentioned as the name of the Hangman is (Bleak House).

Mooney: Stargazer's partner. An astronomer and philosopher who has to be jerked out of his absent-minded ruminations by shocks from a strong battery. Stargazer wants him to marry Emma, but he declines (Lamplighter and 'Lamplighter's Story').

Mopes: The hermit on whom the story centres. By suffering everything about him to go to ruin, and by dressing himself in a blanket and skewer, and by steeping himself in soot and grease and other nastiness, had acquired great renown in all that countryside. . . . He had even blanketed and skewered and sooted and greased himself, into the London papers (Christmas Stories – 'Tom Tiddler's Ground').

Mordlin, Brother: Member of the Brick Lane Branch of the United Grand Junction Ebenezer Temperance Association

who has adapted Dibdin's 'Who hasn't heard of a Jolly Young Waterman?' to the tune of the Old Hundredth, which Anthony Humm invites the meeting to sing. He might take that opportunity of expressing his firm persuasion that the late Mr. Dibdin, seeing the errors of his former life, had written that song to show the advantages of abstinence. It was a temperance song (whirlwind of cheers). The neatness of the young man's attire, the dexterity of his feathering, the enviable state of mind which enabled him, in the beautiful words of the poet, to

'Row along, thinking of nothing at all,'

all combined to prove that he must have been a water-drinker (cheers) (Pickwick).

Morfin: Under-manager at Dombey and Son. Staunch friend of John Carker and later husband to Harriet Carker. A cheerful-looking, hazel-eyed elderly bachelor: gravely attired, as to his upper man, in black; and as to his legs, in pepper and salt colour. His dark hair was just touched here and there with specks of grey, as though the tread of Time had splashed it; and his whiskers were already white. . . . He was a great musical amateur in his way – after business; and had a paternal affection for the violoncello, which was once in every week transported from Islington, his place of abode, to a certain club-room hard by the Bank, where quartettes of the most tormenting and excruciating nature were executed every Wednesday evening by a private party (Dombey).

Morgan: See Jenkins (Young Couples – 'Contradictory Couple').

Morgan, Becky: Deceased old woman about whose age David and the sexton argue in front of Little Nell (Curiosity Shop).

Morgan ap Kerrig: Woodcourt ancestor, lines about whose lineage Mrs. Woodcourt is fond of reciting from the Crumlinwallinwer and the Mewlinwillinwodd (Bleak House).

Mormon Agent: Organiser of the emigrants aboard the Amazon. A compactly-made handsome man in black, rather short, with rich-brown hair and beard, and clear *bright eyes. From his speech, I should set him down as American. Probably, a man who had 'knocked about the world' pretty much. A man with a frank open manner, and unshrinking look; withal a man of great quickness (Uncommercial – 'Bound for the Great Salt Lake').*

Mortair: A vice-president of the anatomy and medicine session at the second meeting of the Mudfog Association *(Mudfog).*

Mortimer: Name under which Micawber finds it expedient to live in Camden Town. *'The truth is,' said Traddles, in a whisper, 'he has changed his name to Mortimer, in consequence of his temporary embarrassments; and he don't come out till after dark – and then in spectacles' (Copperfield).*

Mortimer, Mrs.: A subject for one of Charles and Louisa's recriminations. *'You know as well as I do that I am particularly engaged to Mrs. Mortimer, and that it would be an act of the grossest rudeness and ill-breeding, after accepting a seat in her box and preventing her from inviting anybody else, not to go' (Young Couples – 'Cool Couple').*

Mould: The undertaker who buries Anthony Chuzzlewit. Professionally in league with Mrs. Gamp. *A little elderly gentleman, bald, and in a suit of black; with a note-book in his hand, a massive gold watch-chain dangling from his fob, and a face in which a queer attempt at melancholy was at odds with a smirk of satisfaction; so that he looked as a man might, who, in the very act of smacking his lips over a choice old wine, tried to make believe it was physic (Chuzzlewit).*

Mould, Mrs. and the Misses: Mould's wife and daughters. *Plump as any partridge was each Miss Mould, and Mrs. M. was plumper than the two together. So round and chubby were their fair proportions, that they might have been the bodies once belonging to the angels' faces in the shop below, grown up, with other heads attached to make them mortal. Even their peachy cheeks were puffed out and distended, as though they ought of right to be performing on celestial trumpets (Chuzzlewit).*

Mowcher, Miss: A dwarf and visiting beauty specialist who attends Steerforth. She is instrumental in Littimer's arrest. *There came waddling round a sofa which stood between me and it, a pursy dwarf, of about forty or forty-five, with a very large head and face, a pair of roguish grey eyes, and such extremely little arms, that, to enable herself to lay a finger archly against her snub-nose as she ogled Steerforth, she was obliged to meet the finger half-way and lay her nose against it. Her chin, which was what is called a double-chin, was so fat that it entirely swallowed up the strings of her bonnet, bow and all. Throat she had none; waist she had none; legs she had none, worth mentioning; for though she was more than full-sized down to where her waist would have been, if she had had any, and though she terminated, as human beings generally do, in a pair of feet, she was so short that she stood at a common-sized chair as at a table, resting a bag she carried on the seat (Copperfield).*

Mr. F's Aunt: A strange old lady left to Flora Finching's care by her deceased husband. *An amazing little old woman, with a face like a staring wooden doll too cheap for expression, and a stiff yellow wig perched unevenly on the top of her head, as if the child who owned the doll had driven a tack through it anywhere, so that it only got fastened on. Another remarkable thing in this little old woman was, that the same child seemed to have damaged her face in two or three places with some blunt instrument in the nature of a spoon; her countenance, and particularly the tip of her nose, presenting the phenomena of several dints, generally answering to the bowl of that article. A further remarkable thing in this little old woman was, that she had no name but Mr. F's Aunt. . . . The major characteristics discoverable by the stranger in Mr. F's Aunt, were extreme severity and grim taciturnity; sometimes interrupted by a propensity to offer remarks in a deep warning voice, which, being totally uncalled for by anything said by anybody, and traceable to no association of ideas, confounded and terrified the mind (Dorrit).*

Mudberry, Mrs.: Neighbour quoted by Mrs. Sanders as having told her that Pickwick was engaged to Mrs. Bardell. *Mrs. Mudberry which kept a mangle (Pickwick).*

Muddlebrains: A vice-president at the zoology and botany session of the second meeting of the Mudfog Association *(Mudfog).*

Mudge, Jonas: Secretary of the Brick Lane Branch of the United Grand Junction Ebenezer Temperance Association. *Chandler's shop-keeper, an enthusiastic and disinterested vessel, who sold tea to the members (Pickwick).*

Muff and Nogo, Professors: Vice-presidents of the anatomy and medicine session of the first meeting of the Mudfog Association. They dissect Augustus (q.v.), a lady's pet dog, in their hotel room. *We are all very much delighted with the urbanity of their manners and the ease with which they adapt themselves to the forms and ceremonies of ordinary life. Immediately on their arrival they sent for the head waiter, and privately requested him to purchase a live dog, – as cheap a one as he could meet with, – and to send him up after dinner, with a pie-board, a knife and fork, and a clean plate. It is conjectured that some experiments will be tried upon the dog to-night (Mudfog).*

Mull, Professor: Member of the Mudfog Association *(Mudfog).*

Mullins, Jack: Regular drinker at the Six Jolly Fellowship Porters *(Mutual Friend).*

Mullion, John: Member of the *Golden Mary's* crew. *The man who had kept on burning the blue-lights (and who had lighted every new one at every old one before it went out, as quietly as if he had been at an illumination) (Christmas Stories – 'Golden Mary').*

Mullit, Professor: An American 'professor of education' whom Martin Chuzzlewit meets at Pawkins's Boarding-House, New York. *'He is a man of fine moral elements, sir, and not commonly endowed,' said the war correspondent. 'He felt it necessary, at the last election for* President, to repudiate and denounce his father, who voted on the wrong interest. He has since written some powerful pamphlets, under the signature of "Suturb," or Brutus reversed' (Chuzzlewit).

Muntle: Real name of Alfred Mantalini *(Nickleby).*

Murderer, Captain: Subject of one o the gruesome tales told by the Uncommercial Traveller's childhood nurse. *His warning name would seem to have awakened no general prejudice against him, for he was admitted into the best society and possessed immense wealth. Captain Murderer's mission was matrimony, and the gratification of a cannibal appetite with tender brides (Uncommercial – 'Nurse's Stories').*

Murdstone, Edward: Partner in Murdstone and Grinby, wine merchants. Brother of Jane, second husband to Clara Copperfield, and stepfather to David, whose spirit he tries to break by sending him to Salem House school and then into his own warehouse. He and his sister break Clara's heart, and Murdstone eventually re-marries, with similar results. *He had that kind of shallow black eye – I want a better word to express an eye that has no depth in it to be looked into – which, when it is abstracted, seems, from some peculiarity of light, to be disfigured, for a moment at a time, by a cast. Several times when I glanced at him, I observed that appearance with a sort of awe, and wondered what he was thinking about so closely. His hair and whiskers were blacker and thicker, looked at so near, than even I had given them credit for being. A squareness about the lower part of his face, and the dotted indication of the strong black beard he shaved close every day, reminded me of the wax-work that had travelled into our neighbourhood some half a year before. This, his regular eyebrows, and the rich white, and black, and brown, of his complexion – confound his complexion, and his memory! – made me think him, in spite of my misgivings, a very handsome man. I have no doubt that my poor dear mother thought him so too (Copperfield).*

Murdstone, Mrs. Edward the First:
See **Copperfield, Mrs. Clara** (*Copperfield*).

Murdstone, Mrs. Edward the Second:
Murdstone's second wife, after Clara. '*A charming woman indeed, sir,' said Mr. Chillip; 'as amiable, I am sure, as it was possible to be! Mrs. Chillip's opinion is, that her spirit has been entirely broken since her marriage, and that she is all but melancholy mad'* (*Copperfield*).

Murdstone, Jane: Edward's sister. She is as hard as her brother and Clara Copperfield's death is much attributable to her. *A gloomy-looking lady she was, dark, like her brother, whom she greatly resembled in face and voice; and with very heavy eyebrows, nearly meeting over her large nose, as if, being disabled by the wrongs of her sex from wearing whiskers, she had carried them to that account. She brought with her two uncompromising hard black boxes, with her initials on the lids in hard brass nails. When she paid the coachman she took her money out of a hard steel purse, and she kept the purse in a very jail of a bag which hung upon her arm by a heavy chain, and shut up like a bite. I had never, at that time, seen such a metallic lady altogether as Miss Murdstone was* (*Copperfield*).

Murdstone and Grinby: Firm of wine merchants in which Edward Murdstone is partner, and in whose warehouse he employs and humiliates David Copperfield (*Copperfield*).

Murgatroyd: An undertaker, one of the admiring audience of the gentleman connected with the press at the Green Dragon, Westminster Bridge (*Mudfog* – 'Mr. Robert Bolton').

Mutanhed, Lord: A foppish young nobleman at the ball at Bath Assembly Rooms. '*The one with the long hair, and the particularly small forehead?' inquired Mr. Pickwick* (*Pickwick*).

Mutuel, Monsieur: Friend of Madame Bouclet. *A spectacled, snuffy, stooping old gentleman in carpet shoes and a cloth cap with a peaked shade, a loose blue frock-coat reaching to his heels, a large limp white shirt-frill, and cravat to correspond – that is to say, white was the natural colour of his linen on Sundays, but it toned down with the week* (*Christmas Stories* – 'Somebody's Luggage').

Muzzle: Nupkins's footman and Job Trotter's rival for the cook. *An under-sized footman, with a long body and short legs* (*Pickwick*).

Nadgett: Inquiry agent employed by the Anglo-Bengalee Disinterested Loan and Life Assurance Company to investigate Jonas Chuzzlewit, whose guilt he ultimately proves. *He was born to be a secret. He was a short, dried-up, withered, old man, who seemed to have secreted his very blood; for nobody would have given him credit for the possession of six ounces of it in his whole body. How he lived was a secret; where he lived was a secret; and even what he was, was a secret. In his musty old pocket-book he carried contradictory cards, in some of which he called himself a coal-merchant, in others a collector, in others an accountant: as if he really didn't know the secret himself* (*Chuzzlewit*).

Namby: Sheriff's officer who arrests Pickwick in execution of the judgment in Bardell and Pickwick. *A man of about forty, with black hair, and carefully combed whiskers. He was dressed in a particularly gorgeous manner, with plenty of articles of jewellery about him – all about three sizes larger than those which are usually worn by gentlemen – and a rough great-coat to crown the whole* (*Pickwick*).

Nancy: Member of Fagin's gang and mistress of Bill Sikes. She befriends Oliver Twist and helps him through Rose Maylie and Brownlow, but is overheard by Noah Claypole at a meeting with them, denounced to Fagin for treachery, and savagely murdered by Sikes. *The girl's life had been squandered in the streets, and among the most noisome of the stews and dens of London, but there was something of the woman's original nature left in her still* (*Twist*).

Nandy, John Edward: Mrs. Plornish's father. *A poor little reedy piping old* gentleman, like a worn-out bird; who had been in what he called the music-binding business, and met with great misfortunes, and who had seldom been able to make his way, or to see it or to pay it, or to do anything at all with it but find it no thoroughfare, – had retired of his own accord to the Workhouse.... But no poverty in him and no coat on him that never was the mode, and no Old Men's Ward for his dwelling-place, could quench his daughter's admiration. Mrs. Plornish was as proud of her father's talents as she possibly could have been if they had made him Lord Chancellor. She had as firm a belief in the sweetness and propriety of his manners as she could possibly have had if he had been Lord Chamberlain. The poor little old man knew some pale and vapid little songs, long out of date, about Chloe, and Phyllis, and Strephon being wounded by the son of Venus; and for Mrs. Plornish there was no such music at the Opera, as the small internal flutterings and chirpings wherein he would discharge himself of these ditties, like a weak, little, broken barrel-organ, ground by a baby (Dorrit).

Native, The: Major Bagstock's servant. *A dark servant of the major's, whom Miss Tox was quite content to classify as a 'native', without connecting him with any geographical idea whatever (Dombey).*

Neckett: Sheriff's officer employed to arrest Skimpole. After his death Jarndyce provides for his three children, Charlotte, Tom, and Emma. *In a white greatcoat, with smooth hair upon his head and not much of it, which he was wiping smoother, and making less of, with a pocket-handkerchief (Bleak House).*

Neckett, Charlotte (Charley): Neckett's elder daughter, sister of Emma and Tom. She becomes Esther Summerson's maid. *A very little girl, childish in figure but shrewd and older-looking in the face – pretty-faced too – wearing a womanly sort of bonnet much too large for her, and drying her bare arms on a womanly sort of apron. Her fingers were white and wrinkled with washing, and the soap-suds were yet smoking which she wiped off her arms. But for this, she might have been a child playing*

at washing, and imitating a poor working-woman with a quick observation of the truth (Bleak House).

Neckett, Emma: Neckett's infant daughter, sister of Charlotte and Tom. *A heavy child of eighteen months (Bleak House).*

Neckett, Tom: Neckett's infant son, brother of Charlotte and Emma. *A mite of a boy, some five or six years old (Bleak House).*

Ned: Chimney-sweep who kept his son small, for hiring out on burglary jobs to Bill Sikes and others. *'But the father gets lagged; and then the Juvenile Delinquent Society comes, and takes the boy away from a trade where he was earning money, teaches him to read and write, and in time makes a 'prentice of him. And so they go on,' said Mr. Sikes, his wrath rising with the recollection of his wrongs, 'so they go on; and, if they'd got money enough (which it's a Providence they haven't) we shouldn't have half a dozen boys left in the whole trade, in a year or two' (Twist).*

Neddy: One of Roker's fellow turnkeys in the Fleet Prison. *Of a taciturn and thoughtful cast (Pickwick).*

Neeshawts, Dr.: Member of the Mudfog Association (Mudfog).

Nell, Little: See **Trent, Nell** (Curiosity Shop).

'Nemo': See **Hawdon, Captain** (Bleak House).

Nettingall, the Misses: Principals of a Canterbury school for young ladies attended by Miss Shepherd (Copperfield).

Newcome, Clemency: Dr. Jeddler's maidservant, later married to his man-servant, Benjamin Britain. *She was about thirty years old, and had a sufficiently plump and cheerful face, though it was twisted up into an odd expression of tightness that made it comical. But, the extraordinary homeliness of her gait and manner, would have superseded any face in the world. To say that she had two left legs, and somebody else's arms, and that all four limbs seemed to be out of joint, and to start* from perfectly wrong places when they were set in motion, is to offer the mildest outline of the reality. To say that she was perfectly content and satisfied with these arrangements, and regarded them as being no business of hers, and that she took her arms and legs as they came, and allowed them to dispose of themselves just as it happened, is to render faint justice to her equanimity (*Christmas Books* – 'Battle of Life').

Nicholas: Butler at Bellamy's restaurant in the Houses of Parliament. *A queer old fellow is Nicholas, and as completely a part of the building as the house itself . . . looking as he always does, as if he had been in a bandbox ever since the last session. There he is, at his old post every night, just as we have described him : and, as characters are scarce, and faithful servants scarcer, long may he be there, say we!* (*Boz* – 'Parliamentary Sketch').

Nickleby, Godfrey: Deceased father of Ralph and Nicholas senior (*Nickleby*).

Nickleby, Kate: Sister of Nicholas junior. She marries Frank Cheeryble. *A slight, but very beautiful girl of about seventeen (Nickleby).*

Nickleby, Nicholas, jun.: Son of Mrs. Nickleby and the late Nicholas senior. Brother to Kate and nephew of Ralph. The central figure of the novel, he marries Madeline Bray, whose father he has helped rescue from the financial clutches of Ralph Nickleby and Arthur Gride. *His figure was somewhat slight, but manly and well-formed; and, apart from all the grace of youth and comeliness, there was an emanation from the warm young heart in his look (Nickleby).*

Nickleby, Nicholas, sen.: Deceased son of Godfrey, brother of Ralph, father of Nicholas and Kate (*Nickleby*).

Nickleby, Mrs. Nicholas, sen.: Widow of Nicholas senior and mother of Nicholas junior and Kate. Feckless and absent-minded, she fancies herself wooed by the Gentleman in Small-clothes, but nothing comes of it. *Mrs. Nickleby had begun to display unusual care in the adornment of her person, gradually superadding to those staid and matronly habiliments which had, up to that time, formed her ordinary attire, a variety of embellishments and decorations, slight perhaps in themselves, but, taken together, and considered with reference to the subject of her disclosure, of no mean importance. Even her black dress assumed something of a deadly-lively air from the jaunty style in which it was worn; and, eked out as its lingering attractions were, by a prudent disposal, here and there, of certain juvenile ornaments of little or no value, which had, for that reason alone, escaped the general wreck and been permitted to slumber peacefully in odd corners of old drawers and boxes where daylight seldom shone, her mourning garments assumed quite a new character. From being the outward tokens of respect and sorrow for the dead, they became converted into signals of very slaughterous and killing designs upon the living (Nickleby).*

Nickleby, Ralph: Son of Godfrey, brother of the late Nicholas senior, uncle to Nicholas and Kate. A rich and miserly moneylender who grudgingly helps his late brother's family but tries to humiliate Nicholas. He eventually hangs himself. *He wore a sprinkling of powder upon his head, as if to make himself look benevolent, but if that were his purpose, he would perhaps have done better to powder his countenance also, for there was something in its very wrinkles, and in his cold restless eye, which seemed to tell of cunning that would announce itself in spite of him (Nickleby).*

Nightingale, Christopher: Rosina's uncle and guardian. A hypochondriac who has been paying a regular allowance to Slap, believing the money to be going to his estranged wife, Maria, Slap's sister, who had actually died twelve years ago. He is saved from Slap's ultimate coup by Gabblewig (*Nightingale's Diary*).

Nightingale, Christopher, jun.: An imposture by Tip in aid of Slap's ultimate attempt at extortion from Mr. Nightingale (*Nightingale's Diary*).

Nightingale, Rosina: Nightingale's niece. She wishes to marry Gabblewig, of whom her uncle disapproves, so helps him redeem his character by unmasking Slap, in the course of which she assumes the disguises of Mrs. Poulter and Mrs. Trusty *(Nightingale's Diary)*.

Niner, Margaret: Slinkton's surviving niece, whose murder for her insurance money is narrowly averted by Meltham and Sampson. *She was dressed in mourning, and I looked at her with great interest. She had the appearance of being extremely delicate, and her face was remarkably pale and melancholy; but she was very pretty* ('Hunted Down').

Nipper, Susan: Florence Dombey's maid and support. She marries Toots. *A short, brown, womanly girl of fourteen, with a little snub nose, and black eyes like jet beads (Dombey).*

Nixon, Mrs.: Felix's doting mother. *If you ask Felix how he finds himself to-day, he prefaces his reply with a long and minute bulletin of his mother's state of health; and the good lady in her turn, edifies her acquaintance with a circumstantial and alarming account, how he sneezed four times and coughed once after being out in the rain the other night (Young Gentlemen – 'Domestic Young Gentleman').*

Nixon, Felix: A domestic young gentleman. *Lives at home with his mother, just within the twopenny-post office circle of three miles from St. Martin le Grand. He wears India-rubber goloshes when the weather is at all damp, and always has a silk handkerchief neatly folded up in the right-hand pocket of his great-coat, to tie over his mouth when he comes home at night; moreover, being rather nearsighted, he carries spectacles for particular occasions, and has a weakish tremulous voice, of which he makes great use, for he talks as much as any old lady breathing. The two chief subjects of Felix's discourse, are himself and his mother, both of whom would appear to be very wonderful and interesting persons (Young Gentlemen – 'Domestic Young Gentleman').*

Noakes: A vice-president of the statistics session at the second meeting of the Mudfog Association *(Mudfog).*

Noakes, Mrs.: See **Williamson, Mrs.** *(Strange Gentleman).*

Noakes, Percy: A pleasure-loving law student, of Gray's Inn Square; prime organiser of the steam excursion. *He had a large circle of acquaintance, and seldom dined at his own expense. He used to talk politics to papas, flatter the vanity of mammas, do the amiable to their daughters, make pleasure engagements with their sons, and romp with the younger branches. . . . His sitting-room presented a strange chaos of dress-gloves, boxing-gloves, caricatures, albums, invitation-cards, foils, cricket-bats, cardboard drawings, paste, gum, and fifty other miscellaneous articles, heaped together in the strangest confusion. He was always making something for somebody, or planning some party of pleasure, which was his great forte. He invariably spoke with astonishing rapidity; was smart, spoffish, and eight-and-twenty (Boz –* 'Steam Excursion').

Nobody: Hero of the story. *It matters little what his name was. Let us call him Legion. . . . The story of Nobody is the story of the rank and file of the earth. They bear their share of the battle; they have their part in the victory; they fall; they leave no name but in the mass (Christmas Stories –* 'Nobody's Story').

Nockemorf: Bob Sawyer's predecessor in the medical practice at Bristol *(Pickwick).*

'Noddy': See **Boffin, Nicodemus** *(Mutual Friend).*

Noddy: Friend of Bob Sawyer, present at his supper party. *The scorbutic youth (Pickwick).*

Noggs, Newman: Ralph Nickleby's clerk, a former gentleman. He befriends and serves Nicholas, and is instrumental in Ralph's exposure and ruin. *A tall man of middle age, with two goggle eyes whereof one was a fixture, a rubicund nose, a cadaverous face, and a suit of clothes (if the term be allowable when they suited him not at all) much the worse for wear, very much too small, and placed upon such a short allowance of buttons that it was marvellous how he contrived to keep them on (Nickleby).*

Nogo, Professor: See Muff and Nogo (*Mudfog*).

Norah: Seven-year-old cousin to eight-year-old Harry Walmers, with whom she elopes to Gretna Green, hoping to marry. In adult life she marries a captain and dies in India. *The lady had got a parasol, a smelling-bottle, a round and a half of cold buttered toast, eight peppermint drops, and a hair-brush, – seemingly a doll's* (*Christmas Stories* – 'Holly-Tree').

Normandy: A gaming-booth attendant invited by Chops to join him in entering society. He is the instrument of Chops's ruin. *Had a very genteel appearance* (*Christmas Stories* – 'Going into Society').

Norris Family: A wealthy New York family to whom Martin Chuzzlewit is introduced by Bevan on first arriving there. They drop him hastily when they learn that he had travelled steerage. *There were two young ladies – one eighteen; the other twenty – both very slender, but very pretty; their mother, who looked, as Martin thought, much older than she ought to have looked; and their grand-mother, a little sharp-eyed, quick old woman, who seemed to have got past that stage, and to have come all right again. Besides these, there were the young ladies' father, and the young ladies' brother; the first engaged in mercantile affairs; the second, a student at college* (*Chuzzlewit*).

Norton, Squire: Would-be seducer of Lucy Benson (*Village Coquettes*).

Nubbles, Mrs.: Widowed mother of Kit, Jacob, and a baby. A poor laundress. *Late as the Dutch clock showed it to be, the poor woman was still hard at work at an ironing-table* (*Curiosity Shop*).

Nubbles, Jacob: Kit's small brother. *A sturdy boy of two or three years old, very wide awake, with a very tight night-cap on his head, and a night-gown very much too small for him on his body, was sitting bolt upright in a clothes-basket, staring over the rim with his great round eyes, and looking as if he had thoroughly made up his mind never to go to sleep any more* (*Curiosity Shop*).

Nubbles, Kit: Little Nell's devoted friend and her grandfather's shop-boy at the Old Curiosity Shop. When the couple disapper he goes to work for Garland. Quilp gets him falsely accused of theft, but he is cleared and marries Barbara, the Garlands' maid. *A shock-headed shambling awkward lad with an uncommonly wide mouth, very red cheeks, a turned-up nose, and certainly the most comical expression of face I ever saw. He stopped short at the door on seeing a stranger, twirled in his hand a perfectly round old hat without any vestige of a brim, and, resting himself now on one leg, and now on the other, and changing them constantly, stood in the doorway, looking into the parlour with the most extraordinary leer I ever beheld* (*Curiosity Shop*).

Nupkins, George: Mayor of Ipswich, before whom the Pickwickians are taken on Miss Witherfield's complaint. *As grand a personage as the fastest walker would find out, between sunrise and sunset, on the twenty-first of June, which being, according to the almanacs, the longest day in the whole year, would naturally afford him the longest period for his search* (*Pickwick*).

Nupkins, Mrs. George: Nupkins's wife and mother of Henrietta. *A majestic female in a pink gauze turban and a light brown wig* (*Pickwick*).

Nupkins, Henrietta: The Nupkinses' daughter. *Possessed all her mamma's haughtiness without the turban, and all her ill-nature without the wig* (*Pickwick*).

Oakum-Head: One of the female delinquents in the workhouse visited by the Uncommercial Traveller (*Uncommercial* – 'Wapping Workhouse.).

Obenreizer, Jules: London agent of Defresnier et Cie., Swiss wine merchants, and uncle of Marguerite. Fearing that Vendale is about to discover his frauds, Obenreizer tries to murder him in an Alpine pass. He is eventually killed in an avalanche. *A black-haired young man of a dark complexion, through whose swarthy skin no red glow ever shone. When colour would have come into another cheek, a hardly dicernible beat would come into his,* *as if the machinery for bringing up the ardent blood were there, but the machinery were dry. . . . But the great Obenreizer peculiarity was, that a certain nameless film would come over his eyes – apparently by the action of his own will – which would imprenetrably veil, not only from those tellers of tales, but from his face at large, every expression save one of attention. . . . It was a comprehensive watchfulness of everything that he knew to be, or suspected to be, in the minds of other men* (Christmas Stories – 'No Thoroughfare' and in dramatised version).

Obenreizer, Marguerite: Obenreizer's niece, living with him in London. Courted by Vendale, she saves him after her uncle's murderous attack and eventually marries him. *The young lady wore an unusual quantity of fair bright hair, very prettily braided about a rather rounder white forehead than the average English type, and so her face might have been a shade – or say a light – rounder than the average English face, and her figure slightly rounder than the figure of the average English girl at nineteen. A remarkable indication of freedom and grace of limb, in her quiet attitude, and a wonderful purity and freshness of colour in her dimpled face and bright gray eyes, seemed fraught with mountain air* (Christmas Stories – 'No Thoroughfare' and in dramatised version).

O'Bleary, Frederick: Boarder at Mrs. Tibbs's, with ideas of marrying Mrs. Bloss. *An Irishman, recently imported; he was in a perfectly wild state; and had come over to England to be an apothecary, a clerk in a government office, an actor, a reporter, or anything else that turned up – he was not particular. . . . He felt convinced that his intrinsic merits must procure him a high destiny. He wore shepherd's-plaid inexpressibles, and used to look under all the ladies' bonnets as he walked along the streets* (Boz – 'Boarding-House').

O'Brien: See **Brown and O'Brien** (Boz – 'The River').

Odd Girl, The: One of the maids taken

with them by the party investigating the haunted house. *I have reason to record the attendant last enumerated, who was one of the St' Lawrence's Union Female Orphans, that she was a fatal mistake and a disastrous engagement* (Christmas Stories – 'Haunted House').

'Old Soldier, The: See **Markleham, Mrs.** (Copperfield).

Omer: Yarmouth draper and undertaker, father of Minnie. Employer, and later partner and father-in-law, of Joram. Employer of Little Em'ly before her elopment. *A fat, short-winded, merry-looking, little old man in black, with rusty little bunches of ribbons at the knees of his breeches, black stockings, and a broad-brimmed hat* (Copperfield).

Omer, Minnie: Omer's daughter, marries Joram. *A pretty good-natured girl* (Copperfield).

One Old Man: The Phantom of a hanged man who attends Goodchild in the Lancaster inn and tells his story. *A chilled, slow, earthly, fixed old man. A cadaverous old man of measured speech. An old man who seemed as unable to wink, as if his eyelids had been nailed to his forehead. . . . His cravat appeared to trouble him. He put his hand to this throat, and moved his neck from side to side. He was an old man of a swollen character of face, and his nose was immoveably hitched up on one side, as if by a little hook inserted in that nostril* (Two Apprentices).

Onowenever, Miss and Mrs.: An object of the Uncommercial Traveller's youthful admiration, and her mother. *She was older than I, and had pervaded every chink and crevice of my mind for three or four years. I had held volumes of Imaginary Conversations with her mother on the subject of our union, and I had written letters more in number than Horace Walpole's, to that discreet woman, soliciting her daughter's hand in marriage. I had never had the remotest intention of sending any of those letters; but to write them, and after a few days tear them up, had been a sublime occupation* (Uncommercial – 'Birthday Celebrations').

THE LIKENESS. 'They were sufficiently like each other to surprise everybody' (*A Tale of Two Cities*)

MEEKNESS OF MR PECKSNIFF AND HIS CHARMING DAUGHTERS. 'He was a most exemplary man: fuller of virtuous precept than a copy-book' *(Martin Chuzzlewit)*

MRS GAMP PROPOGES A TOAST. 'My frequent pardner, Betsey Prig!' *(Martin Chuzzlewit)*

BARNABY AND HIS MOTHER. There was something even plaintive in his wan and haggard aspect' (*Barnaby Rudge*)

BARNABY IN NEWGATE PRISON. 'Grip . . . with his head drooping and his deep black plumes rough and rumpled, appeared to comprehend and to partake his master's fallen fortunes' (*Barnaby Rudge*)

FIRST APPEARANCE OF MR SAMUEL WELLER. ' "Ah," said the little man, "you're a wag, an't you?" "My eldest brother was troubled with that complaint," said Sam. "It may be catching." ' (*Pickwick Papers*)

CHRISTMAS EVE AT MR WARDLE'S. 'A scene of general and most delightful struggling and confusion.' *(Pickwick Papers)*

OLIVER INTRODUCED TO FAGIN. 'We are very glad to see you, Oliver, very. Dodger, take off the sausages.' *(Oliver Twist)*

SIKES TRIES TO DESTROY HIS DOG. 'Do you hear me call? Come here!' *(Oliver Twist)*

I AM MARRIED. 'Walking so proudly and lovingly down the aisle with my sweet wife upon my arm.' *(David Copperfield)*

RESTORATION OF MUTUAL CONFIDENCE. 'Mrs Micawber shrieked, and folded Mr Micawber in her embrace.' (*David Copperfield*)

THE GARDEN ON THE ROOF. 'Come up and be dead! Come up and be dead!' (*Our Mutual Friend*)

THE DANCING SCHOOL. 'Prince Turveydrop sometimes played the kit, dancing . . . his distinguished father did nothing whatever, but stand before the fire, a model of Deportment.' (*Bleak House*)

THE GHOST OF CHRISTMAS PRESENT. SCROOGE'S THIRD VISITOR. 'In easy state . . . there sat a jolly Giant, glorious to see.' *(Christmas Books/ A Christmas Carol)*

THE CARRIER AND HIS WIFE. 'It's sure to bring us good fortune, John . . . to have a Cricket on the Hearth, is the luckiest thing in all the world!' (*Christmas Books/A Cricket on the Hearth*)

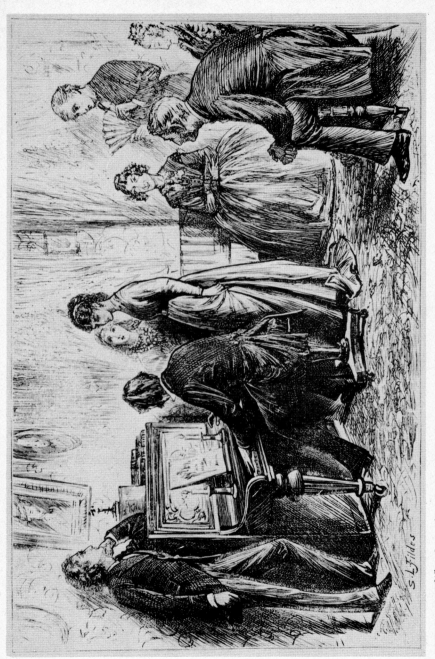

AT THE PIANO. 'When I sing, he never moves his eyes from my lips.' (*Edwin Drood*)

JASPER'S SACRIFICES. 'Reckon up nothing at this moment, angel, but the sacrifices that I lay at those dear feet.' (*Edwin Drood*)

THE OLD CURIOSITY SHOP. 'One of those receptacles for old and curious things which seem to crouch in odd corners of this town.' (*The Old Curiosity Shop*)

Orange, James: Mrs. Orange's 'husband' in Nettie Ashford's romantic tale ('Holiday Romance').

Orange, Mrs. James: A 'truly sweet young creature' in Nettie Ashford's romantic tale who had the misfortune to be sadly plagued by her numerous family of parents and other adults ('Holiday Romance').

'Orfling, The': See Clickett *(Copperfield)*.

Orlick, Dolge: Joe Gargery's journeyman and implacable enemy to Pip, whom he nearly murders at Compeyson's instigation. He is Mrs. Joe Gargery's brutal attacker. *He pretended that his Christian name was Dolge – a clear impossibility – but he was a fellow of that obstinate disposition that I believe him to have been the prey of no delusion in this particular, but wilfully to have imposed that name upon the village as an affront to its understanding. He was a broad-shouldered loose-limbed swarthy fellow of great strength, never in a hurry, and always slouching. He never even seemed to come to his work on purpose, but would slouch in as if by mere accident. . . . He always slouched, locomotively, with his eyes on the ground; and when accosted or otherwise required to raise them, he looked up in a half resentful, half puzzled way, as though the only thought he ever had, was, that it was rather an odd and injurious fact that he should never be thinking (Expectations).*

Overton, Joseph: Solicitor and mayor of Great Winglebury, instructed by Julia Manners to arrange her elopement with Lord Peter. *A sleek man . . . in drab shorts and continuations, black coat, neckcloth, and gloves (Boz – 'Great Winglebury Duel').* He is renamed Owen Overton in the dramatic version, *The Strange Gentleman.*

Overton, Owen: Mayor of a small town on the road to Gretna *(Strange Gentleman).* This is the Joseph Overton (q.v.) of *Boz* – 'Great Winglebury Duel'.

Owen, John: A pupil at Marton's village school. *'A lad of good parts, sir, and frank, honest temper; but too thoughtless, too playful, too light-headed by far. That boy, my good sir, would break his neck with pleasure, and deprive his parents of their chief comfort (Curiosity Shop).*

Packer, Tom: Fellow Royal Marine private of Gill Davis in the sloop *Christopher Columbus. A wild, unsteady young fellow, but the son of a respectable shipwright in Portsmouth Yard, and a good scholar who had been well brought up (Christmas Stories – 'English Prisoners').*

Packlemerton, Jasper: One of Mrs. Jarley's waxwork figures. *'Of atrocious memory, who courted and married fourteen wives, and destroyed them all, by tickling the soles of their feet when they were sleeping in the consciousness of innocence and virtue' (Curiosity Shop).*

Palmer: Amateur actor. *Mister Palmer is to play* The Unknown Bandit *(Boz – 'Private Theatres').*

Pancks: Agent and rent collector for Casby, whom he eventually exposes. *He was dressed in black and rusty iron grey; had jet black beads of eyes; a scrubby little black chin; wiry black hair striking out from his head in prongs, like forks or hairpins; and a complexion that was very dingy by nature, or very dirty by art, or a compound of nature and art. He had dirty hands and dirty broken nails, and looked as if he had been in the coals; he was in a perspiration, and snorted and sniffed and puffed and blew, like a little labouring steam-engine (Dorrit).*

Pangloss: A friend, in an official position, of the Uncommercial Traveller, with whom he visits wounded soldiers from India. *Lineally descended from a learned doctor of that name, who was once tutor to Candide, an ingenious young gentleman of some celebrity. In his personal character, he is as humane and worthy a gentleman as any I know; in his official capacity, he unfortunately preaches the doctrines of his renowned ancestor, by demonstrating on all occasions that we live in the best of all possible official worlds (Uncommercial – 'Great Tasmania's Cargo').*

Pankey, Miss: A fellow-boarder of the Dombey children at Mrs. Pipchin's. *A mild little blue-eyed morsel of a child, who was shampoo'd every morning, and seemed in danger of being rubbed away, altogether* (*Dombey*).

Paragon, Mary Anne: David and Dora Copperfield's first servant. *Her name was Paragon. Her nature was represented to us, when we engaged her, as being feebly expressed in her name. She had a written character, as large as a proclamation; and, according to this document, could do every-thing of a domestic nature that ever I heard of, and a great many things that I never did hear of. She was a woman in the prime of life; of a severe countenance; and subject (particularly in the arms) to a sort of perpetual measles or fiery rash. . . . Our treasure was warranted sober and honest. I am therefore willing to believe that she was in a fit when we found her under the boiler; and that the deficient tea-spoons were attributable to the dustman* (*Copper-field*).

Pardiggle, Egbert, Oswald, Francis, Felix, and Alfred: Sons, in order of seniority, of Mrs. Pardiggle. '*Egbert, my eldest (twelve), is the boy who sent out his pocket-money, to the amount of five-and-threepence, to the Tockahoopo Indians. Oswald, my second (ten-and-a-half), is the child who contributed two-and-ninepence to the Great National Smithers Testimonial. Francis, my third (nine), one-and-sixpence-halfpenny; Felix, my forth (seven), eightpence to the Super-annuated Widows; Alfred, my youngest (five), has voluntarily enrolled himself in the Infants Bonds of Joy, and is pledged never, through life, to use tobacco in any form*' (*Bleak House*).

Pardiggle, O. A.: Philanthropic neigh-bour of John Jarndyce. Father of Egbert, Oswald, Francis, Felix, and Alfred. *An obstinate-looking man with a large waist-coat and stubbly hair, who was always talking in a loud bass voice about his mite, or Mrs. Pardiggle's mite, or their five boys' mites* (*Bleak House*).

Pardiggle, Mrs. O. A.: Pardiggle's wife, a fervent philanthropist and committee woman. *A formidable style of lady, with spectacles, a prominent nose, and a loud voice, who had the effect of wanting a great deal of room. And she really did, for she knocked down little chairs with her skirts that were quite a great way off. As only Ada and I were at home, we received her timidly; for she seemed to come in like cold weather, and to make the little Par-diggles blue as they followed* (*Bleak House*).

Parker: Police constable who accom-panies the narrator and Inspector Field to the Old Mint, Borough. *Parker, strapped and great-coated, and waiting in dim Borough doorway by appointment* (*Reprinted* – 'On Duty with Inspector Field').

Parker, Mrs. Johnson: Rival, with her seven spinster daughters, of the three Miss Browns in charitable endeavours. *A ladies' bible and prayer-book distribution society was instantly formed: president, Mrs. Johnson Parker; treasurers, audi-tors, and secretary, the Misses Johnson Parker* (*Boz* – 'Ladies' Societies').

Parkes, Phil: A ranger at Chigwell and *habitué* of the Maypole (*Rudge*).

Parkins: Friend of Our Bore with some-thing about his wife's sister on his mind (*Reprinted* – 'Our Bore').

Parkins, Mrs.: The narrator's laundress, the porter's widow. *Had particular instructions to place a bedroom candle and a match under the staircase lamp on my landing, in order that I might light my candle there, whenever I came home. Mrs. Parkins invariably disregarding all in-structions, they were never there* (*Re-printed* – 'Ghost of Art').

Parkle: A friend of the Uncommercial Traveller living in chambers in Gray's Inn Square. *They were so dirty that I could take off the distinctest impression of my figure on any article of furniture by merely lounging upon it for a few moments; and it used to be a private amusement of mine to print myself off – if I may use the expression – all over the rooms. It was the first large circulation I had. At other times I have actually shaken a window curtain* *while in animated conversation with Parkle, and struggling insects which were certainly red, and were certainly not lady-birds, have dropped on the back of my hand. Yet Parkle lived in that top set years, bound body and soul to the super-stition that they were clean (Uncommercial – 'Chambers').*

Parksop, Brother: George Silverman's deceased grandfather, a brother of the same Nonconformist congregation as Hawkyard ('Silverman').

Parlour Orator, The: See **Rogers** and also **Snobee** (*Boz* – 'Parlour Orator').

Parsons, Mrs.: Subject of one of the Contradictory Couple's arguments. *Master James, growing talkative upon such prospects, asks his mamma how tall Mrs. Parsons is, and whether she is not six feet high; to which his mamma replies, 'Yes, she should think she was, for Mrs. Parsons is a very tall lady indeed; quite a giantess.' 'For Heaven's sake, Charlotte,' cries her husband, 'do not tell the child such prepos-terous nonsense. Six feet high!' (Young Couples* – 'Contradictory Couple').

Parsons, Gabriel: Tottle's old friend who pays Tottle's debts on condition that he will marry Miss Lillerton and pay him back handsomely from her estate. *A short elderly gentleman with a gruffish voice. . . . He was a rich sugar-baker, who mistook rudeness for honesty, and abrupt bluntness for an open and candid manner (Boz* – 'Watkins Tottle').

Parsons, Mrs. Gabriel (Fanny): Gab-riell's wife, whom he had married against her parents' wishes. *'Our love was raised to such a pitch, and as my salary had been raised too, shortly before, we determined on a secret marriage. . . . Two girls – friends of Fanny's – acting as bridesmaids; and a man, who was hired for five shillings and a pint of porter, officiating as father' (Boz* – 'Watkins Tottle').

Parsons, Lætitia: Pianoforte soloist at the Misses Crumpton's ball. *Whose per-formance of 'The Recollections of Ireland' was universally declared to be almost equal to that of Moscheles himself (Boz* – 'Sentiment').

Parvis, Arson: Resident of Lanrean questioned by Captain Jorgan (*Christmas Stories* – 'Message from the Sea').

Passnidge: A friend with Murdstone at Lowestoft *(Copperfield).*

Patty: John's maiden sister, who moves into the haunted house with him. *I ven-ture to call her eight-and-thirty, she is so very handsome, sensible, and engaging* (*Christmas Stories* – 'Haunted House').

Pawkins, Major: A Pennsylvania-born New Yorker and fraudulent speculator. *Distinguished by a very large skull, and a great mass of yellow forehead; in deference to which commodities, it was currently held in bar-rooms and other such places of resort, that the major was a man of huge sagacity. He was further to be known by a heavy eye and a dull slow manner; and for being a man of that kind who, mentally speaking, requires a good deal of room to turn himself in. But, in trading on his stock of wisdom, he invariably proceeded on the principle of putting all the goods he had (and more) into his window; and that went a great way with his constituency of admirers (Chuzzlewit).*

Pawkins, Mrs.: The Major's wife, pro-prietress of Pawkins's Boarding-House where Martin Chuzzlewit and Mark Tapley stay on arrival in New York. *Very straight, bony, and silent (Chuzzle-wit).*

Payne, Dr.: Surgeon to the 43rd Regi-ment at Rochester. *A portly personage in a braided surtout (Pickwick).*

Pea or Peacoat: Officer conducting the narrator on a night inspection of the Thames Police (*Reprinted* – 'Down with the Tide').

Peak: Sir John Chester's manservant. *Was to the full as cool and negligent in his way as his master (Rudge).*

Peartree: Member of the Royal College of Surgeons and of the Eight Club (q.v.) at Cloisterham. *Mr. Peartree is not accountable to me for his opinions, and I say no more of them here than that he attends the poor gratis whenever they want him, and is not the parish doctor. Mr. Peartree may justify it to the grasp of his* *mind thus to do his republican utmost to bring an appointed officer into contempt. Suffice it that Mr. Peartree can never justify it to the grasp of* mine. (*Drood* fragment).

Pebbleson Nephew: City of London wine merchants to whom Walter Wilding was apprenticed by Mrs. Wilding. When he came of age she transferred her shareholding to him and later bought out the owners, enabling Wilding and Company to come into existence (*Christmas Stories* – 'No Thoroughfare'; not in dramatised version).

Pecksniff, Charity (Cherry): Pecksniff's shrewish elder daughter. She pursues Jonas Chuzzlewit and Moddle, but is evaded by both. *It was morning; and the beautiful Aurora, of whom so much hath been written, said, and sung, did, with her rosy fingers, nip and tweak Miss Pecksniff's nose . . . or in more prosaic phrase, the tip of that feature in the sweet girl's countenance, was always very red at breakfast-time. For the most part, indeed, it wore, at the season of the day, a scraped and frosty look, as if it had been rasped; while a similar phenomenon developed itself in her humour, which was then observed to be of a sharp and acid quality, as though an extra lemon (figuratively speaking) had been squeezed into the nectar of her disposition, and had rather damaged its flavour (Chuzzlewit).*

Pecksniff, Mercy (Merry): Pecksniff's vain younger daughter. Marries Jonas Chuzzlewit. *She was the most arch and at the same time the most artless creature, was the youngest Miss Pecksniff, that you can possibly imagine. It was her great charm. She was too fresh and guileless, and too full of childlike vivacity, was the youngest Miss Pecksniff, to wear combs in her hair, or to turn it up, or to frizzle it, or braid it. She wore it in a crop, a loosely flowing crop, which had so many rows of curls in it, that the top row was only one curl. Moderately buxom was her shape, and quite womanly too; but sometimes – yes, sometimes – she even wore a pinafore; and how charming that was! (Chuzzlewit).*

Pecksniff, Seth: Architect and widower, of Salisbury, and hypocritical schemer after old Martin Chuzzlewit's money. Father of Charity and Mercy. *He was a most exemplary man: fuller of virtuous precept than a copybook. Some people likened him to a direction-post, which is always telling the way to a place, and never goes there; but these were his enemies; the shadows cast by his brightness; that was all. His very throat was moral. . . . It seemed to say, on the part of Mr. Pecksniff, 'There is no deception, ladies and gentlemen, all is peace, a holy calm pervades me.' So did his hair, just grizzled with an iron-grey, which was all brushed off his forehead, and stood bolt upright, or slightly drooped in kindred action with his heavy eyelids. So did his person, which was sleek though free from corpulency. So did his manner, which was soft and oily. In a word, even his plain black suit, and state of widower, and dangling double eye-glass, all tended to the same purpose, and cried aloud, 'Behold the moral Pecksniff!' (Chuzzlewit).*

Pedro: One of Jerry's performing dogs. *One of them had a cap upon his head, tied very carefully under his chin, which had fallen down upon his nose and completely obscured one eye (Curiosity Shop).*

Peecher, Emma: A teacher under Bradley Headstone, whom she loves. *Small, shining, neat, methodical, and buxom was Miss Peecher; cherry-cheeked and tuneful of voice. A little pincushion, a little housewife, a little book, a little workbox, a little set of tables and weights and measures, and a little woman, all in one. She could write a little essay on any subject, exactly a slate long, beginning at the left-hand top of one side and ending at the right-hand bottom of the other, and the essay should be strictly according to rule. If Mr. Bradley Headstone had addressed a written proposal of marriage to her, she would probably have replied in a complete little essay on the theme exactly a slate long, but would certainly have replied yes (Mutual Friend).*

Peepy, The Hon. Miss: A famous figure in the past of our English watering-place.

The Beauty of her day and the cruel occasion of innumerable duels (Reprinted – 'Our English Watering-place').

Peerybingle, John: The carrier on whose hearth the Cricket sings. Husband of Mary. *A sturdy figure of a man . . . this lumbering, slow, honest John; this John so heavy, but so light of spirit; so rough upon the surface, but so gentle at the core; so dull without, so quick within; so stolid, but so good! (Christmas Books – 'Cricket').*

Peerybingle, Mrs. John (Mary, 'Dot'): John's wife, called Dot for her tiny size. *Fair she was, and young: though something of what is called the dumpling shape (Christmas Books – 'Cricket').*

Peffer and Snagsby: The law-stationer's business that is now Snagsby's alone. The deceased Peffer had been Mrs. Snagsby's uncle. *Peffer is never seen in Cook's Court now. He is not expected there, for he has been recumbent this quarter of a century in the churchyard of St. Andrew's, Holborn, with the waggons and hackney-coaches roaring past him, all the day and hálf the night, like one great dragon (Bleak House).*

Pegg (alias Waterhouse): A Liverpool crimp. *'This man's a regular bad one' (Uncommercial – 'Poor Mercantile Jack').*

Peggotty, Clara: Sister to Daniel. David Copperfield's nurse and lifelong friend. She serves his mother at Murdstone's and after Clara Copperfield's death marries Barkis. Eventually widowed, she spends the rest of her days with Miss Trotwood. *'Peggotty!' repeated Miss Betsey, with some indignation. 'Do you mean to say, child, that any human being has gone into a Christian church, and got herself named Peggotty?' . . . Peggotty, with no shape at all, and eyes so dark that they seemed to darken their whole neighbourhood in her face, and cheeks and arms so hard and red that I wondered the birds didn't peck her in preference to apples (Copperfield).*

Peggotty, Daniel: Yarmouth fisherman, bachelor brother to Clara. His household in a converted boat on Yarmouth beach includes his nephew Ham, niece Little

Em'ly, and his partner's widow Mrs. Gummidge. He devotes months to searching for Little Em'ly after her elopement and then takes them all to Australia. *A hairy man with a very good-natured face. . . . He was but a poor man himself, said Peggotty, but as good as gold, and as true as steel – those were her similes. The only subject, she informed me, on which he ever showed a violent temper or swore an oath, was this generosity of his; and if it were ever referred to, by any one of them, he struck the table a heavy blow with his right hand (had split it on one such occasion), and swore a dreadful oath that he would be 'Gormed' if he didn't cut and run for good, if it was ever mentioned again (Copperfield).*

Peggotty, Ham: Son of the late Joe, nephew and adopted son of Daniel. Fiancé of Little Em'ly. Fisherman and boatbuilder. He is drowned trying to rescue his betrayer, Steerforth. *A huge, strong fellow of six feet high, broad in proportion, and round-shouldered; but with a simpering boy's face and curly light hair that gave him quite a sheepish look. He was dressed in a canvas jacket, and a pair of such very stiff trousers that they would have stood quite as well alone, without any legs in them. And you couldn't so properly have said he wore a hat, as that he was covered in atop, like an old building, with something pitchy (Copperfield).*

Peggotty, Joe: Daniel's deceased brother. Father of Ham *(Copperfield).*

Peggy: A housemaid *(Christmas Stories – 'Going into Society').*

Peggy: Lord Chamberlain to King Watkins the First in Alice Rainbird's romantic tale ('Holiday Romance').

Pegler, Mrs.: An old countrywoman who haunts Coketown and is finally revealed as Bounderby's mother. *It was an old woman, tall and shapely still, though withered by time, on whom his eyes fell when he stopped and turned. She was very cleanly and plainly dressed, had country mud upon her shoes, and was newly come from a journey. The flutter of her manner, in the unwonted noise of the streets; the* *spare shawl, carried unfolded on her arm; the heavy umbrella, and little basket; the loose long-fingered gloves, to which her hnads were unused; all bespoke an old woman from the country, in her plain holiday clothes, come into Coketown on an expedition of rare occurrence (Hard Times).*

Pell, Solomon: A seedy attorney at the Insolvent Court who assists the Wellers. *A fat flabby pale man, in a surtout which looked green one minute and brown the next: with a velvet collar of the same cameleon tints. His forehead was narrow, his face wide, his head large, and his nose all on one side, as if Nature, indignant with the propensities she observed in him in his birth, had given it an angry tweak which it had never recovered. Being short-necked and asthmatic, however, he respired principally through this feature; so, perhaps, what it wanted in ornament it made up in usefulness (Pickwick).*

Peltirogus, Horatio: A supposed suitor of Kate Nickleby, whose name is evoked by Mrs. Nickleby in order to intrigue Frank Cheeryble. *She even went so far as to hint, obscurely, at an attachment entertained for her daughter by the son of an old neighbour of theirs, one Horatio Peltirogus (a young gentleman who might have been, at that time, four years old, or thereabouts), and to represent it, indeed, as almost a settled thing between the families – only waiting for her daughter's final decision, to come off with the sanction of the church, and to the unspeakable happiness and content of all parties (Nickleby).*

Penrewen: Resident of Lanrean questioned by Captain Jorgan (*Christmas Stories* – 'Message from the Sea').

Peplow, Mrs. and Master: See Macklin, Walker, and Peplow (*Boz* – 'The Streets – Night').

Pepper ('The Avenger'): Pip's boy servant. *I had got on so fast of late, that I had even started a boy in boots – top boots – in bondage and slavery to whom I might be said to pass my days. For, after I had made this monster (out of the refuse of my washerwoman's family) and had clothed*

him with a blue coat, canary waistcoat, white cravat, creamy breeches, and the boots already mentioned, I had to find him a little to do and a great deal to eat; and with both of these horrible requirements he haunted my existence (Expectations).

Peps, Dr. Parker: Emininent physician who supervises the birth of Little Paul Dombey and is later present at his death. *One of the Court Physicians, and a man of immense reputation for assisting at the increase of great families, was walking up and down the drawingroom with his hands behind him, to the unspeakable admiration of the family surgeon (Dombey).*

Perch: Messenger to Dombey and Son. *When Perch the messenger, whose place was on a little bracket, like a time-piece, saw Mr. Dombey come in – or rather when he felt that he was coming, for he had usually an instinctive sense of his approach – he hurried into Mr. Dombey's room, stirred the fire, quarried fresh coals from the bowels of the coal-box, hung the newspaper to air upon the fender, put the chair ready, and the screen in its place, and was round upon his heel on the instant of Mr. Dombey's entrance, to take his greatcoat and hat, and hang them up (Dombey).*

Perch, Mrs.: Perch's over-fertile wife. *Perch . . . jogging his elbow, begged his pardon, but wished to say in his ear, Did he think he could arrange to send home to England a jar of preserved ginger, cheap, for Mrs. Perch's own eating, in the course of her recovery from her next confinement (Dombey).*

Perker: A Gray's Inn solicitor who acts as election agent for Slumkey at Eatanswill and represents Pickwick in the case of Bardell and Pickwick. *A little high-dried man, with a dark squeezed-up face, and small restless black eyes, that kept winking and twinkling on each side of his little inquisitive nose, as if they were playing a perpetual game of peep-bo with that feature. He was dressed all in black, with boots as shiny as his eyes, a low white neckcloth, and a clean shirt with a frill to it. A gold watch-chain and seals, depended from his fob. He carried his black kid gloves in his hands, not on them; and as* *he spoke, thrust his wrists beneath his coat-tails, with the air of a man who was in the habit of propounding some regular posers (Pickwick).*

Perkins, Mrs.: See **Piper, Mrs. Anastasia** *(Bleak House).*

Perkinsop, Mary Anne: One of Mrs. Lirriper's succession of servants, enticed away for more wages by Miss Wozenham. *Was worth her weight in gold as overawing lodgers without driving them away, for lodgers would be far more sparing of their bells with Mary Anne than I ever knew them to be with Maid or Mistress, which is a great triumph especially when accompanied with a cast in the eye and a bag of bones, but it was the steadiness of her way with them through her father's having failed in Pork (Christmas Stories – 'Mrs. Lirriper's Lodgings').*

Pessell: A vice-president of the anatomy and medicine session at the second meeting of the Mudfog Association *(Mudfog).*

'Pet': See **Meagles, Minnie** *(Dorrit).*

Peter, Lord: Noble suitor of Julia Manners, for her money, who is unintentionally cut out by Alexander Trott. He is killed riding. *Lord Peter, who had been detained beyond his time by drinking champagne and riding a steeple-chase, went back to the Honourable Augustus Flair's, and drank more champagne, and rode another steeple-chase and was thrown and killed (Boz – 'Great Winglebury Duel').*

Petowker, Henrietta: Actress at the Theatre Royal, Drury Lane, and friend of the Kenwigs family. She marries Lillyvick, but deserts him for a half-pay captain. *The great lion of the party, being the daughter of a theatrical fireman, who 'went on' in the pantomime, and had the greatest turn for the stage that was ever known, being able to sing and recite in a manner that brought the tears into Mrs. Kenwigs's eyes (Nickleby).*

Pettifer, Tom: Captain Jorgan's steward, whose hate contains the answer to the mystery. *A man of a certain plump neatness, with a curly whisker, and elaborately nautical in a jacket, and shoes, and all*

things correspondent. *(Christmas Stories – 'Message from the Sea').*

Phib: See **Phoebe** *(Nickleby).*

Phibbs: Haberdasher neighbour of Trinkle who assists Inspector Wield's inquiries in the case of Eliza Grimwood's murder *(Reprinted – 'Three "Detective" Anecdotes').*

Phil: Serving man at Our School. *Our retrospective glance presents Phil as a shipwrecked carpenter, cast away upon the desert island of a school, and carrying into practice an ingenious inkling of many trades. He mended whatever was broken, and made whatever was wanted. . . . We particularly remember that Phil had a sovereign contempt for learning : which engenders in us a respect for his sagacity (Reprinted – 'Our School').*

Phoebe: Crippled daughter of 'Lamps', and exemplar to Jackson. *The room upstairs was a very clean white room with a low roof. Its only inmate lay on a couch that brought her face to a level with the window. The couch was white too ; and her simple dress or wrapper being light blue, like the band around her hair, she had an ethereal look, and a fanciful appearance of lying among clouds. . . . He guessed her to be thirty. The charm of her transparent face and large bright brown eyes was, not that they were passively resigned, but that they were actively and thoroughly cheerful. Even her busy hands, which of their own thinness alone might have besought compassion, plied their task with a gay courage that made mere compassion an unjustifiable assumption of superiority, and an impertinence (Christmas Stories – 'Mugby Junction').*

Phoebe (Phib): The Squeers' maid. *The hungry servant attended Miss Squeers in her own room according to custom, to curl her hair, perform the other little offices of her toilet, and administer as much flattery as she could get up (Nickleby).*

Phunky: Serjeant Snubbin's junior counsel for Pickwick in Bardell and Pickwick. *Although an infant barrister, he was a full-grown man. He had a very nervous manner, and a painful hesitation* in his speech; it did not appear to be a natural defect, but seemed rather the result of timidity, arising from the consciousness of being 'kept down' by want of means, or interest, or connexion, or impudence, as the case might be (*Pickwick*).

Pickles: The fishmonger from whose shop the magic fishbone comes in Alice Rainbird's romantic tale ('Holiday Romance').

Pickleson ('Rinaldo di Velasco'): A giant, exhibited by Mim who leases him from his mother. *This giant when on view figured as a Roman. He was a languid young man, which I attribute to the distance betwixt his extremities. He had a little head and less in it, he had weak eyes and weak knees, and altogether you couldn't look at him without feeling that there was greatly too much of him both for his joints and his mind. But he was an amiable though timid young man (his mother let him out and spent the money)* (*Christmas Stories* – 'Doctor Marigold').

Pickwick, Samuel: General Chairman – Member Pickwick Club and leader of a group of Pickwickians – Snodgrass, Tupman, and Winkle – in a series of travels and adventures. *A casual observer, adds the secretary, to whose notes we are indebted for the following account – a casual observer might possibly have remarked nothing extraordinary in the bald head, and circular spectacles, which were intently turned towards his (the secretary's) face, during the reading of the above resolutions: to those who knew that the gigantic brain of Pickwick was working beneath that forehead, and that the beaming eyes of Pickwick were twinkling behind those glasses, the sight was indeed an interesting one. There sat the man who had traced to their source the mighty ponds of Hampstead, and agitated the scientific world with his Theory of Tittlebats, as calm and unmoved as the deep waters of the one on a frosty day, or as a solitary specimen of the other in the inmost recesses of an earthen jar. And how much more interesting did the spectacle become when, starting into full life and animation, as a simultaneous call for 'Pickwick' burst from his* followers, that illustrious man slowly mounted into the Windsor chair, on which he had been previously seated, and addressed the club himself had founded. What a study for an artist did that exciting scene present! The eloquent Pickwick, with one hand gracefully concealed behind his coat tails, and the other waving in air, to assist his glowing declamation; his elevated position revealing those tights and gaiters, which, had they clothed an ordinary man, might have passed without observation, but which, when Pickwick clothed them – if we may use the expression – inspired voluntary awe and respect (*Pickwick*).

Pidger: Deceased acquaintance of Lavinia Spenlow, believed by her to have been in love with her (*Copperfield*).

Piff, Miss: One of the attendants at Mugby Junction refreshment room (*Christmas Stories* – 'Mugby Junction').

Pigeon, Thomas: See **Thompson, Tally-Ho** (*Reprinted* – 'Detective Police').

Pilkins: The Dombey family physician when Little Paul is born. *The family surgeon, who had regularly puffed the case for the last six weeks, among all his patients, friends, and acquaintances, as one to which he was in hourly expectation day and night of being summoned, in conjunction with Doctor Parker Peps (Dombey)*.

Pinch, Ruth: Tom's sister, governess to a Camberwell family. Marries John Westlock. *She had a good face; a very mild and prepossessing face; and a pretty little figure – slight and short, but remarkable for its neatness. There was something of her brother, much of him indeed, in a certain gentleness of manner, and in her look of timid trustfulness (Chuzzlewit)*.

Pinch, Tom: Pecksniff's ingenuous assistant. *An ungainly, awkward-looking man, extremely short-sighted . . . but notwithstanding his attire, and his clumsy figure, which a great stoop in his shoulders, and a ludicrous habit he had of thrusting his head forward, by no means redeemed, one would not have been disposed (unless Mr. Pecksniff said so) to consider him a bad fellow by any means. He was perhaps* about thirty, but he might have been almost any age between sixteen and sixty : being one of those strange creatures who never decline into an ancient appearance, but look their oldest when they are very young, and get it over at once (Chuzzlewit).

Pip: Friend of Montague Tigg. '*Mr. Pip – theatrical man – capital man to know – oh, capital man !' (Chuzzlewit).*

Pip (Philip Pirrip, jun.): Narrator and central figure of the novel about the rise and fall of his great expectations from a mysterious benefactor. *My father's family name being Pirrip, and my christian name Philip, my infant tongue could make of both names nothing longer or more explicit than Pip. So, I called myself Pip, and came to be called Pip (Expectations).*

Pipchin, Mrs.: Proprietor of the children's boarding-house at Brighton where the Dombey children stay. *A marvellous ill-favoured, ill-conditioned old lady, of a stooping figure, with a mottled face, like bad marble, a hook nose, and a hard grey eye, that looked as if it might have been hammered at on an anvil without sustaining any injury. Forty years at least had elapsed since the Peruvian mines had been the death of Mr. Pipchin ; but his relict still wore black bombazeen, of such a lustreless, deep, dead, sombre shade, that gas itself couldn't light her up after dark, and her presence was a quencher to any number of candles. She was generally spoken of as 'a great manager' of children ; and the secret of her management was, to give them everything that they didn't like, and nothing that they did – which was found to sweeten their dispositions very much. She was such a bitter old lady, that one was tempted to believe there had been some mistake in the application of the Peruvian machinery, and that all her waters of gladness and milk of human kindness, had been pumped out dry, instead of the mines (Dombey).*

Piper, Professor: A boarder at the National Hotel, in America, where Martin Chuzzlewit stays before embarking for Eden (Chuzzlewit).

Pipe, Mrs. Anastasia and **Perkins,**

Mrs.: Neighbours of Krook's and interested onlookers at the events at his house. *The potboy of the Sol's Arms appearing with her supper-pint well frothed, Mrs. Piper accepts that tankard and retires in-doors, first giving a fair good-night to Mrs. Perkins, who has had her own pint in her hand ever since it was fetched from the same hostelry by young Perkins before he was sent to bed (Bleak House).*

Pipkin, Mr., M.R.C.S.: Speaker at the anatomy and medicine session of the second meeting of the Mudfog Association. *Read a short but most interesting communication in which he sought to prove the complete belief of Sir William Courtenay, otherwise Thom, recently shot at Canterbury, in the Homœopathic system (Mudfog).*

Pipkin, Nathaniel: The parish clerk, in the tale of that title, who unsuccessfully loves Maria Lobbs. *A harmless, inoffensive, good-natured being, with a turned-up nose, and rather turned-in legs : a cast in his eye, and halt in his gait (Pickwick).*

Pipson, Miss: Fellow pupil of Master B. at Miss Griffin's school. *Having curly light hair and blue eyes (which was my idea of anything mortal and feminine that was called Fair) (Christmas Stories – 'Haunted House').*

Pirrip, Philip, jun.: See Pip *(Expectations).*

Pirrip, Philip, sen., Georgiana, Alexander, Bartholomew, Abraham, Tobias, and **Roger:** Pip's deceased father, mother, and infant brothers. *My first fancies regarding what they were like, were unreasonably derived from their tombstones. The shape of the letters on my father's, gave me an odd idea that he was a square, stout, dark man, with curly black hair. From the character and turn of the inscription, 'Also Georgiana Wife of the Above, I drew a childish conclusion that my mother was freckled and sickly. To five little stone lozenges, each about a foot and a half long, which were arranged in a neat row beside their grave, and were sacred to* the memory of five little brothers of mine . . . I am indebted for a belief I religiously entertained that they had all been born on their backs with their hands in their trousers-pockets, and had never taken them out in this state of existence (Expectations).

Pitcher: Pupil at Dotheboys Hall who contracts a fever. 'Never was such a boy, I do believe,' said Mrs. Squeers; 'whatever he has is always catching too. I say it's obstinacy' (Nickleby).

Pitt, Jane: A matron at the school, where she is Old Cheeseman's only friend. They marry. She was not quite pretty; but she had a very frank, honest, bright face, and all our fellows were fond of her. She was uncommonly neat and cheerful, and uncommonly comfortable and kind. And if anything was the matter with a fellow's mother, he always went and showed the letter to Jane (Christmas Stories – 'Schoolboy's Story').

Plornish, Thomas: A plasterer, tenant of Casby in Bleeding Heart Yard. He and his wife befriend the Dorrits and Clennam, who lodge Cavelletto with them. He was one of those many wayfarers on the road of life, who seem to be afflicted with supernatural corns, rendering it impossible for them to keep up even with their lame competitors. A willing, working, soft-hearted, not hard-headed fellow, Plornish took his fortune as smoothly as could be expected; but it was a rough one. It so rarely happened that anybody seemed to want him, it was such an exceptional case when his powers were in any request, that his misty mind could not make out how it happened. He took it as it came, therefore; he tumbled into all kinds of difficulties, and tumbled out of them; and, by tumbling through life, got himself considerably bruised. . . . A smooth-cheeked, fresh-coloured, sandy-whiskered man of thirty. Long in the legs, yielding at the knees, foolish in the face, flannel-jacketed, lime-whitened (Dorrit).

Plornish, Mrs. Thomas (Sally): Plornish's wife. A young woman, made somewhat slatternly in herself and her belongings by poverty; and so dragged at by

poverty and the children together, that their united forces had already dragged her face into wrinkles (Dorrit).

Pluck: One of Hawk's followers. A gentleman with a flushed face and a flash air (Nickleby).

Plummer, Bertha: Caleb's blind daughter, Edward's sister. To make her happy, Caleb pretends that their surroundings are not poor, and that Tackleton is not the hard master he is. Bertha comes to love her conception of Tackleton and her father has to reveal his deception. The Blind Girl never knew that ceilings were discoloured, walls blotched and bare of plaster here and there, high crevices unstopped, and widening every day, beams mouldering and tending downward. The Blind Girl never knew that iron was rusting, wood rotting, paper peeling off; the size, and shape, and true proportion of the dwelling, withering away. The Blind Girl never knew that . . . sorrow and faint-heartedness were in the house; that Caleb's scanty hairs were turning greyer and more grey, before her sightless face. The Blind Girl never knew they had a master, cold, exacting, and uninterested – never knew that Tackleton was Tackleton in short (Christmas Books – 'Cricket').

Plummer, Caleb: Father of Edward and Bertha, a poor toymaker employed by Gruff and Tackleton. A little, meagre, thoughtful, dingy-faced man, who seemed to have made himself a great-coat from the sack-cloth covering of some old box; for, when he turned to shut the door, and keep the weather out, he disclosed upon the back of that garment, the inscription G & T in large black capitals. Also the word GLASS in bold characters (Christmas Books – 'Cricket').

Plummer, Edward: Caleb's son, Bertha's brother. Returning after long absence abroad, he finds his sweetheart, May Fielding, about to marry Tackleton. He disguises himself as an old man to test the strength of her affections, and takes her for his own on her intended wedding morning. Had long white hair, good features, singularly bold and well defined for an old man, and dark, bright, *penetrating eyes (Christmas Books – 'Cricket').*

Plunder: One of Miss Flite's birds *(Bleak House).*

Pocket, Alick, Fanny, Jane, and Joe: Four of Matthew and Belinda's children, younger brothers and sisters to Herbert *(Expectations).*

Pocket, Herbert: Matthew's son, elder brother of Alick, Fanny, Jane, and Joe. Pip's close friend. They share lodgings and conspire to hide Magwitch and get him out of England. Through Pip, Herbert gets a partnership in Clarriker and Co. and is enabled to marry Clara Barley. *I had never seen any one then, and I have never seen any one since, who more strongly expressed to me, in every look and tone, a natural incapacity to do anything secret and mean. There was something wonderfully hopeful about his general air, and something that at the same time whispered to me he would never be very successful or rich. . . . He was still a pale young gentleman, and had a certain conquered languor about him in the midst of his spirits and briskness, that did not seem indicative of natural strength. He had not a handsome face, but it was better than handsome : being extremely amiable and cheerful (Expectations).*

Pocket, Matthew: Father of Herbert, Alick, Fanny, Jane, and Joe. Cousin to Miss Havisham. *A gentleman with a rather perplexed expression of face, and with his very grey hair disordered on his head, as if he didn't quite see his way to putting anything straight. . . . By degrees I learnt, and chiefly from Herbert, that Mr. Pocket had been educated at Harrow and at Cambridge, where he had distinguished himself; but that when he had had the happiness of marrying Mrs. Pocket very early in life, he had impaired his prospects and taken up the calling of a Grinder (Expectations).*

Pocket, Mrs. Matthew (Belinda): Matthew's wife, mother of Herbert, Alick, Jane, Joe, and Fanny. *The only daughter of a certain accidental deceased Knight, who had invented for himself a conviction that his deceased father would*

have been made a Baronet but for somebody's determined opposition arising out of entirely personal motives. . . . He had directed Mrs. Pocket to be brought up from her cradle as one who in the nature of things must carry a title, and who was to be guarded from the acquisition of plebeian domestic knowledge. So successful a watch and ward had been established over the young lady by this judicious parent, that she had grown up highly ornamental, but perfectly helpless and useless (Expectations).

Pocket, Sarah: Toadying cousin of Miss Havisham, who leaves her a derisory legacy in her will. *A little dry brown corrugated old woman, with a small face that might have been made of walnut shells, and a large mouth like a cat's without the whiskers (Expectations).*

Podder: A renowned member of the All-Muggleton Cricket Club. *The hitherto unconquered Podder (Pickwick).*

'Poddles': Pet name of one of Betty Higden's charges *(Mutual Friend).*

Podgers, John: Well-to-do widower of Windsor in the time of James I in Mr. Pickwick's tale. *Broad, sturdy, Dutch-built, short, and a very hard eater, as men of his figure often are. . . . He had several times been seen to look after fat oxen on market days, and had even been heard, by persons of good credit and reputation, to chuckle at the sight, and say to himself with great glee, 'Live beef, live beef!' (Humphrey).*

Podsnap, Georgiana: The Podsnaps' only daughter, whom Lammle attempts to manœuvre into marrying Fledgeby. *This young rocking-horse was being trained in her mother's art of prancing in a stately manner without ever getting on. But the high parental action was not yet imparted to her, and in truth she was but an undersized damsel, with high shoulders, low spirits, chilled elbows, and a rasped surface of nose, who seemed to take occasional frosty peeps out of childhood into womanhood, and to shrink back again, overcome by her mother's head-dress and her father from head to foot – crushed by the mere dead-weight of Podsnappery (Mutual Friend).*

Podsnap, John: Father of Georgiana. A complacent businessman. *Two little light-coloured wiry wings, one on either side of his else bald head, looking as like his hair-brushes as his hair, dissolving view of red beads on his forehead, large allowance of crumpled shirt-collar up behind.* || *Mr. Podsnap was well to do, and stood very high in Mr. Podsnap's opinion. Beginning with a good inheritance, he had married a good inheritance, and had thriven exceedingly in the Marine Insurance way, and was quite satisfied. He never could make out why everybody was not quite satisfied, and he felt conscious that he set a brilliant social example in being particularly well satisfied with most things, and, above all other things, with himself (Mutual Friend).*

Podsnap, Mrs. John: Podsnap's wife, Georgiana's mother. *Quantity of bone, neck and nostrils like a rocking-horse, hard features, majestic head-dress in which Podsnap has hung golden offerings (Mutual Friend).*

Pogram, The Hon. Elijah: A rabidly nationalistic American Congressman encountered by Martin Chuzzlewit in his travels. *'One of the master minds of our country.'* || *He had straight black hair, parted up the middle of his head, and hanging down upon his coat; a little fringe of hair upon his chin; wore no neck-cloth; a white hat; a suit of black, long in the sleeves, and short in the legs; soiled brown stockings, and laced shoes. His complexion, naturally muddy, was rendered muddier by too strict an economy of soap and water; and the same observation will apply to the washable part of his attire, which he might have changed with comfort to himself, and gratification to his friends. He was about five-and-thirty; was crushed and jammed up in a heap, under the shade of a large green cotton umbrella; and ruminated over his tobacco-plug like a cow (Chuzzlewit.)*

Polly: Waitress upon Guppy and Jobling at the Slap-Bang dining-house. *The waitress returns, bearing what is apparently a model of the tower of Babel, but what is really a pile of plates, and flat tin dish-covers (Bleak House).*

Polreath, David: Resident of Lanrean questioned by Captain Jorgan (*Christmas Stories* – 'Message from the Sea').

Ponto: Jingle's sagacious dog of former days. *'Surprising instinct – out shooting one day – entering enclosure – whistled – dog stopped – whistled again – Ponto – no go; stock still – called him – Ponto, Ponto – wouldn't move – dog transfixed – staring at a board – looked up, saw an inscription – 'Game-keeper has orders to shoot all dogs found in this enclosure" – wouldn't pass it – wonderful dog – valuable dog that – very' (Pickwick).*

Poddles: A comical mongrel dog found starving at the door of the East London Children's Hospital and adopted there. *Trotting about among the beds, on familiar terms with all the patients. . . . An admirer of his mental endowments has presented him with a collar bearing the legend, 'Judge not Poddles by external appearances' (Uncommercial –* 'Small Star in the East' and 'On an Amateur Beat').

Poor Relation, The: See **Michael** (*Christmas Stories* – 'Poor Relation').

Pordage, Mr. Commissioner and Mrs.: Self-styled 'Government' of Silver-Store Island and his wife. In later years he is officially appointed Governor and a K.C.B., and dies of jaundice. *He was a stiff-jointed, high-nosed old gentleman, without an ounce of fat on him, of a very angry temper and a very yellow complexion. Mrs. Commissioner Pordage, making allowance for difference of sex, was much the same (Christmas Stories –* 'English Prisoners').

Porkenham (Sidney, Mrs. Sidney, and the Misses), Griggs, and Slummintowken Families: Social rivals of the Nupkins family, to whom the latter have boasted of their intimacy with Captain Fitz-Marshall, later unmasked as Jingle (*Pickwick*).

Porter, Emma: Mrs. Porter's daughter, contemptuous of the Gattleton girls for showing off in private theatricals. *Miss P., by the bye, had only the week before made 'an exhibition' of herself for four days, behind a counter at a fancy fair, to all and every of her Majesty's liege sub-*

jects who were disposed to pay a shilling each for the privilege of seeing some four dozen girls flirting with strangers, and playing at shop (Boz – 'Mrs. Joseph Porter').

Porter, Mrs. Joseph: Mother of Emma. A notorious scandal-monger and great rival of the Gattletons, whose private theatricals she contrives to sabotage. *The good folks of Clapham and its vicinity stood very much in awe of scandal and sarcasm; and thus Mrs. Joseph Porter was courted, and flattered, and caressed, and invited, for much the same reason that induces a poor author, without a farthing in his pocket, to behave with extraordinary civility to a twopenny postman (Boz –* 'Mrs. Joseph Porter').

Porters, Mr.: See under **Twinkleton, Miss** *(Drood).*

Potkins, William: Waiter at the Blue Boar, Rochester *(Expectations).*

Pott: Editor of the *Eatanswill Gazette,* of whom Winkle falls foul over a newspaper item linking him with Mrs. Pott. *A tall, thin man, with a sandy-coloured head inclined to baldness, and a face in which solemn importance was blended with a look of unfathomable profundity (Pickwick).*

Pott, Mrs.: Pott's wife. *All men whom mighty genius has raised to a proud eminence in the world, have usually some little weakness which appears the more conspicuous from the contrast it presents to their general character. If Mr. Pott had a weakness, it was, perhaps, that he was rather too submissive to the somewhat contemptuous control and sway of his wife (Pickwick).*

Potter, Thomas and Robert Smithers: Two City clerks who spend their quarter's pay celebrating the receipt of it and paying the resultant fines. *Their incomes were limited, but their friendship was unbounded. They lived in the same street, walked into town every morning at the same hour, dined at the same slap-bang every day, and revelled in each other's company every night. They were knit together by the closest ties of intimacy and* friendship, or, as Mr. Thomas Potter touchingly observed, they were 'thick-and-thin pals, and nothing but it'. There was a spice of romance in Mr. Smithers's disposition, a ray of poetry, a gleam of misery, a sort of consciousness of he didn't exactly know what, coming across him he didn't precisely know why – which stood out in fine relief against the off-hand, dashing, amateur-pickpocket-sort-of-manner, which distinguished Mr. Potter in an eminent degree (Boz – 'Making a Night of it').

Potterson, Abbey: Sister of Job and landlady of the Six Jolly Fellowship Porters. *Miss Potterson, sole proprietor and manager of the Fellowship-Porters, reigned supreme on her throne, the Bar, and a man must have drunk himself mad drunk indeed if he thought he could contest a point with her. Being known on her own authority as Miss Abbey Potterson, some water-side heads, which (like the water) were none of the clearest, harboured muddled notions that, because of her dignity and firmness, she was named after, or in some sort related to, the Abbey at Westminster. But Abbey was only short for Abigail, by which name Miss Potterson had been christened at Limehouse Church, some sixty and odd years before. . . . She was a tall, upright, well-favoured woman, though severe of countenance, and had more of the air of a school-mistress than mistress of the Six Jolly Fellowship-Porters (Mutual Friend).*

Potterson, Job: Abbey's brother, a steward in the ship in which John Harmon travels from Cape Colony to England. *'Lord bless my soul and body,' cried Mr. Inspector. 'Talk of trades, Miss Abbey, and the way they set their marks on men' (a subject which nobody had approached); 'who wouldn't know your brother to be a Steward! There's a bright and ready twinkle in his eye, there's a neatness in his action, there's a smartness in his figure, there's an air of reliability about him in case you wanted a basin, which points out the steward!' (Mutual Friend).*

Pouch, Mrs. Joe: A widow whom Trooper George might have married. *'It* *was a chance for me, certainly,' returns the trooper, half-laughingly, half-seriously, 'but I shall never settle down into a respectable man now. Joe Pouch's widow might have done me good – there was something in her – and something of her – but I couldn't make up my mind to it'* (Bleak House).

Poulter, Mr. and Mrs.: A reformed couple, characters assumed by Gabblewig and Rosina in order to unmask Slap (*Nightingale's Diary*).

Powler Family: An ancient line with which Mrs. Sparsit claims connection through her deceased husband. *Could trace themselves so exceedingly far back that it was not surprising if they sometimes lost themselves – which they had rather frequently done, as respected horse-flesh, blind-hookey, Hebrew monetary transactions, and the Insolvent Debtors Court* (*Hard Times*).

Pratchett, Mrs.: Head chambermaid of the hotel where Christopher works. *Now Mrs. Pratchett was not a waitress, but a chambermaid. Now a chambermaid may be married; if Head, generally is married, – or says so. It comes to the same thing as expressing what is customary. (N.B. Mr. Pratchett is in Australia, and his address there is 'the Bush')* (Christmas Stories – 'Somebody's Luggage').

Precedent: One of Miss Flite's birds (*Bleak House*).

Prentice Knights, later **United Bull-Dogs:** A brotherhood of London apprentices, led by Sim Tappertit, which allied itself with the Protestant cause and joined in the Gordon Riots (*Rudge*).

Price: A prisoner for debt, encountered by Pickwick at Namby's. *A coarse vulgar young man of about thirty, with a sallow face and harsh voice: evidently possessed of that knowledge of the world, and captivating freedom of manner, which is to be acquired in public-house parlours, and at low billiard-tables* (*Pickwick*).

Price, Matilda ('Tilda): Friend of Fanny Squeers. She marries Browdie. *A miller's daughter of only eighteen* (*Nickleby*).

Prig, Betsey: A nurse at St. Bartholomew's Hospital who shares engagements, including the nursing of Lewsome, with Mrs. Gamp until their famous quarrel. *Mrs. Prig was of the Gamp build, but not so fat; and her voice was deeper and more like a man's. She had also a beard* (*Chuzzlewit*).

Priscilla: The Jellybys' maid. *'Priscilla drinks – she's always drinking. It's a great shame and a great story of you, if you say you didn't smell her to-day. It was as bad as a public-house, waiting at dinner'* (*Bleak House*).

Prodgit, Mrs.: Augustus George Meek's nurse. *Stood in the corner behind the door, consuming Sherry Wine. From the nutty smell of that beverage pervading the apartment, I have no doubt she was consuming a second glassful. She wore a black bonnet of large dimensions, and was copious in figure. The expression of her countenance was severe and discontented* (Reprinted – 'Births. Mrs. Meek, of a Son').

Prosee: Member of the Mudfog Association (*Mudfog*).

Pross, Miss: Companion of Lucie Manette, in trying to protect whom she struggles with Madame Defarge and the latter is killed. *A wild-looking woman, whom even in his agitation, Mr. Lorry observed to be all of a red colour, and to have red hair, and to be dressed in some extraordinary tight-fitting fashion, and to have on her head a most wonderful bonnet like a Grenadier wooden measure, and good measure too, or a great Stilton cheese.... ('I really think this must be a man!' was Mr. Lorry's breathless reflection)* (Two Cities).

Pross, Solomon (alias **John Barsad**): Miss Pross's corrupt brother who fleeces her of her possessions and abandons her. An informer in England and later spy and turnkey in France. *Of what profession? Gentleman. Ever been kicked? Might have been. Frequently? No. Ever kicked downstairs? Decidedly not; once received a kick on the top of a staircase, and fell downstairs of his own accord* (Two Cities).

Provis: See **Magwitch, Abel** *(Expectatations)*.

Pruffle: Manservant to the scientific gentleman Pickwick meets at Clifton. *The ingenious Mr. Pruffle (Pickwick)*.

Pubsey and Co.: Moneylending business in the City of London run by Riah for Fledgeby *(Mutual Friend)*.

Puffer, Princess: Keeper of the East End London opium den frequented by Jasper. *'Ah, my poor nerves! I got Heavens-hard drunk for sixteen year afore I took to this; but this don't hurt me, not to speak of. And it takes away the hunger as well as wittles, deary' (Drood)*.

Pugstyles: A constituent of Gregsbury, M.P., and leader of the deputation demanding his resignation. *A plump old gentleman in a violent heat (Nickleby)*.

Pumblechook, Uncle: Joe Gargery's uncle, a well-to-do corn-chandler. A notable hypocrite, he hints that he is Pip's secret benefactor. *A large hard-breathing middle-aged slow man, with a mouth like a fish, dull staring eyes, and sandy hair standing upright on his head, so that he looked as if he had just been all but choked, and had that moment come to. || Besides being possessed by my sister's idea that a mortifying and penitential character ought to be imparted to my diet . . . his conversation consisted of nothing but arithmetic. On my politely bidding him Good-morning, he said, pompously, 'Seven times nine, boy?' (Expectations)*.

Pumpkinskull, Professor: Speaker at the zoology and botany session of the second meeting of the Mudfog Association. *No gentleman attending that section could fail to be aware of the fact that the youth of the present age evinced, by their behaviour in the streets, and at all places of pub'ic resort, a considerable lack of that gallantry and gentlemanly feeling which, in more ignorant times, had been thought becoming. He wished to know whether it were possible that a constant outward application of bears'-grease by the young gentlemen about town had imperceptibly infused into those unhappy persons some-thing of the nature and quality of the bear (Mudfog)*.

Pupford, Miss Euphemia: Principal of an academy for six young ladies of tender years. *One of the most amiable of her sex; it necessarily follows that she possesses a sweet temper, and would own to the possession of a great deal of sentiment if she considered it quite reconcilable with her duty to parents. || Miss Pupford's Assistant has a little more bone than Miss Pupford, but is of the same trim orderly, diminutive cast, and, from long contemplation, admiration, and imitation of Miss Pupford, has grown like her (Christmas Stories – 'Tom Tiddler's Ground')*.

Pupker, Sir Matthew, M.P.: Chairman of the United Metropolitan Improved Hot Muffin and Crumpet Baking and Punctual Delivery Company. *Had a little round head with a flaxen wig on the top of it (Nickleby)*.

Purblind: Member of the Mudfog Association *(Mudfog)*.

Purday, Captain: Ardent supporter of Bung for beadle of 'Our Parish'. *A determined opponent of the constituted authorities, whoever they may chance to be (Boz – 'Election for Beadle')*. Purday is the unnamed 'Half-pay Captain' in the Boz sketch of that title.

Pyegrave, Charley: Son of a duke. Client of Miss Mowcher. *'What a man he is! There's a whisker! As to charley's legs, if they were only a pair (which they ain't), they'd defy competition' (Copperfield)*.

Pyke: One of Sir Mulberry Hawk's followers. *A sharp-faced gentleman (Nickleby)*.

Quale: A philanthropic friend of the Jellybys, wishing to marry Caddy. *A loquacious young man . . . with large shining knobs for temples, and his hair all brushed to the back of his head . . . having a great deal to say for himself about Africa, and a project of his for teaching the coffee colonists to teach the natives to turn piano-forte legs and establish an export trade (Bleak House)*.

Queerspeck, Professor: Speaker at the mechanical science session of the first meeting of the Mudfog Association. *Exhibited an elegant model of a portable railway, neatly mounted in a green case, for the waistcoat pocket. By attaching this beautiful instrument to his boots, any Bank or public-office clerk could transport himself from his place of residence to his place of business, at the easy rate of sixty-five miles an hour, which, to gentlemen of sedentary pursuits, would be an incalculable advantage (Mudfog).*

Quickear: One of the policemen visiting sailors' haunts with the Uncommercial Traveller (*Uncommercial* – 'Poor Mercentile Jack').

Quilp, Daniel: The villain of the story: a money-lender who cheats and ruins people on every hand and ill-treats his wife. Eventually pursued by the police, he drowns in the Thames. *An elderly man of remarkably hard features and forbidding aspect, and so low in stature as to be quite a dwarf, though his head and face were large enough for the body of a giant. His black eyes were restless, sly, and cunning; his mouth and chin, bristly with the stubble of a coarse hard beard; and his complexion was one of that kind which never looks clean or wholesome. But what added most to the grotesque appearance of his face, was a ghastly smile, which, appearing to be the mere result of habit and to have no connection with any mirthful or complacent feeling, constantly revealed the few discoloured fangs that were yet scattered in his mouth, and gave him the aspect of a panting dog. His dress consisted of a large high-crowned hat, a worn dark suit, a pair of capacious shoes, and a dirty white neckerchief sufficiently limp and crumpled to disclose the greater part of his wiry throat. Such hair as he had, was of a grizzled black, cut short and straight upon his temples, and hanging in a frowsy fringe about his ears. His hands, which were of a rough coarse grain, were very dirty; his finger-nails were crooked, long, and yellow (Curiosity Shop).*

Quilp, Mrs. Daniel (Betsey): Quilp's wife and Mrs. Jiniwin's daughter. She re-marries happily after Quilp's death. *A pretty little, mild-spoken, blue-eyed woman, who having allied herself in wedlock to the dwarf in one of those strange infatuations of which examples are by no means scarce, performed a sound practical penance for her folly, every day of her life (Curiosity Shop).*

Quinch, Mrs.: The oldest pensioner at Titbull's. *'Mrs. Quinch being the oldest and have totally lost her head'* (*Uncommercial* – 'Titbull's Alms-Houses').

Quinion: Murdstone and Grinby's manager who introduced David Copperfield to Micawber (*Copperfield*).

Rachael: The Coketown factory hand for love of whom Stephen Blackpool wishes to divorce his drunken wife. *He saw another of the shawled figures in advance of him, at which he looked so keenly that perhaps its mere shadow indistinctly reflected on the wet pavement – if he could have seen it without the figure itself moving along from lamp to lamp, brightening and fading as it went – would have been enough to tell him who was there. . . . She turned, being then in the brightness of a lamp; and raising her hood a little, showed a quiet oval face, dark and rather delicate, irradiated by a pair of very gentle eyes, and further set off by the perfect order of her shining black hair. It was not a face in its first bloom; she was a woman five-and-thirty years of age (Hard Times).*

Rachel, Mrs.: See **Chadband, Mrs.** (*Bleak House*).

Raddle: Mrs. Raddle's husband. *'Oh! If ever a woman was troubled with a ruffi'nly creetur, that takes a pride and a pleasure in disgracing his wife on every possible occasion afore strangers, I am that woman!'* (*Pickwick*).

Raddle, Mrs. (Mary Ann): Raddle's wife. Mrs. Cluppins's sister and Bob Sawyer's landlady at Lant Street, Borough. *A little fierce woman bounced into the room, all in a tremble with passion, and pale with rage (Pickwick).*

Radfoot, George: The seaman whose body is mistaken for Harmon's. Third mate on the ship in which Harmon had been returning to England, he had arranged to exchange with Harmon the clothes in which his body is clothed when found in the Thames by Hexam *(Mutual Friend)*.

Rags: One of Miss Flite's birds *(Bleak House)*.

Rainbird, Alice: 'Bride' of Robin Redforth and author of the romantic tale of Princess Alicia ('Holiday Romance').

Rairyganoo, Sally: One of Mrs. Lirriper's succession of maids. *Which I still suspect of Irish extraction though family represented Cambridge, else why abscond with a bricklayer of the Limerick persuasion and be married in pattens not waiting till his black eye was decently got round with all the company fourteen in number and one horse fighting outside on the roof of the vehicle (Christmas Stories – 'Mrs. Lirriper's Legacy').*

Ram Chowdar Doss Azuph Al Bowlar: Subject of an unlikely anecdote by Captain Helves, interrupted by dinner. *'A devilish pleasant fellow. As we were enjoying our hookahs one evening, in the cool verandah in front of his villa, we were rather surprised by the sudden appearance of thirty-four of his Kit-magars (for he had rather a large establishment there), accompanied by an equal number of Consu-mars, approaching the house with a threatening aspect, and beating a tom-tom (Boz – 'Steam Excursion'.*

Rames, William: Second mate of the *Golden Mary (Christmas Stories – 'Golden Mary').*

Ramsey: Defendant in Bullman and Ramsey, the case discussed at length by Dodson and Fogg's clerks while Pickwick awaits attention *(Pickwick)*.

Rarx: Passenger in the *Golden Mary*. He loses his reason in the long-boat after the wreck. *An old gentleman, a good deal like a hawk if his eyes had been better and not so red, who was always talking, morning, noon, and night, about the gold discovery. But, whether he was making the voyage, thinking his old arms could dig for gold, or whether his speculation was to buy it, or to barter for it, or to cheat for it, or to snatch it anyhow from other people, was his secret (Christmas Stories – 'Golden Mary').*

Ravender, William George: Captain of the *Golden Mary*. He dies in the long-boat after the wreck. *I was apprenticed to the Sea when I was twelve years old, and I have encountered a great deal of rough weather, both literal and metaphorical. . . . I will add no more of the sort than that my name is William George Ravender, that I was born at Penrith half a year after my own father was drowned, and that I am on the second day of this present blessed Christmas week of one thousand eight hundred and fifty-six, fifty-six years of age (Christmas Stories – 'Golden Mary').*

Raybrock, Mrs.: Draper and postmistress of Steepways village, Devon. Mother of Hugh and Alfred. *A comely, elderly woman, short of stature, plump of form, sparkling and dark of eye, who, perfectly clean and neat herself, stood in the midst of her perfectly clean and neat arrangements. (Christmas Stories – 'Message from the Sea').*

Raybrock, Alfred: A fisherman, younger brother to Hugh. Sweetheart and later husband of Kitty Tregarthen. *A young fisherman of two or three and twenty, in the rough sea-dress of his craft, with a brown face, dark curling hair, and bright, modest eyes under his Sou'wester hat, and with a frank, but simple and retiring manner (Christmas Stories – 'Message from the Sea').*

Raybrock, Hugh: Alfred's elder brother, a sailor presumed lost whose message and reappearance clear Tregarthen's name and enable Kitty and Alfred to marry. *A glance at this stranger assured the captain that he could be no other than the Seafaring Man (Christmas Stories – 'Message from the Sea').*

Raybrock, Mrs. Hugh (Margaret): Hugh's presumed widow. *A young widow, sitting at a neighbouring window across a little garden, engaged in needlework, with a young child sleeping on her bosom (Christmas Stories – 'Message from the Sea').*

Raybrock, Jorgan: Son of Alfred and Kitty, named after Captain Jorgan, who made their marriage possible (*Christmas Stories* – 'Message from the Sea').

Raymond: Camilla's husband. Toadying relative of Miss Havisham. *'Cousin Raymond,' observed another lady, 'we are to love our neighbour.' 'Sarah Pocket,' returned Cousin Raymond, 'if a man is not his own neighbour, who is?' (Expectations).*

Red Whisker: Object of David Copperfield's jealousy at Dora Spenlow's birthday picnic. *Red Whisker pretended he could make a salad (which I don't believe), and obtruded himself on public notice. Some of the young ladies washed the lettuces for him, and sliced them under his directions. Dora was among these. I felt that fate had pitted me against this man, and one of us must fall (Copperfield).*

Redburn, Jack: One of Master Humphrey's closest friends and his librarian, steward, and household director. *He is something of a musician, something of an author, something of an actor, something of a painter, very much of a carpenter, and an extraordinary gardener, having had all his life a wonderful aptitude for learning everything that was of no use to him (Humphrey).*

Redforth, Lt.-Col Robin: Alice Rainbird's 'bridegroom' in the romantic tale by this cousin William Tinkling, and himself author of the tale of Captain Boldheart ('Holiday Romance').

Redlaw: Chemist and lecturer who is visited by a phantom on Christmas Eve and endowed with the ability to forget past unhappiness, on condition that he passes the gift on to others. He does, with unhappy results, but Milly Swidger's goodness restores him. *Who could have seen his hollow cheek, his sunken brilliant eye; his black attired figure, indefinably grim, although well-knit and well-proportioned; his grizzled hair hanging, like tangled sea-weed, about his face, – as if he had been, through his whole life, a lonely mark for the chafing and beating of the great deep of humanity, – but might*
have said he looked like a haunted man? (Christms Books – 'Haunted Man').

Refractories: Female delinquents in the workhouse visited by the Uncommercial Traveller. *The oldest Refractory was, say twenty; youngest Refractory, say sixteen. I have never yet ascertained in the course of my uncommercial travels, why a Refractory habit should affect the tonsils and uvula; but, I have always observed that Refractories of both sexes and every grade, between a Ragged School and the Old Bailey, have one voice, in which the tonsils and the uvula gain a diseased ascendancy (Uncommercial – 'Wapping Workhouse').*

Rest: One of Miss Flite's birds (*Bleak House*).

Reynolds, Miss: Inattentive fellow pupil of Rosa Bud at Miss Twinkleton's. *The impropriety of Miss Reynolds's appearing to stab herself in the band with a pin, is far too obvious, and too glaringly unlady-like, to be pointed out (Drood).*

Riah ('Aaron'): The Jew who runs Fledgeby's business for him and bears the odium meant for his master. He helps Lizzie Hexam and finally goes to share a home with Jenny Wren. *An old Jewish man in an ancient coat, long of skirt, and wide of pocket. A venerable man, bald and shining at the top of his head, and with long grey hair flowing down at its sides and mingling with his beard (Mutual Friend).*

Richard: Meg Veck's blacksmith fiancé. *A face as glowing as the iron on which his stout sledge-hammer daily rung. A handsome, well-made, powerful youngster he was; with eyes that sparkled like the red-hot droppings from a furnace fire; black hair that curled about his swarthy temples rarely; and a smile (Christmas Books – 'Chimes').*

Richard: Waiter at the Saracen's Head, Snow Hill (*Nickleby*).

Richards: The name by which Polly Toodle is required to be known while in service with the Dombeys. *Mrs. Toodle . . . dropped a curtsey and replied 'that perhaps if she was to be called out of her name, it would be considered in the wages' (Dombey).*

Rickits, Miss: Fellow pupil of Rosa Bud at Miss Twinkleton's. *A junior of weakly constitution (Drood).*

Riderhood, Roger ('Rogue'): Former partner of Jesse Hexam, whom he implicates in the supposed murder of Harmon. He blackmails Headstone after his attack on Wrayburn, but dies with him, of drowning, in a fight. *A waterside-man with a squinting leer (Mutual Friend).*

Riderhood, Pleasant: Roger's daughter, an unlicensed pawnbroker. She marries Venus. *In her four-and-twentieth year of life, Pleasant was already in her fifth year of this way of trade. . . . Why christened Pleasant, the late Mrs. Riderhood might possibly have been able at some time to explain, and possibly not. Her daughter had no information on that point. Pleasant she found herself, and she couldn't help it. She had not been consulted on the question, any more than on the question of her coming into these terrestrial parts, to want a name. Similarly, she found herself possessed of what is colloquially termed a swivel eye (derived from her father), which she might perhaps have declined if her sentiments on the subject had been taken. She was not otherwise positively ill-looking, though anxious, meagre, of a muddy complexion, and looking as old again as she really was (Mutual Friend).*

Rigaud (alias **Blandois**, alias **Lagnier**): A Frenchman, imprisoned for murdering his wife (see **Barroneau, Madame Henri**). He escapes to England, tries to blackmail Mrs. Clennam for suppressing her husband's uncle's will, but is killed when the house in which he is awaiting her collapses. *His eyes, too close together, were not so nobly set in his head as those of the king of beasts are in his, and they were sharp rather than bright – pointed weapons with little surface to betray them. They had no depth or change; they glittered, and they opened and shut. . . . He had a hook nose, handsome after its kind, but too high between the eyes, by probably just as much as his eyes were too near to one another. For the rest, he was large and tall in frame, had thin lips, where his thick moustache showed them at all, and a quan-* *tity of dry hair, of no definable colour, in its shaggy state, but shot with red (Dorrit).*

'Rinaldo di Velasco': See **Pickleson** (*Christmas Stories* – 'Doctor Marigold').

'Rob the Grinder': See **Toodle, Robin** (*Dombey*).

Robert: Servant to John ('At Dusk').

Robert, Uncle and Aunt Jane: Husband and wife, guests at Christmas dinner (*Boz* – 'Christmas Dinner').

Robinson: Mrs. Tibbs's maid. *By way of making her presence known to her mistress, had been giving sundry hems and sniffs outside the door during the preceding five minutes (Boz* – 'Boarding-House').

Robinson: Husband of the youngest Miss Willis, who has to court her three sisters as well. *A gentleman in a public office, with a good salary and a little property of his own, beside (Boz* – 'Four Sisters').

Robinson: Clerk in Dombey's counting-house (*Dombey*).

Robinson, Mrs.: Robinson's wife, formerly the youngest of the four Misses Willis. *As the four sisters and Mr. Robinson continued to occupy the same house after this memorable occasion, and as the married sister, whoever she was, never appeared in public without the other three, we are not quite clear that the neighbours ever would have discovered the real Mrs. Robinson, but for a circumstance of the most gratifying description, which will happen occasionally in the best-regulated families (Boz* – 'Four Sisters').

Rodolph, Mr. and Mrs. Jennings: Amateur singers who encourage Amelia Martin's belief in her talents. *To hear them sing separately was divine, but when they went through the tragic duet of 'Red Ruffian, retire!' it was, as Miss Martin afterwards remarked, 'thrilling.' And why (as Mr. Jennings Rodolph observed) why were they not engaged at one of the patent theatres? If he was to be told that their voices were not powerful enough to fill the House, his only reply was, that he would back himself for any amount to fill Russell Square (Boz* – 'Mistaken Milliner').

Rogers: The parlour orator. *A stoutish*

*man of about forty, whose short, stiff, black
hair curled closely round a broad high
forehead, and a face to which something
besides water and exercise had communicated a rather inflamed appearance. He was
smoking a cigar, with his eyes fixed on the
ceiling, and had that confident oracular
air which marked him as the leading politician, general authority, and universal
anecdote-relater, of the place. He had
evidently just delivered himself of something very weighty; for the remainder of
the company were puffing at their respective
pipes and cigars in a kind of solemn abstraction, as if quite overwhelmed with the
magnitude of the subject recently under dis-
cussion (Boz* – 'Parlour Orator').

Rogers: Police constable who accompanies Inspector Field and the narrator
to Rats' Castle, Saint Giles's. *Rogers is
ready, strapped and great-coated, with a
flaming eye in the middle of his waist, like
a deformed Cyclops (Reprinted* – 'On
Duty with Inspector Field').

Rogers, Miss: Subject of one of Mrs.
Nickleby's attempted recollections. *'A
lady in our neighbourhood when we lived
near Dawlish, I think her name was
Rogers; indeed I am sure it was, if it
wasn't Murphy' (Nickleby).*

Rogers, Mrs.: Mrs. Bardell's genteel
lodger. *She was more gracious than intimate, in right of her position (Pickwick).*

Roker, Tom: Turnkey at the Fleet
Prison *(Pickwick).*

Rokesmith, John: See Harmon, John
(Mutual Friend).

Rokesmith, Mrs. John (Bella): see
Wilfer, Bella *(Mutual Friend).*

Rolland: Junior partner in Defresnier et
Cie who corresponds with Vendale about
the discovery of fraud *(Christmas Stories
– 'No Thoroughfare').*

Rosa: Lady Dedlock's maid who sup-
plants Hortense. Marries Watt Rouncewell. *A dark-eyed, dark-haired, shy,
village beauty comes in – so fresh in her
rosy and yet delicate bloom, that the drops
of rain, which have beaten on her hair, look
like the dew upon a flower fresh gathered
(Bleak House).*

Rose: The struggling young doctor's
sweetheart. *How happy it would make
Rose if he could only tell her that he had
found a patient at last, and hoped to have
more, and to come down again, in a few
months' time, and marry her, and take
her home to gladden his lonely fireside, and
stimulate him to fresh exertions (Boz –
'*Black Veil').*

Rose: Lucy Benson's cousin, sweetheart
of John Maddox and the object of
Flam's evil designs *(Village Coquettes).*

Ross, Frank: Bachelor friend of Gabriel
Parsons *(Boz – 'Watkins Tottle').*

Rouncewell: Mrs. Rouncewell's son,
brother of George, and father of Watt.
An ironmaster. *Would have been provided for at Chesney Wold, and would have
been made steward in due season; but he
took, when he was a schoolboy, to con-
structing steam-engines out of saucepans,
and setting birds to draw their own water,
with the least possible amount of labour;
so assisting them with artful contrivance of
hydraulic pressure, that a thirsty canary
had only, in a literal sense, to put his
shoulder to the wheel, and the job was
done. This propensity gave Mrs. Rouncewell great uneasiness. She felt it with a
mother's anguish, to be a move in the Wat
Tyler direction (Bleak House).*

Rouncewell, Mrs.: The Dedlocks'
housekeeper at Chesney Wold. Mother
of Rouncewell the ironmaster, and
George, and grandmother of Watt. *She
is rather deaf, which nothing will induce
her to believe. She is a fine old lady, handsome, stately, wonderfully neat, and has
such a back and such a stomacher, that if
her stays should turn out when she dies to
have been a broad old-fashioned family
fire-grate, nobody who knows her would
have cause to be surprised (Bleak House).*

**Rouncewell, George (Mr. George or
Trooper George):** Mrs. Rouncewell's
erratic son who, after serving in the army,
runs a shooting-gallery in London until,
restored to his mother by the Bagnets,
he becomes Sir Leicester Dedlock's
attendant. *A swarthy brown man of fifty;
well-made, and good looking; with crisp*

dark hair, bright eyes, and a broad chest. His sinewy and powerful hands, as sun-burnt as his face, have evidently been used to a pretty rough life. What is curious about him is, that he sits forward on his chair as if he were, from long habit, allowing space for some dress or accoutre-ments that he has altogether laid aside. His step too is measured and heavy, and would go well with a weighty clash and jingle of spurs. He is close-shaved now, but his mouth is set as if his upper lip had been for years familiar with a great moustache; and his manner of occasionally laying the open palm of his broad brown hand upon it, is to the same effect. Altogether, one might guess Mr. George to have been a trooper once upon a time (Bleak House).

Rouncewell, Watt: Son of Rouncewell the iron-master. Marries Rosa. *Perfectly good-humoured and polite; but, within such limits, evidently adapts his tone to his reception (Bleak House).*

Rudge: Barnaby's father. Supposed mur-dered by the slayer (actually himself) of his master, Reuben Haredale, he lives as a fugitive. Found out by Geoffrey Hare-dale, he is eventually executed. *The stranger took off his hat, and disclosed the hard features of a man of sixty or there-abouts, much weather-beaten and worn by time, and the naturally harsh expression of which was not improved by a dark hand-kerchief which was bound tightly round his head, and while it served the purpose of a wig, shaded his forehead, and almost hid his eyebrows. If it were intended to conceal or divert attention from a deep gash, now healed into an ugly seam, which when it was first inflicted must have laid bare his cheek-bone, the object was but indifferently attained, for it could scarcely fail to be noted at a glance. His complexion was of a cadaverous hue, and he had a grizzly jagged beard of some three weeks' date (Rudge).*

Rudge, Mrs. (Mary): Rudge's wife, sup-posed widow, and Barnaby's mother. *She was about forty – perhaps two or three years older – with a cheerful aspect, and a face that had once been pretty. . . . One thing about this face was very strange and startling. You could not look upon it in its most cheerful mood without feeling that it had some extraordinary capacity of express-ing terror. It was not on the surface. It was in no one feature that it lingered. You could not take the eyes or mouth, or lines upon the cheek, or say, if this or that were otherwise, it would not be so. Yet there it always lurked (Rudge).*

Rudge, Barnaby: A simple-minded youth who wanders the roads between Chigwell and London with his raven, Grip. He ingenuously joins the Gordon Rioters, is arrested and sentenced to death, but reprieved through Gabriel Varden's efforts. *He was about three-and-twenty years old, and though rather spare, of a fair height and strong make. His hair, of which he had a great profusion, was red, and hanging in disorder about his face and shoulders, gave to his restless looks an expression quite unearthly – enhanced by the paleness of his complexion, and the glassy lustre of his large protruding eyes. Startling as his aspect was, his features were good, and there was something even plaintive in his wan and haggard aspect. . . . His dress was of green, clumsily trimmed here and there – apparently by his own hands – with gaudy lace; brightest where the cloth was most worn and soiled, and poorest where it was at the best. A pair of tawdry ruffles dangled at his wrists, while his throat was nearly bare. He had ornamented his hat with a cluster of pea-cock's feathers, but they were limp and broken, and now trailed negligently down his back. Girt to his side was the steel hilt of an old sword without blade or scabbard; and some parti-coloured ends of ribands and poor glass toys completed the ornamen-tal portion of his attire. The fluttered and confused disposition of all the motley scraps that formed his dress, bespoke, in a scarcely less degree than his eager and unsettled manner, the disorder of his mind, and by a grotesque contrast set off and heightened the more impressive wildness of his face (Rudge).*

Rugg: A debt collector and agent, and Pancks's landlord. Father of Anastasia. *Mr. Rugg, who had a round white visage,* *as if all his blushes had been drawn out of him long ago, and who had a ragged yellow head like a worn-out hearth broom (Dorrit).*

Rugg, Anastasia: Rugg's daughter. *Miss Rugg, who had little nankeen spots, like shirt buttons, all over her face, and whose own yellow tresses were rather scrubby than luxuriant (Dorrit).*

Ruin: One of Miss Flite's birds *(Bleak House).*

Rumman, Professor: Member of the Mudfog Association *(Mudfog).*

'Rumty': see Wilfer, Reginald *(Mutual Friend).*

Saggers, Mrs.: Oldest but one pensioner at Titbull's and the centre of dissension there. *Has Mrs. Saggers any right to stand her pail outside her dwelling? (Uncommercial – 'Titbull's Alms-Houses').*

St. Evrémonde, Marquis: Elder of twin brothers. Father of Charles Darnay *(Two Cities).*

St. Evrémonde, Marquis: Younger of twin brothers. Uncle of Charles Darnay. Murdered by Gaspard whose child his carriage had killed. *A man of about sixty, handsomely dressed, haughty in manner, and with a face like a fine mask. A face of a transparent paleness; every feature in it clearly defined; one set expression on it. The nose, beautifully formed otherwise, was very slightly pinched at the top of each nostril. In those two compressions, or dints, the only little change that the face ever showed resided. They persisted in changing sometimes, and they would be occasionally dilated and contracted by something like a faint pulsation; then, they gave a look of treachery, and cruelty, to the whole countenance (Two Cities).*

St. Evrémonde, Charles: See Darnay, Charles *(Two Cities).*

St. Julien, Horatio: See Larkins, Jem *(Boz – 'Private Theatres').*

Salcy, the Family P.: Theatrical family appearing in a French–Flemish town visited by the Uncommercial Traveller. *The member of the Family P. Salcy were so fat and so like one another – fathers,*

mothers, sisters, brothers, uncles, and aunts – that I think the local audience were much confused about the plot of the piece under representation, and to the last expected that everybody must turn out to be the long-lost relative of everybody else (Uncommercial – 'In the French–Flemish Country').

Sally: See under **Bill, Uncle** *(Boz – 'London Recreations.)'*

Sally: See **Goldstraw, Mrs. Sarah** *(Christmas Stories –* 'No Thoroughfare').

Sally: Pauper attendant at Oliver Twist's birth. *A pauper old woman, who was rendered rather misty by an unwonted allowance of beer (Twist).*

Sam: Pecksniff's groom *(Chuzzlewit).*

Sam: The cab driver who suspects Pickwick to be an informant. *The cabman dashed his hat upon the ground, with a reckless disregard of his own private property, and knocked Mr. Pickwick's spectacles off, and followed up the attack with a blow on Mr. Pickwick's nose, and another on Mr. Pickwick's chest, and a third in Mr. Snodgrass's eye, and a fourth, by way of variety, in Mr. Tupman's waistcoat, and then danced into the road, and then back again to the pavement, and finally dashed the whole temporary supply of breath out of Mr. Winkle's body; and all in half a dozen seconds (Pickwick).*

Samba, Quanko: See under **Blazo, Colonel Sir Thomas** *(Pickwick).*

Sampson: Chief manager of a Life Assurance Office, who narrates the story. He helps Meltham save Margaret Niner from murder by Slinkton. *I think I have within the last thirty years seen more romances than the generality of men, however unpromising the opportunity may, at first sight, seem. As I have retired, and live at my ease, I possess the means that I used to want, of considering what I have seen, at leisure. My experiences have a more remarkable aspect, so reviewed, than they had when they were in progress. I have come home from the Play now, and can recall the scenes of the Drama upon which the curtain has fallen, free from the glare, bewilderment, and bustle of the Theatre* ('Hunted Down').

Sampson, George: Friend of the Wilfers, admirer first of Bella, then of Lavinia. *The friend of the family was in that stage of the tender passion which bound him to regard everybody else as the foe of the family. He put the round head of his cane in his mouth, like a stopper, when he sat down. As if he felt himself full to the throat with affronting sentiments (Mutual Friend).*

Sanders, Mrs. Susannah: A crony of Mrs. Bardell. *A big, fat, heavy-faced personage (Pickwick).*

Sapsea, Thomas: Auctioneer and Mayor of Cloisterham. *Accepting the Jackass as the type of self-sufficient stupidity and conceit – a custom, perhaps, like some few other customs, more conventional than fair – then the purest Jackass in Cloisterham is Mr. Thomas Sapsea, Auctioneer. . . . Mr. Sapsea has many admirers; indeed, the proposition is carried by a large local majority, even including non-believers in his widsom, that he is a credit to Cloisterham. He possesses the great qualities of being portentous and dull, and of having a roll in his speech, and another roll in his gait; not to mention a certain gravely flowing action with his hands, as if he were presently going to Confirm the individual with whom he holds discourse. Much nearer sixty years of age than fifty, with a flowing outline of stomach, and horizontal creases in his waistcoat; reputed to be rich; voting at elections in the strictly respectable interest; morally satisfied that nothing but he himself has grown since he was a baby; how can dunder-headed Mr. Sapsea be otherwise than a credit to Cloisterham, and society? (Drood).*

Sapsea, the late Mrs. Thomas (Ethelinda, née Brobity): Sapsea's late wife. *'Miss Brobity's Being, young man, was deeply imbued with homage to Mind. She revered Mind, when launched, or, as I say, precipitated, on an extensive knowledge of the world. When I made my proposal, she did me the honour to be so overshadowed with a species of Awe, as to be able to articulate only the two words, "O Thou!" meaning myself. Her limpid blue eyes were fixed upon me, her semi-transparent hands were clasped together, pallor overspread her aquiline features, and, though encouraged to proceed, she never did proceed a word further' (Drood).*

Sarah: See **Mary and Sarah** (*Boz* – 'Seven Dials').

Saunders: The Whifflers' bachelor friend who bears the brunt of their preoccupation with their children. *Whatever the attention of Mr. Saunders is called to, Mr. Saunders admires of course; though he is rather confused about the sex of the youngest branches and looks at the wrong children, turning to a girl when Mr. Whiffler directs his attention to a boy, and falling into raptures with a boy when he ought to be enchanted with a girl (Young Couples – 'Couple Who Dote Upon Their Children').*

Sawyer: A baker who beats his wife and then boils his son in the wash-house copper in a tale the gentleman connected with the press tells his admirers at the Green Dragon, Westminster Bridge (*Mudfog* – 'Mr. Robert Bolton').

Sawyer, Bob: Medical student, lodging at Mrs. Raddle's, Lant Street, Borough. It is intended that he marry Arabella, sister of his fellow student and drinking companion Ben Allen, but Winkle cuts him out. Sawyer and Allen eventually go to begin a new life in Bengal. *Mr. Bob Sawyer, who was habited in a coarse blue coat, which, without being either a greatcoat or a surtout, partook of the nature and qualities of both, had about him that sort of slovenly smartness, and swaggering gait, which is peculiar to young gentlemen who smoke in the streets by day, shout and scream in the same by night, call waiters by their Christian names, and do various other acts and deeds of an equally facetious description. He wore a pair of plaid trousers, and a large rough double-breasted waistcoat; out of doors, he carried a thick stick with a big top. He eschewed gloves, and looked, upon the whole, something like a dissipated Robinson Crusoe (Pickwick).*

Sawyer, late Nockemorf: Medical practice owned by Bob Sawyer in Bristol. '*So snug, that at the end of a few years you might put all the profits in a wine glass, and cover 'em over with a gooseberry leaf (Pickwick).*

Saxby, Long: One of Feenix's many acquaintances. '*Man of six foot ten*' (*Dombey*).

Scadder, Zephania: Agent of the Eden Land Corporation in America who persuades Martin Chuzzlewit to invest in the worthless scheme. *A gaunt man in a huge straw hat, and a coat of green stuff. The weather being hot, he had no cravat, and wore his shirt-collar wide open; so that every time he spoke something was seen to twitch and jerk up in his throat, like the little hammers in a harpsichord when the notes are struck. Perhaps it was the Truth feebly endeavouring to leap to his lips. If so, it never reached them (Chuzzlewit).*

Scadgers, Lady: Mrs. Sparsit's great-aunt. *An immensely fat old woman, with an inordinate appetite for butcher's meat, and a mysterious leg which had now refused to get out of bed for fourteen years (Hard Times).*

Scaley: Co-bailiff with Tix in possession at Madame Mantalini's. *Kate . . . started to hear a strange man's voice in the room, and started again, to observe, on looking round, that a white hat, and red neckerchief, and a broad round face, and a large head, and part of a green coat were in the room too (Nickleby).*

Scarton, Charley: Amateur actor. *Charley Scarton is to take the part of an English sailor, and fight a broadsword combat with six unknown bandits, at one and the same time (one theatrical sailor is always equal to half a dozen men at least) (Boz – '*Private Theatres').

Scientific Gentleman: An elderly gentleman 'of scientific attainments' who mistakes the flashes of Pickwick's lantern at Clifton for an undiscovered phenomenon of nature. *Full of this idea, the scientific gentleman seized his pen again, and committed to paper sundry notes of these unparalleled appearances, with the date, day, hour, minute, and precise second at which they were visible; all of which*

were to form the data of a voluminous treatise of great research and deep learning, which should astonish all the atmospherical sages that ever drew breath in any part of the civilised globe (Pickwick).

Scott, Tom: Quilp's boy. Addicted to standing on his head, he becomes a successful professional acrobat after Quilp's death. *The first object that presented itself to his view was a pair of very imperfectly shod feet elevated in the air with the soles upwards, which remarkable appearance was referable to the boy, who being of an eccentric spirit and having a natural taste for tumbling was now standing on his head and contemplating the aspect of the river under these uncommon circumstances (Curiosity Shop).*

Screwzer, Tommy: One of Feenix's many acquaintances. '*Man of an extremely bilious habit*' (*Dombey*).

Scroo: A vice-president of the display of models and mechanical science session at the second meeting of the Mudfog Association (*Mudfog*).

Scrooge, Ebenezer: Central figure of the story. Surviving partner of the firm of Scrooge and Marley, and a grasping misanthrope, he is visited on Christmas Eve by the ghost of Marley and three Christmas spectres who show him the error of his ways and reform him. *Oh! But he was a tight-fisted hand at the grindstone, Scrooge! a squeezing, wrenching, grasping, scraping, clutching, covetous, old sinner! Hard and sharp as flint, from which no steel had ever struck out generous fire; secret, and self-contained and solitary as an oyster. The cold within him froze his old features, nipped his pointed nose, shrivelled his cheek, stiffened his gait; made his eyes red, his thin lips blue; and spoke out shrewdly in his grating voice. A frosty rime was on his head, and on his eyebrows, and his wiry chin; he iced his office in the dog-days; and didn't thaw it one degree at Christmas (Christmas Books – 'Christmas Carol').*

Scrooge's Niece: Wife of his nephew Fred. *She was very pretty: exceedingly pretty. With a dimpled, surprised-looking,* *capital face; a ripe little mouth, that seemed made to be kissed – as no doubt it was; all kinds of good little dots about her chin, that melted into one another when she laughed; and the sunniest pair of eyes you ever saw in any little creature's head. Altogether she was what you would have called provoking, you know; but satisfactory, too. Oh, perfectly satisfactory* (*Christmas Books* – 'Christmas Carol').

Scuttlewig, Duke of: One of the aristocratic acquaintances claimed by the egotistical couple (*Young Couples* – 'Egotistical Couple').

Seamstress: Sydney Carton's fellow passenger in the tumbril on the way to the guillotine. *A young woman, with a slight girlish form, a sweet spare face in which there was no vestige of colour, and large widely opened patient eyes* (*Two Cities*).

Seraphina: Heroine of Jemmy Lirriper's tale: a schoolmaster's daughter. *The most beautiful creature that ever was seen, and she had brown eyes, and she had brown hair all curling beautifully, and she had a delicious voice, and she was delicious altogether* (*Christmas Stories* – 'Mrs. Lirriper's Lodgings').

Seven Poor Travellers: So styled by the narrator of that story, to comprise himself and the Six Poor Travellers lodging at Watts's Charity, Rochester. *I found the party to be thus composed. Firstly, myself. Secondly, a very decent man indeed, with his right arm in a sling, who had a certain clean, agreeable smell of wood about him, from which I judged him to have something to do with shipbuilding. Thirdly, a little sailor-boy, a mere child, with a profusion of rich dark brown hair, and deep womanly-looking eyes. Fourthly, a shabby-genteel personage in a threadbare black suit, and apparently in very bad circumstances, with a dry, suspicious look; the absent buttons on his waistcoat eked out with red tape; and a bundle of extraordinarily tattered papers sticking out of an inner breast-pocket. Fifthly, a foreigner by birth, but an Englishman in speech, who carried his pipe in the band of his hat, and* *lost no time in telling me, in an easy, simple, engaging way, that he was a watchmaker from Geneva, and travelled all about the Continent, mostly on foot, working as a journeyman, and seeing new countries, – possibly (I thought) also smuggling a watch or so, now and then. Sixthly, a little widow, who had been very pretty and was still very young, but whose beauty had been wrecked in some great misfortune, and whose manner was remarkably timid, scared, and solitary. Seventhly and lastly, a Traveller of a kind familiar to my boyhood, but now almost obsolete, – a Book-Pedler, who had a quantity of Pamphlets and Numbers with him, and who presently boasted that he could repeat more verses in an evening than he could sell in a twelvemonth* (*Christmas Stories* – 'Seven Poor Travellers').

Sexton, The: The old sexton at the village where Little Nell and her gandfather die. *Who peradventure, on a pinch, might have walked a mile with great difficulty in half a dozen hours* (*Curiosity Shop*).

Sexton, The: A deaf old man, one of the characters assumed by Gabblewig in order to unmask Slap (*Nightingale's Diary*).

Sharp: First master at Salem House. *A limp, delicate-looking gentleman, I thought, with a good deal of nose, and a way of carrying his head on one side, as if it were a little too heavy for him. His hair was very smooth and wavy; but I was informed by the very first boy who came back that it was a wig (a secondhand one he said), and that Mr. Sharp went out every Saturday afternoon to get it curled* (*Copperfield*).

Sharpeye: One of the policemen visiting sailors' haunts with the Uncommercial Traveller. *Had a skilful and quite professional way of opening doors – touched latches delicately, as if they were keys of musical intruments – opened every door he touched, as if he were perfectly confident that there was stolen property behind it – instantly insinuated himself, to prevent its being shut* (*Uncommercial* – 'Poor Mercantile Jack').

Sheen and Gloss: Fashionable London mercers. *'To make this article go down, gentlemen,' says Sheen and Gloss the mercers, to their friends the manufacturers, 'you must come to us, because we know where to have the fashionable people, and we can make it fashionable' (Bleak House).*

Sheepskin: One of Miss Flite's birds *(Bleak House)*.

Shepherd, Miss: A boarder at the Misses Nettingall's establishment. One of David Copperfield's first loves. *A little girl, in a spencer, with a round face and curly flaxen hair. . . . I touch Miss Shepherd's glove, and feel a thrill go up the right arm of my jacket, and come out at my hair. I say nothing tender to Miss Shepherd, but we understand each other. Miss Shepherd and myself live but to be united (Copperfield).*

Shepherd, The: One of Mrs. Tony Weller's spiritual comforters, observed by her husband. *'In comes a fat chap in black, with a great white face, a smilin' avay like clockwork. Such goin's on, Sammy! "The kiss of peace," says the shepherd; and then he kissed the women all round. . . . I was just a thinkin' whether I hadn't better begin too – 'specially as there was a wery nice lady a sittin' next to me – ven in comes the tea, and your mother-in-law, as had been makin' the kettle bile downstairs. At it they went, tooth and nail. . . . I wish you could ha' seen the shepherd walkin' into the ham and muffins. I never see such a chap to eat and drink; never' (Pickwick).*

Shepherdson: Thief taken by Sergeant Mith who gains his confidence in the guise of a young butcher *(Reprinted – 'Detective Police').*

Shiny Villiam: Under-ostler at the Bull, Rochester. *So called, probably from his sleek hair and oily countenance (Pickwick).*

'Short' or 'Short Trotters': See Harris *(Curiosity Shop).*

Signal-man, The: The victim in the ghost story titled 'No. 1 Branch Line: The Signal-man' which forms ch. 4. *A dark, sallow man, with a dark beard and rather heavy eyebrows. His post was in as solitary and dismal a place as ever I saw (Christmas Stories – 'Mugby Junction').*

Sikes, Bill: Brutal thief associated with Fagin, lover and murderer of Nancy. He accidentally hangs himself trying to escape a mob hunting him down for the murder. *A stoutly-built fellow of about five-and-thirty, in a black velveteen coat, very soiled drab breeches, lace-up half boots, and grey cotton stockings, which inclosed a bulky pair of legs, with large swelling calves; – the kind of legs, which in such costume, always look in an unfinished and incomplete state without a set of fetters to garnish them. He had a brown hat on his head, and a dirty belcher handkerchief round his neck; with the long frayed ends of which he smeared the beer from his face as he spoke. He disclosed, when he had done so, a broad heavy countenance with a beard of three days' growth, and two scowling eyes; one of which displayed various parti-coloured symptoms of having been recently damaged by a blow (Twist).*

Silverman, The Revd. George: Narrator of the story ('Silverman').

Silverstone, The Revd. and Mrs.: An egotistical couple. *Mrs. Silverstone, who launches into new praises of Mr. Silverstone's worth and excellence, to which he listens in the same meek silence, save when he puts in a word of self-denial relative to some question of fact, as – 'Not seventy-two christenings that week, my dear. Only seventy-one, only seventy-one.' At length his wife has quite concluded, and then he says, Why should he repine, why should he give way, why should he suffer his heart to sink within him? Is it he alone who toils and suffers? What has she gone through, he should like to know? What does she go through every day for him and society? With such an exordium Mr. Silverstone launches out into glowing praises of the conduct of Mrs. Silverstone in the production of eight young children, and the subsequent rearing and fostering of the same; and thus the husband magnifies the wife, and the wife the husband (Young Couples – 'Egotistical Couple').*

Simmery, Frank: Fellow stockbroker and betting friend of Wilkins Flasher. *A very smart young gentleman who wore his hat on his right whisker, and was lounging over the desk, killing flies with a ruler (Pickwick).*

Simmonds, Miss: Employee of Madame Mantalini *(Nickleby).*

Simmons: Parish beadle. *The parish beadle is one of the most, perhaps the most, important member of the local administration. He is not so well off as the churchwardens, certainly, nor is he so learned as the vestry-clerk, nor does he order things quite so much his own way as either of them. But his power is very great, notwithstanding; and the dignity of his office is never impaired by the absence of efforts on his part to maintain it. The beadle of our parish is a splendid fellow. It is quite delightful to hear him, as he explains the state of the existing poor laws to the deaf old women in the board-room passage on business nights* (Boz – 'Beadle'). Simmons's death occurs in Boz – 'Election for Beadle'.

Simmons, Mrs. Henrietta: A neighbour and sympathiser of Mrs. Quilp's *(Curiosity Shop).*

Simmons, William: Van driver who gives Martin Chuzzlewit a ride from Salisbury to London after his dismissal by Pecksniff. *A red-faced burly young fellow; smart in his way, and with a good-humoured countenance (Chuzzlewit).*

Simpson: Boarder at Mrs. Tibbs's. He marries, but is deserted by, Julia Maplesone. *One of those young men, who are in society what walking gentlemen are on the stage, only infinitely worse skilled in his vocation than the most indifferent artist. He was as empty-headed as the great bell of St. Paul's; always dressed according to the caricatures published in the monthly fashions; and spelt Character with a K* (Boz – 'Boarding-House').

Simpson: Fellow prisoner of Pickwick in the Fleet. *Leaning out of window as far as he could without overbalancing himself, endeavouring, with great perseverance, to spit upon the crown of the hat of a personal friend on the parade below (Pickwick).*

Single Gentleman, The: The brother of Nell's grandfather. He goes in search of them, arriving too late. He lodges with the Brass family *(Curiosity Shop).*

Six Poor Travellers: See **Seven Poor Travellers** *(Christmas Stories* – 'Seven Poor Travellers').

Skettles, Lady: Wife of Sir Barnet Skettles, mother of Barnet junior *(Dombey).*

Skettles, Sir Barnet, M.P.: Father of Barnet junior, a pupil at Dr. Blimber's, and host for a time to Florence Dombey at Fulham. *Sir Barnet Skettles expressed his personal consequence chiefly through an antique gold snuff-box, and a ponderous silk pocket-handkerchief, which he had an imposing manner of drawing out of his pocket like a banner, and using with both hands at once. Sir Barnet's object in life was constantly to extend the range of his acquaintance. Like a heavy body dropped into water – not to disparage so worthy a gentleman by the comparison – it was in the nature of things that Sir Barnet must spread an ever-widening circle about him, until there was no room left. Or, like a sound in air, the vibration of which, according to the speculation of an ingenious modern philosopher, may go on travelling for ever through the interminable fields of space, nothing but coming to the end of his moral tether could stop Sir Barnet Skettles in his voyage of discovery through the social system (Dombey).*

Skettles, Barnet, jun.: Son of Sir Barnet and Lady Skettles. A fellow-pupil of Paul Dombey at Doctor Blimber's *(Dombey).*

Skewton, The Hon. Mrs. ('Cleopatra'): Edith Dombey's elderly but coquettish mother. Aunt to Lord Feenix. *The discrepancy between Mrs. Skewton's fresh enthusiasm of words, and forlornly faded manner, was hardly less observable than that between her age, which was about seventy, and her dress, which would have been youthful for twenty-seven. Her attitude in the wheeled chair (which she never varied) was one in which she had been taken in a barouche, some fifty years* *before, by a then fashionable artist who had appended to his published sketch the name of Cleopatra; in consequence of a discovery made by the critics of the time, that it bore an exact resemblance to that princess as she reclined on board her galley. Mrs. Skewton was a beauty then, and bucks threw wine-glasses over their heads by dozens in her honour. The beauty and the barouche had both passed away, but she still preserved the attitude, and for this reason expressly, maintained the wheeled chair and the butting page: there being nothing whatever, except the attitude, to prevent her from walking (Dombey).*

Skewton, Edith: See **Dombey, Mrs. Paul the Second** *(Dombey).*

Skiffins, Miss: Marries Wemmick. *Miss Skiffins was of a wooden appearance. . . . She might have been some two or three years younger than Wemmick, and I judged her to stand possessed of portable property. The cut of her dress from the waist upward, both before and behind, made her figure very like a boy's kite; and I might have pronounced her gown a little too decidedly orange, and her gloves a little too intensely green. But she seemed to be a good sort of fellow (Expectations).*

Skimpin: Serjeant Buzfuz's junior counsel for Mrs. Bardell in Bardell and Pickwick. *Mr. Skimpin proceeded to 'open the case'; and the case appeared to have very little inside it when he had opened it, for he kept such particulars as he knew, completely to himself, and sat down, after a lapse of three minutes, leaving the jury in precisely the same advanced stage of wisdom as they were in before (Pickwick).*

Skimpole, Arethusa, Laura, and Kitty: The Skimpoles' daughters. *'This,' said Mr. Skimpole, 'is my Beauty daughter, Arethusa – plays and sings odds and ends like her father. This is my Sentiment daughter, Laura – plays a little but don't sing. This is my Comedy daughter, Kitty – sings a little but don't play' (Bleak House).*

Skimpole, Harold: Father of Arethusa, Laura, and Kitty. Protegé of John Jarndyce, whom he later estranges by vilifying him for selfishness. *He was a little bright creature, with a rather large head;*

but a delicate face, and a sweet voice, and there was a perfect charm in him. All he said was so free from effort and spontaneous, and was said with such a captivating gaiety, that it was fascinating to hear him talk. . . . He had more the appearance, in all respects, of a damaged young man, than a well-preserved elderly one. There was an easy negligence in his manner, and even in his dress (his hair carelessly disposed, and his neck-kerchief loose and flowing, as I have seen artists paint their own portraits), which I could not separate from the idea of a romantic youth who had undergone some unique process of depreciation. It struck me as being not at all like the manner or appearance of a man who had advanced in life, by the usual road of years, cares, and experiences (Bleak House).

Skimpole, Mrs. Harold: Skimpole's wife, mother of Arethusa, Laura, and Kitty. *Had once been a beauty, but was now a delicate high-nosed invalid, suffering under a complication of disorders (Bleak House).*

Slackbridge: Militant trades-unionist whose oration drives Stephen Blackpool from his work and ultimately to his death. *Judging him by Nature's evidence, he was above the mass in very little but the stage on which he stood. In many great respects he was essentially below them. He was not so honest, he was not so manly, he was not so good-humoured; he substituted cunning for their simplicity, and passion for their safe solid sense. An ill-made, high-shouldered man, with lowering brows, and his features crushed into an habitually sour expression, he contrasted most unfavourably, even in his mongrel dress, with the great body of his hearers in their plain working clothes (Hard Times).*

Sladdery: Fashionable London lending librarian. *'If you want to get this print upon the tables of my high connexion, sir . . . you must leave it, if you please, to me; for I have been accustomed to study the leaders of my high connexion, sir; and I may tell you, without vanity that I can turn them round my finger' (Bleak House).*

Slammer, Dr.: Surgeon of the 97th Regiment at Rochester. Offended by

Jingle, wearing Winkle's coat, he challenges Winkle to a duel. *One of the most popular personages, in his own circle, present was a little fat man, with a ring of upright black hair round his head, and an extensive bald plain on the top of it – Doctor Slammer, surgeon to the 97th. The Doctor took snuff with everybody, chatted with everybody, laughed, danced, made jokes, played whist, did everything, and was everywhere (Pickwick).*

Slammons: A name by which Mrs. Nickleby persists for a time in addressing Smike. *Which circumstance she attributed to the remarkable similarity of the two names in point of sound, both beginning with an S, and moreover being spelt with an M (Nickleby).*

Slang, Lord: One of the aristocratic acquaintances claimed by the egotistical couple (*Young Couples* – 'Egotistical Couple').

Slap: A failed actor (stage name, Formiville) living by writing begging letters and extorting money from gullible people, principally Christopher Nightingale, estranged for many years from his wife, Slap's sister, but still paying a regular allowance, believing her to be alive. Posing as a friend of Mrs. Nightingale, Slap produces a 'Master Nightingale' in an attempt to make a final killing, but is foiled by Gabblewig (*Nightingale's Diary*).

Slasher: Eminent surgeon whose skill is described to Pickwick by Jack Hopkins. '*Took a boy's leg out of the socket last week – boy ate five apples and a gingerbread cake – exactly two minutes after it was all over, boy said he wouldn't lie there to be made game of, and he'd tell his mother if they didn't begin' (Pickwick).*

Slaughter, Lieutenant: Accomplice of the Waters. *Two iron-shod boots and one gruff voice (Boz* – 'Tuggses at Ramsgate').

Sleary: Circus proprietor and father of Josephine. He cares for Sissy Jupe after her father, his clown, has decamped, and helps Tom Gradgrind escape arrest. *A stout man . . . with one fixed eye, and one*

loose eye, a voice (if it can be called so) like the efforts of a broken old pair of bellows, a flabby surface, and a muddled head which was never sober and never drunk (Hard Times).*

Sleary, Josephine: Sleary's daughter. Marries Childers. *A pretty fair-haired girl of eighteen, who had been tied on a horse at two years old, and had made a will at twelve, which she always carried about with her, expressive of her dying desire to be drawn to the grave by the two piebald ponies (Hard Times).*

Sliderskew, Peg: Arthur Gride's housekeeper. By stealing his papers she helps bring about his downfall, and is subsequently sentenced to transportation. *A short, thin, weasen, blear-eyed old woman, palsy-stricken and hideously ugly (Nickleby).*

Slingo: Horse-dealer. One of Tip Dorrit's many employers *(Dorrit).*

Slinkton, Julius: Murderer of one niece and intending murderer of another, Margaret Niner, for their insurance money, he is hunted down by Meltham, who had been in love with the former lady. Believing Meltham to be Beckwith, a drunkard near to death, Slinkton insures and tries to poison him, but is unmasked and kills himself with poison. *About forty or so, dark, exceedingly well dressed in black, – being in mourning, – and the hand he extended with a polite air, had a particularly well-fitting black-kid glove upon it. His hair, which was elaborately brushed and oiled, was parted straight up the middle; and he presented this parting to the clerk, exactly (to my thinking) as if he had said, in so many words : 'You must take me, if you please, my friend, just as I show myself. Come straight up here, follow the gravel path, keep off the grass, I allow no trespassing'* ('Hunted Down').

Slithers: Master Humphrey's barber. Captures Miss Benton from Tony Weller and marries her. *At all times a very brisk, bustling, active little man, – for he is, as it were, chubby all over, without being stout or unwieldy (Humphrey).*

Sloppy: An orphan brought up by Betty

Higden, whom he helps with her laundry work. Boffin has him trained as a cabinet-maker. *A very long boy, with a very little head, and an open mouth of disproportionate capacity that seemed to assist his eyes in staring at the visitors (Mutual Friend).*

Slout: Master of the workhouse of which Mrs. Corney is matron. His death enables Bumble to become his successor and Mrs. Corney's husband. *'Oh, Mrs. Corney, what a prospect this opens! What a opportunity for a jining of hearts and house-keepings!' (Twist).*

Slowboy, Tilly: The Peerybingles' servant and nurse to their baby. *She was of a spare and straight shape, this young lady, insomuch that her garments appeared to be in constant danger of sliding off those sharp pegs, her shoulders, on which they were loosely hung. Her costume was remarkable for the partial development, on all possible occasions, of some flannel vestment of a singular structure; also for affording glimpses, in the region of the back, of a corset, or pair of stays, in colour a dead-green. Being always in a state of gaping admiration at everything, and absorbed, besides, in the perpetual contemplation of her mistress's perfections and the baby's, Miss Slowboy, in her little errors of judgment, may be said to have done equal honour to her head and to her heart; and though these did less honour to the baby's head, which they were the occasional means of bringing into contact with deal doors, dressers, stair-rails, bedposts, and other foreign substances, still they were the honest results of Tilly Slowboy's constant astonishment at finding herself so kindly treated (Christmas Books – 'Cricket').*

Sludberry, Thomas: Defendant in the brawling case of Bumple against Sludberry. *A little, red-faced, sly-looking, ginger-beer seller (Boz – 'Doctors' Commons').*

Sluffen: Speaker at the master sweeps' anniversary dinner at White Conduit House. *Expressed himself in a manner following: 'That now he'd cotcht the cheerman's hi, he vished he might be jolly vell blessed, if he worn't a goin' to have his innings, vich he vould say these here obserwashuns – that how some mischeevus coves as know'd nuffin about the consarn, had tried to sit people agin the mas'r swips, and take the shine out o' their bis'nes, and the bread out o' the traps o' their preshus kids, by a makin' o' this here remark, as chimblies could be as vell svept by 'sheenery as by boys; and that the makin' use o' boys for that there purposs vos barbareous; vereas, he 'ad been a chummy – he begged the cheerman's parding for usin' such a vulgar hexpression – more nor thirty year – he might say he'd been born in a chimbley – and he know'd uncommon vell as 'sheenery vor vus nor o' no use: and as to kerhewelty to the boys, everybody in the chimbley line know'd as vell as he did, that they liked the climbin' better nor nuffin as vos' (Boz – 'First of May').*

Slug: Speaker at the statistics session of the first meeting of the Mudfog Association. *He found that the total number of small carts and barrows engaged in dispensing provision to the cats and dogs of the metropolis was one thousand seven hundred and forty-three. The average number of skewers delivered daily with the provender, by each dogs'-meat cart or barrow, was thirty-six. ... Allowing that ... the odd two thousand seven hundred and forty-eight were accidentally devoured with the meat, by the most voracious of the animals supplied, it followed that sixty thousand skewers per day, or the enormous number of twenty-one millions nine hundred thousand skewers annually were wasted in the kennels and dustholes of London; which, if collected and ware-housed, would in ten years' time afford a mass of timber more than sufficient for the construction of a first-rate vessel of war for the use of her Majesty's navy, to be called 'The Royal Skewer' (Mudfog).*

Slum: A writer of rhyming advertisements and friend of Mrs. Jarley. *A tallish gentleman with a hook nose and black hair, dressed in a military surtout very short and tight in the sleeves, and which had once been frogged and braided all over, but was* now sadly shorn of its garniture and quite threadbare – dressed too in ancient grey pantaloons fitting tight to the leg, and a pair of pumps in the winter of their existence (Curiosity Shop).

Slumkey, The Hon. Samuel: Successful parliamentary candidate against Fizkin at Eatanswill. *The Honourable Samuel Slumkey himself, in top-boots, and a blue neckerchief (Pickwick).*

Slummery and **Fithers:** Artist friends of the Bobtail Widgers. *Mr. Slummery, say they, is unquestionably a clever painter, and would no doubt be very popular, and sell his pictures at a very high price, if that cruel Mr. Fithers had not forestalled him in his department of art, and made it thoroughly and completely his own; – Fithers, it is to be observed, being present and within hearing, and Slummery elsewhere (Young Couples – 'Plausible Couple').*

Slummintowken: See **Porkenham, Griggs,** and **Slummintowken Families** *(Pickwick).*

Slurk: Editor of the *Eatanswill Independent*, rival of Pott's *Gazette. A shortish gentleman, with very stiff black hair cut in the porcupine or blacking-brush style, and standing stiff and straight all over his head; his aspect was pompous and threatening; his manner was peremptory; his eyes were sharp and restless; and his whole bearing bespoke a feeling of great confidence in himself, and a consciousness of immeasurable superiority over all other people (Pickwick).*

Slyme, Chevy: Disreputable nephew of old Martin Chuzzlewit, closely associated with Montague Tigg. Later, as a police officer, he is concerned in Jonas Chuzzlewit's arrest. *Wrapped in an old blue camlet cloak with a lining of faded scarlet. His sharp features being much pinched and nipped by long waiting in the cold, and his straggling red whiskers and frowzy hair being more than usually dishevelled from the same cause, he certainly looked rather unwholesome and uncomfortable than Shakespearian or Miltonic (Chuzzlewit).*

Smalder Girls: See under **Johnson, Tom** *(Dombey).*

Smallweed, Bartholomew (Bart, 'Small', 'Chick Weed'): The Joshua Smallweeds' grandson, twin brother of Judith, and friend of Guppy. *He is a weird changeling, to whom years are nothing. He stands precociously possessed of centuries of owlish wisdom. If he ever lay in a cradle, it seems as if he must have lain there in a tail-coat. He has an old, old eye, has Smallweed : and he drinks and smokes, in a monkeyish way; and his neck is stiff in his collar ; and he is never to be taken in ; and he knows all about it, whatever it is. In short, in his bringing up, he has been so nursed by Law and Equity that he has become a kind of fossil Imp (Bleak House).*

Smallweed, Joshua (Grandfather Smallweed): Grandfather of Bartholomew and Judith. He obtains possession of the letters compromising Lady Dedlock and tries to blackmail Sir Leicester, but is foiled by Bucket. *He is in a helpless condition as to his lower, and nearly so as to his upper limbs; but his mind is unimpaired. It holds, as well as it ever held, the first four rules of arithmetic, and a certain small collection of the hardest facts. In respect of ideality, reverence, wonder, and other such phrenological attributes, it is no worse off than it used to be. Everything that Mr. Smallweed's grandfather ever put away in his mind was a grub at first, and is a grub at last. In all his life he has never bred a single butterfly (Bleak House).*

Smallweed, Mrs. Joshua (Grandmother Smallweed): Grandfather Smallweed's wife, grandmother of Bartholomew and Judith. *There has been only one child in the Smallweed family for several generations. Little old men and women there have been, but no child, until Mr. Smallweed's grandmother, now living, became weak in her intellect, and fell (for the first time) into a childish state. With such infantine graces as a total want of observation, memory, understanding and interest, and an eternal disposition to fall asleep over the fire and into it, Mr. Small-*

weed's grandmother has undoubtedly brightened the family (Bleak House).

Smallweed, Judith (Judy): Bartholomew's twin sister and housekeeper for their grandparents. *Judy never owned a doll, never heard of Cinderella, never played at any game. She once or twice fell into children's company when she was about ten years old, but the children couldn't get on with Judy, and Judy couldn't get on with them. She seemed like an animal of another species, and there was instinctive repugnance on both sides. It is very doubtful whether Judy knows how to laugh. She has so rarely seen the thing done, that the probabilities are strong the other way. Of anything like a youthful laugh, she certainly can have no conception. If she were to try one, she would find her teeth in her way; modelling that action of her face, as she has unconsciously modelled all its other expressions, on her pattern of sordid age (Bleak House).*

Smangle: Fellow prisoner of Pickwick in the Fleet. *A tall fellow, with an olive complexion, long dark hair, and very thick bushy whiskers meeting under his chin. . . . There was a rakish, vagabond smartness, and a kind of boastful rascality, about the whole man, that was worth a mine of gold (Pickwick).*

Smart, Tom: Traveller for Bilson and Slum. Central character of 'The Bagman's Story'. *'Tom Smart, gentlemen, had always been very much attached to the public line. It had long been his ambition to stand in a bar of his own, in a green coat, knee-cords, and tops. He had a great notion of taking the chair at convivial dinners, and he had often thought how well he could preside in a room of his own in the talking way, and what a capital example he could set to his customers in the drinking department' (Pickwick).*

Smauker, John: Angelo Cyrus Bantam's footman who invites Sam Weller to the Bath footmen's soirée. *A powdered-headed footman in gorgeous livery, and of symmetrical stature (Pickwick).*

Smif, Putnam ('America Junior'): American shop assistant who writes to

Martin Chuzzlewit seeking his patronage. *'I am young, and ardent. For there is a poetry in wildness, and every alligator basking in the slime is in himself an Epic, self-contained. I aspirate for fame. It is my yearning and my thirst' (Chuzzlewit).*

Smiggers, Joseph: *Perpetual Vice-President – Member Pickwick Club (Pickwick).*

Smike: Ralph Nickleby's son, abandoned at Dotheboys Hall, befriended and rescued by Nicholas Nickleby, with whom he acts for a time in Crummles's company under the name of Digby. He recovers some of his lost wits, but dies. *Although he could not have been less than eighteen or nineteen years old, and was tall for that age, he wore a skeleton suit, such as is usually put upon very little boys, and which, though most absurdly short in the arms and legs, was quite wide enough for his attenuated frame. In order that the lower part of his legs might be in perfect keeping with this singular dress, he had a very large pair of boots, originally made for tops, which might have been once worn by some stout farmer, but were now too patched and tattered for a beggar. Heaven knows how long he had been there, but he still wore the same linen which he had first taken down; for, round his neck, was a tattered child's frill, only half concealed by a coarse, man's neckerchief. He was lame; and as he feigned to be busy in arranging the table, glanced at the letters with a look so keen, and yet so dispirited and hopeless, that Nicholas could hardly bear to watch him (Nickleby).*

Smith: A London clerk. *He was a tall, thin, pale person, in a black coat, scanty grey trousers, little pinched-up gaiters, and brown beaver gloves. . . . We thought we almost saw the dingy little back-office into which he walks every morning, hanging his hat on the same peg, and placing his legs beneath the same desk: first, taking off that black coat which lasts the year through, and putting on the one which did duty last year, and which he keeps in his desk to save the other. There he sits till five o'clock, working on, all day, as regularly as did the dial over the mantelpiece,* whose loud ticking is as monotonous as his whole existence (*Boz* – 'Thoughts About People').

Smith: Member of the Mudfog Association *(Mudfog)*.

Smith, M.P.: An eager new member. *Seizes both the hands of his gratified constituent, and, after greeting him with the most enthusiastic warmth, darts into the lobby with an extraordinary display of ardour in the public cause, leaving an immense impression in his favour* (*Boz* – 'Parliamentary Sketch').

Smith, Samuel: Real name of Horatio Sparkins (q.v.) (*Boz* – 'Horatio Sparkins').

Smithers, Miss: A boarder at Westgate House school, Bury St. Edmunds, on the night of Pickwick's escapade there. *Miss Smithers proceeded to go into hysterics of four young lady power (Pickwick).*

Smithers, Emily: Pupil of the Misses Crumpton. *The belle of the house* (*Boz* – 'Sentiment').

Smithers, Robert: See **Potter, Thomas** (*Boz* – 'Making a Night of it').

Smithick and Watersby: Liverpool owners of the *Golden Mary. I saw him bearing down upon me, head on. . . . It is, personally, neither Smithick, nor Watersby, that I here mention, nor was I ever acquainted with any man of either of those names, nor do I think that there has been any one of either of those names in that Liverpool House for years back. But, it is in reality the House itself that I refer to; and a wiser merchant or a truer gentleman never stepped* (*Christmas Stories* – 'Golden Mary').

Smithie, Mr., Mrs., and the Misses: A Chatham Dockyard official and his family, present at the charity ball at the Bull, Rochester *(Pickwick).*

Smorltork, Count: A guest at Mrs. Leo Hunter's fancy-dress breakfast at Eatanswill. *'The famous foreigner – gathering materials for his great work on England'* *(Pickwick).*

Smouch: Assistant to Namby at the arrest of Pickwick at the George and Vulture. *A shabby-looking man in a brown great-coat shorn of divers buttons (Pickwick).*

Smuggins: Professional entertainer at a harmonic meeting. *That little round-faced man, with the brown small surtout, white stockings and shoes, is in the comic line; the mixed air of self-denial, and mental consciousness of his own powers, with which he acknowledges the call of the chair, is particularly gratifying. . . . Smuggins, after a considerable quantity of coughing by way of symphony, and a most facetious sniff or two, which afford general delight, sings a comic song, with a fal-de-ral – tol-de-rol chorus at the end of every verse, much longer than the verse itself* (*Boz* – 'The Streets – Night').

Snagsby: Law stationer in Cook's Court, Cursitor Street, who employs Hawdon as a law writer. *A mild, bald, timid man, with a shining head, and a scrubby clump of black hair sticking out at the back. He tends to meekness and obesity. As he stands at his door in Cook's Court, in his grey shop-coat and black calico sleeves, looking up at the clouds; or stands behind a desk in his dark shop, with a heavy flat ruler, snipping and slicing at sheepskin, in company with his two 'prentices; he is emphatically a retiring and unassuming man (Bleak House).*

Snagsby, Mrs.: Snagsby's wife, niece of his deceased partner, Peffer. *Something too violently compressed about the waist, and with a sharp nose like a sharp autumn evening, inclining to be frosty towards the end. The Cook's-Courtiers had a rumour flying among them, that the mother of this niece did, in her daughter's childhood, moved by too jealous a solicitude that her figure should approach perfection, lace her up every morning with her maternal foot against the bed-post for a stronger hold and purchase; and further, that she exhibited internally pints of vinegar and lemon-juice: which acids, they held, had mounted to the nose and temper of the patient (Bleak House).*

Snap, Betsy: Uncle Chill's servant. *A withered, hard-favoured, yellow old woman – our only domestic – always em-*

ployed, at this time of the morning, in rubbing my uncle's legs (Christmas Stories – 'Poor Relation').

Snawley: Stepfather of two boys at Dotheboys Hall. Ralph Nickleby engages him to pose as Smike's father, but he is found out and exposes Nickleby. *The sleek and sanctified gentleman (Nickleby).*

Snawley, Mrs.: Snawley's wife *(Nickleby).*

Snevellici: Theatrical performer and father of Miss Snevellici. *Who had been in the profession ever since he had first played the ten-year-old imps in the Christmas pantomimes; who could sing a little, dance a little, fence a little, act a little, and do everything a little, but not much; who had been sometimes in the ballet, and sometimes in the chorus, at every theatre in London; who was always selected in virtue of his figure to play the military visitors and the speechless noblemen; who always wore a smart dress, and came on arm-in-arm with a smart lady in short petticoats, – and always did it too with such an air that people in the pit had been several times known to cry out 'Bravo!' under the impression that he was somebody (Nickleby).*

Snevellici, Miss: Snevellici's daughter. Member of Crummles's theatrical company. *Could do anything, from a medley dance to Lady Macbeth, and also always played some part in blue silk knee-smalls at her benefit (Nickleby).*

Snevellici, Mrs.: Snevellici's wife and Miss Snevellici's mother. *Still a dancer, with a neat little figure and some remains of good looks (Nickleby).*

Snewkes: A friend of the Kenwigs *(Nickleby).*

Sniff: Employed at Mugby Junction refreshment room, where his wife is chief assistant. *A regular insignificant cove. He looks arter the sawdust department in a back room, and is sometimes, when we are very hard put to it, let behind the counter with a corkscrew; but never when it can be helped, his demeanour towards the public being disgusting servile (Christmas Stories – 'Mugby Junction').*

Sniff, Mrs.: Sniff's wife, chief assistant at Mugby Junction refreshment room. *She's the one! She's the one as you'll notice to be always looking another way from you, when you look at her. She's the one with the small waist buckled in tight in front, and with the lace cuffs at her wrists, which she puts on the edge of the counter before her, and stands a-smoothing while the public foams. This smoothing the cuffs and looking another way while the public foams is the last accomplishment taught to the young ladies as come to Mugby to be finished by Our Missis; and it's always taught by Mrs. Sniff (Christmas Stories – 'Mugby Junction').*

Sniggs: Tulrumble's deceased predecessor as Mayor of Mudfog. *Despite the health-preserving air of Mudfog, the Mayor died. It was a most extraordinary circumstance; he had lived in Mudfog for eighty-five years. The corporation didn't understand it at all; indeed it was with great difficulty that one old gentleman, who was a great stickler for forms, was dissuaded from proposing a vote of censure on such unaccountable conduct. Strange as it was, however, die he did, without taking the slightest notice of the corporation (Mudfog).*

Snigsworth, Lord: First cousin to Twemlow, who dines out upon the relationship *(Mutual Friend).*

Snipe, The Hon. Wilmot: Ensign in the 97th Regiment at Rochester. *'Who's that little boy with the light hair and pink eyes, in fancy dress?' inquired Mr. Tupman. 'Hush, pray – pink eyes – fancy dress – little boy – nonsense – Ensign 97th – Honourable Wilmot Snipe – great family – Snipes – very' (Pickwick).*

Snitchey, Jonathan: Partner in Snitchey and Craggs, Dr. Jeddler's lawyers. *Like a magpie or raven (only not so sleek) (Christmas Books – 'Battle of Life').*

Snitchey, Mrs. Jonathan: Wife of Mr. Snitchey, and friend of his partner's wife, Mrs. Craggs *(Christmas Books – 'Battle of Life').*

Snivey, Sir Hookham: Member of the Mudfog Association *(Mudfog).*

Snobb, The Hon. Mr.: A guest at Ralph Nickleby's dinner party *(Nickleby)*.

Snobee: Parliamentary candidate suggested to the Old Street Suburban Representative Discovery Society by a Mr. Wilson, implacably opposed by Rogers, the Parlour Orator. ' *"The abolitionist of the national debt, the unflinching opponent of pensions, the uncompromising advocate of the negro, the reducer of sinecures and the duration of Parliaments; the extender of nothing but the suffrages of the people,"* says Mr. Wilson, *"Prove it,"* says I. *"His acts prove it,"* says he. *"Prove them,"* says I' *(Boz –* 'Parlour Orator').

Snodgrass, Augustus: A member of the Pickwick Club and one of Pickwick's companions in his travels. He marries Emily Wardle. *The poetic Snodgrass . . . poetically enveloped in a mysterious blue cloak with a canine-skin collar (Pickwick).*

Snore, Professor: President of the zoology and botany session at the first meeting of the Mudfog Association. *Wished to be informed how the ingenious gentleman proposed to open a communication with fleas generally, in the first instance, so that they might be thoroughly imbued with a sense of the advantages they must necessarily derive from changing their mode of life, and applying themselves to honest labour (Mudfog).*

Snorflerer, Dowager Lady: One of the aristocratic acquaintances claimed by the egotistical couple *(Young Couples –* 'Egotistical Couple').

Snow, Tom: Captain Ravender's negro steward in the *Golden Mary (Christmas Stories –* 'Golden Mary').

Snubbin, Serjeant: Pickwick's leading counsel in Bardell and Pickwick. *A lantern-faced, sallow-complexioned man, of about five-and-forty, or – as the novels say – he might be fifty. He had that dull-looking boiled eye which is often to be seen in the heads of people who have applied themselves during many years to a weary and laborious course of study; and which would have been sufficient, without the*

additional eye-glass which dangled from a broad black riband round his neck, to warn a stranger that he was very near-sighted. His hair was thin and weak, which was partly attributable to his having never devoted much time to its arrangement, and partly to his having worn for five-and-twenty years the forensic wig which hung on a block beside him (Pickwick).

Snuffim, Sir Tumley: Mrs. Wititterly's doctor. *'Mrs. Wititterly,'* said her husband, *'is Sir Tumley Snuffim's favourite patient. I believe I may venture to say, that Mrs. Wititterly is the first person who took the new medicine which is supposed to have destroyed a family at Kensington Gravel Pits' (Nickleby).*

Snuffletoffle, Q .J.: Speaker at the umbugology and ditchwaterisics session of the second meeting of the Mudfog Association. *Had heard of a pony winking his eye, and likewise of a pony whisking his tail, but whether they were two ponies or the same pony he could not undertake positively to say. At all events, he was acquainted with no authenticated instance of a simultaneous winking and whisking (Mudfog).*

Snugglewood: One of many doctors consulted by Our Bore *(Reprinted –* 'Our Bore').

Snuphanuph, The Dowager Lady: A whist partner introduced to Pickwick by Bantam at Bath Assembly Rooms. *'Hush, my dear sir – nobody's fat or old in Ba-ath. That's the Dowager Lady Snuphanuph' (Pickwick).*

Soemup, Dr.: President of the anatomy and medicine session at the second meeting of the Mudfog Association *(Mudfog).*

Sophia: Eldest of the Camberwell children to whom Ruth Pinch is governess. *A premature little woman of thirteen years old, who had already arrived at such a pitch of whalebone and education that she had nothing girlish about her (Chuzzlewit).*

Sophia: The Matthew Pockets' housemaid *(Expectations).*

Sophy: The deaf and dumb girl bought by Dr. Marigold from Mim for six pairs of braces. She marries a deaf and dumb man, goes to China with him, and returns with a perfectly normal little daughter. *The way she learnt to understand any look of mine was truly surprising. When I sold of a night, she would sit in the cart unseen by them outside, and would give a eager look into my eyes when I looked in, and would hand me straight the precise article or articles I wanted. And then she would clap her hands, and laugh for joy. And as for me, seeing her so bright, and remembering what she was when I first lighted on her, starved and beaten and ragged, leaning asleep against the muddy cart-wheel, it gave me such heart that I gained a greater heighth of reputation than ever (Christmas Stories – 'Doctor Marigold').*

Sophy: One of Mrs. Lirriper's succession of servants. *The willingest girl that ever came into a house half-starved poor thing, a girl so willing that I called her Willing Sophy down upon her knees scrubbing early and late and ever cheerful but always smiling with a black face (Christmas Stories – 'Mrs. Lirriper's Lodgings').*

Southcote, Mr. and Mrs.: A begging-letter writer, unsuccessfully prosecuted by the narrator, and his wife. *The Magistrate was wonderfully struck by his educational acquirements, deeply impressed by the excellence of his letters, exceedingly sorry to see a man of his attainments there, complimented him highly on his powers of composition, and was quite charmed to have the agreeable duty of discharging him. A collection was made for the 'poor fellow,' as he was called in the reports, and I left the court with a comfortable sense of being universally regarded as a sort of monster (Reprinted – 'Begging-letter Writer').*

Sowerberry: Undertaker to whom Oliver Twist is apprenticed briefly before running away after being thrashed for fighting with the other apprentice, Noah Claypole. *A tall, gaunt, large-jointed man, attired in a suit of threadbare black, with darned cotton stockings of the same colour, and shoes to answer. His features were not*

naturally intended to wear a smiling aspect, but he was in general rather given to professional jocosity (Twist).

Sowerberry, Mrs.: Sowerberry's wife. *A short, thin, squeezed-up woman, with a vixenish countenance (Twist).*

Sownds: Beadle on duty at Little Paul Dombey's christening. *He gave Mr. Dombey a bow and a half-smile of recognition, importing that he (the beadle) remembered to have had the pleasure of attending on him when he buried his wife, and hoped he had enjoyed himself since (Dombey).*

Sowster: Beadle of Oldcastle where the second meeting of the Mudfog Association takes place. *A fat man, with a more enlarged development of that peculiar conformation of countenance which is vulgarly termed a double chin than I remember to have ever seen before. He has also a very red nose, which he attributes to a habit of early rising – so red, indeed, that but for this explanation I should have supposed it to proceed from occasional inebriety (Mudfog).*

Sparkins, Horatio: The name assumed by Samuel Smith, junior partner in the cut-price drapery business of Jones, Spruggins, and Smith, Tottenham-court Road, to take him into wealthy society, such as that of the Maldertons (q.v.), which he captivates by his superior manners and enigmatic air. *Who could he be? He was evidently reserved, and apparently melancholy. Was he a clergyman? – He danced too well. A barrister? – he said he was not called. He used very fine words, and talked a great deal. Could he be a distinguished foreigner, come to England for the purpose of describing the country, its manners and customs; and frequenting public balls and public dinners, with the view of becoming acquainted with high life, polished etiquette, and English refinement? – No, he had not a foreign accent. Was he a surgeon, a contributor to the magazines, a writer of fashionable novels, or an artist? – No; to each and all of these surmises, there existed some valid objection. – 'Then,' said everybody, 'he* *must be* somebody' (*Boz* – 'Horatio Sparkins').

Sparkler, Edmund: Mrs. Merdle's son by her first marriage. He marries Fanny Dorrit and rises high in the Circumlocution Office. *Of a chuckle-headed, high-shouldered make, with a general appearance of being, not so much a young man as a swelled boy. He had given so few signs of reason, that a by-word went among his companions that his brain had been frozen up in a mighty frost which prevailed at St. John's, New Brunswick, at the period of his birth there, and had never thawed from that hour. Another by-word represented him as having in his infancy, through the negligence of a nurse, fallen out of a high window on his head, which had been heard by responsible witnesses to crack. It is probable that both these representations were of ex post facto origin; the young gentleman . . . being monomaniacal in offering marriage to all manner of undesirable young ladies, and in remarking of every successive young lady to whom he tendered a matrimonial proposal that she was 'a doosed fine gal – well educated too – with no biggodd nonsense about her'* (*Dorrit*).

Sparkler, Mrs. Edmund: See **Dorrit, Fanny** (*Dorrit*).

Sparks, Tom: The one-eyed Boots at the St. James's Arms (*Strange Gentleman*).

Sparsit: Mrs. Sparsit's late husband. *He inherited a fair fortune from his uncle, but owed it all before he came into it, and spent it twice over immediately afterwards. Thus, when he died, at twenty-four (the scene of his decease, Calais, and the cause, brandy), he did not leave his widow, from whom he had been separated soon after the honeymoon, in affluent circumstances* (*Hard Times*).

Sparsit, Mrs.: Sparsit's widow and Bounderby's genteel housekeeper. *Here she was now, in her elderly days, with the Coriolanian style of nose and the dense black eyebrows which had captivated Sparsit, making Mr. Bounderby's tea as he took his breakfast* (*Hard Times*).

Spatter, John: Former schoolfriend, and imagined clerk, partner, and relative by marriage of Michael, the Poor Relation (*Christmas Stories* – 'Poor Relation').

Specks, Joe: Former schoolmate of the Uncommercial Traveller, who, revisiting his home town of Dullborough, finds Specks still there, a respected medical practitioner. *Into a room, half surgery, half study, I was shown to await his coming, and I found it, by a series of elaborate accidents, bestrewn with testimonies to Joe. Portrait of Mr. Specks, bust of Mr. Specks, silver cup from grateful patient to Mr. Specks, presentation sermon from local clergyman, dedication poem from local poet, dinner-card from local nobleman, tract on balance of power from local refugee, inscribed* Hommage de l'auteur à Specks (*Uncommercial* – 'Dullborough Town').

Specks, Mrs. Joe: Joe Specks's wife, whom the Uncommercial Traveller discovers to be the former friend of his youth, Lucy Green. *She was fat, and if all the hay in the world had been heaped upon her, it could scarcely have altered her face more than Time had altered it from my remembrance of the face that had once looked down upon me* (*Uncommercial* – 'Dullborough Town').

Speddie, Dr.: The doctor who treats Idle's sprained ankle in a Cumberland village and tells Goodchild the story of the corpse in the hotel bed. *A tall, thin, large-boned, old gentleman, with an appearance at first sight of being hard-featured; but, at second glance, the mild expression of his face and some particular touches of sweetness and patience about his mouth, corrected this impression and assigned his long professional rides, by day and night, in the bleak hill-weather, as the true cause of that appearance* (*Two Apprentices*).

Spenlow, Clarissa: Elder of Francis Spenlow's two maiden sisters, with whom Dora lives after her father's death. *They were dressed alike, but this sister wore her dress with a more youthful air than the other; and perhaps had a trifle more frill, or tucker, or brooch, or bracelet, or some little thing of that kind, which made her look more lively* (*Copperfield*).

Spenlow, Dora: Francis Spenlow's daughter. After his death she lives with her aunts Lavinia and Clarissa, is courted by David Copperfield, and becomes his first wife. Hopelessly immature and impractical, she soon dies. *I don't remember who was there, except Dora. I have not the least idea what we had for dinner, besides Dora. My impression is, that I dined off Dora entirely, and sent away half a dozen plates untouched. I sat next to her. I talked to her. She had the most delightful little voice, the gayest little laugh, the pleasantest and most fascinating little ways, that ever led a lost youth into hopeless slavery. She was rather diminutive altogether. So much the more precious, I thought (Copperfield).*

Spenlow, Francis: Dora's father. A partner in the law firm to which David Copperfield is apprenticed. He dies suddenly. *He was a little light-haired gentleman, with undeniable boots, and the stiffest of white cravats and shirt-collars. He was buttoned up mighty trim and tight, and must have taken a great deal of pains with his whiskers, which were accurately curled. His gold watch-chain was so massive, that a fancy came across me, that he ought to have a sinewy golden arm, to draw it out with, like those which are put up over the gold-beater's shops. He was got up with such care, and was so stiff, that he could hardly bend himself; being obliged, when he glanced at some papers on his desk, after sitting down in his chair, to move his whole body, from the bottom of his spine, like Punch (Copperfield).*

Spenlow, Lavinia: Younger of Francis Spenlow's two maiden sisters. *Miss Lavinia was an authority in affairs of the heart, by reason of there having anciently existed a certain Mr. Pidger, who played short whist, and was supposed to have been enamoured of her. My private opinion is, that this was an entirely gratuitous assumption, and that Pidger was altogether innocent of any such sentiments – to which he had never given any sort of expression that I could ever hear of. Both Miss Lavinia and Miss Clarissa had a superstition, however, that he would have* declared his passion, if he had not been cut short in his youth (at about sixty) by over-drinking his constitution, and over-doing an attempt to set it right again by swilling Bath water (Copperfield).*

Spenlow and Jorkins: Law practice of Doctors' Commons of which Francis Spenlow is a proctor, and to which David Copperfield is articled. Spenlow uses Jorkins's reputed hardness as excuse for his refusal to release him *(Copperfield).*

Sphynx, Sophronia: See 'Marchioness, The' *(Curiosity Shop).*

'Spider, The': See **Drummle, Bentley** *(Expectations).*

Spiker, Henry: Solicitor, fellow dinner-guest with David Copperfield at the Waterbrooks'. *So cold a man, that his head, instead of being grey, seemed to be sprinkled with hoar-frost (Copperfield).*

Spiker, Mrs. Henry ('Hamlet's Aunt'): Spiker's wife. *A very awful lady in a black velvet dress, and a great black velvet hat, whom I remember as looking like a near relation of Hamlet's – say his aunt (Copperfield).*

Spinach: One of Miss Flite's birds *(Bleak House).*

Spottletoe: Relative of the Chuzzlewits with designs on old Martin's money. *Was so bald and had such big whiskers, that he seemed to have stopped his hair, by the sudden application of some powerful remedy, in the very act of falling off his head, and to have fastened it irrevocably on his face (Chuzzlewit).*

Spottletoe, Mrs.: Spottletoe's wife. *Much too slim for her years, and of a poetical constitution (Chuzzlewit).*

Sprodgkin, Mrs. Sally: A pestiferous parishioner of the Revd. Frank Milvey. *A portentous old parishioner of the female gender, who was one of the plagues of their lives, and with whom they bore with most exemplary sweetness and good-humour notwithstanding her having an infection of absurdity about her, that communicated itself to everything with which, and everybody with whom, she came in contact. She was a member of the Reverend Frank's* congregation and made a point of distinguishing herself in that body, by conspicuously weeping at everything, however cheering, said by the Reverend Frank in his public ministration; also by applying to herself the various lamentations of David, and complaining in a personally injured manner (much in arrear of the clerk and the rest of the respondents) that her enemies were digging pitfalls about her, and breaking her with rods of iron. . . . But this was not her most inconvenient characteristic, for that took the form of an impression, usually recurring in inclement weather and at about daybreak, that she had something on her mind and stood in immediate need of the Reverend Frank to come and take it off (Mutual Friend).

Spruggins, Thomas: Defeated by Bung in election for beadle of 'Our Parish'. 'Spruggins for Beadle. Ten small children (two of them twins), and a wife!!!' . . . Spruggins was a little thin man, in rusty black, with a long pale face, and a countenance expressive of care and fatigue, which might either be attributed to the extent of his family or the anxiety of his feelings (Boz – 'Election for Beadle').

Spruggins, Mrs. Thomas: Spruggins's wife. Spruggins was the favourite at once, and the appearance of his lady, as she went about to solicit votes (which encouraged confident hopes of a still further addition to the house of Spruggins at no remote period), increased the general prepossession in his favour (Boz – 'Election for Beadle').

Spyers, Jem: Police officer who arrested Conkey Chickweed in Blathers's anecdote (Twist).

Squeers, Fanny: The Squeers' daughter, sister of Wackford junior, whom Nicholas Nickleby enrages by his indifference. Miss Fanny Squeers was in her three-and-twentieth year. If there be any one grace of loveliness inseparable from that particular period of life, Miss Squeers may be presumed to have been possessed of it, as there is no reason to suppose that she was a solitary exception to a universal rule. She was not tall like her mother, but short like her father; from the former she

inherited a voice of harsh quality; from the latter a remarkable expression of the right eye, something akin to having none at all (Nickleby).

Squeers, Wackford, jun.: The Squeers' small son, brother of Fanny. A striking likeness of his father (Nickleby).

Squeers, Wackford, sen.: Father of Fanny and Wackford junior. The brutal proprietor of Dotheboys Hall school in Yorkshire where Nicholas Nickleby finds work as a master. He is subsequently transported for possessing a will stolen from Gride. He had but one eye, and the popular prejudice runs in favour of two. The eye he had, was unquestionably useful, but decidedly not ornamental; being of a greenish grey, and in shape resembling the fan-light of a street door. The blank side of his face was much wrinkled and puckered up, which gave him a very sinister appearance, especially when he smiled, at which times his expression bordered closely on the villainous. His hair was very flat and shiny, save at the ends, where it was brushed stiffly up from a low protruding forehead, which assorted well with his harsh voice and coarse manner. He was about two or three and fifty, and a trifle below the middle size; he wore a white neckerchief with long ends, and a suit of scholastic black; but his coat sleeves being a great deal too long, and his trousers a great deal too short, he appeared ill at ease in his clothes, and as if he were in a perpetual state of astonishment at finding himself so respectable (Nickleby).

Squeers, Mrs. Wackford, sen.: Squeers's wife. Mother of Fanny and Wackford junior. The lady, who was of a large raw-boned figure, was about half a head taller than Mr. Squeers, and was dressed in a dimity night-jacket; with her hair in papers; she had also a dirty night-cap on, relieved by a yellow cotton handkerchief which tied it under the chin (Nickleby).

Squires, Olympia: A sweetheart of the Uncommercial Traveller's youth. Olympia was most beautiful (of course), and I loved her to that degree, that I used to be obliged to get out of my little bed in the *night, expressly to exclaim to Solitude, 'O, Olympia Squires!'* (*Uncommercial* – 'Birthday Celebrations.'.)

Squod, Phil: George's assistant at the shooting-gallery. *The little man is dressed something like a gunsmith, in a green baize apron and cap ; and his face and hands are dirty with gunpowder, and begrimed with the loading of guns (Bleak House).*

Stables, The Hon. Bob: Cousin to Dedlock. *A better man than the Honourable Bob Stables to meet the Hunt at dinner, there could not possibly be (Bleak House).*

Stagg: Blind keeper of the drinking cellars in London where the Prentice Knights meet. He helps Rudge extort money from his wife and is shot dead as the Gordon Riots ringleaders are being rounded up. *The proprietor of this charming retreat . . . wore an old tie-wig as bare and frouzy as a stunted hearth-broom. . . . His eyes were closed; but had they been wide open, it would have been easy to tell, from the attentive expression of the face he turned towards them – pale and unwholesome as might be expected in one of his underground existence – and from a certain anxious raising and quivering of the lids, that he was blind (Rudge).*

Stakes: See Chops (*Christmas Stories* – 'Going into Society').

Stalker, Inspector: One of the Detective Force officers of Scotland Yard. *A shrewd, hard-headed Scotchman – in appearance not at all unlike a very acute, thoroughly-trained schoolmaster, from the Normal Establishment at Glasgow (Reprinted –* 'Detective Police').

Stalker, Mrs.: Troublesome denizen of the Saint Giles district visited by the narrator and Inspector Field. *'Mrs. Stalker, I am something'd that need not be written here, if you won't get yourself into trouble, in about half a minute, if I see that face of yours again!'* (*Reprinted –* 'On Duty with Inspector Field').

Staple: Dingley Dell cricketer who speaks at the dinner after the match with All-Muggleton. *A little man with a puffy Say-nothing-to-me,-or-I'll-contradict-you sort of countenance, who remained very*

quiet ; occasionally looking round him when the conversation slackened, as if he contemplated putting in something very weighty ; and now and then bursting into a short cough of inexpressible grandeur (Pickwick).

Stareleigh, Mr. Justice: The Judge in Bardell and Pickwick. *A most particularly short man, and so fat, that he seemed all face and waistcoat. He rolled in, upon two little turned legs, and having bobbed gravely to the bar, who bobbed gravely to him, put his little legs underneath his table, and his little three-cornered hat upon it ; and when Mr. Justice Stareleigh had done this, all you could see of him was two queer little eyes, one broad pink face, and somewhere about half of a big and very comical-looking wig (Pickwick).*

Stargazer: Father of Emma and Galileo Isaac Newton Flamstead, and uncle to Fanny Brown. He wishes to marry off his daughter to his partner, Mooney, and predicts by the stars that Fanny is destined to marry Tom Grig (*Lamplighter*). Referred to as Mr. Stargazer in the dramatic version but given no specific name in 'The Lamplighter's Story'.

Stargazer, Emma: Stargazer's daughter, sister of Galileo Isaac Newton Flamstead. Her father wants her to marry his partner, Mooney, but the latter is not interested (*Lamplighter*). She has no surname in the subsequent prose version of this farce, entitled 'The Lamplighter's Story'.

Stargazer, Galileo Isaac Newton Flamstead: Son of Stargazer and brother of Emma. Although he is almost of age, his father regards him still as a child (*Lamplighter*). He has no surname in the subsequent prose version of this farce, entitled 'The Lamplighter's Story'.

Starling, Mrs.: Friend of the Leavers. *A widow lady who lost her husband when she was young, and lost herself about the same time – for by her own count she has never since grown five years older (Young Couples –* 'Loving Couple').

Starling, Alfred: Friend of John, the narrator, who makes one of the party visiting the haunted house. *An uncommonly agreeable young fellow of eight-and-twenty . . . who pretends to be 'fast' (another word for loose, as I understand the term), but who is much too good and sensible for that nonsense, and who would have distinguished himself before now, if his father had not unfortunately left him a small independence of two hundred a year, on the strength of which his only occupation in life has been to spend six* (Christmas Stories – 'Haunted House').

Startop: Fellow boarder with Pip at Matthew Pocket's who assists in the attempt to smuggle Magwitch out of the country. *Startop had been spoiled by a weak mother, and kept at home when he ought to have been at school, but he was devotedly attached to her, and admired her beyond measure. He had a woman's delicacy of feature, and was . . . exactly like his mother* (Expectations).

Steadiman, John: Chief mate of the *Golden Mary.* He assumes command and takes up the narrative after Captain Ravender's death. *At this time of chartering the Golden Mary, he was aged thirty-two. A brisk, bright, blue-eyed fellow, a very neat figure and rather under the middle size, never out of the way and never in it, a face that pleased everybody and that all children took to, a habit of going about singing as cheerily as a blackbird, and a perfect sailor* (Christmas Stories – 'Golden Mary').

Steerforth, Mrs.: Steerforth's mother, an autocrat who, when he seduces Little Em'ly, blames her, and when he is killed cannot accept the fact of his death. *An elderly lady, though not very far advanced in years, with a proud carriage and a handsome face* (Copperfield).

Steerforth, James: Schoolfellow and later friend of David Copperfield, seducer of Little Em'ly, whom he later tries to pass on to his servant Littimer. He is drowned in a shipwreck off Yarmouth. *I was not considered as being formally received into the school, however, until J. Steerforth arrived. Before this boy, who was reputed to be a great scholar, and was very good-looking, and at least*

half a dozen years my senior, I was carried as before a magistrate. || *What is natural in me, is natural in many other men, I infer, and so I am not afraid to write that I never had loved Steerforth better than when the ties that bound me to him were broken. In the keen distress of the discovery of his unworthiness, I thought more of all that was brilliant in him, I softened more towards all that was good in him, I did more justice to the qualities that might have made him a man of a noble nature and a great name, than ever I had done in the height of my devotion to him. Deeply as I felt my own unconscious part in his pollution of an honest home, I believed that if I had been brought face to face with him, I could not have uttered one reproach* (Copperfield).

Stetta, Violetta: See **Thigsberry, Duke of** *(Curiosity Shop).*

Stiggins, The Revd. Mr.: A drunken hypocrite and leading light at the Brick Lane Temperance meetings until exposed by Tony Weller, whose late wife had been one of Stiggins's guillible admirers and providers. *He was a prim-faced, red-nosed man, with a long, thin countenance, and a semi-rattlesnake sort of eye – rather sharp, but decidedly bad. He wore very short trousers, and black-cotton stockings, which, like the rest of his apparel, were particularly rusty. His looks were starched, but his white neckerchief was not, and its long limp ends straggled over his closely-buttoned waistcoat in a very uncouth and unpicturesque fashion* (Pickwick).

Stiltstalking, Lord Lancaster: A high-ranking oversea representative of the Circumlocution Office. *A grey old gentleman of dignified and sullen appearance. . . . This noble Refrigerator had iced several European courts in his time, and had done it with such complete success that the very name of Englishman yet struck cold to the stomachs of foreigners who had the distinguished honour of remembering him, at a distance of a quarter of a century* (Dorrit).

Stiltstalking, Tudor: See under **Barnacle, William** *(Dorrit).*

Stokes, Martin: A small farmer *(Village Coquettes)*.

Strange Gentleman, The: See Trott, Alexander *(Strange Gentleman)*.

Straudenheim: Shopkeeper-owner of a large house in Strasbourg, whose odd behaviour entertains the Uncommercial Traveller one wet Sunday evening. *He wore a black velvet skull-cap, and looked usurious and rich. A large-lipped, pear-nosed old man, with white hair, and keen eyes, though near-sighted (Uncommercial – 'Travelling Abroad').*

Straw, Sergeant: One of the Detective Force officers of Scotland Yard. *A little wiry Sergeant of meek demeanour and strong sense, would knock at a door and ask a series of questions in any mild character you choose to prescribe to him, from a charity-boy upwards, and seem as innocent as an infant (Reprinted – 'Detective Police').*

Streaker: Housemaid at the haunted house. *I am unable to say whether she was of an unusually lymphatic temperament, or what else was the matter with her, but this young woman became a mere Distillery for the production of the largest and most transparent tears I ever met with. Combined with these characteristics, was a peculiar tenacity of holding those specimens, so that they didn't fall, but hung upon her face and nose (Christmas Stories – 'Haunted House').*

Strong, Dr.: David Copperfield's Canterbury schoolmaster, later his employer at Highgate. A temporary rift between him and his young wife, Annie, is healed by Mr. Dick. *Dr. Strong looked almost as rusty, to my thinking, as the tall iron rails and gates outside the house . . . with his clothes not particularly well brushed, and his hair not particularly well combed; his knee-smalls unbraced; his long black gaiters unbuttoned; and his shoes yawning like two caverns on the hearthrug. . . . Outside his own domain, and unprotected, he was a very sheep for the shearers. He would have taken his gaiters off his legs, to give away. In fact, there was a story current among us . . . that on a frosty day, one*

winter-time, he actually did bestow his gaiters on a beggar-woman, who occasioned some scandal in the neighbourhood by exhibiting a fine infant from door to door, wrapped in those garments, which were universally recognised, being as well known in the vicinity as the cathedral (Copperfield).

Strong, Mrs. (Annie): Dr. Strong's wife. A misunderstanding about her relationship with Jack Maldon temporarily estranges them. *A very pretty young lady – whom he called Annie, and who was his daughter, I supposed (Copperfield).*

Struggles: Member of Dingley Dell Cricket Club. *The enthusiastic Struggles (Pickwick).*

Stryver: London barrister who defends Darnay at the Old Bailey. Much of his success is owed to Sydney Carton's 'devilling' for him. *A man of little more than thirty, but looking twenty years older than he was, stout, loud, red, bluff, and free from any drawback of delicacy, had a pushing way of shouldering himself (morally and physically) into companies and conversations, that argued well for his shouldering his way up in life (Two Cities).*

Stubbs: A pony placed at Esther Summerson's exclusive disposal by Lawrence Boythorn. *A chubby pony, with a short neck and a mane all over his eyes, who could canter – when he would – so easily and quietly, that he was a treasure (Bleak House).*

Stubbs, Mrs.: Percy Noakes's laundress. *A dirty old woman, with an inflamed countenance (Boz – 'Steam Excursion').*

Styles: A vice-president of the statistics session at the second meeting of the Mudfog Association *(Mudfog).*

'Suffolk Bantam': See 'Middlesex Dumpling' *(Pickwick).*

Sulliwin, Mrs.: Resident of Seven Dials, the current bone of contention between Mary and Sarah. *'Here's poor dear Mrs. Sulliwin, as has five blessed children of her own, can't go out a charing for one arter-noon, but what hussies must be a comin',* *and 'ticing avay her oun' 'usband, as she's been married to twelve year come next Easter Monday, for I see the certificate ven I vas drinkin' a cup o' tea vith her, only the werry last blessed Ven'sday as ever was sent'* (Boz – 'Seven Dials').

Summerson, Esther ('Dame Durden'): Narrator of much of the story. An orphan, she is adopted by John Jarndyce and becomes companion to Ada Clare. Jarndyce subsequently wishes to marry her, but magnanimously gives her to Allen Woodcourt. She proves to be the illegitimate child of Lady Dedlock and Hawdon. *I am not clever. I always knew that. . . . I had always rather a noticing way – not a quick way, O no! – a silent way of noticing what passed before me, and thinking I should like to understand it better. I have not by any means a quick understanding. When I love a person very tenderly indeed, it seems to brighten. But even that may be my vanity (Bleak House).*

Superintendent: Liverpool police officer who conducts the Uncommercial Traveller on his tour of sailormen's haunts. *A tall well-looking well-set-up man of a soldierly bearing, with a cavalry air, a good chest, and a resolute but not by any means ungentle face. He carried in his hand a plain black walking-stick of hard wood; and whenever and wherever, at any after-time of the night, he struck it on the pavement with a ringing sound, it instantly produced a whistle out of the darkness, and a policeman (Uncommercial – 'Poor Mercantile Jack').*

Susan: Rosina Nightingale's maid *(Nightingale's Diary).*

Susan: Mrs. Mann's maid *(Twist).*

Sweedlepipe, Paul ('Poll'): Bird-fancier and barber. Mrs. Gamp's landlord in High Holborn and great friend of Bailey, whom he eventually takes into partnership. *A little elderly man, with a clammy cold right hand, from which even rabbits and birds could not remove the smell of shaving-soap. Poll had something of the bird in his nature; not of the hawk or eagle, but of the sparrow, that builds in*

chimney-stacks, and inclines to human company. He was not quarrelsome, though, like the sparrow; but peaceful, like the dove. In his walk he strutted; and, in this respect, he bore a faint resemblance to the pigeon, as well as in a certain prosiness of speech, which might, in its monotony, be likened to the cooing of that bird. He was very inquisitive; and when he stood at his shop-door in the evening-tide, watching the neighbours, with his head on one side, and his eye cocked knowingly, there was a dash of the raven in him. Yet, there was no more wickedness in Poll than in a robin (Chuzzlewit).

Sweeney, Mrs.: The Uncommercial Traveller's servant when he is living in Gray's Inn. *In figure extremely like an old family-umbrella, whose dwelling confronts a dead wall in a court off Gray's Inn Lane, and who is usually fetched into the passage of that bower, when wanted, from some neighbouring home of industry, which has the curious property of imparting an inflammatory appearance to her visage. Mrs. Sweeney is one of the race of professed laundresses, and is the compiler of a remarkable manuscript volume entitled 'Mrs. Sweeney's Book,' from which much curious statistical information may be gathered respecting the high prices and small uses of soda, soap, sand, firewood, and other such articles (Uncommercial – 'Chambers').*

Swidger, George: Eldest son of Philip and brother of William. Repentant on his sickbed for his sins, he retracts under Redlaw's influence but later returns to a better frame of mind and appears to be recovering. *Redlaw paused at the bedside, and looked down on the figure that was stretched upon the mattress. It was that of a man, who should have been in the vigour of his life, but on whom it was not likely the sun would ever shine again. The vices of his forty or fifty years' career had so branded him, that, in comparison with their effects upon his face, the heavy hand of time upon the old man's face who watched him had been merciful and beautifying (Christmas Books – 'Haunted Man').*

Swidger, Philip: Father of George and

William. He loses the happiness of his old age under Redlaw's influence, but it is restored through Milly Swidger. '*Superannuated keeper and custodian of this Institution, eigh-ty-seven year old*' (*Christmas Books* – 'Haunted Man').

Swidger, William and Mrs. William (Milly): Redlaw's manservant, Philip Swidger's youngest son, brother of George; and his wife, Denham's ministering angel in his illness. *Mrs. William, like Mr. William, was a simple, innocent-looking person, in whose smooth cheeks the cheerful red of the husband's official waist-coat was very pleasantly repeated. But whereas Mr. William's light hair stood on end all over his head, and seemed to draw his eyes up with it in an excess of bustling readiness for anything, the dark brown hair of Mrs. William was carefully smoothed down, and waved away under a trim tidy cap, in the most exact and quiet manner imaginable. Whereas Mr. William's very trousers hitched themselves up at the ankles, as if it were not in their iron-grey nature to rest without looking about them, Mrs. William's neatly flowered skirts – red and white, like her own pretty face – were as composed and orderly, as if the very wind that blew so hard out of doors could not disturb one of their folds* (*Christmas Books* – 'Haunted Man').

Swillenhausen, Baron and Baroness von: Parents-in-law of Baron von Koëldwethout (q.v.) *(Nickleby).*

Swills, Little: Comic singer at the Harmonic Meetings at the Sol's Arms. *Sensation is created by the entrance of a chubby little man in a large shirt-collar, with a moist eye, and an inflamed nose, who modestly takes a position near the door as one of the general public, but seems familiar with the room too. A whisper circulates that this is Little Swills. It is considered not unlikely that he will get up an imitation of the Coroner, and make it the principal feature of the Harmonic Meeting in the evening (Bleak House).*

Swiveller, Dick: Friend of Fred Trent, who persuades him to give up Sophy Wackles and wait to marry Little Nell for her grandfather's money. Quilp manipulates him into becoming Brass's clerk, but he is repelled by what he discovers and helps to expose Brass and Quilp. He befriends, educates, and marries The Marchioness. *His wiry hair, dull eyes, and sallow face, would still have been strong witnesses against him. His attire was not, as he had himself hinted, remarkable for the nicest arrangement, but was in a state of disorder which strongly induced the idea that he had gone to bed in it. It consisted of a brown body-coat with a great many brass buttons up the front, and only one behind; a bright check necker-chief, a plaid waistcoat, soiled white trousers, and a very limp hat, worn with the wrong side foremost, to hide a hole in the brim. The breast of his coat was orna-mented with an outside pocket from which there peeped forth the cleanest end of a very large and very ill-favoured handker-chief; his dirty wristbands were pulled down as far as possible and ostentatiously folded back over his cuffs; he displayed no gloves, and carried a yellow cane having at the top a bone hand with the semblance of a ring on its little finger and a black ball in its grasp (Curiosity Shop).*

Swoshle, Mrs. Henry George Alfred: See under **Tapkins, Mrs.** *(Mutual Friend).*

Swosser, Captain, R.N.: Deceased first husband of Mrs. Bayham Badger. *Mrs. Badger signified to us that she had never madly loved but once; and that the object of that wild affection, never to be recalled in its fresh enthusiasm, was Captain Swosser (Bleak House).*

Sylvia: Daughter of the farmhouse family at Hoghton Towers where George Silverman is placed by Hawkyard ('Silverman').

Tabblewick, Mrs.: Friend of the Bobtail Widgers. *She is no doubt beautiful, very beautiful; they once thought her the most beautiful woman ever seen; still if you press them for an honest answer, they are bound to say that this was before they had ever seen our lovely friend on the sofa, (the sofa is hard by, and our lovely friend can't help hearing the whispers in which* *this is said) (Young Couples – 'Plausible Couple').*

Tabby: Servant at Miss Griffin's school. *A grinning and good-natured soul called Tabby, who was the serving drudge of the house, and had no more figure than one of the beds, and upon whose face there was always more or less black-lead (Christmas Stories – 'Haunted House').*

Tacker: Mould the undertaker's chief mourner. *An obese person, with his waistcoat in closer connection with his legs than is quite reconcilable with the established ideas of grace; with that cast of feature which is figuratively called a bottle-nose; and with a face covered all over with pimples. He had been a tender plant once upon a time, but from constant blowing in the fat atmosphere of funerals, had run to seed (Chuzzlewit).*

Tackleton: Remaining partner of Gruff and Tackleton, by which name he is still known. He employs Caleb Plummer and is misguidedly adored by blind Bertha Plummer, and almost manages to marry May Fielding, being jilted on the wedding day. *Tackleton the Toy-merchant, was a man whose vocation had been quite misunderstood by his Parents and Guardians. If they had made him a Money Lender, or a sharp Attorney, or a Sheriff's Officer, or a Broker, he might have sown his discontented oats in his youth, and, after having had the full run of himself in ill-natured transactions, might have turned out amiable, at last, for the sake of a little freshness and novelty. But, cramped and chafing in the peaceable pursuit of toy-making, he was a domestic Ogre, who had been living on children all his life, and was their implacable enemy. He despised all toys; wouldn't have bought one for the world; delighted, in his malice, to insinuate grim expressions into the faces of brown-paper farmers who drove pigs to market, bell-men who advertised lost lawyers' consciences, moveable old ladies who darned stockings or carved pies; and other like samples of his stock-in-trade. In appalling masks; hideous, hairy, red-eyed Jacks in Boxes; Vampire Kites; demoniacal Tumblers who wouldn't lie down, and were per-*

petually flying forward, to stare infants out of countenance; his soul perfectly revelled. They were his only relief, and safety-valve (Christmas Books – 'Cricket').

Tadger, Brother: Prominent official of the Brick Lane Branch of the United Grand Junction Ebenezer Temperance Association. *A little emphatic man, with a bald head, and drab shorts (Pickwick).*

Tamaroo: Successor to Bailey as Mrs. Todgers's servant. *An old woman whose name was reported to be Tamaroo – which seemed an impossibility. Indeed it appeared in the fulness of time that the jocular boarders had appropriated the word from an English ballad, in which it is supposed to express the bold and fiery nature of a certain hackney-coachman; and that it was bestowed upon Mr. Bailey's successor by reason of her having nothing fiery about her, except an occasional attack of that fire which is called St. Anthony's. . . . She was chiefly remarkable for a total absence of all comprehension upon every subject whatever. She was a perfect Tomb for messages and small parcels; and when despatched to the Post-office with letters, had been seen frequently endeavouring to insinuate them into casual chinks in private doors, under the delusion that any door with a hole in it would answer the purpose (Chuzzlewit).*

Tangle: Counsel in the suit of Jarndyce and Jarndyce. *Knows more of Jarndyce and Jarndyce than anybody. He is famous for it – supposed never to have read anything else since he left school (Bleak House).*

Tape: Prince Bull's tyrannical old godmother, symbolising the Civil Service Establishment. *She was a Fairy, this Tape, and was a bright red all over. She was disgustingly prim and formal, and could never bend herself a hair's breadth this way or that way, out of her naturally crooked shape. But, she was very potent in her wicked art. She could stop the fastest thing in the world, change the strongest thing into the weakest, and the most useful into the most useless. To do this she had only to put her cold hand upon it, and* *repeat her own name, Tape. Then it withered away (Reprinted – 'Prince Bull').*

Tapkins, Mrs.: One of the first to leave her card on the newly-elevated Boffins. *All the world and his wife and daughter leave cards. Sometimes the world's wife has so many daughters, that her card reads rather like a Miscellaneous Lot at an Auction; comprising Mrs. Tapkins, Miss Tapkins, Miss Frederica Tapkins, Miss Antonina Tapkins, Miss Malvina Tapkins, and Miss Euphemia Tapkins; at the same time, the same lady leaves the card of Mrs. Henry George Alfred Swoshle, née Tapkins; also, a card, Mrs. Tapkins at Home, Wednesdays, Music, Portland Place (Mutual Friend).*

Tapkins, Felix: Bachelor friend of the Lovetowns, who flirts with Mrs. Lovetown *(Is She His Wife?).*

Tapley, Mark: Ostler at the Blue Dragon, Salisbury, renamed The Jolly Tapley after his marriage to its landlady, Mrs. Lupin. Later young Martin Chuzzlewit's servant, bosom friend and travelling companion. *Walked with a light quick step, and sang as he went : for certain in a very loud voice, but not unmusically. He was a young fellow, of some five or six-and-twenty perhaps, and was dressed in such a free and fly-away fashion, that the long ends of his loose red neckcloth were streaming out behind him quite as often as before. (Chuzzlewit).*

Taplin, Harry: Comedian who sings a comic duet with Amelia Martin at White Conduit. *'Go to work, Harry,' cried the comic gentleman's personal friends. 'Tap-tap – tap,' went the leader's bow on the music-desk. The symphony began, and was soon afterwards followed by a faint kind of ventriloquial chirping, proceeding apparently from the deepest recesses of the interior of Miss Amelia Martin (Boz – 'Mistaken Milliner').*

Tappertit, Simon (Sim): Gabriel Varden's apprentice and Joe Willet's rival for Dolly. Leader of the Prentice Knights, later United Bull-Dogs (q.v.), he becomes a leader of the Gordon Riots but has his legs crushed. Discharged from prison, he is helped by Gabriel to set up as a

shoe-black and marries a rag-and-bone man's widow. *An old-fashioned, thin-faced, sleek-haired, sharp-nosed, small-eyed little fellow, very little more than five feet high, and thoroughly convinced in his own mind that he was above the middle size; rather tall, in fact, than otherwise. Of his figure, which was well enough formed, though somewhat of the leanest, he entertained the highest admiration; and with his legs, which, in knee-breeches, were perfect curiosities of littleness, he was enraptured to a degree amounting to enthusiasm. He also had some majestic, shadowy ideas, which had never been quite fathomed by his intimate friends, concerning the power of his eye. . . . As certain liquors, confined in casks too cramped in their dimensions, will ferment, and fret, and chafe in their imprisonment, so the spiritual essence or soul of Mr. Tappertit would sometimes fume within that precious cask, his body, until, with great foam and froth and splutter, it would force a vent, and carry all before it (Rudge).*

Tappleton, Lieutenant: Dr. Slammer's second in the abortive duel at Rochester *(Pickwick).*

Tartar, Lieutenant, R.N.: Former schoolfellow of Canon Crisparkle. Neville Landless's neighbour at Staple Inn, he gives up his rooms to Rosa Bud after her flight from Cloisterham. *A handsome gentleman, with a young face, but with an older figure in its robustness and its breadth of shoulder; say a man of eight-and-twenty, or at the utmost thirty; so extremely suburnt that the contrast between his brown visage and the white forehead shaded out of doors by his hat, and the glimpses of white throat below the neckerchief, would have been almost ludicrous but for his broad temples, bright blue eyes, clustering brown hair, and laughing teeth (Drood).*

Tarter, Bob: First Boy at the school, helped by Old Cheeseman, whom he has always persecuted. *His father was in the West Indies, and he owned, himself, that his father was worth Millions. He had great power among our fellows (Christmas Stories – 'Schoolboy's Story').*

Tatham, Mrs.: Pawnbroker's customer. *An old sallow-looking woman, who has been leaning with both arms on the counter with a small bundle before her, for half an hour previously* (*Boz* – 'Pawnbroker's Shop').

Tatt: Friend of Inspector Wield. His diamond pin is stolen at Epsom Station on Derby Day by the Swell Mob, but ingeniously recovered by Sergeant Witchem. '*A gentleman formerly in the public line, quite an amateur Detective in his way, and very much respected*' (*Reprinted* – 'Three "Detective" Anecdotes').

'Tattycoram': See Beadle, Harriet (*Dorrit*).

Taunton, Captain: Officer commanding Richard Doubledick's company. He is killed, as a Major, at Badajos. *A young gentleman not above five years his senior, whose eyes had an expression in them which affected Private Richard Doubledick in a very remarkable way. They were bright, handsome, dark eyes, – what are called laughing eyes generally, and, when serious, rather steady than severe, – but they were the only eyes now left in his narrowed world that Private Richard Doubledick could not stand. Unabashed by evil report and punishment, defiant of everything else and everybody else, he had but to know that those eyes looked at him for a moment, and he felt ashamed* (*Christmas Stories* – 'Seven Poor Travellers').

Taunton, Mrs.: Widowed mother of Emily and Sophia. They are the great rivals of Mrs. Briggs and her girls (q.v.). *A good-looking widow of fifty, with the form of a giantess and the mind of a child. The pursuit of pleasure, and some means of killing time, were the sole end of her existence. She doted on her daughters, who were as frivolous as herself* (*Boz* – 'Steam Excursion').

Taunton, Mrs.: Captain Taunton's mother. After his death she nurses and virtually adopts Richard Doubledick. *It gradually seemed to him as if in his maturity he had recovered a mother; it gradually seemed to her as if in her bereavement she had found a son* (*Christmas Stories* – 'Seven Poor Travellers').

Tellson's Bank: The London bank served by Jarvis Lorry as confidential clerk and messenger. *Tellson's Bank by Temple Bar was an old-fashioned place, even in the year one thousand seven hundred and eighty. It was very small, very dark, very ugly, very incommodious. It was an old-fashioned place, moreover, in the moral attribute that the partners in the House were proud of its smallness, proud of its darkness, proud of its ugliness, proud of its incommodiousness. They were even boastful of its eminence in those particulars, and were fired by an express conviction that, if it were less objectionable, it would be less respectable* (*Two Cities*).

Testator: Occupant of chambers in Lyon's Inn, who furnishes his rooms with items found in a cellar and is duly visited by their perhaps spectral owner (*Uncommercial* – 'Chambers').

Tetterby, Adolphus: Newsagent husband of Sophia and father of numerous children, including 'Dolphus, Johnny, and Sally. His customary good nature is temporarily lost under Redlaw's influence, but returns. *The small man who sat in the small parlour, making fruitless attempts to read his newspaper peaceably in the midst of this disturbance, was the father of the family, and the chief of the firm described in the inscription over the little shop front, by the name and title of A. TETTERBY AND CO., NEWSMEN. Indeed, strictly speaking, he was the only personage answering to that designation; as Co. was a mere poetical abstraction, altogether baseless and impersonal* (*Christmas Books* – 'Haunted Man').

Tetterby, Mrs. Adolphus (Sophia): Wife of Adolphus, who calls her his 'little woman'. Mother of 'Dolphus, Johnny, Sally and others. *The process of induction by which Mr. Tetterby had come to the conclusion that his wife was a little woman, was his own secret. She would have made two editions of himself, very easily. Considered as an individual, she was rather remarkable for being robust and portly; but considered with reference to her husband, her dimensions became magnificent* (*Christmas Books* – 'Haunted Man').

Tetterby, 'Dolphus: The Tetterbys' eldest son, brother of Johnny, Sally and others. *Was also in the newspaper line of life, being employed, by a more thriving firm than his father and Co., to vend newspapers at a railway station, where his chubby little person, like a shabbily disguised Cupid, and his shrill little voice (he was not much more than ten years old), were as well known as the hoarse panting of the locomotives, running in and out* (*Christmas Books* – 'Haunted Man').

Tetterby, Johnny: The Tetterbys' second son, brother of 'Dolphus, Sally and others. In constant charge of the baby, Sally. *Another little boy – the biggest there, but still little – was tottering to and fro, bent on one side, and considerably affected in the knees by the weight of a large baby, which he was supposed, by a fiction that obtains sometimes in sanguine families, to be hushing to sleep* (*Christmas Books* – 'Haunted Man').

Tetterby, Sally: The baby of the Tetterby family, sister of 'Dolphus, in the constant charge of her brother Johnny. *It was a very Moloch of a baby, on whose insatiate altar the whole existence of this particular young brother was offered up a daily sacrifice. Its personality may be said to have consisted in its never being quiet, in any one place, for five consecutive minutes, and never going to sleep when required. 'Tetterby's baby' was as well known in the neighbourhood as the postman or the pot-boy* (*Christmas Books* – 'Haunted Man').

Théophile, Corporal: A French soldier who cares for the orphan baby Bebelle until his death fighting a fire. *A smart figure of a man of thirty, perhaps a thought under the middle size, but very neatly made, – a sunburnt Corporal with a brown peaked beard. . . . Nothing was amiss or awry about the Corporal. A lithe and nimble Corporal, quite complete, from the sparkling dark eyes under his knowing uniform cap to his sparkling white gaiters. The very image and presentment of a Corporal of his country's army, in the line of his shoulders, the line of his waist, the broadest line of his Bloomer trousers, and*

their narrowest line at the calf of his leg (*Christmas Stories* – 'Somebody's Luggage').

Thicknesse: A baker, one of the admiring audience of the gentleman connected with the press at the Green Dragon, Westminster Bridge. *A large stomach surmounted by a man's head, and placed on the top of two particularly short legs* (*Mudfog* – 'Mr. Robert Bolton').

Thigsberry, Duke of and Stetta, Violetta: Subjects of an anecdote by which Chuckster seeks to impress the Garlands. *Acquainted them with the precise amount of the income guaranteed by the Duke of Thigsberry to Violetta Stetta of the Italian Opera, which it appeared was payable quarterly, and not half-yearly, as the public had been given to understand, and which was exclusive, and not inclusive, (as had been monstrously stated), of jewellery, perfumery, hair-powder for five footmen, and two daily changes of kid-gloves for a page* (*Curiosity Shop*).

Thomas: Dedlock's groom (*Bleak House*).

Thomas: Waiter at the Winglebury Arms. *The waiter pulled down the window-blind, and then pulled it up again – for a regular waiter must do something before he leaves the room – adjusted the glasses on the sideboard, brushed a place that was not dusty, rubbed his hands very hard, walked stealthily to the door, and evaporated* (*Boz* – 'Great Winglebury Duel').

Thomas: Knag's boy. *Nearly half as tall as a shutter* (*Nickleby*).

Thomas: Waiter on the gentleman who killed himself in the cause of crumpet-eating (*Pickwick*).

Thompson, Mrs.: Friend of Fairfax who solicits his opinion of Mrs. Barker (*Young Gentlemen* – 'Censorious Young Gentleman').

Thompson, Bill: Popular performer at the Victoria Theatre. *The inimitable manner in which Bill Thompson can 'come the double monkey', or go through the mysterious involutions of a sailor's hornpipe* (*Boz* – 'The Streets – Night').

Thompson, Julia: A friend of Felix Nixon (*Young Gentlemen* – 'Domestic Young Gentleman').

Thompson, Tally-Ho (alias **Thomas Pigeon**): Notorious horse-stealer, couper, and magsman, taken by Sergeant Witchem (*Reprinted* – 'Detective Police').

Thomson, Sir John, M.P.: Eminent Parliamentarian (*Boz* – 'Parliamentary Sketch').

Tibbs, Mr. and Mrs.: Proprietress of a boarding house in Great Coram Street, London, and her henpecked husband. They eventually separate. *Mrs. Tibbs was somewhat short of stature, and Mr. Tibbs was by no means a large man. He had, moreover, very short legs, but, by way of indemnification, his face was peculiarly long. He was to his wife what the o is in 90 – he was of some importance with her – he was nothing without her. Mrs. Tibbs was always talking. Mr. Tibbs rarely spoke; but, if it were at any time possible to put in a word, when he should have said nothing at all, he had that talent. Mrs. Tibbs detested long stories, and Mr. Tibbs had one, the conclusion of which had never been heard by his most intimate friends. It always began, 'I recollect when I was in the volunteer corps, in eighteen hundred and six,' – but, as he spoke very slowly and softly, and his better-half very quickly and loudly, he rarely got beyond the introductory sentence* (*Boz* – 'Boarding-House').

Tickit, Mrs.: The Meagles' cook and housekeeper. *Cook and Housekeeper when the family were at home, and Housekeeper only when the family were away. . . . When they went away, she always put on the silk-gown and the jet-black row of curls represented in that portrait (her hair was reddish-grey in the kitchen), established herself in the breakfast-room, put her spectacles between two particular leaves of Dr. Buchanan's Domestic Medicine, and sat looking over the blind all day until they came back again* (*Dorrit*).

Tickle: Exhibitor in the display of models and mechanical science at the second meeting of the Mudfog Association. *Displayed his newly-invented spectacles, which enabled the wearer to discern, in very bright colours, objects at a great distance, and rendered him wholly blind to those immediately before him (Mudfog).*

Tiddypot: Vestryman, of Gumption House (*Reprinted* – 'Our Vestry').

Tiffey: Senior clerk at Spenlow and Jorkins. *A little dry man, sitting by himself, who wore a stiff brown wig that looked as if it were made of ginger-bread (Copperfield).*

Tigg, Montague: A confidence-trickster associated with Chevy Slyme. Later, as Tigg Montague, he promotes the fraudulent Anglo-Bengalee Disinterested Loan and Life Assurance Company. Murdered by Jonas Chuzzlewit for knowing too much about his past. *Of that order of appearance, which is currently termed shabby-genteel. . . . His nether garments were of a bluish grey – violent in its colours once, but sobered now by age and dinginess – and were so stretched and strained in a tough conflict between his braces and his straps, that they appeared every moment in danger of flying asunder at the knees. His coat, in colour blue and of a military cut, was buttoned and frogged, up to his chin. His cravat was, in hue and pattern, like one of those mantles which hairdressers are accustomed to wrap about their clients, during the progress of the professional mysteries. His hat had arrived at such a pass that it would have been hard to determine whether it was originally white or black. But he wore a moustache – a shaggy moustache too : nothing in the meek and merciful way, but quite in the fierce and scornful style : the regular Satanic sort of thing – and he wore, besides, a vast quantity of unbrushed hair. He was very dirty and very jaunty ; very bold and very mean ; very swaggering and very slinking ; very much like a man who might have been something better, and unspeakably like a man who deserved to be something worse (Chuzzlewit).*

Tiggin and Welps: City house for which the Bagman's uncle travelled *(Pickwick).*

Tim, Tiny: see **Cratchit, Tim** (*Christmas Books* – 'Christmas Carol').

Timbered: A vice-president of the statistics session at the first meeting of the Mudfog Association *(Mudfog)*.

Timberry, Snittle: Member of Crummles's theatrical company who chairs the farewell supper to the Crummles family. *It is observable that when people upon the stage are in any strait involving the very last extremity of weakness and exhaustion, they invariably perform feats of strength requiring great ingenuity and muscular power. Thus, a wounded prince or bandit-chief, who is bleeding to death and too faint to move, except to the softest music (and then only upon his hands and knees), shall be seen to approach a cottage door for aid, in such a series of writhings and twistings, and with such curlings up of the legs, and such rollings over and over, and such gettings up and tumblings down again, as could never be achieved save by a very strong man skilled in posture-making. And so natural did this sort of performance come to Mr. Snittle Timberry, that on their way out of the theatre and towards the tavern where the supper was to be holden, he testified the severity of his recent indisposition and its wasting effects upon the nervous system, by a series of gymnastic performances which were the admiration of all witnesses (Nickleby).*

Timkins: Candidate for election for beadle of 'Our Parish'. *'Timkins for Beadle. Nine small children!!!' (Boz –* 'Election for Beadle').

Timpson: Proprietor of coaches, including the Blue-Eyed Maid, whose business in Dullborough the Uncommercial Traveller finds taken over, and knocked down, by Pickford *(Uncommercial –* 'Dullborough Town').

Timson, The Revd. Charles: An unctuous friend of Gabriel Parsons, engaged to Miss Lillerton, whom he marries. *Mr. Timson, having conscientious scruples on the subject of card-playing, drank brandy-and-water (Boz –* 'Watkins Tottle').

Tinker, The: A laconic idler questioned by Mr. Traveller on his way to Mopes's. *A short-winded one, from whom no further breath of information was to be derived*

(Christmas Stories – 'Tom Tiddler's Ground').

Tinker, The: A young ruffian who frightens David Copperfield on the Dover Road. *A tinker, I suppose, from his wallet and brazier (Copperfield).*

Tinkler: William Dorrit's valet. *Of a serious and composed countenance (Dorrit)*

Tinkles, Horatio: see **Hunter, Horace** *(Strange Gentleman).*

Tinkling, William: Eight-year-old author of the introductory romantic tale and editor of the others. 'Bridegroom' to Nettie Ashford ('Holiday Romance').

'Tip': see **Dorrit, Edward** *(Dorrit).*

Tip: Gabblewig's servant. He assists Slap in his final attempt to extort money from Nightingale by posing as Nightingale's son Christopher *(Nightingale's Diary).*

Tipkins against Bullock: A case conducted by Spenlow and David Copperfield. *It arose out of a scuffle between two church-wardens, one of whom was alleged to have pushed the other against a pump; the handle of which pump projecting into a school-house, which school-house was under a gable of the church-roof, made the push an ecclesiastical offence (Copperfield).*

Tipkisson: Leading supporter of our honourable friend's opponent for election to Parliament, discredited by religious aspersions. *Our honourable friend being come into the presence of his constituents, and having professed with great suavity that he was delighted to see his good friend Tipkisson there, in his working-dress – his good friend Tipkisson being an inveterate saddler, who always opposes him, and for whom he has a mortal hatred (Reprinted –* 'Our Honourable Friend').

Tipp: Carman at Murdstone and Grinby's warehouse. *Wore a red jacket, used to address me sometimes as 'David' (Copperfield).*

Tippin Family: A theatrical family appearing at Ramsgate. *A short female, in a blue velvet hat and feathers, was led into the orchestra, by a fat man in black* *tights and cloudy Berlins. . . . The talented Tippin having condescendingly acknowledged the clapping of hands, and shouts of 'bravo !' which greeted her appearance, proceeded to sing the popular cavatina of 'Bid me discourse,' accompanied on the piano by Mr. Tippin; after which, Mr. Tippin sang a comic song, accompanied on the piano by Mrs. Tippin : the applause consequent upon which, was only to be exceeded by the enthusiastic approbation bestowed upon an air with variations on the guitar, by Miss Tippin, accompanied on the chin by Master Tippin (Boz – 'Tuggses at Ramsgate').*

Tippins, Lady: Friend of Lightwood from his boyhood, and frequently at the Veneerings' gatherings. *With an immense obtuse drab oblong face, like a face in a tablespoon, and a dyed Long Walk up the top of her head, as a convenient public approach to the bunch of false hair behind. || She has a reputation for giving smart accounts of things, and she must be at these people's early, my dear, to lose nothing of the fun. Whereabout in the bonnet and drapery announced by her name, any fragment of the real woman may be concealed, is perhaps known to her maid; but you could easily buy all you see of her, in Bond Street; or you might scalp her, and peel her, and scrape her, and make two Lady Tippinses out of her, and yet not penetrate to the genuine article. She has a large gold eye-glass, has Lady Tippins, to survey the proceedings with. If she had one in each eye, it might keep that other drooping lid up, and look more uniform. But perennial youth is in her artificial flowers, and her list of lovers is full (Mutual Friend).*

Tisher, Mrs.: Miss Twinkleton's companion and assistant. *A deferential widow with a weak back, a chronic sigh, and a suppressed voice, who looks after the young ladies' wardrobes, and leads them to infer that she has seen better days (Drood).*

Titbull's: A group of east London almshouses visited by the Uncommercial Traveller. *Of Titbull I know no more than that he deceased in 1723, that his Christian name was Sampson, and his social designation Esquire, and that he founded*

these Alms-Houses as Dwellings for Nine Poor Women and Six Poor Men by his Will and Testament. I should not know even this much, but for its being inscribed on a grim stone very difficult to read, let into the front of the centre house of Titbull's Alms-Houses, and which stone is ornamented a-top with a piece of sculptured drapery resembling the effigy of Titbull's bath-towel (Uncommercial – 'Titbull's Alms-Houses').

Tix, Tom: Co-bailiff, with Scaley, in possession at Madame Mantalini's. *A little man in brown, very much the worse for wear, who brought with him a mingled fumigation of stale tobacco and fresh onions (Nickleby).*

Todd's Young Man: Baker's boy, a favourite with housemaids in the Covent Garden district. *Mr. Todd's young man, who being fond of mails, but more of females, takes a short look at the mails, and a long look at the girls (Boz – 'The Streets – Morning').*

'Toddles': Pet name of one of Betty Hidgen's charges *(Mutual Friend).*

Toddyhigh, Joe: Boyhood friend of the Lord Mayor Elect in the Deaf Gentleman's narrative, who overhears Gog and Magog talking in the Guildhall. *Not over and above well dressed, and was very far from being fat or rich-looking in any sense of the word, yet he spoke with a kind of modest confidence, and assumed an easy, gentlemanly sort of an air, to which nobody but a rich man can lawfully presume (Humphrey).*

Todgers, Mrs. M.: Proprietress of the boarding-house where the Pecksniffs lodge in London. *Rather a bony and hard-featured lady, with a row of curls in front of her head, shaped like little barrels of beer; and on the top of it something made of net – you couldn't call it a cap exactly – which looked like a black cobweb (Chuzzlewit).*

Tollimglower, Lady: Subject of obscure anecdotes told by old Mrs. Wardle. *The worthy old soul launched forth into a minute and particular account of her own wedding, with a dissertation on the fashion of wearing high-heeled shoes, and some* *particulars concerning the life and adventures of the beautiful Lady Tollimglower, deceased: at all of which the old lady herself laughed very heartily indeed, and so did the young ladies too, for they were wondering among themselves what on earth grandma was talking about (Pickwick).*

Tom: The struggling young doctor's servant. *A corpulent round-headed boy, who, in consideration of the sum of one shilling per week and his food, was let out by the parish to carry medicine and messages. As there was no demand for the medicine, however, and no necessity for the messages, he usually occupied his unemployed hours – averaging fourteen a day – in abstracting peppermint drops, taking animal nourishment, and going to sleep* (Boz – 'Black Veil').

Tom: Conductor of the 'Admiral Napier' omnibus. *Settled the contest in a most satisfactory manner, for all parties, by seizing Dumps round the waist, and thrusting him into the middle of his vehicle which had just come up and only wanted the sixteenth inside* (Boz – 'Bloomsbury Christening').

Tom: One of the officers who arrest William Warden (Boz – 'Drunkard's Death').

Tom: The Gattletons' servant, co-opted to appear as a fisherman in the private theatricals. *'When the revolt takes place, Tom must keep rushing in on one side and out on the other, with a pickaxe, as fast as he can. The effect will be electrical; it will look exactly as if there were an immense number of 'em'* (Boz – 'Mrs. Joseph Porter').

Tom: Gardener to Gabriel Parsons. *A gardener in a blue apron, who let himself out to do the ornamental for half-a-crown a day and his 'keep'* (Boz – 'Watkins Tottle').

Tom: The Revd. Charles Timson's servant (Boz – 'Watkins Tottle').

Tom: Driver of the train that kills the Signal-man (Christmas Stories – 'Mugby Junction').

Tom: The pavement-artist whose story forms part of this series. He is infatuated with Henrietta, but she leaves him for another pavement-artist. *If there's a blighted public character going, I am the party. And often as you have seen, do see, and will see, my Works, it's fifty thousand to one if you'll ever see me, unless, when the candles are burnt down and the Commercial character is gone, you should happen to notice a neglected young man perseveringly rubbing out the last traces of the pictures, so that nobody can renew the same. That's me* (Christmas Stories – 'Somebody's Luggage').

Tom: Captain Boldheart's cheeky cousin in Robin Redforth's romantic tale ('Holiday Romance').

Tom: Clerk at the employment agency where Nicholas Nickleby first sees Madeline Bray. *A lean youth with cunning eyes and a protruding chin (Nickleby).*

Tom: Wardle's coachman *(Pickwick).*

Tom: Waiter at the St. James's Arms *(Strange Gentleman).*

Tom: Driver of the Dover mailcoach *(Two Cities).*

Tom, Captain: Prisoner in Newgate visited by Pip and Wemmick *(Expectations).*

Tom, Honest: A Member of Parliament. *That smart-looking fellow in the black coat with velvet facings and cuffs, who wears his D'Orsay hat so rakishly is 'Honest Tom', a metropolitan representative* (Boz – 'Parliamentary Sketch').

Tomkins: Pupil at Dotheboys Hall. *A very little boy, habited still in his nightgear, and the perplexed expression of whose countenance as he was brought forward, seemed to intimate that he was as yet uncertain whether he was about to be punished or rewarded for the suggestion. He was not long in doubt (Nickleby).*

Tomkins, Miss: Principal of Westgate House boarding school for young ladies, Bury St. Edmunds *(Pickwick).*

Tomkins, Alfred: Boarder at Mrs. Tibbs's. *A clerk in a wine-house; he was a connoisseur in paintings, and had a wonderful eye for the picturesque* (Boz – 'Boarding-House').

Tomkins, Charles: Fiancé of Fanny Wilson, whom he has arranged to meet at the St. James's Arms in order to elope to Gretna Green. He is confused with the Strange Gentleman, and thought to be mad, but all comes clear eventually and the journey to Gretna proceeds (*Strange Gentleman*).

Tomlinson, Mrs.: Post-office keeper at Rochester, present at the charity ball at the Bull (*Pickwick*).

Tommy: Dissentient to Rogers's opinions. *A little greengrocer with a chubby face* (*Boz* – 'Parlour Orator').

Tommy: A waterman who obtains for Pickwick the cab whose driver, Sam, assaults the Pickwickians. *A strange specimen of the human race, in a sackcloth coat, and apron of the same, who with a brass label and number round his neck, looked as if he were catalogued in some collection of rarities* (*Pickwick*).

Toodle: Polly's husband, father of Robin and four other children. A stoker, later engine-driver. *A strong, loose, round-shouldered, shuffling, shaggy fellow, on whom his clothes sat negligently : with a good deal of hair and whisker, deepened in its natural tint, perhaps by smoke and coal-dust : hard knotty hands : and a square forehead, as coarse in grain as the bark of an oak* (*Dombey*).

Toodle, Mrs. (Polly, 'Richards'): Toodle's wife, and mother of Robin and four other children. Engaged by Dombey as nurse to Little Paul, with the name 'Richards' imposed on her, but dismissed for paying a visit to her own home and children. *A plump rosy-cheeked wholesome apple-faced young woman* (*Dombey*).

Toodle, Robin ('Biler' and 'Rob the Grinder'): The Toodles' eldest son, used as a spy by James Carker and later servant to Miss Tox. *Known in the family by the name of Biler, in remembrance of the steam engine. || Poor Biler's life had been, since yesterday morning, rendered weary by the costume of the Charitable Grinders. The youth of the streets could not endure it. No young vagabond could be* brought to bear its contemplation for a moment, without throwing himself upon the unoffending wearer, and doing him a mischief. . . . *He had been stoned in the streets. He had been overthrown into gutters ; bespattered with mud ; violently flattened against posts. Entire strangers to his person had lifted his yellow cap off his head and cast it to the winds* (*Dombey*).

Toorell, Dr.: A vice-president of the anatomy and medicine session at the first meeting of the Mudfog Association (*Mudfog*).

Tootle, Tom: Regular drinker at the Six Jolly Fellowship Porters (*Mutual Friend*).

'Tootleum-Boots': Mrs. Lemon's baby in Nettie Ashford's romantic tale. *Mrs. Lemon's baby was leather and bran* ('Holiday Romance').

Toots, P.: Dr. Blimber's senior pupil. A friend to everyone, he woos Florence Dombey ardently, but accepts her rejection of him philosophically and eventually marries Susan Nipper. *Possessed of the gruffest of voices and the shrillest of minds ; sticking ornamental pins into his shirt, and keeping a ring in his waistcoat pocket to put on his little finger by stealth, when the pupils went out walking ; constantly falling in love by sight with nursery-maids, who had no idea of his existence ; and looking at the gas-lighted world over the little iron bars in the left-hand corner window of the front three pairs of stairs, after bed-time, like a greatly overgrown cherub who had sat up aloft much too long* (*Dombey*).

Toozellem, The Hon. Clementina: See under Bilberry, Lady Jemima (*Dorrit*).

Tope: Chief verger at Cloisterham Cathedral. Landlord of Jasper and, later, Datchery. *Mr. Tope, Chief Verger and Showman, and accustomed to be high with excursion parties* (*Drood*).

Tope, Mrs.: Tope's wife. *Mrs. Tope had indeed once upon a time let lodgings herself or offered to let them ; but that as nobody had ever taken them, Mrs. Tope's window-bill, long a Cloisterham Institution, had disappeared* (*Drood*).

Topper: A guest at Fred's Christmas dinner. *Topper had clearly got his eye upon one of Scrooge's niece's sisters, for he answered that a bachelor was a wretched outcast* (Christmas Books – 'Christmas Carol').

Toppit, Miss: An American literary lady at Pogram's levee at the National Hotel. *One of the L.L.'s wore a brown wig of uncommon size (Chuzzlewit).*

Topsawyer: Mythical victim of ale-drinking at Yarmouth, invented by William, the waiter, in order to persuade young David Copperfield to let him dispose of his ale for him. *'He came in here,' said the waiter, looking at the light through the tumbler, 'ordered a glass of this ale – would order it – I told him not – drank it, and fell dead. It was too old for him. It oughtn't to be drawn; that's the fact. . . . But I'll drink it, if you like. I'm used to it, and use is everything. I don't think it'll hurt me, if I throw my head back, and take it off quick' (Copperfield).*

Tott, Mrs. Isabella (known as 'Belltott'): A soldier's widow living on Silver-Store Island who fights gallantly against the pirates. *A little saucy woman, with a bright pair of eyes, rather a neat little foot and figure, and rather a neat little turned-up nose. The sort of young woman, I considered at the time, who appeared to invite you to give her a kiss, and who would have slapped your face if you accepted the invitation* (Christmas Stories – 'English Prisoners').

Tottle, Watkins: A bachelor, rescued from imprisonment for debt by his friend Gabriel Parsons, on condition that he marries Miss Lillerton and reimburses him handsomely from her estate. Miss Lillerton proves to be engaged to the Revd. Charles Timson, whom she marries, and Tottle drowns himself in the Regent's Canal. *A rather uncommon compound of strong uxorious inclinations, and an unparalleled degree of anti-connubial timidity. He was about fifty years of age; stood four feet six inches and three-quarters in his socks – for he never stood in stockings at all – plump, clean, and rosy. He looked something like a vignette to one* of Richardson's novels, and had a clean-cravatish formality of manner, and kitchen-pokerness of carriage. . . . *The idea of matrimony had never ceased to haunt him. Wrapt in profound reveries on this never-failing theme, fancy transformed his small parlour in Cecil Street, Strand, into a neat house in the suburbs; the half-hundred-weight of coals under the kitchen-stairs suddenly sprang up into three tons of the best Wallsend; his small French bedstead was converted into a regular matrimonial four-poster; and in the empty chair on the opposite side of the fireplace, imagination seated a beautiful young lady, with a very little independence or will of her own, and a very large independence under a will of her father's* (Boz – 'Watkins Tottle').

'Toughey': See Jo *(Bleak House).*

Towlinson, Thomas: Dombey's footman. Marries Anne, the housemaid. *Adjourning in quest of the housemaid, and presently returning with that young lady on his arm, informs the kitchen that foreigners is only his fun, and that him and Anne have now resolved to take one another for better for worse, and to settle in Oxford Market in the general greengrocery and herb and leech line, where your kind favours is particularly requested (Dombey).*

Tox, Lucretia: Mrs. Chick's close spinster friend. She fails in her design to become the second Mrs. Dombey, but remains loyal throughout his misfortunes. She in turn is much admired by her neighbour, Major Bagstock. *A long lean figure, wearing such a faded air that she seemed not to have been made in what linen-drapers call 'fast colours' originally, and to have, by little and little, washed out. But for this she might have been described as the very pink of general propitiation and politeness. From a long habit of listening admirably to everything that was said in her presence, and looking at the speakers as if she were mentally engaged in taking off impressions of their images upon her soul, never to part with the same but with life, her head had quite settled on one side. Her hands had contracted a spasmodic habit of raising themselves of their own accord as in involuntary admiration. . .*

She was accustomed to wear odd weedy little flowers in her bonnet and caps. Strange grasses were sometimes perceived in her hair; and it was observed, of all her collars, frills, tuckers, wrist-bands, and other gossamer articles – indeed of everything she wore which had two ends to it intended to unite – that the two ends were never on good terms, and wouldn't quite meet without a struggle (Dombey).

Tozer: A room-mate of Paul Dombey at Dr. Blimber's. *A solemn young gentleman, whose shirt-collar curled up the lobes of his ear (Dombey).*

Tpschoffki, Major: See Chops (*Christmas Stories* – 'Going into Society').

Trabb: Obsequious master tailor who attends Pip. *A prosperous old bachelor, and his open window looked into a prosperous little garden and orchard, and there was a prosperous iron safe let into the wall at the side of his fireplace, and I did not doubt that heaps of his prosperity were put away in it in bags (Expectations).*

Trabb's Boy: The tailor's assistant. *The most audacious boy in all that countryside (Expectations).*

Traddles, Thomas: Pupil at Salem House; later a distinguished barrister. David Copperfield's great friend and best man. He marries Sophy Crewler. *Poor Traddles! In a tight sky-blue suit that made his arms and legs like German sausages, or roly-poly puddings, he was the merriest and most miserable of all the boys. He was always being caned – I think he was caned every day that half-year, except one holiday Monday when he was only ruler'd on both hands – and was always going to write to his uncle about it, and never did. After laying his head on the desk for a little while, he would cheer up somehow, begin to laugh again, and draw skeletons all over his slate, before his eyes were dry. I used at first to wonder what comfort Traddles found in drawing skeletons; and for some time looked upon him as a sort of hermit, who reminded himself by those symbols of mortality that caning couldn't last for ever. But I believe he only did it because they were easy, and didn't want any features (Copperfield).*

Trampfoot: One of the policemen visiting sailors' haunts with the Uncommercial Traveller (*Uncommercial* – 'Poor Mercantile Jack').

Traveller, Mr.: Narrator of the story (*Christmas Stories* – 'Tom Tiddler's Ground').

Treasurer: Treasurer of the Foundling Hospital interviewed by Wilding (*Christmas Stories* – 'No Thoroughfare'; not in dramatised version).

Treasury: Whitehall magnate, guest at Merdle's *(Dorrit).*

Tredgear, John: Resident of Lanrean questioned by Captain Jorgan (*Christmas Stories* – 'Message from the Sea').

Tregarthen: Kitty's father, clerk to Dringworth Bros., cleared by the message from the sea of suspicion of theft. *A rather infirm man, but could scarcely be called old yet, with an agreeable face and a promising air of making the best of things (Christmas Stories* – 'Message from the Sea').

Tregarthen, Kitty: Tregarthen's daughter, sweetheart and eventually wife of Alfred Raybrock. *A prettier sweetheart the sun could not have shone upon that shining day. As she stood before the captain, with her rosy lips just parted in surprise, her brown eyes a little wider open than was usual from the same cause, and her breathing a little quickened by the ascent . . . she looked so charming, that the captain felt himself under a moral obligation to slap both his legs again (Christmas Stories* – 'Message from the Sea').

Trent: Name often erroneously ascribed to Little Nell's grandfather (he was her mother's father). Proprietor of the Old Curiosity Shop. A compulsive gambler, he flees with Little Nell to escape his creditor, Quilp. Heartbroken by her death, he dies soon after. *A little old man with long grey hair, whose face and figure, as he held the light above his head and looked before him as he approached, I could plainly see. Though much altered by age, I fancied I could recognise in his spare and slender form something of that delicate mould which I had noticed in the child.*

Their bright blue eyes were certainly alike, but his face was so deeply furrowed, and so very full of care, that here all resemblance ended (Curiosity Shop).

Trent, Frederick: Little Nell's dissolute brother, who tries to marry her off to his friend, Dick Swiveller. *A young man of one-and-twenty or thereabouts; well made, and certainly handsome, though the expression of his face was far from prepossessing, having in common with his manner and even his dress, a dissipated, insolent air which repelled one (Curiosity Shop).*

Trent, Nell (Little Nell): Central figure of the story: the child companion and support of her grandfather (see **Trent**). She wanders the roads with him and dies at a village. *Child she certainly was, although I thought it probable from what I could make out that her very small and delicate frame imparted a peculiar youthfulness to her appearance. Though more scantily attired than she might have been, she was dressed with perfect neatness, and betrayed no marks of poverty or neglect (Curiosity Shop).*

Tresham: Jackson's former colleague and friend, who had taken Beatrice from him and married her. Jackson's visit to Mugby is fortuitously in time to save them and their daughter Polly from the consequences of Tresham's illness and their poverty. *'My husband is very, very ill of a lingering disorder. He will never recover'* (*Christmas Stories* – 'Mugby Junction').

Tresham, Mrs. (Beatrice): A music teacher. Tresham's wife and Polly's mother. Jackson's lost love whom he helps in her poverty. *As you see what the rose was in its faded leaves; as you see what the summer growth of the woods was in their wintry branches; so Polly might be traced, one day, in a careworn woman like this, with her hair turned grey. Before him were the ashes of a dead fire that had once burned bright. This was the woman he had loved. This was the woman he had lost. Such had been the constancy of his imagination to her, so had Time spared her under its withholding, that now, seeing how roughly the inexorable hand had*

struck her, his soul was filled with pity and amazement (*Christmas Stories* – 'Mugby Junction').

Tresham, Polly: Daughter of Tresham and Beatrice, who leads Jackson to his lost love. *A very little fair-haired girl.* || '*A most engaging little creature, but it's not that. A most winning little voice, but it's not that. That has much to do with it, but there is something more. How can it be that I seem to know this child? What was it she imperfectly recalled to me when I felt her touch in the street, and, looking down at her, saw her looking up at me?*' (*Christmas Stories* – 'Mugby Junction').

Trimmers: Friend of the Cheeryble brothers *(Nickleby).*

Trinkle: Son of a noted upholsterer in Cheapside. Inspector Wield's suspect for the murder of Eliza Grimwood, but proved not to be guilty *(Reprinted* – 'Three "Detective" Anecdotes').

Trott, Alexander: An umbrella-maker, rival to Horace Hunter for Emily Brown. Challenged to a duel by Hunter, he plans to save his skin by getting arrested, but is mistaken for Lord Peter, Julia Manners's suitor, and made to elope with her. The mistake revealed, they like one another enough to drive on to Gretna Green and marry. *Mr. Trott was a young man, had highly promising whiskers, an undeniable tailor, and an insinuating address – he wanted nothing but valour, and who wants that with three thousand a year?* (*Boz* – 'Great Winglebury Duel'). He appears as Walker Trott, the Strange Gentleman, in the dramatic version entitled *The Strange Gentleman.*

Trott, Walker: See **Trott, Alexander** *(Strange Gentleman).*

Trotter, Job: Jingle's servant and crony and Sam Weller's adversary. *A young fellow in mulberry-coloured livery . . . who had a large, sallow, ugly face, very sunken eyes, and a gigantic head, from which depended a quantity of lank black hair (Pickwick).*

'Trotters, Short': See **Harris** *(Curiosity Shop).*

Trottle: One of the listeners to the story (*Christmas Stories* – 'Going into Society').

Trotwood, Betsey: David Copperfield's great-aunt and later guardian, to whom he flies from Murdstone and Grinby's. She is actually married, but separated, and lives self-sufficiently, caring for Mr. Dick, David, and then David's successive wives, and combating such people as Jane Murdstone and Uriah Heep, as well as the donkeys which trample the grass in front of her house at Dover. Her husband appears at intervals to demand money, and eventually dies. *My aunt was a tall, hard-featured lady, but by no means ill-looking. There was an inflexibility in her face, in her voice, in her gait and carriage, amply sufficient to account for the effect she had made upon a gentle creature like my mother; but her features were rather handsome than otherwise, though unbending and austere. I particularly noticed that she had a very quick, bright eye (Copperfield).*

Truck: A vice-president of the mechanical science session at the first meeting of the Mudfog Association *(Mudfog).*

Trundle: The young man who marries Isabella Wardle *(Pickwick).*

Trusty, Mrs.: Captain Blower's nurse; one of the characters assumed by Rosina Nightingale to help Gabblewig unmask Slap *(Nightingale's Diary).*

Tuckle: A Bath footman, presiding at the footmen's soirée. *A stoutish gentleman in a bright crimson coat with long tails, vividly red breeches, and a cocked hat (Pickwick).*

Tugby: Sir Joseph Bowley's porter. He marries Mrs. Chickenstalker in Trotty's vision. *The great broad chin, with creases in it large enough to hide a finger in; the astonished eyes, that seemed to expostulate with themselves for sinking deeper and deeper into the yielding fat of the soft face; the nose afflicted with that disordered action of its functions which is generally termed The Snuffles; the short thick throat and labouring chest, with other beauties of the like description (Christmas Books – 'Chimes').*

Tuggs, Charlotte: The Tuggs' only daughter, and Simon's sister. When they come into money she calls herself Charlotta. *Fast ripening into that state of luxurious plumpness which had enchanted the eyes, and captivated the heart, of Mr. Joseph Tuggs in his earlier days (Boz – 'Tuggses at Ramsgate').*

Tuggs, Joseph: Father of Charlotte and Simon. A London grocer who comes into a fortune, determines to live high at Ramsgate, and is duped by the Waterses. *A little dark-faced man, with shiny hair, twinkling eyes, short legs, and a body of very considerable thickness, measuring from the centre button of his waistcoat in front, to the ornamental buttons of his coat behind (Boz – 'Tuggses at Ramsgate').*

Tuggs, Mrs. Joseph: Tuggs's wife, and mother of Charlotte and Simon, in charge of the cheesemongery side of his business. *The figure of the amiable Mrs. Tuggs, if not perfectly symmetrical, was decidedly comfortable (Boz – 'Tuggses at Ramsgate').*

Tuggs, Simon: The Tuggs' only son, and Charlotte's brother. When they come into money he calls himself Cymon. Led on by Belinda Waters, he costs his father £1,500 of his fortune. *As differently formed in body, as he was differently constituted in mind, from the remainder of his family. There was that elongation in his thoughtful face, and that tendency to weakness in his interesting legs, which tell so forcibly of a great mind and romantic disposition. The slightest traits of character in such a being, possess no mean interest to speculative minds. He usually appeared in public, in capacious shoes with black cotton stockings; and was observed to be particularly attached to a black glazed stock, without tie or ornament of any description (Boz – 'Tuggses at Ramsgate').*

Tulkinghorn: The Dedlocks' family lawyer. He makes use of various people to discover Lady Dedlock's secret and is murdered by one of them, Hortense, for refusing to reward her sufficiently. *The old gentleman is rusty to look at, but is reputed to have made good thrift out of* aristocratic marriage settlements and aristocratic wills, and to be very rich. He is surrounded by a mysterious halo of family confidences; of which he is known to be the silent depository. There are noble Mausoleums rooted for centuries in retired glades of parks, among the growing timber and the fern, which perhaps hold fewer noble secrets than walk abroad among men, shut up in the breast of Mr. Tulkinghorn. He is of what is called the old school – a phrase generally meaning any school that seems never to have been young – and wears knee breeches tied with ribbons, and gaiters or stockings. One peculiarity of his black clothes, and of his black stockings, be they silk or worsted, is, that they never shine. Mute, close, irresponsive to any glancing light, his dress is like himself. He never converses, when not professionally consulted. He is found sometimes, speechless but quite at home, at corners of dinner-tables in great country houses, and near doors of drawing-rooms, concerning which the fashionable intelligence is eloquent : where everybody knows him, and where half the Peerage stops to say 'How do you do, Mr. Tulkinghorn?' he receives these salutations with gravity, and buries them along with the rest of his knowledge (Bleak House).

Tulrumble, Nicholas, jun.: The Tulrumbles' son. Couldn't make up his mind to be anything but magnificent, so he went up to London and drew bills on his father; and when he had overdrawn, and got into debt, he grew penitent, and came home again (Mudfog).

Tulrumble, Nicholas, sen.: Mayor of Mudfog in succession to Sniggs. Father of Nicholas junior. Nicholas began life in a wooden tenement of four feet square, with a capital of two and ninepence, and a stock in trade of three bushels and a half of coals, exclusive of the large lump which hung, by way of a sign-board, outside. Then he enlarged the shed, and kept a truck; then he left the shed, and the truck too, and started a donkey and a Mrs. Tulrumble; then he moved again and set up a cart; the cart was soon afterwards exchanged for a waggon; and so he went on like his great predecessor Whittington –

only without a cat for a partner – increasing in wealth and fame, until at last he gave up business altogether, and retired with Mrs. Tulrumble and family to Mudfog Hall, which he had himself erected, on something which he attempted to delude himself into the belief was a hill, about a quarter of a mile distant from the town of Mudfog (Mudfog).

Tulrumble, Mrs. Nicholas, sen.: Tulrumble's wife, mother of Nicholas junior (Mudfog).

Tungay: Porter at Salem House school. A stout man with a bull-neck, a wooden leg, over-hanging temples, and his hair cut close all round his head. . . . I heard that with the single exception of Mr. Creakle, Tungay considered the whole establishment, masters and boys, as his natural enemies, and that the only delight of his life was to be sour and malicious (Copperfield).

Tupman, Tracy: A somewhat elderly member of the Pickwick Club and one of Pickwick's companions in his travels. He wins Rachael Wardle's heart, loses her through Jingle's scheming, and retires to bachelorhood at Richmond. The too susceptible Tupman, who to the wisdom and experience of maturer years superadded the enthusiasm and ardour of a boy, in the most interesting and pardonable of human weaknesses – love. Time and feeding had expanded that once romantic form; the black silk waistcoat had become more and more developed; inch by inch had the gold watch-chain beneath it disappeared from within the range of Tupman's vision; and gradually had the capacious chin encroached upon the borders of the white cravat : but the soul of Tupman had known no change – admiration of the fair sex was still its ruling passion (Pickwick).

Tupple: Guest at the Dobbles' New Year's Eve party. A junior clerk in the same office; a tidy young man, with a tendency to cold and corns, who comes in a pair of boots with black cloth fronts, and brings his shoes in his coat-pocket (Boz – 'New Year').

Turk: John the narrator's bloodhound.

I stationed him in his kennel outside, but unchained; and I seriously warned the village that any man who came in his way must not expect to leave him without a rip in his own throat (Christmas Stories – 'Haunted House').

Turveydrop: Proprietor of a dancing academy in London and a celebrated arbiter of deportment. *A fat old gentleman with a false complexion, false teeth, false whiskers, and a wig. He had a fur collar, and he had a padded breast to his coat, which only wanted a star or a broad blue ribbon to be complete. He was pinched in, and swelled out, and got up, and strapped down, as much as he could possibly bear. He had such a neckcloth on (puffing his very eyes out of their natural shape) and his chin and even his ears so sunk into it, that it seemed as though he must inevitably double up, if it were cast loose. He had, under his arm, a hat of great size and weight, shelving downward from the crown to the brim; and in his hand a pair of white gloves, with which he flapped it, as he stood poised on one leg, in a high-shouldered, round-elbowed state of elegance not to be surpassed. He had a cane, he had an eyeglass, he had a snuffbox, he had rings, he had wristbands, he had everything but any touch of nature; he was not like youth, he was not like age, he was not like anything in the world but a model of Deportment (Bleak House).*

Turveydrop, Prince: Turveydrop's son and assistant, named after the Prince Regent. He marries Caddy Jellyby. *A little blue-eyed fair man of youthful appearance, with flaxen hair parted in the middle, and curling at the ends all round his head. He had a little fiddle, which we used to call at school a kit, under his left arm, and its little bow in the same hand. His little dancing shoes were particularly diminutive, and he had a little innocent, feminine manner, which not only appealed to me in an amiable way, but made this singular effect upon me: that I received the impression that he was like his mother, and that his mother had not been much considered or well used (Bleak House).*

Twemlow, Melvin: Frequent guest at the Veneerings' and elsewhere on the strength of his kinship (cousin) to Lord Snigsworth. *Grey, dry, polite, susceptible to east wind. First-Gentleman-in-Europe collar and cravat, cheeks drawn in as if he had made a great effort to retire into himself some years ago, and had got so far and had never got any farther. || At many houses might be said to represent the dining-table in its normal state. Mr. and Mrs. Veneering, for example, arranging a dinner, habitually started with Twemlow, and then put leaves in him, or added guests to him (Mutual Friend).*

Twigger, Edward ('Bottle-nosed Ned'): The town drunkard, who reduces Tulrumble's Mayor-making procession to chaos. *He was drunk upon the average once a day, and penitent upon an equally fair calculation once a month; and when he was penitent, he was invariably in the very last stage of maudlin intoxication. He was a ragged, roving, roaring kind of fellow, with a burly form, a sharp wit, and a ready head, and could turn his hand to anything when he chose to do it. . . . Notwithstanding his dissipation, Bottle-nosed Ned was a general favourite; and the authorities of Mudfog, remembering his numerous services to the population, allowed him in return to get drunk in his own way, without the fear of stocks, fine, or imprisonment. He had a general licence, and he showed his sense of the compliment by making the most of it (Mudfog).*

Twigger, Mrs. Edward: Edward's wife. *Ned no sooner caught a glimpse of her face and form, than from the mere force of habit he set off towards his home just as fast as his legs could carry him (Mudfog).*

Twinkleton, Miss: Principal of the Nuns' House Seminary for Young Ladies, Cloisterham, attended by Rosa Bud and Helena Landless. *Miss Twinkleton has two distinct and separate phases of being. Every night, the moment the young ladies have retired to rest, does Miss Twinkleton smarten up her curls a little, brighten up her eyes a little, and become a sprightlier Miss Twinkleton than the young ladies have ever seen. Every night, at the same hour, does Miss Twinkleton resume* *the topics of the previous night, comprehending the tenderer scandal of Cloisterham, of which she has no knowledge whatever by day, and references to a certain season at Tunbridge Wells . . . wherein a certain finished gentleman (compassionately called by Miss Twinkleton, in this stage of her existence, 'Foolish Mr. Porters') revealed a homage of the heart, whereof Miss Twinkleton, in her scholastic state of existence, is as ignorant as a granite pillar (Drood).*

Twist, Oliver: Orphan natural son of Edwin Leeford and Agnes Fleming. Apprenticed to crime under Fagin and Bill Sikes, he is rescued and redeemed by Rose Maylie, Brownlow, and others, his identity is established, and Brownlow adopts him. *Oliver Twist's ninth birthday found him a pale thin child, somewhat diminutive in stature, and decidedly small in circumference. But nature or inheritance had implanted a good sturdy spirit in Oliver's breast. It had had plenty of room to expand, thanks to the spare diet of this establishment; and perhaps to this circumstance may be attributed his having any ninth birthday at all (Twist).*

Uncle, The Bagman's: See **Martin, Jack** *(Pickwick).*

Uncommercial Traveller: Narrator of the essays. *I am both a town traveller and a country traveller, and am always on the road. Figuratively speaking, I travel for the great house of Human Interest Brothers, and have rather a large connection in the fancy goods way. Literally speaking, I am always wandering here and there from my rooms in Covent Garden, London – now about the city streets: now, about the country by-roads – seeing many little things, and some great things, which, because they interest me, I think may interest others (Uncommercial – 'His General Line of Business').*

Undery: John the narrator's friend and solicitor who makes one of the party visiting the haunted house. *Plays whist better than the whole Law List, from the red cover at the beginning to the red cover at the end (Christmas Stories – 'Haunted House').*

United Bull-Dogs: See **Prentice Knights** *(Rudge).*

United Grand Junction Ebenezer Temperance Association: Sam and Tony Weller attend a meeting of the Brick Lane Branch in order to expose the Revd. Mr. Stiggins for a drunken hypocrite *(Pickwick).*

United Metropolitan Improved Hot Muffin and Crumpet Baking and Punctual Delivery Company: A company promoted by Bonney of which Ralph Nickleby is a director *(Nickleby).*

Upwitch, Richard: A greengrocer juryman in Bardell and Pickwick *(Pickwick).*

Valentine, Private: Capitaine de la Cour's batman. *Acting as sole housemaid, valet, cook, steward, and nurse . . . cleaning the floors, making the beds, doing the marketing, dressing the captain, dressing the dinners, dressing the salads, and dressing the baby, all with equal readiness (Christmas Stories – 'Somebody's Luggage').*

Varden, Dolly: Gabriel's daughter, loved by Joe Willet and Sim Tappertit. Seized by the mob, with Emma Haredale, during the Gordon Riots, she is rescued by Joe and subsequently marries him. *A roguish face met his; a face lighted up by the loveliest pair of sparkling eyes that ever locksmith looked upon; the face of a pretty, laughing, girl; dimpled and fresh, and healthful – the very impersonation of good-humour and blooming beauty (Rudge).*

Varden, Gabriel: Kindly, honest locksmith, husband of Martha and father of Dolly. *A round, red-faced, sturdy yeoman, with a double-chin, and a voice husky with good living, good sleeping, good humour, and good health. . . . Bluff, hale, hearty, and in a green old age: at peace with himself, and evidently disposed to be so with all the world. Although muffled up in divers coats and handkerchiefs – one of which, passed over his crown, and tied in a convenient crease of his double-chin, secured his three-cornered hat and bobwig from blowing off his head – there was no disguising his plump and comfortable figure; neither did certain dirty finger-*

marks upon his face give it any other than an odd and comical expression, through which its natural good-humour shone with undiminished lustre (Rudge).

Varden, Mrs. Gabriel (Martha): Gabriel's wife and Dolly's mother. *A lady of what is commonly called an uncertain temper – a phrase which being interpreted signifies a temper tolerably certain to make everybody more or less uncomfortable. Thus it generally happened, that when other people were merry, Mrs. Varden was dull; and that when other people were dull, Mrs. Varden was disposed to be amazingly cheerful. . . . It had been observed in this good lady (who did not want for personal attractions, being plump and buxom to look at, though like her fair daughter, somewhat short in stature) that this uncertainty of disposition strengthened and increased with her temporal prosperity; and divers wise men and matrons, on friendly terms with the locksmith and his family, even went so far as to assert, that a tumble down some half-dozen rounds in the world's ladder such as the breaking of the bank in which her husband kept his money, or some little fall of that kind – would be the making of her, and could hardly fail to render her one of the most agreeable companions in existence (Rudge).*

Veck, Margaret (Meg): Toby Veck's daughter, engaged to Richard. *Bright eyes they were. Eyes that would bear a world of looking in, before their depth was fathomed. Dark eyes, that reflected back the eyes which searched them; not flashingly, or at the owner's will, but with a clear, calm, honest, patient radiance, claiming kindred with that light which Heaven called into being. Eyes that were beautiful and true, and beaming with Hope. With Hope so young and fresh; with Hope so buoyant, vigorous, and bright, despite the twenty years of work and poverty on which they had looked (Christmas Books – 'Chimes').*

Veck, Toby ('Trotty'): A ticket-porter, or messenger, whose New Year's Eve dream of spirits inhabiting church bells forms the main theme of the story. *They called him Trotty from his pace, which*

meant speed if it didn't make it. He could have walked faster perhaps; most likely; but rob him of his trot, and Toby would have taken to his bed and died. It bespattered him with mud in dirty weather; it cost him a world of trouble; he could have walked with infinitely greater ease; but that was one reason for his clinging to it so tenaciously. A weak, small, spare old man, he was a very Hercules, this Toby, in his good intentions. He loved to earn his money. He delighted to believe – Toby was very poor, and couldn't well afford to part with a delight – that he was worth his salt. With a shilling or an eighteen-penny message or small parcel in his hand, his courage, always high, rose higher. As he trotted on, he would call out to fast Postmen ahead of him, to get out of the way; devoutly believing that in the natural course of things he must inevitably overtake and run them down; and he had perfect faith – not often tested – in his being able to carry anything that man could lift* (Christmas Books – 'Chimes').

Vendale, George: Partner in Wilding and Co. and head of it after Wilding's death. Courting Marguerite Obenreizer, he comes unwittingly close to discovering her uncle's frauds. Obenreizer tries to kill him in the Alps. He is saved by Marguerite, whom he marries. It transpires that he is the orphan who should have inherited Wilding and Co. in the first place. *A brown-cheeked handsome fellow . . . with a quick determined eye and an impulsive manner* (Christmas Stories – 'No Thoroughfare' and the dramatised version).

Veneering, Hamilton: A self-made rich man, sole remaining partner of Chicksey, Veneering and Stobbles, druggists, of which he had once been a lowly employee. Much given to Society life. He manages to buy a seat in Parliament through a rotten borough. *Forty, wavy-haired, dark, tending to corpulence, sly, mysterious, filmy – a kind of sufficiently well-looking veiled-prophet, not prophesying* (Mutual Friend).

Veneering, Mrs. Hamilton (Anastasia): Veneering's wife. *Fair, aquiline-*

nosed and fingered, not so much light hair as she might have, gorgeous in raiment and jewels, enthusiastic, propitiatory, conscious that a corner of her husband's veil is over herself (Mutual Friend).

'Vengeance, The': Madame Defarge's chief associate among the women revolutionaries. *The short, rather plump wife of a starved grocer, and the mother of two children withal, this lieutenant had already earned the complimentary name of The Vengeance (Two Cities).*

Venning, Mrs.: A resident of Silver-Store Island and mother of Fanny Fisher. *One handsome elderly lady, with very dark eyes and gray hair (Christmas Stories – 'English Prisoners').*

Ventriloquist, Monsieur The: Performer at a Flemish country fair. *Thin and sallow, and of a weakly aspect (Uncommercial – 'In the French-Flemish Country').*

Venus: Taxidermist at Clerkenwell who purchased Silas Wegg's amputated leg and joins in his plot to blackmail Boffin, but repents and betrays Wegg. He marries Pleasant Riderhood, after her long hesitation out of objection to his business. *The face looking up is a sallow face with weak eyes, surmounted by a tangle of reddish-dusty hair. The owner of the face has no cravat on, and has opened his tumbled shirt-collar to work with the more ease. For the same reason he has no coat on : only a loose waistcoat over his yellow linen. His eyes are like the over-tried eyes of an engraver, but he is not that ; his expression and stoop are like those of a shoemaker, but he is not that (Mutual Friend).*

Verisopht, Lord Frederick: A rich young man debauched by Hawk, who kills him in a duel after he has protested about Hawk's treatment of Kate Nickleby. *The gentleman addressed, turning round, exhibited a suit of clothes of the most superlative cut, a pair of whiskers of similar quality, a moustache, a head of hair, and a young face (Nickleby).*

Vholes: Richard Carstone's solicitor who turns him against Jarndyce. *A sallow man with pinched lips that looked as if they were cold, a red eruption here and there upon his face, tall and thin, about fifty years of age, high-shouldered, and stooping. Dressed in black, black-gloved, and buttoned to the chin, there was nothing so remarkable in him as a lifeless manner, and a slow fixed way he had of looking at Richard (Bleak House).*

Villam: Ostler of the Bull, Whitechapel (Pickwick).

Voigt, Maître: Chief notary at Neuchâtel who helps unmask Obenreizer. *A rosy, hearty, handsome old man. . . . Professionally and personally, the notary was a popular citizen. His innumerable kindnesses and his innumerable oddities had for years made him one of the recognised public characters of the pleasant Swiss town. His long brown frock-coat and his black skull-cap, were among the institutions of the place : and he carried a snuff-box which, in point of size, was popularly believed to be without a parallel in Europe (Christmas Stories – 'No Thoroughfare').* Maître Voigt's part in the story is given, in modified form, to Father Francis in the dramatised version.

Vuffin: A showman encountered by Little Nell and her grandfather. *The proprietor of a giant, and a little lady without legs or arms (Curiosity Shop).*

Wackles, Mrs.: Proprietress of a school for young ladies at Chelsea. *Corporal punishment, fasting, and other tortures and terrors, by Mrs. Wackles. . . . An excellent, but rather venomous old lady of three-score (Curiosity Shop).*

Wackles, the Misses Melissa, Sophy and Jane: Mrs. Wackles's daughters, in order of seniority; all teachers in her school for young ladies. Sophy is Dick Swiveller's intended, but he gives her up on hopes of Little Nell and she marries Cheggs. *English grammar, composition, geography, and the use of the dumb-bells, by Miss Melissa Wackles; writing, arithmetic, dancing, music, and general fascination, by Miss Sophy Wackles; the art of needle-work, marking, and samplery, by Miss Jane Wackles. . . .*

Miss Melissa might have been five-and-thirty summers or thereabouts, and verged on the autumnal; Miss Sophy was a fresh, good-humoured, buxom girl of twenty; and Miss Jane numbered scarcely sixteen years (Curiosity Shop).

Wade, Miss: The Meagles' moody friend who persuades Harriet Beadle to leave their service and live with her. *The shadow in which she sat, falling like a gloomy veil across her forehead, accorded very well with the character of her beauty. One could hardly see the face, so still and scornful, set off by the arched dark eyebrows, and the folds of dark hair, without wondering what its expression would be if a change came over it. That it could soften or relent, appeared next to impossible. . . . Although not an open face, there was no pretence in it. I am self-contained and self-reliant; your opinion is nothing to me; I have no interest in you, care nothing for you, and see and hear you with indifference — this it said plainly. It said so in the proud eyes, in the lifted nostril, in the handsome, but compressed and even cruel mouth. Cover either two of those channels of expression, and the third would have said so still. Mask them all, and the mere turn of the head would have shown an unsubduable nature (Dorrit).*

Waghorn: A vice-president of the mechanical science session at the first meeting of the Mudfog Association *(Mudfog).*

Wakefield, Mr. and Mrs.: Participants in the steam excursion, with their small daughter: *about six years old . . . dressed in a white frock with a pink sash and dog's-eared-looking little spencer: a straw bonnet and green veil, six inches by three and a half (Boz – 'Steam Excursion').*

Waldengarver: See Wopsle *(Expectations).*

Walker: A debtor in Solomon Jacobs's sponging-house. *A stout, hearty-looking man, of about forty, was eating some dinner which his wife – an equally comfortable-looking personage – had brought him in a basket (Boz – 'Watkins Tottle').*

Walker, Mrs.: See Macklin, Walker

and **Peplow** *(Boz – 'The Streets – Night').*

Walker, H.: Convert reported to the committee of the Brick Lane Branch of the United Grand Junction Ebenezer Temperance Association. *'Tailor, wife, and two children. When in better circumstances, owns to having been in the constant habit of drinking ale and beer; says he is not certain whether he did not twice a week, for twenty years, taste "dog's nose", which your committee find upon inquiry, to be compounded of warm porter, moist sugar, gin, and nutmeg' (a groan, and 'So it is!' from an elderly female) (Pickwick).*

Walker, Mick: Boy employee with David at Murdstone and Grinby's. *The oldest of the regular boys . . . he wore a ragged apron and a paper cap. He informed me that his father was a bargeman, and walked, in a black velvet head-dress, in the Lord Mayor's Show (Copperfield).*

Walmers: Father of Harry and employer of Cobbs. *He was a gentleman of spirit, and good-looking, and held his head up when he walked, and had what you may call Fire about him. He wrote poetry, and he rode, and he ran, and he cricketed, and he danced, and he acted, and he done it all equally beautiful (Christmas Stories – 'Holly-Tree').*

Walmers, Harry: Eight-year-old cousin of seven-year-old Norah, with whom he elopes to Gretna Green, hoping to marry, in the tale told by Cobbs to Charley. *The gentleman had got about half a dozen yards of string, a knife, three or four sheets of writing-paper folded up surprising small, a orange, and a Chaney mug with his name upon it (Christmas Stories – 'Holly-Tree').*

Walter, Edward M'Neville: See **Butler, Theodosius** *(Boz – 'Sentiment').*

Want: One of Miss Flite's birds *(Bleak House).*

Warden: A hopeless drunkard. His wife dies, one of his sons is killed and another hanged, and his daughter deserts him. He drowns himself in the Thames. *His dress was slovenly and disordered, his face inflamed, his eyes bloodshot and heavy. He*

*had been summoned from some wild
debauch to the bed of sorrow and death. . . .
The time had been when many a friend
would have crowded round him in his
affliction, and many a heartfelt condolence
would have met him in his grief. Where were
they now? One by one, friends, relations,
the commonest acquaintance even, had
fallen off from and deserted the drunkard.
His wife alone had clung to him in good and
evil, in sickness and poverty, and how had
he rewarded her? He had reeled from the
tavern to her bedside in time to see her die*
(Boz – 'Drunkard's Death').

Warden, Henry: Brother of John, William, and Mary. He is killed by a gamekeeper, who is murdered in turn by
William (*Boz* – 'Drunkard's Death').

Warden, John: Brother of William,
Henry, and Mary. He emigrates to
America (*Boz* – 'Drunkard's Death').

Warden, Mary: Sister of John, Henry,
and William. Like her dead mother she
bears her father's excesses in order to
care for him, but eventually deserts him.
*A girl, whose miserable and emaciated
appearance was only to be equalled by that
of the candle which she shaded with her
hand* (Boz – 'Drunkard's Death').

Warden, Michael: A dissolute client of
Snitchey and Craggs. Marion Jeddler
pretends to elope with him, and eventually marries him. *A man of thirty, or
about that time of life, negligently dressed,
and somewhat haggard in the face, but
well-made, well-attired, and well-looking,
who sat in the arm-chair of state, with one
hand in his breast, and the other in his
dishevelled hair, pondering moodily* (Christmas Books – 'Battle of Life').

Warden, William: Brother of John,
Henry, and Mary. He murders a gamekeeper who has killed Henry, hides at his
father's, but is unwittingly betrayed by
his drunken parent, arrested, and hanged.
*A young man of about two-and-twenty,
miserably clad in an old coarse jacket and
trousers* (Boz – 'Drunkard's Death').

Wardle: Owner of Manor Farm, Dingley
Dell, where the Pickwickians enjoy
Christmas sports and festivities. Father

of Emily and Isabella and brother of
Rachael. *A stout old gentleman, in a blue
coat and bright buttons, corduroy breeches
and top boots* (Pickwick).

Wardle, Mrs.: Wardle's mother. *A very
old lady, in a lofty cap and faded silk
gown – no less a personage than Mr.
Wardle's mother – occupied the post of
honour on the right-hand corner of the
chimney-piece; and various certificates of
her having been brought up in the way she
should go when young, and of her not
having departed from it when old, ornamented the walls, in the form of samplers
of ancient date, worsted landscapes of equal
antiquity, and crimson silk tea-kettle
holders of a more modern period* (Pickwick).

Wardle, Emily: One of Wardle's daughters, sister to Isabella. She marries Snodgrass. *'Short girl – black eyes – niece
Emily'* (Pickwick).

Wardle, Isabella: One of Wardle's
daughters, sister to Emily. She marries
Trundle. *A very amiable and lovely girl*
(Pickwick).

Wardle, Rachael: Wardle's spinster sister. Tupman falls in love with her, but
Jingle persuades her to elope with him
and has to be bought off. *There was a
dignity in the air, a touch-me-not-ishness
in the walk, a majesty in the eye of the
spinster aunt* (Pickwick).

'Warwick, The Earl of': One of the
thieves living in Rats' Castle, Saint
Giles's, visited by the narrator and
Inspector Field. *'O there you are, my
Lord. Come for'ard. There's a chest, sir, not
to have a clean shirt on. An't it? Take your
hat off, my Lord. Why, I should be
ashamed if I was you – and an Earl, too –
to show myself to a gentleman with my hat
on!'* (Reprinted – 'On Duty with Inspector Field').

Waste: One of Miss Flite's birds *(Bleak
House)*.

Waterbrook: London solicitor, Wickfield's agent, with whom Agnes stays.
*A middle-aged gentleman, with a short
throat, and a good deal of shirt collar, who*

only wanted a black nose to be the portrait of a pug-dog (Copperfield).

Waterbrook, Mrs.: Waterbrook's wife. *Mrs. Waterbrook, who was a large lady – or who wore a large dress: I don't exactly know which, for I don't know which was dress and which was lady (Copperfield).*

Waterhouse: See **Pegg** (*Uncommercial* – 'Poor Mercantile Jack').

'Waterloo': Toll-keeper on Waterloo Bridge who regales the narrator with tales of suicides there (*Reprinted* – 'Down with the Tide').

Waters, Captain Walter: A confidence trickster, husband of Belinda. *A stoutish, military-looking gentleman in a blue surtout buttoned up to his chin, and white trousers chained down to the soles of his boots* (*Boz* – 'Tuggses at Ramsgate').

Waters, Mrs. Walter (Belinda): Captain Waters's wife and accomplice. By arranging for Simon Tuggs to be found in compromising circumstances in her apartments she enables her husband to extort £1,500 of the Tuggs family's new fortune. *A young lady in a puce-coloured silk cloak, and boots of the same; with long black ringlets, large black eyes, brief petticoats, and unexceptionable ankles* (*Boz* – 'Tuggses at Ramsgate').

Watertoast Association of United Sympathisers: An American association in opposition to the British Lion, presided over by General Choke. *The Watertoast Association sympathised with a certain Public Man in Ireland, who held a contest upon certain points with England ... because they didn't love England at all – not by any means because they loved Ireland much* (*Chuzzlewit*).

Watkins: Kate Nickleby's godfather, recalled to her and Miss Knag by Mrs. Nickleby. *'He wasn't any relation, Miss Knag will understand, to the Watkins who kept the Old Boar in the village; by the bye, I don't remember whether it was the Old Boar or the George the Third, but it was one of the two, I know, and it's much the same – that Mr. Watkins said, when you were only two years and a half old, that you were one of the most astonishing*

children he ever saw. He did indeed, Miss Knag, and he wasn't at all fond of children, and couldn't have had the slightest motive for doing it. I know it was he who said so, because I recollect, as well as if it was only yesterday, his borrowing twenty pounds of her poor dear papa the very moment afterwards' (*Nickleby*).

Watkins the First, King: Father of Princess Alicia in Alice Rainbird's romantic tale ('Holiday Romance').

Watson Family: Friends of Mincin (*Young Gentlemen* – 'Very Friendly Young Gentleman').

Watty: A bankrupt client of Perker. *A rustily-clad, miserable-looking man, in boots without toes and gloves without fingers* (*Pickwick*).

Wedgington Family: A husband-and-wife theatrical act and their infant son. *Mrs. B. Wedgington sang to a grand piano. Mr. B. Wedgington did the like, and also took off his coat, tucked up his trousers, and danced in clogs. Master B. Wedgington, aged ten months, was nursed by a shivering young person in the boxes, and the eye of Mrs. B. Wedgington wandered that way more than once* (*Reprinted* – 'Out of the Season').

Weedle, Anastasia: A Mormon emigrant aboard the *Amazon*. *A pretty girl, in a bright Garibaldi, this morning elected by universal suffrage the Beauty of the Ship* (*Uncommercial* – 'Bound for the Great Salt Lake').

'Weevle': See **Jobling, Tony** (*Bleak House*).

Wegg, Silas: A one-legged balladmonger and fruit-stall holder engaged by Boffin to improve his mind through literature. He finds Old Harmon's will and tries, with Venus, to blackmail Boffin, but is betrayed by his partner. *A knotty man, and a close-grained, with a face carved out of very hard material, that had just as much play of expression as a watchman's rattle. When he laughed, certain jerks occurred in it, and the rattle sprung. Sooth to say, he was so wooden a man that he seemed to have taken his wooden leg naturally, and rather suggested to the fanciful observer,*

that he might be expected – if his develop-
ment received no untimely check – to be
completely set up with a pair of wooden
legs in about six months (Mutual Friend).

Weller, Samuel: Son of Tony senior.
Boots at the White Hart Inn, Borough.
He becomes Pickwick's valet and faithful
aide and eventually marries Mary, Nupkins's housemaid. *He was habited in a*
coarse-striped waistcoat, with black calico
sleeves, and blue glass buttons; drab
breeches and leggings. A bright red hand-
kerchief was wound in a very loose and
unstudied style round his neck, and an old
white hat was carelessly thrown on one
side of his head. || 'I wonder whether I'm
meant to be a footman, or a groom, or a
gamekeeper, or a seedsman. I looks like a
sort of compo of every one on 'em. Never
mind : there's a change of air, plenty to see,
and little to do ; and all this suits my com-
plaint uncommon ; so long life to the Pick-
vicks, say I !' (Pickwick).

Weller, Tony, jun.: Sam Weller's infant
son and Tony's grandson. *'There never*
vos any like that 'ere little Tony. He's
always a playin' vith a quart pot, that boy
is ! To see him a settin' down on the door-
step pretending to drink out of it, and
fetching a long breath artervards, and
smoking a bit of fire-vood, and sayin',
"Now I'm grandfather," – to see him a
doin' that at two year old is better than any
play as vos ever wrote' (Humphrey).

Weller, Tony, sen.: Sam's father, a
stage-coachman. *Among the number was*
one stout, red-faced, elderly man in par-
ticular, seated in an opposite box, who
attracted Mr. Pickwick's attention. The
stout man was smoking with great vehe-
mence, but between every half-dozen puffs,
he took his pipe from his mouth. . . . Then,
he would bury in a quart pot as much of his
countenance as the dimensions of the quart
pot admitted of its receiving (Pickwick).

Weller, Mrs. Tony, sen. (Susan):
Second wife of Tony Weller senior and
formerly the Widow Clarke. She is
landlady of the Marquis of Granby,
Dorking, where she drives Tony to
despair by her infatuation with the
hypocritical Revd. Mr. Stiggins, but

restores him by dying and leaving him
her property. *A rather stout lady of com-*
fortable appearance. || 'Wy, I'll tell you
what, Sammy,' said Mr. Weller, senior,
with much solemnity in his manner; 'there
never was a nicer woman as a widder, than
that 'ere second wentur o' mine – a sweet
creetur she was, Sammy; all I can say on
her now, is, that as she was such an uncom-
mon pleasant widder, it's a great pity she
ever changed her condition' (Pickwick).

Wemmick, sen.: See 'Aged, The' (Expectations).

Wemmick, John: Jaggers's confidential
clerk. He befriends Pip and Herbert
Pocket and helps in the attempt to
smuggle Magwitch out of the country.
He marries Miss Skiffins. *A dry man,*
rather short in stature, with a square
wooden face, whose expression seemed to
have been imperfectly chiselled out with a
dull-edged chisel. There were some marks
in it that might have been dimples, if the
material had been softer and the instru-
ment finer, but which, as it was, were only
dints. The chisel had made three or four of
these attempts at embellishment over his
nose, but had given them up without an
effort to smooth them off. I judged him to
be a bachelor from the frayed condition
of his linen, and he appeared to have sus-
tained a good many bereavements ; for he
wore at least four mourning rings, besides
a brooch representing a lady and a weeping
willow at a tomb with an urn on it. I
noticed, too, that several rings and seals
hung at his watch-chain, as if he were
quite laden with remembrances of departed
friends. He had glittering eyes – small,
keen, and black – and thin wide mottled
lips. He had had them, to the best of my
belief, from forty to fifty years (Expec-
tations).

West, Dame: Grandmother of the child
Harry (q.v.) (Curiosity Shop).

Westlock, John: Pupil of Pecksniff until
he leaves in disgust, after failing to con-
vince Tom Pinch of their master's mal-
practices. Eventually marries Ruth Pinch.
Not the old John of Pecksniff's, but a
proper gentleman: looking another and
grander person, with the consciousness of

being his own master and having money in the bank: and yet in some respects the old John too, for he seized Tom Pinch by both his hands the instant he appeared, and fairly hugged him, in his cordial welcome (Chuzzlewit).

Westwood: See **Adams, Captain** and **Westwood** *(Nickleby).*

Wharton, Granville: Pupil of George Silverman who self-sacrificially induces him to fall in love with Adelina Fareway, and marries them ('Silverman').

Wheezy, Professor: A vice-president of the zoology and botany session at the first meeting of the Mudfog Association *(Mudfog).*

'Whelp, The': See **Gradgrind, Tom** *(Hard Times).*

Whiff, Miss: One of the attendants at Mugby Junction refreshment room *(Christmas Stories –* 'Mugby Junction').

Whiffers: A Bath footman, present at the footmen's soirée, who announces his resignation from his employment because he has been required to eat cold meat. *He had a distinct recollection of having once consented to eat salt butter, and he had, moreover, on an occasion of sudden sickness in the house, so far forgotten himself as to carry a coal-scuttle up to the second floor. He trusted he had not lowered himself in the good opinion of his friends by this frank confession of his faults; and he hoped the promptness with which he had resented the last unmanly outrage on his feelings, to which he had referred, would reinstate him in their good opinion, if he had (Pickwick).*

Whiffin: Town crier of Eatanswill *(Pickwick).*

Whiffler: The doting father. *Mr. Whiffler must have to describe at his office such excruciating agonies constantly undergone by his eldest boy, as nobody else's eldest boy ever underwent; or he must be able to declare that there never was a child endowed with such amazing health, such an indomitable constitution, and such a cast-iron frame, as his child (Young Couples –* 'Couple Who Dote Upon Their Children').

Whiffler, Mrs.: Whiffler's wife, and doting mother of Georgiana, Ned, Dick, Tom, Bob, Mary Anne, Emily, Fanny, Carry and another on the way. *Mrs. Whiffler will never cease to recollect the last day of the old year as long as she lives, for it was on that day that the baby had the four red spots on its nose which they took for measles: nor Christmas-day, for twenty-one days after Christmas-day the twins were born; nor Good Friday, for it was on a Good Friday that she was frightened by the donkey-cart when she was in the family way with Georgiana (Young Couples –* 'Couple Who Dote Upon Their Children').

Whimple, Mrs.: The Barleys' landlady. *An elderly woman of a pleasant and thriving appearance (Expectations).*

Whisker: Garland's pony. *If the old gentleman remonstrated by shaking the reins, the pony replied by shaking his head. It was plain that the utmost the pony would consent to do, was to go in his own way up any street that the old gentleman particularly wished to traverse, but that it was an understanding between them that he must do this after his own fashion or not at all (Curiosity Shop).*

White: A pale, bald, grown-up child in Mrs. Lemon's school in Nettie Ashford's romantic tale ('Holiday Romance').

White: Police constable who accompanies the narrator and Inspector Field to the thieves' kitchen and seminary for the teaching of the art to children in Rotten Gray's Inn Lane *(Reprinted –* 'On Duty with Inspector Field').

White, Betsy: The species of girl preying on Liverpool sailors. *Betsy looks over the banisters . . . with a forcible expression in her protesting face, of an intention to compensate herself for the present trial by grinding Jack finer than usual when he does come (Uncommercial –* 'Poor Mercantile Jack').

White, Tom: The name given for Oliver Twist by a kindly jailer when, shocked and ill, Oliver is unable to give his name to the bullying magistrate, Fang *(Twist)*.

Wickam, Mrs.: Paul Dombey's nurse after Polly Toodle's dismissal. *A waiter's wife – which would seem equivalent to being any other man's widow – whose application for an engagement in Mr. Dombey's service had been favourably considered, on account of the apparent impossibility of her having any followers, or any one to follow (Dombey).*

Wickfield: Betsey Trotwood's Canterbury lawyer; father of Agnes. Brought low by drink, he becomes the tool of Uriah Heep but is eventually rescued by Micawber. *His hair was quite white now, though his eyebrows were still black. He had a very agreeable face, and, I thought, was handsome. There was a certain richness in his complexion, which I had been long accustomed, under Peggotty's tuition, to connect with port wine; and I fancied it was in his voice, too, and referred his growing corpulency to the same cause (Copperfield).*

Wickfield, Agnes: David and Dora Copperfield's friend, and his second wife, by Dora's dying wish. *Although her face was quite bright and happy, there was a tranquillity about it, and about her – a quiet, good, calm spirit, – that I never have forgotten; that I never shall forget. . . . She had a little basket-trifle hanging at her side, with keys in it; and she looked as staid and as discreet a housekeeper as the old house could have. . . . I cannot call to mind where or when, in my childhood, I had seen a stained-glass window in a church. Nor do I recollect its subject. But I know that when I saw her turn round, in the grave light of the old staircase, and wait for us, above, I thought of that window; and I associated something of its tranquil brightness with Agnes Wickfield ever afterwards (Copperfield).*

Wicks: A clerk at Dodson and Fogg's *(Pickwick)*.

Widger, Bobtail and Mrs. Bobtail (Lavinia): A plausible couple. *No less plausible to each other than to third parties. They are always loving and har-monious. The plausible gentleman calls his wife 'darling,' and the plausible lady addresses him as 'dearest.' If it be Mr. and Mrs. Bobtail Widger. Mrs. Widger is 'Lavinia, darling,' and Mr. Widger is 'Bobtail, dearest.' Speaking of each other, they observe the same tender form. Mrs. Widger relates what 'Bobtail' said, and Mr. Widger recounts what 'darling' thought and did (Young Couples – 'Plausible Couple').*

Wield, Inspector Charles: One of the Detective Force officers of Scotland Yard. *A middle-aged man of a portly presence, with a large, moist, knowing eye, a husky voice, and a habit of emphasising his conversation by the aid of a corpulent fore-finger, which is constantly in juxtaposition with his eyes or nose (Reprinted – 'Detective Police' and 'Three "Detective" Anecdotes').*

Wigs: One of Miss Flite's birds *(Bleak House)*.

Wigsby: Speaker at the zoology and botany session of the first meeting of the Mudfog Association. *Produced a cauliflower somewhat larger than a chaise-umbrella, which had been raised by no other artificial means than the simple application of highly carbonated soda-water as manure. He explained that by scooping out the head, which would afford a new and delicious species of nourishment for the poor, a parachute . . . was at once obtained (Mudfog).*

Wigsby: A vestryman, of Chumbledon Square. *Mr. Wigsby replies (with his eye on next Sunday's paper) that in reference to the question which has been put to him by the honourable gentleman opposite, he must take leave to say, that if that honourable gentleman had had the courtesy of giving him notice of that question, he (Mr. Wigsby) would have consulted with his colleagues in reference to the advisability, in the present state of the discussions on the new paving-rate, of answering that question (Reprinted – 'Our Vestry').*

Wilding, Mrs.: The lady who adopts Walter Wilding from the Foundling Hospital and founds his fortunes as a wine merchant, believing him to be another child (*Christmas Stories* – 'No Thoroughfare'; not in dramatised version).

Wilding, Walter: Head of Wilding and Co., City of London wine merchants. Adopted from the Foundling Hospital in mistake for another baby, he had been left the business by Mrs. Wilding. Learning of the mistake from Mrs. Goldstraw, he determines to make restitution to the rightful heir, but dies while trying to trace him. *An innocent, open-speaking, unused-looking man, Mr. Walter Wilding, with a remarkably pink and white complexion, and a figure much too bulky for so young a man, though of a good stature. With crispy curling brown hair, and amiable bright blue eyes. An extremely communicative man : a man with whom loquacity was the irrestrainable outpouring of contentment and gratitude* (*Christmas Stories* – 'No Thoroughfare' and in dramatised version).

Wilfer, Bella: The Wilfer daughter intended under Harmon's will to marry his son. Bereaved before the event by his supposed murder, she marries him unknowingly as John Rokesmith and they have a baby. *A girl of about nineteen, with an exceedingly pretty figure and face, but with an impatient and petulant expression both in her face and in her shoulders (which in her sex and at her age are very expressive of discontent)* (*Mutual Friend*).

Wilfer, Lavinia ('The Irrepressible'): Bella's temperamental younger sister, loved by George Sampson. *'I'm not a child to be taken notice of by strangers'* (*Mutual Friend*).

Wilfer, Reginald ('The Cherub' and 'Rumty'): Father of Bella and Lavinia, a downtrodden clerk to Chicksey, Veneering and Stobbles. *So poor a clerk, through having a limited salary and an unlimited family, that he had never yet attained the modest object of his ambition : which was, to wear a complete new suit of clothes, hat and boots included, at one time. His black hat was brown before he could afford a coat, his pantaloons were white at*

the seams and knees before he could buy a pair of boots, his boots had worn out before he could treat himself to new pantaloons, and by the time he worked round to the hat again, that shining modern article roofed-in an ancient ruin of various periods. . . . His chubby, smooth, innocent appearance was a reason for his being always treated with condescension when he was not put down. A stranger entering his own poor house at about ten o'clock P.M. might have been surprised to find him sitting up to supper. So boyish was he in his curves and proportions, that his old schoolmaster meeting him in Cheapside, might have been unable to withstand the temptation of caning him on the spot (Mutual Friend).*

Wilfer, Mrs. Reginald: Wilfer's wife, mother of Bella and Lavinia. *A tall woman and an angular. Her lord being cherubic, she was necessarily majestic, according to the principle which matrimonially unites contrasts. She was much given to tying up her head in a pocket-handkerchief, knotted under the chin. This head-gear, in conjunction with a pair of gloves worn within doors, she seemed to consider as at once a kind of armour against misfortune (invariably assuming it when in low spirits or difficulties), and as a species of full dress* (*Mutual Friend*).

Wilhelm: German courier who narrates the story of James and John. *The stoutest courier* ('At Dusk').

Wilkins: Boldwig's gardener (*Pickwick*).

Wilkins, Dick: A fellow apprentice of the young Scrooge (*Christmas Books* – 'Christmas Carol').

Wilkins, Samuel: Journeyman carpenter courting Jemima Evans. *Of small dimensions, decidedly below the middle size – bordering, perhaps, upon the dwarfish. His face was round and shining, and his hair carefully twisted into the outer corner of each eye, till it formed a variety of that description of semi-curls, usually known as 'aggerawators'. His earnings were all-sufficient for his wants, varying from eighteen shillings to one pound five, weekly – his manner undeniable – his sabbath waistcoats dazzling. No wonder that,* with these qualifications, Samuel Wilkins found favour in the eyes of the other sex (*Boz* – 'Miss Evans and the Eagle').

Will: Waiter at the St. James's Arms (*Strange Gentleman*).

Willet, Joe: Son of John, whose brow-beating makes him run away. Rejected by Dolly Varden, he joins the army, loses an arm, and returns in time to save Dolly during the Gordon Riots, after which she marries him. *A broad-shouldered strapping young fellow of twenty, whom it pleased his father still to consider a little boy, and to treat accordingly (Rudge).*

Willet, John: Landlord of the Maypole Inn, Chigwell, Essex. Father of Joe. *A burly, large-headed man with a fat face, which betokened profound obstinacy and slowness of apprehension, combined with a very strong reliance upon his own merits. It was John Willet's ordinary boast in his more placid moods that if he were slow he was sure; which assertion could, in one sense at least, be by no means gainsaid, seeing that he was in everything unquestionably the reverse of fast, and withal one of the most dogged and positive fellows in existence – always sure that what he thought or said or did was right, and holding it as a thing quite settled and ordained by the laws of nature and Providence, that anybody who said or did or thought otherwise must be inevitably and of necessity wrong (Rudge).*

William: Young man who kills himself with hard work, copying and translating for publishers to keep himself and his widowed mother. *Night after night, two, three, four hours after midnight, could we hear the occasional raking up of the scanty fire, or the hollow and half-stifled cough, which indicated his being still at work; and day after day, could we see more plainly that nature had set that unearthly light in his plaintive face, which is the beacon of her worst disease (Boz* – 'Our Next-door Neighbour').

William: Yarmouth inn waiter who eats most of young David Copperfield's dinner for him. *It was quite delightful to me to find him so pleasant. He was a*

twinkling-eyed, pimple-faced man, with his hair standing upright all over his head. . . . 'What have we got here?' he said, putting a fork into my dish. 'Not chops?' (*Copperfield*).

William: Driver of the Canterbury coach taking David Copperfield to London. *'Is Suffolk your county, sir,' asked William. . . . 'I'm told the dumplings is uncommon fine down there' (Copperfield).*

William: Waiter at the Saracen's Head inn, where Squeers stays in London (*Nickleby*).

William: Sir Mulberry Hawk's coachman (*Nickleby*).

William, Sweet: A travelling entertainer encountered by Little Nell and her grandfather. *A silent gentleman who earned his living by showing tricks upon the cards, and who had rather deranged the natural expression of his countenance by putting small leaden lozenges into his eyes and bringing them out at his mouth, which was one of his professional accomplishments (Curiosity Shop).*

Williams: Police constable who accompanies the narrator and Inspector Field to sailors' haunts in Ratcliffe Highway (*Reprinted* – 'On Duty with Inspector Field').

Williams, William: Regular drinker at the Six Jolly Fellowship Porters (*Mutual Friend*).

Williamson, Mrs.: Landlady of the Winglebury Arms (*Boz* – 'Great Winglebury Duel'). In the dramatised version, *The Strange Gentleman*, she is renamed Mrs. Noakes.

Willis: A debtor in Solomon Jacobs's sponging-house. *A young fellow of vulgar manners dressed in the very extreme of the prevailing fashion, was pacing up and down the room, with a lighted cigar in his mouth and his hands in his pockets, ever and anon puffing forth volumes of smoke, and occasionally applying, with much apparent relish, to a pint pot, the contents of which were 'chilling' on the hob (Boz* – 'Watkins Tottle').

Willis, the four Misses: Four sisters who move into 'Our Parish', live completely interdependently, and eventually tantalise the neighbourhood with the question of which of them is to marry Robinson. *The eldest Miss Willis used to knit, the second to draw, the two others to play duets on the piano. They seemed to have no separate existence, but to have made up their minds just to winter through life together. . . . The eldest Miss Willis grew bilious – the four Miss Willises grew bilious immediately. The eldest Miss Willis grew ill-tempered and religious – the four Miss Willises were ill-tempered and religious directly. Whatever the eldest did, the others did, and whatever anybody else did, they all disapproved of* (Boz – 'Four Sisters').

Wilson: The Iago of the Gattletons' private presentation of *Othello*. *'Mr. Wilson, who was to have played* Iago, *is – that is, has been – or, in other words, Ladies and Gentlemen, the fact is, that I have just received a note, in which I am informed that* Iago *is unavoidably detained at the Post-office this evening'* (Boz – 'Mrs. Joseph Porter').

Wilson: Contender with Rogers, the Parlour Orator, at an Old Street Suburban Representative Discovery Society meeting over the Parliamentary candidature of Snobee (q.v.) (Boz – 'Parlour Orator').

Wilson, Caroline: Pupil of the Misses Crumpton. *The ugliest girl in Hammersmith, or out of it* (Boz – 'Sentiment').

Wilson, Fanny: Sister of Mary and fiancée of Charles Tomkins (*Strange Gentleman*).

Wilson, Mary: Fanny's sister, on her way to Gretna Green with John Johnson (*Strange Gentleman*).

Wiltshire: A Wiltshire labourer aboard the emigrant ship *Amazon*. *A simple fresh-coloured farm-labourer, of eight-and-thirty* (Uncommercial – 'Bound for the Great Salt Lake').

Winking Charley: A character who frequently enters the narrator's night-thoughts as he drifts to sleep. *A sturdy vagrant, in one of her Majesty's jails* (Reprinted – 'Lying Awake').

Winkle, sen.: Nathaniel Winkle's father. A Birmingham wharfinger. *A little old gentleman in a snuff-coloured suit, with a head and face the precise counterpart of those belonging to Mr. Winkle, junior, excepting that he was rather bald* (Pickwick).

Winkle, Nathaniel: A member of the Pickwick Club and one of Pickwick's companions on his travels. An aspirant to fame as a sportsman, he makes his mark in a very different field by carrying off Arabella Allen as his wife. *The sporting Winkle . . . communicating additional lustre to a new green shooting coat, plaid neckerchief, and close-fitted drabs* (Pickwick).

'Winks': Another name for Deputy (q.v.) (Drood).

Wisbottle: Boarder at Mrs. Tibbs's. *A high Tory. He was a clerk in the Woods and Forests Office, which he considered rather an aristocratic employment; he knew the peerage by heart, and could tell you, offhand, where any illustrious personage lived. He had a good set of teeth, and a capital tailor. . . . It should be added, that, in addition to his partiality for whistling, Mr. Wisbottle had a great idea of his singing powers* (Boz – 'Boarding-House').

Wisk, Miss: Quale's fiancée, a like character and friend to Mrs. Jellyby. *Miss Wisk's mission, my guardian said, was to show the world that woman's mission was man's mission; and that the only genuine mission, of both man and woman, was to be always moving declaratory resolutions about things in general at public meetings* (Bleak House).

Witchem, Sergeant: One of the Detective Force officers of Scotland Yard. *Shorter and thicker-set, and marked with the small-pox, has something of a reserved and thoughtful air, as if he were engaged in deep arithmetical calculations. He is renowned for his acquaintance with the swell mob* (Reprinted – 'Detective Police').

Witherden: The notary to whom Abel Garland is articled. He is instrumental in unmasking Quilp and the Brasses. *Short,* *chubby, fresh-coloured, brisk and pompous (Curiosity Shop).*

Witherfield, Miss: Peter Magnus's fiancée, into whose bedroom Pickwick gets by mistake. *A middle-aged lady, in yellow curl-papers (Pickwick).*

Withers: Mrs. Skewton's page, who propels her invalid-carriage. *The chair having stopped, the motive power became visible in the shape of a flushed page pushing behind, who seemed to have in part outgrown and in part out-pushed his strength, for when he stood upright he was tall, and wan, and thin, and his plight appeared the more forlorn from his having injured the shape of his hat, by butting at the carriage with his head to urge it forward, as is sometimes done by elephants in Oriental countries (Dombey).*

Witterly, Henry: Of Cadogan Place; Julia Witterly's devoted husband. *An important gentleman of about eight-and-thirty, of rather plebeian countenance, and with a very light head of hair (Nickleby).*

Witterly, Mrs. Henry (Julia): Henry's wife, whose companion Kate Nickleby is for a time. *The lady had an air of sweet insipidity, and a face of engaging paleness; there was a faded look about her, and about the furniture, and about the house. She was reclining on a sofa in such a very unstudied attitude, that she might have been taken for an actress all ready for the first scene in a ballet, and only waiting for the drop-curtain to go up (Nickleby).*

Wobbler: Clerk in the Circumlocution Office. *Spreading marmalade on bread with a paper-knife (Dorrit).*

Wolf: Friend of Montague Tigg. *'Mr. Wolf – literary character – you needn't mention it – remarkably clever weekly paper – oh, remarkably clever!' (Chuzzlewit).*

Wood Sawyer, The: A man who conversed with Lucie outside the prison of La Force whenever she went hoping to see her husband. *'See my saw! I call it my Little Guillotine. . . . I call myself the Samson of the firewood guillotine. See here again! Loo, loo, loo; Loo, loo, loo! And off her head comes! Now, a child. Tickle,*

tickle; Pickle, pickle! And off its head comes. All the family!' (Two Cities).

Woodcourt: Mrs. Woodcourt's deceased husband and Allan's father. *'Poor Mr. Woodcourt, my dear,' she would say, and always with some emotion, for with her lofty pedigree she had a very affectionate heart, 'was descended from a great Highland family, the Mac Coorts of Mac Coort. He served his king and country as an officer in the Royal Highlanders, and he died on the field' (Bleak House).*

Woodcourt, Mrs.: Allan Woodcourt's widowed mother. *She was such a sharp little lady, and used to sit with her hands folded in each other, looking so very watchful while she talked to me, that perhaps I found that rather irksome. Or perhaps it was her being so upright and trim; though I don't think it was that, because I thought that quaintly pleasant. Nor can it have been the general expression of her face, which was very sparkling and pretty for an old lady. I don't know what it was (Bleak House).*

Woodcourt, Dr. Allan: The young medical man to whom Jarndyce relinquishes Esther Summerson's hand in marriage. *A gentleman of a dark complexion – a young surgeon. He was rather reserved, but I thought him very sensible and agreeable (Bleak House).*

Wooden, Midshipman, The: Sol Gills's ship's instrument shop in the City of London, based by Dickens on Norie & Wilson's in Leadenhall Street, later Minories. Their original Midshipman sign is now in the Dickens House, London. *Little timber midshipmen in obsolete naval uniforms, eternally employed outside the shop-doors of nautical instrument-makers in taking observations of the hackney coaches. . . . One of these effigies . . . thrust itself out above the pavement, right leg foremost, with a suavity the least endurable, and had the shoe buckles and flapped waistcoat the least reconcilable to human reason, and bore at its right eye the most offensively disproportionate piece of machinery (Dombey).*

Woodensconce: President of the statistics

session at the first meeting of the Mud-fog Association (*Mudfog*).

Woolford, Miss: Popular equestrienne at Astley's. *Another cut from the whip, a burst from the orchestra, a start from the horse, and round goes Miss Woolford again on her graceful performance, to the delight of every member of the audience, young or old* (*Boz* – 'Astley's').

Wopsle: Parish clerk and friend of the Gargerys. He becomes an actor under the name Waldengarver. *Mr. Wopsle, united to a Roman nose and a large shining bald forehead, had a deep voice which he was uncommonly proud of; indeed it was understood among his acquaintance that if you could only give him his head, he would read the clergyman into fits. . . . He punished the Amens tremendously; and when he gave out the psalm – always giving the whole verse – he looked all round the congregation first, as much as to say, 'You have heard our friend overhead; oblige me with your opinion of this style!'* (*Expectations*).

Wopsle's Great-Aunt: *Kept an evening school in the village; that is to say, she was a ridiculous old woman of limited means and unlimited infirmity, who used to go to sleep from six to seven every evening, in the society of youth who paid twopence per week each, for the improving opportunity of seeing her do it* (*Expectations*).

Words: One of Miss Flite's birds (*Bleak House*).

Wosky, Dr.: Mrs. Bloss's physician. *A little man with a red face, – dressed of course in black, with a stiff white necker-chief. He had a very good practice, and plenty of money, which he had amassed by invariably humouring the worst fancies of all the females of all the families he had ever been introduced into* (*Boz* – 'Boarding-House').

Wozenham, Miss: Mrs. Lirriper's rival lodging-house keeper in Norfolk Street, Strand. *Some there are who do not think it lowering themselves to make their names that cheap, and even going the lengths of a portrait of the house not like it with a blot in every window and a coach and four at the door, but what will suit Wozenham's lower down on the other side of the way will not suit me* (*Christmas Stories* – 'Mrs. Lirriper's Lodgings' and 'Mrs. Lirriper's Legacy').

Wrayburn, Eugene: A reluctant barrister who spends his days in indolence and gloom until transformed by marriage with Lizzie Hexham, which he only achieves after nearly being murdered by the jealous Headstone. *'If there is a word in the dictionary under any letter from A to Z that I abominate, it is energy. It is such a conventional superstition, such parrot gabble! What the deuce! Am I to rush out into the street, collar the first man of a wealthy appearance that I meet, shake him, and say, "Go to law upon the spot, you dog, and retain me, or I'll be the death of you"? Yet that would be energy'* (*Mutual Friend*).

Wrayburn, Mrs. Eugene: See Hexham, Lizzie (*Mutual Friend*).

'Wren, Jenny': See Cleaver, Fanny (*Mutual Friend*).

Wrymug, Mrs.: Client of the General Agency Office. *'Pleasant Place, Finsbury. Wages, twelve guineas. No tea, no sugar. Serious family. . . . Three serious footmen. Cook, housemaid, and nursemaid; each female servant required to join the Little Bethel Congregation three times every Sunday – with a serious footman. If the cook is more serious than the footman, she will be expected to improve the footman; if the footman is more serious than the cook, he will be expected to improve the cook'* (*Nickleby*).

Wugsby, Mrs. Colonel: One of Pick-wick's whist opponents at Bath Assembly Rooms. Mother of Jane and another daughter (*Pickwick*).

Yawler: Former Salem House pupil who assists Traddles to enter the law. *'Yaw-ler, with his nose on one side. Do you recollect him?' No. He had not been there with me; all the noses were straight in my day* (*Copperfield*).

York, The Five Sisters of: See Five Sisters of York, The (*Nickleby*).

Youth: One of Miss Flite's birds *(Bleak House)*.

Zamiel: Nickname given to fellow-traveller in his railway compartment by the narrator. *Tall, grave, melancholy Frenchman, with black Vandyke beard, and hair close-cropped, with expansive chest to waistcoat, and compressive waist to coat : saturnine as to his pantaloons, calm as to his feminine boots, precious as to his jewellery, smooth and white as to his linen : dark-eyed, high-foreheaded, hawk-nosed – got up, one thinks, like Lucifer or Mephistopheles, or Zamiel, transformed into a highly genteel Parisian (Reprinted – 'A Flight').*

'Zephyr, The': See Mivins *(Pickwick)*.

THE PLACES

A SELECTED TOPOGRAPHY OF DICKENS'S
WORKS AND LIFE

CONTENTS OF 'THE PLACES'

THE PLACES

PART ONE: THE WORLD, EXCEPT LONDON

Alderbury, Wiltshire: See Salisbury.

Amesbury, Wiltshire: See Salisbury.

Angel Inn: See Bury St. Edmunds.

Australia: Mentioned in several works, principally as a penal settlement for transported convicts (e.g. Magwitch, *Expectations*). Transportation to New South Wales ceased in 1840. Dickens was keenly interested in Australian colonisation as a remedy for bad living conditions in England. He sent the fictional Micawbers and Peggottys there (*Copperfield*), and also his own sons Alfred D'Orsay Tennyson Dickens and Edward Bulwer Lytton Dickens.

Barnard Castle, Durham: The King's Head Inn visited by Nicholas Nickleby on Newman Noggs's recommendation for its ale. Dickens and Hablôt K. Browne stayed at this inn in 1838 while investigating the notorious Yorkshire boarding schools. Opposite the inn were the premises of Mr. Humphrey, a clock-maker, which Dickens recalled when titling *Master Humphrey's Clock*.

Barnet, Hertfordshire: Scene of Oliver Twist's meeting with the Artful Dodger. Also mentioned in *Bleak House*. An important coaching stage on the Great North Road, close to London.

Barnstaple, Devon: Setting of 'A Message from the Sea' (*Christmas Stories.*)

Bastille, The: Notorious Parisian prison, whose seizure by the revolutionaries on 14 July 1789 is a dramatic scene in *A Tale of Two Cities*.

Bath, Somerset: Setting for several episodes in *Pickwick*; for example, the footmen's 'swarry' attended by Sam Weller, and Winkle's escapade with Mrs. Dowler and the sedan chair. Dickens took Pickwick's name from Moses Pickwick, coach proprietor and owner of the White Hart Hotel.

Beckhampton, Wiltshire: The Wagon and Horses Inn on the Marlborough Downs is thought to be the original of the inn of Tom Smart's adventure with the old chair (*Pickwick*).

Birmingham, Warwickshire: Often visited by Dickens, who gave his first public readings there in 1853, and used by him in *Pickwick, Twist, Humphrey, Nickleby, Uncommercial, Reprinted, Dombey*, and *Rudge*.

Blackheath: See under Part Two.

Bleak House: Present-day name of Fort House, Dickens's holiday home at Broadstairs, which has no connection with the novel. The original of the fictional Bleak House is thought to have been either a house in Gombard's Road, St. Albans, or Great Nast Hyde, off the main St. Albans–Hatfield Road.

Blunderstone, Suffolk: David Copperfield's birthplace, based by Dickens on the village of Blundeston which he visited in 1848.

Bonchurch, Isle of Wight: Holiday home of Dickens and family in 1849. He hoped to make it an alternative to Broadstairs for family holidays, but found the climate unsuitable.

Borrioboola-Gha: Fictional African village, the object of Mrs. Jellyby's philanthropic activities (*Bleak House*).

Boulogne, France: Called 'Our French Watering-place' by Dickens, who frequently holidayed there. Mentioned in *Boz* - 'The Boarding-House', *Reprinted* - 'A Flight' and 'Our French Watering-place', and *Two Cities*.

Bowes, Yorkshire: See Dotheboys Hall.

Brentford, Middlesex: Featured in *Expectations, Mutual Friend*, and *Twist*.

Brieg, Switzerland: Township at the foot of the Simplon Pass. Starting-point of

Vendale's and Obenreizer's mountain journey and scene of Vendale's marriage to Marguerite (*Christmas Stories* – 'No Thoroughfare').

Brighton, Sussex: Frequently visited by Dickens, who stayed at the Old Ship and Bedford hotels, and wrote there parts of *Twist*, *Rudge*, and *Bleak House*. Various claims have been made for the sites of Dr. Blimber's school and Mrs. Pipchin's 'Castle' *(Dombey)*.

Bristol, Gloucestershire: Often visited by Dickens, who stayed there first in 1835 as a parliamentary reporter, and gave public readings at Clifton in 1866 and 1869. Bristol is featured in *Pickwick* as the site of Bob Sawyer's and Ben Allen's surgery, and of the Bush Inn (at which Dickens himself had stayed) to which Winkle fled from the wrath of Dowler. Arabella Allen lodged with her aunt in Clifton.

Broadstairs, Kent: Coastal resort, for many years the Dickens family's holiday place. They stayed at the Albion Hotel, Lawn House, and Fort House (now re-named Bleak House and open as a Dickens museum). Much of the work of his middle years was done at Broadstairs. It is 'Our English Watering-place' (*Reprinted*), and the original of Betsey Trotwood is said to have lived in a house on the sea front (now 'Dickens House') which, in *Copperfield*, Dickens transfers to Dover.

Bury St. Edmunds, Suffolk: The Angel Inn is visited by Pickwick and Sam Weller in their pursuit of Jingle, and is the scene of Sam's encounter with Job Trotter and the starting point of Pickwick's adventure at the boarding school for young ladies. The town is also mentioned in *Copperfield*, *Boz* – 'Watkins Tottle', and *Uncommercial*. Dickens stayed there in 1835 while reporting a parliamentary election.

Cairo, Illinois: Probably the original of the barren estate, Eden, to which Martin Chuzzlewit goes in the hope of making his fortune.

Calais, France: Mentioned in *Two Cities*,

Dorrit, *Mutual Friend*, *Uncommercial*, and *Hard Times*. Dickens went there many times when travelling to and from the Continent.

Cambridge, Cambridgeshire: Has associations with several stories, including *Two Cities*, 'Silverman' and *Expectations*.

Canongate, The: See **Edinburgh**.

Canterbury, Kent: David Copperfield attends school at Dr. Strong's (unidentified) and lodges with the Wickfields; the Micawbers lodge at the Sun Hotel, Sun Street, now a shop. Dickens was much attached to Canterbury and enjoyed personally showing his visitors over the Cathedral.

Chalk, Kent: Setting, with Higham, of the early part of *Great Expectations*. The original of Joe Gargery's forge and cottage may still be seen. Dickens spent his honeymoon in this village near Gravesend in 1836 and the neighbourhood was one of his favourites for walking in throughout his life.

Chatham, Kent: A busy naval base at the mouth of the River Medway, Kent. Mudfog of *Mudfog Sketches* and Dullborough of *The Uncommercial Traveller*. In *Pickwick*, the scene of Winkle's abortive duel with Dr. Slammer and of the Pickwickians' first meeting with Mr. Wardle and family. David Copperfield sells some of his clothing there during his walk to his aunt's. Also mentioned in 'Seven Poor Travellers' (*Christmas Stories*). Chatham was Dickens's childhood home, 1817–22, at Ordnance Terrace and St. Mary's Place. His father was a clerk in the Navy Pay Office in H.M. Dockyard. The Mitre Inn is associated with the childhood of Charley in 'Holly-Tree' (*Christmas Stories*) and with Dickens's own childhood: it was where he and his sister used to sing duets on the dining-room table. It is also probably the Crozier, where Datchery stays, in *Drood*.

Chertsey, Surrey: Scene of the attempted burglary of Mrs. Maylie's in which Oliver Twist is wounded and captured.

Chesney Wold, Lincolnshire: Home of

Sir Leicester and Lady Dedlock *(Bleak House)*. The original was Rockingham Castle, Northamptonshire (q.v.).

Chigwell, Essex: The King's Head Inn is the original of the Maypole in *Barnaby Rudge*. Chigwell was a favourite resort of Dickens.

Clifton: See **Bristol**.

Cloisterham: See **Rochester**.

Cobham, Kent: Village near Gad's Hill. The Leather Bottle, one of Dickens's favourite inns, is the setting of Pickwick's discovery of Tupman after his flight from Dingley Dell. The inn contains many items of Dickensian interest, including a reproduction of the stone bearing the mysterious cypher which intrigues Pickwick. The walk through Cobham Park, also mentioned in *Pickwick*, was a favourite of Dickens and the last he ever took. The Hall was the seat of Lord Darnley, a friend of Dickens, and is the scene of a ghost story in 'Holly-Tree' *(Christmas Stories)*.

Coketown: See **Manchester** and **Preston**.

Conciergerie: Parisian prison where Sydney Carton substitutes himself for the condemned Charles Darnay *(Two Cities)*.

Cooling, Kent: Pip's first encounter with Magwitch takes place in the churchyard *(Expectations)*. The Comport graves are used by Dickens as those of Pip's brothers.

Deal, Kent: Richard Carstone is stationed at the Royal Marines barracks *(Bleak House)*. Deal is still a Royal Marines centre, and in Dickens's time was also a thriving naval yard. It was familiar to him in walking between Broadstairs and Dover, and may be the watering place described in *Reprinted* – 'Out of the Season'.

Demerara: A colony in British Guiana where Jingle and Job Trotter are sent by Pickwick to give them a fresh chance in life *(Pickwick)*.

Dijon, France: Rendezvous of Edith Dombey and James Carker in their elopement.

Dingley Dell: The home of Mr. Wardle and family where the Pickwickians spend Christmas and later attend Bella Wardle's wedding festivities. Cob Tree Hall, Sandling, near Maidstone, Kent, is much favoured as the original of Manor Farm.

Dorking, Surrey: Tony Weller and his second wife, Susan, keep the Marquis of Granby Inn, where Tony finally routs the persistent Revd. Mr. Stiggins *(Pickwick)*.

Dotheboys Hall: A Yorkshire boarding school kept by Mr. and Mrs. Squeers where Nicholas Nickleby is employed as a master. Appalled by the conditions, he beats Squeers and escapes to London with the poor drudge, Smike. Dotheboys is the archetype of the notorious Yorkshire schools. The original was William Shaw's school at Bowes, visited by Dickens in 1838. The building survives.

Dover, Kent: The setting for Betsey Trotwood's cottage, where David Copperfield finds refuge after tramping from London. Also featured in *Two Cities*, *Uncommercial*, *Pickwick*, and *Dorrit*. Often visited by Dickens travelling to and from the Continent.

Dullborough: The Uncommercial Traveller's home town. See **Chatham**.

Eatanswill: See **Sudbury**.

Eden: See **Cairo**.

Edinburgh: The Canongate is the setting for the story of the Bagman's Uncle *(Pickwick)*. Dickens had visited the city in 1834 as a reporter. He gave readings there in 1858, 1861, and 1869.

Eel Pie Island, Twickenham: A small island in the Thames where Morleena Kenwigs picnics with friends on 'bottled beer, shrub and shrimps' *(Nickleby)*. Dickens often went there on pleasure outings.

Epping Forest, Essex: Part of the setting for *Rudge*. Chigwell (q.v.) stands on the edge of the forest.

Folkestone, Kent: Summer holiday home of the Dickens family in 1855. Dickens worked on *Dorrit* at 3 Albion Villas,

Folkestone is Pavilionstone of *Reprinted* – 'Out of Town'.

Gad's Hill (also **Gadshill**): Between Gravesend and Rochester, Kent. Dickens first admired Gad's Hill Place as a child, and was told by his father that if he worked hard he might some day own it. In 1855 it became available to him by a coincidence; he bought it, used it as a holiday home until 1860, then made it his permanent home. It was there that he wrote *Two Cities*, *Expectations*, *Mutual Friend*, *Uncommercial*, and the unfinished *Drood*. He died there on 9 June 1870. The Swiss garden chalet in which he wrote is now in the grounds of Rochester Museum. Gad's Hill remained in the Dickens family until 1879 and is now a girls' school.

Glasgow: Dickens opened the Athenaeum in 1847. He gave many successful readings in Glasgow, the first in 1858.

Gravesend, Kent: Busy port on the Thames Estuary, well known to Dickens. He sets a number of scenes there, notably David Copperfield's and Peggotty's farewell to the emigrants for Australia, and the attempt to smuggle Magwitch out of England *(Expectations)*.

Great Winglebury: See **Rochester**.

Greenwich, Kent (now Greater London): Bella Wilfer and her father take two notable meals at The Ship, the second after her wedding to John Rokesmith at Greenwich Church *(Mutual Friend)*. Greenwich Fair is described in a *Boz* sketch of that name.

Greta Bridge, Yorkshire: Squeers and his party alight at the George and New Inn after their journey from London *(Nickleby)*. Probably the original of the 'Holly-Tree' Inn *(Christmas Stories)*. Dickens and H. K. Browne stayed here in 1838.

Gretna Green, Dumfriesshire: Traditional destination for eloping lovers, who could be married by the blacksmith. Featured in 'Holly-Tree' *(Christmas Stories)* and 'Great Winglebury Duel' *(Boz)*.

Groombridge Wells: An amalgam of the neighbouring Groombridge, Sussex, and Tunbridge Wells, Kent. Visited by Walter Wilding in his quest for his true identity *(Christmas Stories* – 'No Thoroughfare')*.

Ham House, near Twickenham, Middlesex: Historic mansion in whose neighbourhood Dickens sets the fatal duel between Sir Mulberry Hawk and Lord Frederick Verisopht *(Nickleby)*.

Hampton, Middlesex: The quarrel between Hawk and Verisopht breaks out at the racecourse *(Nickleby)*. Lightwood and Wrayburn occupy a bachelor cottage near Hampton *(Mutual Friend)*. Sikes and Oliver Twist linger at a public house here on their way to the burglary at Chertsey.

Hatfield, Hertfordshire: Small town near London, site of the former royal palace of Hatfield. Bill Sikes pauses for refreshment at the Eight Bells Inn in his flight after murdering Nancy and helps fight a great fire at a mansion in the neighbourhood *(Twist)*: Dickens was describing the fire at Hatfield House in 1835 when the Dowager Marchioness of Salisbury was burnt to death. Hatfield is also featured in 'Mrs. Lirriper's Legacy' *(Christmas Stories)*.

Henley-on-Thames, Oxfordshire: The Red Lion Inn is probably the Anglers' Inn of *Mutual Friend* where Wrayburn is taken after Headstone's attempt to murder him. Marsh Mill was Paper Mill, where Lizzie Hexam worked. Plashwater Weir Mill Lock in the story is probably Hurley Lock, about six miles down the river.

Higham: See **Chalk**.

Hoghton Tower, Lancashire: Historic house between Preston and Blackburn where Dickens sends George Silverman ('Silverman').

Ipswich, Suffolk: Port and market town, scene of celebrated episodes in *Pickwick*: Pickwick's misadventure with the lady in curl-papers and the Pickwickians' appearance before the magistrate, Nupkins. Sam Weller meets Mary, the housemaid, here. The Great White Horse Inn is the centre of the action: Dickens had stayed there in 1836. Ipswich also features in 'Doctor Marigold' *(Christmas Stories)*.

Kenilworth, Warwickshire: The historic castle ruins are visited by Dombey and Edith Granger on the day when he decides to propose to her. Dickens and H. K. Browne stayed there in 1838.

Kingston, Surrey: Thames-side town mentioned in *Expectations*, *Dombey*, *Mutual Friend*, and *Humphrey*.

Knebworth, Hertfordshire: Home of Sir Edward Bulwer-Lytton, Dickens's close friend. Dickens's theatrical company performed in the Banqueting Hall of Knebworth (now open to the public).

Lancaster, Lancashire: The former King's Arms Inn was the setting for the ghost story in *Two Apprentices*. Dickens and Wilkie Collins stayed there in 1857 while gathering material for the book. Lancaster is also mentioned in 'Doctor Marigold' *(Christmas Stories)*.

Leamington, Warwickshire: Resort and spa, fashionable in Dickens's time. Dombey and Major Bagstock stay at Copp's Royal Hotel, and Bagstock introduces Dombey to Edith Granger.

Liverpool, Lancashire: Major seaport mentioned in several novels. The notorious sailors' haunts are described vividly in *Uncommercial*. Dickens went there in 1838, and again in 1842 when he embarked for America. He and his amateur theatrical company appeared there in 1847 and he read there several times, the last time in 1869.

London: See Part Two.

Lowestoft, Suffolk: Seaside town where Murdstone takes David Copperfield on an excursion.

Maidstone, Kent: County town of Kent. Probably the origin of Muggleton *(Pickwick)*.

Manchester, Lancashire: A principal mercantile centre of the North of England, possibly Coketown of *Hard Times* (but see also **Preston**). Dickens went

there often as a young man. His sister Fanny lived there: he modelled Tiny Tim ('Christmas Carol') and Paul Dombey on her crippled son. Two local Quaker brothers, William and Daniel Grant, were the originals of the Cheeryble brothers *(Nickleby)*.

Margate, Kent: Seaside resort familiar to Dickens and mentioned in several stories.

Marlborough Downs, Wiltshire: At an ancient inn on the Downs Tom Smart has his strange adventure with the chair *(Pickwick)*. There are several claimants to be the original of the inn.

Marseilles, France: Scene of the imprisonment of Rigaud and Cavalletto; also where Arthur Clennam and the Meagles family are kept in quarantine *(Dorrit)*.

Martigny, Switzerland: Scene of Mr. Dorrit's meeting with Mrs. Merdle and Mr. Sparkler.

Medway, River, Kent: The principal river of Kent, at whose mouth stand Chatham and Rochester, towns of much influence upon Dickens's early life and often represented in his works. He observed, 'If anybody present knows to a nicety where Rochester ends and Chatham begins, it is more than I do.' The Medway is referred to in *Pickwick* and the Medway Coal Trade in *Copperfield*.

Mudfog: Venue for the first meeting of the Mudfog Association. See **Chatham**.

Mugby Junction: Setting for 'Mugby Junction' *(Christmas Stories)*. A provincial railway junction with a characteristically bad refreshment room; held by some to have been Rugby.

Muggleton: Scene of the cricket match between All-Muggleton and Dingley Dell *(Pickwick)*. Of many Kentish claimants to be the original of this place, Maidstone is perhaps favourite.

Naples, Italy: Scene of Steerforth's desertion of Little Em'ly and of Peggotty's search for her *(Copperfield)*. Dickens, his wife, and Georgina Hogarth explored the city thoroughly in 1845, ascended Vesuvius, and visited Pompeii and Herculaneum.

New York: Dickens was first there in 1842. His uncomplimentary passages in the subsequent *American Notes* and *Chuzzlewit* earned him much American opprobrium, and copies of the latter were burnt; but by the time he returned to give readings in 1867 all had been forgiven.

'Our English Watering-place': See Broadstairs.

'Our French Watering-place': See Boulogne.

Paper Mill: See Henley-on-Thames.

Paris: Scene of much of *Two Cities*, during the Revolution, and subject of some of the *Reprinted Pieces*. Also featured in *Bleak House*, *Dorrit*, and *Dombey*. Dickens stayed there many times and was lionised by literary and theatrical society.

Pavilionstone: See Folkestone.

Pegwell Bay, Kent: A quiet shrimping bay near Ramsgate visited by the Tuggs family (*Boz* – 'Tuggses at Ramsgate'), and well known to Dickens.

Petersfield, Hampshire: The Coach and Horses is generally accepted to be the original of the unnamed inn where Nicholas Nickleby and Smike meet the Crummles family.

Plymouth, Devon: A major naval port, home of Micawber's in-laws (*Copperfield*). Also mentioned in *Bleak House*.

Portsmouth, Hampshire: Dickens's birthplace, at 1 Mile End Terrace, Portsea: the house, now 393 Commercial Road, is a memorial museum to him. The subsequent family home at 16 Hawke Street no longer exists, but the font in which he was baptised in the now-demolished parish church of St. Mary, Kingston, is preserved in St. Stephen's Church, Portsea. The busy naval city is featured in *Nickleby*: Nicholas and Smike act with the Crummles company at the now-vanished theatre. Associated localities, such as their and the Crummleses'

lodgings, are now unidentifiable, due to wartime destruction.

Preston, Lancashire: Industrial town near Manchester, the birthplace of George Silverman ('Silverman'). There are features of Coketown (*Hard Times*) in Preston that justify stronger identification than with the generally accepted original, Manchester.

Ramsgate, Kent: Seaside setting of *Boz* – 'Tuggses at Ramsgate'. Dickens paid visits there during his stays at the neighbouring Broadstairs.

Richmond, Surrey: A pleasant town on the Thames, much visited by river parties. Tupman retires there (*Pickwick*), and Estella stays at Mrs. Brandley's, a 'staid old house' beside Richmond Green (*Expectations*). The Star and Garter Hotel, where Dickens gave a party to celebrate *Copperfield*, was at the top of the Hill.

Rochester, Kent: Ancient city at the mouth of the River Medway and one of the most significant places in Dickens's life and work. It is bound up with his childhood and he was observed brooding there the day before his fatal seizure. The Royal Victoria and Bull is the Bull of *Pickwick*, the Blue Lion and Stomach Warmer of *Boz* – 'Great Winglebury Duel', and the Blue Boar in *Expectations*. The Crispin and Crispianus, at the foot of Strood Hill, was one of Dickens's own favourite inns, mentioned in *Uncommercial*. Watts's Charity, of 'Seven Poor Travellers' (*Christmas Stories*), stands in the High Street. The original of the homes of Pumblechook (*Expectations*) and Sapsea (*Drood*) is in the High Street. Eastgate House, High Street, is the original of the Nuns' House, Cloisterham (*Drood*): it is the city's museum, and in its grounds stands the Swiss chalet from the grounds of Gad's Hill in which Dickens wrote up to the time of his death. The Cathedral, Minor Canon Row, and Jasper's Gatehouse, feature prominently in *Drood*. Restoration House, Maidstone Road, is Miss Havisham's Satis House *(Expectations)*.

Rockingham Castle, Northamptonshire: Home of Dickens's friends, the
Watsons. He used it as the original of
Chesney Wold (*Bleak House*) and the
local Sondes Arms is the original Dedlock Arms. The Castle is open to the
public.

St. Albans, Hertfordshire: some scenes
in *Bleak House* take place in this cathedral city. A house in Gombard's Road
may have been the original of Bleak
House itself.

St. Antoine, Paris: Setting for most of the
Parisian scenes of *Two Cities*.

Salisbury, Wiltshire: Cathedral city.
Home of Pecksniff and setting for many
scenes of *Chuzzlewit*. The Blue Dragon
Inn has been identified with the George,
Amesbury, the Green Dragon, Alderbury, and the Lion's Head, Winterslow, all places nearby.

Sandling, Kent: A village near Maidstone, generally accepted as the original
of Dingley Dell *(Pickwick)*.

Satis House: Miss Havisham's home
(Expectations). The original is Restoration
House, Maidstone Road, Rochester.

Sens, France: Small cathedral town
where Mrs. Lirriper and Jemmy visit the
dying Edson *(Christmas Stories* – 'Mrs.
Lirriper's Legacy').

Shanklin, Isle of Wight: Dickens visited
the resort in 1849. He set the scene of
the Lammles' mutual disillusionment on
Shanklin sands *(Mutual Friend)*.

Stevenage, Hertfordshire: Visited by
Dickens in 1861 for the purpose of meeting a local eccentric known as Mad Lucas
(used as Mopes in *Christmas Stories* –
'Tom Tiddler's Ground'). The White
Hart Inn is the Peal of Bells in the same
story.

Sudbury, Suffolk: Original of Eatanswill *(Pickwick)*.

Tewkesbury, Gloucestershire: the Hop
Pole Inn is the hostelry where Pickwick,
Ben Allen, and Bob Sawyer dine on their
way to Birmingham.

Tong, Shropshire: Village near Shifnal:
scene of the deaths of Little Nell and her
grandfather *(Curiosity Shop)*.

Towcester, Northamptonshire: The
Pomfret Arms is the inn (the Saracen's
Head) where Pickwick and his party stay
on their return from Birmingham and
meet the rival editors, Pott and Slurk,
who fight there.

Tunbridge Wells, Kent: An inland spa
where one of Dickens's sons was educated. Scene of Miss Twinkleton's early
romance with 'foolish Mr. Porters'
(Drood), and of one of Mr. Finching's
many proposals to Flora *(Dorrit)*.
Groombridge Wells (*Christmas Stories* –
'No Thoroughfare') is a combination of
Tunbridge Wells and the nearby Groombridge, Sussex.

Twickenham, Middlesex: Dickens
stayed there during the summer of 1838.
He made it the setting of the fatal duel
between Sir Mulberry Hawk and Lord
Frederick Verisopht *(Nickleby)*, and of
the Meagles' home *(Dorrit)*.

Venice, Italy: The first place visited by
the newly-rich Dorrits. Mr. Sparkler
courts Fanny Dorrit there. It was one of
Dickens's favourite continental cities.

Warwick, Warwickshire: Visited by
Dickens and H. K. Browne in 1838. Its
historic castle delights Mrs. Skewton on
the outing arranged by Dombey. It is
open to the public.

Windsor, Berkshire: Scene of John Pod-
ger's adventures in Pickwick's story
(Humphrey). Childhood home of Esther
Summerson *(Bleak House)*.

Winterslow, Wiltshire: See **Salisbury.**

Yarmouth, Norfolk: Seaside town visited
by Dickens in 1848. Daniel Peggotty
lives in an inverted boat on the beach,
and Yarmouth is the setting for many
other scenes in *Copperfield*.

York, Yorkshire: Dickens stayed at the
Black Swan in 1838. This cathedral city
is the setting for the story of 'The Five
Sisters of York' *(Nickleby)*. Visited by
John Chivery in search of a clue to the
Dorrit fortune.

Adelphi: Residential terrace built by the Adam brothers just east of Charing Cross in 1768; now demolished. One of Dickens's favourite districts during his boyhood employment at the blacking warehouse. The vanished Adelphi Hotel, at the corner of John Adam Street, was Osborne's, Wardle's favourite London hostelry (*Pickwick*). 'Mrs. Edson' attempts suicide from the Adelphi Terrace (*Christmas Stories* – 'Mrs. Lirriper's Lodgings'). David Copperfield lodges near the Adelphi, presumably at 15 Buckingham Street (demolished) where Dickens himself lodged briefly in youth. The Adelphi is the scene of Miss Wade's meeting with Blandois (*Dorrit*) and Martin Chuzzlewit lodges in a public house nearby.

Albany: Residential chambers near Burlington House in Piccadilly, where Fascination Fledgeby lives *(Mutual Friend)*.

Aldersgate Street, City: Site of the warehouse of Chuzzlewit and Son. John Jasper stays in a lodging house here on his London visits *(Drood)*.

Aldgate, City: Pickwick starts for Ipswich by coach from the Bull Inn. David Copperfield arrives at the Blue Boar, near the Bull, on his way to school at Salem House. Recognising that Florence Dombey's affections lie with Walter Gay, Toots consoles himself with a walk to Aldgate Pump, at the junction of Fenchurch and Leadenhall Streets.

'All the Year Round' Offices: The site is 26 Wellington Street, at the corner of Tavistock Street, Strand. Dickens occupied bachelor chambers above his editorial premises.

Angel, Islington: Famous tavern, now vanished, featured in *Twist*. The neighbourhood retains the name.

Arundel Street, Strand: No. 2 is the site of Chapman & Hall's former publishing premises (then 186 Strand) where Dickens bought the magazine containing his first story.

Astley's Royal Equestrian Amphitheatre stood on the site of 225–33 Westminster Bridge Road. The leading place of entertainment featuring equestrian acts, mentioned in *Curiosity Shop*, *Bleak House*, *Boz*, and elsewhere.

Athenaeum Club, Waterloo Place: Club founded in 1824, with a distinguished membership of learned men, to which Dickens was elected at the age of twenty-six. He and Thackeray ended their long estrangement there a few days before the latter's death.

Austin Friars, City: Old Martin Chuzzlewit's solicitor, Phipps, lives here.

Balls, Pond, north London: Home of the Perches (*Dombey*) and the Butlers (*Boz* – 'Sentiment').

Bank of England: Established 1694 and located in Threadneedle Street since 1734. Mentioned in *Boz*, *Pickwick*, *Uncommercial*, *Chuzzlewit*, *Mutual Friend*, *Dombey*, and *Dorrit*.

Barbican, City: The inn where Sim Tappertit and the Prentice Knights hold their meetings (*Rudge*) is placed in the Barbican area, which has been virtually rebuilt since the Second World War. Also mentioned in *Twist*, *Chuzzlewit*, and *Dorrit*.

Barnard's Inn, Holborn: A now-vanished Inn of Chancery where Herbert Pocket and Pip share chambers *(Expectations)*.

Barnet: See under Part One.

Bartholomew's Close, adjoining St. Bartholomew's Church, Little Britain: Pip sees Jaggers dealing with some of his importunate clients outside his office here *(Expectations)*.

Battle Bridge: The old name for King's Cross. Nearby stood Boffin's Bower

(*Mutual Friend*). Also mentioned in *Dombey*, *Twist*, and *Boz*.

Bayham Street, Camden Town: No. 16, now demolished, was the home of Dickens's parents and family in 1823. Probably the original of Bob Cratchit's (*Christmas Books* – 'Christmas Carol') and the lodging Traddles shares with the Micawbers (*Copperfield*).

Bedford Street, Strand: Warren's Blacking Warehouse was moved from Hungerford Stairs to the site of the present Civil Service Stores. This is where Dickens was humiliated by having to work in public view.

Bedlam: Actually Bethlehem Hospital, the lunatic asylum formerly in Moorfields, moved in Dickens's youth to Lambeth where the Imperial War Musuem now stands. Referred to in *Uncommercial* – 'Night Walks'.

Bell Alley, Coleman Street (now Mason's Avenue): Pickwick is taken to the house of Namby, sheriff's officer, here before being put in the Fleet.

Bell Yard, Carter Lane: Dickens rented an office at No. 5 while reporting for one of the Proctors' offices in Doctors' Commons.

Bell Yard, Fleet Street: see **Cursitor Street**.

Belle Sauvage Inn, Ludgate Hill: Now-vanished headquarters of Tony Weller (*Pickwick*).

Bentinck Street, Portland Place: The home of John Dickens and family was here in 1833–34.

Berners Street, Oxford Street: Scene of Dickens's encounter with an eccentric woman in white, disappointed in marriage, who may have been the original of Miss Havisham in *Expectations*.

Bethnal Green: In Dickens's day a squalid East End region where Sikes and Nancy first kept house (*Twist*), and Eugene Wrayburn is spied on by Bradley Headstone (*Mutual Friend*).

Beulah Spa, Norwood: Opened in 1831 as a fashionable resort, but its popularity was short-lived (*Boz* – 'Watkins Tottle').

Bevis Marks, City: Sampson and Sally Brass live at No. 10; and Dick Swiveller enjoys 'exceedingly mild porter' at the Red Lion (*Curiosity Shop*).

Billingsgate: London's centuries-old fish market in the City features in *Dorrit*, *Expectations* and *Uncommercial*.

Bishopsgate: City terminus for eastern counties coaches where Brogley, the broker, keeps shop (*Dombey*).

Black Bull Inn: See Holborn.

Blackfriars Bridge: One of the Thames bridges: the bridge referred to by Dickens was demolished in 1863. As a child he had crossed it frequently, going from the blacking warehouse to the Marshalsea.

Blackfriars Road: Southern approach to the Blackfriars Bridge. In this road David Copperfield was robbed of his luggage and thus compelled to walk to Dover.

Blackheath: Residential district of southeast London where Dickens places Salem House School attended by David Copperfield (but see **Salem House School**). David shelters behind the school for a night on his walk to Dover. John and Bella Rokesmith have their first married home in Blackheath (*Mutual Friend*). The Dover Mail is ascending Shooter's Hill, Blackheath, as *A Tale of Two Cities* opens. Harry Walmers's father lives at the Elms, Shooter's Hill (*Christmas Stories* – 'Holly-Tree'). Tony Weller retires to a public house in the district at the end of *Pickwick*.

Bleeding Heart Yard, near Hatton Garden: The Plornish family lives here, and it contains the factory of Doyce and Clennam (*Dorrit*).

Bloomsbury: A residential part of Holborn. Dickens's last London home, **Tavistock House** (q.v.) was here. Mr. and Mrs. Kitterbell live at 14 Great Russell Street, and their 'Bloomsbury Christening' takes place at the church of St. George, Hart Street, now Bloomsbury Way (*Boz.*) No. 29 Bloomsbury Square, burnt by the Gordon Rioters, was the home of Lord Mansfield, the Judge *(Rudge)*.

Boffin's Bower: Name given by Mrs. Boffin to the house where she and Boffin lived before coming into their fortune *(Mutual Friend)*. It was in Maiden Lane (now York Way), north London.

Bond Street: Fashionable West End shopping thoroughfare. The Uncommercial Traveller lodges here for a time in 'Arcadian London'.

Boot Tavern, Cromer Street, Bloomsbury: The present public house stands on the site of its former namesake, headquarters of the Gordon Rioters *(Rudge)*.

Borough: District immediately south of London Bridge, incorporating Southwark. At the White Hart (now demolished, though its yard remains) Pickwick meets Sam Weller, and Pickwick and Wardle discover Jingle and Rachael after their elopement. Bob Sawyer lives in Lant Street (q.v.). The first half of *Dorrit* is set in and around the Marshalsea Prison, of which there are visible remains adjoining the churchyard of St. George's, the church where Little Dorrit is christened and married. The George, London's only surviving galleried inn, features in *Dorrit*. David Copperfield lodges in Lant Street. The King's Bench Prison (q.v.) stood at the corner of the Borough Road.

Bouverie Street: A street off Fleet Street where, in 1846, Dickens was editor of the *Daily News* for less than three weeks.

Bow: In Dickens's day a rural district of east London where the Cheeryble brothers let a cottage to Mrs. Nickleby and her family.

Bow Street Police Court, Covent Garden: The Artful Dodger appears before the Bow Street magistrate *(Twist)*. Barnaby Rudge is questioned here after his arrest in the Gordon Riots. The page employed by David and Dora Copperfield is charged here with stealing Dora's watch. Bow Street Runners – London's first regular detective force, operating

from Bow Street – appear in the characters of Blathers and Duff *(Twist)*, and in *Expectations*, and Bow Street is the scene of *Boz* – 'Prisoners' Van'.

Brentford: See under Part One.

Brick Lane, Shoreditch: A mission hall here is the meeting place of the Brick Lane Branch of the United Grand Junction Ebenezer Temperance Association *(Pickwick)*.

Bridewell: Workhouse and reformatory near Blackfrairs, now demolished. Miss Miggs is appointed female turnkey *(Rudge)*.

Brig Place, India Docks: Captain Cuttle lodges with Mrs. MacStinger at No. 9 *(Dombey)*.

Britannia Theatre, Hoxton: Described in *Uncommercial* – 'Two Views of a Cheap Theatre'. Destroyed in 1940.

Brixton: In Dickens's time a prosperous suburb of south London where Pickwick carries out some of his researches.

Broad Court, off Bow Street, Covent Garden: Snevellici lives here *(Nickleby)*.

Brook Street, Grosvenor Square: Mrs. Skewton borrows a house belonging to a Feenix relative for Edith's wedding to Dombey. Mr. Dorrit stays at a hotel here.

Buckingham Street, Strand: David Copperfield lodges with Mrs. Crupp at No. 15, now demolished, where Dickens lodged in his youth.

Burlington Arcade: A fashionable shopping arcade off Piccadilly (*Uncommercial* – 'Arcadian London').

Camberwell: In Dickens's time a rural south London suburb. Home of the Malderton family (*Boz* – 'Horatio Sparkins'). Pickwick pursues researches there. Wemmick and Miss Skiffins are married at St. Giles's Church (*Expectations*). Ruth Pinch is employed as governess in the house of a brass and copper founder *(Chuzzlewit)*.

Camden Town: A rural area of northwest London, fast becoming urbanised in Dickens's time. His parents lodged at 16 Bayham Street (q.v.) and elsewhere.

Dickens lodged with Mrs. Roylance, the original of Mrs. Pipchin, in Little College Street in 1824, when his father was committed to the Marshalsea. The Evans family live in Camden Town (*Boz* – 'Miss Evans and the Eagle'). The effect of the new railway on the district is described in *Miscellaneous Papers* – 'Unsettled Neighbourhood'. See also **Staggs's Gardens.**

Carnaby Street, behind Regent Street, near Oxford Circus: The Kenwigs family lives here (*Nickleby*).

Castle Street, Holborn (now Furnival Street): Traddles lodges here (*Copperfield*).

Cateaton Street, City (now Gresham Street): Tom smart travels for Bilson and Slum's warehouse here (*Pickwick*).

Cavendish Square, Marylebone: Madame Mantalini's showroom and workrooms are in this neighbourhood (*Nickleby*). Silas Wegg has his pitch near the square (*Mutual Friend*).

Cecil Street, Strand: The Dickens family lodged here in 1832. Watkins Tottle has a lodging here (*Boz* – 'Watkins Tottle').

Chancery, Court of: Before the building of the Law Courts in the Strand, 1874, Chancery cases were heard at Lincoln's Inn Hall or Westminster Hall. Jarndyce and Jarndyce (*Bleak House*) was heard largely at the former but ended at the latter.

Chancery Lane, off Fleet Street: Much of the action of *Bleak House* is set here, old Tom Jarndyce having blown out his brains in a local coffee house. In Cook's Court (actually Took's Court) the Snagsbys live. Chichester Rents is the site of Krook's shop and the Sol's Arms. Watkins Tottle is imprisoned for debt in Cursitor Street (*Boz* – 'Watkins Tottle'). Pickwick is approached by a bail tout at Serjeant's Inn (now demolished).

Charing Cross: Regarded as the central point of London, it adjoins Trafalgar Square (laid out in 1829), formerly streets of houses, shops and, notably, the Golden Cross Hotel where Pickwick and

his friends begin their travels. David Copperfield also stays there and takes Peggotty there after meeting him on the steps of St. Martin-in-the-Fields (*Copperfield*).

Cheapside, City: Mould, the undertaker, lives here (*Chuzzlewit*). Pickwick meets Tony Weller for the first time at an inn in Grocers Hall Court to which he is taken by Sam (*Pickwick*).

Chelsea: Residential quarter of west London, on the river; semi-rural when Dickens married Catherine Hogarth in the Parish Church of St. Luke, 2 April 1836, Mr. and Mrs. Bayham Badger live here and Richard Carstone studies law under Mr. Badger's supervision (*Bleak House*). Dick Swiveller visits Sophia Wackles here before she throws him over for Mr. Cheggs (*Curiosity Shop*). Crummles shows Nicholas Nickleby a newspaper cutting: 'Crummles is NOT a Prussian, having been born in Chelsea'. The Royal East London Volunteers, in which Gabriel Varden is a sergeant, march to the Chelsea bun-house (*Rudge*). Bucket's aunt lives next-door-but-two to the bun-house (*Bleak House*).

Chichester Rents: See **Chancery Lane.**

Children's Hospital, Great Ormond Street, Bloomsbury: Probably the hospital to which Betty Higden's grandson Johnny is taken to die by Mrs. Boffin (*Mutual Friend*). Dickens took a keen interest in this hospital and helped to raise funds for it.

Church Street, Smith Square, Westminster (now Dean Stanley Street): Jenny Wren lives here with her drunken father (*Mutual Friend*).

City of London Theatre, Norton Folgate, Spitalfields, is featured in *Boz* – 'Making a Night of it'.

City Road, north London: The Micawbers lodge at Windsor Terrace (*Copperfield*). See also **Eagle Inn.**

Clapham: Residential quarter of south London. Mr. Gattleton lives at Rose Villa, Clapham Rise, and presents the ill-fated amateur theatricals there (*Boz*

– 'Mrs. Joseph Porter'). The Poor Relation lives in Clapham Road (*Christmas Stories* – 'Poor Relation').

Clare Market, Holborn: The market no longer exists but a building survives as an antique shop, calling itself The Old Curiosity Shop and erroneously imagined by most visitors to be the original referred to in the novel. However, Dickens is said to have done business with a bookbinder there. This area may have been the site of the slum, Tom-all-Alone's (*Bleak House*). The local gin shops are referred to in *Boz* – 'Gin-shops'. The area also features in *Pickwick* and *Rudge*.

Clerkenwell: A north London borough. Gabriel Varden lives at his locksmith's premises, the Golden Key; prisoners are released from the New Gaol by the Gordon Rioters (*Rudge*). Jarvis Lorry lives here (*Two Cities*). Mr. Venus has his taxidermist's business here (*Mutual Friend*), and Phil Squod plies his trade as a tinker (*Bleak House*). Near Clerkenwell Green Mr. Brownlow has his pockets picked outside a bookshop by Charley Bates and the Artful Dodger, and Oliver Twist is arrested; and it is near here that he is later recaptured for Fagin by Nancy.

Clifford's Inn, Fleet Street: Oldest of the Chancery Inns, established 1345. It figures in one of Jack Bamber's stories of the Inns of Court (*Pickwick*). Melchisedech, Old Smallweed's legal adviser, practises here (*Bleak House*). Tip Dorrit works here for a year as a clerk, John Rokesmith takes Mr. Boffin to Clifford's Inn to discuss his secretaryship *(Mutual Friend)*.

Cock Lane, Snow Hill, Holborn: Scene in 1762 of the Cock Lane Ghost manifestations; referred to in *Nickleby* and *Two Cities*.

Coldbath Fields, Islington: Site of the present Mount Pleasant post office, where formerly stood one of the harshest London prisons, mentioned in *Boz* – 'Prisoners' Van'.

Commercial Road, Whitechapel: Where Captain Cuttle buys a 'ballad of con-

siderable antiquity' about 'the courtship and nuptials of a promising coal-whipper with a certain "Lovely Peg" ' (*Dombey*). Also mentioned in *Uncommercial* – 'Wapping Workhouse'.

Cook's Court: See **Chancery Lane**.

Coram Street: See **Great Coram Street**.

Cornhill, City: Setting of several scenes in *Pickwick*. Freeman's Court, where Dodson and Fogg have their office, is now the Royal Exchange. The George and Vulture (q.v.) where Pickwick lodges is accessible from Cornhill. Bradley Headstone makes his appeal to Lizzie Hexam in St. Peter's churchyard (*Mutual Friend*). Bob Cratchit here slides down the ice 'at the end of a lane of boys, twenty times' on Christmas Eve (*Christmas Books* – 'Christmas Carol').

Covent Garden: One of Dickens's favourite districts from childhood. The Uncommercial Traveller always begins his journeys from here, and Dickens's own offices were at 26 (originally 11) Wellington Street. Pip stays at Hummums Hotel, at the corner of Russell Street, when warned by Wemmick not to go home, and it was probably the meeting place of 'the Finches of the Grove' (*Expectations*). Tom Pinch strolls here with Ruth (*Chuzzlewit*). Sikes remarks that fifty boythieves could be obtained every night in Covent Garden (*Twist*). David Copperfield lodges temporarily in the area with Miss Trotwood, buys a bouquet for Dora in the Market, and attends the theatre. Job Trotter spends the night before Pickwick's release in a vegetable basket here. John Dounce sometimes attends Covent Garden Theatre for half price 'to see two acts of a five-act play' (*Boz* – 'Misplaced Attachment').

Craven Street, Strand: Brownlow and Rose Maylie meet in a lodging-house here before the rescue of Oliver *(Twist)*.

Cross Keys Inn, Wood Street, Cheapside: A large coaching-office at which Dickens first arrived in London. Pip arrives here with Estella (*Expectations*), and Cavalletto is run over here (*Dorrit*). Also mentioned in *Uncommercial* and *Boz*.

Crown Inn, Golden Square: The favourite inn of Newman Noggs, now rebuilt and named the New Crown Inn (*Nickleby*).

Cursitor Street, Chancery Lane: John Dounce lives here with his three spinster daughters (*Boz* – 'Misplaced Attachment'). Watkins Tottle is detained in Solomon Jacobs's sponging-house (*Boz* – 'Watkins Tottle'). Skimpole takes Jarndyce, Ada, and Esther to 'Coavinses Castle', Bell Yard, the home of the late Neckett, to see Neckett's orphaned children (*Bleak House*). See also **Chancery Lane**.

Custom House, Lower Thames Street: Place of work of the late Mr. Bardell (*Pickwick*). Peepy Jellyby gets work here and prospers (*Bleak House*). Pip leaves his boat at a wharf nearby as part of the scheme to get Magwitch out of England (*Expectations*). Mrs. Clennam lives nearby (*Dorrit*). Florence Dombey reaches a wharf belonging to her father in Thames Street after her abduction by Good Mrs. Brown.

Cuttris's Hotel, James Street, Covent Garden, (now the Tavistock): This was Dickens's lodging when he came to London from Italy to give the first reading of 'The Chimes' to friends in 1844.

Deptford: A Thames dockside area where Toby Magsman recounts the story of Chops, the dwarf (*Christmas Stories* – 'Going into Society').

Devonshire Terrace, Marylebone Road: Dickens lived at No. 1 from 1839 to 1851. It was demolished in 1962, but the present office block incorporates a commemorative mural.

Doctors' Commons, City: The College of the Doctors of Law, founded 1768 and demolished 1867 to make way for the present Queen Victoria Street. Dickens rented an office in his reporting days at 5 Bell Yard, leading into the Commons. David Copperfield becomes

an articled clerk here. Jingle applies for his licence to marry Rachael Wardle, and Tony Weller obtains his second wife's legacy here (*Pickwick*). It is featured in *Boz* – 'Doctors' Commons'.

Doughty Street, Bloomsbury: Dickens lived at No. 48 from 1837 to 1839. *Pickwick* and *Twist* were finished here, *Nickleby* written, and *Rudge* begun. It is now the headquarters of the Dickens Fellowship and a Dickens library and museum.

Dover Road: The road starting from Blackheath taken by David Copperfield on the walk to his aunt's house in Dover.

Drummond Street, Euston: Miss Martin lives at No. 47 (*Boz* – 'Mistaken Milliner'). Dickens and other boys from Wellington House Academy used to pretend to be beggars here.

Drury Lane: Dickens recalled ordering a small plate of beef during his blacking warehouse days at Johnson's alamode beef house, Clare Court, now vanished; and David Copperfield relates the same experience. Dick Swiveller lodges over a tobacconist's shop here (*Curiosity Shop*). Crown Court, Russell Street, leads into Drury Lane Garden, once a graveyard, where Hawdon is buried in *Bleak House*. Miss Petowker, of the Crummles company, is 'of the Theatre Royal, Drury Lane' (*Nickleby*), and John Dounce frequents the theatre at half-price in *Boz* – 'Misplaced Attachment'.

Duke Street, St. James's: Twemlow lodges over a livery stable (*Mutual Friend*).

Dulwich: An old residential district south of the Thames to which Pickwick retires at the end of his adventures.

Eagle Inn, City Road, north London: It stands on the site of the former Eagle Pleasure Gardens featured in *Boz* – 'Miss Evans and the Eagle'.

Ely Place, Charterhouse Street, City: Agnes Wickfield stays here with the Waterbrooks, and David Copperfield calls on her to apologise for his drunken behaviour at the theatre.

Essex Street, Strand: Pip finds a lodging here for Magwitch, under the name of Provis *(Expectations)*.

Fenchurch Street, City: Bella Wilfer waits here in the Boffin coach for her father on her visit to his office *(Mutual Friend)*.

Fetter Lane, Holborn: Augustus Cooper lives here *(Boz* – 'Dancing Academy').

Field Lane, Holborn: Slum area cleared for the building of Holborn Viaduct in 1867. Fagin's den is nearby *(Twist)*.

Finchley: A north London suburb. After their escape from Newgate, Barnaby Rudge and his father spend a night here in a shed in a field. Toots journeys to Finchley to get some chickweed for Florence Dombey's bird. Kit Nubbles is employed by Mr. and Mrs. Garland at Abel Cottage *(Curiosity Shop)*. Dickens lodged at Cobley's Farm in 1843 while writing *Chuzzlewit* and got the idea for Mrs. Gamp there: the site is now occupied by No. 70 Queen's Avenue, which bears a commemorative tablet.

Fitzroy Street, Marylebone: Dickens lived with his parents at No. 15 (now 25) for part of 1832–3.

Fleet Prison. This stood in Farringdon Street, between Fleet Lane and the corner of Ludgate Hill. It was destroyed in the Gordon Riots *(Rudge)*, rebuilt, and used until 1842, when debtors were removed to the Queen's Bench. Pickwick is imprisoned in the Fleet for refusing to pay Mrs. Bardell's damages and costs.

Fleet Street: It is prominent in Dickens's writings, and was a neighbourhood he knew intimately. Like David Copperfield he used to haunt it when he had no money, to look in food shops. David takes Peggotty to see Mrs. Salmon's waxworks here. When going to Doctors' Commons with his aunt he pauses to watch the giant figures outside the church of St. Dunstan's-in-the-West striking the hours on the bells. St. Dunstan's is the church of 'The Chimes' *(Christmas Books)*. Jarvis Lorry works for Tellson's Bank by Temple Bar (actually Child's Bank) in *Two Cities*.

Fleet Street in the early morning is described in *Christmas Stories* – 'Holly-Tree'.

Folly Ditch: See Jacob's Island.

Foster Lane, City: No. 5 is considered to be the original of the home of Anthony and Jonas Chuzzlewit.

Foundling Hospital, Bloomsbury: Now demolished, it stood north of Guilford Street, on a site now known as Coram's Fields. Walter Wilding's story largely revolves round it *(Christmas Stories* – 'No Thoroughfare'). On a Sunday morning, while listening to the foundlings singing, the Meagles family decide to adopt Tattycoram *(Dorrit)*.

Fox under the Hill, near Charing Cross: This former riverside inn, where the Hotel Cecil now stands, was one of Dickens's haunts during his blacking warehouse days. He relates how he went there to watch the coal-heavers dancing.

Freeman's Court: See Cornhill.

Freemasons' Hall, Great Queen Street, Holborn: The scene of *Boz* – 'Public Dinners'. Dickens attended a farewell dinner here in 1867 before leaving for America.

Fresh Wharf, near London Bridge: Mrs. Gamp stands here, hoping to see Jonas and Mercy Chuzzlewit boarding the 'Ankwerks package'.

Fulham: Riverside district adjoining Chelsea. Florence Dombey stays here for a time at the home of Sir Barnet and Lady Skettles.

Furnival's Inn, Holborn: Former Inn of Court, demolished 1898. Dickens's chambers 1834–7, and first married home, were here. He began *Pickwick* here. Wood's Hotel sends meals by 'flying waiter' to Grewgious, across at Staple Inn, and Rosa Bud stays at the hotel on the night after her flight from Jasper *(Drood)*. John Westlock has chambers at the Inn *(Chuzzlewit)*.

Garraway's, Change Alley, Cornhill: One of the oldest City coffee houses, it was demolished in 1874 but is commemorated by a plaque. Pickwick writes his famous 'chops and tomata sauce' letter to Mrs. Bardell from here. Nadgett keeps watch on Jonas Chuzzlewit from Garraway's. The Poor Relation sits here every day (*Christmas Stories* – 'Poor Relation'), and it is where Jeremiah Flintwinch transacts his business (*Dorrit*). The Uncommercial Traveller describes it on a Sunday, 'bolted and shuttered hard and fast'.

George Inn, Southwark: See **Borough.**

George and Vulture Inn, Lombard Street: Pickwick is 'at present suspended' at the George and Vulture when dealing with the legal business of Bardell and Pickwick. The Pickwickians are served with subpoenas here and Pickwick is arrested, to return after his eventual release from prison. Winkle and Arabella stay at the George and Vulture after their marriage and are visited by Winkle's father. The inn still exists, much as Dickens knew it.

Gerrard Street, Soho: Dickens's uncle, Thomas Barrow, lived at No. 10 over a bookseller's. Jaggers lives at a stately, if dingy, house probably based on Barrow's *(Expectations)*.

Golden Cross: See Charing Cross.

Golden Square, Soho: It was going down in the world when Ralph Nickleby lived there, possibly at No. 7, now demolished. David Copperfield and Martha Endell find Little Em'ly at a house in a street off the square.

Goswell Road, City: Known in Dickens's time as Goswell Street, this is where Pickwick lodges in Mrs. Bardell's house and the misunderstanding occurs which leads to the breach of promise suit.

Gower Street, Bloomsbury: Dickens's parents lodged at No. 4 Gower Street North in 1823–4 and Mrs. Dickens unsuccessfully tried to conduct a young ladies' school.

Gray's Inn, Holborn: Dickens was a solicitor's clerk at 6 Raymond Buildings, 1828. Pickwick's legal adviser, Perker, has chambers in Gray's Inn Square, and Phunkey's chambers are in South Square,

where Dickens's employers were previously located. David Copperfield stays in Gray's Inn after his return to England, in a room over the archway. Flora Finching makes a rendezvous with Arthur Clennam in Gray's Inn Gardens (*Dorrit*). The Inn is disparagingly described in *Uncommercial* – 'Chambers'.

Great Coram Street, Bloomsbury (now Coram Street): Mrs. Tibbs has her boarding-house in the neatest house in the street (*Boz* – 'Boarding-House').

Great Marlborough Street, Soho: The police court here is probably that to which Bucket takes Esther Summerson before his search for Lady Dedlock (*Bleak House*).

Great Queen Street, Holborn: Dick Swiveller buys a pair of boots on credit here, thus closing his last-but-one avenue to the Strand (*Curiosity Shop*). The Freemasons' Hall (q.v.) stands here.

Great Russell Street, Bloomsbury: Charles Kitterbell (*Boz* – 'Bloomsbury Christening') lives at No. 14, now marked by a plaque.

Great Tower Street, City: Joe Willet enlists in the army through a recruiting sergeant at the Crooked Billet inn (*Rudge*).

Green Dragon, Westminster: The public house near Westminster Bridge where Robert Bolton, the 'gentleman connected with the press', regales his regular audience with anecdotes (*Mudfog* – 'Mr. Robert Bolton').

Green Lanes, Marylebone: The name by which the area now covered by Cleveland Street and the northern end of Newman Street was known in the late eighteenth century. The Gordon Rioters are meeting here when Gashford arrives (*Rudge*).

Greenwich: See under Part One.

Grocers Hall Court: See **Cheapside.**

Grosvenor Square, Mayfair: Tite Barnacle lives at 24 Mews Street (*Dorrit*). Lord Rockingham's house was one of those defended against the Gordon Rioters (*Rudge*).

Guildhall, City: The Court of Common Pleas (since rebuilt) is the scene of the Bardell and Pickwick trial. The giant figures of Gog and Magog figure prominently in *Master Humphrey's Clock*.

Guy's Hospital, Southwark: Bob Sawyer is a student at Guy's (*Pickwick*), where Mrs. Gamp's late husband died (*Chuzzlewit*).

Hammersmith: A south London riverside district. Matthew Pocket and his family live here; Pip is brought to study; Clara Barley completes her education at a school here and meets Herbert Pocket (*Expectations*). The Misses Crumpton's finishing establishment, Minerva House, is the setting for *Boz* – 'Sentiment'.

Hampstead: A village on the northern heights of London. Dickens stayed in lodgings in North End in April or May 1832. After the death of his sister-in-law, Mary Hogarth, in 1837, Dickens and his wife spent most of the summer at Collins's Farm (now Wyldes Farm) on the Heath. Hampstead was a favourite place for Dickens, who rode out with friends to Jack Straw's Castle, an inn overlooking the Heath. David Copperfield likes to walk to Hampstead after bathing in the Roman bath in the Strand. Dick Swiveller and Sophronia live in a little cottage at Hampstead 'which had in the garden a smoking-box, the envy of the civilised world', where he is visited by Chuckster with news from London (*Curiosity Shop*). One of Pickwick's papers for the Pickwick Club was 'Speculations on the Source of the Hampstead Ponds'; and Mrs. Bardell and friends are enjoying tea at the Spaniards Inn beside the Heath when she is lured by Jackson into custody in the Fleet Prison. The Gordon Rioters march to Ken Wood House (then the seat of Lord Mansfield) intending to destroy it, but are foiled (*Rudge*). Bill Sikes crosses the Heath on his flight after the murder of Nancy (*Twist*). Mrs. Griffin's establishment, in 'Haunted House' (*Christmas Stories*), is near Hampstead Ponds.

Hampstead Road (then New Road): In a terrace at the Mornington Crescent end stood Wellington House Academy, now demolished, attended by Dickens after his period at the blacking warehouse (see also **Pancras Road**). George Cruikshank's house, marked by a plaque, is at the end of the remaining part of the terrace.

Hampton: See under Part One.

Hanging Sword Alley, Whitefriars Street, Fleet Street: Jerry Cruncher and his family live here (*Two Cities*). Mr. George sees possibly fatal symbolism in the alley's name as he passes on his way to the Bagnets' (*Bleak House*).

Hanover Square, off Regent Street: At the Hanover Square Rooms, on the site of the present No. 4, several performances were given of Bulwer-Lytton's play *Not so Bad as we Seem* by Dickens's amateur company, and he later gave some of his readings here. Dickens's sister Fanny attended the Royal Academy of Music, then in Tenterden Street off the Square.

Harley Street, Marylebone: The Merdles live at the handsomest house in the Street (*Dorrit*).

Hart Street: See **Bloomsbury.**

Hatton Garden, Holborn: The Metropolitan Police office presided over by Fang was the Hatton Garden police court, of which one of the magistrates was a Mr. Laing. Oliver Twist is taken there on suspicion of robbing Mr. Brownlow. The Garden forms part of Phil Squod's beat as a tinker, and the Jellybys take furnished lodgings here (*Bleak House*).

Haymarket, off Pall Mall: Turveydrop is fond of dining at a French restaurant in the Opera Colonnade, now Royal Opera Arcade; Mr. George's shooting gallery is hereabouts (*Bleak House*).

Highgate: A village on the northern heights of London. Dickens and his parents lodged here in 1832 at a house next to the old Red Lion Inn. The inn has disappeared but a house near the site bears a plaque. Dickens's parents and his daughter Dora are buried in

Highgate Cemetery. Much of *David Copperfield* is set in the village: Mrs. Steerforth's house is said to be Church House, South Grove; Dr. Strong and Annie live in a cottage on the other side of the village, and David brings Dora here as his bride, while his aunt, Miss Trotwood, settles into the cottage next door. At the Archway toll Bucket first picks up the trail of Lady Dedlock on her last flight (*Bleak House*). Pickwick undertakes some of his unwearied researches in the area. Noah Claypole and Charlotte enter London under the old Archway; Bill Sikes strides up Highgate Hill on his way north after the murder of Nancy (*Twist*). In *Rudge*, Joe Willet, after his farewell to Dolly Varden, walks out to Highgate and meditates, 'but there were no voices in the bells to bid him turn' (a reference to Dick Whittington: Highgate is the place where he heard the bells of London summoning him back).

Hockley-in-the-Hole: A slum area now replaced by Clerkenwell Road and Rosebery Avenue. The Artful Dodger brings Oliver Twist through it on their way to Fagin's.

Holborn: A district deriving its name from a major thoroughfare running from Tottenham Court Road to the western boundary of the City of London. Mrs. Gamp lived in Kingsgate Street, High Holborn, above Poll Sweedlepipe's. At the now-vanished Black Bull, Holborn, she and Betsey Prig nurse Lewsome; Chicken Smivey lodges in Holborn (*Chuzzlewit*). Job Trotter runs up Holborn Hill to summon Perker when Mrs. Bardell is taken into the Fleet Prison; and Oliver Twist walks the same way with Sikes en route for the crib at Chertsey. Langdale's warehouses on Holborn Hill are burnt by the Gordon Rioters (*Rudge*). Esther Summerson sees her first 'London particular' (fog) in Holborn when conducted by Guppy to Thavies Inn (*Bleak House*).

Holloway: Holloway Road was the old route into London from the North, approaching Islington. Some of it was still semi-rural in the 1860s, but the

Wilfers lived between Holloway Road and the dustheaps at Battle Bridge (now King's Cross), 'a tract of suburban Sahara' (*Mutual Friend*).

Horn Coffee House: The Horn Tavern, 29 Knightrider Street, City, now occupies the site of the coffee house to which Pickwick sends out for 'a bottle or six' to celebrate Winkle's visit to the Fleet Prison.

Hornsey: A northern district of London where Pickwick conducts some of his unwearied researches. Betsey Trotwood's husband was born and buried here (*Copperfield*).

Horse Guards, Whitehall: After the loss of his legs Sim Tappertit is established by Gabriel Varden as a shoeblack under the archway near the Horse Guards (*Rudge*). Peggotty takes Mr. Dick to see the mounted guards (*Copperfield*).

Horsemonger Lane, Borough: Now Union Road. The notorious Horsemonger Lane gaol stood where there is now a recreation ground. In 1849 Dickens and 500,000 others witnessed the execution of the Mannings here, and he wrote a notable letter to *The Times* (13 November 1849) which helped to bring about the abolition of public hangings. He later based the character of Hortense on the French-born Mrs. Manning (*Bleak House*). Young John Chivery's mother keeps her 'snug tobacco business' at 5 Horsemonger Lane (*Dorrit*).

Hummums Hotel: See **Covent Garden.**

Hungerford Market: This stood on the site of Charing Cross station, was rebuilt in 1833, and demolished 1862. Hungerford Stairs, site of Warren's Blacking Warehouse, where the child Dickens worked, adjoined it. Mr. Dick lodges over a chandler's shop in the old market; the Micawbers leave from Hungerford Stairs to board their ship for Australia (*Copperfield*).

Hyde Park: The largest of London's parks. Dickens stayed briefly at several addresses in the neighbourhood: 16 Hyde Park Gate (1862), 16 Somers

Place (1865), 6 Southwick Place (1866), and 5 Hyde Park Place (1870), his last London address.

Inns of Court: The old English meaning of inn was lodging, rather than tavern, and the Inns of Court take their names from their former owners whose London abodes they were – e.g. Lincoln's Inn, residence of the Earls of Lincoln. They became associated with the law as the premises of the four societies with the exclusive right to call persons to the Bar – Inner Temple, Middle Temple, Lincoln's Inn, and Gray's Inn. There were also nine Chancery Inns – Clifford's, Clement's, Lyon's, Strand, New, Furnival's, Thavies, Staple, and Barnard's. For story references see under individual Inn names.

Iron Bridge: Popular name for Southwark Bridge, built 1818, replaced 1921. Little Dorrit liked to walk here.

Islington: A northern district of London, once the site of numerous tea-gardens and places of entertainment, and the ancient Angel Inn (q.v.). Porter and Smithers live here (*Boz* – 'Making a Night of it'). Tom Pinch settles here with Ruth, possibly at a house in Terrett's Place, Upper Street (*Chuzzlewit*). Morfin lives here (*Dombey*). Mrs. Lirriper's first lodgings are here. Characters in several stories pass through Islington, e.g. Joe Willet and Barnaby Rudge, the Artful Dodger and Oliver Twist, Oliver Twist and Mr. Brownlow, John Browdie (*Nickleby*), Esther Summerson and Bucket (*Bleak House*), and Nicholas Nickleby's coach, *en route* to Yorkshire, stops at the Peacock Inn (now demolished).

Jack Straw's Castle: See **Hampstead**.

Jacob's Island, Bermondsey: Known as an island because it was cut off by Folly Ditch, since filled in, it was a slum district in Dickens's day. Escaping over the roof-tops from Toby Crackit's home here, Bill Sikes is accidentally hanged (*Twist*). A housing estate here is named after Dickens.

Jerusalem Chambers, Clerkenwell: Site of Tetterby's house and shop, possibly in the vicinity of the present Jerusalem Passage (*Christmas Books* – 'Haunted Man').

Johnson Street, Somers Town, north London (now Cranleigh Street): Dickens lived with his parents at No. 29 in 1825, while a pupil at Wellington House Academy. A modern building occupies the site of their home.

Johnson's Court: The *Monthly Magazine* had its offices at 166 Fleet Street. Into its letter-box in the side door in Johnson's Court Dickens 'stealthily, one evening at twilight, with fear and trembling,' put his first submitted story.

Ken Wood: See **Hampstead**.

Kensington: Fashionable district of west London, where Gabriel Parsons and his sweetheart meet secretly in the Gardens (*Boz* – 'Watkins Tottle').

Kent Street (now Tabard Street): The start of the London–Dover Road, referred to by the Uncommercial Traveller as one of the worst-kept parts of London.

Kentish Town: Populous district of north London, whose oldest inhabitant David Copperfield declares Mrs. Kidgerbury, his charwoman, to have been. Also mentioned in *Rudge*.

King's Bench Prison: Debtors' prison, at the junction of Newington Causeway and Borough Road, demolished 1869. Micawber is imprisoned there (*Copperfield*). Madeline Bray and her father live in the Rules of the King's Bench, an adjoining area where more favoured debtors lodged (*Nickleby*). The Uncommercial Traveller contemplates the prison in 'Night Walks'. The earlier building was destroyed by the Gordon Rioters (*Rudge*). (See also **Borough**.)

King's Bench Walk: An open space in the Temple (q.v.) where Sydney Carton strolls before commencing his work for Stryver *(Two Cities)*.

Kingsgate Street: See **Holborn**.

Kingston: See under Part One.

Lambeth: Former slum district across the river from Westminster, where Peg

Sliderskew hides after stealing Gride's papers, and is tracked down by Squeers (*Nickleby*).

Lant Street, Borough: Dickens lodged here as a boy while his father was imprisoned in the Marshalsea nearby, and later used his room as the model for Bob Sawyer's lodging with Mrs. Raddle (*Pickwick*). David Copperfield also lodges in Lant Street. There is a Charles Dickens school there today.

Leadenhall Market, City, near Cornhill and Gracechurch Street: The Green Dragon in Bull's Head Passage is believed to have been the original of the Blue Boar, where Sam Weller writes his Valentine to Mary (*Pickwick*). Sol Gills's shop, the Wooden Midshipman (*Dombey*), is said to have been 157 Leadenhall Street, since demolished, and the offices of Dombey and Son are also conjectured to have been in the street.

Leather Lane, Holborn: Barnaby and Hugh escape along it from the mob burning Langdale's Distillery (*Rudge*).

Leicester Square: Known as Leicester Fields at the time of the Gordon Riots, provoked by the Catholic Relief Bill of Sir George Saville, whose mansion was here (*Rudge*). Mr. George's shooting gallery was nearby (*Bleak House*), and the original Old Curiosity Shop may have been in Green Street (now Orange Street) connecting the Square with Castle Street, near Charing Cross Road. Dickens celebrated the completion of *Pickwick* by giving a dinner at the former Prince of Wales Hotel in Leicester Place, north of the Square.

Limehouse: Dockside quarter of east London. Dickens's godfather, Christopher Huffam, or Huffham, lived here. The Six Jolly Fellowship Porters Tavern was The Grapes, in Narrow Street, and Rogue Riderhood and the Hexams live nearby in Limehouse Hole (*Mutual Friend*). Near here Captain Cuttle encounters Jack Bunsby on his way to marry Mrs. MacStinger (*Dombey*). The Uncommercial Traveller describes the leadmills near Limehouse Church.

Lincoln's Inn: One of the oldest Inns of Court. *Bleak House* opens in the Court of Chancery, held here at the time, and this is the scene of the interminable Jarndyce and Jarndyce lawsuit; the offices of Kenge and Carboy are in Old Square; Krook's Rag and Bottle Warehouse is in Chichester Rents, near New Square (*Bleak House*). Pickwick and Perker visit Serjeant Snubbin in Old Square. Dickens was a clerk to a solicitor named Molloy in New Square. At No. 58 Lincoln's Inn Fields John Forster, Dickens's biographer and close friend, lived: his house, still standing, is Tulkinghorn's in *Bleak House*. Betsey Trotwood lodges at a private hotel in the Fields (*Copperfield*).

Little Britain: See **Bartholomew Close.**

Little College Street: See **Camden Town.**

Little Russell Street, Bloomsbury: The Albion Hotel is the scene of the bibulous celebrations of Potter and Smithers (*Boz* – 'Making a Night of it').

Lombard Street, City: Maria Beadnell, Dickens's first love, lived with her parents next door to the bank of Smith, Payne, and Smith, where her father was manager. The George and Vulture (q.v.) can be approached from Lombard Street. Barbox Brothers' office was in the vicinity (*Christmas Stories* – 'Mugby Junction').

London Bridge: In his days at Warren's Blacking Warehouse Dickens was fond of passing his spare time on London Bridge, an experience he relates through the young David Copperfield: 'I was wont to sit in one of the stone recesses, watching the people go by.' This was old London Bridge, the second being designed by Rennie and not opened for traffic until 1831; it has now been transported to America, and replaced by a new bridge. David Copperfield first sees the bridge when travelling to school at Blackheath, with Mr. Mell, whose old mother lived in an almshouse across the bridge. On the bridge, later, David meets 'the Orfling', a little servant who may have been based on the same original as 'the Marchioness' in *Curiosity Shop*, and tells her stories mostly proceeding from his own imagination about the riverside area. The Pickwickians, accompanied by Ben Allen, return across London Bridge after Bob Sawyer's memorable supper party in Lant Street. Pip crosses old London Bridge on his way from the interview in which he opens Miss Havisham's eyes to the wreck she has made of his life and Estella's (*Expectations*). Nancy has her fatal conversation with Rose Maylie on the steps of the new bridge, on the Surrey bank, near St. Saviour's Church (*Twist*). From the steps at the opposite end, on the Middlesex side, Jonas Chuzzlewit sinks the bundle of bloodstained clothes after murdering Tigg. Haredale, while in hiding, travels from Westminster to London Bridge by water, to avoid possible encounters in the busy streets (*Rudge*). London Bridge Station, built in 1851 on the site of St. Thomas's Hospital, is mentioned in *Reprinted* – 'A Flight'.

London Coffee House: This was on the site of 42 Ludgate Hill. Here Arthur Clennam stays on the dreary Sunday evening after his return to England, listening to the monotonous sound of church bells (*Dorrit*).

London Docks: Described in *Uncommercial* – 'Bound for the Great Salt Lake.' Mortimer Lightwood combs the docks for news of John Harmon (*Mutual Friend*).

London Hospital, Whitechapel: Founded 1741. Sally Brass buys Dick Swiveller an office-stool in an open street market just opposite the Hospital (*Curiosity Shop*).

London Tavern, Bishopsgate Street (now Bishopsgate): Now demolished. The first annual dinner of the General Theatrical Fund was held here in 1836, chaired by Dickens, who was also in the Chair at a similar dinner in 1841. The public meeting of the United Metropolitan Improved Hot Muffin and

Crumpet Baking and Punctual Delivery Company is held here (*Nickleby*).

London Wall, City: Clennam and Doyce share a house near London Wall (*Dorrit*). Tom Pinch loses himself here when seeking Furnival's Inn, and finds himself at the Monument (*Chuzzlewit*).

Long Acre, stretching between St. Martin's Lane and Great Queen Street: Dick Swiveller finds himself unable to pay for a meal he has eaten here, and is obliged to regard the street as being henceforth closed to him (*Curiosity Shop*). Dickens gave his first series of paid public readings at the former St. Martin's Hall in 1858.

Long's Hotel, 15 New Bond Street: Cousin Feenix stays here (*Dombey*).

Ludgate Hill: Until 1864, when it was widened, only the lower part was known as Ludgate Hill, the upper being Ludgate Street. David and his aunt are accosted here by her renegade husband (*Copperfield*).

Lyon's Inn: One of the Inns of Chancery, in Newcastle Street, Holborn, it was demolished in 1863. Mentioned in *Uncommercial* – 'Chambers'.

Magpie and Stump: The meeting-place of Lowten and his friends (*Pickwick*) may have been the George IV (demolished in 1896 and later rebuilt) or the Old Black Jack, both in Portsmouth Street, Lincoln's Inn Fields. Another Magpie and Stump stands opposite the Old Bailey.

Maiden Lane, near Battle Bridge, now King's Cross: See **Boffin's Bower**.

Maiden Lane, Strand, between Bedford Place and Southampton Street: See **Strand**.

Manchester Buildings, Westminster: Gregsbury, M.P., lives in this block of chambers and Nicholas Nickleby applies to him here for a situation as secretary.

Mansion House, City: During the Gordon Riots the Lord Mayor is visited at the Mansion House by Haredale, who needs his help to get Rudge imprisoned; Langdale, the distiller, also arrives for aid, fearing the destruction of his premises (*Rudge*). Kit Nubbles, arrested on a false charge, is taken to the Mansion House police court (*Curiosity Shop*). Nicodemus Dumps leaves the Mansion House en route for the Kitterbells' in the Admiral Napier omnibus (*Boz* – 'Bloomsbury Christening').

Marshalsea Prison: See **Borough.**

Marylebone Church: Next door to the site of Dickens's home at No. 1 Devonshire Terrace stands St. Marylebone Parish Church, built in 1817. This is generally considered to be the church at which Paul was christened and Dombey married to Edith Granger (*Dombey*).

Mile End, east London: The scene of Tony Weller's remarks to Pickwick on the life of tollpike keepers. Mrs. Jellyby has 'Borrioboolan business' at Mile End (*Bleak House*).

Millbank: The riverside thoroughfare between Lambeth and Vauxhall Bridges. Lambeth Bridge is on the site of the horse-ferry, and the Penitentiary site is now occupied by the Tate Gallery. The ultimate destiny of the mutilated Sim Tappertit is to marry the widow of a rag-and-bone merchant of Millbank (*Rudge*).

Mincing Lane, City: Herbalists and tea-merchants abounded here in Dickens's time. Rumpty Wilfer works here in the firm of Chicksey, Veneering and Stobbles (*Mutual Friend*).

Monmouth Street: Continuation of St. Martin's Lane. In Dickens's day the headquarters of second-hand clothing shops. Described in *Boz* – 'Meditations in Monmouth-street'.

Montague Place, Bloomsbury: The home of Perker (*Pickwick*).

Montague Square, Marylebone: Jorkins, Spenlow's partner, lives in a dilapidated house here (*Copperfield*).

Monument: Erected in 1667 as near as possible to the place where the Fire of London had broken out. Dickens (and David Copperfield) used to gaze at the golden flame on the top of it from Lon-

don Bridge. Mrs. Todgers's boarding-house is almost in the shadow of the Monument, and Tom Pinch is disillusioned on hearing the comments of the guide (*Chuzzlewit*). John Willet's idea of a pleasant day in London is to go to the top of the Monument and sit there (*Rudge*). Dorrit's solicitors, Peddle and Pool, have their premises in Monument Yard.

Mount Pleasant, Islington: The way to Mr. Brownlow's house at Pentonville lay through Mount Pleasant (*Twist*). The Smallweed family lived nearby, 'in a rather ill-favoured and ill-savoured neighbourhood' (*Bleak House*).

Mutton Hill, often known as Mutton Lane, was the part of Vine Street between Hatton Garden and Clerkenwell Green. The back door of the police court to which Oliver Twist was taken was beneath an archway leading out of Mutton Hill. The Field Lane Ragged School, one of Dickens's favourite charities, was here.

New River Head, Islington: Off the present Rosebery Avenue. Uriah Heep lodges in the district (*Copperfield*).

Newgate, City: Newgate Market was the main meat market for London until the Central Meat Market was opened at Smithfield in 1855. Peepy Jellyby gets lost here (*Bleak House*). The old Newgate prison was destroyed by fire in the Gordon Riots (*Rudge*). Rebuilt in 1782, it provided the attraction of public executions. Lord George Gordon died there in 1793. Fagin has his last interview with Oliver Twist in the condemned cell, and is later executed here. Kit Nubbles is imprisoned here on a false charge (*Curiosity Shop*), Wemmick takes Pip into the prison (*Expectations*), which is described in detail in *Boz* – 'Visit to Newgate' and 'Criminal Courts'. In Newgate Street Sam Weller tells Pickwick the story of the sausage steam-engine inventor.

Newman Street, north of Oxford Street: Turveydrop lives at No. 26, and is joined there by Prince and Caddy after their marriage (*Bleak House*).

Norfolk Street, off Fitzroy Square, Marylebone (now Cleveland Street): The Dickens family lodged at No. 10 (now 22) in 1829–31 and, more briefly, in Dickens's infancy.

Norfolk Street, Strand: Here are the boarding-houses of Mrs. Lirriper and Miss Wozenham (*Christmas Stories* – 'Mrs. Lirriper's Lodgings and 'Mrs. Lirriper's Legacy').

Norwood: A residential district south of London, semi-rural in Dickens's youth. James Carker lives here in an unpretenious but tasteful house (*Dombey*). Spenlow also lives here, and here David Copperfield first meets Dora. Gabriel Parsons has a pleasant villa at Norwood (*Boz* – 'Watkins Tottle').

Obelisk: A south London landmark which once stood at the centre of St. George's Circus, now in the grounds of the Imperial War Museum, Lambeth Road. Dickens had his clothes valued for debt repayment at a house near the Obelisk when the Dickens home was sold up and his father imprisoned. At the same point David Copperfield's luggage and money are stolen by a young man with a donkey-cart as he travels towards Dover. The Gordon Rioters gather at St. George's Fields (*Rudge*). Solomon Pell lives in the area favoured by the attorneys to the Commissioners of the Insolvent Court, more or less within a radius of one mile from the Obelisk (*Pickwick*).

Old Bailey: The street runs from Ludgate Hill to Newgate Street. At the Old Bailey Court (now the Central Criminal Court) Charles Darnay is tried (*Two Cities*). Bailey Junior is said to have become thus nicknamed 'in contradistinction perhaps to the Old Bailey' (*Chuzzlewit*).

Old Black Jack Inn: See Magpie and Stump.

Old Curiosity Shop: See Leicester Square and Clare Market.

Old Kent Road: David Copperfield's way to Dover lies through it. At Dolloby's shop he sells his waistcoat to buy food. In the New Kent Road, set in a public garden, is a modern reconstruction, placed there by the Dickens Fellowship, of the Triton statue at which David made his first halt. Dr. Marigold takes the child Sophy to the Asylum for the Deaf and Dumb for training (*Christmas Stories* – 'Doctor Marigold').

Old Square: See Lincoln's Inn.

Old Street: Formerly called Old Street Road. Between City Road and Shoreditch Church. Mrs. Guppy, mother of Esther Summerson's admirer, lives at 302 Old Street Road (*Bleak House*).

Olympic Theatre: In Wych Street, Strand, it was opened in 1806 and burnt down in 1849. Madame Vestris, dancer and actress-manager, controlled it when Dickens wrote *Young Gentlemen* – 'Theatrical Young Gentleman'. The Olympic was known as the 'Pic', as the Victoria was the 'Vic'.

Opera Colonnade: See Haymarket.

Osnaburgh Terrace, Regent's Park: Dickens stayed at No. 9 in 1844.

Oxford Market: This was north of Oxford Street between Great Tichfield Street and Great Portland Street. Towlinson, Dombey's footman, aspires to lead 'an altered and blameless existence as a serious greengrocer' there (*Dombey*).

Oxford Street: Known in Dickens's day as the Oxford Road, and largely residential for much of the nineteenth century. Esther, Ada, Richard, and John Jarndyce have a 'cheerful lodging' nearby (*Bleak House*). Gabriel Parsons walks up and down the street for a week, in tight boots, hoping to meet his sweetheart (*Boz* – 'Watkins Tottle'). Micawber fancies a lodging at the west end, facing Hyde Park (*Copperfield*). Clennam and Meagles search the streets nearby for Miss Wade (*Dorrit*). Nicholas Nickleby first sees Madeline Bray at the General Agency Office, and meets Mr. Charles Cheeryble at the same spot. Mrs. Nickleby relates how Kate's grandmama once, turning into Oxford Street, collided with her hairdresser escaping from a bear: or it may have been the other way round.

Palace Yard, Westminster: Julius Handford (John Harmon) gives the Inspector the address of the Exchequer Coffee House, Old Palace Yard *(Mutual Friend)*.

Pall Mall: Nearby are the offices of the Anglo-Bengalee Disinterested Loan and Life Assurance Company, whose chairman, Tigg Montague, lives in Pall Mall *(Chuzzlewit)*. Twemlow spends a day in the window of his club here canvassing for Veneering *(Mutual Friend)*. Chops, the dwarf, lodged in Pall Mall and 'blazed away' his fortune *(Christmas Stories* – 'Going into Society').

Pancras Road: Running northward between St. Pancras and King's Cross Stations, neither of which existed in the first half of the nineteenth century. At old St. Pancras Church (still to be seen) Jerry Cruncher digs up what he imagines to be the coffin of Roger Cly *(Two Cities)*. The churchyard contains the tombstone of Dickens's schoolmaster at Wellington House Academy (see **Hampstead Road**).

Paper Buildings: See **Temple**.

Park Lane, Mayfair: Clennam and Meagles lodge nearby while searching for Tattycoram and Miss Wade *(Dorrit)*. Outside a hotel off Park Lane Nicholas Nickleby assaults Sir Mulberry Hawk for insulting language used about Kate.

Parliament, Houses of: The old Houses of Parliament were burnt down in 1834, with the exception of Westminster Hall. In 1855 Dickens, in his only political speech, attributed the fire to 'the burning up of the discarded notched sticks upon which exchequer accounts were kept . . . worn-out, worm-eaten bits of wood.'

Parliament Street, Westminster: Dickens recalled how, during his blacking warehouse days, he went into the Red Lion public house in Parliament Street and ordered a glass of ale, which was served to him with kindness. David

Copperfield does the same. The Red Lion still stands.

Peacock Inn, Islington: The narrator of 'Holly-Tree' *(Christmas Stories)* starts off from the Peacock (now demolished) on his journey to the North. Nicholas Nickleby leaves London with Squeers from the same point, a depot for the York coaches.

Peckham: South London district east of Camberwell. Feeder, in order to study 'the dark mysteries of London', proposes to stay with two maiden ladies in Peckham; Walter Gay is a weekly boarder at a Peckham school *(Dombey)*.

Penton Place: Between Kennington Park Road and Newington Butts. Guppy lives at No. 87 *(Bleak House)*.

Pentonville: A new and fashionable residential district of north London in the early nineteenth century. Brownlow lives here *(Twist)*. Pancks lodges at Rugg's Agency *(Dorrit)*. Nicodemus Dumps rents a first floor furnished which commends itself to him because it commands 'a dismal prospect of an adjacent churchyard' *(Boz* – 'Bloomsbury Christening'). Micawber's lodging is presumbly in the part of Pentonville fronting the City Road *(Copperfield)*.

Petersham: In Dickens's day a rural district, adjoining Richmond and Ham. Dickens spent the summer of 1839 at Elm Cottage, now Elm Lodge, and had lodged in Petersham in 1836 while writing *The Village Coquettes*. He gave his address there as 'Mrs. Denman's', which was perhaps the Dysart Arms, whose landlord was John Denman.

Piccadilly: Largely a fashionable residential area in Dickens's day. Piccadilly Circus was known as Regent's Circus. Fascination Fledgeby lives at Albany (q.v.) and the Lammles are married at St. James's Church *(Mutual Friend)*. Micawber, in a burst of optimism, envisages himself and his family 'in the upper part of a house, over some respectable place of business – say in Piccadilly' *(Copperfield)*. The White Horse Cellar, a coaching inn, stood at the corner of

Dover Street. Esther Summerson meets Guppy at the inn (*Bleak House*). On the site of the present Piccadilly Hotel stood St. James's Hall, where Dickens gave his last reading in March 1870.

Polygon, Somers Town: A down-at-heel block of north London houses (now demolished) where John Dickens and his family lived in the late 1820s at No. 17. Harold Skimpole lives here *(Bleak House)*.

Portland Place, Marylebone: The large family of Tapkinses live here and are 'At Home, Wednesdays, Music' *(Mutual Friend)*.

Portman Square, Marylebone: The Podsnaps live 'in a shady angle' adjoining the Square *(Mutual Friend)*.

Putney: South of Fulham, on the Surrey side of the Thames, a rural district in Dickens's time. Dora Spenlow's aunts, with whom she goes to live after her father's death, reside here, and Dora and David Copperfield may have been married in St. Mary's Church, on the riverside. Arthur Clennam strolls over Putney Heath en route for the Meagleses', to enjoy sunshine and exercise *(Dorrit)*.

Quadrant, The: The curve of Regent Street between Vigo Street and Piccadilly Circus. Its arcades (demolished 1848) are mentioned in *Boz* – 'Misplaced Attachment'.

Queen Charlotte's Hospital: In Marylebone Road in Dickens's time, now removed to Goldhawk Road. It is applied to by Miss Tox for a suitable wet nurse for little Paul Dombey.

Queen Square, Bloomsbury, behind the present Southampton Row: John Jarndyce places Richard Carstone in a furnished lodging here *(Bleak House)*.

Quilp's Wharf: Unidentified precisely by Dickens, it has been speculated that it may have been old Butler's Wharf, below Tower Bridge on the Surrey side *(Curiosity Shop)*.

Ratcliff: East End riverside district, notable for crime in the early nineteenth century. Nancy lives there before moving to Field Lane (*Twist*). The *Cautious Clara* is lying hard by Ratcliff when Florence visits Captain Bunsby *(Dombey)*.

Raymond Buildings: See **Gray's Inn.**

Red Lion, Highgate: See **Highgate.**

Red Lion, Parliament Street: See **Parliament Street.**

Red 'Us: The Red House, a popular pleasure resort of Londoners, it was a riverside tavern, on the Battersea shore (*Boz* – 'The River').

Regent Street: Completed in 1820, two years before Dickens came to London. Lord Frederick Verisopht lives here *(Nickleby)*.

Regent's Canal, Regent's Park: Watkins Tottle may have drowned himself here after his disappointment in love (*Boz* – 'Watkins Tottle').

Regent's Park: Dickens lived for a time at 3 Hanover Terrace, writing part of *Great Expectations*; and 1 Devonshire Terrace (q.v.), his home for many years, was almost opposite the York Gate to the park.

Richmond: See under Part One.

Rolls Yard, Symond's Inn: Now demolished, this opened out of Chancery Lane, and was a spot where Snagsby 'loved to lounge about of a Sunday afternoon' *(Bleak House)*.

Roman Bath, Strand Lane, Strand: More likely of seventeenth century origin, it was popular with gentlemen who had dined too well the night before, or who wanted a refreshing dip. Dickens often used it, as does David Copperfield.

Rookery of St. Giles's: There were many 'rookeries' in London, haunts of filth and vice, but that of St. Giles's was the most notorious. Removed when New Oxford Street was made in 1844–7, it is described in *Reprinted* – 'On Duty with Inspector Field'.

Royal Exchange: The old Exchange was burnt down in 1838 and rebuilt in 1844. Pip is surprised by the 'fluey' men sitting there, whom he takes to be great merchants; Herbert Pocket frequents 'Change *(Expectations)*.

Sackville Street, off Piccadilly: Lammle's bachelor home and temporary married quarters *(Mutual Friend)*.

Saffron Hill: A notorious criminal district, obliterated by the development of Holborn. The Three Cripples Inn, patronised by Fagin and his associates, stood here until about 1860 *(Twist)*. Phil Squod has a tinker's round here *(Bleak House)*.

St. Andrew's Church, Holborn: One of the old City churches still in existence, mentioned in *Twist, Copperfield*, and *Bleak House*.

St. Bartholomew's Hospital, Smithfield: The oldest London hospital. Jack Hopkins is a student here *(Pickwick)*. Betsey Prig nurses here *(Chuzzlewit)*. Cavalletto is taken to Bart's after being run over *(Dorrit)*.

St. Clement Dane's Church, Strand: Scene of Mrs. Lirriper's wedding *(Christmas Stories – 'Mrs. Lirriper's Lodgings')*.

St. Dunstan's-in-the-West: Church of 'The Chimes' *(Christmas Books)*. See also Fleet Street.

St. George's Church, Southwark: See Borough.

St. George's Church, Hart Street, Bloomsbury: See Bloomsbury.

St. Giles's: Criminal slumland incorporating the Rookery (q.v.) and Seven Dials (q.v.).

St. James's Church, Piccadilly: Alfred Lammle marries Sophronia Akersham here *(Mutual Friend)*.

St. James's Park: One of the Royal parks, adjoining Buckingham Palace. Ralph Nickleby is accosted by Brooker while sheltering here in a thunderstorm. Mark Tapley arranges a meeting here between young Martin Chuzzlewit and Mary Graham. It was 'darkly whispered' that Sally Brass, enlisted as a private in the Guards, had been seen on sentry duty in the Park *(Curiosity Shop)*.

St. James's Square, off Pall Mall: Twemlow frequently meditates here on his social status *(Mutual Friend)*. The Gordon Rioters threw loot, including the keys of Newgate, into the pond then in the centre of the Square *(Rudge)*.

St. James's Street, off St. James's Square: In chambers on the Piccadilly side lives the narrator of the Trial for Murder *(Christmas Stories – 'Doctor Marigold')*. In a hotel here Mrs. Sparsit tells Bounderby of Louisa's elopement *(Hard Times)*.

St. James's Theatre: Now vanished from a corner of St. James's Square, it was the scene of the productions of Dickens's early plays, *The Strange Gentleman* and *The Village Coquettes* (1836) and *Is She his Wife?* (1837).

St. John's Church, Smith Square, Westminster: A fine and rare exercise in early Georgian baroque, Dickens thought it 'a very hideous church . . . generally resembling some petrified monster, frightful and gigantic, on his back with its legs in the air.' See also **Church Street.**

St. Luke's Church, Chelsea: See Chelsea.

St. Martin-in-the-Fields, Trafalgar Square: On the church steps, before Trafalgar Square was completed in 1841, David Copperfield encounters Peggotty returning from his search for Little Em'ly. Some of Dickens's childhood recollections of this neighbourhood, notably of a special pudding shop, are worked into the novel. The Uncommercial Traveller has a horrifying experience with a pauper on the church steps *(Uncommercial – 'Night Walks')*.

St. Mary Axe, City: Now a modern commercial area, it held the ancient office of Pubsey and Co., supervised by Riah. Lizzie Hexam and Jenny Wren often sit in the roof-garden *(Mutual Friend)*.

St. Mary-le-Strand Church: Dickens's parents were married here in 1809, when John Dickens was a clerk in Somerset House near the church.

St. Olave's Church, Hart Street: Referred to by the Uncommercial Traveller as St. Ghastly Grim; nevertheless, one of his favourite London churchyards (*Uncommercial* – 'The City of the Absent').

St. Pancras Church: See Pancras Road.

St. Paul's Cathedral: It features in passing in several of the novels, including *Nickleby*, *Two Cities*, *Copperfield*, *Mutual Friend*, *Rudge*, *Expectations*, *Dombey*, etc. Doctors' Commons (q.v.) was joined to St. Paul's Churchyard by Paul's Chain.

St. Peter's Church, Cornhill: Bradley Headstone pleads with Lizzie Hexam in the churchyard to marry him *(Mutual Friend)*.

Salem House School: It is sited near Blackheath (*Copperfield*), but was based on Wellington House Academy (q.v.).

Saracen's Head, Snow Hill: The inn where Squeers has his London headquarters, adjoining St. Sepulchre's Church (*Nickleby*). Demolished in 1868: the site is now occupied by a police station.

Scotland Yard, Westminster: Headquarters of the Metropolitan Police from 1829 until 1967. Its earlier appearance is described in *Boz* – 'Scotland-yard'.

Serjeant's Inn, Chancery Lane: Now demolished: Pickwick is taken there for commission to the Fleet prison after refusing to pay Mrs. Bardell's costs and damages.

Seven Dials: Once a notorious criminal slum district, where seven streets converge on St. Giles's Circus. Described in *Boz* – 'Seven Dials' and 'Meditations in Monmouth-street'. Mantalini is last discovered here by Nicholas and Kate Nickleby, turning a mangle.

Shadwell: Dockside district of low repute in Dickens's time. He visited an opium den here, and made it the setting for Princess Puffer's (*Drood*). The Mormon emigrant ship *Amazon* lies near Shadwell Church in *Uncommercial* – 'Bound for the Great Salt Lake'.

Shooter's Hill: See Blackheath.

Six Jolly Fellowship Porters: See Limehouse.

Smith Square, Wesminster: See Church Street and St. John's Church.

Smithfield: London's wholesale meat market, near Holborn Viaduct. It is referred to in *Twist*, and it is in this neighbourhood that Barnaby helps his father to get rid of his fetters after his release from Newgate by the Gordon Rioters.

Snow Hill: Once a busy route from Holborn down into Farringdon Street. The Saracen's Head (q.v.) stood at the top. It is referred to principally in *Twist*, *Nickleby*, *Dorrit*, and *Rudge*.

Soho: A cosmopolitan district, bounded by Regent Street, Oxford Street, Charing Cross Road, and Shaftesbury Avenue. Houses in Carlisle Street and Greek Street have been claimed as the original of Dr. Manette's (*Two Cities*). Obenreizer's house is on the north side of Soho Square (*Christmas Stories* – 'No Thoroughfare'). Caddy Jellyby and Esther Summerson have a rendezvous in the Square (*Bleak House*). At Carlisle House, near Carlisle Street, Emma Haredale encounters Gabriel Varden at a masquerade *(Rudge)*.

Sol's Arms: The Old Ship, on the corner of Chancery Lane and Chichester Rents, was the original of this tavern where Little Swills entertains in *Bleak House*.

Somers Town: A cosmopolitan district north of Euston Station. See also Polygon.

Somerset House, Strand: Built in the eighteenth century for a ducal palace, it has long housed government record departments. Dickens's father and uncle, Thomas Culliford Barrow, were clerks there, as is Minns in *Boz* – 'Mr. Minns and his Cousin'.

Southampton Street, now Southampton Place, connecting High Holborn with Bloomsbury Square: Grewgious finds lodgings for Miss Twinkleton and Rosa Bud at Billickins's, possibly at No. 20, next to the archway leading to Barter Street *(Drood)*.

Southwark: See **Borough**.

Southwark Bridge: One of the Thames bridges, built of iron in 1815–19. John Chivery proposes to Little Dorrit on it. Southwark Bridge and London Bridge mark the limits of Gaffer Hexam's river beat in search of corpses *(Mutual Friend)*.

Spa Fields: Once the name for an open area near the present Mount Pleasant post office, used as winter quarters by travelling showmen. Old Maunders keeps his eight dwarfs and eight giants in a cottage here *(Curiosity Shop)*.

Spaniards, Hampstead: An historic inn, little changed from the day of Dickens, who used to walk there across the Heath. Its tea garden is where Jackson, of Dodson and Fogg, finds Mrs. Bardell and lures her away to the Fleet Prison *(Pickwick)*.

Staggs's Gardens: A fictitious part of Camden Town (q.v.), typical of the district at the time, featured in *Dombey*, as home of the Toodle family.

Staple Inn, Holborn: This ancient Inn of Chancery was established in the fourteenth century. The Tudor shops which form its frontage – a unique one in central London – date from about 1545. Grewgious lives in chambers here, entertains Rosa Bud after her flight from Cloisterham, and conspires with Tartar and Crisparkle to outwit Jasper; while in another set of chambers, near Tartar's, Neville and Helena Landless lodge *(Drood)*. Staple Inn received severe damage in the Second World War, but has been largely restored – the restorations including the inscription on the building lived in by Grewgious – 'P.J.T. 1747', standing for 'President James Taylor' (President of the Society of Antients of Staple Inn). Snagsby enjoys the countrified atmosphere of the Inn's courtyards in summertime *(Bleak House)*.

Stock Exchange, City: Here Tony Weller receives from Wilkins Flasher a

cheque for £530, the proceeds of his late wife's investments *(Pickwick)*.

Strand: This thoroughfare appears very frequently in the stories. Warren's Blacking Warehouse was at Hungerford Stairs, at the western end of the Strand, and Dickens knew the whole area well when he worked there. Dickens worked as a reporter at the offices of the *Morning Chronicle*, and had a lodging in Buckingham Street (now demolished) which he described as Mrs. Crupp's house where David Copperfield has rooms. The editorial offices for *All the Year Round* were at No. 26 (formerly 11) Wellington Street, and those of *Household Words* opposite the Lyceum Theatre in the same street. Rule's Restaurant, in Maiden Lane, running parallel with the Strand off Bedford Street, was a favourite resort of Dickens, and still keeps a Dickens Corner. Miss La Creevy has her lodgings and studio in the Strand, conjecturally at No. 11 *(Nickleby)*. Young Martin Chuzzlewit and Mark Tapley find lodgings in a court in the Strand, near Temple Bar.

Sun Court, Cornhill: Dickens places the George and Vulture here, when Dodson and Fogg's clerk goes to the inn to inquire for Pickwick.

Surrey Theatre: Now demolished, this stood at the end of the Blackfriars Road, near the original site of the Obelisk (q.v.). It was built in 1782 for Charles Dibdin, and was in Dickens's day the rival of Sadler's Wells for its presentations of legitimate drama. It is probably the theatre where Frederick Dorrit plays 'a clarinet as dirty as himself', and Fanny Dorrit is a dancer. Dickens and John Forster attended a performance of a dramatisation of *Oliver Twist* there in 1838, but Dickens was unable to watch it and 'laid himself down upon the floor in a corner of the box and never rose from it until the drop-scene fell.'

Symond's Inn: On the eastern side of Chancery Lane, backing on to Breams Buildings, it was most given over to private solicitors. Dickens probably worked there as a young clerk with a solicitor named Molloy. Vhole's offices 'in this dingy hatchment commemorative of Symond' (*Bleak House*) may be based on Molloy's.

Tavistock House, Tavistock Square, Bloomsbury: Dickens moved his household here from Devonshire Terrace in 1851, having bought the lease from Frank Stone, A.R.A. It stood in private gardens and had adapted its commodious schoolroom as a theatre for his amateur dramatic productions. Tavistock House was demolished about 1900. The offices of the British Medical Association on the site bear a commemorative plaque.

Tellson's Bank: See **Fleet Street.**

Temple: Extending from Fleet Street to the river in Dickens's day, before the building of the Embankment, this ancient area of Inns and chambers and quiet precincts figures frequently in the stories. Badly damaged in the Second World War, it has now been restored. Pip has chambers in Garden Court, where he is visited by Magwitch and learns the truth about his fortune. At Temple Stairs he keeps the boat used for the attempted escape of Magwitch (*Expectations*). Sir John Chester (*Rudge*) has chambers in Paper Buildings, where Maypole Hugh calls on him. (These Paper Buildings were burnt down in 1838.) Tom Pinch is installed in chambers in Pump Court, to work as librarian for his mysterious benefactor, and in Fountain Court takes place the courtship of Ruth Pinch and John Westlock (*Chuzzlewit*). Tartar keeps his boat at Temple Stairs (now vanished), at the end of King's Bench Walk, and rows Rosa up the river from there (*Drood*). Mortimer Lightwood and Eugene Wrayburn have chambers on the site of Goldsmith's Buildings, near Temple Church (*Mutual Friend*). Stryver has chambers in the Temple, in which Sydney Carton works for him (*Two Cities*).

Temple Bar: This London landmark, dividing the Strand from Fleet Street, seems to have been unpopular with Dickens. In *Bleak House* he calls it 'that leaden-headed old obstruction' and remarks that in hot weather it is 'to the adjacent Strand and Fleet Street, what a heater is in an urn, and keeps them simmering all night.' Tom Pinch retires under it to laugh about Ruth's beefsteak pudding (*Chuzzlewit*). The 'Prentice Knights swear not to damage Temple Bar during any rising they may instigate (*Rudge*). Temple Bar was removed in 1878 to Sir Henry Bruce Meux's estate of Theobalds Park, near Waltham Cross.

Tenterden Street: See **Hanover Square.**

Thames Street: Running from Blackfriars to the Tower of London, it is probably the location of the dilapidated house owned by Ralph Nickleby, where he lodges his sister-in-law and Kate; and of the decaying home of Mrs. Clennam in *Dorrit*. See also **Custom House.**

Thavies Inn: One of the Inns of Chancery, near Holborn Circus, it was destroyed in the Second World War. In *Bleak House* the Jellybys live here.

Threadneedle Street, City: The offices of the brothers Cheeryble are in a courtyard off the street *(Nickleby)*. See also **Bank of England.**

Titbull's Almshouses: Described in *Uncommercial* – 'Titbull's Almshouses', they were probably the Vintners' Almshouses, in Mile End Road.

Took's Court: See **Chancery Lane.**

Tottenham Court Road: In Dickens's time it was noted for the number of its drapers' shops. Horatio Sparkins serves in one, Jones, Spruggins and Smith (*Boz* – 'Horatio Sparkins'). The table, flowerpot, and stand belonging to Traddles and Sophy, taken with Micawber's furniture when his Camden Town lodgings are seized by a broker, are found in a broker's shop at the top of Tottenham Court Road (*Copperfield*). Miss Knag's brother, who keeps a stationer's shop and circulating library, lives in a by-street *Nickleby*). A wedding-party in Tottenham Court Road is described in *Boz* – 'Hackney-coach Stands'.

Tower of London: Lord George Gordon was imprisoned here. At the Crooked

Billet in Tower Street (now demolished)
Joe Willet enlists for the Army (*Rudge*).
Quilp lives on Tower Hill *(Curiosity Shop)*.

Turnham Green: District of west London where the Lord Mayor is held up and robbed by a highwayman *(Two Cities)*.

Turnstile, Holborn: Once a centre of the tailoring trade, it is a passage leading from Holborn to Lincoln's Inn. Snagsby recalls to his apprentices that he has heard of a crystal-clear brook once running down the middle of Holborn, when Turnstile was actually a stile leading into meadows *(Bleak House)*.

Twickenham: See under Part One.

Tyburn: Place of public execution sited near the present Marble Arch, used until 1783, after which executions took place outside Newgate Prison. Dickens recounts the tragic story of a young mother's death at Tyburn in the Preface to *Rudge*, and Dennis, hangman at Newgate, recalls when he held the same office at Tyburn.

Vauxhall Bridge: The bridge Dickens knew was replaced in 1906. It is referred to in *Boz*, *Mutual Friend*, and *Christmas Stories* – 'Someboy's Luggage'.

Vauxhall Gardens: Famous pleasure resort in the eighteenth and early nineteenth centuries, sited on the Surrey side of Vauxhall Bridge and closed in 1859. The gardens are described in *Boz* – 'Vauxhall-gardens by Day'.

Victoria Theatre, Waterloo Road: Referred to in *Boz* – 'The Streets – Night' and *Miscellaneous Papers* – 'Amusements of the People'. Built in 1817 as the Coburg Theatre, it is now the Old Vic.

Walcot Square, Kennington: Guppy offers his house in Walcot Square as an attraction when proposing to Esther *(Bleak House)*.

Walworth: Now a populous district south of the Borough, in Dickens's day it was a semi-rural area into which speculative builders were beginning to

find their way. Wemmick lives with his aged father in 'Wemmick's Castle' *(Expectations)*. The Uncommercial Traveller records the high incidence of windy weather ('Refreshments for Travellers'). Walworth at the turn of the nineteenth century is described in *Boz* – 'Black Veil'.

Wapping: East London riverside district, described in *Uncommercial* – 'Wapping Workhouse'.

Waterloo Bridge: The bridge Dickens knew was opened in 1817 and demolished in 1939. Described in *Uncommercial* – 'Night Walks'. A suicide from the bridge steps is recounted in *Boz* – 'Drunkard's Death'. Sam Weller tells Pickwick how in his youth he had 'unfurnished lodgings for a fortnight' under 'the dry arches of Waterloo Bridge'.

Welbeck Street, Marylebone: Lord George Gordon lived at No. 64 (now rebuilt) *(Rudge)*.

Wellington House Academy: See **Hampstead Road** and **Salem House School.**

Wellington Street: See **Strand.**

West India Docks: Captain Cuttle's lodgings are 'on the brink of a little canal near the India Docks . . . a first floor and a top story, in Brig Place' *(Dombey)*. This was probably a reminiscence of Dickens's visits to his godfather, Christopher Huffan, at Church Street, Limehouse.

Westminster Abbey: Pip and Herbert Pocket go to a morning service at the Abbey *(Expectations)*. David and Daniel Peggotty follow Martha from Blackfriars, hoping she may lead them to Little Em'ly, and lose her at the Abbey *(Copperfield)*. Some of Miss Abbey Potterson's customers think (that she is 'named after, or in some way related to, the Abbey at Westminster' *(Mutual Friend)*. Dickens was buried in Poets' Corner in the Abbey on 14 June 1870.

Westminster Bridge: The first stone bridge, built in 1739–50, was the one Dickens knew. It was demolished and replaced in 1862. Pickwick and his party cross it on their way to Kent by coach. Morleena Kenwigs is invited to a pleasure trip on Eel Pie Island (q.v., Part One) starting by steamer from Westminster Bridge *(Nickleby)*.

Westminster Hall: The only survivor of the fire which destroyed the old Houses of Parliament (q.v.). The old Law Courts, where the Jarndyce case was concluded, adjoined the Hall on the western side. Lord George Gordon was tried in the old Courts for high treason *(Rudge)*. John Harmon, under the name of Julius Handford, gives as his address the Exchequer Coffee House, Old Palace Yard.

White Conduit House: An inn with pleasure-grounds, it was a popular resort in Pentonville, on the fringes of Islington. It deteriorated and was demolished in 1849. The May Day procession of sweeps was exchanged for a formal anniversary dinner at White Conduit House *(Boz – 'First of May')*.

White Hart Inn: See **Borough.**

White Horse Cellar: See **Piccadilly.**

Whitechapel: East End district, containing many coaching inns in Dickens's day. Joe Willet has meals on credit at the Black Lion. Whitechapel Road, begrudged by his father *(Rudge)*. Pickwick and Mr. Peter Magnus travel to Ipswich from the Bull. David Copperfield arrives in London for the first time at the Blue Boar. Sam Weller observes that poverty and oysters invariably go together, and points out to Pickwick that the Whitechapel streets are lined with oyster stalls *(Pickwick)*. After being recaptured by Sikes and Nancy, Oliver Twist is taken to a house in the Whitechapel district.

Whitefriars Street: See **Hanging Sword Alley.**

Whitehall: Jingle comments on the Banqueting Hall of Whitehall Palace as the coach containing himself and the Pickwickians sets out for Rochester. 'Fine place – little window – somebody else's head off there – eh, sir ?'

Windsor Terrace, City Road: David Copperfield lodges with the Micawbers, and Mrs. Micawber advertises on a brass plate her Boarding Establishment for Young Ladies.

Wood Street, City: The Cross Keys inn (q.v.), a Rochester coaching house, is mentioned in *Expectations, Uncommercial, Dorrit,* and *Boz.* Mould, the undertaker, has premises near a small shady churchyard *(Chuzzlewit)*.

Wyldes Farm: See **Hampstead.**

CHARLES DICKENS: A TIME CHART

A TIME CHART

Year	Date	Life	Career	General Events
1812	February 7	Dickens born at 387 Mile End Road (also known as 1 Mile End Terrace), Landport, Portsmouth, son of John Dickens, employed in Navy Pay Office, Portsmouth Dockyard, and Elizabeth Dickens, *née* Barrow; and brother of Frances Elizabeth, born 1810.		(George III on throne of England since 1760. Due to his illness the Prince of Wales had become Regent in 1811.) Assassination of Spencer Perceval, Prime Minister; Lord Liverpool succeeds him. Viscount Castlereagh is Foreign Minister. Napoleon invades Russia; Battle of Borodino; French enter Moscow, then retreat. In the Peninsular War Wellington advances to Madrid after the Battle of Salamanca, but is forced to retreat. War breaks out between Britain and U.S.A. Early steamship *Comet* launched on the Clyde by Henry Bell. Gas Light and Coke Company developed by F. A. Winsor. Painless amputation developed by Napoleon's surgeon, Baron Larrey. Anti-machinery 'Luddite' riots break out in England. Beethoven's 7th and 8th symphonies first performed. Elgin Marbles brought to England. Discovery of Great Temple of Abu Simbel in Egypt.
	March	Dickens baptised Charles John Huffam (sometimes spelt Huffham) in Parish Church, Portsea.		
	June 24	John Dickens family moves to Hawke Street, Kingston, Portsea.		Publications: Grimms' *Fairy Tales*; first two cantos of Byron's *Childe Harold*.

1813	Alfred Dickens born. Died in infancy.	War of Liberation breaks out in Prussia. Prussia joins Russia against France; French retreat to the Elbe; Sweden joins Russia and Prussia; Napoleon defeats allied army but is defeated at Leipzig; Wellington's victory at Vittoria drives France out of Spain. 'Puffing Billy' locomotive built in England by William Hedley. Last golden guineas issued in England. Publications: William Blake's *Day of Judgment*; Southey's *Life of Nelson*; Shelley's *Queen Mab*; Jane Austen's *Pride and Prejudice*; Scott's *Rokeby*.
1814 June 24	John Dickens transferred to a London post, probably at Somerset House. John Dickens family moves to Norfolk Street, St. Pancras, London.	Washington D.C. burnt by British; Treaty of Ghent ends Anglo–U.S. war. Allies invade France and capture Paris; Napoleon abdicates; Louis XVIII ascends French throne; first Treaty of Paris; Congress of Vienna. Tsar of Russia visits England. Construction of first efficient steam locomotive near Newcastle-upon-Tyne by George Stephenson. Development of steam cylinder-press printing. Term 'birth-control' first used. Publications: Jane Austen's *Mansfield Park*; Scott's *Waverley*; Wordsworth's *The Excursion*; Byron's *The Corsair and Lara*.

Year	Date	Life	Career	General Events
1815		Catherine Hogarth, later Mrs. Charles Dickens, born.		Napoleon escapes from Elba and regains Paris; Louis XVIII flees; Ney and Murat executed; Congress of Vienna dispersed; Napoleon's army defeated by Wellington at Waterloo; Napoleon abdicates; Louis XVIII returns; Napoleon banished to St. Helena and Congress of Vienna reassembles. Corn Law passed by British Parliament and income tax abolished. Schubert's 3rd symphony performed. Publications: Scott's novel *Guy Mannering* and poem *The Lord of the Isles*.
1816		Letitia Mary Dickens born.		Corn Law causes widespread hardship in England. U.S.A. introduces protection against British imports. Transatlantic packet service begins. First performance of Rossini's *The Barber of Seville*. Schubert's 4th and 5th symphonies performed. Publications: Coleridge's 'Kubla Khan' and 'Christabel'; Scott's *The Antiquary* and *Old Mortality*; Byron's *The Prisoner of Chillon*; Jane Austen's *Emma*.

1817	John Dickens reappointed to Chatham. John Dickens family moves to temporary lodgings in Chatham. John Dickens family moves to 2 Ordnance Terrace, Chatham.	Continued unrest in England: riots and marches. Death of Princess Charlotte, Prince Regent's daughter and heir, after him, to the English throne. Constable paints *Flatford Mill*. Rennie's Waterloo Bridge opened in London. Publications: Scott's *Rob Roy*; John Keats's *Poems*; Thomas Moore's *Lalla Rookh*; Byron's *Manfred*; Hazlitt's *Characters of Shakespear's Plays*; Coleridge's *Biographia Literaria*. *Blackwood's Magazine* founded.
1818		Count Bernadotte ascends Swedish throne as Charles XIV. Attempts to find the North-West Passage by Ross, Parry, and others. First iron passenger ship launched on the Clyde. Foundation of Bonn University. Publications: Keats's *Endymion*; Scott's *The Heart of Midlothian*; Mary Shelley's *Frankenstein*; Jane Austen's *Northanger Abbey* and *Persuasion*.
1819 August	Harriet Ellen Dickens born. Died in infancy.	Peterloo Massacre of Corn Law protesters in Manchester. First macadam roads laid in England. S.S. *Savannah* crosses Atlantic in 26 days. Factory Act protecting child workers in English cotton

Year	Date	Life	Career	General Events
1819— *contd*				mills passed. Singapore founded by Raffles. Publications: Scott's *Ivanhoe*; Shelley's *The Cenci*; Byron's *Don Juan* and *Mazeppa*.
1820	July	Frederick William Dickens born.		Death of George III, Prince Regent succeeds him as George IV and brings unsuccessful divorce action against Queen Caroline. Constable paints *Dedham Mill*. Venus de Milo discovered on Greek Island of Melos. Publications: Shelley's *Prometheus Unbound*; Keats's *Hyperion* and 'Lamia'; Washington Irving's *Sketch-Book*.
1821		Dickens begins education at William Giles's school, Chatham. John Dickens in reduced circumstances due to improvidence. Family moves to 18 St. Mary's Place, Chatham.	Dickens writes a tragedy, *Misnar, the Sultan of India*.	Greek independence declared. Gold Coast becomes British Crown Colony. John Keats dies in Rome. Faraday demonstrates principle of electric motor. Wheatstone demonstrates sound reproduction. Weber's *Der Freischütz* performed. Constable paints *The Hay Wain*. Publications: De Quincey's *Confessions of an Opium-Eater*; Scott's *Kenilworth*; Shelley's 'Adonais' and *Defence of Poetry*.

1822	December (probably)	Alfred Lamert Dickens born. John Dickens transferred to London. John Dickens family moves to London: 16 Bayham Street, Camden Town, leaving Dickens in Chatham with William Giles.	English Foreign Secretary, Lord Castlereagh, commits suicide. Home Secretary, Lord Sidmouth, resigns; Lord Liverpool's Ministry re-formed. First railway locomotives used in Durham. Foundation of Royal Academy of Music, London. Shelley dies. Publications: Scott's *The Fortunes of Nigel*.
	December (late)	Dickens rejoins family.	
1823	October	John Dickens family moves to 4 Gower Street North. Mrs. Dickens opens school for young ladies, but no pupils arrive. Dickens living at home.	Home Secretary, Robert Peel, institutes penal reforms. First Ashanti war breaks out. World's first iron railway bridge built by Stephenson for Stockton and Darlington Railway. Foundation of Mechanics' Institutes in London and Glasgow. Present British Museum building erected. Schubert's *Rosamunde* performed. Publications: Scott's *Quentin Durward*; Lamb's *Essays of Elia*.
1824	February	John Dickens arrested for debt. Imprisoned first in King's Bench, later transferred to Marshalsea. Mrs. Dickens and younger children join John Dickens in Marshalsea. Dickens lodging with Mrs. Roylance in Little College Street, Camden Town. Then moves to Lant Street, Borough,	Poor Law Act of 1662 repealed. Byron dies at Missolonghi. Death of Louis XVIII of France; succeeded by Charles X. Beethoven's 9th symphony and *Missa Solemnis* performed. Blake paints *Beatrice Addressing Dante*. Athenaeum Club founded in London.

Year	Date	Life	Career	General Events
1824— contd		and employed through the agency of his cousin James Lamert at Warren's Blacking Warehouse.		Publications: Scott's *Redgauntlet*; Mary Russell Mitford's *Our Village*.
	May 28	On release of John Dickens, family moves to lodging in Camden Town, then to Seymour Street, Camden Town. Fanny Dickens resident at the Royal Academy of Music, Tenterden Street, off Hanover Square.		
	June	Dickens removed from Warren's and sent to Wellington House Academy, Hampstead Road.		
1825		John Dickens family moves to 29 Johnson Street, Somers Town. John Dickens retired with small pension.		Suppression of Irish Catholic Association. Factory Act passed in Britain. Tsar Alexander I of Russia dies; succeeded by Nicholas I. Stephenson builds his first locomotive 'The Rocket' and opens his first passenger line, the Stockton and Darlington Railway. John Nash begins to re-build Buckingham Palace. Publications: Pepys's *Diary*; Scott's *The Talisman*.
1826		Dickens at Wellington House Academy. John Dickens writing for the *British Press* as city correspondent. The paper fails at the end of the year.		Telford's bridge over Menai Straits, Wales, opened. Berlioz's *Symphonie Fantastique* performed. Mendelssohn's *Midsummer Night's Dream* overture performed. Weber's *Oberon* performed.

		Schubert's String Quartet in D minor ('Death and the Maiden') performed. Constable paints *The Cornfield*. Publications: J. Fenimore Cooper's *The Last of the Mohicans*; Hölderlin's *Gedichte*.
1827	Augustus Dickens born. John Dickens family evicted for non-payment of rates. Dickens removed from Wellington House Academy, and Fanny from Royal Academy of Music.	Lord Liverpool resigns British Premiership. George Canning succeeds him, but dies and is succeeded by Viscount Goderich. Turks capture the Acropolis at Athens. Turkish fleet destroyed by British, French, and Russians at Navarino.
March	Dickens joins Ellis & Blackmore, 5 Holborn Court, Gray's Inn, as solicitor's clerk.	Publications: First parts of Audubon's *Birds of North America*; Heine's *Buch der Lieder*; John Clare's *The Shepherd's Calendar*; Manzoni's *I Promessi Sposi*; first Baedeker travel guide.
1828	Ellis & Blackmore move to 6 Raymond Buildings, Gray's Inn. Dickens employed for a time at this period by Charles Molloy, solicitor.	Duke of Wellington succeeds Goderich as Prime Minister. Daniel O'Connell debarred from standing for Parliament for County Clare because he is Catholic. Turks evacuate Greece; Greek independence declared. Schubert's 7th symphony performed. Constable paints *Salisbury Cathedral*.
November	John Dickens has learnt shorthand and is working as a reporter for the *Morning Herald*.	Publications: Webster's *Dictionary*; Casanova's *Mémoires*; Bulwer-Lytton's *Pelham*.

Year	Date	Life	Career	General Events
1829		John Dickens family moves to 10 Norfolk Street, Fitzroy Square.	Dickens has learnt shorthand and become a freelance reporter at Doctors' Commons, sharing Thomas Charlton's box to report legal proceedings.	Robert Peel establishes Metropolitan Police, London. Catholic Emancipation Act passed: O'Connell re-elected for County Clare. Colonisation of Western Australia begins. Horse-drawn omnibuses introduced in London. Louis Braille perfects his reading method for the blind. First boat race between Oxford and Cambridge Universities.
				Publications: Mérimée's *Mateo Falcone*; Balzac's *Les Chouans*, his first successful novel.
1830	February		Dickens admitted reader at British Museum.	George IV dies; succeeded by Duke of Clarence as William IV. Wellington resigns Premiership; succeeded by Earl Grey. Agricultural workers riot in Southern England ('Captain Swing' Riots). Plymouth Brethren founded. Charles X of France overthrown in 'July Revolution'; succeeded by Louis Philippe. Royal Geographic Society founded in London. Mendelssohn's *Reformation* symphony performed. Auber's *Fra Diavolo* performed. Corot paints *Houses at Honfleur*.
	May	Dickens meets Maria Beadnell.		
				Publications: Tennyson's *Poems, chiefly Lyrical*; Hugo's *Ernani*; Musset's *Poems*; Cobbett's *Rural Rides*.

1831		Forster sees Dickens for the first time.	Dickens working for John Henry Barrow, his uncle, reporting for the *Mirror of Parliament*.	Reform Bill passed by House of Commons but vetoed by Lords. Agricultural riots continue. Twelve-hour working day for persons under 18 in cotton mills becomes compulsory. Leopold of Saxe-Coburg becomes first King of Belgium. Charles Darwin sails as naturalist in *H.M.S. Beagle*. Chloroform discovered by von Liebig. Faraday discovers electro-magnetic induction. British Association for the Advancement of Science founded. New London Bridge opens. Meyerbeer's *Robert le Diable* performed. Publications: Pushkin's *Boris Godunov*; Stendhal's *Le Rouge et le Noir*; Balzac's *La Peau de Chagrin*; Hugo's *Nôtre Dame de Paris*.
1832	Dickens courting Maria Beadnell. John Dickens family living at 15 Fitzroy Street. Family lodges in Highgate for a fortnight in late summer.	Dickens reporting for evening paper, the *True Sun*.		First Parliamentary Reform Act. Irish 'Tithe Strikes'. Anti-slavery movement begins in Boston, U.S.A. First U.S. railway built. Donizetti's *L'Elisir d'Amore* performed. Publications: George Sand's *Indiana*; Balzac's *Contes Drolatiques*; Hugo's *Le Roi s'amuse*.
? March		Dickens seeks audition at Covent Garden Theatre but is ill on the day.		
April or May	Charles Dickens lodges briefly in Cecil Street, Strand.			
1833 January	John Dickens family moves from Fitzroy Street to 18 Bentinck Street.			First session of reformed House of Commons. Tories adopt name

Year	Date	Life	Career	General Events
1833— *contd*	May	Dickens's romance with Maria Beadnell broken off.		Conservative. S.S. *Royal William* first vessel to cross Atlantic by steam alone. Mendelssohn's *Italian* symphony performed. Turner exhibits first Venetian paintings. Donizetti's *Lucrezia Borgia* performed.
	December 1		Dickens's first story, 'A Dinner at Poplar Walk', published in the *Monthly Magazine*. It was later re-titled 'Mr. Minns and his Cousin'.	Publications: Carlyle's *Sartor Resartus*; Balzac's *Le Médecin de Campagne*.
1834	January–February 1835		8 more stories published in *Monthly Magazine*.	Melbourne succeeds Grey as Prime Minister; is dismissed and succeeded by Peel. Poor Law Amendment Act passed.
	August		Dickens becomes a reporter on the *Morning Chronicle*.	'Tolpuddle Martyrs' transported for attempting to form a union. Establishment of Central Criminal
	September–December	Dickens meets Catherine Hogarth.	'Street Sketches' 1–5 published in the *Morning Chronicle*.	Court in London. Slavery abolished in all British possessions.
	November	John Dickens arrested for debt and detained at sponging-house. Family home at 18 Bentinck Street broken up. On release John Dickens goes to lodgings in North End, Hampstead.	George Hogarth, Catherine's father, commissions 'Sketches of London' for his new paper, the *Evening Chronicle*.	Faraday expounds laws of electrolysis. Hansom Cab patented by Joseph Hansom. Old Houses of Parliament destroyed by fire.
	December	John Dickens family moves to 21 George Street, Adelphi. Dickens moves to 13 Furnival's Inn, Holborn.		Publications: Bulwer-Lytton's *The Last Days of Pompeii*; Balzac's *Père Goriot*; Captain Marryat's *Peter Simple*.
1835	January–August		'Sketches of London' 1–20 published in *Evening Chronicle*.	Peel resigns; replaced by Melbourne. Municipal Reform Act for England and Wales passed.
	? May	Dickens engaged to Catherine Hogarth. He takes lodgings at		Gas first used for cooking.

September–January 1836	11 Selwood Terrace, Queen's Elm, Brompton.	'Scenes and Characters' 1-12 published in *Bell's Life in London*.	Darwin studies Galapagos Islands, with important future results. Foundation of Melbourne, Australia. Schumann's *Carnaval* performed. Madame Tussaud's waxworks opens in London. Donizetti's *Lucia di Lammermoor* performed.	Publications: Gautier's *Mademoiselle de Maupin*; Browning's *Paracelsus*; John Clare's *The Rural Muse*.
1836 February 8		*Boz*, 1st series, published.	Boers make Great Trek from Cape Colony to found Republic of Orange Free State. Republic of Texas founded by Mexicans. Siege of El Alamo and Battle of San Jacinto, Births, Deaths, and Marriages Registration Act passed in Britain. Mendelssohn's *Saint Paul* performed. Meyerbeer's *Les Huguenots* performed. Glinka's *Life for the Czar* performed.	
February 10		First idea of *Pickwick* proposed to Dickens by Chapman & Hall.		
February 17	Dickens moves to chambers at 15 Furnival's Inn, with brother Fred.	Dickens writing *Pickwick*.		
March 31		*Pickwick* begins publication in 20 monthly parts (Chapman & Hall).		Publications: Gogol's *The Inspector General*; Marryat's *Midshipman Easy*.
March–May		2 sketches published in the *Library of Fiction*.		
April 2	Dickens marries Catherine Hogarth at St. Luke's Church, Chelsea. They go to Chalk, near Gravesend, for honeymoon, returning to live at Furnival's Inn, with Fred Dickens and Catherine's sister Mary Hogarth.			
April 20		Robert Seymour, illustrator of *Pickwick*, commits suicide. Succeeded by Hablôt K. Browne ('Phiz').		

Year	Date	Life	Career	General Events
1836— contd	June		'Sunday under Three Heads' published.	
	August 6		'Hospital Patient' published in the *Carlton Chronicle*.	
	August–September	Dickens and Catherine staying at Petersham.		
	September 29		*Strange Gentleman*, adapted from 'Great Winglebury Duel', begins run at St. James's Theatre of 60 nights.	
	November 4		Dickens agrees with Richard Bentley to edit *Bentley's Miscellany*.	
	November		Dickens leaves the *Morning Chronicle*.	
	December 6		*Village Coquettes* produced at St. James's Theatre.	
	December 17		*Boz*, 2nd series, published.	
	December 22		*Village Coquettes* published.	
	? December 25	Dickens introduced to Forster by Harrison Ainsworth.		
	? December (or January 1837)		*Strange Gentleman* published.	
1837	January 1		First number of *Bentley's Miscellany* appears. The first of three pieces dealing with 'Mudfog' appears in it this month.	William IV dies. Victoria becomes Queen. Samuel B. Morse develops telegraph in U.S.A. Berlioz's *Requiem* performed. Isaac Pitman introduces his shorthand system. Joe Grimaldi dies, May 31.
	January 6	Charles Culliford Boz (Charley) Dickens born.		

Date	Event	Publications
January 21	Dickens elected member of Garrick Club.	
January 31		*Twist* begins publication in *Bentley's Miscellany*, February issue (24 monthly instalments).
February 4–? March 6	Dickens and family at Chalk.	
March 6		*Is She His Wife?* produced at St. James's Theatre.
March	Dickens and family in lodgings at 30 Upper Norton Street.	
April (first week)	Dickens and family move to 48 Doughty Street.	
May 3		Dickens speaks in public for the first time at the Literary Fund Anniversary Dinner.
May 7	Mary Hogarth dies suddenly after a visit to the theatre. Dickens, Catherine, and Charley retire to Collins's Farm, Hampstead.	Writing of *Pickwick* and *Twist* suspended for a month.
June 16	Dickens introduced to William Charles Macready by Forster.	
July 2–? 8	Dickens holidays in France and Belgium with Catherine and H. K. Browne.	
August 31–September ? 8/12	Dickens and family at 12 High Street, Broadstairs.	
September		First authoritative statement that 'Boz' is Dickens.
October 30		Last parts of *Pickwick* appear.
October 31–November 7	Dickens and Catherine at the Old Ship Hotel, Brighton.	

Publications: Carlyle's *The French Revolution*.

Year	Date	Life	Career	General Events
1837— *contd*	November 17 November 18		Dinner to mark publication of *Pickwick*. *Pickwick* appears in book form.	
1838	January 30– ? February 6	Dickens on expedition to examine the Yorkshire schools with H. K. Browne.		Anti-Corn Law League founded in Manchester. First Afghan War breaks out. People's Charter (demanding universal suffrage, etc.) published at Glasgow, followed by several years of riots in its support. Daguerre perfects Daguerreotype system of photography. Regular Atlantic steamship service begins. Publications: Hugo's *Ruy Blas*.
	February 10		*Young Gentlemen* published.	
	February 26		*Memoirs of Grimaldi* published.	
	March 6	Mary (Mamie) Dickens born.		
	March 29	Dickens takes Catherine to the Star and Garter Hotel, Richmond, to convalesce and to celebrate their wedding anniversary.		
	March 31		*Nickleby* begins publication in 20 monthly instalments. (First issue dated April.)	
	June 21	Dickens elected member of the Athenaeum Club.		
	June–July	Dickens rents cottage at Twickenham.		
	September ? 3–12	Dickens and family in the Isle of Wight, staying at the Needles and Ventnor.		
	October 29– November 8	Dickens tours the Midlands and North Wales with H. K. Browne. Forster joins them at Liverpool on November 5.		
	November 9		*Twist* published in 3 vols.	
	November		*Lamplighter*, a play, written but not acted.	

1839			Queen Victoria becomes engaged to Albert of Saxe-Coburg. First Opium War between Britain and China breaks out. Fox Talbot introduces photographic paper. First Henley Regatta takes place. First Grand National run. Turner paints *The Fighting Téméraire*. Berlioz's *Roméo et Juliette* performed.
January		Dickens begins writing *Rudge*.	
January 12–17	Dickens visits Manchester with Harrison Ainsworth and Forster.		
January 31		Dickens relinquishes editorship of *Bentley's Miscellany*.	
March 4–11	Dickens visits Exeter to find a home for his parents. He stays at the New London Inn, and settles on Mile-End Cottage, Alphington.		
March 13		Dickens elected to Literary Fund Committee.	
March		Last part of *Twist* appears.	
April 30–August 31	Dickens and family at Elm Cottage, Petersham.		
June		First complete edition of *Boz* published.	
September 3–? 1/2 October	Dickens and family at 40 Albion Street, Broadstairs.		
October 1		Dickens completes *Nickleby*.	
October 23	Kate Macready Dickens born.		
October 29	Dickens enrolled a student of Middle Temple, but does not 'eat dinners' there until many years later.	Serialisation of *Nickleby* completed.	
December 6		*Nickleby* published in 1 vol.	
December (early)	Dickens and family move to 1 Devonshire Terrace, Regent's Park.		

Publications: Stendhal's *La Chartreuse de Parme*; Bradshaw's first railway timetable.

Year	Date	Life	Career	General Events
1840	February 10		*Young Couples* published.	Queen Victoria and Prince Albert marry. Princess Royal born (November). Act passed forbidding employment of boy chimney-sweeps in Britain, but proves ineffectual. Rowland Hill introduces a penny post in England. First bicycle produced. Captain Hobson, first Governor of New Zealand, lands there and signs Treaty of Waitangi, acquiring land rights from Maoris. Barry builds new Houses of Parliament and Palace of Westminster in London. Nelson's column erected in Trafalgar Square. Donizetti's *La Fille du Régiment* performed. London Library opens.
	February		Dickens writing *Humphrey*.	
	February 29–March 4	Dickens at Bath with Forster, visiting Walter Savage Landor. They stay at York House Hotel.		
	March		Dickens writing *Rudge* and *Curiosity Shop*.	
	April 3–? 7	Dickens, Catherine, and Forster visit Birmingham, Stratford-upon-Avon, and Lichfield.		
	April 4		First part of *Humphrey* appears.	
	April 25		*Curiosity Shop* begins publication in the fourth number of *Humphrey* and runs for 40 instalments, sporadically up to June 20 and weekly thereafter.	
	June 1–? 28	Dickens and family at 37 Albion Street, Broadstairs.		Publications: Browning's *Sordello*; W. Harrison Ainsworth's *The Tower of London*.
	June 29–30	Dickens, Forster, and Maclise visit Rochester and Cobham.		
	July 27–August 4	Dickens visits his parents in Devon.		
	August 30–October ? 10/11	Dickens at Lawn House, Broadstairs, with family.		
	October 15	*Humphrey*, vol. 1, published.		

Date	Dickens	Works / Publications	World events
1841 January		Dickens completes *Curiosity Shop*. End of serialisation of *Curiosity Shop*.	Melbourne resigns; Peel becomes Prime Minister. Albert Edward, Prince of Wales, born. New Zealand becomes separate British colony. Union of Upper and Lower Canada. Hong Kong founded as British settlement by British refugees from Canton. Schumann's 1st symphony performed. Thomas Cook's travel agency founded. German national anthem, *Deutschland, Deutschland Uber Alles*, first heard. Publications: Carlyle's *On Heroes and Hero-Worship*; Browning's *Pippa Passes*; *Punch* founded; *New York Tribune* founded.
February 6	Walter Landor Dickens born.		
February 8			
February 13		*Rudge* begins publication in 42 weekly instalments in *Humphrey*.	
February 24–March 3	Dickens and Catherine at the Old Ship Hotel, Brighton.		
April ? 12/15		*Humphrey*, vol. II, published.	
May 29	Dickens is invited to be Liberal parliamentary candidate for Reading. He declines.		
June 19	Dickens and Catherine set off for Scotland.		
June 22–July 4	They stay at the Royal Hotel, Edinburgh.	Dickens writing *Humphrey*.	
June 25	Dinner at Waterloo Rooms, Edinburgh, in Dickens's honour.		
June 29	Dickens is granted the Freedom of the City of Edinburgh.		
July 4–16	Dickens and Catherine tour Scotland, with the sculptor Angus Fletcher.		
July 18	Dickens and Catherine return to London.		
August 1–October 2	Dickens and family at Lawn House, Broadstairs.		
August 9		*The Pic Nic Papers* published, containing 'Lamplighter's Story'.	
October 2–5	Dickens and Forster visit Rochester, Cobham and Gravesend.		

Year	Date	Life	Career	General Events
1841—contd	October 8	Dickens undergoes an operation for fistula. He is convalescent during the following weeks.		
	October 24	Death of George Thomson Hogarth, Dickens's brother-in-law		
	November 6–20	Dickens, still unwell, goes to Windsor to rest at the White Hart Hotel.	Dickens finishes *Rudge*.	
	November 27		End of serialisation of *Rudge*.	
	December 4		End of serialisation of *Humphrey*.	
	December 15		*Humphrey*, vol. III, published. *Curiosity Shop* and *Rudge* published in single-volume editions.	
1842	January 4	Dickens and Catherine sail on their first visit to America.		House of Commons rejects second Chartist petition; renewed rioting. South Australia becomes a Crown Colony and wide-scale immigration commences. Women and children prevented from working in English collieries. Income tax reintroduced in Britain. Reformation of Corn Laws by Peel and beginning of Free Trade policies. American surgeon, Crawford Long, first to use anaesthetic for operation. Glinka's *Russlan and Ludmilla* performed. Wagner's *Rienzi* performed. Verdi's *Nabucco* performed.
	January	Dickens and Catherine in Boston. Dickens meets Longfellow and R. H. Dana.	Dickens speaks on international copyright in Boston.	
	February	Dickens and Catherine in Worcester, Springfield, Hartford, and New Haven.	Dickens speaks on international copyright at Hartford.	
		Dickens and Catherine in New York. Dickens meets Washington Irving.	Dickens speaks on international copyright and investigates gaol conditions.	
	March	Dickens and Catherine in Philadelphia, Washington, Richmond, Baltimore, York, and Harrisburgh.	Dickens investigates gaol conditions in Philadelphia, and criticises slavery in Richmond.	

April	Dickens and Catherine in Pittsburgh, Cincinnati, Louisville, St. Louis, Sandusky, and Buffalo.	Publications: Tennyson's *Poems*; Macaulay's *Lays of Ancient Rome*; Samuel Lover's *Handy Andy*; Gogol's *Dead Souls*; *Illustrated London News* founded.
May	Dickens and Catherine at Niagara, Toronto, Kingston, and Montreal, where Dickens performs in private theatricals with guards officers.	
July 1	Dickens and Catherine arrive back in England, stay briefly at 37 Albion Street, Broadstairs, then return to their London home, 1 Devonshire Terrace, where Georgina Hogarth joins the household.	
August	Dickens and family at Broadstairs.	Dickens writing *American Notes*.
October 18		*American Notes* appears.
October–November	Dickens, Forster, and Maclise make a 'bachelor' excursion to Cornwall.	
December (or January 1843)		Dickens begins writing *Chuzzlewit*.
1843		
January	Dickens rents Cobley's Farm, Finchley, for a month's concentrated work on *Chuzzlewit*.	First part of *Chuzzlewit* appears.
June		Princess Alice Maud Mary born to Queen Victoria. Establishment of Free Church of Scotland. Natal proclaimed a British possession. Irish government prohibit meeting in support of Daniel O'Connell's movement for repeal of Irish Act of Union. S.S. *Great Britain* is first screw-steamer to cross Atlantic. First public telegraph line established in
August	Dickens and family at Albion Street, Broadstairs.	
October 4–6	Dickens presides at opening of Athenaeum Club, Manchester, with Richard Cobden and Benjamin Disraeli.	

Year	Date	Life	Career	General Events
1843— *contd*	October–November		Dickens writing 'Christmas Carol'.	England. Mendelssohn's music for *A Midsummer Night's Dream* performed. Donizetti's *Don Pasquale* performed. Wagner's *The Flying Dutchman* performed. First printed Christmas cards designed.
	December		'Christmas Carol' appears.	Publications: George Borrow's *The Bible in Spain*; Thomas Hood's 'The Song of the Shirt'; John Stuart Mill's *System of Logic*; *News of the World* newspaper founded; vol. I of Ruskin's *Modern Painters*.
1844	January		Dickens successfully takes proceedings in Chancery against pirates of his works.	Trial and sentence of O'Connell for sedition, later reversed by Lords. Tsar Nicholas I makes state visit to England. Retail Co-operative Movement founded by Rochdale Pioneers. Prince Alfred Ernest born to Queen Victoria. Polka introduced into Britain. Turner paints *Rain, Steam and Speed*. Verdi's *Ernani* performed.
	January 15	Francis Jeffrey (Frank) Dickens born.		
	February 26	Dickens takes the chair at the Mechanics' Institute, Liverpool.		
	February 28	Dickens takes the chair at the Polytechnic Institution, Birmingham.		Publications: Disraeli's *Coningsby*; Dumas's *Les Trois Mousquetaires* and *Monte Cristo*; Heine's *Neue Gedichte*; Kinglake's *Eothen*.
	May	Dickens family move to 9 Osnaburgh Terrace, having let 1 Devonshire Terrace for their forthcoming visit to Italy.		
	June		Dickens leaves Chapman & Hall for Bradbury & Evans. He completes *Chuzzlewit*.	

July		*Chuzzlewit* completes serialisation and appears in book form.
July	Dickens family leave for Italy.	
July 16	They arrive at Albaro, suburb of Genoa.	
October	They rent rooms in the Palazzo Peschiere, Genoa.	
October 10–November 3		Dickens writing 'Chimes'.
November 6	Dickens starts alone for England, visiting *en route* Parma, Modena, Bologna, Ferrara, Venice, Verona, Mantua, the Simplon Pass, Fribourg, Strasbourg, and Paris.	
December 3	In London, Dickens reads 'Chimes' to a group of friends at Forster's house, Lincoln's Inn Fields. He leaves a few days later for Paris where he meets many literary celebrities.	
December		'Chimes' published as Chapman & Hall's Christmas Book for 1844.
December 13	Dickens leaves Paris. Returns to Genoa by December 22.	
1845		
January 20	Dickens and Catherine leave Genoa for Rome via Carrara, Pisa, and Siena.	Peel resigns over Corn Laws but is recalled. British agricultural holdings reformed by General Enclosure Act. Evangelical Alliance formed to oppose Roman Catholicism in Britain. First Sikh War breaks out. Faraday expounds electro-magnetic theory of light. Wagner's *Tannhäuser* performed. Mendelssohn's Violin Concerto performed.
January 30	They arrive at Rome.	
February–April	Dickens and Catherine visit Naples, where they are joined by Georgina Hogarth. From Naples, they return to Rome, then visit Florence in March, leaving on April 4 for Genoa.	

Year	Date	Life	Career	General Events
1845— contd	April 9	They return to Genoa.	Dickens conceives idea for 'Cricket'.	Publications: Disraeli's *Sybil*; Dumas's *La Tulipe Noire*; Engels's *The Condition of the Working Class in England*; Poe's *Tales of Mystery and Imagination*.
	June	Dickens, Catherine, and Georgina Hogarth leave Genoa for England via Switzerland. They are joined in Brussels by Maclise, Douglas Jerrold, and Forster, and arrive back at 1 Devonshire Terrace at the end of June.		
	July	Dickens engages Fanny Kelly's theatre, Dean Street, Soho, for amateur productions.		
	August	Dickens family at Broadstairs for three weeks.		
	September 21	Jonson's *Every Man in his Humour* produced at Fanny Kelly's theatre, Dickens playing Bobadil.		
	October		Dickens writing 'Cricket'.	
	October 28	Alfred D'Orsay Tennyson Dickens born.		
	December	Performance of Beaumont and Fletcher's *The Elder Brother* at Fanny Kelly's theatre.	'Cricket' appears. Dickens begins writing *Pictures from Italy*.	
1846	January 21		First issue of Daily News appears, with Dickens as editor. *Pictures from Italy* begins publication in it.	Peel, defeated after repeal of Corn Laws, is succeeded by Russell. Princess Helena Augusta Victoria born to Queen Victoria. American Richard March Hoe designs rotary printing press. Fleet Prison in London pulled down. Elizabeth Barrett marries Robert Browning. Mendelssohn's *Elijah* performed.
	February 9		Dickens resigns editorship of *Daily News*.	
	March 2		Serialisation of *Pictures from Italy* ends. It appears in volume form later in the month.	

May 31	Dickens goes with his family to Switzerland, settling at the Villa Rosemont, Lausanne. Becomes interested in Swiss prison reform and Haldimand's work for the blind.	Dickens writing *Life of Our Lord* (it was not published until 1934).	Smithsonian Institute founded in Washington. Pneumatic tyre patented. First submarine cable laid across English Channel. Publications: Thackeray's *The Book of Snobs*; Edward Lear's *Book of Nonsense*; *Poems* by 'Currer, Ellis, and Acton Bell' (Charlotte, Emily and Anne Brontë).
June 27		Dickens begins *Dombey*.	
September		Dickens interrupts *Dombey* to write 'Battle of Life'.	
October		Dickens completes 'Battle of Life'. First monthly part of *Dombey* appears.	
November 20	Dickens family arrive in Paris for a three month stay *en route* for England. They stay at the Hotel Brighton and then rent 48 rue de Courcelles, home of the Marquis de Castellane.		
December		'Battle of Life' appears.	
December 15–23	Dickens in London, He attends rehearsals of a dramatic version, by Albert Smith, of 'Battle of Life', then returns to Paris.		
1847 January–February	Dickens and family in Paris.	Dickens writing *Dombey*.	Mormons emigrate to Utah, establishing themselves at Salt Lake City. Britain undergoes financial crisis. Chloroform used successfully for first time in operation by James Y. Simpson. Verdi's *Macbeth* performed. Flotow's *Martha* performed. Berlioz's *The Damnation of Faust* performed.
February	Dickens and family return to London prematurely because Charley, at King's College School, has scarlet fever. They stay at the Victoria Hotel, Euston Square. Their own house is still let, so they rent, furnished, 3 Chester Place, Regent's Park, for three months.		
April 18	Sydney Smith Haldimand Dickens born.		Publications: Disraeli's *Tancred*;

Year	Date	Life	Career	General Events
1847— contd	May	Dickens and Catherine, Georgina Hogarth, and Charley holiday at Brighton, staying at 148 King's Road.		Charlotte Brontë's *Jane Eyre*; Emily Brontë's *Wuthering Heights*; Marryat's *The Children of the New Forest*; Tennyson's *The Princess*.
	June–September	Dickens and family at the Albion Hotel, Broadstairs.	Dickens writing *Dombey*. Begins 'The Haunted Man', but lays it aside until winter 1848.	
	July	Dickens appears at Manchester and Liverpool in *Every Man in his Humour* with a cast of friends and relatives, for benefit of Leigh Hunt and John Poole. The play proper followed on alternate nights by farces: *A Good Night's Rest*, *Turning the Tables* and *Comfortable Lodgings, or Paris in 1750*	Dickens writes an account of the Tour, 'a new Piljians Projiss', in the character of Mrs. Gamp, to be sold to augment the benefit fund. This never appeared because of the failure of the artists to provide illustrations.	
	September	Dickens and family return to Devonshire Terrace.		
	December 1	Dickens chairs a meeting of Leeds Mechanics' Society.		
	December 28	Dickens in Scotland, opening the Glasgow Athenaeum. Visits Edinburgh, where Catherine is taken ill, and they stay over the New Year period.		
1848	March	Dickens and his company give eight performances in London in aid of the purchase and	Last part of *Dombey* finished.	Revolution in Paris; Louis Philippe abdicates. Second Republic formed, and Louis Napoleon becomes Prince
	April		Last part of *Dombey* appears and the work is published in book form.	

Date	Dickens	Dickens's work	Historical events
	preservation of Shakespeare's birthplace, Stratford-upon-Avon: *The Merry Wives of Windsor*, Dickens playing shallow, and a farce, *Love, Law and Physick*.		President. Revolutions break out in Berlin, Vienna, Venice, Rome, Milan, Naples, Prague, and Budapest. Francis Joseph becomes Emperor of Austria. Princess Louise Carolina Alberta born to Queen Victoria. Cholera epidemic breaks out in England. Successful steam-powered model aircraft flown by Strongfellow. First official settlers in California. First official settlers arrive at Dunedin, New Zealand. Spiritualist movement begins with experiences of the Fox Sisters in New York. Pre-Raphaelite Brotherhood founded in England.
April–July	They tour with the plays, visiting Manchester, Liverpool, Birmingham, Edinburgh and Glasgow.		
Summer	Dickens and family at Broadstairs on holiday.		
August	Fanny Burnett, Dickens's sister, dies.		
November	Dickens at the Bedford Hotel, Brighton.	Dickens writing 'Haunted Man'.	
December		'Haunted Man' appears.	Publications: Mrs. Elizabeth Gaskell's *Mary Barton*; Thackeray's *Pendennis* begun (completed 1850); J. S. Mill's *Political Economy*; Anne Brontë's *The Tenant of Wildfell Hall* and *Agnes Grey*; first two vols. of Macaulay's *History of England*.
December 31	Dickens, John Leech, Mark Lemon, and Forster visit Norwich and Yarmouth for several days.		
1849			
January 15	Henry Fielding Dickens born.		Britain annexes the Punjab. Dr. David Livingstone begins exploration of Central and South Africa, crossing the Kalahari Desert and reaching Lake Ngami. Discovery of reinforced concrete by J. Monier. 'Bloomers' introduced as women's wear by Amelia Jenks Bloomer.
February–June	Dickens and family at Brighton, in lodgings and the Bedford Hotel.	Dickens writing *Copperfield*.	
May		First number of *Copperfield* appears.	
July	Dickens and family at Fort House, Broadstairs.		
July–October	Dickens, family, and friends at Bonchurch, Isle of Wight.		Publications: Charlotte Brontë's

Year	Date	Life	Career	General Events
1849— *contd*	October 1	His original enthusiasm for the Isle of Wight having waned suddenly, Dickens takes his family back to Broadstairs, to the Albion Hotel.		*Shirley*; Matthew Arnold's *The Strayed Reveller and other Poems*; first publication of *Who's Who*.
	October 7		In a letter to Forster, Dickens outlines the details of the proposed journal *Household Words*, an often-recurring idea which he has worked out at Bonchurch and Broadstairs.	
	November	Dickens and Catherine make first visit to Rockingham Castle, Northamptonshire.		
1850	March 30		First number of *Household Words* appears with Dickens as editor.	Death of Sir Robert Peel. Factory Act passed to define legal working hours.
	April	Dickens and Catherine and Georgina Hogarth spend a week at Knebworth to discuss with Bulwer-Lytton his scheme for creating a Guild of Literature and Art to assist needy writers and artists.		Revival of trade unionism. Catholic hierarchy in Britain inaugurated. Prince Arthur William Patrick Albert born to Queen Victoria. Gold discovered in Australia. Meteorological Office established in England. Petrol refining first used. Pre-Raphaelite paintings include William Holman Hunt's *Claudio and Isabella* and
	June	Dinner at Star and Garter, Richmond, in honour of *Copperfield*.		John Everett Millais's *Christ in the House of His Parents*. Jean-François Millet paints *The Sower*.
	June	Dickens visits France with Maclise to see plays and pictures.		Schumann's 3rd symphony (The
	July	Dickens and family at Fort House, Broadstairs.		

August 16	Dora Annie Dickens born in London. Dickens, who had joined his wife there for the event, then re-joins Georgina and his children at Fort House, Broadstairs.		Rhenish) performed. Wagner's *Lohengrin* produced at Weimar. Sydney University, Australia, founded. Wordsworth dies.
October	Dickens back at Devonshire Terrace.	*Copperfield* finished.	Publications: Elizabeth Barrett Browning's *Sonnets from the Portuguese*; Nathaniel Hawthorne's *The Scarlet Letter*; Charles Kingsley's *Alton Locke*; Dante Gabriel Rossetti's *The Blessed Damozel*; Tennyson's *In Memoriam*; Ivan S. Turgenev's *A Month in the Country*; Wordsworth's *The Prelude*.
November	Rehearsals at Knebworth for *Every Man in his Humour*, to be given in aid of the Guild of Literature and Art. Three private performances of *Every Man* given in the hall at Knebworth, followed by the farces *Animal Magnetism* and *Turning the Tables*, Dickens acting and directing.	Dickens writing *A Child's History of England*. Serialisation of *Copperfield* completed, and it appears in book form.	
1851 January	Performances of *Animal Magnetism* and *Used Up* at Rockingham Castle.	*A Child's History of England* begins in *Household Words*.	Palmerston dismissed from office as Foreign Secretary. Louis Napoleon gains control of all France. Crystal Palace built in Hyde Park, London, and Great Exhibition opens there. Isaac M. Singer markets first practical sewing-machine. Submarine cable links Dover and Calais. New York yacht *America* wins Royal Yacht Squadron cup, hence-forward known as the America's Cup. Verdi's *Rigoletto* performed.
February	Dickens visits Paris with Leech and the Hon. Spencer Lyttleton.		
March	Catherine Dickens suffers a nervous collapse and goes to Malvern to recover. Dickens visits her, but is recalled to London to his father		
March 31	John Dickens dies in London.		Publications: Borrow's *Lavengro*; Herman Melville's *Moby Dick*; Harriet Beecher Stowe's *Uncle Tom's Cabin*; Henri Murger's
April 14	Dickens takes the chair at the General Theatrical Fund meeting. Forster withholds the news until afterwards that Dickens's daughter Dora Annie has died at Devonshire Terrace.		

Year	Date	Life	Career	General Events
1851—contd	May 16	Dickens directs and plays in Bulwer-Lytton's *Not so bad as we Seem* at Devonshire House, Piccadilly, home of the Duke of Devonshire.		*Scènes de la Vie de Bohème*; Ruskin's *Stones of Venice*.
	May 27	A second presentation at Devonshire House, at which Dickens plays in his own farce, *Nightingale's Diary*. The play is published privately this year, exact date unknown.		
	May–June	Dickens decides to move his family to a larger house on the expiration of the Devonshire Terrace lease. He decides on Tavistock House, Bloomsbury, and supervises improvements during these months.		
	May (late)	Dickens and family at Fort House, Broadstairs, for the last time, Dickens being driven out by the incessant noise of German bands and other street musicians.		
	November	The Dickens family and Georgina Hogarth move into Tavistock House.	Dickens begins writing *Bleak House*.	
	November	Catherine Dickens's only publication, a cookery book *What Shall We Have for Dinner?* appears under the pseudonym Lady Maria Clutterbuck.		

1852	March	First part of *Bleak House* appears.		Fall of Russell: coalition government. Duke of Wellington dies. New Zealand and Transvaal made self-governing. Wells Fargo & Co. founded in U.S.A. Holman Hunt paints *The Light of the World*. Millais paints *Ophelia*. Crystal Palace transferred to permanent site at Sydenham. Victoria and Albert Museum opened.
	March 13		Edward Bulwer Lytton Dickens born.	
	July–October	Dickens writing *Bleak House*.	Dickens's children staying at Camden Crescent, Dover, while he, accompanied by Catherine and Georgina Hogarth, tours in performances of Bulwer-Lytton's *Not so Bad as we Seem* at Derby, Sheffield, Nottingham, Sunderland, Newcastle, Manchester and Liverpool. Deaths of his friends, Count D'Orsay, in August, and Mrs. Macready, in September.	Publications: Thackeray's *Henry Esmond*; Dumas *fils*'s *La Dame aux Camélias*; Matthew Arnold's *Empedocles on Etna and other Poems*.
	October	Dickens working on *Bleak House*; also on 'To be Read at Dusk' for *The Keepsake* at about this time.	Dickens and Catherine and Georgina Hogarth in Boulogne, experimenting with it as a holiday place, after which they return to London for the rest of the year.	
	December	First bound volume of *A Child's History of England* appears. *Christmas Books* appears.		
1853	January	Dickens writing *Bleak House*, and *A Child's History of England*, and editing *Household Words*.	Dickens receives ovation and presentations at Birmingham for his services to Mechanics' Institute. At Twelfth Night banquet Dickens makes offer to give two public readings at Christmas in aid of the New Midland Institute. Charley Dickens leaves Eton and goes to study at Leipzig.	Gladstone's first Budget: Death Duty introduced. Napoleon III marries Eugénie. Russo–Turkish War breaks out. Queen Victoria allows use of chloroform during birth of Prince Leopold. Smallpox vaccination compulsory in England. Balmoral Castle rebuilt. Verdi's *Il Trovatore* and *La Traviata* performed.

Year	Date	Life	Career	General Events
1853— contd.	June 13	Dickens returns to Boulogne to escape nervous breakdown. Catherine and Georgina Hogarth accompany him and the family follow three weeks later. They have rented the Château des Moulineaux.		Publications: Charlotte Brontë's *Villette*; Mrs. Gaskell's *Cranford*; Nathaniel Hawthorne's *Tanglewood Tales*; Thackeray's *The Newcomes*; Matthew Arnold's *Sohrab and Rustum*.
	August		Dickens completes *Bleak House*.	
	September		Dickens completes *A Child's History of England*. Last monthly part of *Bleak House* appears, and it is published in volume form.	
	October–December	Dickens sends family home and goes on trip to Italy with Wilkie Collins and Augustus Egg. Revisits Haldimand's institution. Revisits Genoa, Naples, Rome, Florence, Venice.		
	Mid-December	Dickens returns to London.		
	December 10		*A Child's History of England* ends in *Household Words*. Second bound volume appears.	
	December 27		Dickens gives his first public reading, 'Christmas Carol', at Birmingham Town Hall, followed on December 29 by 'Cricket', and 'Christmas Carol' again on December 30. Henceforth, reading from his works in London and the provinces occupies much of his time and energy.	

1854	January 6	Twelfth Night celebrations at Tavistock House with *Tom Thumb* performed by the family.	Crimean War breaks out: Battles of Alma, Balaclava, Inkerman; siege of Sebastopol begins. Commodore Perry forces Japan to make trade treaty with U.S.A. W. P. Frith paints *Ramsgate Sands*. Millet paints *The Reapers*. Wagner begins composing *The Ring*.
	January	Dickens in Preston.	
	April 1	First instalment of *Hard Times* in *Household Words*. Dickens collecting material for *Hard Times*, which he begins.	
	June–October	Dickens at Boulogne at the Villa Camp de Droite.	Dickens writing *Hard Times*
	August 12		Last instalment of *Hard Times* appears. It appears this month in volume form. Publications: Tennyson's 'The Charge of the Light Brigade'; Thoreau's *Walden*.
	October	Dickens returns to Tavistock House.	
	December		Third and last bound volume of *A Child's History of England* appears.
1855	January 6	Twelfth Night celebrations at Tavistock House: performance of *Fortunio and His Seven Gifted Servants*.	Crimean setbacks cause resignation of Aberdeen; succeeded by Palmerston. Queen Victoria and Prince Albert make state visit to France. Sebastopol falls; Britain and Turkey ally against Russia. Florence Nightingale becomes household name for her nursing work in the war. Death of Tsar Nicholas I; accession of Alexander II. Victoria Falls discovered by Livingstone. Liszt's *Faust* symphony performed. Ford Madox Brown paints *The Last of England*.
	February	Dickens spends fortnight in Paris with Wilkie Collins.	
	May	Dickens meets again Maria Winter, *née* Beadnell, and suffers disappointment in her.	Dickens begins writing *Dorrit*, first called *Nobody's Fault*.
	June	Amateur theatricals at Tavistock House: *The Lighthouse*, *Nightingale's Diary*, and *Animal Magnetism*.	

Year	Date	Life	Career	General Events
1855—contd	July	Dickens at 3 Albion Villas, Folkestone.	Dickens writing *Dorrit*.	Publications: Kingsley's *Westward Ho!*; Longfellow's *Hiawatha*; Motley's *Rise of the Dutch Republic*; Browning's *Men and Women*; Trollope's *The Warden*; Tennyson's *Maud*; Whitman's *Leaves of Grass*; *Daily Chronicle* and *Daily Telegraph* newspapers first appear.
	November	Dickens and family winter in Paris at 49 Avenue des Champs-Elysees.		
	December	Dickens sits for Ary Scheffer for his portrait and meets the *élite* of Paris, including George Sand.	First monthly part of *Dorrit* appears.	
1856	March 14	Dickens pays the purchase money for Gad's Hill Place. Returns to Paris until May.	Dickens writing *Dorrit*.	Crimean War ends with Treaty of Paris. Second Anglo-Chinese war breaks out. Holman Hunt paints *The Scapegoat*. Millais paints *Autumn Leaves*. Victoria Cross instituted. Royal Opera House, Covent Garden, burns down.
	June–August	Dickens at Boulogne with family.		
	September	Dickens returns to London.		
	November	Rehearsals at Tavistock House for Collins's melodrama *The Frozen Deep*.		Publications: Flaubert's *Madame Bovary*; Kingsley's *The Heroes*; J. A. Froude's *The History of England*.
1857	January 6, 8, 12, 14	*The Frozen Deep* acted at Tavistock House, followed by farces *Animal Magnetism* and *Uncle John*.		Chinese fleet destroyed by British: British enter Canton. Indian Mutiny: Siege of Lucknow, Cawnpore Massacres, relief of Lucknow, capture of Delhi. Transportation for crime ends. Princess Beatrice born to Queen
	February	Dickens gets possession of Gad's Hill Place.		
	June		Last instalment of *Dorrit* appears, and it appears in volume form.	

June 8	Douglas Jerrold, journalist and friend of Dickens, dies.	Victoria. Millet paints *The Gleaners*. Sir Charles Hallé founds Hallé concerts in Manchester.
July 4	*The Frozen Deep* given as benefit performance for widow of Douglas Jerrold at Gallery of Illustration in Regent Street.	Publications: Charlotte Brontë's *The Professor*; Borrow's *The Romany Rye*; Elizabeth Barrett Browning's *Aurora Leigh*; Baudelaire's *Les Fleurs du Mal*; Thomas Hughes's *Tom Brown's Schooldays*; Herbert Spencer's *Essays*; Thackeray's *The Virginians*; Trollope's *Barchester Towers*; Mrs. Craik's *John Halifax, Gentleman*.
July 20	Walter Dickens leaves for India.	
July	Marital discord between Dickens and Catherine growing at this period.	
August	Dickens meets Ellen Ternan and she goes with his troupe to Manchester to play in the benefit performances of *The Frozen Deep* on August 21 and 22.	
September	Dickens tours through the North of England with Wilkie Collins.	Dickens and Collins acquire material for *Two Apprentices*.
October 3–31		*Two Apprentices*, by Dickens and Wilkie Collins appears in *Household Words*.
1858 February	Dickens throws himself into work for Hospital for Sick Children.	Palmerston resigns; succeeded by Derby. Jews admitted to Parliament. Irish Republican Brotherhood, the Fenians, founded in U.S.A. Indian Mutiny suppressed, East India Company abolished and government transferred to British Crown. First recorded miracle at Lourdes. Lake Tanganyika, source of Nile, discovered. Suez Canal Company formed. Cathode rays discovered.
April 15	Dickens gives reading in aid of Hospital.	
April 29	First of the many public readings for Dickens's own benefit given at St. Martin's Hall, London.	
[Date unknown]	*Reprinted Pieces* collected in 8th volume of Library Edition of Dickens's works (Chapman & Hall).	

Year	Date	Life	Career	General Events
1858— *contd*	May	Dickens and Catherine separate.		First European oil well found. First Atlantic cable laid. Offenbach's *Orpheus in the Underworld* performed. Brahms's 1st piano concerto performed. Present Royal Opera House, Covent Garden, opened. Big Ben cast at Whitechapel Bell Foundry. Frith paints *Derby Day*.
	June 12		Dickens makes unwise public statement in *Household Words* and quarrels with publishers Bradbury & Evans.	
	August 2– November 13		87 readings, beginning Clifton, ending Brighton, taking in Ireland and Scotland; 44 places altogether.	Publications: George Eliot's *Scenes from Clerical Life*; Frederic W. Farrar's *Eric, or Little by Little*; Oliver Wendell Holmes's *The Autocrat at the Breakfast-Table*; William Morris's *Defence of Guenevere and other Poems*; Longfellow's *The Courtship of Miles Standish*; Trollope's *Doctor Thorne*; Ibsen's *The Vikings in Heligoland*; Carlyle's *Frederick the Great*; first publication of *Crockford's Clerical Directory*.
1859	January 28		Dickens chooses title of *All the Year Round* for a new weekly journal.	Disraeli, Chancellor of the Exchequer, introduces Reform Bill, which is defeated. Derby's Government falls and Palmerston becomes Prime Minister for second term of office. Growth of Fenian activity. First American oil wells drilled in Pennsylvania. T. B. Bishop composes *John Brown's Body* to commemorate raid at
	February		Takes office at 11 Wellington Street, Strand.	
	March		Dickens begins writing *Two Cities*.	
	April 30		First number of *All the Year Round* appears, containing opening instalment of *Two Cities*.	

331

May 28	As owner-editor, Dickens contributed to it throughout the remainder of his life, and willed his share in it to his son Charley. Chapman & Hall agree to publish the remainder of his books. Last number of *Household Words* appears. *Dickens finishes Two Cities.*	Harper's Ferry. Gounod's *Faust* performed. Millet paints *The Angelus.* Vauxhall Pleasure Gardens, London, closed. Publications: Charles Darwin's *The Origin of Species;* Edward FitzGerald's translation of *The Rubáiyát of Omar Khayyám;* George Eliot's *Adam Bede;* George Meredith's *The Ordeal of Richard Feverel;* Samuel Smiles's *Self-help;* J. S. Mill's *On Liberty;* Tennyson's *Idylls of the King.*
Summer	Dickens at Gad's Hill with daughters, younger sons, and Georgina Hogarth as housekeeper. Moves to Broadstairs for a week at the end of the summer.	
August 20	*First part of Hunted Down* (in three parts) *published in New York Ledger.*	
November 26	*Last instalment of Two Cities appears.*	
December	*Two Cities appears in volume form.*	
1860 January 28	*Uncommercial begins in All the Year Round.*	Free Trade Budget introduced by Gladstone. Cobden makes Free Trade Treaty with France. First Italian National Parliament formed at Turin. Capture of Sicily and Naples by Garibaldi. Publications: Wilkie Collins's *The Woman in White;* George Eliot's *The Mill on the Floss;* Thackeray's *The Four Georges.*
July 17	Katey Dickens marries Charles Allston Collins.	
July 27	Alfred Lamert Dickens dies in Manchester.	
July	Tavistock House given up.	
September	Dickens settles at Gad's Hill as his permanent residence.	
October	Dickens begins writing *Expectations.*	

Year	Date	Life	Career	General Events
1860— contd	November	Dickens and Wilkie Collins visit Devon and Cornwall.		
	December 1		First instalment of *Expectations* appears in *All the Year Round*.	
	December		First collection of *Uncommercial* pieces in book form appears.	
1861	March	Dickens takes 3 Hanover Terrace, Regent's Park, as London base.	Dickens writing *Expectations*,	Death of Albert, Prince Consort. Abraham Lincoln elected President of U.S.A. American Civil War breaks out: Battles of Bull Run and Lexington. Italian unity (except for Roman Venice) achieved under Victor Emmanuel of Savoy.
	March	Sydney Dickens appointed to H.M.S. *Orlando*.		
	March–April		Second series of readings begins at St. James's Hall, ending April 18.	Serfdom abolished in Russia. London's first horse-drawn tramcars.
	June	Dickens at Gad's Hill.	Dickens finishes writing *Expectations*.	
	August 3		Last instalment of *Expectations* appears, and the work is published in 2 vols. this month.	Publications: Mrs. Beeton's *Book of Household Management*; Palgrave's *Golden Treasury*; Charles Reade's *The Cloister and the Hearth*; Turgenev's *Fathers and Sons*; Dostoievsky's *The House of the Dead*; George Eliot's *Silas Marner*.
	October 28		A long series of provincial readings opens at Norwich, taking in Berwick-on-Tweed, Lancaster, Bury St. Edmunds, Cheltenham, Carlisle, Hastings, Plymouth, Birmingham, Canterbury, Torquay, Preston, Ipswich, Manchester, Brighton, Colchester, Dover, and Newcastle.	
	October	Dickens's tour manager, Arthur Smith, dies. Henry Austin, Dickens's brother-in-law, dies.		

Date			
November	Charley Dickens marries Bessie Evans, daughter of Dickens's one-time publisher.	Provincial readings end at Chester.	American Civil War: Battles of Mill Springs and Williamsburg. Bismarck becomes Prime Minister of Prussia. Frith paints *The Railway Station*; Julia Ward Howe's 'Battle Hymn of the Republic' sung by Union forces in America; Berlioz's *Beatrice and Benedict* performed.
1862 January			Publications: Hugo's *Les Misérables*; Mrs. Henry Wood's *The Channings*; Christina Rossetti's *Goblin Market and other Poems*; George Eliot's *Romola*; Flaubert's *Salammbô*; Herbert Spencer's *First Principles*; Ruskin's *Unto This Last*; Borrow's *Wild Wales*; Elizabeth Barrett Browning's *Last Poems*.
February	Dickens takes 16 Hyde Park Gate for three months.		
March	Georgina Hogarth seriously ill.		
March–June		Series of London readings at St. James's Hall, ending in mid-June.	
October–December	Dickens takes Georgina Hogarth and Mamie Dickens to Paris, where they rent 24 rue du Faubourg St. Honoré.		
December	Dickens home for Christmas.		
1863 January	Dickens returns to Paris with Georgina Hogarth and Mamie.	Dickens gives four readings at the British Embassy, Paris, for British Charitable Fund.	Edward, Prince of Wales, marries Princess Alexandra of Denmark. Abolition of slavery in U.S.A. American Civil War: Battles of Nashville, Winchester, Gettysburg, etc. Lincoln delivers Gettysburg Address. Work begins on London's underground railway, world's first. Bizet's *The Pearl Fishers* performed. Manet paints *Le Déjeuner sur l'Herbe*. Liszt's Symphony in A performed.
February	Dickens and his companions return to London.		
June		Dickens gives 13 readings at the Hanover Square Rooms.	
September 12	Death of Dickens's mother.		
November	Dickens at Gad's Hill.	Dickens begins writing *Mutual Friend*.	

Year	Date	Life	Career	General Events
1863— *contd*	December 24 December 31	Death of Thackeray. Death of Walter Dickens in India.		Publications: Kingsley's *The Water Babies*.
1864	January February	Frank Dickens starts for India. Dickens moves London base to 57 Gloucester Place.	Dickens writing *Mutual Friend*.	First Trade Union Conference. Chimney Sweeps Act forbidding employment of children; proves ineffective. International Red Cross founded by Henry Dunant. Offenbach's *La Belle Hélène* performed. Bruckner's Symphony in D Minor performed.
	May 1		First part of *Mutual Friend* appears.	
	June	Dickens leaves 57 Gloucester Place and returns to Gad's Hill for the remainder of year.		Publications: Le Fanu's *Uncle Silas*; Tennyson's *Enoch Arden*; Ségur's *Les Malheurs de Sophie*; Ibsen's *The Pretenders*; John Henry Newman's *Apologia pro Vita Sua*.
	October 29	Death of John Leech.		
	December	Swiss chalet arrives at Gad's Hill, the gift of Fechter.		
1865	February	Dickens attacked by pain and lameness in left foot, probably early symptoms of thrombosis.		Death of Palmerston. Russell becomes Prime Minister. President Lincoln assassinated. First concrete roads laid in Britain. Queensberry Rules controlling boxing drawn up. Wagner's *Tristan and Isolde* performed. Whistler paints *Old Battersea Bridge*. Rimsky-Korsakov's Symphony in E Flat Minor performed.
	March	Dickens takes furnished house at 16 Somers Place, Hyde Park, until June.		
	June	Dickens takes short holiday in Paris, possibly accompanied by Ellen Ternan and her mother.	Dickens writing *Mutual Friend*.	
	June 9	Dickens and companions in serious railway accident at Staplehurst, Kent. Dickens uninjured but permanently affected by shock.		Publications: Lewis Carroll's *Alice in Wonderland*; Newman's

	November	Last part of *Mutual Friend* appears, and the work is published in book form.	*Dream of Gerontius*; Ouida's *Strathmore*; Ruskin's *Sesame and Lilies*; Swinburne's *Atalanta in Calydon*; Tolstoy's *War and Peace*.
	December	Second collection of *Uncommercial* pieces appears in book form.	
1866	March	Dickens accepts offer from Chappells of Bond Street to undertake 30 readings.	Defeat of Gladstone's Reform Bill and resignation of Government. Derby becomes Prime Minister. Austria defeated by Prussia in Seven Weeks' War at Sadowa. Mary Baker Eddy formulates first ideas of Christian Science.
		Dickens takes furnished house, 6 Southwick Place, Hyde Park. Suffers from heart trouble and general ill-health.	
	April	Reading tour begins at Liverpool	Offenbach's *La Vie Parisienne* produced. Suppé's *Light Cavalry* produced.
		Dickens shocked by news of death of Jane Welsh Carlyle.	
	June	Tour ends.	Publications: Paul Verlaine's *Poèmes saturniens*; Dostoievsky's *Crime and Punishment*; Kingsley's *Hereward the Wake*; Ruskin's *Crown of Wild Olive*; C. M. Yonge's *The Dove in the Eagle's Nest*; Emile Gaboriau's *L'Affaire Lerouge*; George Eliot's *Felix Holt*.
	June	Dickens complains to various correspondents of exhaustion, and pain in left eye, hand, and foot. Returns to Gad's Hill for remainder of year.	
	October 6	Augustus Dickens dies impoverished in Chicago.	
	December	'Mugby Junction' published in *All the Year Round*.	
1867	January	Dickens begins new series of 50 provincial readings at Liverpool, taking in Scotland and Ireland.	Fenian rising in Ireland. Garibaldi invades Papal States. Emperor Maximilian executed by Mexican rebels. South African diamond fields discovered. Alfred B. Nobel produces dynamite. Lister demonstrates the use of carbolic antiseptic. Gounod's
	January 15	Dickens complains of exhaustion and faintness, and of nervousness produced by rail travel.	
	May	Death of Dickens's close friend Clarkson Stanfield.	

Year	Date	Life	Career	General Events
1867— *contd*	May 14		Tour ends. After it, Dickens tells Forster of American offers, and that he is tempted to undertake an American tour.	*Roméo et Juliette* produced. Johann Strauss's *The Blue Danube* performed. Sullivan provides music for Morton and Burnand's *Cox and Box*. Wagner's *Die Meistersinger von Nürnberg* performed. Bizet's *La Jolie Fille de Perth* performed.
	August	Dickens suffers severely from pain and swelling in foot, and is unable to walk. Forster tries to dissuade him from undertaking the American project.	Dolby sails for America to reconnoitre.	Publications: Zola's *Thérèse Raquin*; first volume of Karl Marx's *Das Kapital*; Dostoievsky's *The Gambler*; Ibsen's *Peer Gynt*; Swinburne's *Song of Italy*.
	September		Dolby reports favourably on American conditions.	
	September 30		Dickens telegraphs acceptance to J. T. Fields in Boston.	
	? October–November		Dickens writes his last Christmas piece (with Wilkie Collins) 'No Thoroughfare', for *All the Year Round*. This and other Christmas pieces from *Household Words* and *All the Year Round* are now familiar as Christmas Stories.	
	November 9	Dickens sails for America.		
	November 19	Dickens arrives in Boston.		
	December 2	Dickens writes home of severe weather and trials of travelling, but enjoys warm hospitality in New England.	Dickens gives first reading in Boston. Is now making a clear profit of £1300 a week.	
	December 9		Gives first reading in New York.	
	December 26		First production of *No Thoroughfare*.	
	December 27	In New York, Dickens calls in doctor to treat persistent cold and catarrh.		

Date			
1868			
January–February	Dickens continues ill. Comments on improvements in American conditions since his first visit.	Dickens reads in New York, Brooklyn (in Ward Beecher's chapel), Philadelphia, Baltimore, Washington (where he meets President Andrew Johnson).	Disraeli's first ministry, followed by Gladstone's first ministry. Ku Klux Klan founded in southern states of U.S.A. following the Civil War. Monet paints *Argenteuil-sur-Seine*; Renoir paints *Sisley and his Wife*; Moussorgsky's *Boris Godounov* performed; Rimsky-Korsakov's Symphony Number 2 performed. Maxim Gorky born.
February		'Silverman' published in *Household Words*.	
January–March		'Silverman' published in *Atlantic Monthly*.	
January–May		'Holiday Romance' simultaneously begins publication in *Our Young Folks* (U.S.A.) and *All the Year Round*.	Publications: Browning's *The Ring and the Book*; Wilkie Collins's *The Moonstone*; Louisa May Alcott's *Little Women*; William Morris's *Earthly Paradise*; Queen Victoria's *Leaves from a Journal of Our Life in the Highlands*; Dostoievsky's *The Idiot*; first publication of *Whitaker's Almanac*.
March	Dickens revisits Niagara. Complains of being 'nearly used up'.	Dickens reads in Rochester, Syracuse, Buffalo, Springfield, Utica, Portland, New Bedford, etc. Returns to Boston.	
April	Public dinner given for Dickens at Delmonico's.	Dickens gives farewell readings in Boston and New York.	
April 22	Dickens sails for England.		
May 1	Dickens arrives in England. Appears in better health.		
Summer	Throughout summer Dickens entertains American and other friends at Gad's Hill.		
September	Dickens's youngest son, Edward Bulwer Lytton Dickens, sails for Australia.		
October 5		Dickens starts reading tour for Chappells.	

Year	Date	Life	Career	General Events
1868— *contd*	October **20**	Dickens's only surviving brother Fred dies.		
	November		Reading tour interrupted for anticipated general election. Dickens works up his 'Murder of Nancy' reading and first presents it privately at St. James's Hall, London, on November 14.	
1869	January		Readings resume; first public hearing of the 'Murder of Nancy' is on January 5.	Imprisonment for debt abolished. Irish Church Disestablishment Act. Suez Canal opened by Empress Eugénie. Union Pacific Railway completed. Blackfriars Bridge, London, built. *Cutty Sark*, tea-clipper, launched. Girton College for Women founded. Borodin's 1st Symphony performed; Manet painted *Portrait of Berthe Morisot*; Brahms completed *Ein Deutsches Requiem*.
	April 22		At Preston, Dickens is ordered by Dr. Beard and Sir Thomas Watson to discontinue readings, as paralysis threatens. The audience's money is returned and Dr. Beard escorts Dickens back to London. He continues unwell, but promises Chappells a series of London farewell readings.	
	July		Dickens conceives first ideas of *Drood*.	Publications: R. D. Blackmore's *Lorna Doone*; W. S. Gilbert's *Bab Ballads*; Mark Twain's *Innocents Abroad*; Flaubert's *L'Education Sentimentale*; Verlaine's *Fêtes Galantes*; Daudet's *Lettres de Mon Moulin*.
	October	Dickens at Gad's Hill.	Dickens begins writing *Drood*.	

1870			
January	Dickens takes a furnished house, 5 Hyde Park Place, and visits Ellen Ternan regularly at Windsor Lodge, Peckham. Suffers much pain in left hand and failure in left eye.	Dickens writing *Drood*.	Irish Land Act passed. Outbreak of Franco-Prussian War; French defeated at Sedan; Siege of Paris. Second Empire ends, and Third Republic proclaimed. First Elementary Education Act results in the establishment of Board Schools. First Caesarean operation performed. Millais paints *The Boyhood of Raleigh*. Delibes's music for *Coppélia* performed. Smetana's *The Bartered Bride* performed.
January 11		Dickens begins 12 farewell readings at St. James's Hall.	
March 9	Dickens received by Queen Victoria at Buckingham Palace.		Publications: Spencer's *Principles of Psychology*; D. G. Rossetti's *Poems*.
March 15		Dickens gives final reading at St. James's Hall.	
April 1	Daniel Maclise dies.	First number of *Drood* appears.	
April 30	Dickens attends Royal Academy Dinner and returns thanks for 'Literature', paying tribute to the recently-dead Maclise.	Dickens writing *Drood*.	
May	Dickens dines with Motley, American Minister, meets Disraeli at dinner at Lord Stanhope's, breakfasts with Gladstone. He is obliged to refuse invitation to attend Queen's ball with Mamie, because of illness. Dines with Lord Houghton, in company with Prince of Wales and King of the Belgians.		
May 29	Dickens writes last letter to Forster.		
June 7	Dickens drives from Gad's Hill to Cobham with Georgina Hogarth and walks in Cobham Park; expresses to her his desire to be buried at Rochester.		

Year	Date	Life	Career	General Events
1870—contd	June 8	Dickens taken ill after a day of writing *Drood*.		
	June 9	Dickens dies of cerebral haemorrhage.	*Drood* is left unfinished.	
	June 14	(Buried in Poets' Corner, Westminster Abbey.)		
	August 12		First bound publication of *Drood*.	
	September		Sixth and last extant part of *Drood* appears.	

DICKENS AND HIS CIRCLE

THE FAMILY, FRIENDS AND ASSOCIATES
MOST INFLUENTIAL UPON DICKENS'S
WORKS AND LIFE

Agassis, Jean Louis Rodolph (1807–73): Swiss-American naturalist, geologist and teacher, the son of the Protestant pastor of Motier, Switzerland. At Erlangen he took the degree of Doctor of Philosophy and at Munich that of Doctor of Medicine. The study of fish-forms became his life-work, and he travelled widely to gather material for his important works *Recherches sur les Poissons Fossiles* and *Études Critiques sur les Mollusces*, and other volumes of scientific research. When Dickens visited America on his last reading tour Agassis was one of the notabilities introduced to him, and was present, with other American friends, when he left Boston for New York in December 1867.

Ainsworth, William Harrison (1805–82): Trained for the law, he became a publisher in 1826. His first novel, *Rookwood*, 1834, was an immediate success. He edited *Bentley's Miscellany*, 1840–2, and was the first professional writer to invite Dickens to his house as a fellow-author. His afternoon parties were a meeting-point for celebrities from the worlds of art and literature, and were often attended by Dickens. He wrote thirty-nine novels, mainly historical.

Andersen, Hans Christian (1805–75): After a varied career in Denmark as singer, dancer, and schoolmaster, he turned to literature and produced a successful novel in 1835. Later that year the first instalment of his *Fairy Tales* was published in Copenhagen and continued to appear until 1872, bringing him fame throughout Europe. In 1847 and 1857 he stayed with the Dickens family in England, and was one of Dickens's most ardent admirers.

Austin, Henry (d. 1861): Architect, and husband of Dickens's sister Letitia, he surveyed and gave advice on Dickens's purchases of Tavistock House and Gad's Hill. Skilled as an artist, he painted portraits of Maria Beadnell during Dickens's courtship of her.

Austin, Mrs. Henry (Letitia Mary, *née* **Dickens)** (1816–93): Younger sister of Dickens, she was a delicate child, subject to fits. In 1837 she married Henry Austin, architect and artist. Her husband's death left her in straitened circumstances, and Dickens obtained for her a pension of £60 a year as widow of the Secretary to the London Sanitary Commission. After Dickens's death his sister-in-law, Georgina Hogarth, continued to help Letitia.

Barham, Richard Harris (1788–1845): Author of *The Ingoldsby Legends* under the pen-name of Thomas Ingoldsby; minor canon of St. Paul's, 1821, divinity lecturer at St. Paul's and vicar of St. Faith's, London, 1842. Literary adviser to Bentley, 1839–43. The *Legends* were printed in *Bentley's Miscellany* and the *New Monthly Magazine*. Barham, born in Canterbury, was a friend of Dickens and Forster – 'the cordial Thomas Ingoldsby' – and shared Dickens's love for the supernatural, appreciating particularly 'The Chimes', of which, at his request, Dickens gave a second private reading in 1844.

Barrow, Charles (1759–1826): Father of Elizabeth Barrow and father-in-law of John Dickens. At the time of John Dickens's marriage to his daughter, Barrow was 'Chief Conductor of Monies in Town' at the Navy Pay Office, being responsible for the conveyance of money under armed guard to the ports of Plymouth, Portsmouth, Sheerness, and Chatham. Suspicion of dishonesty led to criminal proceedings being brought against him, and he admitted his guilt, pleading the heavy expenses of a family of ten children and his own ill-health. In 1810 he left England without repaying the sum he had embezzled.

Barrow, Edward (1798–1869): Son of

Charles Barrow, younger brother of John Henry Barrow, and uncle of Charles Dickens. He married Janet Ross the miniaturist, who possibly provided some of the characteristics of Miss La Creevy in *Nicholas Nickleby*. She painted the earliest authentic portrait of Dickens.

Barrow, Elizabeth: See Dickens, Mrs. John.

Barrow, John Henry (1796–1858): Brother of Elizabeth Barrow (1789–1863). A Barrister-at-Law of Gray's Inn, he founded and edited the *Mirror of Parliament*, for which his brother Edward Barrow, his brother-in-law John Dickens and his nephew Charles became parliamentary reporters. He taught Dickens shorthand by the Gurney system. He was the author of *The Battle of Talavera*, an epic poem in the style of Scott, was a specialist in Indian affairs, and at the time of the trial of Queen Caroline was a Doctors' Commons reporter on the staff of *The Times*. When Charles Dickens became editor of the *Daily News* he appointed his uncle sub-editor.

Barrow, Thomas Culliford (?1793–1857): Uncle of Dickens. In 1805, aged 12, he became a clerk in the Navy Pay Office, and became friendly with a colleague, John Dickens, who later married Barrow's sister Elizabeth. He became head of the Prize Branch at a salary of £710 a year.

Beadnell, Anne: Second daughter of George Beadnell, she married Dickens's friend Henry Kolle in 1833.

Beadnell, Maria (1810–86), later Mrs. Henry Winter: Youngest daughter of George Beadnell. Dickens was introduced to her family about 1830. He fell violently in love with Maria, but her parents disapproved of him as being young and irresponsible, and he was forbidden the house, while Maria was sent to a finishing school abroad. The courtship was later resumed, but ended by Maria. Dickens portrayed her as Dora in *David Copperfield* and, after meeting her again in 1855, when she had become middle-aged and matronly, as the ridiculous Flora Finching of *Little Dorrit*.

Beard, Dr. Francis Carr (1814–93): Thomas Beard's youngest brother; studied medicine at London University, M.R.C.S. in 1838, F.R.C.S. 1853. Dickens does not appear to have written to or consulted him much between the 1830s and 1859, after which date Beard became his regular medical attendant; he was at Dickens's death-bed.

Beard, Thomas (1807–91): Journalist, sometimes called Dickens's oldest friend; their friendship lasted until Dickens's death. Beard came of a family of brewers. A fellow shorthand-writer of Dickens when he entered the gallery of the House of Commons, he joined the *Morning Herald* about 1832 and in 1834 moved to the *Morning Chronicle*, where he was soon joined by Dickens. The two travelled the country widely as reporters, and Beard thought that 'there never *was* such a short-hand writer' as Dickens. He was best man at Dickens's wedding, godfather to Charley, Dickens's eldest son, and close friend of the family. To Dickens he was always 'Tom'.

Bentley, Richard (1794–1871): Publisher who went into partnership with Henry Colburn in 1829, but subsequently became his professional rival. He started *Bentley's Miscellany* with Dickens as editor in 1837. After some dissension over contractual matters Dickens agreed to edit a life of Grimaldi for Bentley. Despite other differences between them, the two men remained personally friendly, according to Forster, but it seems probable that Dickens never got over a certain dislike and distrust of Bentley, whom he had once called 'a nefarious rascal who expected to publish serials for his own benefit and authors to acquiesce in toiling to make him rich'. He founded the firm of Richard Bentley & Son.

Blackmore, Edward: Partner in the firm of Ellis & Blackmore, Gray's Inn, and Dickens's first employer. 'I was well acquainted with his parents,' Blackmore wrote, 'and being then in practice in Gray's Inn, they asked me if I could find employment for him. He was a bright, clever-looking youth, and I took him as a clerk.' Dickens worked for a salary of 13s. 6d., rising to 15s. a week. Blackmore noticed several incidents which had taken place in his offices making their appearance in *Pickwick* and *Nickleby*, and well recalled Dickens's passion for acting at minor theatres.

Blessington, Marguerite, Countess of (1789–1849): Born Margaret Power, she married in 1804 Captain Maurice St. Leger Farmer, separating from him after a few unhappy months. In 1818, after his death, she married Charles John Gardiner, first Earl of Blessington, and travelled with him on the Continent, returning, a widow once more, to London in 1831, after living in Paris for some time and making the acquaintance of Byron. She was accompanied by Alfred, Count D'Orsay, who had been married to and separated from Lady Harriet Gardiner, her stepdaughter. Their *ménage* at Gore House, Kensington, gave rise to widespread scandal, and they were cold-shouldered by many leaders of London society, though arists, wits, dandies, politicians, scholars and men of letters flocked around them. Dickens was one of these, and met at her salon Walter Savage Landor, the young Disraeli, Bulwer-Lytton, Macready, and Harrison Ainsworth, among many others. He first met her about 1836, soon becoming a close friend of both her and D'Orsay. She edited the *Book of Beauty* and *The Keepsake* and wrote novels and memoirs. Ruined by extravagant entertaining, she was bankrupted in 1849 and fled to Paris with Count D'Orsay, dying there that summer. In July 1856 Dickens wrote to Landor, 'There in Paris . . . I found Marguerite Power and little Nelly (Lady Blessington's nieces) living with their mother and a pretty sister, in a very small, neat apartment, and working (as Marguerite told me) very hard for a living. All that I saw of them filled me with respect, and revived the tenderest remembrances of Gore House.' Brilliant and beautiful, she was one of the most notable of London hostesses. Her portrait by Lawrence is in the Wallace Collection, Manchester Square, London.

Boyle, Mary (1810–90): Daughter of the Commissioner of Sheerness Dockyard, and niece of Lord Cork and of Mrs. Richard Watson of Rockingham Castle. A socialite and wit, her love of the theatre brought her into the Dickens circle of amateur players and she acted in many of his productions, often playing opposite him. To Dickens she was dearest 'Meery' for the twenty years of their close friendship.

'Boz': See **Dickens, Charles John Huffam.**

Bradbury & Evans: William Bradbury and Frederick Mullet Evans became partners in 1830 in the London publishing firm who replaced Chapman & Hall as Dickens's publishers in 1844. He broke with them in 1858 because of the refusal of *Punch*, of which they were the proprietors, to publish his 'separation document' denying the rumours of his attachment to Ellen Ternan. Bessie, Evans's daughter, married Charles Dickens junior.

Brown, Anne: Later Anne Cornelius. Maid in Dickens family from 1842 to sometime in the 1860s, she was held in great affection by Dickens. Before his separation from his wife she was personal maid to Catherine Dickens. After her marriage she asked Georgina Hogarth and Mamie Dickens for financial help during her husband's illness, and they raised a handsome subscription for her.

Brown, Hablôt Knight ('Phiz') (1815–82): Water-colour painter and book illustrator. His first illustration for Dickens was for 'Sunday under Three Heads' in 1836, followed by *Pickwick*. He continued to illustrate for Dickens for twenty-three years, ten of the novels being illustrated by him in etching or in wood-engraving. *A Tale of Two Cities* was the last book for which he drew, before being succeeded by Marcus Stone. His drawings are notable for grotesquerie and strong characterisation – caricatures rather than depictions of real life. His pseudonym 'Phiz' was chosen to match with the author's 'Boz'.

Bulwer, Edward: See Lytton.

Burdett-Coutts, Angela Georgina (1814–1906): Youngest daughter of Sir Francis Burdett, fifth Baronet, and his wife Sophia Coutts, in 1837 she assumed the additional surname of Coutts upon inheriting the great fortune of her maternal grandfather, the banker Thomas Coutts. Her father's social circle, as an eminent politican and reformer, included such famous men as Byron, Samuel Rogers, Moore, Wordsworth, and Dickens. The young heiress, who later became Baroness Burdett-Coutts, devoted her life to philanthropy, giving her time and wealth to such causes as education of the poor, the prevention of cruelty to children and animals, and the reclamation of prostitutes, in which cause she worked closely with Dickens. Their friendship lasted from about 1835 until his death, and their collaboration in good works until 1855, Dickens acting as unofficial almoner and secretary.

Burnett, Henry (1811–93): Singer, music teacher, and brother-in-law of Dickens. His character was influenced by his early life in the care of a deeply religious dissenter grandmother. Later he lived with his father in Brighton, and at the age of ten or thereabouts sang before George IV and his court at the Pavilion. Studied music with the organist of the Chapel Royal, entered the Royal Academy of Music in March 1832, met Fanny Dickens, with whom he sang in several concerts 1835–6, and married her in 1837. He took over from Braham the part of Squire Norton in *The Village Coquettes*, and in 1838 joined Macready's company at Covent Garden, but his inbred religious scruples soon made him doubt the propriety of the professional stage, and he left it in 1841, never afterwards entering a theatre.

Burnett, Mrs. Henry: See Dickens, Frances Elizabeth.

Carlyle, Mrs. Jane Baillie Welsh (1801–66): Born at Haddington, Scotland, she was a brilliant and beautiful young woman with a talent for versifying. She married Thomas Carlyle in 1826. Their home in Cheyne Row, Chelsea, became a centre for the literary ladies of her time and for literary society in general. Dickens admired her immensely and said of her 'none of the writing women come near her'.

Carlyle, Thomas (1795–1881): Essayist and historian. Scots-born, he came to London in 1831 with his wife Jane Welsh Carlyle. He first met Dickens in 1840 and a warm friendship began which lasted until Dickens's death, in spite of Carlyle's occasional criticisms. His *French Revolution* published in 1837, made his reputation, and his Collected Works appeared in 1857–8.

Cattermole, George (1800–68): Painter, exhibited at the Royal Academy 1819–27. A prolific book-illustrator, he was invited by Dickens to illustrate, together with 'Phiz', *Master Humphrey's Clock*. This was followed by *The Old Curiosity Shop* and *Barnaby Rudge*, the best-known of these drawings on wood being the church (Tong, Shropshire) which saw the end of Little Nell's travels, the scene of her deathbed, and the Maypole Inn in *Barnaby Rudge*. Cattermole was notable for his romanticism of style and the quaint elaboration of detail with which he fantasised ordinary buildings and scenes. From 1850 onwards he painted in oils, chiefly Biblical subjects.

Chapman, Edward (1804–80): With William Hall, of 186 Strand, bookseller and publisher from 1830. Chapman, son of a Richmond solicitor, was the more literary of the partners. It was he who commissioned Dickens to write the series of sketches which became *Pickwick Papers*. Also published *Nicholas Nickleby*, first complete edition of *Sketches by Boz*, *Master Humphrey's Clock*, incorporating *The Old Curiosity Shop* and *Barnaby Rudge*, *American Notes*, *Martin Chuzzlewit*, and 'The Chimes'. After this Dickens broke with the firm and became associated with the printers Bradbury & Evans. Chapman & Hall also published works for the

Brownings, Lord Lytton, Trollope, and Meredith.

Chapman, Frederic (1823–95): Publisher, and cousin of Edward Chapman. He became a partner in the house of Chapman & Hall in 1847 and head of the firm in 1864.

Clarke, Mrs. Charles Cowden (Mary Victoria) (1809–98): Daughter of Vincent Novello, married Charles Cowden Clarke in 1828. Produced the *Complete Concordance to Shakespeare*, published in monthly parts 1844–5. Lived in Italy from 1856. She became a friend and admirer of Dickens through amateur theatricals and wrote of him in her *Recollections of Writers*, 1878.

Colburn, Henry (d. 1855): Publisher and magazine proprietor. He started a number of London magazines, 1814–29, kept a circulating library in 1816, and brought out a library of modern standard novelists, 1835–41. After an unsatisfactory partnership with Richard Bentley, he went into competition with him. Forster married Colburn's widow Eliza Ann in 1856, to Dickens's amused astonishment: 'I have the most prodigious, overwhelming, crushing, astounding, blinding, deafening, pulverising, scarifying secret, of which Forster is the hero . . . after I knew it (from himself) this morning, I lay down flat as if an engine and tender had fallen on me.'

Collins, Charles Allston (1828–73): Son of William Collins, R.A., and brother of Wilkie Collins. Became a Pre-Raphaelite, exhibited at the Royal Academy, published essays and novels. Married Dickens's daughter Katey in 1860, and designed the famous green cover for *Edwin Drood* and some sample illustrations, but was prevented by ill-health from continuing the work.

Collins, Mrs. Charles Allston: See Dickens, Kate Macready.

Collins, William Wilkie (1824–89): Called to the bar in 1851, but turned to authorship. Contributed to *Household Words* from 1855. Collaborated with Dickens in *The Lazy Tour of Two Idle Apprentices* and 'A Message from the Sea'; contributed *The Woman in White* to *All the Year Round*. Wrote, with Dickens, 'No Thoroughfare', 1867, by which time he had become a close friend of, and a strong influence upon, Dickens. His later novels include *Armadale* and *The Moonstone*.

Cornelius, Mrs.: See Brown, Anne.

Cornwall, Barry: See Procter, Bryan Waller.

Cruikshank, George (1792–1878): Artist and caricaturist, son of Isaac Cruikshank, and brother of Robert, also artists. After an early career of caricaturing contemporary events and illustrating books, including the Grimms' *Popular Tales*, he was commissioned to illustrate *Sketches by Boz*, and later *Oliver Twist*. His drawings were essentially caricatures rather than portraits, comedy and drama being more conspicuous in them than beauty. Dickens, in an 1847 revival of the adventures of Mrs. Gamp, published in Forster's *Life*, made her speak of 'the great George'. Mrs. Gamp sees 'the wery man a-making pictures of me on his thumb nail, at the winder . . . a gentleman with a large shirt-collar and a hook nose, and an eye like one of Mr. Sweedlepipes's hawks, and long locks of hair, and wiskers that I wouldn't have no lady as I was engaged to meet suddenly a-turning round a corner.' In 1847 Cruikshank published *The Bottle*, and in 1848 *The Drunkard's Children*, a series of propagandist illustrations of the dangers of drink, against which he was now campaigning hotly. His *magnum opus* (1862) was *The Worship of Bacchus: or, the Drinking Customs of Society*. Dickens admired and remained friendly with him, in spite of Cruikshank's strange claims to have written *Oliver Twist* and originated *Pickwick*.

Dickens, Alfred D'Orsay Tennyson (1845–1912): Dickens's fourth son. 'A chopping boy' was his father's description of him at birth. Count D'Orsay and Tennyson stood godfathers to him. He was soon nicknamed 'Skittles'. Dickens attempted to press him into an army career, for which he was manifestly unsuited. After two years of work in a London China house he sailed for Australia at the age of 20, leaving a pile of unpaid bills behind him and confirming his father's fears that his sons were irresponsible and extravagant. In 1875 he married the 'Belle of Melbourne', Jessie Devlin who was tragically killed in a carriage accident in 1879, leaving two daughters. Alfred did 'extremely well in the money way' with the London and Australian Agency Company Ltd., and after his father's death travelled in England and America lecturing on Dickens's life and works. He suffered from a weak heart and died suddenly in New York at the end of a lecture tour.

Dickens, Alfred Lamert (1822–60): Dickens's younger brother. Trained as a civil engineer, he became a sanitary inspector. His death left his widow Helen and her five children in straitened circumstances, for Alfred had been a bad manager of money. Dickens, despite other pressing commitments, undertook the support and housing of the family, and found a house for them on Haverstock Hill. Finding responsibility for Helen too much, he turned to his sister-in-law Georgina Hogarth for help with her and her affairs for, he said, 'I really can not bear the irritation she causes me.'

Dickens, Augustus (1827–66): Dickens's youngest brother. It was he whom Dickens, in honour of the Vicar of Wakefield, had nicknamed 'Moses', which facetiously pronounced through the nose became 'Boses', and ultimately 'Boz'. 'Boz was a very familiar household word to me, long before I was an author, and so I came to adopt it', Dickens told Forster. Augustus's life proved a disappointment to his brother: Thomas Chapman, of Chapman & Hall, found him 'City employment' about 1847, but he gave it up and deserted his blind wife to elope to America with another woman. From there he wrote to Dickens for funds, and died impoverished in Chicago, leaving his relict and several

children penniless. 'Poor fellow! a sad business altogether,' said Dickens, and undertook the support not only of them but of Augustus's deserted wife. Until Dickens's death Augustus's eldest son, Bertram, received £50 a year.

Dickens, Charles Culliford Boz (1837–96): Dickens's eldest son and first child, known as Charley. For a time he worked in Baring's Bank. In 1860 he went to China to buy tea, and on his return in 1861 set himself up as an Eastern merchant. Dickens, hypercritical of his sons, thought Charley 'wanting in a sense of perseverance', and strongly disapproved of his marriage to Bessie Evans, daughter of one of the partners in the firm of Bradbury & Evans, with whom Dickens had quarrelled. In 1868 the papermill company which Charley had been running in association with Evans failed, and he was bankrupted. Dickens took him into the offices of *All the Year Round* as sub-editor. He attended Dickens during the final public readings when his health was rapidly failing. After his father's death Charley bought Gad's Hill, but was forced to give it up because of illness. He undertook reading tours in imitation of his father, whose works he edited, and died, as his father had done, of a stroke.

Dickens, Charles John Huffam ('Boz'): Born 1812 in Landport, Portsmouth; married Catherine Hogarth in 1836; died at Gad's Hill Place, Kent, in 1870. (See Time Chart.)

Dickens, Mrs. Charles John Huffam (Catherine) (1815–79): Eldest daughter of George and Georgina Hogarth, she was born in Scotland and came to England with her family in 1834. Through her father's journalistic connections she was introduced to Dickens, who was then writing sketches for the *Morning Chronicle*, of which her father was music critic. In April 1836 they were married. Dickens found Kate an incompatible partner, blamed her, somewhat unreasonably, for the birth of their ten children, and turned over the housekeeping to her sister Georgina. In 1858 their widely-publicised separation took place. From that time until Dickens's death they remained estranged, Catherine living with her eldest son, Charley, but she remained attached and loyal to her husband and to his memory until her own death from cancer.

Dickens, Dora Annie (1850–1): Dickens's youngest daughter. Born at Devonshire Terrace, she was named after David Copperfield's wife. Frail from birth, she died of convulsions aged only eight months, while her mother was recuperating from illness at Malvern. She is buried, with Dickens's parents, in Highgate cemetery.

Dickens, Edward Bulwer Lytton ('Plorn') (1852–1902): The tenth and last child of Dickens and Catherine, he was nicknamed 'the Plornishgenter' or 'Plornishmaroon tigunter', later shortened to 'Plorn.' Sensitive and shrinking by nature, he found Rochester High School too large and confusing, and was sent for private tuition at Tunbridge Wells. In 1868 he sailed for Australia to join his brother Alfred, but never prospered, having inherited his grandfather's spendthrift and unworldly nature.

Dickens, Frances Elizabeth (Fanny) (1810–48): Dickens's elder sister. In 1823 she became a pupil at the Royal Academy of Music. Dickens, working at the blacking warehouse, was both proud and jealous at seeing her receive a prize there. She studied the piano under Moscheles and singing under Crivelli, winning the Academy's silver medal in June 1824. John Dickens found himself unable to pay her fees, and she was forced to leave the Academy in 1827, but later returned as pupil-teacher. About 1832 she met Henry Burnett, also studying there, and married him in 1837. On leaving the Academy in 1834 she was made Associate Honorary Member, a distinction kept for ex-students of exceptional ability. Performed at public concerts 1835–7. Her delicate, deformed son was the model for Tiny Tim and Paul Dombey, and she appears as Scrooge's sister in 'A Christmas Carol' and as herself in 'A Child's Dream of a Star'. She died of consumption aged only thirty-eight.

Dickens, Francis Jeffrey (Frank) (1844–86): Charles Dickens's third son. He aspired to become doctor, gentleman farmer and journalist, but none satisfied him and he joined the Bengal Mounted Police. Returning to England on leave in 1871, he overstayed, fell into debt, and after some drifting joined the Northwest Mounted Police. He resigned his commission in 1886 and died the same year.

Dickens, Frederick William (1820–68): Dickens's younger brother. Lived with Dickens before his marriage, and afterwards at Doughty Street. Dickens procured a clerkship for him in the Secretary's office of the Custom House. He joined the Dickens family on a Continental tour in 1844, and narrowly escaped drowning at Albaro. After Frederick's death Dickens commented, 'It was a wasted life, but God forbid that one should be hard upon it, or upon anything in this world that is not deliberately and coldly wrong.'

Dickens, Henry Fielding (1849–1933): Dickens's sixth son, known as Harry. Educated at Boulogne and Rochester, he edited with his brother 'Plorn' a small newspaper called *The Gad's Hill Gazette*, learning to operate a printing-press in the process. More robust and enterprising than his brothers, he became a notable sportsman. His early manifestations of a poetic gift were suppressed by his father. He became Head Censor at Wimbledon, organised the Higham Cricket Club, entered Trinity Hall, Cambridge, and to his father's delight won two scholarships and an essay prize. In 1873 he was called to the bar and started on a brilliant career. In 1876 he married Marie Thérèse Louise Roche. He undertook readings of his father's works for charity in 1904 with considerable success. The last years of Georgina Hogarth were cheered by Harry and his wife and two daughters.

Dickens, John (1785–1851): Charles Dickens's father. He married Elizabeth Barrow in 1809, when a clerk in the Navy

Pay Office at Portsmouth Dockyard. Later he was transferred to London, and in1817 to Chatham, transferring again to Somerset House in 1822. Described by a biographer as 'a jovial opportunist with no money sense', he was repeatedly in debt and in 1824 was arrested and imprisoned in the Marshalsea, to his son's humiliation. He returned to the Navy Pay Office, but in 1828 became a parliamentary reporter for the *Morning Herald*, and for the *Mirror of Parliament* of which his brother-in-law J. H. Barrow was editor. His recklessness in money matters continued to be a worry and annoyance to Charles, whose parents spent many years in shabby lodgings until in 1839 he found a cottage for them at Alphington, Devon. Dickens retained throughout his life warm affection and respect for his father, though deploring his unthrifty habits, and depicted him in the character of Wilkins Micawber in *David Copperfield*.

Dickens, Mrs. John (Elizabeth) (1789–1863): Daughter of Charles Barrow. She married John Dickens in 1809 and became the mother of Charles Dickens and seven other children. Although she appears to have devoted much time to cultivating her eldest son's mind and teaching him in early years, her attitude to his employment at Warren's Blacking Warehouse caused him to turn against her, and cool relations seem to have existed between them until her death. Dickens caricatured her as Mrs. Nickleby.

Dickens, Kate Macready (1839–1929): Dickens's second daughter; the actor Macready stood godfather to her. Pretty and spirited, she earned herself the nickname of 'Lucifer Box' because of her fiery temper. She had a talent for art and attended Bedford College for art lessons. The only one of his children to stand up to Dickens, she sided with her mother over the separation in 1858, and when she married Charles Allston Collins Dickens broke down and declared that 'but for me Katey would not have left home'. She appears to have entered upon

the marriage more as a means to independence than because she loved Collins. She was the last person to talk at length with her father on the day before his death, and afterwards recorded something of the conversation. After Charles Collins's death she married Carlo Perugini, a painter, as Collins had been. At the age of thirty-seven she gave birth to a son, who died aged seven months. She lived to a ripe and lively old age, and was the only member of Dickens's family to disclose any semi-intimate information about him to a biographer.

Dickens, Letitia Mary: See Austin, Mrs. Henry.

Dickens, Mary (1838–96): Dickens's eldest daughter. Always known as 'Mamie', she was called after Mary Hogarth, who had died tragically the year before her birth. Dickens's nickname for her was 'Mild Glo'ster', a tribute to her gentleness, a strong contrast to her sister Katey's fire. She remained with Dickens until his death, taking second place to Georgina Hogarth as housekeeper and companion, and lived with Georgina afterwards. She left a book of memoirs, *My Father as I Recall Him*, and collaborated with Georgina in the editing and publication of Dickens's letters.

Dickens, Sydney Smith Haldimand (1847–72): Dickens's fifth son, nicknamed 'Ocean Spectre', later modified to 'Hoshen Peck', because of his curiously unchildlike way of gazing out to sea during his first holiday at Broadstairs. He may have contributed something to the character of Paul Dombey. Always a favourite with his father, he delighted Dickens by embarking on a naval career and returning from a successful examination 'all eyes and gold buttons', to be referred to thereafter as 'The Admiral'. In 1861 he gave Dickens further satisfaction by obtaining an excellent appointment in H.M.S. *Orlando*, but later showed ominous signs of the extravagance characteristic of his grandfather and brothers. While in America he appealed to his father for financial help, but Dickens, exasperated into sternness, refused and informed Sydney that he would not be received at Gad's Hill on his return to England. Aged only twenty-five, he died at sea aboard the *Malta* on his way home for sick leave. Georgina Hogarth wrote that 'poor Sydney's life was his Father's most bitter trial and grief for several years before his death.'

Dickens, Walter Landor (1841–63): Dickens's second son, and the first he was to name after a literary celebrity, though he was facetiously known as 'Young Skull' in childhood. Educated at Boulogne and Wimbledon, he was nominated at the age of sixteen, through the influence of Angela Burdett-Coutts, to a cadetship in the East India Company. Two years later he was promoted to the rank of lieutenant in the 42nd Highlanders, but got into debt, jeopardising his career. Soon after his family heard that he was being sent home on sick leave the news arrived that he was dead of an aortic aneurysm. Later in the year unpaid accounts were received from India, for the harassed Dickens to settle.

Dolby, George: Dickens's reading manager from 1866 to 1870. Devoted to Dickens, he was a large, amiable, highly competent man hampered in his business dealings by a speech impediment. He sustained the ailing Dickens through the English tours of 1866 and 1867, the arduous American tour of 1867–8, and the 'Final Farewell' tour in the United Kingdom of 1868–70. After Dickens's retirement from his touring life Dolby was a frequent visitor to Gad's Hill, and left a detailed and rapturous account of his friendship with his beloved 'Chief', and of the tours, in the book *Charles Dickens as I Knew Him*, published in 1885.

D'Orsay, Alfred Guillaume Gabriel, Count (1801–52): Artist; served in the Bourbons' bodyguard in France, visited England for the coronation of George IV, 1821, became a leader of fashion in London, and gave rise to scandal because of his *ménage à trois* with Marguerite, Countess of Blessington, and her hus-

band. After Blessington's death he presided at her fashionable soirées at Gore House, Kensington, becoming the friend of other dandies such as Bulwer and the young Disraeli. When Lady Blessington became bankrupt in 1849 she and D'Orsay fled to France. He was appointed director of the fine arts by Prince Louis Napoleon in 1852, shortly before his death. Dickens, in youth 'a highflyer at fashion', modelled himself on the elegantly flamboyant D'Orsay, to whom he had probably been introduced by Serjeant Talfourd in 1836.

Doyle, Richard (1824–83): Artist and caricaturist, son of John Doyle ('H.B.'), also famous for his political caricatures. He designed the cover of *Punch*, contributed cartoons and *Manners and Customs of ye Englyshe* to it, but resigned in consequence of its hostility to Roman Catholicism in 1850. With other artists he illustrated 'The Chimes' in a typically delicate and fantastic manner, and later illustrated Thackeray's *The Newcomes*. He was the uncle of Sir Arthur Conan Doyle.

Egg, Augustus Leopold (1816–63): Subject-painter, student at the Royal Academy, 1836, later an exhibitor. He acted in amateur theatricals with Dickens and designed some costumes for them. A comfortably-situated bachelor, he developed an attachment to Dickens's sister-in-law Georgina Hogarth, and Dickens did what he could to recommend Egg to Georgina. But Georgina declined to 'brighten up a good little man's house' as Dickens wished, and both died unmarried. Egg painted a charming portrait of Georgina sewing, commissioned by Dickens.

Ellis & Blackmore: See **Blackmore, Edward.**

Emerson, Ralph Waldo (1803–82): American poet and essayist, born in Boston of a family containing seven New England church ministers. After studying divinity at Cambridge, Mass., he was 'approbated to preach' by the Middlesex Association of Ministers; but doubts about the sacramental validity of the

Lord's Supper caused him to abandon the formal ministry, though he continued to preach throughout his life. Thomas Carlyle introduced Emerson's essays into England, and Emerson published Carlyle's books in America. He turned to a lecturing career, and became leader of the transcendental school of philosophy – 'the Sage of Concord'. When Dickens visited America on his last reading tour Emerson was one of the famous men to become acquainted with him.

Evans, Bessie: See under Dickens, Charles Culliford Boz.

Evans, Frederick Mullet: See Bradbury & Evans.

Fagin, Bob: A boy who worked at Warren's Blacking Factory with Dickens in 1824. An orphan, he lived with his brother-in-law, a waterman. Dickens was at first deeply humiliated to find himself in the company of Bob and other boys of his kind, but grew to like him for his good nature. When Dickens had a bad attack of the pain in his side which troubled him, 'Bob filled empty blacking-bottles with hot water, and applied relays of them to my side, half the day.' Bob then insisted of escorting Dickens home, but Dickens, too proud to let his friend know that his father was in the Marshalsea, 'shook hands with him on the steps of a house near Southwark Bridge on the Surrey side, making believe that I lived there. As a finishing piece of reality in case of his looking back, I knocked at the door . . . and asked, when the woman opened it, if that was Mr. Robert Fagin's house.'

Fechter, Charles (1822–79): Swiss actor-manager, first seen by Dickens in London when he was playing in *Hamlet* and *Ruy Blas*. In Paris Dickens was immensely impressed by the actor's performances in *Le Maître de Ravenswood* and *La Dame aux Camélias*. 'By Heavens!' he exclaimed, 'the man who can do that can do anything.' He was equally enthusiastic about Fechter's Othello, though his opinion was not that of many people,

who considered him a mediocre player. Fechter became lessee of the Lyceum Theatre in London in 1863 with Dickens, by now his personal friend, as financial backer. In 1868 he played the leading role of Jules Obenreizer in Wilkie Collins's and Dickens's drama *No Thoroughfare*, adapted from the Christmas story written by them in collaboration. It was Fechter who presented Dickens with the Swiss chalet which became his writing-place in the garden at Gad's Hill (it is now preserved at Rochester Museum).

Field, Inspector Charles F.: Inspector in the R. Division (Greenwich) of the Metropolitan Constabulary in 1833, subsequently promoted to the Detective Force. Dickens portrays him as Detective Wield in *Reprinted Pieces*: 'The Detective Police', 'Three "Detective" Anecdotes', and 'On Duty with Inspector Field' (by this time his thin disguise had been abandoned). He took Dickens on conducted tours of London's underworld. Dickens drew a fairly close portrait of him as Inspector Bucket in *Bleak House*.

Fields, James T. (d. 1880): American publisher and editor, who appears to have met Dickens for the first time in 1859, when he attempted to persuade him to undertake reading tours in America, a project which was realised in 1867. Dickens stayed with Fields and his family in Boston and became friendly with his wife, Annie. After Dickens's return to England the Fields, with other American visitors, were lavishly entertained by Dickens in London and at Gad's Hill.

Fields, Mrs. James T. (Annie): Wife of Dickens's American publisher. When Dickens met Annie Fields at her Boston home she impressed him as 'a very nice woman, with a rare relish for humour and a most contagious laugh'. They became warm friends, Dickens being encouraged by Annie's sympathetic nature to confide in her to an unusual degree, his confidences apparently including his relationship with Ellen Ternan. When the Fields visited England

Annie and Georgina Hogarth became equally friendly, and remained so for the rest of their lives. Annie wrote a biography of her husband after his death. Her unpublished diaries, containing accounts of Dickens's visits, are owned by the Massachusetts Historical Society at Boston.

Fildes, Sir Luke, R.A. (1844–1927): Subject-painter of great popularity in the last quarter of the nineteenth century, his most famous picture was *The Doctor*. When Charles Collins, through illness, was forced to abandon the illustrations for *Edwin Drood*, Fildes was called in and given by Dickens some guarded information about the solution of that mystery. Dickens had set the story in the earlier years of Victoria's reign, but Fildes dressed his characters in contemporary (i.e. 1870) clothing.

Fitzgerald, Percy: One of 'Dickens's young men' and among his most ardent admirers and disciples, the Irish Fitzgerald was a frequent visitor to Gad's Hill in the 1860s and left glowing accounts of life there in his *Life of Charles Dickens*, published in 1905, and *Memoirs of an Author*, published in 1895. He was romantically interested in Mamie Dickens but, Dickens lamented, 'I am grievously disappointed that Mary can by no means be induced to think as highly of him as I do.' His Catholicism may have been a possible barrier to marriage with him in Mamie's eyes. After Dickens's death Fitzgerald drew upon himself the anger of the Dickens family by publishing a Dickens letter connecting John Dickens with Micawber, and an article speculating on the relationship between Dickens and his sister-in-law Mary Hogarth. In 1900 Fitzgerald founded the Boz Club, which met annually on Dickens's birthday, the celebration taking the form of a gala dinner.

Forster, John (1812–76): Historian and biographer, he was one of Dickens's closest friends. In 1843 he was a barrister of the Inner Temple, but had already embarked on a literary career, being dramatic critic to *The Examiner* and con-

tributing *Lives of the Statesmen of the Commonwealth* to Lardner's *Cyclopaedia*. Editor of several journals, friend of Lamb, Leigh Hunt, and many of the Dickens circle, he constituted himself Boswell to Dickens's Johnson, and in 1872–4 produced *The Life of Charles Dickens*, dedicated to his god-daughters, Mamie and Katey Dickens. A detailed and valuable record of Dickens's life, providing essential material for later biographers, it slides over all remotely scandalous episodes, omitting much from the 'letters of unexampled candour and truthfulness' which he had received from his friend, thus presenting an idealised rather than an accurate portrait. In the later years of Dickens's life Forster maintained a somewhat jealous attitude to Wilkie Collins, by then an intimate of, and a strong influence upon, Dickens. Forster proof-read for Dickens, and claimed to know the truth of Dickens's solution to *The Mystery of Edwin Drood*. A large, bluff, vociferous man, Forster was known to Dickens and other friends as 'Fuz'. He was probably the original of Podsnap in *Our Mutual Friend*.

Gaskell, Mrs. Elizabeth Cleghorn (1810–65): Brought up by her aunt at Knutsford, Cheshire, she later immortalised the town in her novel *Cranford*. She married William Gaskell, a Unitarian minister, in 1832, and wrote her first novel, *Mary Barton*, in 1848. Dickens thought her a very original writer, for whose powers he had a high admiration. She contributed to the first number of *Household Words* in 1850, and continued to be a contributor while writing her later novels and engaging in charitable works in the North of England.

Giles, The Revd. William, F.R.G.S. (1798–1856): Baptist minister and Dickens's first schoolmaster. Educated at St. Aldate's School, Oxford, he took over the 'classical, mathematical, and commercial school' at Chatham, attended by Dickens 1821–2. In 1831 he opened a boarding-school at Patricroft, near Manchester, and after 1837 opened schools in

Manchester, Liverpool, and Chester. His scholars in Chatham were locally known as Giles's Cats. He was a liberal, intelligent man who recognised Dickens's quality, christened him 'The Inimitable', and remained friendly with him in later years. Dickens inscribed copies of *Sketches by Boz* and *Pickwick* to Giles, 'from his old and affectionate pupil'.

Grant, William and Daniel: The originals of the Cheeryble brothers in *Nicholas Nickleby*. Scots by birth, in youth the brothers had kept a shop in Bury St. Edmunds, but migrated to Manchester, where they became leading wool- and linen-drapers, famous for their philanthropy. Dickens met them in 1838 when he and Forster were the guests of Gilbert Winter of Stocks House, Manchester, but from Percy Fitzgerald's account it seems that John Dickens knew them much earlier and held them up as an example to his son.

Grip: Dickens admitted that the remarkable raven of *Barnaby Rudge* was based on 'two great originals, of whom I was at different times the proud possessor. The first was in the bloom of his youth when he was discovered in a modest retirement in London by a friend of mine, and given to me. He had from the first . . . "good gifts", which he improved by study and attention in a most exemplary manner.' Grip the First died of eating lead paint left about by workmen. Grip the Second, of Yorkshire origin, was a strong character who specialised in stable language, had no respect for anybody but the cook, and was once met by Dickens 'walking down the middle of a public street, attended by a pretty large crowd, and spontaneously exhibiting the whole of his accomplishments. His gravity under these most trying circumstances I can never forget, nor the extraordinary gallantry with which, refusing to be brought home, he defended himself behind a pump, until overpowered by numbers.' After some years Grip the Second died: 'he kept his eyes to the last upon the meat as it roasted, and suddenly turned over on his back with a sepulchral cry of

"Cuckoo!" ' Maclise sketched *The Apotheosis of Grip* (the First) depicting him lying dead, a bird-soul emerging from his beak and ascending to a Heaven full of welcoming bird-angels. Both Grips lived at Devonshire Terrace.

Haldimand, William (1784–1862): Philanthropist, direct of the Bank of England, M.P. for Ipswich 1820–6. He gave financial support to the cause of Greek independence, founded the Hortense Hospital at Aix-les-Bains and a blind asylum at Lausanne, where he met Dickens, who was deeply interested in the institution and visited it often.

Hall, William: See **Chapman, Edward.**

Harte, Francis Brett (1836–1902): American author who wrote under the name of Bret Harte. His early career was varied, and it was not until he was appointed secretary of the U.S. Mint in California in 1864 that he found time to devote himself to writing. In 1868 he became editor of the *Overland Monthly*, to which he contributed his famous western tale 'The Luck of Roaring Camp', the first of his vivid stories of pioneer life. It was just before this period that he was introduced to Dickens, then on his last American reading tour. After Dickens's death Harte paid him a poetical tribute in the verses 'Dickens in Camp'.

Hogarth, Catherine: See **Dickens, Mrs. Charles John Huffam.**

Hogarth, George (1783–1870): Father of Catherine, Mary, and Georgina Hogarth (and many other children), and father-in-law of Dickens. Educated for the law in Edinburgh, he was admitted to the practice in 1810. In 1814 he married Georgina Thomson, daughter of a musician friend of Burns. The couple moved in musical and literary circles, and when Sir Walter Scott was bankrupted by the failure of his publishing firm, Hogarth became his legal adviser. A violoncellist and composer, he served as joint secretary for the first Edinburgh Musical Festival in 1815, and was music critic for the Edinburgh *Courant*. In 1830 he abandoned the law for journalism, moved to Yorkshire and launched the *Halifax Guardian*, besides founding the Halifax Orchestral Society. In 1834 he moved his family to London and joined the staff of the *Morning Chronicle* as music critic. Here he met the young Dickens, who was writing a series of 'Street Sketches' for that paper, and when an offshoot, the *Evening Chronicle*, was launched, Hogarth asked Dickens for a contribution to the first issue: thus some of the earlier *Sketches by Boz* were commissioned by him. Hogarth also helped him to sell his libretto for *The Village Coquettes*. After a short courtship Dickens married the eldest of the Hogarth girls, Catherine, in 1836. George Hogarth died aged eighty-six, but still active in journalism.

Hogarth, Mrs. George (Georgina) (1793–1863): Wife of George Hogarth. In 1854, when Dickens's marriage was beginning to deteriorate, his relationship with his in-laws did likewise; he complained of Mrs. Hogarth's 'imbecility' and sluttishness, announced himself to be 'dead sick of the Scottish tongue' and found that the sight of his father-in-law at breakfast 'undermined his constitution'. He later became estranged from Mrs. Hogarth and her daughter Helen on the matter of his separation from Catherine.

Hogarth, Georgina (1827–1917): The youngest of the three elder Hogarth sisters introduced to Dickens by their father in 1834. From 1839, when Dickens, his wife and family removed to Devonshire Terrace, Marylebone, Georgina frequently visited them to play with the children. When Dickens and Catherine sailed for America in 1842 Georgina took such a part in the care of the young family they had left behind that Dickens invited her to come a member of the household. She remained with them as housekeeper, organiser, adviser and friend until her brother-in-law's death, and afterwards remained in close touch with his surviving relatives. She has been much blamed for the rift between Dickens and Catherine, and rumours were abroad at the time of

the separation in 1858 that Georgina, as well as Ellen Ternan, was Dickens's mistress. Her relationship with Catherine seems to have been ambiguous, but it is supposed that any differences between them were made up before Catherine's death. With Mamie Dickens she edited Dickens's letters for publication, and the rest of her life was dedicated to the clearing of Dickens's reputation and the perpetuation of his memory. To the family she was always 'Aunt Georgy'.

Hogarth, Mary Scott (1819–37): Next in age to Catherine, and seven years older than Georgina, Mary was a pretty, lively girl, with whom Dickens may have been subconsciously in love, although he married her sister. She joined him and his bride when they set up house at Furnival's Inn in 1836, and moved with them to 48 Doughty Street in 1837. Her sudden death after a theatre outing in May of that year shattered Dickens's happiness. He grieved inordinately for her: 'the peace and life of our home – the admired of all for her beauty and excellence . . . she has been to us what we can never replace.' He took a ring from her dead finger and slipped it on his own, wearing it to the end of his life. She haunted his imagination, an ideal of youth and pure beauty, and his undying grief found expression in literary portraits of her as Rose Maylie, Little Nell, and other youthful victims. Her tombstone at Kensal Green bears Dickens's epitaph for her: 'Young, beautiful and good, God in his mercy numbered her with his angels at the early age of seventeen.'

Hood, Thomas (1799–1845): Poet and wit, he began his literary career with contributions to the *London Magazine*, which brought him the acquaintance of Lamb, Hazlitt, and De Quincey. He issued *Whims and Oddities* in 1826–7, became editor of the *Gem*, began the *Comic Annual*, 1830, lived at Coblenz and Ostend for a time, edited the *New Monthly Magazine*, and founded *Hood's Own* and *Hood's Magazine*. He was very friendly with Dickens, of whom he wrote in 1840, 'Boz is a very good fellow'. All his life he was dogged by ill-health and poverty. Dickens often wrote of him as 'poor Hood', and when he received Hood's book *Up the Rhine* for review he told Forster, 'It is rather poor, but I have not said so, because Hood is too, and ill besides.' Hood's most famous poem is 'The Song of the Shirt' and he wrote many punning ballads such as 'Faithless Nellie Gray'.

Huffam, Christopher: Godfather of Dickens. He lived at Limehouse Hole, and was an oar- and block-maker and rigger to His Majesty's Navy. He had come to the notice of the Prince Regent for fitting out a privateer against the French during the Napoleonic Wars, and was reputed to have been rewarded with an honour. He lived, said Forster, 'in a substantial handsome sort of way', and visits to him were among the young Dickens's greatest treats while he was living at Bayham Street in 1822–3. The atmosphere of Limehouse coloured the boy's imagination strongly, familiar as he was with shipping from his days at Chatham, and Huffam himself (sometimes spelt Huffham) probably contributed something to Captain Cuttle's character. Dickens's accomplishment of entertaining the company with comic songs, frequently nautical, was the admiration of one of his godfather's guests, who pronounced the child a 'progidy'.

Hunt, James Henry Leigh (1784–1859): Essayist and poet, friend of Keats, Byron, Moore, Shelley, and Lamb in his youth, and later of Dickens. He edited the *Examiner*, 1808, and the *Reflector*, 1810; was sentenced, with his brother John, to a fine and two years' imprisonment in 1813 for derogatory remarks about the Prince Regent. His literary career was versatile and distinguished and his personal charm considerable. The fellowship with Dickens suffered when Hunt heard gossip to the effect that Dickens had based the character of Harold Skimpole in *Bleak House* upon him. Dickens wrote to him explaining that his intention was not to be offensive; he had certainly taken some of Hunt's

characteristics and way of speaking in creating Skimpole, but had no intention of identifying him in any way with Skimpole's irresponsibility and dishonesty in money matters. After Hunt's death he published in *All the Year Round* a vindication of himself in the same connection, praising Hunt highly and denying any intention of hurting him.

Irving, Washington (1783–1859): American man of letters, born of an English mother and an Orcadian father. Trained for the law, he deserted it for literature, and when the family business in which he was a sleeping partner was bankrupted he turned to writing as a livelihood. Arriving in England, he became friendly with several prominent literary figures, and was introduced to the publishing firm of John Murray. His many works show a strong English influence, particularly in their style of humour. On his return to America, after extensive foreign travel, he found his name a household word. Dickens first met him on his American visit of 1842, when at the City Hotel, New York, Irving gave the toast of 'Charles Dickens, the Nation's guest, coupled with International Copyright', and observed, 'It is but fair that those who have laurels for their brows should be permitted to browse on their laurels.' (Irving realised, as did few American authors, the importance of the copyright question which so exercised Dickens.) Their correspondence had begun after the publication of *The Old Curiosity Shop*, on which Irving wrote to congratulate Dickens. Many letters between them were destroyed when Dickens embarked upon the ritual burning of his private correspondence. Dickens's summing-up of Irving, after their first meeting, was 'Washington Irving is a *great* fellow. We have laughed most heartily together. He is just the man he ought to be.'

Jerrold, Douglas William (1803–57): Author and noted wit, he practised journalism while still a printer's assistant. He made his reputation as a playwright with *Black-eyed Susan* in 1829.

By 1841 he was a constant contributor to *Punch*, and founded *Douglas Jerrold's Shilling Magazine* and *Douglas Jerrold's Weekly Newspaper* in 1845–6. He was on terms of the closest friendship with Dickens, who greatly admired his wit and charm, calling him 'one of the gentlest and most affectionate of men . . . in the company of children and young people he was particularly happy . . . he never was so gay, so sweet-tempered, and so pleased as then.' Many other tributes were paid to him by contemporaries, but against his charm was offset the bitter and biting quality of his satire. Dickens organised performances of *The Frozen Deep*, Wilkie Collins's play, for the benefit of Jerrold's widow.

Jones, William (1777–1836): Headmaster of Wellington House Academy, Mornington Crescent, London, which Dickens attended from 1824 to 1827. A Welshman, he appears to have been something of a tyrant: Dickens says that he 'was always ruling ciphering books with a bloated mahogany ruler, smiting the palms of offenders with the same diabolical instrument, or viciously drawing a pair of pantaloons tight with one of his large hands and caning the wearer with the other.' He was probably the model for Creakle in *David Copperfield*.

Kent, William Charles: Editor of the *Sun* newspaper and friend of Dickens. He was a particular admirer of Dickens's readings, and after the Final Farewell Reading on 15 March 1870, suggested to him that an accurate record should be made of all the readings given over the years. Dickens agreed, giving Kent *carte blanche* to compile such a record. (The resulting book, *Charles Dickens as a Reader*, published in 1872, was not entirely accurate, and it was left to Walter Dexter to provide a correct one. His 'Mr. Charles Dickens will Read' was published in *The Dickensian*, vols. 37–9, in 1941–3.) One of the last two letters written by Dickens was to Kent: dated 'Wednesday eighth June 1870', it is an apology for not calling on Kent, because of pressure of business, on the following

day – the day on which, in fact, his fatal seizure occurred.

Kolle, Henry William (1808–81): Bank clerk. Son of a calico printer and manufacturer of household goods. He and Dickens met at the Beadnells' house about 1830. Kolle became engaged to Anne Beadnell, and Dickens strongly attracted to Maria, Kolle acting as go-between during the courtship. In 1833 he married Anne and by 1846 was a manufacturer of stoves, grates, and ranges in Jermyn Street, St. James's, painting in his spare time. Anne died in May 1836.

Lamert, James: Cousin of Dickens in a step-relationship. Dickens's mother's sister Mary married as her second husband Dr. Matthew Lamert, an army surgeon of Chatham, having joined the Dickens family there after her first husband's death. Lamert's son James, older than Dickens and with a passion for amateur theatricals, infected Dickens with his own enthusiasm and introduced him to the professional theatre at Chatham. In 1822 James was lodging with Dickens and his family at Bayham Street, Camden Town, and was responsible for Dickens's entry into Warren's Blacking Warehouse, which his cousin George Lamert had bought. A quarrel between Dickens's father and James Lamert resulted in Dickens being allowed to leave his hated employment. James's father Dr. Lamert was probably the model for Dr. Slammer in *Pickwick*.

Landon, Letitia Elizabeth ('L.E.L.') (1802–38): Poetess, she published under her initials and enjoyed a certain amount of popularity. In 1831 and 1834 she produced novels, and in 1836 a supposedly autobiographical novel, *Traits and Trials of Early Life*. A member of Lady Blessington's circle, she was frequently at Gore House at the time when Dickens visited there. At one time she was engaged to John Forster, but scandalous rumours about her ended this. In 1838 she married George Maclean, governor of Cape Coast Castle, West

Africa, joined him there, and died mysteriously of poisoning.

Landor, Walter Savage (1775–1864): Poet and prolific author of belles-lettres, traveller, and godfather of Dickens's son Walter. In 1840 Dickens and Forster visited Landor at Bath, and Dickens there conceived the idea that was to develop into the character of Little Nell. Landor was immensely charmed by Nell, who became his favourite personage in fiction and, said Forster in his *Life of Landor*, in 'one of those whimsical bursts of comical extravagance out of which arose the fancy of Boythorn' (Dickens is supposed to have modelled Boythorn in *Bleak House* on Landor), he regretted that he had not purchased the house in Bath where the idea came to Dickens 'and then and there . . . burnt it to the ground, to the end that no meaner association should ever desecrate the birthplace of Nell. Then he would pause a little, become conscious of our sense of his absurdity, and break into a thundering peal of laughter.'

Landseer, Sir Edwin Henry (1802–73): Best known for his paintings of animals, he was a favourite of Queen Victoria and Prince Albert and frequently painted their portraits. He received a knighthood in 1850, and completed the lions for Nelson's monument in Trafalgar Square in 1866. A friend of Dickens's from Devonshire Terrace days, he grieved deeply over Dickens's death, somewhat to the surprise of Georgina Hogarth, who felt that 'Edwin was fonder of Charles than Charles of him'. Landseer drew the dog Boxer for 'The Cricket on the Hearth'.

La Rue, Mrs. Emile de: The English wife of a Swiss banker carrying on business in Genoa during the Dickens family's stay there in 1844. Dickens felt a 'magnetic attraction' towards this 'affectionate, excellent little woman', who confided to him that she suffered from alarming delusions. Dickens attempted to cure them by hypnotism, with Mr. de la Rue's co-operation but to the jealous anger of Catherine Dickens, who quarrelled with her husband about

his visits to the lady's apartments. Mrs. de la Rue's phantom persecutors may have lent something to 'The Chimes: a Goblin Story', upon which Dickens was engaged at the time.

Layard, Sir Austen Henry (1817–94): Excavator of Nineveh, politician, world traveller, Lord Rector of Aberdeen University, 1855, and Liberal M.P. for Aylesbury, 1852–7; author of several books, mainly on art. A friend of Dickens, the correspondence between them was made available for publication in 1881, and printed in the third volume of the edition of Dickens's letters published by Chapman and Hall 1879–82. This was the first selection of Dickens's letters ever to appear.

Leech, John (1817–64): Humorous artist, made famous by his drawings for *Punch*, 1841–64. A schoolfellow at the Charterhouse was Thackeray, who became his life-long friend. After an interlude studying medicine Leech turned to art and offered himself, unsuccessfully, as illustrator of *Pickwick* after Seymour's death. In 1843 he married Annie Eaton, who was often his model. He became a personal friend of Dickens, contributed illustrations to all the *Christmas Books*, and was the sole illustrator of 'A Christmas Carol'. Leech was noted for his personal charm: George du Maurier said that he was 'the most charming companion conceivable', and Dean Hole of Rochester, meeting him in 1858, described his 'slim, elegant figure, over six feet in height, with a grand head, on which nature had written "gentleman" with a wonderful genius in his ample forehead; wonderful penetration, observation, humour, in his blue-gray Irish eyes, and wonderful sweetness, sympathy and mirth about his lips'.

Lemon, Mark (1809–70): Lifelong friend of Dickens; first editor of *Punch*, author of farces, melodramas, and operas, contributor to *Household Words* and *Illustrated London News* among other periodicals. In 1849 he adapted 'The Haunted Man' for the stage, in 1851 collaborated with Dickens in the farce *Mr. Nightin-*

gale's Diary, and his children acted with the Dickens family in theatricals at Tavistock House. Dickens, in his continuation of Mrs. Gamp's adventures, published in Forster's *Life* makes her describe Lemon as 'a fat gentleman with curly black hair and a merry face, a-standing on the platform rubbing his two hands over one another, as if he was washing of 'em, and shaking his head and shoulders very much'. In the same year, inviting Lemon to Brighton after an illness, he sent his friend a poetical effusion, to be sung to the air of 'Lesbia hath a beaming eye', and beginning:

> *Lemon is a little hipped,*
> *And this is Lemon's true position –*
> *He is not pale, he's not white-lipped,*
> *Yet wants a little fresh condition.*
> *Sweeter 'tis to gaze upon*
> *Old Ocean's rising, falling billers,*
> *Than on the Houses every one*
> *That form the street called Saint Anne's*
>   *Willers.*
>   *Oh my Lemon, round and fat,*
>   *Oh my bright, my right, my tight 'un,*
>   *Think a little what you're at –*
>   *Don't stay at home, but come to*
>   *Brighton!*

Lewes, George Henry (1817–78): Author and contributor to quarterlies, he co-operated with Thornton Leigh Hunt in the *Leader*, 1850, wrote a play, two novels, and miscellaneous works. From 1854 to the end of his life he lived with Mary Ann Evans ('George Eliot') as her husband. Dickens had 'an old and great regard' for him, says Forster. A year after Dickens's death Lewes published a paper on 'Dickens in Relation to Criticism', which greatly annoyed Forster because of some implied depreciation of the man who had been his friend.

Linda: One of the St. Bernard dogs kept at Gad's Hill for protection against the vagrants who roamed the Dover Road. On Dickens's return from America in 1868 Linda, he said, 'was greatly excited; weeping profusely, and throwing herself on her back that she might caress my foot with her great forepaws'. Mamie

Dickens recorded that she was soft-eyed, gentle, and good-tempered.

Linton, Mrs. Eliza Lynn (1822–98): Self-described 'a woman of letters', she wrote novels from 1845 onwards, was a member of the staff of the *Morning Chronicle*, contributed to *All the Year Round*, and married W. J. Linton in 1858 but soon separated from him. A protégée of Walter Savage Landor in her youth, she moved in Dickens's circle for many years. She was a somewhat formidable and plain-spoken lady, disliked Forster and reviewed his books with venom, but thought Dickens bright, gay, and charming, except when he blue-pencilled her contributions to *All the Year Round*. It was through her that Dickens gained possession of Gad's Hill Place, the house he had admired from boyhood: her father had left it to her and she could not afford to live in it.

Longfellow, Henry Wadsworth (1807–82): American poet, born in Portland, of an ancient New England family. Entering the world of literature against his father's wishes, he was offered in 1836 the Smith chair of modern languages at Harvard, which he accepted, and went abroad to study in England, Sweden, Denmark, and other countries. Dickens met him during the first American visit in 1842, and thought him a 'noble fellow'. On Dickens's return to England he invited Longfellow to become his guest at Devonshire Terrace. Longfellow accepted and Forster has left an amusing account of mild law-breaking at Rochester on the part of Dickens and Longfellow, and a tour of the haunts of tramps and thieves in London. The poet visited Dickens again in 1856 and 1868. Dickens, during his last American tour, was struck by the beauty of Longfellow's eldest daughter Alice, who with her sisters Edith and Allegra stayed at Gad's Hill during their father's 1868 visit. Of this Dickens wrote, 'Nothing can surpass the respect paid to Longfellow here, from the Queen downward. He is everywhere received and courted, and finds the working men at least as well acquainted with his books as the classes socially above them.'

Lowell, James Russell (1819–91): American author and diplomatist. His earliest work to be published was a collection of poems in 1843, followed by *Conversations on Some of the old Poets.* He became a regular contributor to the *National Anti-Slavery Standard* of New York, and was made editor of the *Atlantic Monthly* in 1857. In 1877 he was appointed minister resident at the court of Spain. Dickens met him when visiting Boston on his last American reading tour, 1867–8.

Lytton, Edward George Earle Lytton Bulwer-Lytton, first Baron (1803–73): Novelist, poet, playwright, writer for various periodicals, reformer in politics and supporter of authors' copyrights and the removal of taxes upon literature. His novels include *Falkland, Paul Clifford, Eugene Aram, The Last Days of Pompeii, Rienzi,* and *The Coming Race,* a remarkable prophecy of life in the twentieth century. Dickens, his friend and admirer, said of him, 'Some of you will connect him with prose, others will connect him with poetry. One will connect him with comedy, and another with the romantic passions of the stage, and his assertion of worthy ambition and earnest struggle against

> *Those twin gaolers of the human heart, Low birth and iron fortune.'*

With Dickens, he founded the Guild of Literature and Art, to improve the lot of impoverished writers. The scheme failed, but provided Dickens with the opportunity of producing and acting in a series of plays in London and at Knebworth, Lytton's home, with his amateur company. The repertoire included Lytton's comedy *Not so Bad as we Seem.* His marriage to Rosina Wheeler was a failure, and after their separation in 1836 she devoted herself to a series of verbal and literary attacks on him.

Maclise, Daniel (1806–70): Irish-born artist, close friend of Dickens from 1838, he painted the famous portrait of Dickens aged 27 which was exhibited at the Royal Academy in 1840, and several portraits of his family. Forster says, 'A greater enjoyment than the fellowship of Maclise at this period [1838] it would be difficult to imagine. Dickens hardly saw more than he did, while yet he seemed to be seeing nothing; and the small esteem in which this rare faculty was held by himself, a quaint oddity that in him gave to shrewdness itself an air of Irish simplicity . . . combined to render him attractive far beyond the common.' Dickens's last words to be spoken in public, at the Royal Academy Dinner of 1870, were a eulogy of the recently-dead Maclise: 'in wit a man, simplicity a child'.

Macready, William Charles (1793–1873): Distinguished actor. Made his first appearance as Romeo in 1810, and became famous for his Richard III. Manager of Drury Lane 1841–3. Forsook the stage in 1851, his last part being Macbeth at Drury Lane. Bulwer-Lytton gave him a farewell dinner, at which Dickens spoke; he and 'dear old gallant Macready' were friends for many years, and Macready's declining health was a constant anxiety to Dickens in the last year of his own life. Among his last words was an inquiry about Macready's son. A mutual friend recorded of Macready that 'When time and sorrow pressed him down, Dickens was his most frequent visitor; he cheered him with narratives of bygone days; he poured some of his own abundant warmth into his heart; he led him into new channels of thought . . . he conjured back his smile and his laugh.'

Macrone, John (1809–37): A Manx-born publisher, he met Dickens in 1836, introduced by Harrison Ainsworth, and persuaded him to sell the copyright of *Sketches by Boz* for £100. A dispute over the reissue of the *Sketches*, Macrone demanding £2,000 from Dickens and Chapman & Hall to relinquish the rights, ended the association. Dickens edited the *Pic Nic Papers,* 1841, which were published for the benefit of Macrone's family, left destitute by his sudden death.

Millais, Sir John Everett (1829–96): President of the Royal Academy, one of the founders of the Pre-Raphaelite movement, painter of such famous works as *Isabella*, *The Huguenot*, *The Boyhood of Raleigh*, *The Princes in the Tower* and *The Order of Release*. He was teacher of painting to Dickens's daughter Katey, and thought her talented. The day after Dickens's death he went to Gad's Hill to make a sketch of the dead face, which was later given to Katey. Millais had forgiven, if not forgotten, Dickens's slashing attack on the Pre-Raphaelites, and particularly Millais's *Christ in the House of his Parents*, in *Household Words*. He found Dickens personally amiable, and Katey sat to him for a figure in his painting *The Black Brunswicker*.

Milner-Gibson, Thomas (1806–84): Conservative M.P. for Ipswich, 1837-9, resigned on changing his views and became an active member and speaker of the Anti-Corn Law League; became Vice-President of the Board of Trade and Privy Councillor. His wife was a close friend of Mrs. Benjamin Disraeli, with whose husband Milner-Gibson had been at school. Early in 1870 Milner-Gibson briefly leased Dickens his Bays-water house, 5 Hyde Park Place.

Milnes, Richard Monckton, first Baron Houghton (1809–85): Politician and literary man, he was Conservative M.P. for Pontefract in 1837, and did much to secure the passing of the Copyright Act, to the pleasure of Dickens. He and his wife frequently entertained Dickens, and were entertained by him, from Tavistock House days onwards.

Mitton, Thomas (1812–78): He met Dickens in boyhood, possibly about 1827. Both were law-clerks in Lincoln's Inn, and he later became a solicitor. He remained friendly with Dickens through-out his life, and seems to have transacted the legal business of obtaining for Dickens the lease of 1 Devonshire Ter-race.

Mrs. Bouncer (1859–74): A white Pomeranian dog belonging to Mamie Dickens at Gad's Hill. On her death Georgina Hogarth recalled how 'very, very kind and sweet to her' Dickens had been.

Nash, Mrs.: Landlady at the cottage at Chalk, Kent, where Dickens and Kate spent their honeymoon.

Ouvry, Frederic (1814–81): Dickens's friend and solicitor, who acted for him in the separation from his wife which occurred in 1858, and was still handling his affairs up to the drawing-up of the contract for *Edwin Drood* in 1870. He afterwards acted for Georgina Hogarth. In 1883, two years after his death, selec-tions from Dickens's correspondence with Ouvry were published in America, unauthorised by Georgina, Dickens's executrix. But she refused to blame Ouvry, 'one of the most delicate, most discreet and judicious of men'.

Perugini, Carlo (c. 1839–1918): Artist, Italian by birth, a naturalised English citizen. He became Katey Dickens's second husband in 1874, after the death of Charles Collins. Georgina Hogarth described him as 'a most sensible, good, honourable and upright man, and devotedly attached to Katey'. In 1875 their only child was born, and christened Leonard Ralph Dickens Perugini, but died at the age of seven months. Perugini became a moderately well-known painter, exhibiting a series of genre pictures at the Royal Academy.

Perugini, Mrs. Carlo: See **Dickens, Kate Macready**.

'Phiz': See **Browne, Hablôt Knight**.

Proctor, Bryan Waller (1787–1874): Poet and playright, biographer of Charles Lamb, he started life as a soli-citor and built up a large connection as conveyancer. In 1815 he began to con-tribute to the *Literary Gazette*. His tragedy *Mirandola* was produced at Covent Garden in 1821 under the pseu-donym of Barry Cornwall. He was a close friend of both Dickens and Leigh Hunt, and was instrumental in reducing the likenesses between Hunt and the irre-sponsible Harold Skimpole of *Bleak House*.

Rogers, Samuel (1763–1855): Banker, poet, wit, and entertainer, his wealth enabled him to write poetry for pleasure. His 'breakfasts' were famous, gathering together luminaries of the arts and politics. Dickens was numbered among his friends, though he was not an 'out-and-out' admirer of the novelist's work, and brought his mordant wit to bear on 'A Christmas Carol'. Forster tells an amusing story of a dinner-party given by Dickens at which Rogers and another guest were taken ill, and Dickens was chaffingly accused of poisoning them.

Sala, George Augustus Henry (1828–96): Journalist. Once an artist and scene-painter, he wrote regularly for *Household Words*, and was sent to Russia by Dickens at the close of the Crimean War to write descriptive articles for it. *When All the Year Round* was founded he became a contributor. Dickens wrote of him to Forster in 1851, 'I find him a very conscientious fellow. When he gets money ahead, he is not like the imbecile youth who so often do the like in Wellington Street [the office of *Household Words*] and walk off, but only works more industriously. I think he improves with everything he does.'

Seymour, Robert (1800–36): Artist and illustrator, he was famous for his sporting prints, usually of a slightly vulgar kind. He was engaged on a journal called the *Figaro in London*; practised art with a fellow-student at Canonbury Tower, Islington, and as a result produced an enormous picture representing scenes of German diablerie, rife with 'goblin incidents'. It was not a success, and he devoted himself to humorous sketches. In November 1835 Chapman & Hall published a small book called the *Squib Annual*, with plates by Seymour, and he expressed to them a wish to do a series of Cockney sporting prints of a superior kind. This was to deal with the adventures of the 'Nimrod Club', amateurs of shooting, fishing, and the like, who would get themselves into laughable difficulties. Chapman & Hall approached Dickens to write the text. He expressed

no enthusiasm for it, regarding it as hackneyed and of no particular interest to himself, a non-sportsman. 'I would like to take my own way, with a freer range of English scenes and people,' he said; but such was the genesis of *The Pickwick Papers*. Dickens conceded the sporting Mr. Winkle as a sop to Seymour. Between the first and second numbers of *Pickwick* Seymour committed suicide, working to the last on his illustration for 'The Stroller's Tale', the original version of which Dickens had criticised slightly.

Shaw, William (?1783–1850): London-born schoolmaster, of Bowes, Yorkshire from 1822. Dickens had been much impressed in youth by reports of the trial of Shaw in 1823 for cruelty to his pupils, one of whom died. In 1838 he travelled up to Yorkshire to investigate the notorious Yorkshire boarding-schools or 'boy farms' to which unwanted boys were sent to be boarded, without holidays and under conditions of privation and brutality (Shaw's curriculum expressly stated 'No Vacations'). Shaw may have been no worse than the rest of his kind, and was apparently well regarded in Bowes, but Dickens made a scapegoat of him and caricatured him as Wackford Squeers, the one-eyed monster who rules Dotheboys Hall in *Nicholas Nickleby*. 'I have kept down the strong truth and thrown as much comicality over it as I could, rather than disgust and weary the reader with its fouler aspect,' said Dickens of the Dotheboys episodes in the book.

Smith, Arthur (1825–61): Manager of Dickens's first major reading-tour in 1858. He had been introduced to Dickens by his brother, Albert Smith, an entertainer, renowned for his one-man shows: travelogues interspersed with comic songs and sketches, and illustrated by dioramic views. Arthur Smith took over all the business details of the tour and Dickens was impressed by his efficiency. 'He is all usefulness and service,' he told Wilkie Collins. 'I never could have done without him.' Smith died in 1861, to

Dickens's great grief, plans for the readings on his mind to the last. Dickens composed an inscription for his gravestone.

Smith, Sydney (1771–1845): Canon of St. Paul's, he took orders in 1794 but became famous in a lay capacity as writer, campaigner, Whig reformer, and brilliant wit. Dickens probably met him at Gore House in the 'Blessington Set', and he became a friend and frequent guest. He accepted one of Dickens's invitations in these words: 'If I am invited by any man of greater genius than yourself or by one in whose works I have been more completely interested I will repudiate you and dine with the more splendid phenomenon of the two.'

Smith, Dr. Thomas Southwood (1788–1861): Studied medicine while a Unitarian minister in Edinburgh; helped to found the *Westminster Review*, 1824, the Useful Knowledge Society, the *Penny Cyclopaedia*, the Health of Towns Association; wrote valuable works on epidemics and sanitary improvements. Dickens first met him when Smith was Commissioner on the Employment of Young People early in the 1840s. The Commission's report on the conditions of children working in factories and mines aroused Dickens's indignation, though he seems to have held himself off from campaigning against these because he could not reconcile the necessary mighty change with the consequent reduction in income of poor families. However, Smith's influence led him to realise that good housing was essential if the terrible sanitary conditions of slum dwellings were to be banished; a conviction strengthened by the cholera outbreak of 1850, and an even worse one in 1854. Dickens's article 'To Working Men' published in *Household Words* called on the working classes to 'turn their intelligence, their energy, their numbers, their power of union . . . in this straight direction in earnest' in order that they might by Christmas find a worthy government in Downing Street.

Stanfield, Clarkson (1793–1867): Marine and landscape painter. He was pressed into the navy in 1812, but left the sea six years later. He became scene-painter at Drury Lane Theatre and painted the scenery for Dickens's productions of *The Lighthouse* and *The Frozen Deep*, the act-drops for which were used as hall-decorations at Gad's Hill. Stanfield contributed some illustrations to 'The Battle of Life'. Dickens had a warm affection for 'old Stanny', whom he called 'the soul of frankness, generosity, and simplicity, the most loving and most lovable of men'. The act-drop for *The Lighthouse* is preserved in the Dickens House, London.

Stone, Frank (1800–59): Painter, first exhibiting at the Royal Academy in 1837 and becoming A.R.A. in 1851. Dickens took Tavistock House from him in 1851 and they were close friends for many years, Stone painting several portraits of the Dickens children and taking part in Dickens's amateur theatricals. He made three of the drawings for 'The Haunted Man', and provided some extra illustrations for *Nicholas Nickleby* and *Martin Chuzzlewit*. He was the father of Marcus Stone, R.A., illustrator of *Our Mutual Friend*.

Stowe, Mrs. Harriet Elizabeth Beecher (1811–96): American writer and philanthropist, brought up in the intellectual society of New England, she devoted herself to the cause of anti-slavery and wrote her famous propagandist novel *Uncle Tom's Cabin*, published in 1852. Her travels brought her to England the year after, and she met Dickens at a banquet. 'Directly opposite me was Mr. Dickens, whom I now beheld for the first time, and was surprised to see looking so young. Mr. Justice Talfourd made allusion to the author of *Uncle Tom's Cabin* and Mr. Dickens, speaking of both as having employed fiction as a means of awakening the attention of the respective countries to the condition of the oppressed and suffering classes.'

Stroughill, George: Dickens's neighbour and playmate during Ordnance Terrace days. George, somewhat older than

Dickens and of a bold and fearless nature, probably reappeared as the young Steerforth of *David Copperfield*.

Stroughill, Lucy: George's sister and Dickens's childhood sweetheart, the 'peach-faced creature in a blue sash' of 'Birthday Celebrations' and Golden Lucy of 'The Wreck of the Golden Mary'. Dickens uses the name Lucy five times in the novels.

Sultan: A St. Bernard-bloodhound cross given to Dickens by Percy Fitzgerald. Dickens remarked that he must be a Fenian, for no non-Fenian dog would have made such a point of rushing at and bearing down with fury anything in scarlet with the remotest resemblance to a soldier's uniform. Sultan had eventually to be shot for savagery.

Talfourd, Sir Thomas Noon (1795–1854): Judge and author, he published *Poems on various Subjects*, 1811, contributed articles and dramatic criticisms to numerous journals, and met the literary celebrities of the day. He was made Serjeant, 1833, and Justice of the Common Pleas, 1849; M.P. for Reading, 1835, 1837, and 1841; introduced the Custody of Infants Bill and the Copyright Bill, the latter particularly endearing him to Dickens and earning him the dedication of *The Pickwick Papers*. When he was made a judge Dickens was 'really quite enraptured at his success'. Forster observes that 'such small oddities or foibles as he had made him secretly only dearer to Dickens, who had no friend he was more attached to'. He was known among his friends as 'Ion', the title of a tragedy of his produced in 1836.

Tennyson, Alfred, first Baron Tennyson (1809–92): Author of *Maud, Idylls of the King, In Memoriam, The Princess*, 'The Charge of the Light Brigade', *Enoch Arden*, and many other poems, lyrical and heroic, who became Poet Laureate on the death of Wordsworth in 1850. He and Dickens had a reciprocal admiration. Forster says that in Dickens's brilliant middle years Tennyson gave him 'full allegiance and honoured welcome'. He appears as a young man in Frank Stone's painting *The Duet*, showing the Dickens family and guests at a musical evening in their Villa Rosemont, Lausanne. He was godfather to Dickens's son Alfred.

Ternan, Ellen Lawless (1839–1914): Presumed mistress of Dickens, she was a young actress whom he met in 1857, when she was appearing in Talfourd's play *Atalanta*. Dickens engaged her and her actress mother and sister, Frances Eleanor and Maria Ternan, for his next amateur production, *The Frozen Deep*, followed by a farce, *Uncle John*. The meeting, and Dickens's subsequent infatuation, appear to have turned him finally against his long-suffering wife. In 1858 a separation was arranged, Catherine going to live with her eldest son Charley, while Dickens published an unwise and uncalled-for refutation of the supposed rumours and slanders that were flying about. Everyone, including Catherine, subscribed meekly to his will except Katey, who defied him and took her mother's part. It would seem (though the facts will never be known) that Ellen Ternan held out against him for some time after this date, but finally succumbed and entered with him into a furtive and somewhat unsatisfactory relationship, which added to the stresses of his last ten years. They apparently lived intermittently together at Peckham and Slough. Persistent legend says that a son was born to them, but no confirmation of this has ever been found. Ellen Ternan received £1,000 under Dickens's will, was present at his deathbed, and later remained on friendly terms with Georgina Hogarth and Mamie Dickens. In 1876 she married George W. Robinson, a clergyman who later became headmaster of a school in Margate.

Thackeray, William Makepeace (1811–63): Novelist. Born in India, he came to England in 1817; studied for the law, but abandoned it; failed in the management of a journal; studied drawing in Paris; and turned to miscellaneous literature and novel-writing, his most famous books being *Vanity Fair, Henry Esmond, The Newcomes,* and *The Virginians. Vanity Fair* completely established his reputation, which was enhanced by the later *Pendennis.* Dickens and he met in *Pickwick* days, when Dickens was in search of an illustrator, and Thackeray always remembered offering him some drawings 'which, strange to say, he did not find suitable'. In 1858 the two quarelled over a critical comment on Thackeray by Edmund Yates, published in *Town Talk.* Thackeray tried to get Yates removed from membership of the Garrick Club; Dickens defended Yates, and the two literary giants remained estranged until a week before Thackeray's death. Dickens was deeply shocked by the death, and paid warm tribute to Thackeray's genius, learning, and humour.

Thompson, Mrs. T. J.: See Weller, Christiana.

Timber: A white spaniel who was a pet of Dickens's during Devonshire Terrace days. He travelled on the Continent with the family and was such an attraction to Italian fleas that he 'had to be clipped in lion style'. He survived into the 1850s. His original name was Mr. Snittle Timbery, later changed to Mr. Timber Doodle.

Turk: A mastiff owned by Dickens at Gad's Hill, and a great favourite; 'a noble animal', according to Forster, 'full of affection and intelligent'. By a strange coincidence he died as a result of a railway accident in 1865, shortly after his master had been involved in the Staplehurst disaster.

Victoria, Queen (1819–1901): When the Queen was married in 1840 to Prince Albert Dickens affected to be 'raving with love' for her, and wrote such lyrics on the subject as:

> *My heart is at Windsor,*
> *My heart is not here,*
> *My heart is at Windsor,*
> *A following my dear.*

He managed, however, to watch the wedding procession calmly enough. In 1857 when Dickens applied to the Queen for the Douglas Jerrold Memorial Fund, for which he was repeating his production of *The Frozen Deep,* she replied that she never patronised benefits for individuals, but would like to see the play, and invited Dickens to bring his troupe to the Palace. He replied that he preferred not to take the ladies of his company there 'in the quality of actresses', and the Queen accepted his invitation to a private presentation for herself and party at the Gallery of Illustration in Regent Street. They 'made a most excellent audience', reported Georgina Hogarth, '. . . cried and laughed and applauded'. In 1870 Dickens made his first appearance at Buckingham Palace, to receive Her Majesty's thanks for some American photographs he had sent at her request. He found her 'strangely shy . . . and like a girl in manner . . . but with a girlish sort of timidity which was very engaging'. He informed her that in his opinion the division of classes would gradually cease and, she commented in her journal, 'I earnestly hope it may'. On leaving he was presented with a copy of her book *Our Life in the Highlands,* given with the modest remark that she was really ashamed to offer such a book to such a writer. After Dickens's death the Queen telegraphed from Balmoral to Catherine, 'Deepest regret at the sad news.' A specially bound copy of his *Letters* was sent to her in 1879. There have been rumours that Dickens was offered a baronetcy, and accepted it, shortly before his death; but there seems to be no absolute proof of this. He certainly did not tell Forster about it, if it happened.

Warren, Jonathan: Original proprietor of the blacking warehouse in which Dickens worked in 1824, he sold out to the Lamerts his interest in the premises at 30 Hungerford Stairs, Strand, where he had set up a business in opposition to Robert Warren at 30, Strand. Both Jonathan and Robert claimed to hold the recipe for the blacking, and as no copyright law then existed, one firm exactly copied the pictorial advertisements of the other. Dickens's experience at Warren's is re-lived in David Copperfield's employment at Murdstone and Grinby's warehouse, and there are frequent glancing references to Warren in the novels.

Watson, The Hon. Richard (d. 1852): Owner of Rockingham Castle, Northamptonshire, and brother of Lord Sondes. Dickens first met Watson and his wife and family at the house of William Haldimand, former M.P. for Ipswich, who was living in Lausanne when the Dickenses lodged there in 1846. He formed a lasting friendship with them, cemented by Watson's strong Liberal views which chimed with Dickens's political sympathies. Invitations to Rockingham followed, and there, in 1849, Dickens met Mrs. Watson's niece, Mary Boyle, who became one of his closest friends. They acted together at Rockingham for the first time, in a farce called *Used Up*. Another production there was planned for 1852, but Watson died abroad before the plans could be implemented. Dickens wrote to Forster, 'I was so fond of him that I am sorry you didn't know him better. I believe he was as thoroughly good and true a man as ever lived; and I am sure I can have no greater affection for him than he felt for me. When I think of that bright house, and his fine simple honest heart, both so open to me, the blank and loss are like a dream.' As a tribute to Watson's memory he gave a reading of 'A Christmas Carol' in Peterborough. Chesney Wold, the home of the Dedlocks in *Bleak House*, is probably based on Rockingham Castle.

Weller, Christiana: On 26 February, 1844, Dickens took the chair at a soirée of the Mechanics' Institute in Liverpool. It included music, and as chairman Dickens announced, 'I am requested to introduce a young lady whom I have some difficulty and tenderness in announcing – Miss Weller – who will play a fantasia on the pianoforte.' The name Weller raised a great laugh, but Dickens's own amusement was tempered by his immediate infatuation with Christiana Weller, who possibly reminded him of Mary Hogarth. He wrote to his friend T. J. Thompson, 'I cannot joke about Miss Weller; for she is too good; and interest in her (spiritual young creature that she is, and destined to an early death, I fear) has become a sentiment with me.' Some days later Thompson confessed that he himself was in love with Miss Weller, to Dickens's shocked surprise, although he urged Thompson to win and marry her. Thompson did so, and far from being destined to an early death, Christiana became the mother of two daughters, one of whom became Lady Butler, the genre painter, and the other, Alice Meynell, the poet and essayist. Dickens visited them in Italy in 1853 and disapproved markedly of Christiana's Bohemian methods of running her household, and of the 'singularly untidy' state of her little girls.

Weller, Mary: Nurse to Dickens when the family lived at Ordnance Terrace, Chatham, she was an accomplished tale-spinner whose stories of ghosts, goblins, murders, and other ghoulish subjects stimulated the child's mind as well as frightening him a great deal; but it is not easy to reconcile the portrait in the essay 'Nurse's Stories' with the 'smart young girl' who looked after the Dickens family and remembered her young charge with such kindness in her old age. Dickens gave Mary's name to the immortal Sam. She married Thomas Gibson, a shipwright in Chatham Dockyard.

Williamina: Dickens's cat at Gad's Hill, the only one permitted there because of his fondness for bird-life. She had been presented to Georgina as a pretty white kitten, but became devoted to Dickens and was allowed, with her kittens, to live in his study. Her son, a completely deaf cat, was allowed to remain when homes were found for the others, and became known simply as The Master's Cat, following Dickens about like a dog and sitting beside him while he wrote. Mamie Dickens tells a charming anecdote about him in *My Father as I Recall Him*.

Wills, William Henry (1810–80): Appointed assistant editor of *Household Words* in 1850. It was Wills who in 1855 excitedly told Dickens, 'It is written that you were to have that house at Gad's Hill!' for the previous night he had learnt from Mrs. Lynn Linton that she wanted to sell the house Dickens had admired since boyhood. When Dickens's sons, Harry and 'Plorn', started their private newspaper *The Gad's Hill Gazette*, Wills presented the young journalists with a 'manifold writer' and a printing-press. In company with Forster and Georgina Hogarth he opposed Dickens's intention of embarking on the American tour of 1867–8, but Dickens pointed out the immense profits to be made from it, and made light of his growing ill-health. It appears from the correspondence of this date that Wills was privy to the liaison with Ellen Ternan: he received letters from Dickens written on Ellen's stationery, and among his instructions was a memorandum containing a code message for her by which she was to know whether or not to follow Dickens to America. After Dickens's death Wills sold out his one-eighth share in *All the Year Round* to Charley Dickens, with whom he quarrelled over money.

Dickens had written to him in 1862, 'we doubt whether any two men can have gone on more happily, and smoothly, or with greater trust and confidence in each other', a passage which Wills was gratified to see in print when Dickens's *Letters* were published.

Winter, Mrs. Henry: See Beadnell, Maria.

Yates, Edmund (1831–94): Novelist and founder of the journal *The World*, he began his career as a post office worker. He was drama critic and reviewer of the *Daily News*, 1854–60, wrote several plays, and was editor of various periodicals as well as contributing to *All the Year Round*. Dickens took a great interest in him and in 1872 Yates followed Dickens's example by touring America, giving a series of literary lectures containing many reminiscences of his friendship with Dickens. Georgina Hogarth was disapproving of Yates's venture, fearing that some undesirable facts might come out during the lectures, for she though Yates 'a harum-scarum creature', and it was he who had been the cause of the estrangement between Dickens and Thackeray.

SELECTIVE INDEX

SELECTIVE INDEX

compiled by Ann Hoffmann

This is an index to the TIME CHART (excluding the *General Events* column) and to information concerning publishers, dates and places of publication contained in the preambles under each title in THE WORKS. Finding references (in bold figures) are also given for all entries in DICKENS AND HIS CIRCLE.

The letters *l* and *c* after a page number refer to the *Life* and *Career* columns of the TIME CHART respectively.

In order to avoid overloading the entry for Charles Dickens, personal sub-headings only have been included there and the rest, together with titles of his works, placed in their alphabetical sequence.

Sub-headings are arranged chronologically rather than alphabetically, except in the case of addresses of Dickens in London, titles of works and theatrical productions.

The following abbreviations of names have been used: CD, for Charles Dickens; D, for Dickens; H, for Hogarth.

Where titles of works by Dickens appear more than once in the same column on the same page of the TIME CHART, one entry only will be found in the index. A series of sub-headings to cover the writing, completion, serialisation and book publication of each work, followed by identical page references, would merely add bulk to the index, and the reader should have no difficulty in locating these references. A similar rule applies where the names of journals, publishers and places occur more than once in the same column.